Rising Road

Rising Road

SHARON DAVIES

A True Tale of Love,

Race, and Religion

in America

Dear Will,
Thank you for your support
of the Moritz College of Law.
May the road rise up to
meet you.

Sharon Davies

OXFORD
UNIVERSITY PRESS

2010

OXFORD
UNIVERSITY PRESS

Oxford University Press, Inc., publishes works that further
Oxford University's objective of excellence
in research, scholarship, and education.

Oxford   New York
Auckland   Cape Town   Dar es Salaam   Hong Kong   Karachi
Kuala Lumpur   Madrid   Melbourne   Mexico City   Nairobi
New Delhi   Shanghai   Taipei   Toronto

With offices in
Argentina   Austria   Brazil   Chile   Czech Republic   France   Greece
Guatemala   Hungary   Italy   Japan   Poland   Portugal   Singapore
South Korea   Switzerland   Thailand   Turkey   Ukraine   Vietnam

Published by Oxford University Press, Inc.
198 Madison Avenue, New York, New York 10016

www.oup.com

Oxford is a registered trademark of Oxford University Press

Library of Congress Cataloging-in-Publication Data
Davies, Sharon L., 1960–
Rising road : a true tale of love, race, and religion in America / Sharon Davies.
p. cm.
Includes bibliographical references and index.
ISBN 978-0-19-537979-2
1. Interracial marriage—Alabama—Birmingham—History—20th century.
2. Anti-Catholicism—Alabama—Birmingham—History—20th century.
3. Murder—Alabama—Birmingham—History—20th century.   I. Title.
HQ1031.D37 2010
306.84'60976178109042—dc22   2009018486

9 8 7 6 5 4 3 2 1

Printed in the United States of America
on acid-free paper

For Alan, Heather, and Tyler

May the road rise up to meet you.
May the wind be always at your back.
May the sun shine warm upon your face;
the rains fall soft upon your fields and until we meet again,
may God hold you in the palm of His hand.

—Traditional Irish Blessing

CONTENTS

THE EVENTS DESCRIBED in this book are true. To remain true to them, throughout, I use the terms for African Americans and others that the nation used at the time, words like "Negro" and "colored," or worse. I hope that readers will understand that I intend no offense by using the outdated and sometimes deliberately hurtful terms so frequently used when these events occurred.

About the Book's Title

The inspiration for the title *Rising Road* was the aged Irish blessing set out at the front of the book. It seemed an appropriate homage to the life of Father James Coyle, native son of Ireland. More broadly though, the title is offered as a reminder of our very human (if at moments largely aspirational) journey away from fears that can divide us. Perhaps it is always in hindsight that we are best able to see the failings of our prejudices. If so, may the road continue to rise before us, bringing us closer to the day when it is our commonalities rather than our differences that we see most clearly.

Rising Road

Prologue

THE SOREST MISFORTUNE of Ruth Stephenson's young life was not that she was born (and died) a decade or more too soon to ever really enjoy the promises women's suffrage would bring. Nor was it that she was born into a region of the country that could be relied on to be particularly unpliant when it came to the concern of women's liberation. Nor even that she was born into a household ruled by an ordained Methodist minister with a taste for discipline and guns and a love for the robes of the Ku Klux Klan. The sorest misfortune of Ruth Stephenson's young life was that she was raised an only child.

Ruth's mother had given birth to one other child, but the baby had not survived, which left only Ruth. Perhaps had Edwin and Mary Stephenson had other children (as their parents before them had done, and their closest neighbors to boot), maybe even a pack of them, as was the habit of their day, Ruth's parents might have developed that special resilience of those too outnumbered and beleaguered to worry over nonfatal threats to their offspring. Or perhaps if they had had just one more besides her, the inevitable perplexing contrast between the two children would have convinced Edwin and Mary that the flaws they observed in them must be the children's own. For if the parents and their rearing habits had not varied, only the inherent character and character flaws of the children themselves could explain such differences. And with that realization Edwin and Mary Stephenson might have relaxed, and let Ruth's missteps (if missteps they were) be her own.

But for whatever reason, and though it was not the custom of the time, Ruth Stephenson was Edwin and Mary Stephenson's only child, and as such, they dutifully showered on her every suffocating over-protection, every unrelenting expectation, every crushing judgment they could muster, in the loving expectation that through these lessons she would come to share their loves and convictions, as well as their hates and fears. So when the girl began to think differently, her flaws (if flaws they were) must have seemed like Mary's and Edwin's own—defects in *their* house, which of course needed to be cleansed.

ONE | # Resistance

Birmingham, Alabama, 1921

There was little to distinguish Thursday, August 11, 1921, from any of the other days that choked Birmingham that week beneath a blanket of heat, with the exception that Ruth Stephenson and Pedro Gussman chose it as their wedding day. And likely the unremarkable character of the day was part of the couple's plan, as they would have wanted a day with as little to commend itself as possible. A day less apt to stand out; one that would draw no attention. As if only on a day so pedestrian, and by a strategy uncluttered by its particulars, could they ever hope to bring the thing off.

The trouble was not that the law prevented Ruth Stephenson and Pedro Gussman's union, though in 1921, like most states, Alabama had a great deal to say about who could marry whom, and who could not. At minimum, most states specified the age at which couples became free to make the decision to wed by themselves, without the consent of a parent. Alabama set it at twenty-one for men and eighteen for women. Younger lovers than that could marry, provided their parents concurred, but to protect against fraud in such cases the state gave the youths only two choices: either present their ostensibly "consenting" parents to the probate judge in person, or produce the guardians' assent in writing, the authenticity of which the couple was required to guarantee by agreeing to pay the state the mammoth sum of $200 if the consent of any of their parents was proven false.[1]

Both Pedro and Ruth had cleared the state's age hurdles. Pedro long before; he was forty-two. And Ruth had celebrated her eighteenth birthday on August 29th the year before; she would be nineteen by the end of the month. Though some in Birmingham might have disapproved of the twenty-four-year gap between them, there was ample precedent for such generational chasms. The critical thing was that no law precluded it.

On the question of how Pedro Gussman had snared a fiancé twenty-four years his junior, pictures of him in 1921 provided one answer: Pedro enjoyed a distinctly youthful appearance. His draft registration card, filled out in 1919, described his height as "medium" and his build "slender," the naturally lean frame of a man accustomed to muscle-straining work. Since his arrival in Birmingham about fourteen years before, Pedro had made his living by hanging wallpaper for Sherwin Williams in homes around the city. He was undoubtedly strong and fit. Born in "Porto Rico" (the accepted spelling at the time), his complexion was smooth and tanned, and his dark clear eyes sloped ever-so-slightly downward, giving him a faint look of sadness and a vague vulnerability with its strong romantic appeal. Even if other men his age could no longer attract the attention of young women like Ruth, apparently Pedro Gussman had little trouble.[2]

When it came to state tinkering on the question of appropriate and inappropriate marriage partners, however, age restrictions were only the tip of the iceberg. Far more serious constraints were state laws based on race. At one time or another, most of the states had passed laws that banned marriage and sexual intimacy between the races, albeit with a robust disagreement around the question of precisely which racial partners needed to be kept apart. In many states the answer took on a decidedly regional cast, varying with the types and numbers of racial "undesirables" with which they happened to be cursed. For most of the northern Atlantic seaboard states, therefore, simple demographics seemed to make the threat of whites marrying anyone but Negroes pretty much a minor concern. The most common cross-race ban in that part of the country prohibited whites from marrying or fornicating with Negroes or the offspring of Negroes, but no one else. California, by contrast, with its significant "Chinese problem," banned whites from marrying or laying with Negroes, Mulattoes, or *Mongolians*.[3]

The rules did not always follow such an easily understood path, of course. As is so often the case with laws that nest within fear, demographic logic sometimes slipped away when lawmakers dwelled on the threat that the amalgamation of the races posed to the "integrity and purity" of the white race—that "abominable mixture," that "spurious issue." Even states blessed with overwhelmingly white populations seemed to fear that a failure to prohibit interracial unions would attract them, like fleas. Taking no chances, the state of Nebraska banned whites from marrying or laying with Negroes despite the fact that according to the 1920 census, only 1 percent of its population was black, and Idaho, with a defilement of only 920 Negroes in the entire state—a meager 0.2 percent of its population—thought it wise nonetheless to declare marriage between whites and Mongolians, Negroes, or mulattoes "illegal and void."[4]

But no part of the country could out worry the Deep South, where the numbers of Negroes were greater, and attention to skin color bordered on hysteria.[5] Long before Ruth Stephenson and Pedro Gussman decided to wed, lawmakers in Alabama had declared the marriage of any white person to any "Negro or any descendant of a Negro" to be a crime. Yet voters in the state seemed to lack confidence that the law was sufficiently indelible. As if living in fear that their elected representatives might someday reverse themselves and decide that marriage between whites and Negroes was tolerable after all, white voters decided an additional precaution was necessary, and they fashioned a section of the state's constitution to provide it: "The Legislature shall *never* pass any law to authorize or legalize any marriage between any white person and a Negro, or a descendant of a Negro," the Alabama charter read.[6]

Occasionally, a couple would attempt to buck the rules, of course, but even if the lovers managed somehow to procure a marriage certificate and someone to take their vows, upon discovery, the anti-miscegenation states regarded their union a nullity—without binding effect, a colossal waste of time. If the newlyweds thought they might escape this fate by fleeing to a sister state without an anti-miscegenation ban, they would quickly be disabused of the notion upon their return. The home states considered themselves under no obligation to honor such out-of-state liberalities. Worse, offenders of the racial marriage rules were not just ignored, they could be unceremoniously tossed in jail, including anyone who had knowingly helped them. For it was common for such states to threaten not only the cross-race couples with criminal punishment, but the clerks who issued them licenses, and any cleric foolish enough to perform their ceremony as well.

Ruth Stephenson and Pedro Gussman would have been aware of these restrictions when they decided to marry; Birmingham authorities kept it no secret that offenders of the state's anti-miscegenation rules would be promptly prosecuted. There was a need for vigilance. The roots of the laws, their proponents claimed, could be traced back to the Bible. God himself had decreed the separation of the races.[7] The lawbreakers could expect no lenience. Thus, earlier that year, the grand jury had indicted Edith Labue, a married Italian immigrant, and Jim Rollins, a Negro, for having sex when it became clear that Rollins had fathered a child with the married woman. For a time, Edith LaBue had explained her baby's dark complexion by claiming she had been scared by a Negro man during her pregnancy, as if it were possible for such an emotional trauma to actually defile a child's appearance. Labue's husband, who worked late driving a taxi down at the Metropolitan Hotel, seemed to accept the story, especially after his wife's doctors told him that "it was possible that she could have got scared at a Negro." But something caused the police to be suspicious, as one night in early March 1921, while her husband was off at work, the police arrived at the Labue home at 2216 Avenue F, kicked the door in, and found Edith Labue and the Negro Jim Rollins "standing up right close to one another" in the back kitchen. The baby looked just like Rollins, one of the officers said, and the Negro eventually confessed his paternity.[8]

But as far as Ruth Stephenson and Pedro Gussman were concerned, the fact that no white person could marry or have sexual contact with a Negro had nothing to do with them. Ruth was the white daughter of Edwin and Mary Stephenson, and Pedro was Puerto Rican, an ethnic group that state and federal authorities had tended to classify as "white," or at least not "Negro," since Spain had ceded Puerto Rico to the United States at the conclusion of the Spanish-American War in the Treaty of Paris of 1898. Like many of the other immigrant groups that flooded into the country in the beginning of the twentieth century, newcomers like Pedro Gussman may have arrived at their ports of entry without a "racialized" world view of themselves, but if so they quickly learned to develop one. And not surprisingly the race that all preferred to lay claim to in America was "white."[9]

In truth, many of the "native whites" considered the waves of immigrants spilling into the country as only slightly more palatable than the Negroes; an antipathy that for a time made the newcomers from southeastern Europe and elsewhere, with their darker complexions and their foreign tongues, perhaps best considered the nation's "in-between peoples." But that was enough to spare them the Negro's special degradations, a species of disadvantages lost on no one. For if in the world of social interaction Puerto Ricans, Mexicans, Italians, Greeks, and Jews (and even at one time the Irish) were considered by their white Anglo-Saxon neighbors as not precisely "white," they could take solace in the thought that neither were they deemed "black or belonging to a race proscribed by law." Although the process would take some time, they were becoming "white by default,"[10] a status that seemed to suit them, for as one historian later put it, the "new immigrants and their children quickly learned that 'the worst thing one could be in this Promised Land was 'colored.' "[11]

This meant that even if Pedro Gussman's tan complexion and noticeable Spanish accent put off some of the "native white stock" of Jefferson County, when it came to his marriage to Ruth Stephenson, they could keep it to themselves. For legal and social purposes, he counted as white, just like Ruth. And if anyone cared to look for proof of Gussman's racial *bona fides*, evidence in color-conscious Birmingham was abundant. He roomed in all-white boardinghouses, and he ate in sections of restaurants cordoned off for white patrons. Some years before, he had married a white woman without objection. The U.S. Census of 1920 listed him as white, as did his voter registration card, which meant that he was entitled to vote in the primaries in which only whites could vote—a strategy devised to disenfranchise Negroes near the turn of the century. Years later, Pedro Gussman's death certificate again would list his race as white, and throughout the years he lived and worked in the city, he was spared the letter *c* for "colored" next to his name in the *Birmingham City Directory*—the equivalent of today's phone book—an ignominy all the Negroes in Birmingham silently endured, as if, even in print the need to segregate whites from blacks could not be overemphasized.[12]

With no racial bans standing in their way, once Ruth Stephenson reached the age of majority on her eighteenth birthday, the law of Alabama had little to say about the wisdom of her decision to wed Pedro Gussman. There was no *legal* obstacle to the marriage. If there was trouble with the union, therefore, the problem lay outside the state—with her church or her household—for quite naturally, Ruth's family or neighbors might be less keen about the coupling for reasons of their own.

———

It is difficult to know just how much Ruth Stephenson really liked Pedro Gussman when she agreed to marry him. She might have liked him very much, as Pedro was the kind of man capable of capturing the hearts of women. He had certainly done so before. A woman from Nashville had hoped to make a life with him after he arrived in the states as a young man, and she married him—mute testimony to his appeal—but then she died, leaving Pedro without a mate. After her burial, Pedro found a fresh start in Birmingham, where women continued to take notice of him.[13] Besides his dark good looks and fit physique, Pedro Gussman was soft-spoken and dependable. He had a reputation for kindness and for working hard. It is not difficult to understand his appeal. So it is entirely possible that Ruth Stephenson was drawn to Pedro for many of the same reasons other women had been.

But it is also possible that what Ruth Stephenson saw in Pedro Gussman was more a convenient means of escape than a lifetime of happiness. By their wedding day, though the couple had known each other for nearly five years, they could not have spent a lot of time alone together. Ruth was only thirteen years old when the two first met, when her parents hired Pedro to hang some wallpaper at their home. It must have taken some time to complete the job, as Pedro later said that the family permitted him to board in the house while he worked. But Mary Stephenson, as the matriarch and homemaker, would usually have been somewhere about the house, and it seems unlikely she would have left her teenage daughter alone with Gussman for long. Even if the two managed to talk now and then, their conversations could not have been many. Yet Pedro came to like the girl, enough to ask her to marry him, despite her youth.

Many years later, Ruth told others about Pedro's proposal, but never in a way that made it seem as though she had considered it seriously. Perhaps she realized that there was no sense in entertaining the idea, for even if she had been tempted, at age thirteen the law would have required her parents' consent, surely a nonstarter. If Ruth was flattered by the attention of the hardworking paperhanger with the doleful eyes, the prospect of their spending a life together must have appeared unlikely.[14]

The best evidence, then, that Ruth was actually attracted to Pedro, and that she might actually have taken his marriage proposal seriously, is the fact that, after he completed his work at the Stephenson house, the two stayed in contact with each other. Sometimes they met by accident, on the street on their way to somewhere else. When they did, Pedro would pass Ruth little slips of paper with his current telephone number so that she would know how to reach him. The numbers changed over the years, as Pedro boarded with the families for whom he worked, or roomed at one of the many boardinghouses in the city when his patrons were unable to make room for him. No matter where he happened to be, with Pedro's slips of paper, Ruth could reach him if she liked. And it seems she did use them, for according to Ruth, sometimes the two met by design rather than accident.

In a city with few secrets, it is difficult to think that these meetings could have been frequent. But occasionally, Ruth said, she and Pedro would slip away and meet each other at a picture show, where a romance kindled at age thirteen could have been reignited under the theater's soothing cloak of darkness. Over those years, Ruth told a reporter later, Pedro renewed his proposal of marriage more than once. So it is possible that Ruth and Pedro's romance was true in fact, a simmering attraction that built slowly, fueled by hidden smiles and stolen scraps of time alone as Ruth approached the age of majority. But it is also possible that Ruth had reasons besides love to accept Pedro Gussman's offer of marriage, six years after they met. Perhaps on August 11, 1921, her chosen wedding day, she was just tired of waiting for things in her life to change.[15]

———

Had things been different, Ruth and Pedro would probably have preferred to be married in Birmingham, at the magnificent St. Paul's Catholic Church on

Third Avenue, where Pedro had long been a parishioner. But St. Paul's was only two doors down from the Jefferson County Courthouse, Ruth's father's preferred base of operations, and the odds of running into him there were simply too great. They could not risk it.

The irony of having to travel out of the city to be married to avoid crossing paths with Reverend Edwin R. Stephenson, of all people, could not have escaped the couple. In Birmingham, Stephenson was well known as the "Marrying Parson," a moniker he had earned for his daily traipses to the Jefferson County Courthouse, and the great number of runaway couples he had married there. Every day of the week, Ruth's father would stand on the courthouse steps "on the lookout for business," or linger about the probate court, where youngsters came to obtain marriage licenses. The minister was tall and slim, dressed all in black, and had a mustache so full it hid his top lip almost entirely from view. And he was the picture of helpfulness. *Are you looking to get married?* he would ask the couples solicitously, before explaining that he was an ordained minister. He would guide them to the office that could issue them a license. Why should they know how to find it? He would help them find witnesses. Did they need someone to perform the ceremony? He could do it for a small fee.[16]

Once the state of Alabama had seen fit to issue such couples a license to wed, Edwin Stephenson was not one to stand in the way of love. Though he must have known that many of the young men and women he approached chose haste over pomp out of fear of interference with their plans, there is no evidence to suggest that he ever refused to perform the rites, or probed for information about their families' feelings about the union, or inquired about the couples' preparedness. On occasion he was known to delay the nuptials, but only long enough to lecture the young lovers about the seriousness of marital vows, as if a sermon by the willing minister was somehow needed to lend the occasion solemnity.

As for venue, the weddings took place where they had to under such circumstances, as Stephenson was what was known at the time as a "local preacher": he had preached to audiences on special occasions, but he had no regular pastorate. With no pulpit or altar to offer the young couples, he married them in stealth, secluded from the protestations of their families, in the only place he could: a darkened corner of the Jefferson County Courthouse—"near the end of the hall on the second floor."[17]

My father should have been the person best able to understand our decision to wed the way we did, Ruth must have thought.

———

Edwin Stephenson had not always been the city's "Marrying Parson." When the Stephensons moved from Georgia to Birmingham in 1909, Edwin took a job at a barbershop on Twenty-second Street, and for the next five years, whenever he was asked about the nature of his work, he answered that he was a "barber." Entries in multiple issues of the *Birmingham City Directory* confirmed this as his professed trade through 1918. The idea of trying his hand at any other work might never have occurred to Stephenson, had he not shot a bullet through his foot while cleaning his pistol one day. The wound was not fatal, nor even life threatening, but it never healed properly and it pained him greatly. When he could no longer stand on it for hours on end as barbers must do, he was forced to put up his shears and look for other work.[18]

There is no record of how Edwin Stephenson first thought to use the ministerial credentials he had brought with him to Birmingham when he moved his family there. Even then he had claimed his ordination into the Methodist ministry—back in Newnan, Georgia, he said, in 1905 at the age of thirty-five—but it wasn't until after the shooting accident that he began to claim the ministry as his vocation. In contrast to the description he had given the census taker in 1910 of his work—"barber" he had said—by the time the 1920 census taker came to call, Edwin Stephenson had routinely begun to refer to himself as "the Rev. E. R. Stephenson," even without a pulpit from which to preach. Entries in subsequent issues of the *Birmingham City Directory* listed him that way as well, and soon he was known as the city's "Marrying Parson."[19]

It can no longer be known precisely when it was that the Reverend Robert Echols, presiding pastor of the First Methodist Episcopal Church, South (M.E.C., South), first learned that Edwin Stephenson was "hanging around the courthouse" marrying people. But some time around August 1920, Reverend Echols decided he had to take action, and he asked his parishioner to come to the church for a meeting. The M.E.C., South had had no trouble with Edwin Stephenson up to that time. When Stephenson had moved his family to Birmingham years before, he had mentioned his ordination within the ministry to Echols, but the newcomer had never been awarded a pastorate, and he had seemed to understand that the M.E.C., South had no post to offer him. There had never been a question about the man's real trade; and the church had been happy to welcome the barber and his family into its fold.[20]

Reverend Echols probably thought to himself that the whole mess could have been avoided had Stephenson just been a little more careful with his gun. But, as far as Rev. Echols was concerned, the fact that Stephenson had shot himself in the foot did nothing to enhance his pastoral standing. Had his parishioner sought Echol's advice about what he might do to support his family after his injury, Echols might not have had many good ideas, but he certainly would have counseled Stephenson against marrying runaway couples for a fee. Weddings were solemn events, and a Methodist minister who rummaged after misguided lovers in the hallways of Birmingham's courthouse was a rank embarrassment. So when the two men met, Echols told Stephenson that the business just had to stop.[21]

The meeting of the two ministers took place sometime around Ruth's eighteenth birthday in August 1920 at the Methodist Episcopal Church, South, which stood proudly on the corner of Nineteenth Street and Sixth Avenue. The handsome building was built of rustic stone in the American Romanesque style invented by Mr. Henry Hobson Richardson, the widely acclaimed architect of Trinity Church in Boston. Work on the M.E.C., South had been finished nearly twenty years before, after much hand-wringing over the spiraling costs of its construction. In August 1890, church planners had thought $80,000 would surely be enough, but only a month later they raised the figure to $100,000. By January 1891, the prediction had jumped again, to $125,000, then to $150,000 in June. When the church finally opened its doors later that year, the final cost of the project totaled $160,000, twice the original estimate (an amount that excluded the value of the land on which the church stood, which Colonel James W. Sloss had generously donated to the parish free of charge).

Despite the steep price tag, the congregation must have been pleased. The M.E.C., South was the very picture of the Protestant break from the Gothic architectural style so favored by the Catholics. Unlike the soaring interior arches, haunting stone sculptures, and "distant altar" of St. Paul's Catholic Church on Third Avenue, the "reform" architecture of the M.E.C., South enclosed a grand auditorium that seated twenty-four hundred, juxtaposing a massive, circular balcony over the square footprint of the sanctuary below. Every seat in the house enjoyed the same focal point—the pastor's pulpit—enabling Reverend Echols to deliver his sermons and read passages from the scriptures literally surrounded by his congregants, for the circular design of the room situated the parishioners "always immediately before him, gathered in the community of prayer." Grand, rounded stained-glass windows echoed the chamber's circular themes and let in filtered light.[22]

It is not hard to imagine the wave of resentment Edwin Stephenson must have felt during that meeting with his pastor that day, as Robert Echols demeaned the services he had provided to couples in the courthouse. He was an ordained minister just like Echols, Stephenson probably thought to himself, even if he had never enjoyed the same comforts: the pleasures of a devoted congregation; the privileges of a lectern from which to preach. As an ordained member of the clergy, the laws of Alabama plainly authorized him to perform marriages wherever and whenever he chose. Did Robert Echols imagine himself wiser than the state?

There can be little doubt that part of Stephenson's reaction to his pastor's scolding that day was due to the fact that he had already grown accustomed to the privileges of the cloth. It must have felt good to be able to refer to himself and his profession as "minister" or "preacher" instead of "barber" when people came to call. Imbued with inherent stature, the position even seemed to demand that its bearer don a particular look to carry it off. So Stephenson had begun to wear the garb of the ministry—the all-black suit and crisp white shirt—and he must have liked the deference and respect the uniform seemed to evoke. Admittedly, the shift did not move him into the top-ranking stratum of Birmingham elites: that top 1 percent dominated by the owners of the iron and steel companies, coal mines, and railroad or banking interests. But it did place him in tier of men just below: the realm occupied by the city's attorneys, engineers, journalists, physicians, clergymen and teachers. The workforce of Birmingham could be sorted into three fairly distinct classes at the time: the industrialists plainly ranked at the top. As James Bowron put it after moving to the city to oversee the financial operations of the Tennessee Coal, Iron and Railroad Company: "I found on coming to Birmingham that to be in the iron trade was to be respectable; to be an officer of an iron making corporation was to have the entree to the best of society; but to be the chief residential officer of the largest corporation was to carry the key to the Kingdom of Heaven."[23] Though not in that revered company, Edwin Stephenson's metamorphosis to "minister" situated him within the group of professional men in the "middle-ranking set," and dissociated him from the lowly company of the city's "wage earners"—the men who comprised the bottom 80 percent of the city's workers—where barbers were lumped unapologetically alongside farmers, grocers, saloon dealers, and worse, coal miners.[24]

So when Echols demanded that his parishioner cease his marriage practices in the Jefferson County Courthouse, Edwin Stephenson simply refused. He and Mary would sooner switch churches, the Marrying Parson told his pastor coldly. And that is exactly what they did.[25]

———

Edwin and Mary Stephenson considered themselves good parents. They took seriously the need to cabin the influences to which their daughter Ruth was exposed. So as the list of dangers that threatened Ruth seemed to grow larger with every passing day, Edwin Stephenson sought comfort in the fellowship of men of like mind: the brotherhood of the hooded empire.

The crosses of the revived Ku Klux Klan had burned with renewed intensity since the chilly Thanksgiving night in 1915 when William Simmons and a small troupe of white-robed men had climbed the slopes of Stone Mountain in nearby Atlanta and heralded the return of the secret brotherhood. Although it would take some time for the Imperial Wizard to reignite the country's passion for the furtive (and at one time, disgraced) organization, by the 1920s Simmons's dreams for the revived Klan had begun to ripen, and the fruit in Birmingham seemed especially promising. Within a year of the Klan's revival, Simmons had chosen Birmingham as the site of Alabama's first chapter, naming it the "Robert E. Lee Klavern No. 1" after the Confederacy's greatest war hero. It quickly lived up to its name, becoming the Klan's most active affiliate and a potent disseminator of the organization's dire warnings. Although Negroes would forever remain "the foremost Klan target," during this period Catholics, Jews, and foreigners were added to its list as well, and the brotherhood's literature made clear why the members of each of these groups created dangers against which every loyal American should be on guard. On the question of Catholics, the Klan leadership in Alabama "accused the Pope of making secret treaties to bring on World War I" and "of stockpiling arms for an imminent Catholic takeover of Washington," and circulated "ghastly tales about the carnal lust of priests and the evils of parochial education."[26]

A subscriber to such views, Edwin Stephenson had sworn the brotherhood's eternal vow of secrecy upon his initiation, pledging never to disclose its confidences. Yet despite the Klan's code of secrecy, Mary and Ruth were well aware of Edwin's membership. Evidently, within his home he did not bother to hide it. Neither did he trouble about putting the telltale sign of his allegiance to the brotherhood—a set of the empire's signal white robes—out of sight of his curious daughter. One Halloween, Ruth surprised Edwin and Mary Stephenson by fetching the robes and donning them as her chosen costume. Her parents' peals of laughter, Ruth said later, exhibited their approval.[27]

It is unlikely that Mary and Edwin Stephenson saw Charles Sweeny's article published in the *Nation* in November 1920 reporting that death threats had been made against the life of Father James E. Coyle, the presiding pastor of St. Paul's Catholic Church and Birmingham's most prominent Catholic leader. Ruth's parents would have disliked the progressive bent of the *Nation*. They tended to rely on the local papers for their news, and if they considered other reading materials at all, periodicals with an anti-Catholic bent would have been more in keeping with their way of thinking. There were plenty to pick from. The country was awash in anti-Catholic literature at the time, and not only in the South. Publications like Tom Watson's *Jeffersonian* and Wilbur Phelps's *Menace* crowded the newsstands everywhere one looked.

Tom Watson of Georgia had begun his wildly popular series of articles denouncing the Roman papist threat in 1910, beneath such irresistible titles as "The Roman Catholic Hierarchy: The Deadliest Menace to Our Liberties and Our Civilization," or "How the Confessional Is Used by Priests to Ruin Women," and "What Happens in Convents." Other installments played on his audience's racial fears as well, like: "The Sinister Portent of Negro Priests." Watson's readers loved them.

Capitalizing on his success, Watson launched a new series in 1912: a string of open letters to James Cardinal Gibbons, the Archbishop of Baltimore and public face of the nation's Roman Catholics. The letter-writing campaign ran uninterrupted in every issue of the *Jeffersonian* that Watson published over the next decade, which according to noted historian C. Vann Woodward, gave it the feel of a "deliberately planned crusade," "matchless in its insulting offensiveness." In one of the letters, Watson lamented the inadequacy of the English language itself to capture the depths of his scorn for the Catholics' beliefs: there simply "is no discoverable vocabulary" that will ever "adequately express the profundity of my loathing and contempt for your stupid, degrading faith," Watson wrote to Cardinal Gibbons. The thirst of his readers for such loutish messages appeared unquenchable: after completing each series, Watson's articles were bundled together, bound into books or pamphlets, and sold again.

Tom Watson had not always displayed such antipathy for Catholics and Negroes. When running for political office as a younger man, Watson had bucked the crowd. At a time when demands for white supremacy were the currency of the day, Watson called instead for an "alliance" with Negroes, as the only way to protect the interests of poor farmers and the working class. In hindsight, this populist message was almost certainly strategic—demanding not so much *social* equality for Negroes, as political equality—for if the votes of the great number of freed Negroes living in Alabama at the time could be added to those of poor and laboring whites, their champion (whom Watson hoped to be) would be unbeatable. For a short time, the calculation proved right, and Watson was swept into the U.S. Congress as an "Alliance Democrat" in 1890. But his victory was fleeting. Only two years later, Watson lost his bid for a second term, and he was defeated again in 1894. Sorely embittered, Watson attributed these defeats to the manipulations of big-city corporate elites who had co-opted, he thought, the votes of "easily duped"

Catholics and Negroes. Years later, these bigoted resentments exploded raw and ragged in the columns of his *Jeffersonian:* soulless Southern industrialist elites were determined to crush America's most glorious, agrarian traditions, Watson warned. Catholics were "laying in guns and ammunition" in preparation for their plot to seize power, "working day and night, spending money like water to 'Make America Catholic!'" Negroes "simply [had] no comprehension of virtue, honesty, truth, gratitude and principle," he wrote, making it necessary to lynch or flog them occasionally to show "that a sense of justice yet lives among the people."[28]

With such venom-filled messages filling the pages of the *Jeffersonian,* Wilbur Franklin Phelps was inspired to launch his own anti-Catholic weekly, *The Menace,* in Aurora, Missouri in 1911. Following in Watson's footsteps, Phelps and his staff railed against the encroaching Catholic threat in each issue, exalting the patriotism personified by the simple, honest lives of rural Americans. The nationally-circulated "patriotic" weekly plainly struck a chord. Within three years the *Menace* boasted a circulation of over a million subscribers, and employed a staff of 135, who ran a fully-equipped publishing plant that, in addition to the paper, churned out a slew of anti-Catholic booklets and "arranged engagements for anti-Catholic lecturers" as well.[29]

Even if Edwin and Mary Stephenson had not read the *Nation*'s article about the death threats against Father James Coyle and the pledges to burn his church to the ground, they certainly would have heard word of the threats buzzing around town. But there is no reason to think the news would have troubled them. Ruth Stephenson had known her whole life that her parents hated Catholics, she said later. Although their feelings on the matter could not have been clearer to their daughter, knowing how children sometimes reject the good guidance of their elders, and perhaps especially that of their parents, Mary and Edwin directed Ruth's attention to the wealth of evidence that existed to support their view of the "Romanists." Couldn't she see? The better part of Birmingham feared that Catholics were plotting to overthrow the government. The fear had fueled the resurgence of the Klan, and set the agendas of other secret fraternal anti-Catholic organizations as well: groups like the Masons, the Knights of Pythias, the Odd Fellows, the Guardians of Liberty (G.O.L.s), and the True Americans, or "T.A.s," as they were popularly known around town. Mary Stephenson told her daughter many times that she wished she could put the bomb beneath St. Paul's Catholic Church herself.[30]

The beliefs fomented by these groups were hardly confined to the South, although there were some particularly loud voices in that region dedicated to getting the anti-Catholic message out into the public. Learning from earlier miscalculations, Tom Watson in nearby Georgia, one of the "chief instigators of southern anti-Catholicism," had gotten himself elected to the United States Senate running on an anti-Catholic platform.[31] In 1916, Florida voters signaled their concern about the Catholic menace as well, by electing Baptist minister Sidney Johnston Catts governor after he vowed to roll back the papist tide. On the campaign trail, the dark horse candidate had deliberately exploited the voters' anti-Catholic fears to outmatch his more experienced opponents. "Nothing in Florida above the Nation's flag," one of Sidney Catts's campaign ads bellowed with patriotic bluster: "As Roman Catholicism puts her allegiance to the pope above the flag, Mr. Catts stands against the invasion of the state of Florida in her politics!" Winning the election by a margin of over nine thousand votes, Catts promptly made good on his campaign promise to pass a law that had been defeated twice before: an act that empowered the state to inspect convents and monasteries without a warrant.[32]

Through these and other sources, Protestants of good will like Edwin and Mary Stephenson had been put on the alert: the Catholics worshiped idols, the messengers warned. They kidnapped young women and children, and enslaved them in their monasteries and convents. They opposed the public school system. Their white nuns ran schools for Negro schoolchildren, which threatened the dominance of the white race. The Knights of Columbus, supposedly a benevolent Catholic fraternal organization, were actually trained soldiers; men who had sworn an oath to wage "a war of extermination and mutilation of all heretics."[33] They were planning to take over the country, it was said. They were storing arsenals of weapons and ammunitions in the basements of their buildings, just waiting for the moment when their foreign leader, the pope, directed the insurrection to begin.[34]

It would thus be hard to overstate the supreme disappointment Edwin and Mary Stephenson must have felt when their daughter, still a child, began to exhibit clear, undeniable signs of being seduced by that hated religion. Despite all they had tried to teach her, their daughter was beguiled by the deceptions of popery! So Edwin warned Ruth that if she continued her childish fantasies about the Catholic Church she would end up getting someone killed.[35]

Despite his warning, Edwin Stephenson discovered Ruth at age twelve sitting and talking with Father James Coyle on the porch of St. Paul's rectory one day, as if her being there was the most natural thing in the world. The sight of his daughter sitting with a Catholic priest in full public view must simply have stunned the man. And James Coyle was not just any priest; he was Birmingham's leading "Romanist." He was the priest who defended the indefensible through his endless letters to the editors of the city's newspapers; editors who, for reasons beyond Stephenson, seemed never to decline to print them. Letters plainly designed to lure the gullible, to ensnare the foolish, and there with him on the porch sat Stephenson's own daughter, not even a teenager, with her fingers just inches from that fire!

Stephenson did not condescend to enter the gated yard of the rectory when he saw his daughter on the porch with Father James Coyle that day. He offered the priest no greeting. He simply barked the child's name from the sidewalk where he stood, enough to cause the girl to scurry off the porch and out to the walk. At age thirty-nine, over six feet tall, he would have towered over her—years later, when the Birmingham newspapers described Ruth, they consistently referred to her as "petite"—and as the Stephensons lived less than a block away, the walk home would not have taken long. But for little Ruth Stephenson each step must have been like torture. She knew her parents' feelings about Father Coyle and the Catholic Church, even if she was inclined to disagree. Her father had said many times that Coyle was "one of humanity's biggest enemies" and that he wished Coyle was dead.[36]

Ruth said later, without elaboration, that her father's punishment was "severe."[37]

———

The proximity of the Stephenson household to St. Paul's Church and its rectory might well have been part of the problem. The Stephenson family lived at 2231 Third Avenue, on the south side of the street. The Catholic Church and the home of its priest sat in the middle of the next block on the north side. So despite her parents' warnings, or perhaps in spite of them, Ruth was able to take stock of the Catholics for herself.[38]

Rather than repulsing her, what she saw of the Catholics simply stoked the embers of her curiosity. There always would have been something to see. Some of the Catholics, especially the women, came to church every day, with their hats, and gloves, and rosary beads, in time for the morning mass. Others came to make confession, or to stand for unimaginable stretches of time before the stations of the cross, reciting in rhythmic repetition, just under their breath, the Lord's Prayer, the Hail Mary, and the Glory Be—the three centerpieces of the Holy Rosary. On occasion, Ruth slipped unnoticed into the church; where she must have been delighted by its dimly lit interior and the hushed, respectful whispers of its visitors. The women's prayers would have been just barely audible to one who had slipped quietly into a pew, lending a balletic warmth to the forbidding tableaux before which they murmured their meditations.[39]

Not all of the Catholics were so daily observant, of course. Most would have come only on Sunday, and judging from the pleas Father Coyle injected into the *Catholic Monthly,* the parish's newspaper, others not even that. But enough of them came often enough to give young Ruth the chance to try to reconcile the reverential faces of St. Paul's parishioners with her parents' vilifications, and what she saw in those faces did not frighten her at all. Ruth later insisted that it had been her ability to see folks coming in and out of St. Paul's Church from her home on Third Avenue that first aroused her curiosity about Catholicism, and being a girl given to independent thinking, she arrived at her own conclusions about them.

So if her parents had given it more thought, they might simply have chosen another avenue on which to set up house and home, and saved themselves a lot of trouble. For in Birmingham, Alabama, there was an unwritten code known to all good people of strong conviction: the firm and universal understanding that familiarity breeds not contempt but *converts.* Who in Birmingham did not know how important it was to keep one's loved ones segregated from the forces that threatened their physical and spiritual well-being?

But Mary and Edwin Stephenson could not conceive of the possibility that their daughter had come to admire the Catholic Church on her own. The persuasion had to have come from an external source. The only explanation was that the Catholics had deliberately seduced their daughter, they thought, for what else could have planted such ideas in her head and poisoned her against her true and noble Protestant roots? After all, everyone knew that that was what Catholics did best.[40]

When nothing of significance changed in the Stephenson household on August 29, 1920, the day Ruth turned eighteen, some part of the teenager must have been devastated. Who could have blamed the girl for seeing something magical in the number? An expectation that the age would confer some additional liberty, some leeway not enjoyed before? The signs of change must have seemed all around her; she was living in an age flush with change. Just eleven days before, the country had ratified the Nineteenth Amendment, giving women the right to vote. Unlike generations of women before her, once she turned twenty-one (the voting age for everyone at the time), Ruth Stephenson would not be denied that fundamental right of citizenship. From the vantage point of a young woman of the 1920s, the world might easily have appeared full of opportunities, regardless of gender. It is therefore entirely possible that Ruth did not fully appreciate how poorly her family would regard her independent spirit, especially when that spirit bumped too hard against the norms they and their kinspeople held most dear. As feminist scholars would later have been able to show Ruth, women in the 1920s might have been enfranchised, but they were hardly liberated.

So if Ruth Stephenson had been tempted to think of the age of eighteen as holding a great number of advantages not previously enjoyed, her disappointment must have been great. In truth, she was anything but emancipated. She was still living in the home of Edwin and Mary Stephenson, and her parents' ideas about the matter over which she wished most to exercise control had not changed from the time she was twelve. If anything, their fears had only deepened with the passage of those years. In their view, the case against the Catholics had actually worsened, a fact they no doubt had hoped that their impressionable daughter would grasp for herself as she matured. For pity's sake, a person needed only to read the *New Menace* (the successor to the *Menace,* based in Branson, Missouri, after the printing plant for its predecessor in Aurora was destroyed by an accidental fire) or the detailed response Dr. O. T. Dozier had published after Father Coyle had challenged the critics of his religion to offer some proof of the charges routinely made against the Catholics. The proof was everywhere one looked, Ruth Stephenson's parents thought. The girl had simply to open her eyes.

The battle for Ruth's soul thus raged more or less quietly inside the Stephenson household for another eight months after her eighteenth birthday, until Ruth decided she would wait no longer. As Easter approached, she found her way to the Convent of Mercy to speak with the sisters about her desire to convert. She had reached the age when the law said she could decide for herself, she told them. *Are you sure you know what you are doing?* they asked her. She was certain, Ruth assured them. So over the next couple of weeks, the nuns provided Ruth with instruction about the Catholic baptism and way of life, and on April 10, 1921, she slipped away from her home and made her way to a small church on Birmingham's south side, a "beautiful red brick building trimmed with white stone"—Our Lady of Sorrows, which had served the needs of the city's German-speaking Catholics since its dedication in 1905; and from whose name the girl might have taken a warning, had she been any less determined about her course.[41]

When Ruth arrived, Aileen Cronan and Mr. Fred Bender were waiting for her. Aileen Cronan and Ruth both worked at the time as sales clerks for Loveman, Joseph & Loeb, the popular downtown department store where Ruth's parents had permitted her to take a job the previous fall. During breaks or quieter moments, the two young women sometimes had the chance to talk, and occasionally their conversations turned to Catholicism, Cronan's religion. Fred Bender was the owner of a furniture store very close to the Stephensons' home on Third Avenue. Ruth had asked Cronan and Bender to witness her conversion and to serve as her godmother and godfather, and they had agreed. So on the appointed day, Ruth stood with her two witnesses before Father John O'Kelly and was baptized a Catholic.[42]

Ruth might have been willing to defy her parent's wishes, but she was not foolish enough to think they would condone her conversion. So she shared her secret with some friends, but otherwise kept the news to herself. The date for her first communion was set for May 10, and in the lead-up to that important event it appears that she practiced her Catholicism in the shadows, out of sight of her parents. In this state of secrecy, it is unclear how often she managed to fulfill the Catholic Church's expectation that she attend weekly mass, or even whether she was able to attend Easter Sunday services on May 1, 1921, at the close of Holy Week. After Ruth had turned fourteen, in an effort to keep her out of the grip of the Catholics, Ruth's parents had agreed to let her join one of the Baptist churches in Birmingham. So they might not have been accustomed to escorting her to church on Sundays. But given her history of defiance, it seems unlikely that Mary and Edwin would have waved their daughter off to the Baptist parish house without somehow verifying that she had actually gotten to where she said she was going.

As May and the date of her First Communion approached, Ruth's day of reckoning could no longer easily be avoided, and in her excitement or worry, she must have shared the news of her conversion with someone less circumspect about the need for secrecy, for somehow her parents got word that their daughter had been baptized a Catholic. They were livid, a friend warned Ruth; her father was threatening "to kill her" when he caught up with her. By age eighteen, Ruth knew better than to take the threat lightly. Her father might wear the garb of the clergy, but he was "no model of Christian forgiveness." He "came from the old school of strictness," one relative of the family told a prominent writer some years later; "the very old school."[43]

Too frightened to face her parents, Ruth caught the bus to Fred Bender's two-story home on Milner Heights Road. Bender had not yet gotten home from work, but his wife, Anna, was there. She invited Ruth to have supper with them and phoned her husband at his downtown store. Miss Ruth Stephenson had stopped over, Anna told him. The news must have come as a surprise; Ruth had never paid a social visit to his home before. Weeks earlier, Bender had witnessed Ruth's baptism and agreed to be her godfather, but the duties of the position were usually nominal when the person baptized was above the age of eighteen, and although he had known Ruth and her family from the neighborhood where he ran his business since she was a young girl, mostly they traveled in different circles. Bender assured his wife he would be home shortly.[44]

The Benders' sense of trepidation must have grown as they listened over dinner to Ruth's fears about returning home. After considering her plight, they urged her to call home and let her parents know she was there. *They will be worried about you,* they told her. And although Fred Bender may not have said so out loud, he must have felt a little knot of anxiety beginning to form on the question of his new goddaughter. With all of the accusations whirling around Birmingham about Catholics kidnapping Protestant children, it would not do for Edwin and Mary Stephenson to think their daughter had been whisked away by some imagined child robber.

It could not have been easy, but after dinner Ruth took the Benders' advice and telephoned home, and when her father got on the line, she told him she knew that he and her mother had learned that she had been baptized a Catholic. She knew they were not happy about it, she said, but she wanted to come home, if he would just promise not to punish her when she got there. It is hard to know what Ruth expected her father to say. Perhaps it was more a hope than an expectation; the hope that he and her mother would accept her decision once they understood the deed was done. But if Ruth entertained such a hope, her father's response quickly disabused her: "I'll fix you when you get home," he vowed through the telephone line. She would get no other promises from him than that.

It is not precisely clear how many days passed before Ruth got up her nerve to return home after that call. Not more than two, according to her recollection; and then she stayed at home, she said, until she could bear things no longer.

It was not long after the girl's departure from their home that Fred Bender began to worry out loud to his wife that Edwin Stephenson was harboring a grudge against him over the incident. It might have been his imagination, but when Fred Bender passed Stephenson on the street a day or so after Ruth returned home, he was sure that Stephenson had refused to meet his eye. Bender told his wife that they had best take care with Edwin Stephenson and his daughter. His agreement to stand up for the girl at her conversion had become messy, even dangerous. Bender wanted nothing more than to put the whole episode behind them.[45]

He had no way of knowing that the trouble over his goddaughter had only just begun. Ruth showed up at the Benders' doorstep again a week or so later.

———

Birmingham's chief of police, Thomas J. Shirley, first learned about Edwin Stephenson's problems with his daughter, he said, sometime in 1920, when Stephenson came to his office at City Hall looking for his help. Ruth had run off, Stephenson told him. She was already eighteen, but unless she married, Alabama law made Edwin and Mary Stephenson her guardians until she turned twenty-one, and her father wanted her back. Somehow, Edwin

Stephenson had discovered that his daughter had fled to Chattanooga, and having no friends on that city's police force, he wanted Chief Shirley to write him "a letter of introduction that would get him the courtesies of the police department up there in catching her."

T. J. Shirley had no qualms about Stephenson's request. "I gave him the letter," he said later, and the Chattanooga Police Department was happy to help out. Stephenson "went up there and brought her back" without any trouble, Shirley said.

It is possible that Shirley's willingness to help Edwin Stephenson went beyond his commitment to the performance of his official police duties. Like Stephenson, Shirley was a member of Birmingham's Robert E. Lee Klavern No. 1—apparently seeing no contradiction between his oath to uphold the city's laws and the oaths the sheeted order demanded as a requisite of its membership. In very little time, T. J. Shirley proved himself such a devoted initiate that the hierarchy-conscious klavern awarded him a seat on its Imperial Council.[46] The police chief was not alone, according to Glenn Feldman, a leading scholar on the Alabama Klan in the 1920s. The rosters of the city's police force and the rolls of the Klan enjoyed considerable overlap. By some estimates, at least half of the police officers in Birmingham were members. A good number of judges and city and county officials had also joined up. Some of the Klan's parades even sported police escorts. As Feldman later put it: "The line between hooded vigilantism and official law enforcement was sometimes a fine one."[47]

Some months after Stephenson hauled his daughter back from Chattanooga, he marched into Shirley's office again, claiming "the Catholics" had got his daughter, and that he needed the police chief's help getting her back. He was sure that the girl was being kept locked up in Fred Bender's house. He had learned the whereabouts of his daughter from a friend, he said, a man named Baskin who worked as a manager for Loveman, Joseph & Loeb, the department store where Ruth worked. Baskin had overheard a store clerk, Aileen Cronan, saying that she had been appointed Ruth's "godmother," and knowing that Ruth had gone missing, Baskin asked her where the girl was. At Fred Bender's house, Cronan had told him.

Fred Bender said later that he had never tried to keep the fact that Ruth was at his home a secret; that he had even sent a woman by the name of Miss Dill to tell Mary Stephenson her daughter was safe at the Benders' home. Edwin and Mary Stephenson knew full well the girl was there and that she had come on her own accord, Bender said. But Stephenson told the police chief that the Catholics were holding his daughter captive, so Shirley sent four of his detectives over to the Benders' to extract her.

It would still have been daylight when Stephenson and the detectives piled into their cars and headed for the Benders' home that day. When they arrived, the doors were locked; if the girl was inside, she was not saying. Two of the detectives drove back to the furniture dealer's store in search of Fred Bender to come and let them in. Before long they were back, with the uneasy Bender in tow. At their direction, he unlocked the door and let the officers in. They found the girl inside, and the detectives handed her over to her father.

Later that night, according to Chief Shirley, Fred Bender approached an officer newly assigned to the Birmingham Police Department and complained that Reverend Edwin Stephenson had his daughter locked up in their house on Seventh Avenue, and was beating her. Bender could hear the girl's screams from outside the house, he said. He asked the officer to arrest Stephenson and "make him turn her out." Later Ruth Stephenson described the horrors Fred Bender had overheard unfolding inside the house: that her father had nailed shut the windows of her room to prevent her escape; that he had lashed her to the bedposts and beat her with a leather razor strap; that her mother had stuffed a rag in her mouth to smother her screams for help.

It could not have been a comfortable moment for the young lawman. Bender's complaint involved a man and his daughter. The rookie officer was unsure of the best way to handle the situation, so he contacted the police chief back at the station. Chief Shirley told the officer that he knew all about the matter. "They weren't punishing the girl, they were [just] keeping her in the house," Shirley said. *Don't worry about Bender's report,* the chief instructed him, *just stay away from the place:* Stephenson had asked some friends to stand guard outside the house that night, thinking the Catholics would try to "come in there and take her away." If anyone tried to take the girl from the Stephenson home that night, they would "meet their Waterloo."[48]

―――――

It is unclear who first suggested the idea to Edwin Stephenson that he have his daughter involuntarily committed to the insane asylum in nearby Tuscaloosa. Perhaps he came to the idea himself, as a great number of other families appear to have done in the closing decades of the nineteenth century and the early decades of the next. After the death of the asylum's first superintendent, Dr. Peter Bryce, in 1892, Alabama legislators changed the institution's name from Alabama Insane Asylum to Alabama Bryce Insane Hospital, and then later simply to Bryce Hospital, in his honor. The treatment method utilized by Dr. Bryce and his staff, developed well before Sigmund Freud's "talking therapies" began to attract American attention in the 1920s, was generally referred to simply as "moral treatment."[49] This method was still in use at Bryce Hospital when Stephenson contemplated sending his daughter there, over her objections.

It was not unusual at the time for patients to be referred to as "inmates," a word that signaled better than most that a patient's resistance to being committed would not necessarily have kept her out of Bryce Hospital. Although by 1921 the state had passed some criteria for involuntary commitments, with the concurrence of two supportive physicians, the deed could be achieved no matter how loudly the admittee protested. "Virtually all of the Hospital's inmates came against their will," one expert wrote. In order to effect such transfers with as little of a scene as possible, some families duped their loved ones into thinking they were just stopping off "to see" Bryce Hospital, ostensibly on the way to somewhere else. Once on the premises, Dr. Bryce would advise the admittee "in the frankest but kindest manner . . . that [her] mind was disturbed through derangement," and that the hospital had the legal authority to confine her. She would have no choice but to stay.[50]

Naturally, the staff was prepared for a protest in such circumstances. The attendants would forcibly separate the patient from all of her possessions, then cart her to a ward of the asylum known simply as the "cross hall." The ward had earned the name from the great number of the patients who, hauled to its rooms, were "at least 'cross,'" wrote one scholar, if not entirely "enraged" by the sudden news that they were to be prisoners. The therapeutic idea behind employing the cross hall as the primary residence for the asylum's newest (and angriest) inmates was to exhaust an admittee's anger in a cell where she could do little harm to herself or others. These rooms were "without chair, stool, or furniture of any description, without water or anything save a mattress on the floor and a box in the corner for necessary purposes," and in them it was expected that the inmate would eventually learn to conform her behavior to the institution's highly disciplined regime.[51]

As for the more stubborn patients, the asylum had other ways of persuading them to adjust their nonconforming behaviors. The "moral treatment" method looked unkindly on the physical restraints and bleeding techniques that had been used so freely in the past, but it was open to the use of pharmaceuticals to control unruly inmates. Doses of hyoscyamine were forcibly injected into the arms of strapped-down, screaming patients through "crude hypodermic syringes" that resembled "a veterinarian's device more than an implement used to inject human beings."[52] If that failed to do the trick, hushed threats of removal to the asylum's infamous "back wards" might do better—the mysterious rooms tucked behind the main building where the most demented of the institution's patients were housed.[53]

By the early 1900s, the Bryce asylum was the largest single building in the state of Alabama. Eventually its overcrowded wards, and an exposé written after the release of an inmate still seething from his involuntary incarceration and treatment there, spurred a formal investigation by the state legislature. In August and September 1907, the testimony of 125 witnesses was taken in three cities in the state, including Birmingham, and two of the city's leading newspapers covered the hearings closely. The hospital was ultimately exonerated, but the tales of mistreatment recounted by former inmates and staff would have stayed in the memories of residents of Birmingham long after the close of the hearings.[54]

So even without the well-meaning advice of friends or family, Stephenson might have thought of the Bryce asylum as a solution to his problems with his daughter on his own, especially when the prospect of changing Ruth's mind about the Catholics by appealing to her common sense seemed particularly remote. Ruth said later that her father had little trouble coming up with affidavits from two physicians to have her sent to Bryce against her will. The two doctors had never examined her, she said. Apparently what they had heard from her father was enough to convince them of her derangement: she persisted in her desire to join the Catholic Church despite her parents' efforts to persuade her otherwise.

The records disclosing the identities of the two physicians no longer exist, but they most certainly would not have been trained in modern psychiatry. In 1921, there were no psychiatrists in the United States, and even the doctors who administered treatment to Bryce Hospital's patients were known simply as "insanity specialists." Instead, the hospital routinely relied on the opinions of family physicians—today's general practitioners—about the need for a patient's commitment.

Although which two of Birmingham's medical professionals were willing to swear to Ruth Stephenson's insanity without the benefit even of examining her remains a secret of history, it is clear that a number of the city's doctors harbored the same suspicions about Catholics as Edwin and Mary Stephenson. Dr. Orion T. Dozier was one example. In early 1917, Dozier wrote, published, and sold (for 25 cents each) thousands of copies of a soft-covered, 160-page booklet addressed directly to Father Coyle. Dozier pulled no punches regarding his views of the despised religion:

> No man who is loyal to the Roman Catholic Church can at the same time be loyal to the government of these United States, and therefore, no member of that Church should be permitted to vote or hold public office under the Stars and Stripes, and no Roman Catholic should be allowed to teach in, or Jesuit permitted to come in touch with, our public schools, to poison and pollute them with their papalistic ideals.[55]

Stephenson would not have had to work very hard to convince a physician disposed to such views that Ruth's attraction to the Catholic Church was a sign of mental illness. Dr. Dozier's son, Bryon Dozier, also a licensed physician, possessed the same animosities as his father. Had he tried, Stephenson might have been able to acquire the signatures of both doctors in support of his daughter's commitment in the course of a single office visit.

After obtaining the affidavits of the physicians that he needed, Stephenson took a trip to the Tuscaloosa asylum to see the place for himself. It can no longer be known what horrors he saw or heard during his visit, but it was enough to make him pause before having his daughter sent there. Her behavior may have infuriated her parents, but she was still their daughter. Stephenson decided to keep the commitment papers in reserve.

––––––

By July 1921, the tension between Ruth and her parents was nearly unbearable. A stream of her parents' friends had visited the home to counsel Ruth about the deep degradations of Catholicism, her daughterly duties, and heeding her parents' guidance. Edwin and Mary had even begun to threaten to arrange a suitable marriage for her, a union with a man who would be certain to return their daughter to her rightful religious path. The realization that there would be no escape from her parents' dominance, no changing their minds on the question of her religious independence, finally sank in. Ruth sent Pedro Gussman a letter. She would marry him, the letter said.

Pedro dropped by the Stephenson house a few days later to make some plans.[56]

––––––

Their plan was simple, and they would share it with no one. They would begin the day just like any other, and avoid any changes in their routines that might arouse suspicion. They would do their best to act naturally: Pedro by reporting to Sherwin Williams, where he picked up his supplies each day, and Ruth by clocking in at Loveman, Joseph & Loeb, where she worked as a salesclerk. They would attend to their duties, slipping away only at lunchtime so no one would wonder why Ruth was away from her station. They would meet outside the store and catch the nearest streetcar to the county's satellite courthouse in nearby Bessemer, fifteen or so miles away. There they would get a marriage license from the probate office, and then hike three city blocks to St. Aloysius, on the corner of Fifth Avenue and Seventeenth Street, a modest wood-frame church that provided mass for a largely Italian congregation. If all went well, Ruth and Pedro could walk the distance from the courthouse to the church in under five minutes, and Father George Callahan, St. Aloysius's residing pastor, would have them married before anyone at Loveman, Joseph & Loeb even noticed that Ruth had failed to return from lunch.[57]

TWO | A Parish to Run

FATHER COYLE FINISHED each day on the swing that hung at the end of the rectory porch, reading or writing and returning the greetings of those who strolled by the gated yard. "Hundreds of persons had grown accustomed to speaking to him as they passed," one parishioner said, so constant was his practice of sitting there. With a Birmingham congregation that had grown to over one thousand, and his additional responsibilities over the entire northern region of the state of Alabama, there was always plenty of work to do. So after he finished his supper each day, he would retire to the porch with his breviary, and his hat, and whatever unfinished work continued to tug at him, and sitting on the swing, he would accomplish what he could.[1]

At some moments of the day, the distractions of the street would have made any work there all but impossible. The rectory faced south onto Third Avenue, which pulsed with life. Private motorcars, electric streetcars, pedestrians, and the ubiquitous jitney jockeyed endlessly for position. By 1921, 70 percent of the city's residents still relied on public transports to get them back and forth, but over twelve thousand were able to afford their own cars. The result was a daily slog through gridlock.

Accidents were common, complicating things further. The early automobiles were ill equipped to avert sudden hazards, leaving their occupants and pedestrians vulnerable to mishap and injury. The city had devoted some resources to the problem, but many of the streets were still in poor condition. And the lack of a system of traffic lights to govern right-of-way created a lethal prescription for collisions, causing one writer for the city's Chamber of Commerce to call the private motorcar Birmingham's "number one menace."[2]

Two massive red-brick buildings flanked the northeast and northwest corners of the busy block. To the rectory's left, on the corner of Third and Twenty-second streets, stood the towering, Gothic-style St. Paul's Catholic Church, its dimensions so majestic that it would soon be declared a cathedral. A thousand people could be seated within, ten times the number the original Catholic parish house had been able to accommodate. Its vaulted ceiling stretched skyward nearly seventy feet beneath peaked arches resting atop ten granite columns that spanned the 140-foot length of the edifice. Along the side walls of the church, an orderly row of stained-glass windows admitted filtered light into its interior, in somber hues of purple, blue, red, orange and gold. Each window featured a different celestial figure or scene: Saint Paul, the church's patron saint; Saint Patrick, the bishop and missionary to Ireland, whence a great many of the parishioners or their ancestors hailed; the Holy Family at Nazareth; the Assumption of the Blessed Mother into Heaven; and more. A last, massive stained-glass window, the largest in the state, hung above the heavy wooden doors at the church's front, ushering light into the choir gallery and cheerily greeting parishioners as they entered. A pair of tall, elegant steeples framed the window on both sides, easily visible over rooftops by passengers stepping down from their trains at the Birmingham Terminal Station on Twenty-sixth Street, four blocks away.[3]

Anchoring the opposite end of the block, at the corner of Third Avenue and Twenty-first Street, loomed the Jefferson County courthouse and jail. In 1889, Father John J. Browne, the first permanent pastor of St. Paul's, had sold the courthouse's lot to the city to defray the costs of building the larger church for his growing congregation, as the number of Catholics in and around Birmingham had exploded after a cadre of new steel plants and coal mines moved into the area with their promise of jobs and prosperity. Romanesque in style, and dwarfing all of the other buildings in Birmingham at the time, the courthouse had as its most outstanding feature a central clock tower, flanked by two large square towers with pyramidal roofs. In addition to its courtrooms, the back of the building was attached to the county jail, a squat, square edifice entirely devoid of adornment. Within the jail, social conventions were observed: until the inmates could be tried, completed their sentences, or in the most unhappy cases, hanged, white prisoners were housed on one end, Negroes on the other. Some of the cells overlooked the back of the rectory and the old Catholic parish house, which Father Patrick O'Reilly (Father Coyle's predecessor) had had converted into a Church Goods Supply House when the new church opened its doors. Between classes, Catholic schoolchildren sometimes played around and behind the two church buildings, and on occasion prisoners would shout unpleasantries at them through open cell windows. If bothered, the children had learned to ignore such taunts. In the early decades of the twentieth century, in Birmingham and elsewhere, even the youngest Catholics knew the value of keeping their heads low.[4]

———

James Coyle was only thirty-one when he first stepped off the train from Mobile, Alabama, in September 1904, onto the platform of the Birmingham Passenger Station on Twentieth Street and Powell Avenue. Plans for the construction of a far grander railroad station along Twenty-sixth Street were already under way, but that terminal would not open for another five years. So newcomers like Coyle had to make do with the more minimal comforts of the "station shed," a vaulting, open-sided structure of steel and wood trusses erected to protect passengers as they climbed onto or descended from the trains. The structure was more functional than pretty, but it provided some shelter from the rain and the sun, no small blessing in a city where temperatures were known sometimes to top one hundred degrees.[5]

At the time of his arrival, many would have taken James Coyle for younger than his thirty-one years. His frame was slender and fit, and still possessed that look of youth. He had lived and worked in Mobile for the last eight years, but his complexion was still fair and uncreased, somehow untaxed by the southern sun. No doubt part of the explanation was that very little of the cleric ever appeared uncovered. In keeping with the custom of the priesthood, he always wore black; not even the buttons on his jackets and vests escaped the somber color; the small strip of white that circled his neck being the only exception. His face was cleanly shaven and his dark hair neatly trimmed, but almost always it, too, was hidden beneath one of the hats so popular with men of the time; in cooler months, a fedora of soft grey felt; in the summer, a breezier top hat of pale yellow straw.

The young priest had a look of confidence and kindness. Faint grooves, barely noticeable, framed his mouth pleasantly, betraying the frequency of his smiles, for he had the wry, quick sense of humor possessed by so many from his homeland of Ireland. His nimble mind and sharp wit were known to work to others' considerable disadvantage, particularly when the subjects of his ire had somehow cast aspersions on his faith. But judging from pictures of the young priest at the time, it was James Coyle's eyes that people would have noticed about the newcomer first. Kind and intelligent eyes, in a shade of blue so impossibly pale that they rivaled the daybreak sky.[6]

Confidence aside, some of the parishioners of St. Paul's probably thought Father Coyle too young, at age thirty-one, to handle the job Bishop Edward

Allen of Mobile had sent him to do in Birmingham in 1904. The bishop had placed on the young priest's shoulders the unenviable task of replacing Father Patrick O'Reilly, the handsome and hugely popular former pastor of St. Paul's. Two months before, Father O'Reilly had suffered a grievous head injury while serving as chaplain for the Alabama National Guard. During a routine review of the troops at the state fairgrounds, something had frightened his horse, and it threw him. The summer-warmed ground was far from its hardest, but he landed badly, and the force of the impact cracked his skull. Horrified onlookers rushed the priest's broken body to St. Vincent's Hospital, which, ironically, O'Reilly had founded himself four years before. He had first proposed building a hospital in Birmingham following one of the city's annual summer bouts with typhoid fever. Unsanitary conditions made epidemics of cholera, diphtheria, typhoid, smallpox, and tuberculosis a perpetual hazard, and when they occurred the fatalities were devastating. Following a particularly distressing episode of typhoid one summer, Father O'Reilly sent a letter to the sisters of the Daughters of Charity at St. Vincent's de Paul in Maryland asking that they come to Birmingham to run a hospital. They considered the request and came. Shortly after the hospital opened its doors, Father O'Reilly announced he would build an orphanage as well, and his reputation in the city as a doer of good deeds was cemented.[7]

A squadron of doctors and nuns at St. Vincent's Hospital ministered tirelessly over their beloved founder, doing all they could to save him, as word spread among the city's Catholics that Father O'Reilly was hurt and in need of their prayers. Perhaps the chorus of supplications that answered that call slowed his exit; for he hovered between life and death for nearly a week. But finally, on July 28, 1904, he died, at the age of forty-nine.[8]

Bishop Allen considered the matter for over a month before asking the thirty-one-year-old Father Coyle to take up Father O'Reilly's post. Like O'Reilly, Coyle hailed from Ireland originally, and many of St. Paul's parishioners had either emigrated from Eire as well or were the offspring of mothers or fathers born there. Father O'Reilly had fared well among these kinspeople in Birmingham, and likely Bishop Allen hoped that Father Coyle would do the same. Bishop Allen had watched over James Coyle and his compatriot Michael Henry from the day they two had arrived in Mobile fresh from their ordinations in Rome when not even twenty-five years old. And over the years Father Coyle had impressed him greatly. The parishioners may not have remembered, but Patrick O'Reilly had also been young when he became St. Paul's second permanent rector, only thirty-three. Father Coyle was just two years younger, and despite his youthful appearance, he was by that point already eight years into his priesthood. Bishop Allen was confident he had chosen well.

───

Owen Coyle and Margaret Durney Coyle had raised a family of a size fairly common for young Catholic couples of their day: six children in all, two boys and four girls. James Edwin was their second son. He was born at home on March 23, 1873, a cold early spring day, in his parents' snug, thatch-roofed cottage in the parish of Drum, Ireland, four miles southwest of Athlone. The entire parish of Drum occupied slightly less than 9,000 acres on the river Shannon in County Roscommon, where its inhabitants did their best to till the generally poor soil and to reclaim the bog, which by some accounts was "considerable." March temperatures in Drum were generally quite bitter, and the parents might have been forgiven had they been tempted to delay the ceremony that would christen the new baby boy into their faith. But James Edwin was baptized within two days of his birth, a hasty bestowal of the first sacrament, and a sign no doubt of his parents' acceptance of the Church's teaching that an unbaptized infant could not attain salvation in the event of untimely death. If James should perish, Margaret and Owen would at least have had the comfort that they had done their parental duty to him.[9] They need not have feared, however, for their baby boy thrived.[10]

With no scarcity of children in the parish of Drum, the Coyle children had many playmates to choose among. From early on, James befriended one in particular, Michael Henry, a boy not a year James's senior. At play, the boys amused themselves with the games that come so easily to the minds of the young, and at the Drumpark National School, their studies proceeded apace under the watchful gaze of James Coyle's father, Owen, the school's headmaster.[11]

All of the schoolchildren at Drumpark were required to take their studies seriously, but none suffered the expectation more keenly than Owen and Margaret Coyle's own six. Owen Coyle had come from a long line of educators. For decades, men in the Coyle family had served as teachers and professors in schools and colleges across Ireland, and Margaret Durney Coyle was the daughter of an academic as well. Her father, Francis Durney, had served as headmaster of the Cornafulla National School when she and her siblings were children. "Naturally," James Coyle wrote many years later, his mother and father expected him "to make a better showing in classes and examinations than the other boys."[12] He did his best not to disappoint them.

If his parents' expectations were a burden during his youth, he reaped the benefits of their close attentions later in life. Under their tutelage, he developed a fervent love of reading and a penchant for writing prose and poetry, a diversion that would bring him both comfort and a measure of influence as an adult. Dickens became a staple; James Coyle read at least one work by the writer each year. For poets, he preferred Shakespeare and Tennyson.

The literary habits James Coyle formed as a youth must have been a great help when he and Michael Henry left Drum at eighteen to attend the Jesuit School of Mungret College of Royal University in Limerick County, where they labored over their books for the next two years.[13] They received their bachelor's degrees in 1893, and then traveled together to the Collegia Americano del Nord in Rome, where they studied theology in preparation for the priesthood. Three years later, on May 26, 1896, at St. John Lateran's Basilica, Cardinal Parrocchi ordained the two men into the priesthood. At the age of 23, continuing to defy separation, Father James Coyle and Father Michael Henry received the news that their futures lay in America. They were to be dispatched to the southern port city of Mobile, Alabama, to serve as missionaries to the state's growing Catholic population. They had only about three months to prepare for the journey and bid their families and homeland goodbye.[14]

The two arrived in Mobile on September 1, 1898, ready to begin their mission work under the watchful supervision of Bishop Edward Allen at the Cathedral of the Immaculate Conception. It took James Coyle very little time to earn his superior's respect. After just three years of mission work, Bishop Allen sent for Coyle and asked him to take on the post of rector, and then director, of the new McGill Institute, a Catholic school for boys in Mobile. With his strong family background in education, the role was custom-made for the young priest, and if left to his own devices, he probably would have opted to stay there. His father had toiled as the principal of the same local school in Drum for forty years; no doubt his son regarded such work as service of the highest order. But the sudden death of Father Patrick O'Reilly in Birmingham and the need for an able replacement caused Bishop Allen to prevail on the young priest again, and James Coyle found himself headed to a new city to head the congregation of St. Paul's in a land he had only just begun to think of as his own.[15]

The parishioners of St. Paul's did their best to welcome their new pastor when he arrived at the Birmingham depot in September 1904, but it was plain they still grieved. And Father Coyle, aware of their anguish, must have wondered more than once what chance any priest would have to win the hearts of the congregation when succeeding such a one as Father Patrick O'Reilly. As he looked into the grief-stricken faces of his parishioners from the pulpit for the first time, he gave voice to their sadness. He remembered out loud the great number of ways Father O'Reilly had served the congregation, their faith, and the city of Birmingham, before turning to the matter of his appointment as their new pastor. He had not come to Birmingham with the expectation that he would take the place of Father O'Reilly in their hearts. "When I received the letter of appointment to the pastorate of this Church," he told them, "my first thought was not one of jubilation at the promotion" or "elation that of the many worthy priests of the diocese, I was deemed worthy by my ecclesiastical superior to assume charge of this congregation and this Church." The task of leading a church such as St. Paul's was not truly performed solely by the one blessed with such an honor, he said, or "I should have begged that shoulders stronger than mine should assume the burden and the care of this parish. But I knew that not unaided was I assuming this charge."[16]

With this humble introduction, the newcomer commenced his job, and for his first several years in the city, it was almost all he could do just to get to know his parishioners and attend to St. Paul's most pressing needs. The church's financial footing seemed a constant concern in those early years, and almost immediately the pastor decided something had to be done to convince the congregation to be more diligent in their payment of their "pew dues"—the rent that was charged at the time for the privilege of sitting in pews preassigned to parishioners for church services. Somehow the matter of collecting pew dues had been permitted to lapse, but St. Paul's substantial financial obligations made the need for their collection acute. One invoice in particular was especially large—the bill for an elaborate white marble altar that Father O'Reilly had commissioned for the new church. The altar was to be dedicated in Father O'Reilly's memory, and Father Coyle was loathe to permit financial worries mar the event, so he pleaded with the congregation to be more punctual with their pew rents.[17]

When the response was underwhelming, and the communicants failed to rush to the rectory with their outstanding pew debts in hand, Father Coyle's parishioners got their first taste of the forcefulness of his displeasure over matters that placed the standing of St. Paul's in jeopardy. After weeks of repeated pleas, and then more weeks of warnings, he finally announced to the parish that he would open the seats of the unpaid pew holders to new tenants. "As ample warning has been given old pew holders to retain their seats if they cared to," he wrote in the *Catholic Monthly,* "the large number who have not [declared their pews and paid their dues] need not be offended to see rent signs on the pews next Sunday."[18]

The threat appeared to have its desired effect. At least for a time, little more needed to be said in the *Catholic Monthly* about delinquent dues.

———

The climate of relative religious tolerance that had existed in the city when Father Coyle first arrived in 1904 noticeably began to dissipate over the next decade, as waves of new immigrants flooded into the country in response to the industrial age's promise of jobs.

In southern cities like Birmingham, this influx of darker-skinned newcomers from southeastern Europe—Italians, Jews, Slavs, and Greeks—triggered the region's "acute color phobias." According to one historian, the immigrant's "in-betweenness" seemed a double threat to the southern Anglo-Saxon. Although generally recognized as non-Negroid, the immigrants' swarthy complexions stood in stark contrast to the paler skin of the region's "native" white stock, and even the fair skin tones of earlier generations of migrants from Germany and Ireland. The very real possibility that interbreeding among these "whites" would occur, caused some to openly worry about the "purity" of the white race. At the same time, the new immigrants seemed to threaten white solidarity as well, as the immigrants lacked a sufficient understanding of "southern traditions and values," and it was feared as a result that they might desire to "relax the pattern of white supremacy" rather than think of themselves as the natural beneficiaries of it.[19]

To make matters worse, by the mid-1910s, as the country began to debate whether to enter the Great War, and demands for absolute "patriotism" and "100-percent Americanism" intensified, nativists seemed to come out of the woodwork. The loyalty of all but the country's "native" population began to be questioned, and old slurs against Catholics—their vows of obeisance to the foreign pope; their plot to "Make America Catholic"—popped up in Sunday sermons, public speeches, and letters to the local papers.

It was against this backdrop of growing ethnic and religious tension that Robert L. Durant, pastor of the First Baptist Church in Pratt City, a Birmingham suburb, mailed out a bulletin in March 1916 inviting the city's residents to a sermon he would deliver the following Sunday. His topic would be "Romanism vs. Americanism," Durant's flyer announced—not "Catholicism versus Protestantism" or even "Catholicism versus Christianity" (for some critics of the papists insisted that their creed was not even Christian), but "Romanism vs. Americanism"—signaling that Durant intended to address why Catholics were un-American. Birmingham positively buzzed with anticipation. To ensure a full house, Durant sent a follow-up letter to the *Birmingham Age-Herald,* extending an open invitation to anyone who cared to attend the sermon, but the paper declined to publish it on the ground of a standing policy against unpaid advertisements. Durant was indignant, certain that the *Age-Herald*'s refusal to print his invitation had more to do with the Catholics' success in inhibiting a free and open press than any evenhanded policy.

If fear of a low turnout played a part in Durant's annoyance, he needn't have worried. When the appointed day arrived, a reporter for the *Age-Herald* got to the church early, determined to secure a seat. He found the chapel filled to the rafters—its "largest gathering in months," he wrote later—and not just with its own congregants; a full third of the audience had come from other houses of worship to hear what Durant had to say. The newsman scribbled furiously, determined to record as many of the minister's words as he could, and the *Age-Herald* published a two-page spread about the sermon the next morning based on what he heard.

It was not unusual at the time for men like Tom Watson of Georgia and Sidney Catts of Florida to toss around inflammatory words like "Romanism" or "papism" in denigration of the Catholics' reverence for their Roman pope. But men of the ministry—like Robert Durant—might have been expected to do better, out of professional courtesy, if not doctrinal respect. Yet Durant sprinkled the word "Romanism" lavishly throughout his talk, pounding two principal themes: the suspicion that the Roman Catholic Church intended to dominate not only the nation's religious traditions but its political ones as well, and a sizzling Protestant resentment of the insulting way the Catholics regarded the religious beliefs of other faiths. *Romanism* taught that men were not free to embrace religions outside of Catholicism, Durant fulminated from the pulpit, whereas *Americanism* insisted that men could worship God (or not) according to the dictates of their own consciences. *Romanism* labeled non-Catholics as heretics, he said, and treated marriages performed by Protestant ministers as not worthy of recognition, whereas *Americanism* recognized all lawfully consecrated unions whether performed in front of a Romanist altar or not. *Romanism* sought to stifle free press and to make newspapers like the *Age-Herald* an arm of the church, Durant said pointedly, while *Americanism* ensured an unfettered press.

Protestants loyal to the country had better wake up, the pastor solemnly warned them, or they would soon find themselves strangers in their own homeland. The Catholic Church was aggressively pursuing its goal to "Make America Catholic." The signs of its imperialism were everywhere: it was training an army of soldiers, the so-called Knights of Columbus. It was stockpiling arms. It was currying favor with President Woodrow Wilson—a full "70 percent of Mr. Wilson's appointments have been to Catholics!" Durant claimed—all determined to undermine the sacred traditions of Baptists, Methodists, and Presbyterians. Every Sunday they defiled "the Christian Sabbath" with their golf-playing, and moviegoing, and drinking! It was time to awake.

As Durant's audience filed out of his church, his cautionary message probably still rang in their ears: Catholicism was not simply an alien religion in their midst, it was a danger to the nation's very security; it was time for patriotic Americans to take defensive action. The Catholics had "already got a big piece of the pie," Durant had said, "and while they have not the supreme authority here yet, they may get it if we don't fight against it." The only way to stem the tide was "true, red-blooded Americanism!"[20]

Durant must have known that his words would offend the Catholics of Birmingham when they read about his sermon in the next day's morning paper. There was nothing particularly subtle about his message. But he offered no olive branch to his Catholic brothers. There would have been no warrant for such niceties, by his way of thinking—he was a patriot, not a religious bigot. Men were not "anti-Catholic" simply because they were "pro-American," men like Robert Durant were known to say at the time. They were the conscience of a nation; the front line of its defense; and men who were "100 percent American" owed apologies to no one. Bigotry had nothing to do with it.

Father James Coyle thought that Catholics tolerated the brand of patriotic logic dished out by folks like Reverend Robert Durant far too quietly, and every now and then, when the pressure caused by sermons like Durant's became too much to bear, Coyle would let his parishioners hear his true feelings on the matter. Just a few weeks before Durant's diatribe in Pratt City, Father Coyle had exhorted his own congregation at St. Paul's "not to be sheep" in the face of attacks on their faith. "Preparedness is essential," the priest told them. Not "preparedness" in the way Catholics' critics flung about the word, he said. Not the type of preparedness of which Catholics were so often accused—the supposed stashes of weapons in church basements or the training of the Knights of Columbus as the pope's alleged foot soldiers—but rather preparedness in the sense of being watchful for signs of religious bigotry, and being ready to stand up bravely against such assaults when they occurred.

Many of the parishioners of St. Paul's shrank from the idea of such resistance, and probably Father Coyle read their apprehension on their faces as they listened to his words. There was no dishonor in the type of preparedness he was prescribing, he reassured them. Just as the nation had been forced to prepare itself for the possibility of war, he said, so, too, Catholics needed to prepare themselves for the "new spirit [that was] entering American life and thought"—the spirit that slandered a man's patriotism on the sole basis of his religion; the spirit that called Catholics enemies of the flag and tools of the pope. Catholics made a mistake when they stood silent in the face of such assaults. Secret societies had been formed with the express purpose of boycotting Catholic businesses and driving Catholics from positions of trust and authority, and for "too long have we put up with [these] studied affronts."

Contrary to the claims of its critics, "the Church was not a political machine, but an institution founded by Christ to save men's souls," but when we Catholics are assailed as unfit purely because of our religion, he exhorted them, we *must* protest, or "we are mere jellyfish, unworthy of the name of men."[21]

By 1916, the parishioners of St. Paul's were accustomed to their priest's fiery defiance. Since his arrival thirteen years before, Father Coyle had become the Catholic community's most visible spokesman. Newsmen filled their columns with descriptions of his sermons, and Coyle himself, with his literary flair, was given to writing long letters to the local papers explaining the actual tenets of Catholicism whenever false claims about the faith were made, which in the 1910s was often. But much as the St. Paul's congregation admired its priest's bravery, many (perhaps even most) of his parishioners preferred simply to let the insults against themselves and their faith pass by without answer. It just seemed the safer course—the Catholics of Birmingham being so greatly outnumbered. The Catholics in and around the city exceeded ten thousand by 1916, but in relative terms they still only comprised a meager 10 percent of the city's churchgoers. So while they agreed with what their pastor said that Sunday about the new spirit infecting America, many remained doubtful about the wisdom of calling more attention to themselves at such a time. Some even wished their pastor would speak a littler more quietly, too.

But as he had once written about himself, James Coyle came from a "race of fighters." Owen and Margaret Coyle had raised their son to defend what he believed was right, just as both branches of his lineage had done in their uncompromising opposition to English rule over Ireland. The battle for Irish home rule had been mother's milk to both the Coyle and Durney clans—men from both his father's and mother's families had joined in nearly every major effort to overthrow English rule at the risk of their lives. During the insurrection of 1798, the two families had backed the patriots who rose in rebellion against the English, though the odds of their success were paltry. And when England crushed the insurrection, seized the lands of the families, and hung two of James Coyle's great-great-great-uncles, the brutality of the defeat only seared the spirit of opposition even deeper into the Coyle bloodline, so that each succeeding generation passed to the next the sense of duty to fight for right.[22]

There was little reason to think that James Coyle would be any less fierce when it came to defending his faith and its people in the service of his God. We must fight, he told his congregation, to be worthy of the name of men.

It could not have been easy for men like Father Coyle, after years of rigorous theological study, to watch his faith slandered so effectively by men very often lucky to have graduated from high school. Unlike the Catholic,

Episcopalian, and Presbyterian churches, which generally demanded both a college degree and successful completion of a course of study at a seminary for ordination into the clergy, many Baptists and Methodists at the time doubted that years of formal religious study conferred any special competence within the ministry. Formal schooling was seldom demanded for ordination into the Baptist and Methodist ministries; the qualification most esteemed was rather "a call from God."[23] On occasion, a demand would be heard for steeper academic credentials—the churches were inviting derision on themselves, some argued—but the greater weight of opinion, at the end of the nineteenth century and the beginning of the next, was to the contrary. As one defender of the antidiploma forces put it: "Whenever the day comes that the Methodist Church requires a college course as conditional to admittance to the traveling [ministry], that day will sound the death-knell of the Church."[24]

On such reasoning, the M.E.C., South asked only three things before bequeathing "provisional" ministerial status on would-be preachers like Edwin Stephenson: that they be "familiar with the Bible," that they be acquainted with two sermons written by John Wesley, the religion's founder, and that they be associated in one way or another with "the ordinary branches of an English education." The provisional preachers could then win full ordination privileges four years later simply by satisfactorily completing a correspondence course.[25] By the late 1920s, only four out of every one hundred members of the clergy of the M.E.C., South had spent time in a seminary, only 11 percent had finished college, and a full one-third had terminated their education after grade school.[26] As put by one critic of the church's slim commitment to intellectualism: the "itinerant ranks" of the Methodist ministry were littered with roving preachers who could neither "write a complex sentence, [n]or understand it when written."[27]

As for that elite sliver of the Baptist and Methodist clergy who could boast of diplomas, it was not always clear whether their academic achievement was a benefit or a curse. Although higher education was not a prerequisite at the time, both denominations sponsored theological seminaries—the Methodists had Vanderbilt University in Nashville, and the Baptists supported the Southern Baptist Theological Seminary in Louisville, Kentucky—but the educators who oversaw the issuance of the diplomas at them so regularly tripped over their own credentials that some wondered if they did their pupils more harm than good. Alexander Winchell, a special lecturer at Vanderbilt with an advanced degree in geology, ran into trouble of this sort in 1878 when he wrote a book suggesting that men might actually have existed before Adam, contradicting the creation story in Genesis.[28] Displeased by the heresy, Vanderbilt "discreetly asked for his resignation," and when Winchell stood firm on the claim of academic freedom, the Board of Trustees devised a reason to cancel his lectureship anyway and tossed him out on his ear.[29]

The president of the Baptist Theological Seminary, William H. Whitsitt, likewise became embroiled in a controversy when he wrote a book that challenged a powerful orthodoxy of the church, claiming there was historical evidence that some early Baptist leaders had baptized their communicants by sprinkling rather than by full immersion.[30] Sprinkling, like the Catholics! It was an article of faith that Baptist congregations had participated in an unbroken practice of immersion from the time John the Baptist had submerged the Savior beneath the surface of the River Jordan. An editor of the *Memphis Baptist,* James R. Graves, howled in protest: "We do not want [such]...infidelity taught to our young ministers." For a time, Whittsitt survived the brouhaha, though the seminary's board decided it would be prudent to install a special committee to watch over the school under his leadership, and eventually he was moved to tender his letter of resignation.[31]

To those who resisted the necessity of academic credentials among the clergy, the cause of the problems suffered by educators like Winchell and Whitsitt was obvious; sometimes educational instruction aroused an insouciant openness to biblical *investigation;* an irksome tendency to question things that should have defied all questioning. Communicants looking "to the pulpit for spiritual guidance want[ed] the authoritative statement of infallible truth," a group of M.E.C., South bishops stated in 1906, "not the methods of critical research or the varied phases of theological inquiry."[32] Far better was the approach taken by less well educated preachers more accepting of biblical authoritativeness—"men whose hearts were hot with love to God," one wrote—those "earnest," "extempor[aneous] preachers,"—men like Robert L. Durant, perhaps—whose unquestioning mien and unbending certitude, like "steel against flint," made "sparks fly in all directions."[33]

When Father Coyle read the coverage of Durant's sermon "Americanism v. Romanism" in the *Age-Herald* in March 1916, he could not resist penning a letter to the editor that dripped with sarcasm and openly mocked Durant's message, taking a swipe at his poor grammar along the way. Reverend Durant had "wanted to deliver [his sermon] 'real bad' (*sic*)," Coyle quoted, and "[h]aving gotten it out of his system, let me...express the hope that now he feels...let us say, 'real good.'" Father Coyle wrote that he had been unaware until the Baptist minister had informed him by his sermon that the Catholic Church "was so intimately wound into affairs of state." And how strange, Coyle wrote, that despite being a dues-paying "charter member of the Knights of Columbus council," he had "not yet been supplied with [the] Krag rifle" that Reverend Durant insisted was standard issue. He would make sure to have the oversight remedied at the council's next meeting, Coyle quipped, and demand an explanation for why he had been denied "all of the knightly equipment."[34]

But then, as if aware that some readers of the *Age-Herald* might be persuaded by Durant's accusations and offended by his lighthearted tone, Father Coyle's letter turned serious, continuing on to explain that the Baptist minister was mistaken about the Catholic Church's view of marriages secured elsewhere. On the question of the legitimacy of the marriages of non-Catholics, the Catholic Church "presumes that all such marriages are lawful," Coyle wrote; such marriages "not being her business she does not pass judgment." Only Catholics were expected to abide by the Church's rules. "The Catholic church legislates for her own subjects solely," he wrote, like the rule that Catholics be wed only by the Church's own priests. But from Durant's accusation that Catholics wished to make "America Catholic," Coyle did not flinch. It was true, he admitted, but not in the way Reverend Durant was suggesting. The wish was no different, he imagined, from the wish held by members of any other faith. "Every true Catholic would gladly see his fellow man live holily and die happily with the hope of a glorious resurrection," Coyle conceded, but "[m]ust not every true Baptist who believes that his faith possesses wonderful spiritual help for life and death wish America Baptist? Must not every Methodist wish it Methodist, and every Presbyterian, Presbyterian?...If they sincerely profess and practice their belief they most assuredly do."

It probably was no surprise to the Catholic community in Birmingham that a good number of the subscribers of the *Age-Herald* who read James Coyle's letter that day were not at all satisfied by the priest's reassurances, nor pleased by the decision of the newspaper to continue to give him a platform from which to pontificate. Reverend Durant had complained earlier that it was the *Age-Herald*'s decision not to print one of his earlier letters about the Catholics that had spurred his decision to print and distribute the bulletin that advertised his sermon. After seeing Coyle's letter, one outraged reader in Tuscaloosa, Mr. L. E. Brice, took Durant's side, chiding the paper for publishing Coyle's letter but not Durant's: "The manner in which you willingly allow a Catholic priest to attack a Protestant minister through the columns of your paper...makes me know that your paper is owned and controlled by a bunch of Catholics," Brice railed. "You can discontinue my subscription at once."[35] Soon flooded by a wave of like correspondence, the *Age-Herald* replied in its own defense that its policy was to print letters to the editor as space permitted—"the views of all sides alike"—provided the sentiments of the writers "were expressed in parliamentary language and signed by responsible persons." But the paper said it had "no patience with any set of narrow-minded people of whatever denomination or creed who accuse a newspaper of being controlled by one church because it gives that church the same fair treatment it accords to others." And as if to prove its evenhandedness, the next day the paper printed a letter from Durant himself, who, despite the two-page article the *Age-Herald* had devoted to his sermon, accused the paper of giving his talk only a "partial report," and went on to renew his assault on the Catholic Church and to decry the utter inadequacies of Father Coyle's response to the charges he had made in his sermon.[36]

By 1916, this type of back-and-forth between Coyle and critics of his faith had become a familiar pattern. Every time that the priest wrote a letter to one of the local papers to correct some perceived misstatement or outright slur, for days afterward the papers would be besieged by irate letters in response, demanding equal time, and more often than not repeating the accusations leveled against the Catholics in the first place.

Somewhere around this time, Father Coyle began to feel some pressure to make his defenses of this congregation and religion less public. For a time his letters slowed, and when they came at all, they were shorter and milder in tone; when he felt compelled to defend his faith, he was as apt to do it by pointing to the remarks of other well-regarded Catholic or non-Catholic leaders rather than by putting himself on the front-line.[37] It may be that Bishop Allen of Mobile had something to do with quieting the priest. The bishop had a good number of sources in the city who kept him posted on the upsurge in the anti-Catholic rhetoric occurring in Birmingham. It is reasonable to think that he would have counseled Father Coyle against fanning the flames any more than necessary.

But maintaining such reserve became all but impossible for James Coyle toward the end of 1916, after an obscure but overtly anti-Catholic candidate Sidney Catts was elected governor of Florida over a slate of more prominent opponents with long-standing roots in the state. Still celebrating his success, Catts, an Alabama native, traveled back to Birmingham to visit some family members before picking up the gubernatorial reins, and the city all but gave him a hero's welcome. When Dr. O. T. Dozier learned that the governor-elect of Florida was in the city, he invited him to speak about his campaign experiences. Catts happily accepted. On the evening of December 13, 1916, before a standing-room-only crowd at Cable Hall, Catts lugged his "massive frame" back and forth across the stage and gloated about his win. No one in Florida had given him a chance, Catts crowed. Compared to his opponents, he had been a relative newcomer to Florida. He had never held public office there, while each of his challengers had; he had only left Alabama to become a preacher in DeFuniak Springs, Florida, six years before. With no machine to back him or war chest to fund his campaign, his opponents' response to his announced candidacy had been more amused than fearful.

"But they failed to reckon with the Guardians of Liberty, and the prohibitionists!" Catts told the appreciative gallery. They failed to understand the determination of those opposed to the stranglehold that the Roman Catholics had exerted over the state, he said, despite constituting only one-fifth of its population.[38]

Running for office hadn't always been his plan, Catts told them. He had heard the voice of God one night telling him to enter the race, but had lain awake, uncertain, until he found the courage he needed from the warnings provided by the nation's "greatest leader of our cause of Americanism, Tom Watson!" The audience roared at the mention of Watson's name, and "for several moments" Catts could not be heard as applause filled the chamber. When a semblance of order returned, Catts continued: "I felt as if God was on my side and that he was giving me eloquence and ability so that I might win." Something told him to avoid the cities that were sapping most of his opponents' time; to speak to plain folk instead—in the churches and schoolhouses that dotted the state's countryside, where the menace of the Roman Catholic Church was better understood. And on Election Day he had stunned them all.

Catts's listeners could not get enough. His hour-and-a-half-long talk had itself been preceded by a full hour of introductory speeches by Orion T. Dozier and Dr. A. J. Dickinson, but the delighted assemblage "called for more," a local reporter wrote the next day. When the orator finally brought the lecture to a close, the time must have seemed right to cash in on the successful event's returns. "A meeting of the Ku Klux Klan was called to follow immediately after adjournment," reported the *Age-Herald*.[39]

A man's patience can be tested too many times, and the "double report" of Catts's lectures that the *Age-Herald* published the next day proved too much for Father Coyle to bear in silence. He dashed off a letter to the editor protesting the lavish coverage the paper had given the politician's harangue. There were those among the *Age-Herald*'s readership who would be amazed by the paper's decision "to give such undue prominence to...stuff that has heretofore found place and space only in the malodorous gutter press of Georgia and Missouri," Coyle wrote icily in plain allusion to Tom Watson's *Jeffersonian* and Wilbur Phelps's *Menace*. It is hard to think that the editors of the *Age-Herald* could have been happy to be compared to these well-known anti-Catholic sheets. But maybe they consoled themselves with the thought that if their paper had angered both Father Coyle and the friends of Reverend Durant, it had to be doing something right.

Under the pressure of Catts's speech and his audience's feverish reaction at Cable Hall, something in Father Coyle finally seemed to snap. It was high time for the hatemongers like Catts and Durant to "put up or shut up," Coyle wrote heatedly.[40] A national Catholic publication, the *Sunday Visitor,* had deposited $1,000 into an account in the First National Bank of Huntington, Indiana, and issued a challenge agreeing to pay the full amount to any person able to produce hard evidence that substantiated all *or even any* of the thirteen charges most commonly lodged against the Catholic Church, which Father Coyle then listed one by one in turn.[41]

A thousand dollars!—to most people in 1921, the sum would have been enormous.

Orion T. Dozier considered the priest's challenge for less than a day before deciding to accept it. "[I]nasmuch as I feel that I was possibly the one most responsible for the meeting that called forth the challenge," Dozier replied in his own letter to the *Age-Herald* the next day, "I do now accept," though not "with any expectation of receiving the $1,000," he added. Compensation was entirely unnecessary—he would do it for "the sole purpose of discharging an American's patriotic duty to his God, home and country," Dozier wrote, and he thanked James Coyle for furnishing him the "excuse" to do it.[42]

Dozier delivered on his promise with impressive rapidity, publishing in early 1917 his 160-page soft covered booklet, addressed directly to his antagonist: "Response of Doctor O.T. Dozier to Priest James E. Coyle, Pastor, St. Paul's Roman Catholic Church," read its title. Its contents purported to lay out a great number of proofs of the disloyalty of Catholics to the country— the pope's plan for a takeover, the immorality running rampant in monasteries and convents, the means by which girls were forced into the "Sisterhood" and kept in it against their will, and more. The work of a great number of "brave American patriots" who had already given thought to the Catholic question had facilitated the speed of his response, Dozier wrote, naming Tom Watson and Augustus E. Barnett among them.[43] He had scarcely finished his letter accepting James Coyle's challenge, he wrote, before countless strangers had flooded him with materials they thought he might use to make his case. They "deluged me with a perfect Niagara torrent of anti-Catholic literature. . . . I have, in fact, been so completely overwhelmed with such data that I have found it utterly impossible to use more than a very small part of the material contributed by them."[44]

The opus Dozier proudly created with such help was what one might fairly have predicted: a regurgitation of the usual slurs, grounded on "proofs" supplied by the usual sources. A bill of particulars capable of convincing only those already convinced; enough to satisfy Orion Dozier and his ilk that Coyle's challenge had been ably met, perhaps, but few more. And even Dozier seemed to understand that the target of his publication would not likely share his own estimation of the work: "Whether or not I am entitled to the thousand dollars so generously offered in Mr. Coyle's challenge," he wrote, "I leave to him to decide."[45]

If payment was ever made, there is no record of it.[46]

James Coyle tried to keep Bishop Allen in Mobile abreast of the growing anti-Catholic hostilities in Birmingham. Over the years, he sent the bishop letters and clippings from the local papers that painted a picture of a community increasingly under siege. At times, the priest's letters had the feel of a man swimming upstream, as when, three days after Orion T. Dozier accepted the challenge issued by the *Sunday Visitor,* the local paper denied Father Coyle the chance to have the last word:

> Dec., 1916
> Rt. Rev. and dear Bishop,
>
> ...We are presently in an anti-Catholic atmosphere here. The T.A.'s [True Americans] and the G.O.L.'s [Guardians of Liberty] are stirring up trouble and harassing everyone who is a Catholic, or has anything to do with Catholics. Even the Press seems tainted and unfair. The *Age Herald* wouldn't publish a reply of mine to Dr. Dozier's late letter, though indeed it hardly called for a reply. I expect the town will soon be flooded with all sorts of nasty literature....
>
> I am, Rgt. Rev. and dear Bishop, yours sincerely in Deo,
>
> James E. Coyle

Not long after, one of Birmingham's most active and influential Catholics, Sterling Wood, wrote Bishop Allen asking for his help in convincing Father Coyle of the need for greater discretion when it came to responding to the Catholics' detractors. Publicly upbraiding religious bigots only made matters worse, Wood thought, as the widely publicized answer Dozier had recently given to Father Coyle's challenge seemed plainly to establish. Dozier had been delighted by Father Coyle's offer, using it as an excuse to publish a virulent tract that simply rehashed the anti-Catholics' favorite harangues against the church, Wood wrote. The more prudent course was not to rise to their bait to begin with.[47]

In his own letter to Bishop Allen around the same time, Father Coyle acknowledged that he might have made a mistake in providing a platform for Dozier's onslaught. After reflecting on the advice of Wood (who had shared a copy of his letter to the bishop with him, Father Coyle wrote), he had been persuaded to hold his fire—after the *Age-Herald* only that week had published another letter from Durant, this one criticizing a statement that Henry M. Edmonds, pastor of Birmingham's Independent Presbyterian church, had submitted to the *Age-Herald* pleading for greater religious tolerance in the city.

Over the years, James Coyle and Henry Edmonds had become friends, and from time to time the Presbyterian minister spoke up in a Sunday sermon or a letter to one of the local papers about his concern over the oppressive anti-Catholic atmosphere existing in Birmingham. Shortly after the release of Dozier's highly publicized response to Father Coyle, Edmonds had sent a statement to the *Age-Herald* challenging the untruths routinely circulated about the Catholics: "In our dealings with the Roman Catholic Church, I fear that some of us have gone beyond rightful criticism and have ascribed views [to the church] not really held and accused of actions not really committed." There was a danger, Edmonds said, when one began to "leap over all questions of evidence" to "straightway begin persecuting Catholics as if these things were proven." For his part, Edmonds concluded, "I consider intolerance of Roman Catholicism not only un-American but un-Christian."[48]

Edmonds had named no names, but it could have been no surprise when Durant took offense at Edmonds's insinuations. The criticism of Catholics was not owing to their religious beliefs, Durant angrily answered Edmonds in his own letter to the *Age-Herald*—they could worship any way they pleased "so long as their practice does not interfere with the rights of others." The real question that "apologists for the Roman hierarchy" like Edmonds failed to address was whether the Catholics were intent on "usurping the functions of civil government in this country." And on that score, Edmonds knew full well that "the record of the Roman Catholic Church [was] most unsavory." The patriotism of those who insisted "upon America for Americans," Durant seethed, should not be questioned by the likes of Henry Edmonds.[49]

It could not have been easy for Father Coyle to let Durant's assault on his friend pass without a public defense. But in his letter to Bishop Allen, Father Coyle informed his superior that he had stayed his hand. But he also made clear to the bishop that he had not yet given up hope that Catholics would one day defend themselves when confronted with hatred and injustice on account of their faith:

Feb., 1917
Rt. Rev. and dear Bishop,

....The anti-Catholic spirit is still with us. It is quiescent just now but there is liable to be an ebullition any moment. I realize that

I was guilty of bad judgment in noticing that old quack Dozier against the advice of Sterling Wood who . . . sent me a copy of his letter to you. For that reason I didn't want to be guilty of a second one by noticing Durant's latest in reply to Dr. Edmond's sermonette. I was glad you sent him (Edmonds) the note you did. . . . This persecution will, I hope, give Catholics up here some backbone. . . .
I am, Rt. Rev. and dear Bishop,

Yours sincerely in Deo,
James E. Coyle

If Bishop Allen and Sterling Wood had hoped to convince the son of Irish freedom fighters that a posture of passivity in the face of aggression was the wisest course, it seemed they yet had some work to do. At age forty-four, Father James Coyle may have been chastened, but he was not cowed.

By August 1921, some of Coyle's parishioners likely worried about the openness of their pastor's habit of ending each day on the swing on the rectory porch. It was no secret that threats had been made on the priest's life. Just eight months before, a reporter for the *Nation* had written about them. No one seemed to know precisely who had made the threats. But authorities in Washington, D.C., had taken them seriously enough to send word about them to Bishop Edward Allen in Mobile. Federal agents had learned of a plot to kill Father James Coyle, they told the bishop. There was also talk of burning his Birmingham church to the ground. It was best to take precautions.[50]

In the early decades of the 1900s, such threats were often followed through. On December 9, 1917, in Pratt City, not far from where Durant had given his sermon "Romanism v. Americanism," St. Catherine of Siena Church and its adjacent one-room school for Catholic children had been destroyed by fire. Built on "Irish Hill," St. Catherine's had been the second Catholic church erected in the Birmingham area. It had held masses primarily for the miners who worked Pratt Mine No. 1, and their families. The day after the fire, the local press reported the cause as a faulty furnace, but many believed that night riders of the Ku Klux Klan were responsible. In the realm of small blessings, the fire had raged in the middle of the night, so no one was hurt. But by the time the flames were extinguished, both buildings were completely consumed, and the Catholics in the area could not have failed to get the message.[51]

As the invisible empire increased its rolls, public appearances by Klansmen in Birmingham became more and more commonplace. On "a cold, wet January evening in 1921," at the state fairgrounds in downtown Birmingham, one thousand Klansmen participated in the Klan's first publicly witnessed initiation ceremony, scheduled to coincide with the fifty-fourth anniversary of the initiation of General Nathan Bedford Forrest, the first imperial wizard of the Klan of Reconstruction days. A group of newsmen were permitted to witness the proceedings from atop a building inside the fairgrounds, where white-robed Klansmen grasping fiery torches formed a blazing, living cross. A column of initiates "four abreast" approached a throne placed at the foot of the pulsating cross, the reporters later recounted, where the Klan's imperial wizard William Simmons sat waiting in a robe of brilliant purple, the "sole relieving note in the monotony of white." By the end of the night, more than five hundred men had sworn the Klan's eternal vow of loyalty. The ceremony was held publicly, its organizers later stressed to the newsmen, not for the praise that flowed from the successful event but simply to remind Birmingham that the Klan was there. "That they were here yesterday, and that they will be here forever."[52]

Alabama Klansmen stepped up their activities during the spring of 1921, urging residents to boycott Catholic-owned businesses, and pressuring employers to fire or refuse to hire Catholic workers. Placards appeared in windows across the city reminding white Anglo-Saxon Protestants to "TWK," or Trade with the Klan, a slogan the Birmingham klaverns later chose for the masthead of their monthly publication.

Resistance to such messages was risky, as one Catholic professional learned the hard way. In April 1921, a group of Klansmen in nearby Talladega County seized longtime resident Pearce H. DeBardeleben, a successful Catholic druggist. They hauled him to a secluded spot in the woods, stripped off his clothes, tied him to a tree, and beat him to "a bloody pulp," breaking his jaw and knocking out most of his teeth. During the attack, the hooded terrorists demanded that DeBardeleben give up his business and get out of town, but he had long-standing roots in Alabama and refused to be scared off. When the Talladega County solicitor brought no charges against the men DeBardeleben believed to be responsible, he hired an attorney of his own to sue the local klavern, arguing that the attack was part of its plan to rid the area of all Catholics and Jews. The suit failed miserably, and DeBardeleben never collected a cent. Some years later, DeBardeleben's own lawyer swore the Klan's eternal vow of membership and became one of its most respected strategists.[53]

A month after the attack on DeBardeleben, members of the Birmingham klaverns took to the streets once again, parading on Flag Day, 1921, from downtown Birmingham to the steel centers of Ensley and Bessemer. Their identities firmly concealed under peaked white hoods, the Klansmen spilled out of their car windows, steering a line of motorcars that stretched many miles long.[54] A reporter of the *Birmingham Post* estimated that "about 60 cars carrying over 250 robed and masked figures, preceded by several motorcycle scouts, silently threaded [through] the business district" before moving off toward Ensley. Even as the Klansmen themselves remained mute, the signs they hung from their cars broadcast the aims of the hooded brotherhood with perfect clarity. "White Supremacy," "dominance of the American flag," and "protection to womanhood," the placards read. A final sign touted the merits of a pro-Klan film playing in a downtown theater, *The Face at the Window,* and according to the reporter for the *Post,* when the parade ended, throngs "flocked from the curb to the picture show" to see it. Afterward, the moviegoers were met by speakers for the Klan who used the film with great success to recruit new members. The speakers praised the Klan's emphasis an unqualified allegiance to the United States, the flag, and the Constitution, and its pursuit of members dedicated to "100 percent Americanism." New members were welcome, the recruiters said, so long as one was white, native born, and a "Christian gentile without foreign allegiance." Negroes, Catholics, Jews, and immigrants, in other words, needn't bother to apply.[55]

The Klan was not the only candidate for suspicion of being the source of the death threats against Father Coyle. After World War I, people had rushed to join a host of "patriotic" societies that virtually pledged "to distrust anything and everything foreign." Postwar America was no time for moderation in one's patriotism. Drys, anti-Darwinists, self-appointed defenders of the moral order, haters of Negroes, Catholics, and Jews found in the American flag the perfect tool to achieve their goals: they "wrapped themselves in Old Glory and the mantle of the Founding fathers" and demanded from their neighbors unflagging patriotism, "100 percent Americanism." To the nativists, "intolerance became an American ideal," and vigilantism seemed a natural way to defend the nation from its enemies.[56]

In Birmingham, members of a secret political organization fitting this description referred to themselves simply as the "True Americans." Like the nativist Know-Nothings of the 1850s, the True Americans were trained to deny, or at least avoid confirming, the existence of their organization. But stealth had its drawbacks. To win new recruits and attract the attention of city officials in order to influence their policy-making, people had to be aware of the group and to fear crossing its members. So for all of their talk of furtiveness, the True Americans were in fact the best-unkept secret in town. There appeared no real question in anyone's mind that the organization was active in the city, or even who headed it. Its reputed leader was Dr. A. J. Dickinson, pastor of Birmingham's First Baptist Church.

In 1917, the True Americans endorsed the candidacy of Dr. Nathaniel A. Barrett for City Commission president, over the incumbent, George Ward. Ward had angered the city's moralists when he refused to join their crusade against Sunday movies, one of the many corrupting forces that Dickinson and Barrett believed would be the downfall of the country. Vowing to run the incumbent out of office, Barrett accused his opponent, an Episcopalian, of being "a tool of the Catholics," and the leader of the True Americans lent his support. A bulletin printed and circulated around town by Dickinson's church denounced Ward's support of Sunday movies and hinted that a close relationship existed between Ward and Father Coyle. George Ward was in league with the Roman Catholic Church and its "Dago pontiff" to desecrate the Christian Sabbath by the showing of movies, Dickinson's flyer charged. "The Baptist, Methodist, Presbyterian and other Christian pastors are determined that with the help of their brethren, the Christian Sunday shall be preserved, Messrs. Coyle [and] Ward . . . to the contrary notwithstanding."[57]

Father Coyle tried to shrug the insult off, saying only that he had "no bull or brief from his holiness of Rome" on the question of Sunday movies, but Ward understood the effort that was being made to associate him with the Catholics. The strategy could have come only from the True Americans, he thought. Going on the offense, he attempted to prove his opponent's close association with the leaders of the True Americans—Dickinson, Orion Dozier, and others—with the hope of then outing him as a religious bigot. The first step was to get Dickinson to admit that he set the secretive True Americans' agenda. But his quarry proved slippery. Even when Ward cornered Dickinson in public one day and challenged him to answer flat out whether he was or was not a member of the True Americans, the pastor refused to be pinned down.

"Why do you think I am a member of the T.A.s?" Dickinson dodged.

"Because I saw you and Dr. Dozier come out of 1811 ½ Fourth Avenue, the meeting place of that organization," George Ward answered matter-of-factly.

Dickinson continued to skirt. "I might have been in some other room. You do not know that I was in any T.A. meeting."

"Well, I believe you are a member of that society," Ward pressed, "and I ask you again if you are."

"Well, that isn't any of your business," Dickinson replied smoothly.[58]

Ward decided to act even without Dickinson's admission. At a final rally held at the Jefferson Theatre shortly before election day, Ward warned voters that his opponent had the backing of Dickinson's True Americans, and that if Barrett was elected, his intention was to see every Catholic then working for the city fired. But Barrett, without confirming a relationship with the T.A.'s, had no qualms about publicly admitting his distaste for Catholics: "If the principles as laid down in what is said to be the T.A. platform are anti-Catholic, well, I declare without hesitation I am anti-Catholic," Barrett crowed, to the delight of his audience.[59]

Barrett's unabashedly anti-Catholic strategy worked. On Election Day, a wave of support from voters in the city's outlying areas swept him into office and Ward out. Barrett wasted no time showing his appreciation. As Ward had warned, Barrett's first official act took aim at the last remaining Catholic holding high city office—Birmingham's police chief, Martin Eagan. Barrett demoted Chief Eagan to patrolman and then, adding salt to the wound, appointed Thomas J. Shirley, an open member of the Imperial Council of the Ku Klux Klan, to replace him. Rather than endure the humiliation of his demotion, Eagan resigned from the force, without a word of thanks from Barrett for his many years of service.[60]

In such an atmosphere, the St. Paul's congregation no doubt understood that they could not take lightly the threats that had been made against Father Coyle's life. Some of his friends might even have considered their pastor's daily vigil on the porch to be a bit reckless. Why broadcast to those who wanted to do you harm precisely where they might find you when they finally got around to doing it? For his own part, Father Coyle was not complacent about the threats: he hired guards to patrol St. Paul's, and in the *Catholic Monthly* he urged his congregation to exercise caution. Those who insisted on misunderstanding or misrepresenting the Catholic Church's teachings posed genuine threats to the parish's safety and well-being, he warned them.[61]

But when it came to modifying his own routine, James Coyle drew the line. If any of his enemies truly wanted to, they knew where they could find him.

———

Over the years, the congregation of St. Paul's came to appreciate what they could not have known about Father Coyle when he first stepped off the train in 1904 to replace their beloved Father O'Reilly. The cumulative years of his daily work on their behalf, his steady presence in their lives, and his dogged defense of their faith had finally won the hearts of his congregants. In the spring of 1921, his parishioners tried to communicate their gratitude by surprising him with a gift in celebration of his Silver Jubilee, the twenty-fifth anniversary of his ordination into the priesthood. The night before the festivities, Bishop Allen had given his blessing to Father Coyle to travel home to Ireland. He had not been back to the land of his birth for a number of years, and his friends knew his heart ached to see it. His congregation presented him with $25,000 to be used on his return to fund his plans for the new rectory, and "a small purse" of $1,000, which they hoped he would spend in Ireland "in the resting" so that he might "come back refreshed and ready to do battle for them in Birmingham yet again."[62]

"Let it help you stay in the church militant," they teased him gently. "We want to keep you out of heaven just as long as we can." It had taken some time, but it was clear that James Coyle had earned his parishioners' love.[63]

———

He tried to think, during his days away from them, when it had happened. Precisely when was it that Birmingham, Alabama, had become home, and Drum simply the place he drawn first breath? Ireland was so dear to him, and the home rule its people struggled for seemed an obvious, incontestable right. But Birmingham and St. Paul's were dearer to him yet, and the realization surprised him. James Coyle, that fierce lover of Ireland, missing his home and friends in Birmingham! When the thought occurred to him, like other matters of importance, the priest gave it a voice. During his time away, he sent letters and cards "to more than one friend" back in the States, one parishioner recalled later.

"I shall come home gladly," Father Coyle wrote to one, plainly refreshed. "It *is* home. I find I love St. Paul's and I am coming back to give my life and its poor heart to Birmingham."[64]

| Until Death Do Us Part

THE EARLY SETTLERS of Birmingham called their home "The Magic City," and perhaps there was something magical or divine about it. For what else save the intervention of some mighty invisible force could have seen to it that the plans of a few entrepreneurial spirits to build a new city in the shadow of Red Mountain, plans that were but the wisp of an idea at the outbreak of the Civil War, would survive the hostilities to evolve from fancy to fact? And what force but magic, or the favor of God himself, could have stopped the first pioneers of the young city from fleeing after it was decimated, first by cholera and then economic disaster, all within two years of its founding? But if some magical presence did in fact trouble itself about the fledgling city when it was first incorporated in late 1871, by the time Birmingham prepared to celebrate its fiftieth anniversary in 1921, some of its residents would have been entitled to wonder whether the spirit was of darkness or the light.

It was the decision to cross the railroads just northeast of Elyton, Alabama, rather than through Elyton itself that sealed the birth of the city of Birmingham. That and the related fact that threading through the hills, fields, and valleys of Jefferson County were unthinkable deposits of coal, limestone, and iron ore, all of the raw ingredients needed to make pig iron and steel. No doubt the decision to bypass Elyton in favor of a stretch of land consisting mostly of "swampy farmland"[1] was both a surprise and a disappointment to those Elyton landowners who had believed the rumors—that tracks were to be laid straight through Elyton's center—and had allowed themselves to fantasize about the resulting jump in their property values. These men were not fools; their vision of easy money was not ill founded. If railroad tracks were to be laid down anywhere, Elyton was the logical choice. About forty years before the war, Alabama law-makers had named Elyton the seat of Jefferson County, and despite the losses suffered during the hostilities, by 1870 the city's population topped a thousand, while the county's overall number exceeded eleven times that: twelve thousand. There were also signs of more invigorated commerce, despite the general isolated state of the region. Pony express and stage lines stretched north, south, east, and west, connecting the county seat to Huntsville, Selma, Tuscaloosa, and Montgomery, and a system of roads, though still rudimentary, had transformed Elyton into the region's "transportation hub." Wagons loaded with mail, cotton, corn, and goods on route to two of the state's primary waterways—the Warrior River to the west and the Cahaba River to the east—wended their way through the city streets, then off-loaded their freight onto boats to be hauled elsewhere.[2]

Admittedly, the changes were modest in comparison to other regions, but they represented dramatic and promising growth for residents of Jefferson County. In the early decades of the nineteenth century, only the most stouthearted had ventured to set up homes there. Unlike the fertile soil of Alabama's famed Black Belt region, the land in Jefferson County could not support any serious production of cotton and corn, the state's primary cash crops. While a few households propitiously situated alongside the region's creek beds were able to yield a respectable crop, large-scale harvests were out of the question for the bulk of the county's residents. Most could scarcely wring their family's yearly needs from the hilly, heavily timbered soil.[3] This meant that it was likely that Jefferson County's sheer isolated beauty, rather than the promise of agricultural fortunes, was what had drawn the first settlers there—its dense woods of pine, hickory, oak, and chestnut, its rolling hills, and its quiet, underpopulated countryside. Word about the region got a boost, the locals liked to claim, after David Crockett, the famed Tennessee frontiersman, found his way there on an exploration and returned home with memories of the eventful trip. According to Crockett's notes, he took ill while exploring a part of the county called Jones Valley, which General Andrew Jackson had largely (but luckily for Crockett, not completely) rid of its native Creek inhabitants. For a time, his recovery was in grave doubt. But for the help of some Indians, who happened on him and carted him to the home of Jesse Jones, the valley's namesake, Crockett might well have died. After returning home, he described the valley's charms in a chronicle of his expedition, and Jefferson County residents liked to think that by doing so the much-admired frontiersman had dispatched not a few settlers their way.[4]

Certainly its vast hidden mineral treasures could not have been the lure. State officials ordered the region surveyed and discovered its bounty of natural resources only shortly before the war. In the mid-1800s, Alabama legislators paid two professors at the University of Alabama in Tuscaloosa to survey the central part of the state. They reported back that the region was laced with mineral riches—deposits of inestimable value, the depths of which would only fully be known after excavation and mining. Later, when the locations and dimensions of the mineral deposits became better known, the veins of iron ore and the region's coalfields were given names like Browne Seam, Pratt Seam, and Warrior Field.

When the surveyors first filed their reports, however, very few people were privy to their findings, and those who were must have been daunted by the impediments that appeared to stand in the way of profiting from the information. Even after the precise locations of the ore, limestone, and coal deposits were identified, the minerals still had to be pulled from their resting places, and without the capacity to process them nearby, an infrastructure for carting it elsewhere would be necessary as well. The extremely limited access into and out of the area created a formidable obstacle. Said one senator from Calhoun County: "The country up there is so poor that a buzzard would have to carry provisions on his back or starve to death on his passage."[5] Railroads were the obvious answer.

John T. Milner was one of the select group of men who had come to know of the untapped fortunes of ore and coal that blessed the hills and valleys of Jefferson County. Born in Pike County, Georgia, in 1826, Milner was the son of a railroad contractor. Understanding that untold fortunes could be made in the areas of the country yet to be gifted with steel rails and steam engines, Milner's father sent him to the University of Georgia to receive training in the field of civil engineering. In the 1850s, the South & North Railroad Company hired the young engineer, not yet in his thirties, to plot a route for a railroad line cutting through the hilly central area of the Alabama. The state's law-makers had granted a charter to two companies to lay down track: the South & North Railroad Company and the Alabama & Chattanooga Railroad Company. The Alabama & Chattanooga's track, bisecting the state east to west, would connect Chattanooga, Tennessee, to Meridian, Mississippi, and because Meridian had already laid track running south to New Orleans, the addition of the new track through Elyton would enable Tennessee commerce to reach the Louisiana gulf. Likewise, the South & North's railroad line would link the commercial business of Decatur's Tennessee River to that of Montgomery's Alabama River, broadening access to the Mobile gulf. The plan was to cross the two tracks somewhere in between, likely in Elyton, the seat of Jefferson County, where the state's surveyors had reported finding untold mineral riches.

The two companies began to lay track straightaway, but when the war started, their work stalled. Alabama needed its "full complement of men" for the Confederate army, state officials decided. The railroad workers could not be spared. For another decade, while the Civil War and Reconstruction taxed the state's fiscal and human resources, any hope of uncovering the bounties that lay beneath the red clay of Jefferson County remained a dream.[6]

Finally, in December 1871, with the traumas of the war and the irritations of Reconstruction sufficiently behind them, a group of ten land speculators formed the Elyton Land Company, with the stated purpose of creating a new industrial city in the heart of Jefferson County, and quietly began to buy up 4,150 acres of marshy countryside just northwest of Elyton. Josiah Morris, a personal friend of John Milner, was named the company's banker, and Colonel James R. Powell, its president, became its most colorful booster. If the men worried about the future profitability of their speculation, there is little to suggest it. No doubt the fact that most of them were connected in one way or another with the South & North Railroad Company helped brace their nerve, especially as their chum, John Milner, would be the man to determine the exact location for the crossing of the railroad lines that would run through the area.

A person innocent of the way fortunes are made might reasonably have predicted that, having named their company the Elyton Land Company, the men's plan was to make the city of Elyton the site of their ambitious new venture. After all, the railroad tracks Milner had designed before the war had been plotted to run directly through Elyton's center, where they would intersect with the Alabama & Chattanooga line. By the late 1860s, the Alabama & Chattanooga had already laid its rails, cutting "through the trough of Jones Valley" and straight on through Elyton.[7] The residents of Elyton had little reason to guess, therefore, that between December 1870 and December 1871, the investors in the Elyton Land Company had purchased huge tracts of land lying just outside of Elyton, and that Milner had devised the railroads to cross not through the city as originally planned but just to its east, through the swath of land owned by his friends, who had already given it a name—Birmingham.[8] By the time these entrepreneurs' intentions became clear, there was little the Elytonians could do but watch their dreams pass by.

Before long, rumors were flying that the promoters of the Elyton Land Company had plans to poach the county seat from Elyton as well. By 1873, the politically astute Colonel Powell had seen to it that a referendum would be held to decide whether to build the proposed new county courthouse in Elyton (where it currently stood) or in Birmingham, the newcomer that had not even existed before the war! Reportedly, on Election Day, through the use of wit and trickery, the fifty-seven-year-old white-haired colonel persuaded a majority of the county's voters to opt for Birmingham, thereby creating a new county seat.[9]

The founders decided on Birmingham as the name for their new city not so much out of respect for the iron-manufacturing maven of the same name across the Atlantic, as braggadocio that their metropolis would surely match it. Even as the last nail was driven into the railroad ties that sealed its birth, the promoters brashly predicted that Birmingham, Alabama, would become "the Pittsburgh of the South"—the very exemplar of the new industrial South. In those early days, however, there was scant visible evidence to vouch for their bluster. When the town was first incorporated in November 1871, there was scarcely a building there—one early resident recalled only four, and that number included a toolhouse for the railroads, the town grocery, and a saloon.[10]

Yet even before the fledgling city's street plans were finalized, word was plainly spreading that a new city would be built in the shadow of Red Mountain. Settlers began to pour into the area—they "came faster than the building[s]," one city historian wrote—and, lacking houses, put up tents on Village Creek, where years later the Thomas Furnace would stand, while they waited for Major William P. Barker, a civil engineer, to finish the painstaking task of "laying off the streets, avenues, alleys."[11] When finished, Barker's checkerboard of thoroughfares covered nearly 2,000 acres. A double-lane artery bisected and grounded the center of the grid—Powell Avenue, in honor of the Colonel—and a complex of blocks, intersecting in sharp right angles, emanated outward from it, a series of sequentially numbered avenues and streets stretching outward in a dense grid of highly disciplined, broad, straight lines. The avenues ran east to west, the streets north to south; each a spectacular 100 feet wide, as if space was as limitless as the founders' vision of the city's promise. Narrow alleyways running parallel to the avenues sliced through each city block, creating shortcuts and room for the houses of Negro servants.[12] Although the city got off to a rocky start—cholera and a depression threatened its existence within its first two years—it soon lived up to the founders' forecasts. Homes, businesses, churches, and parks appeared along the lines of Barker's penciled plan so quickly that the trained engineer himself might have been tempted to wonder whether some magical force was at play.

Indeed, if anything characterized the city of Birmingham, Alabama, as it approached its fiftieth anniversary in 1921, it was its spectacular growth. Between 1900 and 1910, the central city grew nearly 250 percent. Soaring office buildings, elegant homes, and a hodgepodge of commercial establishments occupied much of the downtown area. But the real source of the booming town's prosperity rested on its periphery, in the vast complex of coal mines, furnaces, ironworks, rolling mills, and steel plants that circled the downtown district. After residents voted to annex a number of the communities that serviced the mines and plants on the outskirts of town, the population of Birmingham rose to over 310,000, over 200,000 of whom lived in the central city area alone.[13]

It was around this time that someone hoisted a massive sign outside the railway terminal to greet visitors to Birmingham with the boast of its adopted nickname—"The Magic City"—as if to suggest the role of some benevolent enchantment in the prosperity of the place.[14] In truth, the transformation of the muddy town of the 1870s into a bustling, twentieth-century industrial powerhouse had been accomplished by the wave of no illusionist's hand. Rather, clear-eyed entrepreneurial calculation deserved the credit. One of the first acts of the men of the Elyton Land Company after obtaining their charter had been to donate land to each of the five religious denominations claiming parishioners in the area—the Baptists, Methodists, Presbyterians, Catholics, and Episcopalians—and the founders' generous gift was not entirely altruistic. In its earliest days, Birmingham had qualities not unlike those of the untamed West. Saloons abounded; some of them never closed their doors, bestowing a vague, unwanted seediness on the inner city. The easy access to liquor these establishments facilitated, combined with the fact that men carried guns freely, made the streets little safer than the frontier. Shootouts, frequent brawls, and other acts of violence erupted without warning—hardly the atmosphere needed to attract newcomers to aid the city's growth.[15] To the developers of the Elyton Land Company the solution to this profit-inhibiting reality appeared clear, and His name was God.[16]

———

As Father Coyle sat on the swing on Thursday, August 11, 1921, St. Paul's Church still looked the grand dame of Third Avenue, but the rectory porch was showing its age. The two-story, five-room house was over forty years old, and years of heat and rain and wind had weathered it. Inside, the house was filled to the brim. By 1921, the rectory sheltered five adults: three priests—Father Coyle, Father Thomas F. Brady, and Father Edward O'Shea—and two women—Stella Caruthers, the rectory's sixty-year-old housekeeper, and Marcella Coyle, James Coyle's unmarried younger sister and constant companion. Whenever a transient priest stopped over on his way to one of the missions in areas outside Birmingham or in northern Alabama, the group occupying the rectory was squeezed even further.[17]

For all of its shortcomings of space, the exterior of the rectory was still inviting. During the warmer months in particular, passers-by were treated to a panoply of colors set off against the modest patch of neatly trimmed grass that stretched from the porch to the sidewalk. A black wrought-iron gate, about thigh-high, separated the yard from the street just beyond, and along both sides of the walk that led from the house to the gate, red bricks worn by time enclosed two flowerbeds, like toppled dominoes. More flowers cascaded from low-slung wooden boxes that flanked the outer edges of the porch. On the eastern border of the yard loomed the majestic church, and on its west, a low hedge ran the length of the property, separating the rectory yard from that of the aging church goods supply store that occupied the small wood-framed building that had once served as the parish's first church.[18]

By the summer of 1921, the city's more careful observers would have noted with some surprise a hint of neglect in the maintenance of the rectory. If it had ever been painted, evidence of the fact was no longer observable on the graying wood planks of its exterior. Jagged, smoke-colored water stains, the product of decades of rain, streaked the boards at the corners of the house beneath the roof, and a gaping hole marred the wooden latticework that ran the length of the porch just under its edge. Instead of shielding the dark shadows of the crawlspace, the lattice opened into a great, yawning hole—like a silent, prescient scream.[19]

It was not like Father Coyle to let broken planks and peeling paint go unattended. But even to him, there must have seemed little point in fussing over the rectory's decline. Bishop Allen had consented to let the rectory and the church goods supply store be razed "to make way for a larger rectory, a school for the children of the parish, and a convent" for the nuns who would run it. Demolition was set to begin within the month.[20]

As the demolition date approached, Father Coyle must have wanted to preserve some record of the parish's original church, for he arranged to have its picture taken on the morning of August 11, 1921. As the photographer snapped the shot, James Coyle stood side-by-side with Bill Fex, the church's business manager, at the top of the well-worn wooden steps that led into the building, their elbows nearly touching. The air was hot, and Fex wore no jacket or hat. He stood on the priest's right, facing Third Avenue, in a crisp white shirt and tie, hands tucked casually into the pockets of his slacks. Despite the heat, Father Coyle wore his customary black suit. His stiff roman collar gleamed in the sun, and a straw hat was perched high on his head. Neither man had any way of knowing that only one of them would live to see the building torn down, or even the end of that day.[21]

———

Sometime after 6:30 P.M., a man pushed open the iron gate and headed up the rectory walk. The man was tall, over six feet. Despite the day's oppressive temperatures, he wore the black suit of the ministry. His dark hair, streaked with gray, had thinned since the day he had found his daughter on the porch with the priest nearly seven years before. At 51, he was still trim. He was given to walking, though it took some effort, as his foot pained him. Most days he carried a cane, but on that day, none of the people who noticed him out on the streets mentioned it, making it possible that he had decided for some reason to leave it at home. Something else was different as well. The man normally wore a mustache, thick and full. But on that day it was gone, making the lines that had settled on his face over the years more noticeable. The furrow between his eyes had become more deeply etched, and his mouth arched downward, as though life itself had been a disappointment.[22]

Had Father Coyle been on the rectory porch earlier that day, he might have noticed the minister walking back and forth along Third Avenue and found his movements curious. First west, then east, then west again, as if working through some intractable problem. Certainly others had wondered about it. But the witnesses, unaware at the time that they were witnesses, did what so many do at such times. They put the observation aside and let their thoughts flow to other things.

Thus, Rufus E. Hammett, an ambulance driver for Lige Loy's Undertaking and Funeral Service, which was located only a half a block away from the rectory, thought that there was something odd about Reverend Stephenson that Thursday, but it was only later that Hammett tried to put into words what it was about the minister that had seemed strange. There was something about his weaving, the way he had walked up Third Avenue, turned around, and walked back again, Hammett later told Joe Tate, as if that explained it. And perhaps it did. A summer heat wave had propelled temperatures into the midnineties every day that week. As soon as the morning sun had chased the shadows from the corners of Callahan Park, the mercury climbed steadily. By midafternoon, the streets nearly sizzled in the heat.

By the time Stephenson hiked from his home on Seventh Avenue to Loveman, Joseph & Loeb, after receiving a phone call that his daughter had failed to return from lunch, the temperatures would have been punishing. His walk from there to City Hall, where he talked to his friends at the Birmingham Police Department, and from there to the sheriff's office at the county courthouse, where he registered a request that they search for the girl, must have been stultifying.

Rufus Hammett knew that most folks in Birmingham would try to stay out of the sun on such days. But Reverend Stephenson had walked back and forth as though immune to the blistering heat. And there was something about the look in his eyes, Hammett told the prosecutor. "He had just a stare."[23]

As the sun began to tilt toward the horizon, two coal miners, twenty-five-year-old William Chiles and his brother-in-law Edwin McGinty, stood across the street from the Jefferson County Courthouse, waiting for the "Jitney"—one of the smaller, gasoline-powered passenger vehicles that darted in and out among the less agile streetcars, like flies. Chiles and McGinty had spent the day trudging up and down the streets of Birmingham looking for other work. The search had been rough. The air that Thursday had been brutally hot. The men had stopped several times for icy drinks. By the end of the day of fruitless searching, they had little to show for their trouble and must have felt dispirited. By 6:30 they had given up, resigned to return to work in the mines, back to the house they shared with some other miners in a company town in neighboring Walker County. The mining town bordered the Jefferson County line, outside Birmingham's city limits; because the streetcars that looped through the downtown district stopped at the city's edge, men who worked beyond that boundary, like Chiles and McGinty, were forced to rely on the Jitney to get them home. It would take them some time to make the trip.[24]

There were authorities whom, had they seen the two coal miners out on the street that day, would have happily reminded them that Birmingham had not always looked kindly on men who skipped out on a days work to idle the hours away, especially men whose labor was needed to keep the district's coal mines, iron foundries, rolling mills, and blast furnaces up and running. As early as 1891, the city had enacted strict vagrancy ordinances that could be used to lock up any man who "habitually neglect[ed] his employment" or "habitually loaf[ed] or loiter[ed] about disreputable places," and the penalties for such activity were strengthened in the first decade of the next century.[25]

Mostly the vagrancy laws were aimed at controlling the labor and general whereabouts of Negro men, of course, not white miners like Chiles and McGinty. Before the war, the sparse population of Jefferson County had been largely white, but by 1920, Negroes accounted for nearly 40 percent of the area's residents.[26] After the turn of the century, thousands of Negroes across the South had left their homes in the country for the region's cities. The hope of better paying jobs, schools for their children, and an end to the cycle of debt and dependency created by ubiquitous sharecropping arrangements gave them the courage to uproot their families and leave their homes.

It is not hard to imagine the disappointment of these hopeful travelers when they arrived in cities like Birmingham and found themselves shuttled into the baggage and waiting rooms reserved "for Coloreds only" as soon as they stepped off the train. And if they had dared to dream of finding stouter homes to live in than the "loosely constructed sharecropper cabins" they had just left behind, they must have been sorely discouraged when they learned that, like the pattern of other cities of the time,[27] the neighborhoods of Birmingham shifted from "areas of neat middle-class residence" to "modest workingmen's cottages" to bands of houses "three-to-five blocks-wide...dominated by Negro quarters, crowded with monotonous gray rows of narrow, unpainted shacks, blighted by smoke and coal dust from the nearby railroads and industries."[28] Most of the Negroes lacked the money to buy these shacks, so they rented them instead, clustered near the places where they worked, in the city's "vacant spaces"—areas shunned by whites—along soggy creek beds, noisy railroad lines, or narrow and darkened alleyways. Some found their way to the city's Northside as well, near the Alice furnace. Others set up home in the East End, or the alley section of the Southside, near one of the furnaces operated by the Sloss-Sheffield Steel and Iron Company.[29] Still others crowded into shacks that elbowed for space along the city's many muddy, rutted back alleys, situated like the antebellum slave quarters behind the grander homes of the whites. A last group occupied the rows of dingy houses that made up the company towns that dotted the city's outskirts near the mines.[30]

Birmingham had never shown much tolerance for the sight of unoccupied Negroes on its streets, and its impatience with such idlers intensified during World War I, when business elites experienced unprecedented labor shortages. By 1900, Negro men made up better than half of the area's coal miners and about 65 percent of its iron and steel workers. And while whites frequently claimed that Negroes no longer dedicated themselves to their work the way they had during the days of slavery, in truth, the city's industries would have shut down without them. Just as rigid social custom made sure that they were steered into the "right" neighborhoods away from whites, once there they were expected to abide by the city's other racial norms as well: to be content with their lot in life, to understand their place, to show up for work. With such a great number of Negroes about, Birmingham could ill afford to tolerate fissures in the social fabric. If Negroes were to be free, and whites forced to live in close proximity to them, rules about interactions between the races had to be set and adhered to.

At minimum, the industrialists thought, all able-bodied men could be expected to work. In April 1918, after the beginning of World War I, twenty-five irate representatives of the city's leading iron and steel industry appeared before the City Commission and demanded more vigorous enforcement of the vagrancy laws to counteract the "acute labor shortage." The group urged the adoption of a stricter vagrancy rule—one that would place the burden on any man discovered "wandering or strolling about, or remaining in idleness during any workday" to show why he was not a vagrant subject to arrest. And as every American could be expected to support "full-capacity wartime production," the businessmen argued, opposition to such an ordinance would be unpatriotic—"pro-German," they said. The ordinance passed by unanimous agreement.[31]

In addition to aiding the capitalists, aggressive enforcement of the vagrancy laws helped soothe white fear of the "menace" of black criminality. Almost as soon as the Negro migrants began to arrive, the whites of Birmingham began to look on their neighborhoods as centers of crime and depravity. Before the county voted to become dry in late 1907 (a full year before the state passed its own prohibition law effective January 1, 1909), the Negro wards were home to some of the city's most famous dives—ramshackle bars with names like "Buzzard's Roost, Pigeon Roost, Scratch Ankle, Dry Brunch and Beer Mash"—and a great number of shootings, stabbings, and general acts of drunkenness and debauchery occurred in them. When Birmingham earned the label of "Murder Capital" of the country, something had to be done. Stepped-up enforcement of the vagrancy laws helped reassure the fearful that the Negroes were being kept under control.[32]

While the vagrancy laws of Birmingham were used primarily as a means to regulate the activities of Negro men during this period, white men like Chiles and McGinty were sometimes arrested under their authority as well. As anti-Catholic hostilities increased in the Age of Prohibition, the perceived drinking habits of Irish men had become a frequent source of ridicule. It would not have been above some in the city to doubt the excuse Chiles and McGinty offered for not reporting for work.

————

From where Chiles and McGinty stood waiting for the Jitney to pull up, they could see the porch of St. Paul's rectory across the street. Chiles noticed Father Coyle sitting on the swing before his attention was drawn to the frustrated sounds of a man trying to crank up a one-seated Ford.[33] At that time, the sight of this man's cranking calisthenics would have seemed increasingly anachronistic. Some years earlier, Charles F. Kettering had invented an integrated starter system for automobiles, complete with ignition, electrical system, and rechargeable battery,[34] and Henry Leland, the head of Cadillac Motors, had had Kettering's ignition system installed in the 1912 Cadillac model after one of Leland's friends had injured himself while cranking his car and died of the complications. Within a few years, Kettering's design had saturated the market, and hand cranks were becoming obsolete.[35]

The searing temperatures must have made the motorist's job even more unpleasant than usual, but as he yanked the iron shaft up and down, the two miners might have been forgiven if they felt pangs of envy, notwithstanding his labors. The man at least had a car. Once he succeeded in turning the engine over, he would be on his way—not baking in the heat, like Chiles and McGinty, waiting for a Jitney that would take at least another hour to get them home.[36]

———

After the arrival of the private motorcar in Birmingham, it was a rare day when city officials could declare a day accident-free,[37] and Thursday, August 11, 1921, was not one of those days. Sometime around 6:00 P.M., two cars had crashed into each other at the corner of Twenty-second Street and Third Avenue, about a block away from where Chiles and McGinty waited for the Jitney. Both drivers had survived without injury, but neither was prepared to take the blame for the collision. Their argument quickly drew a crowd. For the McClellan brothers, who shared an apartment a block away, the commotion proved too much to resist, even though the temperature still hovered near ninety. They slipped into the crowd to take in the show.[38]

Officer Henry Harrison Weir of the Birmingham Police Department was finishing up his regular beat on Second Avenue a block away, when a Negro boy ran up and told him that two motorcars had collided on the corner near the Mabson Hotel and St. Paul's Catholic Church. The site was close enough that Weir knew he had to investigate. His grey eyes may have darkened at the thought. The idea of something new coming up so late in the day would have irritated most officers. It was already almost 6:00 P.M., and Weir must have known that if he got drawn in to sorting out an accident, he could be at it for hours. On day so hot, the heat would have felt like it was coming at the officer from both directions, first pelting down from above and then ricocheting back up again, like the inside of one of the city's blast furnaces. At age thirty-two, Weir was no longer in the best of shape. His World War I registration card described him as "stout" for his "medium height" frame. The extra pounds would not have made the hours out in the sun any easier.[39] Weir asked the boy if there wasn't a traffic officer already there, and the child replied that there was. It must have been welcome news. If another officer was already attending to the mess, who could blame Weir if he took his time getting there?

When Weir finally reached the site of the accident, he saw the source of the trouble straightaway. Two motorcars were tangled near the busy intersection, and one of the drivers, a woman, was raising Cain, insisting that the other motorist should pay for the damage. Weir took stock of the situation from a safe distance away and decided that the traffic officer at the scene had matters under control. He phoned a quick report about the incident into police headquarters at City Hall from a telephone outside a small grocery on Third Avenue. As Weir stood near the phone, a "big, fleshy man"—one of the McClellan brothers—approached him and began to wax on about which driver he thought was at fault. Evidently, McClellan knew the woman driver and had a very strong opinion about the motorists' respective liabilities. Weir was still standing near the phone, trying to tune McClellan out, when he heard the shots.[40]

———

Richard W. Gayle and his son, Dick, were known to disagree, and they were doing a lot of it that afternoon. Part of the problem was likely that the two men just spent too much time together. Although an adult himself, Dick Gayle still lived in his parents' home, and each morning, he and his father went off to work together besides.[41] Richard Gayle was a plumber, and his son had followed in his footsteps. When the two plumbers called it quits for that day, neither of them was in the mood to agree about much of anything, including what time it was when they had finally knocked off work. They were still arguing about it when they reached the "Dago stand" across the street from St. Paul's Church on the corner. It was around 6:30, and both men wanted to be home.[42]

Though the pair stopped in the store nearly every day on their way home from work, neither of them showed signs of knowing the proprietor's name or any sense that he might take offense at their use of such a phrase to refer to his business. They said it casually—"We stopped in at the Dago stand" or "we were over at the Dago shop"—in the same way one might refer to stopping off at the bank or the park, or O'Brien's Opera House. The grocery stand was small, but the owner kept the icebox stocked with icy bottles of soda pop, and Richard and Dick liked to stop in at the end of the workday for a Coca-Cola and a cigar. Some days, one of them would pull a watermelon rind or two from the slop pail at the back of the store to bring home to the family cow.[43] There were other patrons in the store when they arrived there that day, and one of them ribbed the elder Gayle when he moved to the icebox and helped himself to a bottle of pop. Richard Gayle paid him no mind. He had been pulling Coca-Cola bottles from the icebox of the Dago stand for far too long to worry over social etiquette. Age and patronage conferred certain privileges, and, rather than waiting for service, Gayle was one to use them.

Sometime around 6:30, he noticed a uniformed police officer standing outside the door of the store next to the telephone post. The officer was talking "to a fat man," Richard remembered later. It was about the last thing he noticed before he heard the shots.[44]

Officer Weir whipped his head in the direction of the shots, west up Third Avenue. The shots appeared to have come from the porch of St. Paul's rectory. A black cat startled by the noise darted beneath the hedge that separated the rectory's yard from that of the old church goods house. Weir stood motionless for a second, confused about why someone would be shooting at a cat. Then he heard a woman scream.[45]

———

By August 1921, Stella Caruthers had lived and worked as the housekeeper at St. Paul's rectory for six years. Some days it was a struggle to keep up, even with the help of Marcella Coyle and the Negro woman Father Coyle had hired to help with the cooking. But by 6:30, Caruthers and the other women had completed most of the day's tasks. A short time before, Stella had served Father Coyle and Father Brady their dinner in the rectory dining room. Then Father Coyle retired to the porch, and Father Brady left the rectory to fill his car with gas. He had to travel to a mission outside the city early the next morning, and he wanted to be ready to go without delay when he awoke.

Once the priests were fed, it was possible to relax, and Stella and Marcella were able to sit and eat their own dinner undisturbed. By 6:30, they had finished their meal and moved to the housekeeper's room at the rear of the house. It was their custom to visit together in Stella's room, reading a book or enjoying some other pastime, where they could hear the Negro woman leave for the night. She always left through the back door, of course; she would not have been permitted to enter or exit the house any other way. Normally, Stella and Marcella heard her leave without trouble.

On that night, however, Stella Caruthers and Marcella Coyle never did hear the cook leave. The sound that tore through the house instead was the unmistakable crack of gunfire. They heard two shots, fired in quick succession; a brief pause; and then one more—three shots in all—and then the awful silence that always follows such a thing. The housekeeper's heart must have sunk. Even without seeing the source of the trouble, she knew—"The shots were too close."[46]

Marcella Coyle moved first, flying from her seat in the back room and whirling into the corridor that led to the front of the house. From the end of the hall, she could see clear to the porch. The back of a man was visible through the screen door, and he was moving away. Without a word, Marcella raced down the hall and punched open the door.

Gripped by panic, Stella Caruthers moved more slowly. "Don't run," she called after the retreating woman. It was not fear that caused Caruthers to shout the warning. It was dread. There was no mistaking the sounds she had heard. Someone had been shooting a gun. And the gunshots had been too close. Then, as though the reverberations of gunfire had not been bad enough, an equally chilling sound sliced through the house: Marcella Coyle's scream.

By the time the housekeeper reached the door, the younger woman was rushing back inside, where she yanked the telephone earpiece from its cradle. Send a doctor, Marcella yelled into the receiver, and a priest, she sobbed.[47]

Stella Caruthers hurried out onto the porch. A tall man dressed in black was walking away from the porch. His pace was strangely slow. And instead of heading to the sidewalk beyond the front gate, he moved toward the low-lying hedge that separated the yard of the rectory from that of the church goods supply house.

Stella Caruthers wrenched her attention back to the porch. Father Coyle was sprawled awkwardly on the floorboards to the left of the door, his head against the wall. A pool of blood was welling beneath it. People raced to the rectory from all directions when the housekeeper swung back toward the retreating man and screamed. "Stop him!" she shouted. "He shot Father Coyle!"[48]

The man walked across the rectory lawn in a path parallel to the porch, his back to the steeples of St. Paul's Church. He stepped over the hedge and crossed the yard, passing within a few feet of the spot where Bill Fex and Father Coyle had stood posing for their photograph just hours before. The sidewalk might have provided a quicker egress, or the shadows of the alley-way behind the rectory an escape more concealed. But if the man desired to escape, his method was nonsensical. He walked, rather than ran, his pace unhurried and deliberate. And he steered an unveering path toward the courthouse, which everyone knew housed the sheriff's office and the passage-way to the Jefferson County jail.[49]

As Officer Weir ran toward the rectory, a man named M. L. Easter, who was standing almost directly across the street from where the shots had been fired, gestured to him. Easter was pointing toward a man in a black suit who was crossing in front of the church goods supply house, with a revolver in his hand. "There he goes!" Easter shouted to Weir. "Shoot him!" Even had Officer Weir been so inclined, there would have been no easy way to comply with Easter's wish. Right after the shots were fired, a streetcar speeding along Third Avenue had screeched to a stop in the middle of the avenue. The car blocked Weir's path, forcing him to go around it. After he did so, he could see that the man had reached the side of the county courthouse and was climbing the stairs on its east side, and another officer was in hot pursuit. The strange thing was, it looked to Officer Weir as if the shooter "knew right where he was going."[50]

———

Dick Gayle had just removed two cigars from the case at the front of the Dago store when he heard the shots: two shots fired quickly, a pause, and then a third. Dick jerked his head toward the sound. It had come from the rectory porch across the street. Smoke from the last shot still lingered in the air. The porch swing was shaking slightly. A man in dark clothes stood on the porch, his body angled toward the wall, stooped slightly downward. He lowered the gun he was holding, turned, and headed down the steps. A woman then rushed out onto the porch from inside the rectory. "Shoot him!" she shouted. "He shot Father Coyle!"—as if any of the number of the people rushing toward the rectory porch would have happened to be carrying a gun.[51]

"They're shooting a man over there!" Dick yelled to his father as he bolted out the front door. Richard rushed to see. Smoke from the gunshot was still barely visible, and the man who had fired the shots was moving down the rectory steps. His pace seemed oddly "leisurely," Richard told to the prosecutor later—for once he and his son agreed.[52]

Birmingham traffic officer W. L. Snow was standing in the middle of the intersection of Third Avenue and Twenty-first Street guiding traffic when he heard the shots. Even at that late hour, cars continued to choke the busy intersection, and Officer Snow was doing what he could to maintain some order. Not long before, at the other end of the block, two cars had collided. Snow did not want the same thing to happen on his watch. The city government had responded to the growing traffic problems by adding police officers specifically assigned to traffic direction and control. In 1921, the city stationed eighteen of these traffic officers at the busiest intersections of the downtown district. The measure was not a complete solution, but city officials hoped that it would provide relief to the most hopelessly congested areas. By the end of the decade the numbers of traffic officers grew to nearly sixty as the glut of motorcars that clogged key downtown intersections reached a crisis level. The city's traffic code reflected the strain as well, growing heavier by the year, and including for the first time provisions for one-way streets, new parking restrictions, speed limits, and restrictions on the popular Jitney, whose nimbleness made safety and congestion a constant concern.[53]

Without warning, the sound of gunshots exploded around Traffic Officer Snow, drowning out the competing sounds of traffic. One shot, followed rapidly by another. A momentary pause, then a third. All from the direction of the Catholic Church one block away. Officer Snow looked toward the church, confused, as a small flock of pigeons darted into the air and out of sight. Who would be shooting at pigeons? Officer Snow wondered; but when he heard a woman scream, he ran.[54]

Snow reached the front of the Jefferson County Courthouse in just a few seconds. Dick Gayle, who was standing in the street, pointed wildly at the courthouse, shouting, "There he goes!"[55] Dick had bolted after the shooter as soon as he stepped down from the porch and began to stride away. Dick reached the corner of the courthouse just as the gunman turned inward, along the building's east wall. Officer Snow came running from the opposite direction. Dick gestured to the police officer to let him know that the retreating man had moved along the side of the courthouse. It must have been a relief to relinquish the pursuit. Unlike Dick Gayle, the officer had a gun. If the shooter had ideas of any more violence, at least it would be a fair fight.[56]

Still running, Officer Snow slid his gun from its holster, vaguely aware that another officer, Weir, had fallen in behind him. The gunman, dressed in black, had climbed the stairs on the right side of the courthouse, turned a corner on the landing, and moved out of sight. The officers tore up the stairs, Officer Snow in the lead. When Snow reached the landing and rounded the corner, the man was jerking at the knob of the door. It was locked. He turned back toward the officers, outnumbered and trapped. The man moved slowly then, as if aware that the officers might feel threatened by the gun he still gripped in his hand. But Snow had a wife and children at home, and he took no chances. He leveled his gun on the man's chest.[57]

"That's all right, gentlemen," the gunman said evenly. "I know what I am doing. I want to be locked up."

"Put your gun down then," Snow replied coolly, keeping his gun squared at the man's chest.

The gunman lowered his arm, and Officer Weir stepped forward and pulled the gun from his hand, while Officer Snow took hold of him.

The prosecutor asked Snow later about the gun's caliber, but looking back through the haze of adrenalin, the officer could not be sure. Either a .38 or .45, he answered, uncertain. Definitely an automatic. The officer was sure of one thing: "It was big," Snow remembered grimly.[58]

———

By several accounts, Fred Bender was one of the first to reach the rectory porch. Bender's furniture store—F. J. Bender's Furniture & Fixture Store—at 2211 Third Avenue, was just a half of a block away from the rectory on the opposite side of the street. He had been sitting in his car just outside the store when he heard the gunfire.

For his height, the businessman was stout—the sign of a man who had done well for himself. His furniture store had grown over the years, despite the pressures the Klan and the True Americans had put on the community not to do business with Catholics. The path to prosperity could not have been easy—although he was still a month shy of his forty-fifth birthday, according to his registration card, Bender's hair had been gray for years. But it seems that the businessman could still get around, despite his girth. When Fred Bender heard the shots and the women's screams, something must have told him to run, fast.[59]

In 1921, Lige Loy's Ambulance and Funeral Company and the rectory of St. Paul's were only a half of a block away from each other. Lige Loy's was located between Twenty-second and Twenty-third streets on Third Avenue, directly across the street from Fred Bender's furniture store. When waiting for a call, the employees of the undertaking and ambulance business liked to carry their chairs outside and place them on the sidewalk in front of the building. The sidewalk was a fine spot to be social, and in the world of an undertaker, where everyone was a potential customer, it paid to be known.

By 6:30 that day, the sun was low enough in the sky to seduce the owner's son, Lige Loy, Jr., and one of the company's ambulance drivers, Rufus (Harry) Hammett, outside with their chairs. They couldn't have been there long before they heard the gunfire. The shots, so close, left little room for confusion, and if they needed any confirmation that someone needed help, the screams of two women provided it. Someone had been shot, and not a block away. The two men sprang to their feet. Lige Jr. scooped up a cot and scrambled into the ambulance, just as Hammett pulled the car away from the curb.[60]

The ambulance workers arrived at the rectory within a minute or so of the shots. The light of the day was beginning to wane, but as they rushed up the walk to the rectory porch, they could see the injured man lying on the floorboards. A crowd of people had already gathered around the porch. Lige Jr. and Hammett had to navigate their way through them. The man down was unconscious, but Lige Jr. and Hammett immediately recognized him. It was Father James Coyle. The priest had fallen onto the floor of the porch; his head pitched toward the wall of the house, just beneath one of the windows. His feet were stretched out toward the front of the porch, beneath the swing. Blood flowed from a hole in his temple. Lige Jr. pulled one of the porch chairs out of the way to make more room.[61]

One of the men in the crowd who saw the blood must have doubted the injured man's chances. There was blood splattered against the wall, M. L. Easter remembered later. More blood streamed from the wound in the priest's head running in a torrent across the floorboards "halfway between the steps and the end of the porch and swing."[62]

The ambulance workers wasted no time. Fred Bender helped Hammett and Lige Jr. hoist the injured priest onto the stretcher. The workers heaved the cot up between them, and headed through the crowd. People were everywhere. They swarmed around the porch and filled the yard. Another group pressed against the fence, covering the sidewalk and spilling out into the street.[63]

Marie E. Brantley stood among the horde on the sidewalk. Brantley had been seated on the Highland Avenue streetcar proceeding along Third Avenue when shots rang out and the streetcar jerked to a stop. She might have kept her seat and watched the commotion from a distance, but when she heard a woman scream, she recognized the voice. It was Marcella Coyle. The shots had come from the rectory porch. Brantley dashed down the steps of the streetcar and squeezed into the crowd that milled around the rectory fence. When the ambulance workers eased a stretcher through the crowd, Brantley saw that it carried Father Coyle. Blood poured from his temple. Marie Brantley knew Hammett and Lige Jr. She had been on her way to St. Vincent's Hospital, in fact, when the streetcar had stopped in the middle of the street. She asked the men if she could ride along with them to the hospital. They must have been eager for an extra set of hands; they agreed straightaway. In 1921, Lige Loy's ambulances were motorized, but they had yet to be fitted with sirens. A bell fastened to the inside of the emergency vehicle was the only means the men had to urge pedestrians and other motorists out of the way, and it had to be operated manually. Marie Brantley clanged the hard metal insides of the ambulance bell from the moment Hammett wheeled the car away from the curb until it arrived at St. Vincent Hospital's front door.[64]

———

What Reverend Edwin Stephenson thought to himself as the city rushed to assist the fallen priest only he knew. Maybe he was irritated by the clang of the ambulance bell—for the speedy response of Lige Loy's men offered his victim a hope of life, even if his chances were small. Or maybe the minister's unhurried step showed that he knew what the others did not: that Father Coyle was lost; that he could tell it from the way the priest had slumped to the floor.

Or maybe it was not death but life that occupied Stephenson's thoughts on his solitary walk to the courthouse. Not the life of his victim—for the spirit of James Coyle was indeed draining away into wood and paint and dust—but his own life. For there were laws in Alabama that policed the fates of men who killed, and in 1921, more often than not they involved a hangman's noose.

FOUR | A City Reacts

DUSK GATHERED IN the corners and alleyways of the city as word spread that Father Coyle had been shot, and with the proliferation of commercial radio and television still years away, people hurried from their homes and their workplaces in search of more news. They descended on the most obvious places. One crowd rushed to Third Avenue and clogged the yard of St. Paul's rectory. Another group trailed Lige Loy's ambulances to St. Vincent's Hospital, where they huddled together outside the main entrance. It would have been close to 7:00 P.M. by the time many of them arrived, and they must have known that there was little they could do to help. But helping was plainly not the point. The crowds simply hoped "against hope," wrote one who was there, that the ominous portent of "the first message would be reversed."[1]

A fifty-year-old baker named Thomas A. McGough was one of the men who rushed from his workplace in the hunt for more news. Shortly after 6:30 P.M., Fred Bender had dashed through the door of Tom McGough's bakery on Second Avenue, only a block away from St. Paul's, his entry so sudden that it jolted the attention of the baker's twelve-year-old twin daughter, Helen, away from the day's comics. Although young, one look at the furniture salesman was all Helen needed to know that something was seriously wrong. The man had raced in without his hat; only an emergency could have explained the omission. In the early decades of the twentieth century, men instinctively reached for their hats before they went anywhere, even when they were going no farther than their own front porches. But Mr. Bender was both bareheaded and "breathless" when he "burst through the door and rushed up to [her] father in the rear of the store," where he spoke to the baker "in a low but excited voice." The youngster was unable to hear Mr. Bender's words, but their visitor's message must have been dire—a "look of grief and shock" contorted her father's face. Almost by reflex, the baker turned and took a step toward the rear of the shop, as if he needed a moment to think what to do. A second later, he swung around and ran after Bender out the front door. Like his companion, her father was without a hat.

Helen McGough bolted after the two men, but when she reached the street, a friend of the family pulled the child to a stop. Father Coyle had been shot, the friend explained. The priest was badly hurt. It was best to let her father alone.[2]

If there was the smallest hope of a reversal of that awful news, it would have been due to the speedy response of the employees of the Lige Loy Ambulance and Funeral Company. For by more than one account, Rufus Hammett and Lige Jr. had the wounded priest from the rectory to the St. Vincent's Hospital in under ten minutes, the ambulance's bell noisily dispersing all obstacles from its path. And likely the medical staff had received advanced warning of their arrival, for a troupe of doctors, nurses, and interns rushed the unconscious priest's body to the operating table as soon as the car jerked to a stop. The medics went straight to work. They applied stimulants. They took x-rays of the wound. They even began surgery. But hope was quickly extinguished. The bullet that had plowed its way through their patient's brain had blown a hole through the base of his skull. There was no metal to remove; no way to save him; all they could do was to get Father Coyle his last rites before he died.[3]

The records no longer show the identity of the courier who, not long after, stepped outside to share the unhappy news with the crowd of men and women clustered around the hospital's front doors. It could have been Dr. James M. Mason, or Dr. Edward O'Connell, as both worked on the wounded priest.[4] The assignment could not have been pleasant. The shadows of the hospital building had lengthened with the approaching nightfall, but the air was still hot, enveloping the throng in a sweltering gloom. Father Coyle has died, the messenger told them.

It is not hard to imagine the force of the awful news—that sudden metamorphosis of dejection to anguish—for there is something about the human spirit that clings to hope until every chance is gone. And as if to prove it, it was only after hearing the doctor's final word that "the crowds quietly disperse[d]," Mrs. Isabel Beecher remembered many years later, to begin their grieving in the privacy of their homes.[5]

———

A press dispatch reporting that the head priest of St. Paul's Catholic Church in Birmingham had been shot arrived at the offices of the *Mobile Register,* the leading newspaper in Mobile, late that night. Word of the priest's killing spread across the port city like contamination from a tidal surge. Father Coyle had taken his first steps in the priesthood in Mobile, at the age of only twenty-three, and eight years later, he still had a great number of friends there. "A large number of Mobilians feel the greatest regret in hearing of the tragic death of the Very Rev. James E. Coyle" wrote the editors of the *Mobile Register* the next day, for Father Coyle had become "well and favorably known in the community" through his mission work and his leadership at the McGill Institute. "He was liked particularly for his evident kindliness of heart and his invariable thoughtfulness of others." The apparent cause of the shooting, the paper reported grimly, was the marriage ceremony that Father Coyle performed "between Stephenson's daughter and Pedro Gussman, a Catholic."[6]

When Bishop Allen received the news that Father Coyle had been killed, he stopped work on everything else and focused on the crisis in Birmingham. The news must have been a vicious blow. Father Coyle was more than a priest in the diocese; over the years the bishop and he had developed a close, respectful friendship, even if the two men had not always agreed on the best way to deal with the rantings of religious bigots. By 1921, they had known each other for seventeen years, and for a good number of those they had shared a home in Mobile, where Bishop Allen had guided James Coyle during the earliest days in his priesthood. Bishop Allen had worried about the death threats that had been made against Father Coyle's life in Birmingham, but even with the mounting influence of the Ku Klux Klan and organizations like the True Americans, the bishop could not have been prepared when news of the shooting reached him. And if such a thing were possible, the bishop's horror must have deepened with the information about the identity of the killer—a fellow man of the cloth, an ordained Methodist minister.

It is hard to think how the prelate managed to set his despair aside to attend to the many things that had to be done. A great number of people needed to be informed, and as the bishop spread the word, messages of disbelief, grief, and support poured into the diocese from near and distant corners.[7]

The records do not indicate how Father Michael Henry learned of the death of his lifelong friend and compatriot, but it is possible that the bishop was the unfortunate harbinger of the sorrowful news, for shortly after being advised of Father Coyle's death, Bishop Allen asked for Father Henry's audience. No doubt during their meeting the bishop extended his condolences to the priest. Bishop Allen understood better than most the special kinship between James Coyle and Michael Henry. Before the bishop had asked Father

Coyle to go to Birmingham to lead St. Paul's, the two priests had scarcely been apart. Maybe it was for that reason—out of compassion rather than actual need—that Bishop Allen asked Father Henry to take an early train to Birmingham the next morning to carry some messages to the St. Paul's community. Though a simple telegram could have conveyed the information just as well, he asked Father Henry to tell Father Brady at St. Paul's that Bishop Allen and several other high dignitaries would arrive in Birmingham later in the day, and that final plans for the funeral would be announced at that time. It is possible that the bishop sent other messages as well, of course—more private ones, to which the Birmingham papers did not have access. So it might have been genuine need that motivated Bishop Allen's request for Father Henry's help. But even if it was more kindness than need, there can be no doubt that his second appeal was made out of a sincere desire for Father Henry's help. Would he deliver the sermon at Father Coyle's funeral service? Bishop Allen asked.

The grief-stricken priest replied that he would.

———

In 1921, as the city's only morning daily, the *Birmingham Age-Herald* enjoyed a competitive edge when it came to reporting an event that broke too late in the day for its two nearest competitors—the *Birmingham News* and the *Birmingham Post*—to have covered it in their evening editions. On the morning of Friday, August 12, 1921, the *Age-Herald* made optimal use of its advantage with an attention-grabbing headline that spanned the width of the front page—"Father Coyle Killed by Minister," the banner read; "Rev. E. R. Stephenson in County Jail"—beneath which followed a jumble of articles, each dissecting a different slice of the scandal: the shooting, the shooter, the victim, and the couple at the heart of the confusion, until in combination the journalists' reports filled every line of every column of the paper's first two pages. The paper's editors must have been pleased. By the time the *Age-Herald* went to press, the writers had managed to file eight full-length articles, a good night's work by any measure (even if by the end of the day the reporters for the *Birmingham News* had managed not only that number but two more besides).[8]

Some days in the world of journalism, heaven must have seemed to intervene, for even as word raced through the offices of the *Age-Herald*—shots had been fired at St. Paul's rectory, a building only a few short blocks away—and even as its reporters flew to the streets, the shooter was already being led to a cell over at the county jail. The more seasoned newsmen among them might have taken a moment to give thanks for the blessing. In an age when beatings were sometimes inflicted by men in hoods, questions about the identity of the person or persons responsible could prove endless. Even in cases where the identity of a culprit was thought to be known, other commitments sometimes interfered with a witness's ability to recall who he had seen do what to whom. (The identities of the men who had beaten Pearce DeBardeleben bloody in the middle of a darkened wood, for example, had never been proved, even though the victim himself believed that he could pick them out.) Suspecting the identity of a criminal was one thing, the writers knew; proving it another.

But when the identity of a perpetrator was certain, additional leads could be pursued more easily. Blessedly, the identity of the killer of Father Coyle seemed a nonissue. Everyone who knew anything about it appeared to be of the same mind: Reverend Stephenson shot Father Coyle, said Deputy Sheriff Steven Wiggins, when a crush of reporters rushed to the sheriff's office in search of information about the prisoner. Stephenson had confessed to shooting the priest as soon as he "turned himself in," Wiggins told them.

In other circumstances, the reporters might have pressed Wiggins about his characterization of the minister's "surrender." Minutes after the shooting, eyewitnesses outside the courthouse were reporting that two policemen had chased the man down with guns drawn, and that they had physically escorted him to the sheriff's office; hardly the typical description of a suspect voluntarily giving himself up. And while witnesses were also saying that the officers had come upon the man tugging at one of the courthouse doors, everyone knew that the adrenalin-spiking effects of an act of lethal violence could cloud a man's thinking. Perhaps the minister had simply found himself trapped up against the courthouse wall in the throes of a crime-induced daze.[9]

But Stephenson's first words to the policemen who cornered him on the courthouse stairs—"It's all right, gentlemen. I know what I am doing."—seemed in their very succinctness to rule out the possibility that somehow, unwittingly, he had found himself caught, in the wrong place at the wrong time. So did the eyewitnesses' descriptions of his movements in the seconds just after the blast of his last shot: the shooter had made a beeline for the jail, they said, right after he stopped firing the gun. He had moved straight to the side door of the courthouse. And while it was true that someone less versed in the layout of the city's public buildings might have steered in that direction without knowing any better, *this man,* Reverend Edwin R. Stephenson, knew the courthouse on the corner of Twenty-first Street and Third Avenue like the back of his hand. The "Marrying Parson" had prowled its hallways for years. So when the witnesses concluded that Stephenson had been trying to reach the sheriff's office in order to surrender, and Deputy Sheriff Wiggins reported that in his view the minister had effectively "turned himself in," the reporters were inclined to agree, and in their stories the next day they described the man's surrender as entirely free-willed. Only two things had foiled the minister's plan to deliver himself up to the authorities unassisted, they reported: the fleet reactions of Officers Snow and Weir and the misfortune of a locked door.

If further evidence was needed that Stephenson had been thinking clearly enough to decide to hand himself over to the authorities, his first words to the deputy sheriff seemed to supply it. Deputy Wiggins had been manning the front desk when Officer Weir and Officer Snow pushed through the door with Stephenson in tow. "I'm in trouble," Stephenson told the surprised duty officer. "I want to be locked up."

When the minister asked to be taken into custody, Wiggins told the newsmen, he was unsure at first whether the sheriff's office had jurisdiction over the case. There was professional courtesy to consider. Two officers of the Birmingham Police Department had Stephenson by the arm. It was clear that the man was already in their custody. The Jefferson County Sheriff's Office had overlapping jurisdiction with the Birmingham Police Department, and decisions about which one of them should take control over a particular case could create tension and resentment. Although as a matter of law, the sheriff was authorized to investigate any felony that occurred inside the county lines, in cities like Birmingham, which could afford to hire their own police forces, it would have been Sheriff Hartsfield's policy to exercise only secondary authority over crimes committed within the municipal borders.[10] Deputy Sheriff Wiggins knew that if the man in the custody of Officers Snow and Weir had in fact committed a crime, it was unlikely that he had done so *outside* of Birmingham.

Both Stephenson and his wife Mary had been in the sheriff's offices talking with the sheriff and Deputy Wiggins not an hour before, complaining about the Catholics and their missing teenager. Sometime before 6:00 P.M., Mary Stephenson had phoned Sheriff Hartsfield with a frantic plea for help, but their telephone connection was so bad that the sheriff could hardly make out what the woman was saying—"some trouble about a girl," he told Joe Tate later. Hartsfield had asked her to come by the office to talk about it, either that night or the next morning, he added. She replied that she would be there "in ten minutes."[11]

When the woman arrived, she explained to the sheriff that her daughter, Ruth, had gone missing, and she and her husband were sure that it was the Catholics who had her locked away somewhere. They wanted the sheriff to help look for the girl, she said.[12] Accusations of kidnapping were no trivial matter in Jefferson County, Alabama, in 1921. Under state law, a conviction for that offense could put a man in prison for up to ten years.[13] If he did it for ransom money, he could be hung.[14] But Hartsfield had been the sheriff of Jefferson County for two and a half years, long enough to know that when an eighteen-year-old girl vanished, she was more likely a willing runaway than the victim of a kidnapping. Disappearances had a way of resolving themselves, given a little time.

The hour was late, and Hartsfield was due home to his family, but Mary Stephenson was worked up over her daughter, so he ushered her over to the desk of one of his deputies, Paul C. Cole, and asked her to provide Cole with a description of her daughter. Deputy Cole would do what he could for her, Hartsfield reassured her as he prepared to leave them. The last thing the sheriff remembered hearing that day as he pulled the office door closed behind him was the woman's statement to his deputy that "she thought that they had her locked up somewhere around the Catholic church."[15]

Shortly after Hartsfield had left for home, Edwin Stephenson arrived at the office, and seeing that his wife was with Deputy Cole, Stephenson cornered Deputy Wiggins and started in on him. Immediate action was needed to prevent the papists from absconding with their girl, the pair told the lawmen. There was no time to waste. They had to search *that night*. If they waited until morning it might be too late. By then the girl might be gone. They needed to search "every Catholic institution in town," Mrs. Stephenson said—St. Paul's, the rectory, the convent over on the Westside, "and every other place she could think of."[16]

Deputy Cole scribbled some notes as he listened to the woman, probably as much to placate her as to record her suspicions. But the longer Mary Stephenson went on, the more the deputy must have doubted that Ruth had had been abducted at all. It was far more likely she had run off on her own. Alabama law made it clear that a person was only considered kidnapped if someone had *forcibly* enticed the person away with the intent to secretly confine or imprison the person *against the person's will*.[17] And although Mrs. Stephenson was careful to intersperse her philippic with phrases like "some Catholic had her" or the claim that Fred Bender "had decoyed her off" before, the deputy could not have helped but notice the equal number of times she let it slip that her daughter "was run away," and that the girl "had run away once before."

Deputy Cole dutifully jotted down Fred Bender's name and assured Mary Stephenson that they would look into it, but he also explained to the woman that the sheriff's office would not be able to search all of the Catholic buildings in town. "I would have to have a search warrant," he said apologetically, and the deputies needed more facts that pointed to the Catholics' involvement before they could get a judge to issue one.[18]

Deputy Wiggins and Deputy Cole were both still in the office about fifteen minutes later when the shots rang out. The lawmen must have propped open the windows to let in whatever breeze was about, for they heard the gunfire from where they sat. Wiggins rose to the window to locate the source of the sound but, unable to get a clear view, sank back down into his desk chair. He never said if he thought of the distraught minister and his wife as he speculated about the origin of the blasts. If so, he hadn't long to wait for verification. A few minutes later, the two city officers walked in, one of them grasping Stephenson tightly by the arm. The other handed Wiggins a gun.[19]

Stalling for time, Wiggins told the prisoner he could not put him in jail without a charge. But then one of the policemen said that Stephenson had just shot a man.

"So I locked him up," Wiggins told the reporters.[20]

As he led Stephenson to the jail located at the rear of the courthouse, Wiggins asked the minister who he had shot.

"[T]hat man over there," Stephenson gestured.

"The priest?" Wiggins asked.

"Yes sir, Father Coyle."[21]

Did Reverend Stephenson say why he shot the priest? the newsmen asked the deputy.

He said that Father Coyle had married "his daughter, Ruth, to a Catholic man," the deputy replied. Stephenson said that they quarreled about it, and the priest had hit him, so he had shot the priest in self-defense.

It is not clear whether any of the journalists bought the story, or asked the lawman what he thought about the minister's excuses. Certainly the eyewitnesses outside had described no scuffle between the two men. The only sounds they had described were the blasts from Stephenson's gun.

Would the prisoner speak to the reporters? they asked.

No, Deputy Wiggins said, the minister said that he wanted to be left alone.[22]

———

With all of Birmingham roused by news of the killing, reporters from the city's three leading daily newspapers fanned out across the city in search of the bride and groom. But when morning sun eased into view, the reporters were still empty-handed on the question of the newlyweds' whereabouts. Their difficulty must have grated. Rumors of Ruth and Pedro "sightings" circulated everywhere around them. The newlyweds had celebrated their nuptials by dining with friends, one source said. They were seen together over on Twenty-fourth Street at a store buying some drinks, said another. They may have spent their wedding night hidden away at a rooming house where Pedro used to stay over on Fifth Avenue, a third source offered. But when the reporters rushed to each spot, they found the couple gone, as if the Magic City had lived up to its nickname and made the bride and groom disappear.[23]

Yet even without the help of the couple at the heart of the scandal, the reporters rapidly pieced together a skeleton of the story's critical facts. The sheriff's office had identified the killer as Reverend Edwin Stephenson, and contrary to the prisoner's self-defense story, rumors buzzing around town identified the marriage of Stephenson's daughter Ruth to a Catholic man named Pedro Gussman as the cause. One needed a license to be lawfully married in Alabama. A reporter for the *Age-Herald* rang the Probate Office in the Jefferson County Courthouse to see if one had been issued there. No, an employee of the office said, Ruth Stephenson and Pedro Gussman had not been there. The couple's license to marry must have come from somewhere else. The reporter thought quickly. If the couple had sidestepped Birmingham, they could have sought a license in Bessemer and then returned to St. Paul's to be married. The newsman placed a second call.

It is not difficult to imagine the trepidation the Bessemer probate judge must have felt when he took the call and realized that a license from his office was at the center of a maelstrom. Once the confirmation was given—yes, Miss Ruth Stephenson and Mr. Pedro Gussman had applied for a license there, said the judge, and they had left with a license in hand—no doubt the jurist retraced his steps. Alabama law-makers had set steep penalties for a knowing violation of the state's marriage laws. Even a judge could be thrown into jail if he failed to heed them. But a quick review of the paperwork suggested that everything was in order: the application that certified that Pedro Gussman was forty-two and Ruth Stephenson eighteen, both the age of majority, both white; the signed bond that guaranteed the truth of their certifications. Unless the judge had purposely ignored something obvious about the applicants, some physical feature that rendered the couple's certifications unworthy of his belief, there would have been no reason to deny them a license to wed, and apparently he had seen nothing of the sort. So on the afternoon of August 11, 1921, Miss Ruth Stephenson and Mr. Pedro Gussman had walked out of the Bessemer Probate Office with a piece of paper embossed with the seal of the great state of Alabama—a document that endowed "any Licensed Minister of the Gospel" with the full and legal authority to solemnize their marriage.[24]

––––––

Like the probate judge in Bessemer, the leaders of the two branches of the Methodist Episcopal Church in Birmingham—the M.E.C. South and the M.E.C., North—suddenly found themselves thrust into the center of the commotion over the shooting of Father Coyle, as local reporters scrambled for facts about the priest's acknowledged shooter. It was no secret around Birmingham that Edwin Stephenson was an ordained member of the Methodist ministry. Over the years he had developed a reputation as the city's "Marrying Parson." A reporter from the *Age-Herald* raced to beat out his rivals to get a comment about the shooting from Stephenson's spiritual leader. In his haste, the newsman must have guessed that Stephenson was more likely to be affiliated with the M.E.C., South than the M.E.C., North. He contacted its pastor first.

The guess proved wrong, and Reverend Robert Echols let him know about it, hinting that Echols considered any suspicion of a connection between his parish and the actions of such a man a grievous insult. Stephenson was not a minister of the *southern* Methodist church, said Echols. Neither was he a member of the southern Methodist congregation. He and his family had "formerly affiliated" with the church, Echols allowed. But they had chosen to leave the M.E.C., South about a year before, after Echols had "remonstrated" with Stephenson over the unseemly business of his "constantly hanging around the courthouse" marrying couples for a fee, Echols said. When Echols had demanded that Stephenson stop, he refused, and unable to come to a meeting of minds, the two men had agreed that Stephenson and his family would be happier elsewhere, Echols said. Echols wanted to be clear: "It is a very deplorable affair, but I should like to have it made clear that Mr. Stephenson was not a minister of the Southern Methodist church," he repeated. Then, taking no chance that the newsman would misunderstand: "He went to the *Northern* Methodist church, and I understand became affiliated with them."[25]

It can no longer be known how the district head of the M.E.C., North, Reverend W. I. Powell, first heard about Echols's remarks. Likely Powell saw them as so many others in the city did that morning, splayed across the front page of the *Birmingham Age-Herald*. However he heard of them, Powell did not miss the insults Echols had directed at the M.E.C., North. It was not so much what Echols had said to the *Age-Herald* reporter. Everything he had said was technically true. It was more a matter of what he had purposely left out. For as everyone knew, the truth—the *whole* truth—could be hidden by facts a person deliberately chose to omit. It was the impression that Echols's omissions had created that irked Powell the most: Echols's intimation that Stephenson's decision to shoot a priest was somehow more appropriately linked to the M.E.C., North church than Echols's own.

Something had to be done.

By the time the papers hit the newsstands that afternoon, Powell had penned a sharply worded rebuke that the editors of the *Birmingham Post* were delighted to print. The *Birmingham Post* was the city's youngest daily. Unlike the *Age-Herald,* which could trace its roots back to before the city's incorporation in 1871, the fledgling *Birmingham Post* had printed its first issue in January 1921, scarcely six months earlier.[26] Lacking its rival's long lineage, the *Post* would have had to scramble for readers, and nothing sold newspapers faster than a good controversy. A head-to-head clash between the district head of the M.E.C., North and the presiding elder of the M.E.C., South fit the bill.

"Rev. Robert Echols is quick to say the Rev. Mr. Stephenson, who did the shooting, was not a member of the Southern Methodist Church," Powell's statement began, icily. "So he was not, *at the time he did the shooting,"* the pastor conceded, "but that is where he came from a very short time ago." "My dear brother, he has not been long from you," Powell continued, as if speaking directly to Echols himself, adding: "If he had stayed with you, I have no idea you could have prevented it." A fuller, fairer rendition of the facts by Reverend Echols might have mentioned that "Rev. Stephenson had been a member of and local preacher in the First Methodist Church, South, for *many* years," Powell went on, unlike the M.E.C., North, which Stephenson had joined only a year ago. Powell's tone darkened even further: "About one year ago, [Stephenson] came with papers showing his *good standing* in that church." The M.E.C., North could hardly be faulted for relying on Reverend Echols's own endorsement of the man. It was the M.E.C., South that had sent Edwin Stephenson to the M.E.C., North, neither disclosing the reasons behind the family's move nor Reverend Echols's apparent disapproval of the man. If the northern Methodists had been fooled, Robert Echols was primarily responsible for their hoodwinking: "It is the law and custom of the Methodist Episcopal Church to receive members from other churches in the same standing they are in the church from which they come, according to the papers they present."[27]

More knowledgeable observers of the spat between the two pastors probably suspected that the heat in their exchange had as much to do with the long-standing disagreements between the M.E.C., South and the M.E.C., North as anything relating to the man sitting in the county jail. Members of the Methodist Episcopal Church had had a tendency to disagree, even before the church had dramatically split in two before the Civil War. Fears concerning the continued unity of the M.E.C. over the slavery question had festered for decades before erupting in earnest in May 1844, after 180 delegates to the General Conference convened their meeting "on the floor of the large, barnlike Greene Street Chapel" in New York City.[28] By far the most contentious question to be discussed at the month long meeting was whether to demand that Bishop James Osgood Andrew of Georgia resign his clerical post. The delegates had debated the fate of Bishop Andrew once before—at their last convening in 1840—after the bishop had inherited a twelve-year-old Negro slave girl named Kitty, and then refused to free the child in violation of church policy. Andrew claimed in his own defense that he could not emancipate the girl because Georgia law prohibited it, and after a tense debate, the 1840 conference of delegates had declined to order his expulsion. By the time the delegates reconvened four years later, however, Bishop Andrew had acquired a second slave, a young Negro boy bequeathed to him through the estate of his first wife. Then, adding fuel to the fire, the widowed bishop had married a woman with even more slaves of her own, all of whom he and his new bride declined to manumit.[29]

The Georgian cleric's slave-holding brought back to the surface the contentious issue that the Methodists had been squabbling about for decades. Back in England, the founding father of the religion, John Wesley, had vehemently opposed American slavery, and when the M.E.C. was launched in the United States in 1784, the church had at first taken an official stance against the practice. That opposition weakened over time, however, as wealthy southerners began to exert more and more influence over church policy. By the early 1800s, the rift among the membership on the question was so great that a bargain was struck to save the church from ripping in two: lay members of the church could hold slaves, but the clergy must desist.

In the years that followed, as the north-south divide on the question of slavery worsened, the two warring camps within the church just barely managed to abide by their truce, and by 1844, the accommodation that had secured the church's unification was shakier than ever. The report that Bishop Andrew of the Southern Conference had taken possession of even more slaves threatened to be the last straw.

The argument between the delegates to the 1844 conference raged for days, as "[t]hrongs of strangers poured into the visitors' gallery" of the Greene Street church to watch the show—"an actual debate over slavery between Northerners and Southerners."[30] Bishop Andrew's defenders argued that Georgia law prevented him from freeing the slaves, and thus the kindest course of action toward the Negroes would be to allow him to continue his ownership, despite the policy of the M.E.C. that prohibited it. More fundamentally, the southerners argued, the question of slave ownership was never an issue in which the church should rightly have interfered to begin with. They trotted out the well-worn passages from the scriptures that (they thought) lent support to the institution: Paul himself had dispatched the slave of Philemon back to his owner with the message not that he and his fellow slaves be freed but that he be treated as "more than a slave, as a beloved brother."[31] More compelling was the story of Noah's son, Ham, who had sinned, and from whom the Negro race descended. The Old Testament made clear that Ham's progeny would forever live in servitude as punishment for his sin. Slaveholders were simply "vindicating the righteous law of God,"[32] the southerners argued, and if the church had a role to play in its regulation, it was simply to teach the master to be kind, and the slave submissive.

The fight grew uglier by the day, and the longer the battle raged, the more apparent it became that the church hovered on the precipice of disaster. In a last-ditch effort to stop the question from being called, one of the delegates made a motion to end the debate and to postpone a decision until the delegates met again four years later, but the motion failed, and the matter of Bishop Andrew's continuing status within the Episcope was called. By a tally of 110 to 69, the conference voted to demand that Bishop Andrew "desist from the exercise of his office so long as [the] impediment [of his slave ownership] remains." He was to cease all clerical functions until he freed his slaves, a clear majority decided.[33]

The defeated southern delegates were outraged; they would have none of it. They quickly announced that their northern brethren's "continued agitation on the subject of slavery and abolition" and actions against Bishop Andrew rendered the General Conference's continued jurisdiction over them "inconsistent with the success of the ministry in the slaveholding states."[34] They would sooner secede from the church than brook such imperious interference. Early the next year at a special convention held in Louisville, Kentucky, the southerners still fumed, and they made good on their threat: the M.E.C., South was born. Decades later—well after the ending of the Civil War— rumblings about the reunification of the church were sometimes heard. But the antagonisms that had split the M.E.C. into two continued to smolder long after the fate of the Union and the question of slavery were resolved. It would take nearly a century before the M.E.C., North and the M.E.C., South were prepared to bury the hatchet and reunite, long after Edwin Stephenson had left the M.E.C., South in a huff over his disagreement with Reverend Robert Echols, and Echols and Powell tussled over which of the two branches was more responsible for him.

By late in the afternoon on the day after the shooting, Echols must have been feeling some heat over the comments he had made to the *Age-Herald* reporter, as he was moved to offer an olive branch. He issued a statement to soften the edge of his earlier remarks; to remedy any misimpression that he harbored any ill will toward the Northern Methodists. "This is no time to stir up denominational differences or to air church animosities," Echols said in a statement printed in the *Birmingham News*. He had not meant to cast aspersions on Edwin Stephenson or his church when he stated that man was no longer a member of the M.E.C., South. "The mere matter of his church affiliation has no bearing on his guilt or innocence, a jury of his peers will say whether he is guilty or not." Then, as if hoping to take the focus off of his disagreement with the M.E.C., North, and fix it on the more pertinent religious disagreement that had motivated Stephenson's act, Echols continued: "[W]hile everyone knows that there are very wide differences between the Methodist Church and the Roman Catholic Church," he wrote, "every good citizen of every creed and of no creed will join together in lamenting this awful tragedy."[35]

In the days immediately following the shooting, a number of Birmingham's religious leaders repeated this sentiment, announcing that they would preach sermons related to the shooting at their Sunday services and penning letters to the local newspapers expressing distaste for the act of a man who would shoot another man over a religious quarrel. Even the presiding elder of Stephenson's own church issued a statement that signaled a reluctance to endorse his act. "Our church believes in constituted authority as the means by which difficulties should be settled," the pastor of the M.E.C., North told the reporters. "There must be some other and better way for setting difficulties."

In a show of support for this supposed newfound unity, a headline in the *Birmingham News* trumpeted optimistically: "Catholics and Protestants United in Sympathy Over Slaying of Father Coyle."[36]

———

News of the killing of Father Coyle raced beyond the borders of Alabama. Within hours, the Associated Press picked up the story and transmitted it across the country.[37] The next day, the story's headline blared from the pages of several of the country's leading newspapers, each identifying the motive for Stephenson's act as fury over the fact that the priest had married Stephenson's daughter to a Catholic. "Minister in Jail for Shooting Priest, Angered by Marriage of Daughter to Catholic," the front page of the *New York Herald* shouted. "Marriage of Minister's Daughter by Father Coyle Cause of Alabama Shooting," echoed the *New York Times*. "Minister Held After Killing of

Dixie Priest, Shooting Follows a Marriage Dispute" was the front-page banner headline in the *Chicago Tribune*.

Despite the shock the headlines suggested, tucked into the seams of the reporters' lines it was possible to detect a noticeable lack of surprise over the slaying of an unarmed priest, as if the newsmen were openly acknowledging that members of the Catholic clergy were becoming something of a moving target. Maybe the reporters were still reeling from the news about the gruesome killing of another priest—Father Patrick E. Heslin of the Holy Angels Catholic Church in Colma, California, whose mangled body had been recovered from a makeshift grave only two days before the word broke of the murder of Father Coyle. Father Heslin had been missing since August 2, after an unidentified man had knocked on the door of the Holy Angels rectory. The man had begged the priest to come with him—a friend was near death, he said—and the two rushed off into the night. Father Heslin was never seen alive again. Frantic, the church offered a reward of $11,000 to anyone who could supply solid information about his whereabouts. William A. Hightower showed up to collect it a day or so later, with a cockamamie story that some woman had told him that some man had told her that he had shot and buried a man on a nearby beach. Suspicious, the police played along as Hightower led them to the gravesite the woman had supposedly identified. Hightower's story began to unravel when he started to dig in the sand, and the officers warned him to take care not to strike the decedent's face with the shovel, and the dolt replied that they needn't worry because he was digging near the priest's feet—a fact only the killer could have known!

After Hightower's arrest, the evidence against him mounted quickly: the priest's housekeeper identified him as the man who had knocked at the rectory door and lured Father Heslin off, and the suspect's blood pressure spiked by a reported thirty-two points when he was asked during an old-style lie detector test if he had murdered the priest. An acquaintance of the prisoner later informed the authorities that Hightower had a motive as well—he had been quite vocal about his hatred for the Catholic Church, the acquaintance said. The priest's wounds corroborated the depth of his attacker's hatred: after the police pulled the priest's body from the makeshift grave, an autopsy showed that Father Heslin had been shot twice, but only after suffering massive injuries to the head; his skull and brain had been literally crushed by the force of the blows inflicted.[38]

Charles P. Sweeney, a freelance writer for the *Nation* living in New York City, had been warning his readers for some time about the deepening anti-Catholic sentiments in the country, particularly in the south. After learning about the anonymous death threats that had been made on the life of Father James Coyle, Sweeney had begun to track the worsening situation for Catholics there. Birmingham's ten thousand Catholics were living in a state of siege, Sweeney reported in 1920. Egged on by men like Georgian Senator Tom Watson whose favorite pastime was spewing anti-Catholic venom, and the bigoted tropes of publications like the *Menace* which southerners purchased unabashedly, wrote Sweeney, anti-Catholicism stood "second only to the hatred of the Negro as the moving passion of entire Southern communities." Birmingham was a prime example, Sweeney told his readers. The writer recounted the deep suspicions about the Klan's involvement in the midnight burning of St. Catherine's Church, the passage by Alabama lawmakers of a "convent inspection law," the purging of Catholics from public office, and the anti-Catholic literature overflowing every city newsstand. Sweeney wrote further about the machinations of the so-called True Americans, a "vast and rapidly growing secret organization having the extermination of Catholicism as its sole object." " 'No Catholics in public office' is its watchword," Sweeney told readers of the *Nation*. Men and women of good will could not remain silent, he counseled: "Intolerance when it joins so many citizens in a common hatred, and dominates the politics of whole American states, is a proper and immediate subject for serious reflection by the whole people."

Charles Sweeney was not at all surprised when he got the news that Father Coyle had been killed some months later. In a follow-up article in the *Nation* on August 31, 1921, under the headline: "Bigotry Turns to Murder," the writer described Coyle's murder and openly worried about the prospects of bringing his killer to justice in the "American hotbed of anti-Catholic fanaticism" that Birmingham had become. In the week following the killing, rumors had already begun to circulate that the grand jury would refuse even to indict Stephenson, Sweeney wrote, and a letter had been sent to the editor of the *Birmingham Age-Herald* that "appeal[ed] for consideration of the murder on its own merits as a crime against the law of the land" without regard to the priest's Catholic religion. "Where else in America but in the gallant Southland would it be necessary that such an appeal would have to be made when a good man was murdered on his front porch?" Sweeney asked, outraged. But Stephenson had culpable company, Sweeney thought. The local press in Birmingham was also at least partly to blame—their willingness to "give full play to the mad utterances of the bigots" earned them partial responsibility for the atmosphere of "ignorance and hatred" that thrived there, he charged. Then he ventured a prediction for the days to come. The stench of bigotry had not yet dissipated in Birmingham, he warned. "Let the country watch Birmingham during the progress of the case against Stephenson...for the appearance of forces that will seek to put the murderer on a pedestal of patriotic heroism."[39]

Probably many in Birmingham did not put much stock in the opinions of a Yankee journalist like Charles P. Sweeney, who heaped judgments on their city in the pages of the *Nation*. But the local press in Birmingham plainly shared some of Sweeney's misgivings. Even as the three Birmingham papers published editorials lamenting the loss of Father Coyle—one so literate and accomplished, "a man of unusual scholarly attainments," "a writer of prose and poetry of a high order," a man of "literary taste and scholarship," they wrote—so, too, did they acknowledge that the city was not of one mind about the killing. There were those in town who were merely holding their tongues, being in that school that hesitated to speak ill of the dead, the papers hinted, and others who failed to manage even that. The editors of the *Birmingham News* were moved to comment that "in view of the strong politico-religious prejudice that has been prevalent in Birmingham the past few years," it might be necessary "to appeal to the sane common sense of the people of Jefferson County." Even before the *News* had circulated an "extra edition" of its paper the day after the killing, the editors wrote, "the comment was heard everywhere from Protestant and Catholic alike: 'The man who killed him will be acquitted.'" "That is a terrible thing to say of any community," the editorial protested; "that jurors drawn from the ranks of its citizens are going to acquit the slayer of a Catholic priest, regardless of the circumstances. The *News,* for one, hopes and believes that it is not true." Stephenson deserved a fair trial, the paper conceded, but if his claim of self-defense was destroyed by the facts, the *News* hoped he would be punished "regardless of the faith of his victim," it wrote—as if it was not a given that one could take for granted such a conviction when the person killed was a Catholic.[40]

George Ward, the former president of the City Commission who had not long before been run out of office on the crest of an anti-Catholic uprising, took the time to pen a letter to the editor of the paper echoing this concern. He urged a quick official response to the shooting to quell the "religious discord" festering in the city. "Swift action is needed to vindicate the good name of Birmingham," Ward wrote.[41]

———

The summer sun was high in the sky when the Louisville & Nashville train from Mobile pulled into the Birmingham Terminal Station around noon the day after the shooting, and the journalists who crowded the platform could read the grief on the arriving priests' faces as they stepped down from the train.

The Birmingham Terminal Station on Twenty-sixth Street and Fifth Avenue had opened to great acclaim in 1909. The "new station," as it was sometimes still called, had immediately taken its place in the company of that great group of passenger stations constructed during the first decade of the twentieth century in those bustling southern metropolises—cities like Columbia, South Carolina, Savannah, Georgia, New Orleans, and Chattanooga—whose increased rates of passenger travel, and Jim Crow laws demanding the segregation of white and colored riders, had combined to necessitate the redesign of the train terminals of the past. At the time it opened, the new station in Birmingham was considered "the most extensive of the stations so far built in the South."

Massive reinforced concrete pillars and a series of arches and beams supported the roof of its train shed, providing needed cover for five separate platforms and ten sets of railroad tracks. Stairways directed passengers downward from the platforms to walkways running beneath the tracks that led toward the center of the terminal station building and prevented the travelers from cutting across the busy rails. Signs to the waiting rooms located in the terminal—the main waiting room for "Whites Only" and a separate waiting room for "Coloreds"—let passengers know which way to head, Negroes to the right, and whites to the left, with a ticket office and baggage room located in between, so as to be accessible to both. The main waiting room was particularly grand—the centerpiece of the station. Its ceiling was made "of four barrel vaults intersecting with a central dome sixty-four feet in diameter" and covered a room nearly seventy-six hundred square feet in area. Panels of Tennessee marble "in a soft shade of gray" lined the walls of the room, stretching upward sixteen feet. Copper cornices and flashings and copper-glazed skylights decorated with wired glass completed the look and reduced the chance of fire, as "no combustible materials were used" anywhere in the building, save the wood necessary to frame the windows and doors, and the dark oak benches that provided seating throughout the terminal. Telephone and telegraph booths, a barbershop, a dining hall, refreshment stands, newsstands, and restrooms with marble tile floors and matching wainscoting supplied passengers with amenities as they waited for or exited their trains.[42]

On that Friday afternoon it is unlikely that the arriving Catholic officials noticed the grandeur of the place, however. It was all they could do to keep their emotions in check. "Mobile is greatly shocked over the tragedy," Father Henry told the crowd of reporters as the clerics made their way through the terminal. The bishop would be arriving later that evening, he told them. Monsignor Dennis Savage of Montgomery, the eldest in the group, was well known to the reporters; he had ministered in the state for over a half century.

Unlike the other priests, who filed past the reporters as if in a daze, the monsignor seemed to understand the newsmen's desire for some further comment from the churchmen. *What did you think when you heard the news?* one of the reporters asked Savage, and he paused briefly to face them. The man's body shook noticeably and his lip trembled when he replied, a reporter for the *Birmingham Post* wrote later. "I could hardly believe it," he said. "It seems so hard a blow that I can hardly express myself." Then he and the others were whisked away to the rectory of St. Paul's.[43]

Saying the 6:30 A.M. Mass had been among Father Coyle's daily duties, but rarely did he recite it to a large crowd. Only the most devout of the St. Paul's congregation found their way to the church for early morning Mass during the week; that "little group in the habit of beginning the day with that quiet hour before the altar."[44] The cavernous cathedral that could seat over one thousand must nearly have swallowed them up, but there were small advantages for those who made the effort to attend the weekday services. No doubt the faithful few would have felt licensed to sit wherever they pleased on such days—gravitating toward the front, in pious proximity to the priest who led them—their modest numbers rendering the question of pew assignments inconsequential.

On the morning after the shooting, Father Brady, St. Paul's assistant priest, recited the morning Mass to a group "augmented" in its usual numbers, though the assemblage was far smaller than the crowds that would pour into the church in the hours and days to come. "[P]ale with sleeplessness," the adherents took their seats in silence, "exchanging no word," remembered one of the parishioners who was there. The youthful priest wore the vestments that had belonged to Father Coyle, his friend and mentor, and his face displayed his grief.

> *Gloria Patri, et Filio, et Spiritui Sancto.*
> *(Glory be to the Father, and to the Son, and to the Holy Spirit.)*
> *Sicut erat in principio, et nunc, et semper, et in saecula saeculorum. Amen.*
> *(As it was in the beginning, is now, and ever shall be, world without*
> *end. Amen.)*

With every chorus of the Mass, the finality of the events of the preceding day seemed to sink deeper into the consciousness of the company, "as one memory crowded another in that place permeated with the personality of the friend that they had lost." Memories of Father Coyle christening their newborns and leading their children in their catechism lessons. Father Coyle taking their confessions. Father Coyle offering words of consolation and guidance as loved ones departed. Father Coyle offering them the Bread of Life from the sacred chalice at the rail of the altar.[45]

> Ostende nobis, Domine, misericordiam tuam.
> (Show us, Lord, Thy mercy.)
> Et salutare tuum da nobis.
> (And grant us Thy salvation.)

The rhythms of the Mass—so familiar and internalized—must have been both a blessing and curse, for the parishioners' ability to recite their replies from memory required no act of thinking, leaving them time to think about the one no longer there. And according to one, the "church soon became a house of grief," the pain washing over them in successive waves of loss.

> Dominus vobiscum.
> (The Lord be with you.)
> Et cum spiritu tuo.
> (And with thy spirit.)

It is hard to imagine when the congregants' expected reply could ever have tasted so bitter. The contrast between their heartbreak and the Mass's words of hopeful faith must have been nearly too much to bear.

When the Mass was finished, Father Brady walked quietly out of the sanctuary, and the church's lights were dimmed, a signal to the churchgoers that it was time to depart. But the "kneeling company did not stir." Maybe it was the cold flicker of the flames from the altar candles that kept them in their seats, or the soothing quiet of the chamber, or the realization that only by remaining motionless would they manage to contain their pain. Finally, when the intention of the congregants to remain in the hall grew clear, Father Brady returned to the altar, and looking out upon them, he began to speak, keeping his words personal then, not rote. Gentle, loving words that openly acknowledged their shared sorrow: "He tried to recall to his mind and to ours the attitude of spirit with which Father Coyle met life, how simple and entire had been his conformity to the will of God," Isabel Beecher remembered later. And as for what could have possessed the man sitting in the jail cell not one block away—that "wretched creature guilty of the blood of this just man," Beecher wrote—the priest ended simply with a prayer for God's mercy. "God forgive them," he said, "for they know not what they do."[46]

———

The papers did not say whether Marcella Coyle attended that 6:30 Mass the morning after her brother was killed, so it was likely that she was not there. She had collapsed shortly after Lige Jr. and Rufus Hammett had carried her brother off the porch the day before. Friends had transported her to St. Vincent's Hospital not long after, where one of the doctors ordered sedatives to blunt Marcella's pain. The staff was still attending to her when workers from Lige Loy's funeral home removed her brother's body from the hospital and brought it to the back to the undertaker's workrooms on Third Avenue. In keeping with Catholic tradition, plans had been made to have the priest's remains lie in state at St. Paul's beginning the next afternoon. People would want a last chance to view the body. The gaping wound in his left temple needed to be camouflaged.[47]

Throughout that afternoon, trains continued to arrive in Birmingham from all directions, and priests and laypersons filed off of them and made their way to the Third Avenue Church. Sometime around 3:00 P.M., the hush of the church's chamber grew deeper still, when the coffin cradling the body of Father Coyle was carried in and positioned in front of the altar rail, and its lid gently lifted. For the next two days, volunteers of the Knights of Columbus took turns guarding the casket, one man at the head of the bier, another at its foot, as mourners waited in line to say their final goodbyes. Before long, the queue was a chain of living grief, silently coiling through the center of the church and out into the street, where the August sun, indifferent to their misery, beat down on those forced to wait outside, the temperature near ninety. Still, the callers were not deterred—they numbered in the "thousands," one paper reported. The wait must have seemed interminable.[48]

Most of the parents who stood in the line had left their children at home. Younger ones had trouble standing quietly for so long, and no doubt many parents must also have worried about the effect that seeing a dead man might have on them. But here and there a child could be spotted in the line, including Francis, the six-year-old daughter of Frank and Helen Mahon. The wait could not have been easy for the child, but Helen Mahon was determined that her daughter would see the fallen priest. She pulled Francis close as they edged nearer to the casket, and when their turn finally came to stand before it, the mother bent down and lifted the girl so that she could see him. "Remember this, Francis," Helen Mahon whispered to the little girl, "for you are looking at a saint."[49] As night approached, and the line continued to grow, someone must have realized that steps would have to be taken to ensure that the callers still waiting had not come in vain. An announcement was made that the church would be kept open; everyone who had come would have a chance to look on the priest one last time.

———

The funeral Mass in the Catholic tradition is generally held the day after the wake. But in light of the great number of people who wanted to view the casket of Father Coyle, and the scores of churchmen who continued to make their way to Birmingham from distant parts, St. Paul's Church announced a delay in the recitation of the funeral Mass: Bishop Allen would celebrate a Solemn Pontifical Mass at 9:30 A.M. Saturday, and Father Michael Henry, a lifelong friend of Father Coyle, would deliver the final funeral Mass preceding the burial at 3:00 P.M. the following afternoon.

When Saturday arrived, the spacious St. Paul's was quickly "taxed to capacity." Well before the time the bishop was scheduled to speak, every pew in the hall was filled. "Scores were unable to gain admission," the *Birmingham News* reported, and hundreds chose to stay anyway, just outside the church doors, as the bishop delivered his sermon. When Bishop Allen stepped up to the pulpit to begin the Mass, a heavy silence descended on the gathering, broken only occasionally by a stifled sob,[50] and even the bishop had to stop several times to regain his composure. In his sermon, he puzzled aloud about the changes that had occurred in the city of Birmingham, a place that had opened its doors to Catholics in its early days, he said. After his appointment, the bishop told them, many good people in Birmingham had extended him a cordial welcome, including members of other faiths. But over the years, that climate of tolerance had changed. A relentless campaign of "propaganda of hatred" had been aimed at the Church, and Father Coyle had borne the brunt of it on their behalf. "Over and over again there were threats of death made against him," and although the city was home to many people of goodwill, "a few unprincipled politicians" had permitted an environment of abuse and intolerance to thrive. "What a terrible indictment of the community that does not put such men where they belong and teach them the principles of right and justice."[51]

————

The massive numbers who had come to view the casket and who had attended (or tried to attend) the bishop's requiem Mass provided some warning about what might be expected the day Father Coyle was to be buried. But the scene outside St. Paul's on the day of the funeral itself must nonetheless have stunned those there to witness it. The church itself with its thousand-plus capacity was filled to its limit long before the beginning of the 3:00 P.M. service, and "thousands" more who were unable to enter the hall stood quietly outside in the afternoon sun. A cameraman from one of the Birmingham newspapers attempted to photograph the horde from a spot across the street, but the throng was so mammoth—the largest funeral gathering in state's history, it was thought—that his lens could only capture a fraction of it. And judging from the angle of the shot, the photographer probably put himself at some risk to get even that: he must have been leaning out of the upper floor window of one of the buildings on the south side of Third Avenue when his flashbulb went off. The picture looked down and over a multitude of mourners who, despite the heat, stood tightly bunched, silently facing the church—a veritable sea of top hats, fedoras, and dark suits and dresses, dotted here and there with an occasional umbrella thrown open to ward off the light rain that fell off and on that day.

A reporter inside the church described the proceeding within the chamber: "a retinue of priests and assistants entered from a side entrance," followed closely by a group of friends and relatives of the priest, who took the seats at the front of the church that had been kept open for them. Banners and flags encircled the coffin, none more prominently than the American flag—a silent answer to those who continued to question Catholics' patriotism. When Father Henry, "tall, and white-haired," stepped behind the podium, a "great hush fell on the audience."[52] It is not likely that those who were there would have been offended had the priest's address been tinged with bitterness. Most of the parishioners understood that the two men had shared their boyhood. But Father Henry's sermon was given instead in a "spirit of charity," one wrote later, and although his voice broke now and then as he took some time to describe the keenness of his loss, otherwise he delivered his message with calm deliberation. Father Henry told the assemblage that he and Father Coyle had first come to America as young men, "carried by the same desire to work at the call of Jesus," and he beseeched them not to forget all of the good work that his friend, their pastor, had done in pursuit of that goal during his years among them. "Remember, dear brethren, the interest Father Coyle took in you" and the hopes he had for you, Father Henry said to them. For "if he were with us now, it would be his wish that each be faithful to His trust, that we continue steadfastly in the faith." Turning to the matter of his friend's killer, Father Henry challenged the gathering to scrutinize their own feelings of anger and desires for revenge: "Would you have Father Coyle change places with his murderer?" he solemnly asked them before answering his own question. No, not one among them could believe the "unfortunate man who [was then] sitting in prison with the stain of blood on his hands" was in a better place than the man whose life he took. "The Catholic Church does not call for vengeance," he reminded them gently. "We believe in law and order, and the institutions of the land which uphold these." Then, as if realizing that his audience might lack confidence that Birmingham authorities would commit themselves to sorting right from wrong, Father Henry finished: "It is in the hands of the law."[53]

When Father Henry concluded the service and stepped back from the pulpit, a "request was made that the center aisles be cleared of the multitude that had thronged into them for the service" so that the coffin could be withdrawn from the chamber. Six pallbearers gently hoisted the casket from its bier and shepherded it through the hall and out the front doors. They eased their way down the broad concrete steps, forging a narrow channel through the assemblage of mourners waiting outside. Their passage could not have been easy. The crowd was so thick that, were it not for the vehicle that stood waiting with its back doors flung wide to receive their load, the men would scarcely have been able to tell when they had reached the curb. When the task was accomplished, the pallbearers passed the casket into the hearse, and a slow convoy of cars soon headed to the Southside Cemetery. So great was the host of people that "[a]utomobiles were still leaving the church when the head of the procession had reached the cemetery, nearly three miles away."[54]

As the line of cars snaked away, one was spied among the crowd whose horror must have surpassed even that of her neighbors, for sorrow and guilt form a formidable pair even if borne undeservedly. Eighteen-year-old Ruth Stephenson Gussman, dressed all in black, stood in the midst of the crowd, recognized by only a few acquaintances, the papers reported later, her cheeks wet with tears.[55]

| A Killer Speaks

AFTER EXCHANGING VOWS in the nearly empty St. Paul's, Pedro and Ruth Stephenson Gussman did what most happy newlyweds do: they allowed themselves a little time to celebrate. They bypassed Ruth's home and the rooming house Pedro had moved into a few weeks before, and they headed for the home of friends. Homer Eugene Badger and his wife Louise had just finished their dinner when a cab pulled up to the curb at 1005 North Twenty-fourth Street. A man and a woman climbed out of the livery; Homer recognized Pedro Gussman at once. Like so many who came to the United States at the tail end of the nineteenth century and start of the next, Pedro let his friends "Americanize" the Latin sounds of his name: although he invariably scrawled "Pedro Gussman" whenever writing his signature, Homer and Louise Badger always called him "Pete."

It is doubtful that that was the first thing to change about Pedro's name. Born in Guayama, Puerto Rico, Pedro's last name was almost certainly Guzman with a *z*, not Gusman with an *s*. But when he entered the United States at age eighteen, it was recorded as Gusman, and the paperhanger probably found it wise not to press the point. Later, after the shooting, the Birmingham papers began to refer to him in their daily stories as "Pedro Gussman" with a second *s*—diluting the Spanish strains of his surname even further. He told the reporters that they were spelling it wrong, that it was "Gusman" with one *s*, not "Gussman" with two; but day after day the papers continued to insert the double consonant, until it must have seemed that it was Pedro himself who needed to learn how to spell: that Gussman was correct, and Gusman simply some foreign relic from which the migrant should have been pleased to flee. After some time, it seems that Pedro decided to let the matter rest; even his death certificate and gravestone some years later included the second *s*.[1]

Homer Badger and Pedro Gussman had been friends for years. Both men made their livings with their hands, Homer as a painter, Pedro as a paper-hanger. It might even have been their brother trades that brought the two men together—the kind of honest, hard work that can dissolve differences, toiling side by side in some patron's home in the torrid Alabama heat. Or maybe their introduction was more basic still, during one of those times when Pedro was in search of housing. Some years earlier, when Homer and Louise Badger had taken in boarders at their Fifth Avenue flat, they had invited Pete to live in one of their rooms. He had become a member of their household, and was still a welcome guest.

But Homer and Louise were surprised to see their visitor piloting a young woman behind him when he climbed out of the cab in front of their house that afternoon. The Badgers said later that they knew Ruth Stephenson by sight, but they did not know her well, and Pete had never mentioned that he was acquainted with the girl. Nor had Homer and Louise ever seen them together before that day. Their astonishment grew when Pedro and Ruth announced that they were married. Unfathomable! Pete had not said a word about his plans.

The shadows of evening were just beginning to descend on the city, and the next day was a workday, but the bride and groom's news was cause for celebration. Though the Badgers had already eaten their supper, Louise quickly laid out a meal for the pair, and she and Homer listened enthralled as Ruth and Pedro laughingly described how they had slipped away from their jobs in the middle of the day and caught the train to Bessemer to be married, without anyone knowing their plans.[2]

———

Ruth and Pedro had taken the precaution of arranging to meet up at noon-time. A couple of weeks earlier, Edwin and Mary Stephenson had agreed to let Ruth resume her work as a sales clerk for the popular downtown department store, Loveman, Joseph & Loeb, but only after extracting a promise from their daughter that she would abandon her intention to practice Catholicism. Ruth gave the promise, she told a reporter later, but only because she was coerced to do so. A few months before, she had slipped off to Our Lady of Sorrows without her parents' knowledge, and had been baptized as a Catholic there. But, Ruth said, when her father discovered her conversion, before the scheduled date of her First Communion, he locked her in a room and "mistreated me terribly," imprisoning her in the house for days, while his friends from the Birmingham Police Department guarded the house to prevent her escape.

After it was all over, Ruth would sometimes mention those days, but rarely in a way that brought the horror back to life. The girl displayed behavior very common for those whose distress has involved members of their own families: she disclosed the general outlines of her ordeal in hazy terms, letting phrases like "he mistreated me terribly" to substitute for a more vivid accounting. "I hate to talk about my people," she once explained to a reporter, but then seemed to consider the irony of directing such a statement to a person whose job it was to broadcast everything she said to the world. "I might as well be frank," she added weakly. "I still have nightmares about those nights."[3]

When the fury over Ruth's conversion receded in her household, her parents held out an olive branch—an excursion. They would pay for her to travel to Texas, they said, to visit with one of her uncles who lived there, though Mary Stephenson would go along, of course. The motivation underlying the offer must have been apparent to the girl: an out-of-state trip would separate Ruth from the people her parents were certain were influencing her, and maybe her Texas kindred would succeed where Ruth's parents had failed in reconnecting the girl with her Protestant roots. But if Ruth was annoyed by her parents' manipulations, she set her resentment aside. From time to time, stories from the Lone Star State would make their way into the Birmingham papers, bigger than life, like the former republic itself. The thought of traveling there, or anywhere, must have been exciting to the eighteen-year-old; she could not have had many occasions to travel outside the city of her youth. So she accepted her parents' offer, ignoring for a time the unhappy truth that the rewards of such deals are rarely lasting. Indeed, when the trip neared its end, the women's time in the Texas sun seemed only to have hardened their differences, and when the time came for them to return to Birmingham, the tension between the mother and daughter was worse than ever before.[4]

The twin cities of Texarkana, Texas, and Texarkana, Arkansas, nestled up to a single shared border separating the two states, outdoing the more famous "Twin Cities" to the north. Whereas Minneapolis–St. Paul maintained a united municipal boundary within a single state, Texarkana managed the same feat in two. Knit together by the aptly dubbed State Line Avenue, their main street stretched out with surveyor-like precision directly along the cities' shared border—Bowie County, Texas, to the west of the street, Miller County, Arkansas, to the east. A federal building housing a United States Post Office with a joint zip code—the only one of its kind—was later erected, with exactly half of its rooms in one state and half in the other, making it possible for amused visitors to stand before its front door with a foot in each.

Local lore abounded on the question of the ancestry of the cities' peculiar name—Texarkana. One popular explanation was that it hailed from a favorite regional cocktail, the "Texarkana Bitters," coined by a general store owner from Bossier Parish, Louisiana. Others claimed that it derived from an old steamboat named the *Texarkana* that carried passengers and goods up and down the Red River in the late 1800s. Perhaps the most persuasive claim was that "Texarkana" was simply an amalgam of the names of the two states that State Line Avenue yoked together—"Tex" for Texas, "ark" for Arkansas, with a respectful "ana" added in a hospitable nod to Louisiana, their neighbor less than thirty miles to the south.[5]

Ruth Stephenson would not have known a soul in Texarkana, but when the train ferrying her and her mother back to Birmingham stopped at its railroad depot, the girl slipped off it unseen, silently proclaiming with her flight that a life among a city of strangers trumped one with those whom she knew back home. Perhaps the relative smallness of the place bolstered the teenager's nerve. The growth of Texarkana had been steady and promising almost from the moment, in 1874, when the railroad lines of the Cairo & Fulton forded the Red River and intersected with those of the Texas & Pacific just across the Texas state line. But on the night Ruth Stephenson stepped noiselessly off the train at the Texarkana Union Station in 1921, the Texarkana had a combined reported population of only 14,118 whites, 5,614 Negroes, and 6 amorphous "Others"—which made it less than a fifth the size of the Magic City to its east. Still, though smaller than her hometown, with no familiar landmarks to guide her, Ruth had to use her wits, so she made her way to a Catholic hospital and sought help.[6] In 1909, a Catholic Irishman named Michael Meagher had left his entire estate to the city of Texarkana, to build a hospital. With the help of the Sisters of Charity of the Incarnate Word, the hospital had opened its doors in 1916, only five years before Ruth Stephenson walked through them.

It is not hard to imagine the sense of betrayal Mary Stephenson must have felt when she realized her daughter had gone from the train. At the next opportunity, Mary followed suit, circling back around and enlisting the help of some local authorities. Although the records no longer exist to show precisely who came to the woman's aid, in a city with two police forces and two county sheriffs, there would have been a number of officials from which to choose. Maybe it was A. J. Lummus, the Texarkana-Arkansas chief of police, or his counterpart the police chief of Texarkana-Texas. Or it might have been Lish Barber, the sheriff of Miller County, Arkansas, or G. A. Richardson, the sheriff of Bowie County, Texas, or even one or more of their deputies. Whomever she talked to, Mary Stephenson must have told the lawmen that her daughter would seek refuge with the Catholics, for not long after Ruth's disappearance from the train, a group arrived at the Michael Meagher Memorial Hospital on the corner of Fifth and Walnut Streets in search of the girl.[7]

It is hard to think what the Sisters of Charity must have thought when the companionless youngster arrived unannounced, only to be followed not long after by a group of lawmen and her furious mother. The authorities made it clear that the teenager was to be turned back over to her parent, Ruth told a reporter later, and Mary Stephenson dragged her back to Birmingham more convinced than ever that she could not be trusted. For the next two weeks, Ruth recalled, she was "mistreated many times" and kept "under constant watch," until finally her parents relented a bit and allowed her to return to her job. But even then it was clear that they believed she would run off again. Every morning Edwin Stephenson walked her to the front door of the department store just to be sure.

That was why Ruth and Pedro had agreed to make August 11, 1921 look like a normal workday. They had agreed to meet at noon, with a plan to take the streetcar to Bessemer where they would apply for their license to avoid running into Ruth's father at the courthouse in Birmingham. But when the time came for Ruth to meet Pedro that day and she moved toward the front door of the store, one of her uncles was just walking in. She was sure she would be caught, she said later, but by some act of heaven the man failed to see her, and Ruth willed her feet to keep moving until she reached the spot outside where Pedro was waiting.[8]

In Bessemer, they were nearly foiled again. After they had obtained their license from the probate judge, they walked the few blocks to the local Catholic church, St. Aloysius, and asked to speak with Father Callahan, its presiding priest. But the priest was out. He would not be back in time to perform their rites, they were told. How strange the things that can unravel a plan—the possibility that Father Callahan might be away had obviously not occurred to them. After formulating a secret meeting place, dodging Ruth's relative, sidestepping the place her father was most likely to be, and obtaining the state's official permission to wed, the last critical ingredient needed to accomplish their plan—a priest!—was missing.

It could not have been easy for the couple to decide to return to Birmingham. The Bessemer marriage license authorized any official pastor in the state to marry them, so if they could make it to St. Paul's unseen, they could ask Father Coyle for his help. But the rectory was terrifyingly close to the courthouse where Ruth's father conducted marriages in the hallways. If Stephenson happened to step outside as they were approaching the rectory, all would be lost. Worse, had Ruth and Pedro known the full truth—that Edwin Stephenson was already on the lookout for his daughter, that he had been canvassing the streets all afternoon, that he and Mary Stephenson had alerted the police there, and a private detective as well, all of whom were making efforts to find the girl—the prospect of returning to the city would likely have been unthinkable. But the couple labored under that great advantage of ignorance, and being unaware of the determined multiplicity of efforts already underway in the city to discover her, Ruth and Pedro resolved to double back to Birmingham to be married at St. Paul's.

And somehow they managed it. When the streetcar arrived back in the city, Pedro and Ruth stepped off it and moved toward the towering twin steeples that guarded the entrance of St. Paul's. The bustle of the downtown streets must have conferred some soothing frenetic cover, helping them pass undetected, even across Third Avenue and straight up the walkway to the rectory door. But there luck failed them again. Father Coyle was out, Father Brady told them; he was visiting with Father Malone at the rebuilt St. Catherine's Church in nearby Pratt City, and because Ruth and Pedro had posted no "bans" at St. Paul's announcing their plans to marry in advance, by church rule only its presiding priest (Father Coyle) possessed the authority to take their vows. It might have seemed that heaven itself was testing their firmness.

Later, no doubt, with the maddening benefit of hindsight, Father Brady must have wished that he had just sent the twosome away. But at that moment, as he looked at the couple standing on the threshold of the rectory, no doubt he read the desperation on their faces. The urge to assist them must have been strong. He could call St. Catherine's to see if Father Coyle could be reached, Father Brady offered.

Ruth and Pedro said they would wait.

———

After it was all over, Father Joseph Malone told a reporter that he and Father Coyle were deep in conversation when the telephone rang that day. A call from St. Paul's for Father Coyle: Ruth Stephenson and Pedro Gussman were waiting to be married, the caller said. Father Coyle never lived to tell what passed through his mind when he received that message, but something deep inside him must have urged caution. Probably the priest remembered the Methodist minister's fury some six years before when he found his twelve-year-old daughter sitting and talking with the priest on the rectory porch. Or maybe Father Coyle experienced one of those premonitions people sometimes have, before moving toward the very danger about which they have just been warned. It is impossible to know for sure.

But Father Malone would never forget the words his friend said to him as he prepared to return to St. Paul's that day: "Stephenson will probably kill me for this," Father Coyle said.[9]

———

It would not have taken the priest long to get back to St. Paul's from Pratt City. The distance was only about seven miles, and the parish had recently surprised their pastor with a gift of a new Model T Ford. Even with the afternoon traffic, he would have made the trip easily in less than half an hour. When he arrived, Pedro and Ruth showed him the marriage license they had obtained in Bessemer. After checking to see that everything was in order, Ruth told a reporter later, Father Coyle invited her and Pedro to stand with him before the enormous white marble altar that dominated the front end of the church. The soaring arches and columns of the hall would have dwarfed the small group. Ruth and Pedro had arrived without friends or family, so Father Brady and Father Coyle's sister, Marcella, stood quietly nearby, the only witnesses, as Father Coyle led them through their vows.[10]

The fact that Ruth and Pedro were permitted to stand before the altar as they exchanged their pledges—to love and honor each other, in sickness and in health, until death parted them—meant more to the girl than she could say. Of all people, she understood the significance of the setting. The Catholic Church imposed a number of rules when it came to marriage in 1921, like the command that offended so many Protestants that the Church would recognize as legitimate only those unions officiated by a Catholic priest. If a Catholic was married by anyone else, say, a justice of the peace, or a minister of another faith, the Church considered the ceremony a nonevent in the eyes of God. Catholics were to be married only by Catholic priests. Another canon involved the treatment of interfaith marriages—marriages between a Catholic and a person outside the faith. Catholics and non-Catholics could marry under the Church's doctrine, but the unions were not considered ideal. In the eyes of the Church, the question of the religious upbringing of the unborn children of such spouses seemed to hang over the heads of the lovers like a hatchet. Thus, though the marriages could occur, priests were forbidden to take such a couple's vows in front of the holy altar. Interfaith couples would be shuffled off into the sacristy—the changing room, where the priests and altar boys put on and off and stored their vestments—an unspoken rebuke aimed to communicate to the couple that the situation needed to be remedied.

Ruth and Pedro were spared that little indignity as a result of the girl's conversion to the faith a few months before. The bride had paid dearly for the privilege, and later she tried to explain to a reporter the sense of pride she felt as she and Pedro stood before the grand altar of St. Paul's and exchanged their vows; how much it had meant to her to be able to stand there, rather than in the sacristy, as though that sanctum itself were capable of shouting her status to the world—that Ruth Stephenson was a Catholic. That she had married a Catholic man, and that never again would her father, or mother, or anyone else have anything to say about it. It would not have taken long, that humble exchange of promises, without a lengthy Catholic Mass to delay the *denouement,* and before long they were married—Mr. and Mrs. Pedro Gussman— victors over the myriad panicked moments the day had tossed their way. But as the triumphant couple prepared to leave, Father Coyle delayed them for a moment and spoke directly to the bride, the last words she would ever hear him say: "You've got a good boy," the priest told Ruth. "The right thing for you to do is to notify your parents that you are married at once."[11]

A reporter asked her later if she had followed this advice. Yes, she said, she had called home not long after the ceremony.

Even with the deed done, the teenager must have had to brace her nerve, and when it was Ruth's cousin who picked up the receiver instead of one of her parents, she must have breathed a sigh of relief. Ross Campbell, the thirty-two-year old son of Edwin Stephenson's eldest sister, Alice, told his cousin that her parents were not at home. The papers never said what had brought Ross Campbell to his uncle's house. Maybe Edwin and Mary had beseeched their families for help, after learning that Ruth was missing, just as they had urged the sheriff, and Police Chief Shirley, and their men to launch a hunt for their girl.

Ruth asked her cousin to give her parents a message when they returned: "I am married to a Catholic boy," she told him.

The reporter asked her later if she knew whether Ross Campbell had relayed the message, but Ruth did not know. It was possible that he had, or that her father learned it when he confronted Father Coyle on the porch, as he was saying from his jail cell. The girl could not say.[12]

———

After Pedro and Ruth had relayed their adventures to Homer and Louise and polished off the last of their dinner, the four friends decided to prolong the festivities a bit longer. They strolled two doors down to the corner store, bought some cold drinks, and carried them back to Homer and Louise's home. They were still celebrating when a man walked up—Thomas Cartwright, a detective in the Birmingham Police Department. The detective had stopped in at the corner store just after they had left. When the store owner overheard him talking on the phone about Stephenson and the shooting, he told Cartwright that the minister's daughter had only just been there. The detective could probably still catch up with her. She was with Homer and Louise Badger, who lived up the street. It is impossible to know whether the detective regretted breaking the spell of cheer that must have surrounded the two couples when he found them. The new spouses must nearly have sparkled—"They were in high spirits," said Louise Badger later, ruefully. But Cartwright forged ahead: Ruth's father was under arrest at the county jail, he told them. He had shot and killed Father Coyle. It was plain from their reactions, the detective said later, that before that moment the group had not heard the news—the Stephenson girl burst into tears, he said. After asking them a few questions, the detective saw no reason to hold them any longer. Ruth and Pedro called a livery cab, and still reeling from the news, they disappeared into the summer night.[13]

Early the next morning, Pedro Gussman slipped unnoticed into his rooming house on Twenty-second Street and threw his few belongings into a suitcase. "I'm in a bad fix," Pedro told a fellow boarder named Parks. "I'm not sure how it will turn out." Then he melted off into the streets.

Did he say where he was headed? a journalist pressed Parks later.

No, Parks said. He had not thought to slow Pedro's exit with questions.

Did he mention where he and his wife had stayed the night before?

No, nothing besides being in a fix.

Only later did the local reporters learn where Pedro had headed: the man had simply gone to work! Someone spotted him later that morning, at Sherwin Williams, purchasing his day's supplies, just as he always did, as if the event of his wedding and the shooting of his pastor had provided no occasion to deviate from his usual routine.[14] It is impossible to think that the groom could have been unaffected by the news that his father-in-law, now sitting in jail, had killed the priest who had married him to Ruth. But Pedro Gussman went about that day as though it was a Friday like any other, a move that had plainly taken the reporters off guard. Yet maybe the explanation for the paperhanger's industry had nothing to do with indifference to the awful news. Maybe it was no more complicated than that the wages of a day laborer did not confer a lot of leeway. Pedro Gussman, at age forty-two, had a young wife to support, which required work, whether standing in the shadow of a crisis or not.

———

At age fifty, Joseph R. Tate, the circuit solicitor for Jefferson County, cut a commanding figure. His dress was dignified and imposing—a dark three-piece suit, white shirt, and tie, even on the steamiest days—and his intelligent eyes were framed by a pair of round, steel-rimmed glasses. The prosecutor's hair was full and dark, but he kept it closely cropped, and when he went out in public, a fedora derby of muted grey felt hid most of it from sight. From time to time, the local papers printed photographs of him; his expression was invariably somber—not scowling, but certainly without a smile—as if mirth was somehow unprofessional, or in warning, perhaps, to the offenders who crossed his path that the prosecutor was nobody's fool.

The public image only told part of the story though. Joe Tate laughed often, one of his grandson's recalled years later, especially when he was at home, surrounded by the happy noises of his family, or submerged in the boisterous energy of his grandchildren.[15] A photograph taken of him later in life, when the need for reserve felt perhaps less acute, captured deep laugh lines radiating from the corners of his eyes, a silent witness to this lighter side. Joe Tate and his wife, Eula, kept their family close, in a veritable family compound "up on the hill" on Ninth Avenue, where Tates young and old could trip into and over each other at will. Joe and Eula's home, at 904 Ninth Avenue West, housed at least six members, according to the 1920 census taker, while Paul Tate, the couple's eldest son, built a house for himself, his wife Catherine and their two children, Mildred and Joe Allen, just a couple of doors down. As late as 1930, four of the couple's six children, ranging in age from seventeen to twenty-seven, still lived in Joe and Eula's home. Even the marriage of twenty-five-year-old Bernice Tate Cohron failed to sever the familial tie—the bride simply steered her husband, Ralph, and later their daughter Louise, into the family home instead. Some years later, when the brood of Tates began to spread out across Birmingham, the patriarch's home on Ninth Avenue still remained the family's center of gravity. Eula Tate was reputedly an excellent cook; grandchildren arrived to the smells of fried corn and okra, pickled watermelon rind, and an assortment of other southern delicacies. And if Joe Tate was not already there in the kitchen savoring his wife's fares, more often than not the youngsters would find their grandfather outside, tending his garden—a favorite occupation—where he would stake off flowers and vegetables in row after perfect row.[16]

There is no record of where Joe Tate was when he received word that Father Coyle had been shot, but considering the lateness of the hour, maybe a call to his home pulled the prosecutor back to work. The circuit solicitor's office was located in the Jefferson County Courthouse, just steps away from St. Paul's rectory, and not long after the shooting, a local reporter spotted Joe Tate on the rectory's blood-splattered porch. The prosecutor was talking with a group of officers who were scooping up discarded cartridges and taking measurements of the damages Stephenson's gun had inflicted on the house and church. The sky was beginning to darken, and the scene was chaotic—the kind of confused bedlam that can sink a prosecutor's case if not contained. A throng of men and women jammed the front yard, spilling onto the sidewalk just beyond. Some, gripped by curiosity or horror, leaned against the edge of the porch in hope of a better view. Crime scenes can easily be corrupted, even by those whose interest is earnest and benign. If the prosecutor expected to make any use of what the lawmen were finding, order needed to be restored—enough calm to let the officers record their observations: the pathway of Stephenson's slugs, the location of the victim's blood. Memories of such specifics fade fast—without written records of their findings, the officers would be lost when asked to recall them later. No doubt, Joe Tate trusted the police to know all that, and acting in the hectic shadow of the shooting, it appears that he spent very little time making certain of it.

The prosecutor had his own set of concerns. Edwin Stephenson was sitting in a jail cell two doors down, and even as Tate asked the lawmen to brief him about what they knew, a feeling would have begun to gnaw at him. All veteran prosecutors know there are advantages to questioning a prisoner quickly—striking while the metal is hot—before he or she has time to concoct a story, or think better of talking at all. Joe Tate needed to get to the jail.

Thus, Tate may not have given much thought, at the time, to the odd mishmash of lawmen rooting about on the porch, the motley jumble of deputies and police officers peering at this, measuring that, or generally just milling about. Normally the sheriff's office and the Birmingham Police Department would divvy up their cases. Over the years, the two offices had developed a loose arrangement to keep from feuding when their jurisdictions overlapped. But that day, notwithstanding that Stephenson had plainly surrendered himself to Sheriff Chris Hartsfield, officers from the outfit of Police Chief Shirley were on the porch as well, as if the matter of who was running the case had yet to be resolved. If Joe Tate noticed it, he probably thought he could sort the puzzle out later, when the need to press forward was less urgent, without worrying about the possibility that at least some of the men he left gathering evidence on the porch were more likely to sympathize with the man whose crime they were investigating than the priest he had killed. For Stephenson was both a Klansman and a Methodist minister, and Coyle had married his daughter to a Catholic against his wishes, perhaps reason enough for a fellow Klansman to be less than fastidious with the evidence he was gathering or precise about his observations of Stephenson's crime.

Joe Tate could have sent one of his assistants to conduct the interrogation of the prisoner. By 1921, Tate had hired three able associates: John Morrow, John P. McCoy, and James Davis, any of whom could have handled the questioning. But from the start, it must have been clear that the Coyle homicide belonged in that special, unwritten category of cases that demanded Joe Tate's personal attention—whose delegation the public would not tolerate, no matter how competent his assistants might be. Sometimes it was the prominence of the victim or status of the offender that demanded the chief prosecutor's hands-on involvement. Other times, when a homicide's motive was especially explosive or tensions over a crime threatened to flare out of control, Tate's particular notice or seasoned perspective would have been desired to defuse the situation. The Coyle homicide had it all. A Catholic priest shot by a Methodist minister, and not just any priest but the appointed dean of Northern Alabama, the Catholics' most famous local champion. And if there was any question that Tate's personal interest would be required in the case, the publicity about the shooting before the end of the next day would have put the question to rest—when newspapers across the country spread the news that an Alabamian preacher had slayed a priest over the marriage of his daughter to a Catholic. Even for Birmingham, which had once been dubbed the "Murder Capital" of the nation, it was plain that this killing was no everyday event. Joe Tate decided to handle the prisoner's questioning himself.[17]

It is doubtful that Joe Tate expected Stephenson to deny that he was the man who had shot Father Coyle when he entered his cell that night. Stephenson had already admitted to Deputy Wiggins and Officers Snow and Weir that he shot the priest. So chances were good that he would not suddenly deny it. Still, Joe Tate would have wanted to hear the admission from Stephenson himself, in the presence of an officer or other witness whom Tate could later call before the grand jury or at trial to testify about what Stephenson had said. Criminal defendants could not be forced to testify at their own trials, Tate knew, even if they had confessed earlier. At trial, Stephenson could remain silent and force Tate to prove his guilt without any help from Stephenson himself. Moreover, in such a case, the judge would be obligated to instruct the jury that it could not penalize the defendant for his decision not to testify. The jurors could not infer from the man's silence that Stephenson was guilty, the judge would tell them, even if they were tempted to believe that an innocent man would have had no reason to shun the witness stand. In short, no matter what Stephenson had already said to the officers who took him into custody, there was no way to force him to repeat those admissions at a later trial. This made the time between arrest and the arrival of defense counsel a critical window of opportunity for a prosecutor—the time to get the defendant to make a confession in front of an officer, or a stenographer, or in writing, from whom or which the jury could later learn what the accused had said. For this reason, when Joe Tate entered Stephenson's cell in the early evening hours of August 11, 1921, he brought two men with him: Chief

Deputy Sheriff Fred McDuff of the Jefferson County sheriff's office and Assistant Coroner George C. Moore. Dr. R. H. Hammrick, the jail physician, may have been present as well. The key was to get the defendant talking.

In the 1920s and early 1930s, quarrels broke out about the line between acceptable and unacceptable interrogation techniques. Police forces across the country used threats, fear, and even bodily pain to obtain the desired confessions, for nothing, it was thought, served as well as a defendant's own admission of guilt. In the hunt for such confessions, the moral limits of tolerable questioning sometimes appeared blurred. Stories of brutality were legion, and perhaps not surprisingly, as in so many other aspects of life at the time, Negro men suffered the worst of it. For example, in 1930, after police officers in Marion, Indiana had arrested three Negroes, including sixteen-year-old James Cameron, for the murder of a white man, one of the officers stomped on the boy until he agreed to sign a confession he had not even been allowed to read. Later, a mob gathered, stormed the jail where Cameron and the other men were being held, pulled the Negroes from their cells, and hanged two of them from a tree. It may have been only horticultural fortuity—the tree lacked a sufficiently stout third limb—that won the younger man a temporary reprieve, but while the mob lynched the other two, they beat James Cameron senseless. Just as they were about to hang him as well, an unidentified voice in the crowd called out that he had committed no crime, and the mob relented and turned him back over to the authorities. Despite the brutal means employed to obtain the boy's confession, the trial judge said he saw no reason to exclude it, and the jury no reason to question it. The boy was guilty of murder, their verdict said.

Such stories of police brutality in extracting confessions abounded in the 1920s, finally provoking calls for reform. Near the end of the decade, President Hoover would convene a commission to study the police practice led by George Wickersham. A couple of years later, the Wickersham Commission published a scathing critique of such "third degree" tactics. Torture was a sure sign of laziness and lack of initiative, it concluded, and only an officer who lacked confidence in his ability to reason his way through an investigation would resort to such brute force.[18]

Change was not immediate, however. It took the barbaric facts of another case in Mississippi four years later to finally move the nation's highest court to rule on the question. In 1934, three black men suspected of murdering a white man in Mississippi were dragged from their homes by local deputies and ordered to confess. When slow to comply, one of the men was hanged by a rope from a tree before being let down, gasping for breath. When he still would not confess, he was hoisted up a second time, to allow him more time to think it over. The Negro survived the mock lynching, though as the deputies' noose dug into his air pipe cutting off his oxygen supply, he must have doubted that he would. And his ordeal was far from over. Determined to obtain the desired confession, the man was then tied to the tree and whipped until he confessed. The other two Negro suspects fared similarly; back at the station, their backs were ripped raw with a leather strap while the deputy assured them that the beatings would continue until they confessed. They did. Three days later, the Negroes were led limping into a county courtroom to stand trial, where they testified that the confessions were false; they had been beaten until they made the statements. The prosecutor, in his rebuttal case, called to the stand the deputy who had lashed the men's backs. He admitted the whippings without reserve, and when asked how severe the beatings had been, languidly replied, "Not too much for a Negro; not as much as I would have done if it were left to me." Untroubled by the deputy's admission, the trial judge accepted the confessions into evidence, and the men were convicted.

In 1936, when the case appeared before the United States Supreme Court, the normally deferential justices had finally had enough. In the landmark case, *Brown v. Mississippi,* the Court ruled that the three men's convictions had been derived from confessions obtained by torture, an unconstitutional failure of due process. And while loath, as a general matter, to interfere with a state's authority to set the procedures for its own courts, the Court admonished the Mississippi court for allowing the confessions to be used. There are "some principles of justice...so rooted in the traditions and conscience of our people as to be ranked as fundamental," the Supreme Court scolded, and the trial court's decision to admit the confessions obtained by methods "so revolting to the sense of justice, was a wrong so fundamental that it made the whole proceeding a mere pretense of a trial and rendered the conviction and sentence wholly void."[19]

It can hardly be doubted that the privileges of whiteness and the clerical credentials of Reverend Edwin Stephenson virtually guaranteed him a line of questioning far more civil than that given James Cameron, the Negro defendants in *Brown v. Mississippi,* or countless others like them. But there were other dangers. Brutality aside, criminal interrogations follow a certain rather predictable trajectory. The goal of the process is to defeat a soul's natural impulse to deny wrongdoing—like the instinctive cry of a six-year-old: "I didn't eat it!" despite the telltale crumbs of the missing treat still clinging to his lips. Interrogators were trained to ignore such protestations of innocence, and doggedly to assert the facts that pointed to guilt. Interrogation was, in short, a relentless wearing-down of the suspect, a studious rejection of all of his denials—until even he could see that the jig was up, the prosecutor had the goods, and further claims of innocence were futile. Or until maybe he was just too exhausted to continue to mouth them.

In the throes of such questioning, it would not have been unusual for a prisoner like Edwin Stephenson to be blind to the fact that by the end of the opening cordialities, he was already teetering on the edge of a precipice. For threading through the usual pleasantries—soothing, respectful, seemingly inconsequential words, like "Good evening, Reverend Stephenson, I am Joe Tate" and "I would like to ask you a few questions"—lurked an almost irresistible bait: to speak when one is spoken to, normally a harmless etiquette. In an interrogation room, however, that deeply engrained rule of civility could wreck havoc. With everything to hide, a guilty man could easily conclude that answering a few questions was the smart thing to do—the path out of his difficulties—somehow unmindful that the odds of talking his way out of trouble in such a setting were, in fact, house odds.

Many decades later, when contemplating evidence of the criminal pastimes of a man named Ernesto Miranda, the United States Supreme Court grappled with the paradoxical tendency of suspects to talk with their interrogators, and interpreted the Constitution to require that an interrogator like Joe Tate not only forgo using torture, but pause to warn a prisoner like Edwin Stephenson of his right not to incriminate himself—to tell him that he had a right to remain silent and a right to an attorney, that an attorney could be appointed for him if he could not afford one, and that anything he said could be used against him. These things needed to be explained to suspects who were about to be interrogated, the Supreme Court finally decided, to counteract the inherent compulsion they would otherwise feel to talk.[20]

In 1921, however, when Tate and the others made their way to Stephenson's cell, the famed *Miranda* warnings were still some forty-five years away. Thus, nothing prevented the prosecutor from questioning the minister at will. Neither did the law require Tate to caution Stephenson that, before speaking, he might want to talk with a lawyer first, or, for that matter, that he might not want to talk to Tate at all—that talking to the man responsible for his prosecution was about as smart as cleaning a loaded gun.

No transcript or other record was made that night of Reverend Edwin Stephenson's interrogation. Likely the prosecutor thought he could rely on Chief Deputy Fred McDuff, Assistant Coroner George Moore, or Dr. Hammrick to remember the conversation well enough. It was a risky assumption. Even in the best of circumstances, where the objectives of the observers are in agreement, it is not uncommon for witnesses to the same event later to remember its details differently. When such discrepancies occur, it is helpful to have a written record to clear up the disagreements.

In fact, the memories of the men in that room that night would turn out to differ in certain respects, but all of them agreed on one thing: Stephenson had been willing to admit that he shot Father Coyle; and he showed little remorse for it He claimed he had shot the priest in self-defense. Without a verbatim transcript, the prisoner's exact words about what happened on the rectory porch were forever lost, but the men who questioned him that night later recalled his principal assertions in similar ways: when he was passing by the rectory, Stephenson told them, the priest had called out to him and invited him up to the porch. So he took a seat in one of the chairs and they began to talk. After a minute or two, the priest excused himself and went into the house. He returned a little while after, and then asked Stephenson what objection he had to his daughter becoming a Catholic. Then the priest told him that he had married Ruth to a Catholic man named Pedro Gussman earlier that day. Stephenson was enraged at the news, he said, and he shouted at the priest: "You're a dirty dog!" or "You've treated my family like a dirty dog!" or words to that effect, until Father Coyle warned him not to repeat it. But Stephenson claimed that he did repeat it, which caused the priest to hit him, and to grab his belt, said Stephenson, and to knock him down. During the attack, the priest hurt Stephenson's side, he said, and his sore foot as well. He had been forced to defend himself, he told Joe Tate and the others. Either that or be killed. So he had shot.[21]

Joe Tate let the minister talk, but he could not have believed him. The man's claims defied reason. According to his story, none of the day's events had had anything to do with his meeting with Father Coyle on the porch—not his midday discovery that his daughter was missing, or his certainty that the Catholics had taken her, or his request that the sheriff raid the Catholics' strongholds in search of her. Stephenson wanted them to believe that his conversation with the priest was a pure coincidence, a cordial chat. The suggestion was ludicrous. And other parts of the story were far too convenient as well: the priest's supposed trip inside the house shortly before their purported brawl—a claim plainly designed to suggest that the priest had gone inside to arm himself for a battle. No weapon had been found on the fallen priest, or anywhere near the porch. None besides Stephenson's own had been recovered. And Stephenson's claim that he had shot in self-defense after being knocked down, clashed with the physical evidence left behind on the porch as well. Tate had just been there, before he entered Stephenson's cell, and he had seen the pathway of the minister's bullets, moving downward, not up, as if in pursuit of a man diving desperately out of harm's way. Nor did any of the statements taken from witnesses that night comport with the story of an attack by the priest on Stephenson. Witnesses had heard shots, but seen no brawl. They had heard the screams of the two women who flew to the porch immediately after the shooting, but no shouts between Stephenson and the priest in the seconds before it. The man's story made no sense.

Once Stephenson offered his version of the events, Tate had a decision to make. No doubt, some prosecutors would have pressed the man, confronting him with facts that made his story unconvincing. Hadn't he had a grievance against the priest before they met on the porch? Tate could have asked. Hadn't he and his wife Mary asked the sheriff earlier that day to send his deputies into the rectory to search for Ruth? Why had no one seen the fight Stephenson was claiming took place between him and Father Coyle? Why had no one mentioned the protracted conversation between the two men Stephenson claimed took place? Why had no one seen the priest strike Stephenson, as Stephenson claimed? The kind of questions that can confound a suspect, prodding him to offer additional explanations, each less plausible than the last, backing him into a corner, shutting off, one by one, all avenues of escape, until the prosecutor, almost kindly, offers the suspect a way out: telling him that his story just did not hold up—that no one would believe it—and that the best thing he could do was to just tell the truth.

But after Joe Tate heard Edwin Stephenson out, for reasons that remain a secret of history, it appears he decided not to push. Maybe the explanation was no more, or less, than that because the suspect was an ordained minister; a man with status, whose friends would surely come to his defense. Or maybe Tate thought it best to go back over the evidence before trying to contradict the man's story; to double-check his facts, and go back over the measurements of the bullet tracks on the rectory porch, to comb the witnesses' statements more carefully than he had had time to do before entering Stephenson's cell. But later, others would wonder, after hearing about the shooter's kid-glove treatment, whether Joe Tate's heart was really in the case, a suspicion that would continue to haunt the prosecutor even beyond the grave.

———

On the night of the shooting, after Tate and the others had gone, a group of local reporters were led to the hospital ward of the jail to see Reverend Stephenson. Sometime after he had turned himself in, Stephenson had begun complaining that his head hurt, the newsmen were told. He had been taken to see Dr. Hammrick, the jailhouse doctor. They found Stephenson lying on a cot. Though earlier that day he had let it be known that he wanted no visitors, the newsmen gently asked if he would speak with them.

"I am not myself," he told them.

Would he at least give some background information about himself and his family, they asked. How long had the family been in Birmingham? What was the nature of his acquaintance with Father Coyle?

The man was visibly nervous, one of the reporters wrote later. He ran his hand repeatedly through his hair. For a long moment it must have seemed that he would adhere to his vow of silence, but then he began to talk. He had moved his family to Birmingham twelve years before, he said.

What was his occupation?

He was "a local preacher of the Northern Methodist church."

With an official charge?

No, he "had never held a charge."

Did he know the priest?

"We were speaking acquaintances," Stephenson said stiffly.

How were their prior relations?

"Heretofore friendly."

"How did the affair start?" one of them asked.

Too much. Stephenson burrowed back into his cot. The reporter had moved too quickly. "I would rather not talk about it," he muttered.

It must have been an awful moment—just when it had seemed that the man was warming up. But before the newsmen had time to regroup, Stephenson turned back toward them, as if it had occurred to him that the benefits of offering something more necessitated a bit more patience with the journalists: "I will state this much," he said. "It was purely a case of self-defense. I did not shoot until Father Coyle had struck me in the head twice and knocked me to my knees."

The newsmen scribbled furiously; they would take what they could get.

"I regret the occurrence very much," Stephenson continued, "but I had to protect myself. I was passing by Father Coyle's residence. He was sitting on the porch and called me in and asked me to sit down. We started to talk about my daughter's marriage, and finally I told Father Coyle he had acted a dirty dog, or words to that effect."

He told me not to repeat the remark, Stephenson continued, but I ignored the warning and repeated it anyway—telling Coyle that he "was a dirty dog"—and he hit me. "He struck me twice and run his hand in his pocket. Then I shot."

The minister eyed the reporters. Surely they understood the significance of what he was saying. That he had acted only when forced to do so—*after* the priest had assaulted him, *after* Coyle had reached inside his pocket. Maybe it was the newsmen's lack of reaction that made Stephenson think that something more was needed, some additional piece of information to bolster his claim that despite killing a priest he had acted with restraint.

"I did not empty my revolver," he said pointedly, and then turned his back for good. "I won't say anymore."[22]

———

A few days later, the editors of the Birmingham papers could not have been pleased when they learned that the reporters they had sent to cover Father Coyle's funeral Mass had failed to detect Ruth Stephenson Gussman in the crowd. For days, the papers had been forced to admit that their staffs had yet to locate Ruth and Pedro Gussman, and a slight edge had begun to creep into their reports about the couple's whereabouts. The *Age-Herald* in particular seemed disinclined to accept any responsibility for the newlyweds' disappearing act. Its reporters had not been idle, the paper made clear—Ruth Stephenson Gussman had simply avoided all of the places they could rightly have expected to find her. On the night of the shooting, members of the *Age-Herald's* staff had camped outside the doorstep of the Stephenson's home at 2126 Seventh Avenue, the paper said in its own defense. It had set up watch at the entrance to the county jail as well, and dispatched a third crew to Pedro Gussman's rooming house on Twenty-second Street. But the couple had never showed up.[23]

The papers seemed confounded, even offended, by the girl's behavior: "One of the most pitiful aspects of the story of the killing of Father James E. Coyle," wrote a reporter for the *Age-Herald,* is that "the girl, formerly Ruth Stephenson . . . has preferred to stay away from her mother and her home," and "has not been to see her father at the jail." "She has chosen, instead, to remain with her husband, Pedro Gussman, to whom Father Coyle married her and the fact of which, because he was a Catholic, is said to have caused the trouble between the priest and the girl's father which brought on the tragedy."[24] The insinuation seemed clear: surely the fact that Ruth Stephenson Gussman had failed to console her parents displayed some fundamental defect in the girl, or the undue influence of someone else.

It can no longer be known whether the *Age-Herald* spent any time fussing over the scant objectivity of such reports—that it was "pitiful" that the bride had not hurried to the jail to give comfort to her father, and bewildering that she had "preferred" to stay with her husband rather than to rush home to the woman who had given her life. The paper's editors may have seen no need, at least not if they were able to convince themselves that the paper was doing no more than reporting the facts. The girl *hadn't* bothered to check on her mother or father, after all. It may hardly have seemed editorializing to say so.

But if the behavior of Ruth Stephenson Gussman confounded the Birmingham journalists, they seemed to experience no similar difficulty when they dwelled on the subject of the bride's mother. A squadron of newsmen rushed to the Stephensons' home on Seventh Avenue shortly after the shooting, where they found the older woman. Her distress could not have been more evident.

"Could you blame him?" Mary Stephenson cried when she saw them, and she buried her face in her handkerchief. "We have endured so much from the whole terrible Catholic question."[25]

It seems unlikely that the reporter consciously determined to side with Mary Stephenson over her daughter; it must simply have seemed the natural thing to do. For unlike the perplexing choices of the eighteen-year-old—her conversion, her elopement, her abandonment of her parents—Mary Stephenson fulfilled every expectation: devoted wife, loving mother.

The mother of Ruth Stephenson was "just a wisp of a woman," one reporter wrote for the *Birmingham Post,* plainly sympathizing with her plight. "Perhaps none have suffered from the tragedy . . . as she has." One look was all one needed to see "that life at no time has dealt kindly with her."[26] "She is not strong physically," echoed the *Birmingham News,* "and the double burden [of a jailed husband and missing daughter] is telling upon her."[27] The woman "is so small and thin," the *Age-Herald* tenderly concurred, "so frail and nervous."[28] Who could say if she would weather the storm?

It was impossible not to detect the journalists' admiration for the woman—the way she was pushing on despite her troubles: "She has the woman's role to play," wrote one of the reporters un-self-consciously. "She must smile and cheer her husband with her optimism, and she must fold her hands and wait, praying that each ring of the telephone means that her daughter is at the other end." (*So powerless, yet so fierce in her defense of her husband!*)

This portrait was repeated by the reporters so consistently that soon it seemed clear that Mary Stephenson was the biggest victim of all—bigger even than the priest whose life her husband had taken—as if she had played no part in the drama that enfolded her, but rather had simply been *acted on* by forces outside her control, driftwood tossed on the waves of her husband's and daughter's making.

So taken were the newsmen with Mary Stephenson's piteous state that they seemed entirely to miss the import of the statement she had shouted out in defense of her jailed husband when they first arrived at her door. Five simple but revealing words—"the whole terrible Catholic question!"—pinpointed quite precisely what Mary Stephenson believed had motivated her husband's act. Nothing about some supposed, sudden attack against which Edwin must have been forced to defend himself. Not: "Could you blame him? The priest attacked him!" or "Could you blame him? He was about to be killed!" But:

"Could you blame him? We have endured so much from the whole terrible Catholic question!"

In fairness, of course, Mary Stephenson uttered the cry shortly after her husband was jailed, before she had had a chance to speak with Edwin. But perhaps especially without the benefit of such a meeting, the reporters might have considered it significant that the first unrehearsed explanation the minister's wife offered of her husband's act centered not on any suspicion that he must have been viciously assaulted to have done such a thing, but solely on the protracted, simmering antagonisms that had smoldered within the Stephenson household for years: "We have endured so much from the whole terrible Catholic question!" she cried.

And Mary Stephenson was not alone in the view that it was the "Catholic question" that was responsible for Edwin Stephenson's act. When she could no longer hold up under the assault of the journalists' questions—"I am in no condition to talk," she pleaded at one point[29]—other members of the minister's family stepped in as her surrogates, and lacking, like Mary, the advantage of a meeting with Edwin himself, they, too, tendered explanations remarkably similar to that given by his wife. Thus, Mrs. Amanda Alice (Stephenson) Danforth, of 732 West Twentieth Street, Edwin's elder sister, leapt to her brother's defense with the cry "Isn't it just terrible? They have had so much worry over Ruth's attraction toward the Catholic church that I presume my poor brother just didn't think of what he was doing."[30] And from one of Mary Stephenson's sisters, Mrs. J. M. Chadwick of Gadsen, Alabama: "Mary and Edwin had been upset for two years or more.... [T]hey believed their daughter was unduly influenced by the Catholic churchman." It was their "objection to that influence that had led to the killing," Chadwick said authoritatively.[31]

The newsmen reported the women's comments, but without any follow-up, leaving it to others to reconcile the women's explanations with Stephenson's own. There must have seemed so many other more important things to ask them about. Like what they knew about Ruth's relationship with Pedro Gussman. Had they been seeing each other for long?

One of the reporters asked Mary Stephenson what she was planning to do.

"I must wait, that is all," Mary Stephenson replied. Or, as she headed off to Edwin's cell: "I am going out now to my husband." *(But never: "I wish Edwin had not done it." Or "Perhaps, we were too hard on Ruth.")*[32]

"Would Ruth be welcome to return?" another asked her.

"No matter what she has done, whether she is married or just run away, she knows my house is always open to her," Mary Stephenson replied stoically.

"But how about her husband, who is a Catholic?" the newsman pressed harder. "Would he be welcome?"

"I cannot say. I cannot say," Mary Stephenson answered, as if the question had suddenly cast her into a sea of helpless confusion—completely unaware that her reply left the matter perfectly clear.[33]

––––––

Eventually the press discovered them, of course. Indeed, the *Age-Herald's* reporter H. W. Schaefer was hot on the bride's heels even as troops of city newsmen managed to miss her at the Coyle funeral. It can no longer be known who tipped Schaefer off, but he had plainly heard from someone where Ruth and Pedro had been staying since their wedding night, for he phoned the house and caught the bride on the other end of the line. Cornered, Ruth agreed to give the reporter an interview, but she asked Schaefer not to reveal her whereabouts to anyone else. She feared that her "relatives might attempt to take her away by force" if they knew where she was staying, she told him. The concession could not have been onerous; Schaefer willingly agreed not to broadcast it. No doubt he wanted the scoop.

It is not hard to picture the reporter's excitement as he made his way to the flat on Twenty-fourth Street where he and Ruth had arranged to meet. But when Ruth let Schaefer into the house, a quick look around told him that Pedro Gussman was not there. Her husband was working, Ruth explained. She had only just arrived back herself. The reporter took stock of his subject: the teenager was "pretty" and "little," he wrote later, but "her eyes showed traces of tears." He asked if she had been crying.

Yes, at the funeral services for Father Coyle, she said.

Aside from sadness, the girl's demeanor was calm enough, Schaefer thought. He decided to press on, making quick work of the preliminaries. The day before, the *Birmingham News* had printed a story claiming that one of its reporters had actually spoken with her. Schaefer wanted to establish that the *Age-Herald's* interview was an exclusive. He asked if she could confirm it.

Yes, said Ruth. The claim made by the *Birmingham News* was false. She had not spoken with any other reporter. All of the statements printed in the article had come from other people who had happened to be at a house that she visited that day, she explained, and only some of the statements attributed to her were true.

Schaefer could scarcely have asked for anything better. He asked her what the *Age-Herald's* rival had gotten wrong.

"[T]he statement attributed to me . . . that my husband and I are going to leave town," she said.

Rumors that Ruth and Pedro Gussman were planning to flee the city had appeared in a number of articles after the shooting. The girl seemed anxious to put the speculation to rest. "Pedro and I are very, very happy," she said. "We are going to stay in Birmingham where all our friends are."

The reporter made note of it, then steered the interview back to the shooting. He asked how Ruth had felt when she heard the news.

"I am mighty sorry my father killed Father Coyle," she said. The news had shocked her. "Father Coyle was such a wonderful and noble man." And as to her father's claim of self-defense—that Father Coyle had struck him—she just didn't believe it, Ruth Stephenson said flatly. "Neither do other Catholics."

The comment may have startled Schaefer, stripped of all embellishment. Four short words—"Neither do other Catholics"—communicating far more than the bride's certainty that the priest had not incited the shooting. With the remark, Ruth Stephenson had identified herself as a Catholic, an alignment Schaefer knew had not started with the girl's birth, an association that was purely voluntary, and evidently unshaken even by the ferocity of her father's act of violence. Schaefer must have ached to interrogate her further, to ask the questions on the minds of so many of his readers: Hadn't she been raised a Methodist? What in heaven could have led her to convert? Who had persuaded her? Had Father Coyle been behind it? But something must have told the newsman not to push. Ruth Stephenson had already gone underground once; he needed to keep the girl talking. So Schaefer eased ahead, like a swimmer in icy waters, asking instead how she and Pedro had managed it, how they had gotten married without being discovered. The reporter's instincts paid off, and a description of the remarkable day's events gushed forth from the girl, as if through a ruptured dam—the trouble in her household, her secret plan with Pedro, their midday flight to Bessemer, the absent St. Aloysius priest, their undetected return to Birmingham, the missing Father Coyle—a fast-paced chain of misses and near misses, ending almost improbably in the success of the couple's plan.

As Schaefer listened to Ruth recount the couple's travails, he detected an air of self-satisfaction in the teenager, a certain pride about the way she and Pedro had managed things, how they had negotiated each of the hurdles thrown their way. Something about the girl's mien irked him. "The young bride was very much pleased with the way in which she had matched wits against 'everybody in town,'" Schaefer wrote later—"her escape to Bessemer, returning to get married and evading all lookouts." Maybe what bothered him most was the way Ruth Gussman smiled when she remarked: "'It would have been a thrilling elopement if it had not been for the deplorable tragedy.'"

Maybe the newsman thought that only the most ridiculously thoughtless *child* would use the words "thrilling" and "deplorable tragedy" in the same sentence, or that when a man was dead and the girl's own father could be hanged for it, there was no room for cheerfulness, even if the girl was still celebrating her nuptials. Schaefer made sure to include a reference to the way she had smiled in his later report of their interview, and he followed the bride's blithe-sounding statement with a tag line laden with unspoken meaning—"said, the girl wife"—a phrase that accentuated Ruth Gussman's youth.[34] Not for the last time would a Birmingham newsman communicate his disdain for the girl's apparent happiness and her unfathomable indifference to her father's fate.

As the interview drew to a close, Schaefer must have felt on more solid ground. He turned to the question of Ruth's feelings toward her parents. The papers were reporting that she had not been home or over to the jail. Didn't she want to see her father?

"I do not wish to see my father," the teenager answered unapologetically. "He has done a terrible thing for which there is no excuse. I care nothing about seeing him after the deed which he has committed," she said.

Didn't she love her father? the newsman asked.

The girl could not have missed the chill in Schaefer's question. "I love my father as much as a daughter could who has received such treatment as I have been accorded," she said, guardedly.

What about Mary Stephenson? Would Ruth return home to see her mother?

Ruth must have wondered after all that she had just told Schaefer about the way her parents had mistreated her that the answer to his question was not obvious. The papers kept writing that her mother wanted Ruth to come back home, but it was perfectly clear to her that Mary Stephenson had no intention of welcoming her husband Pedro. The woman's proclaimed desperation to have Ruth back would thus come at a steep price. "I can't go back there," Ruth answered. "After people marry they should live for each other and have their own home," she added weakly.[35]

Maybe the justification sounded contrived even to her own ears, or maybe Ruth realized that the only way to convince the reporter was to let him come to know Mary Stephenson better himself. She asked Schaefer if he would carry a request to her mother on her behalf. Since the shooting the local papers had published countless stories about sightings of the bride, here and there about town, always "stylishly" or "smartly" dressed," always in some pleasing shade of blue—as if she hadn't a care in the world. But the reporters had failed to put two and two together: that Ruth had not been home since the morning of the shooting, that she had left the house with only the clothes on her back and had been wearing the same blue dress and hat for days.

Would Schaefer ask her mother if she would allow some of her things to be sent to her? Ruth asked.

Later that day, at the Stephenson's home on Seventh Avenue, the reporter relayed the request. He would be pleased to take the clothes back to her daughter if Mary Stephenson agreed, Schaefer told Ruth's mother. "He was met with a refusal."

When he delivered news of the rebuff to Ruth, the girl had simply said, "All right,"[36] as if only he, and not she, had ever expected anything more.

| The Building of a Defense

J ESSE DANIEL RUSSUM was exactly one month shy of his forty-seventh birthday on the day Father Coyle was shot, younger than the priest himself. As the coroner for Jefferson County, Russum was one of the first people to get the news. People in Birmingham generally referred to him by his first two initials, "J.D.," rather than his full name, and as the reporters peppered him with questions about how he planned to proceed, Russum proved he knew how to get to the point.

The coroner's office would hold its inquest behind closed doors, he told them.

The pronouncement could have been no surprise. One of the first things Russum had announced when he had commenced his duties as coroner earlier that year was that he would hold all of his investigations in secret, and he had held to the pledge despite the protests of the press. The policy was indefensible, the newsmen had argued.[1] The coroner's investigations involved the most grievous acts of violence in the county. Russum only got a call when someone's death was suspicious or unexpected—homicides of greatest interest to the county's residents. These were the cases in which there was reason to think that, as the law put it, the victim's death might have been "occasioned by the act of another by unlawful means."[2] The people of Jefferson County had a right to know how the coroner was conducting such inquests on their behalf, the reporters said.

But eight months into his term, Russum had not budged, so after the shooting at the rectory, a reporter for the *Birmingham News* tried a more diplomatic tack: might not the killing of Father Coyle warrant an exception to the closed-door policy—considering the victim's prominence and the community's demand for a fair and speedy resolution of the case?

The coroner was not persuaded. There would be no exception, came Russum's answer. He would conduct the Coyle inquest behind closed doors, just as he always did.

The newsmen were furious—the rookie official's honeymoon had plainly lasted long enough. By the afternoon of August 12, the papers took aim at Russum's shrouded procedures: "In accordance with his usual custom in the investigation of homicide cases, Russum excluded newspaper men and the public," the *Birmingham News* fired off. The paper demanded that the coroner "abandon his star chamber proceedings and open the doors to the press."[3] The *Birmingham Post* agreed: "An inquest is, in a way, a trial," wrote its editors indignantly; "it should be open to the fullest public scrutiny."[4] As the clamor for a reversal of the coroner's policy mounted, Joe Tate tried to blunt the media onslaught on his friend. Russum was not the first coroner to come down on the side of closed-door proceedings, Tate reminded the reporters. Several of his predecessors had followed the same policy. The law of Alabama left the decision up to him alone. The journalists remained unswayed.[5]

Unlike Joe Tate, J. D. Russum appeared remarkably unbothered by the racket being raised over his policy. He simply went about his work, speaking with witnesses, visiting the rectory porch, as though the reporters' campaign against his closed-door practices hardly even registered. It is hard to know whether the coroner's repose was merely for show. It might have been. But it is also possible that the din over his policy had exactly the effect on the man's equilibrium that it appeared to have, which was none at all. As his friends could have explained, by 1921, J. D. Russum had faced down far greater challenges in his life than the fleeting estimations of a disgruntled press corps—including living the better part of his days on earth with no feet and only half of his legs.

Jesse Daniel Russum was born in Elbert County, Georgia, early in the autumn of 1874, the oldest of the seven children James and Mary (Daniel) Russum. Like their neighbors, the Russum family would not have had a lot of luxuries, as James Russum supported his wife and children on the modest wages of a mechanic. Later he branched into farming, and the family lived from the land's bounty. For a time that seemed enough. James and Mary Russum were even able to send their children to the local public school. But at some point, the needs of the family of nine must have grown too large. While still in his teens, J.D. began to work as well, on a farm like his father, and when he turned fifteen, he took a job at a nearby furniture factory, no doubt for the higher wages. Less than a year later, the move proved disastrous, when the boy suffered an accident at the plant "that necessitated the amputation of both his feet and his legs to the knees."[6]

Maybe it was the love of his family that saved him, or some core strength buried deep within himself—a full-grown man could hardly have been faulted for "throwing himself upon the charity of his fellow citizens" after suffering an injury so great, one acquaintance wrote years later. But when J.D.'s wounds had sufficiently healed, the teenager took stock of his future, and as if to prove something to himself and the world, he resolved to make the best of his lot, and took up the hard (if improbable) life of a traveling salesman.[7]

The choice, as it turned out, was inspired, as apparently J.D. possessed those special, intangible gifts of a man made for business, and "he made an excellent living" at it, against all odds. Before long, he had accumulated a bevy of devoted customers, and his reputation for "business astuteness [became] universally recognized" throughout the region. By age twenty-nine, he had made such a success of his trade that he was able to turn some of his attention to other pursuits. In 1904 (the same year that Father Coyle arrived in Birmingham to assume the lead pastorate at St. Paul's Catholic Church), J.D. married Miss Mary Della Tribble of Granada, Mississippi, and the two started a family. A year later, they welcomed their first child into their home, J.D., Jr., and before long they added three more: George, Walter and Roy. In 1907, Russum moved his wife and sons to Birmingham,[8] where the special qualities that had won him so many admirers over the years impressed his new neighbors as well. The man's self-reliant and cheerful approach to life, wrote one, was enough to make others "ashamed of complaining against small discouragements." Thirteen years after J.D. and his family put down roots in Birmingham, the voters of Jefferson County signaled their admiration by electing him to be their coroner.[9]

No matter what the papers were saying, J. D. Russum had his reasons for preferring to hold the inquest into the death of Father Coyle in private. Contrary to his critics' view, an inquest was not a trial. At times it could be the state's first step toward a trial, but the opposite was true as well. Some deaths were simply accidents, and if evidence led to the reasonable conclusion that a decedent's passing had not been occasioned by an unlawful act, the coroner's obligation was to recommend that no charges be brought. In such cases J. D. Russum could spare the innocent targets of his investigations a great deal of anxiety by concluding without fanfare that they had played no culpable role in the deaths. Other times, where the deaths were more suspicious and Russum worked to sort things out, his witnesses tended to speak more freely when they knew that their words would not be splayed across the next day's front pages, perhaps especially in those instances when the witnesses' friends and neighbors preferred them to be less than forthcoming about what they knew. Russum's closed-door policy provided such a witness needed cover.

Despite the misgivings of the press, no one could deny that J.D. Russum made quick work of the Coyle investigation. Within hours of the shooting, the coroner and his deputy, George Moore, had listened to Stephenson's excuses, examined the priest's fatal wound at Lige Loy's funeral parlor, and talked with the doctors who had treated the priest when he was rushed to St. Joseph's Hospital. The day after the shooting, Russum ordered subpoenas served on about seventy-five people, the *Birmingham News* reported, and although he conducted his interviews in private, the newsmen had ways of discovering many of the highlights. Even distant papers like the *New York Times* were able to verify what was transpiring behind the closed doors. Sheriff Hartsfield testified about the minister's visit to his office on the afternoon of the shooting, reported the *Times*, and records from the Birmingham Police Department revealed that the minister had been there as well, asking Police Chief Shirley to search a number of Catholic buildings for the girl. The journalists' sources also told them that, contrary to Stephenson's claim that he had shot Coyle while under attack, the absence of powder marks on the priest's body suggested that the two men had been standing some distance apart when the minister fired his gun.

In the end, J. D. Russum needed to hear the testimony of just a small number of the witnesses he had subpoenaed before making up his mind—the *New York Times* reported only eight—and two days after the shooting, he stood before a judge at the Jefferson County Courthouse and swore out a warrant for premeditated murder: "Edwin R. Stephenson, unlawfully and with malice aforethought did kill James E. Coyle by shooting him with a pistol," the coroner's warrant charged. Later that evening, a headline from the evening edition of the *Birmingham News* trumpeted news of the minister's deepening legal troubles: "Stephenson Now Faces a Formal Murder Charge."[10]

―――――

Whispers were heard around town almost as soon as its residents learned that Father Coyle had not survived: grumblings that Joe Tate and his men could not be trusted to do the job. The case demanded the appointment of someone who would see to it that Edwin Stephenson was aggressively prosecuted, some said.

It is unlikely that the skeptics' foreboding stemmed from any legitimate concern about the circuit solicitor's competence. A look at Joe Tate's public record would have resolved any doubt about whether he knew how to run a homicide investigation. In the month before the shooting of Father Coyle alone, the prosecutor had asked the grand jury to indict thirteen different men on the charge of murder, and it had happily complied each time. So probably the calls for the appointment of "special counsel" were explained by no more (or less) than the fact that neither Joe Tate nor any of his assistants were Catholic. Predispositions could slow an official's steps, and even if Joe Tate had escaped the anti-Catholic fervor that gripped so many others in Birmingham at the time, he still served at the pleasure of his constituents, and his term would be up the next year. The highly publicized prosecution of a man like Edwin Stephenson could doom a prosecutor's chances for reelection if his decisions were out of step with the opinions of the electorate, and Joe Tate must have known it. The prosecutor's safest course must have seemed plain—to defer to those urging engagement of special counsel.[11]

Yet five days after the shooting, the *Birmingham News* still could not verify that an outside prosecutor would be employed, and whatever Tate thought about the suspicion being directed at himself and his men, he let the insults pass in silence. Probably he understood that little profit could be gained from responding to such distrust, at least not with words. He could have tried to refute them, but those who harbored doubts would scarcely have been convinced by his pledges of neutrality. Neither would his public denials have worried those who quietly hoped that the Catholics were right. If Joe Tate meant to throw the case, no member of the town's furtive fraternities would have expected him to confess it.

To minimize the disruption to their lives, grand jurors for Jefferson County served for only three months at a time. The first grand jury of each year sat from January through March; the second from April through June; the third from July through September; and the last from October through December. Judging from the attendance records kept by the county, it was rare for the jurors to meet for more than a total of twelve to fifteen days, spread out relatively evenly across their three months of service—four to five days of deliberations in one month, four to five days in the next, and so on. But August 1921 had been a busy month for crime. By the close of business on Wednesday, August 10, the day before Father Coyle was shot, the grand jury had already deliberated for four days running; they were due for a break. With no way of predicting the next day's events, Joe Tate had advised the men that they would not have to meet again until almost two weeks later, on August 23.[12]

When news of the shooting broke the next afternoon, reporters rushed to the prosecutor to see if he planned to reconvene the grand jury sooner. Joe Tate said that he needed to talk with the grand jury foreman, Lynn R. Patton, but that he was inclined to call them back: "The importance of the case and the interest manifested by both Protestants and Catholics seems to demand an immediate threshing out of the tragedy."

When will they return to work? the reporters asked him.

If the grand jury foreman agrees with my recommendation, by next Wednesday, said Joe Tate hopefully, maybe even sooner.[13]

But by the next day, Tate had changed his mind—"No Special Grand Jury to Investigate Killing," announced a headline of the evening edition of the *Birmingham Post*—and when reporters asked him why, the prosecutor said simply that "developments in the case" had made it less urgent to recall the men sooner, and that he had decided to "let the affair take its regular course."

Those who doubted that Joe Tate and his men were serious about the prosecution of Reverend Edwin Stephenson could not have been reassured when the prosecutor pulled this about-face on the question of calling the Jefferson County grand jury immediately back to work so that they could hear evidence about the case. The explanation was opaque, but the newsmen seemed scarcely to notice, maybe because the "developments" to which Joe Tate alluded seemed clear. J. D. Russum's swift action against Stephenson the day before had guaranteed that the minister would remain jailed until the grand jury had a chance to hear evidence about the shooting. The reporters might reasonably have concluded, therefore, that the coroner's warrant made a "special session" of the grand jury less urgent, especially after Joe Tate reminded them that the grand jurors would be back in just ten days, and reassured them that Stephenson's case would be the first matter they discussed.[14]

Still, Joe Tate's sudden reversal could have been thought puzzling. Maybe his change of heart had something to do with the prosecutor's conversation with the grand jury foreman, Patton. Although no more was written about the conference between the two men, it was reasonable to surmise that the consultation did not go well. Maybe Patton's reaction to the idea of a special session carried just enough of a chill to make the prosecutor pause. Or maybe the foreman was clearer still: that the grand jury that had just indicted thirteen men for murder at Tate's request would be less obliging when it came to indicting a Methodist minister whose daughter had been married against his will to a Catholic Puerto Rican.

What was clear was that Joe Tate decided not to rush. Later some would second-guess Joe Tate's choice not to reconvene the grand jury in special session, hinting that the delay was a blunder. But it is doubtful that the prosecutor himself regretted the decision until days later—after Stephenson disclosed the identity of the man who would lead his defense.

Stephenson started to look for counsel within hours of surrendering to the sheriff's men, but nearly a week passed before the names of the members of his defense team were finally revealed. For a time, the Birmingham papers were sure that the minister meant to hire Ernest Mathews, a named partner of the downtown law firm Ellis & Mathews. Stephenson had sent for Ernest Mathews the morning after the shooting, and the two men, closeted away in a private room at the county jail, conferred for hours. Although by the end of the day the reporters still were unable to confirm that the lawyer had been hired, one paper felt confident enough to speculate that Mathews's retainer was all but certain.[15]

The prediction proved erroneous, though judging from the shift in Stephenson's approach to the press after talking with Ernest Mathews, the meeting between the two men had not been wasted time. No doubt Mathews told Stephenson what any experienced defense attorney would have told him in Mathews's shoes: he had to stop talking! A talking client was a defense lawyer's worst nightmare, even (maybe especially) when he thought he was doing himself some good. It was not hard to understand why Stephenson might have believed there was no downside to speaking to the prosecutor and the reporters, not when all he was saying was that he had shot the priest in self-defense. According to the papers, Stephenson had begun making such statements almost as soon as two officers cornered him on the courthouse steps, probably never considering that every comment he made was backing him farther into a cage from which he (or his attorneys) might later wish to escape.

Certainly Ernest Mathews would have known that it mattered not at all that the bulk of Stephenson's comments were claims that he had shot the priest justifiably, in an act of self-defense. There were only three possibilities in such a situation—the self-defense claim was true; the defendant believed it in error to be true; or the claim was a desperate deceit, the first thing that came to Stephenson's mind as he trekked to the courthouse to turn himself in. No matter which, prudence counseled against the prisoner's chatter. Even if what Stephenson asserted was true—and perhaps especially if he only mistakenly *believed* it to be true—Ernest Mathews would have known that the legal definition of self-defense was quite precise. A claim could be lost in an instant if a defendant failed to describe the threat he had faced in a way that satisfied its requirements. Until his lawyers had time to steer Stephenson through the thicket of the law's demands, there were good reasons for the prisoner to keep the facts to himself.

Worse, if Stephenson's explanation of his conduct was simply a lie, more often than not the prosecutor's witnesses would be able to refute it, again leaving his lawyers wishing that he had not spoken in the first place. For naturally Stephenson's claim that he had shot Father Coyle to save his own life made it tricky for them to suggest later on that something else had in fact caused the violence. At least, not without it looking like they would say anything to save their client's life.

Ernest Mathews would also have known that community perception of a criminal defendant was critically important—in some cases, important enough to influence the outcome of a case—and that the public's perception of an accused was dramatically impacted by the way the press chose to portray the accused. For that reason, whenever possible, defense attorneys tried to control the conditions under which journalists and their clients met. But Stephenson had jumped the gun. Although reticent in the hours immediately after his surrender, a good night's sleep seemed to have conferred on the minister a strengthened resolve, and on the morning after the shooting, when a reporter for the *Birmingham Post* appeared outside his cell, the preacher rewarded the newsman's perseverance with a passel of publishable comments.

Evidently, someone had given Stephenson a copy of the morning edition of the *Age-Herald*—possibly Mary Stephenson, for she was there as well, the reporter wrote—and the minister was visibly "agitated" over the things that he read in it. Especially the comments of Reverend Robert Echols: that Stephenson had been asked to leave the M.E.C., South; that he was not a fully ordained minister within the Methodist church; that he held no regular pastorate. Echol's remarks had plainly stung Stephenson's pride.

"It seems they are trying to hurt me saying that I have not always been an ordained minister," Stephenson protested. "They are saying things that are untrue. I *am* an ordained minister and have been since 1905." The prisoner rose from his chair and moved closer to the reporter. "I was ordained in 1905 in Newnan, Georgia, by Bishop William Wallace Dunn." The newsman could verify the facts for himself. "I have married 1,140 couples over the last two years."

"We have the papers showing that my husband was ordained," Mary Stephenson chimed in. There could be no questioning Edwin's credentials.

If Stephenson's figure was accurate, the implications were startling: 1,140 marriages in just two years meant the minister would have had to have married over three couples a day, seven days a week, including the Sabbath and holidays. The reporter asked if the weddings had occurred at the courthouse, rather than a church.

About half of them, Stephenson replied, without elaboration.

Edwin and Mary Stephenson were so wrapped up in their defense of the man's clerical status, the reporter wrote later, that they seemed hardly to notice the bigger threats to Stephenson's reputation—like his arrest for murder. Did someone need to remind them that things far worse were being said about the prisoner than that he was not a fully ordained minister? That he was in jail for gunning down an unarmed priest? That he might be hanged?

The newsman changed the subject. Would the Reverend consent to be photographed? he asked.

Stephenson "was reluctant" at first, wrote the reporter. Probably he worried how it would look—a prisoner insisting on the *bona fides* of his ordination in the ministry while dressed in prison garb! But after a bit of coaxing, he was persuaded—on one condition, he said: that the cameraman let him stage the setting of the picture himself.

Fifteen minutes or so later, adorned once again in "his customary dark suit," Reverend Edwin R. Stephenson stood tall and erect in the center of the county jail's courtyard. The reporter had voiced a preference for a shot in front of the bars of his cell, but Stephenson insisted on a change of venue to a spot less conspicuously incarceratory, and someone, perhaps Mary, had arranged a cluster of pretty potted flowers to serve as an attractive backdrop. Stephenson stepped carefully in front of them, clasping, chest high, several sheets of paper, to make it appear as though the photographer had caught him in the midst of delivering some important sermon. It can no longer be known what the papers really were, or how Stephenson came to the idea of using them as a prop, or by whose authority he was removed from his cell and permitted to change back into his clerical clothes. The day before, a reporter for the *Age-Herald* had overheard Stephenson tell Sheriff Hartsfield that he had never expected to be there, and having grown accustomed to the privileges and prerogatives of the ministry, he asked the lawman to "look after" him. Sheriff Hartsfield "told him not to be uneasy, he would be taken care of."[16] Perhaps for similar reasons, Stephenson had not truly feared that the *Birmingham Post* reporter would litter his article about their meeting with trifles that would cast the minister in an unflattering light: like minutiae about flower pots, references to imaginary lecture notes, or digressions into the little accommodations the prisoner had insisted on before he would agree to have his picture taken.

"I hope you will say some little nice things about me," Stephenson had said to the reporter hopefully, as the flash from the photographer's camera suffused the yard with light. "It is just as easy to say the nice things as it is to say the bad ones."[17]

———

After his meeting with Ernest Mathews, Reverend Edwin Stephenson went quiet, making it almost certain that the lawyer had counseled him against making any further statements about the shooting, or himself. Stephenson asked the warden to confine the list of persons permitted to visit him: some ministers and family members were granted entry. His wife, Mary, of course, came regularly, and was even permitted to brighten Edwin's cell with "a little vase of fresh flowers," one paper reported. Undoubtedly Ruth's name would have been on the list as well. But over the next several days, before the names of his attorneys were finally revealed, very few others succeeded in winning a word from the prisoner. Stephenson passed the time in quiet contemplation of his Bible, one reporter wrote, or "gazing for a long, long time" at the wasting petals of his wife's gift. No word from his daughter.[18]

It can no longer be known who first mentioned the name Hugo Lafayette Black to Stephenson. Perhaps he thought of the lawyer himself. At age thirty-five, Black was still some years away from his greatest achievements— election to the United States Senate in 1926, and eleven years after that, appointment to the United States Supreme Court. But in Birmingham, the young lawyer was already quite well known. Decades later, various biographers would plumb Black's formative years in the state, looking for portents that might have telegraphed his future successes. But little predicted them. Black was born in late February 1886 at his parent's home in Clay County, Alabama, near Ashland, the youngest of eight children. His father, William LaFayette Black, once a volunteer in the Confederate Army, supported Hugo, his mother, Martha Toland Black, and his siblings on the hard-won yields of a small family farm. When Hugo turned three, his father bought a general store in Ashland, the county seat, adding his large family to the town's 350 or so other residents. Hugo grew up there, attending the public schools and the Baptist church, and internalizing his father's "strict moral code" proscribing dancing, gambling, and most of all drinking "as a demon which lured good men to their destruction."[19]

Interest in the law came early to Hugo, thanks to the Clay County courthouse, which stood at the center of Ashland's main square, and provided some of the small town's best entertainment. Even as a boy, Hugo was drawn to it, seduced by the antics of the lawyers on full public display: "The dramas enacted in Ashland's suffocating courtrooms intrigued young Hugo far more than such boyish pastimes as pitching silver dollars or horseshoes, playing croquet, or fishing," wrote biographer Virginia Van der Veer Hamilton some years later. As he watched the lawyers argue their cases, he fantasized about how he could have outmatched them—"how he might have asked a shrewder question or more cleverly won the jury's sympathy"— exhibiting that innate competitive spirit that marked so many men destined for a career in the law.[20] Some years later, after one of his older brothers became a physician, Hugo toyed with the idea of a profession in medicine instead. But in 1904, the same year Father Coyle arrived in Birmingham, eighteen-year-old Hugo enrolled in the entering law class at the University of Alabama in Tuscaloosa. He graduated two years later and returned to Ashland, opening a law office. The welcoming faces of family and friends and the familiar rhythms of the Clay County courthouse must have been gratifying, but small-town life was not his destiny. Within a year, a fateful fire destroyed his office and all of its contents. Lacking the insurance to recoup his losses, Black risked a move he had not dared to make before then—to the "Magic City" of Birmingham.[21]

Fourteen years later, when he was still trim and wiry and approaching thirty-five, people must have begun to wonder whether any woman would ever persuade the busy lawyer to forgo his bachelorhood. The years since Hugo's arrival in Birmingham had been crammed with professional achievements—a flourishing law practice, a one-year stint as a magistrate judge for the raucous city police court, two and a half years as the county solicitor, another two and half years of military service during World War I at the rank of captain providing instruction at training camps in California and Oklahoma, and after that a return to his law practice in Birmingham. Somewhere along the way, Black had developed into a formidable trial lawyer and something of a ladies' man. The only thing he appeared to lack was a family of his own.

But 1921 was a year for love, and Miss Josephine Foster, "a girl of striking good looks" and thirteen years Hugo's junior, accomplished what no other woman had been able to do. According to his biographers, Hugo had noticed Josephine about town—always stylishly dressed, in a long flowing skirt here, or a bathing suit there, or after the war, in a smart, blue Yeomanette uniform, with its flowing cape and sailor's hat, at a formal dance thrown by the Southern Club—and the lawyer was caught. In February 1921, barely five months before Ruth Stephenson and Pedro Gussman exchanged their vows in the nearly empty St. Paul's Cathedral, Hugo and Josephine were married in an intimate ceremony with family and friends in the parlor of the bride's home on Niazuma Avenue. Later in the year, the happy couple took a month-long trip to Colorado, escaping the Alabama heat in the dog days of August, where they visited with a friend who had moved there. They had not been there long when Crampton Harris, Hugo's law partner, called from Birmingham: Reverend Edwin Stephenson had been arrested for killing Father Coyle, the head priest of St. Paul's Catholic Church, Harris told him. The minister wanted Hugo Black to represent him.[22]

Father James E. Coyle, as a young priest in Mobile, Alabama c. 1904.
Erik Overbey Collection, University of South Alabama Archives

Father James E. Coyle and his sister Marcella Coyle. Courtesy of Annie Bracken, niece of Fr. Coyle. Fr. James E. Coyle Memorial Project, Birmingham

Father Coyle in formal vestments, Birmingham. Courtesy of Birmingham Public Library Archives.

Father Coyle and Bill Fex early on the day Coyle was killed.
Courtsy of Bill Dudley, Bill Fex Collection

FROM LEFT TO RIGHT

Ruth Stephenson Gussman, Birmingham 1921

Pedro Gussman, Birmingham 1921

The Rev. Edwin R. Stephenson, August 1921. *The Birmingham News*

Porch of St. Paul's Rectory where Coyle was shot. Photographer unknown,
Fr. James E. Coyle Memorial Project, Birmingham

Crowd at St. Paul's Cathedral for Fr. Coyle's funeral Mass, Aug. 15, 1921.
Photographer unknown, Fr. James E. Coyle Memorial Project, Birmingham

Klan gathering in Birmingham, Alabama in the 1920s.
Courtesy Birmingham Public Library Archives, Catalog #816.13.79c

Jefferson County Courthouse and St. Paul's on Third Avenue, Birmingham.
Courtesy Birmingham Public Library Archives, Catalog #3.14

FROM LEFT TO RIGHT

Circuit Solicitor Joseph R. Tate, Birmingham. Courtesy of Robert Greye Tate

Birmingham Chief of Police, T.J. Shirley. Courtesy Birmingham Public Library Archives

Hugo Black, lawyer, Birmingham, Alabama. Courtesy Birmingham Public Library Archives

Stephenson on witness stand in Judge William Fort's courtroom October 1921. Courtesy Birmingham Public Library Archives, Catalog #49.81

It was a subtle thing, easily missed: the point at which the focus of the public slid away from the depravity of the killing to fix on the exoneration of the killer. It occurred in an instant. Almost as soon as the names of Stephenson's lawyers were revealed, praise for his choice crowded the columns of the local papers: "Four of the best known criminal lawyers in Birmingham will defend Rev. Edwin R. Stephenson," applauded the *Birmingham Post*. Law partners Hugo Black and Crampton Harris had agreed to take the case, joined by two other lawyers, John C. Arnold and Fred Fite, the paper reported. Black would lead the team. Stephenson's splendid choices virtually guaranteed that that his defense would "be one of the most brilliant in the history of Alabama," another paper chimed in.[23]

The defense of Reverend Edwin Stephenson had begun.

———

Joe Tate could not have been pleased when he learned the name of the man who had agreed to lead Stephenson's defense, though there is no record of how the prosecutor came to hear the news. There was no love lost between Joe Tate and Hugo Black; the two men had a history. Only four years earlier, they had been locked in a duel for prosecutorial power—and their battle had played out for the public's enjoyment on the front pages of the city's leading newspapers. Neither of them could have forgotten it.

Probably neither realized it, but the showdown between them in 1917 actually had its roots in a decision made by state law-makers three decades earlier, when Joe Tate was still a teenager, and Hugo Black in cloth diapers. Hugo was just nine days away from his first birthday when, on February 18, 1887, in the frenzy of judicial expansion that characterized the middle and late nineteenth century, the General Assembly in Montgomery, Alabama, approved the creation of a new court—the Criminal Court of Jefferson County. The newcomer arrived with the swagger of a playground bully. Until that time, criminal cases originating in Birmingham or the surrounding county were prosecuted either in the police court at City Hall or before the Circuit Court in the Jefferson County Courthouse. But by 1887, the law-makers were persuaded that a new court empowered to referee all of the county's criminal cases in one spot would be more efficient. So they bestowed on the new Criminal Court "exclusive jurisdiction" over all such cases and directed that all criminal matters then pending before either the city police court or the Circuit Court be transferred to the new court "at once." Under a separate law, the legislators approved the position of a new prosecutor as well, one who would carry the title "county solicitor" and who would thereafter exercise all prosecutorial authority within the county limits.[24]

The effect of these two new laws on the circuit solicitor of the Tenth Judicial Circuit at the time, a man named Charles W. Ferguson, could hardly have been more dramatic. Instead of exercising power over all of the civil and criminal cases arising in the circuit, Ferguson's authority had just been sliced in half! It was not hard to imagine the man's annoyance. But resistance must have seemed futile. Alabama law-makers had done the same thing to the circuit solicitor in the neighboring Ninth Judicial Circuit a year before, a man by the name of John Lusk, transferring all of Lusk's criminal powers to DeKalb County's new county solicitor. But Lusk decided to fight back. The next time the clerk called the criminal docket, both Lusk and the newly appointed county solicitor stood up and asked to be recognized, to the presiding judge's chagrin. A few months later, the dispute found its way to the Alabama Supreme Court. The judgment, for Lusk at least, was not good: as long as the General Assembly had left Lusk's constitutional office with *some* authority, the court held, the law-makers were free to transfer the remainder of his powers to the new county solicitor if they thought that was best.[25] Thus the next year, when Charles Ferguson, the circuit solicitor for the Tenth Circuit, suffered the same treatment, he must have realized that there was little he could do.[26]

It could not have been much comfort to men like John Lusk and Charles Ferguson that minds began to change on the wisdom of court expansion not long after their powers were slashed. By the beginning of the twentieth century, the states' prior infatuation with diversification, and their decisions to overload their court systems with a hodgepodge of competing tribunals, were considered by some to have been a sorry mistake.

One summer evening in 1906, in the Capitol Building in St. Paul, Minnesota, an up-and-coming star in the legal field said as much. Roscoe Pound, the thirty-six-year old dean of the University of Nebraska Law School at the time, took the podium that evening at the annual gathering of the American Bar Association. Earlier that day, Pound's audience had sat patiently through a string of not entirely riveting talks. No doubt by the time the young dean was called up to the lectern to give the dinner address, most of the gallery expected something lighter—a pleasant morsel to mull over as they contemplated a good night's sleep. Instead, Pound delivered a bombshell lecture, one that legal scholars and policy-makers would continue to talk about over a century later. Calling his talk "The Causes of Popular Dissatisfaction with the Administration of Justice," Pound rattled off the leading ills of the judiciary, including among them the "archaic" multiplicity of the American courts. This overabundance of tribunals, and fragmentation of judicial responsibility, the young dean charged, was "sheer waste": a throwback to the antiquated and long-since-abandoned Anglo-Saxon system, where one could apply for judicial relief from any of a slew of adjudicators—"the Hundred, the Shire, the Witan, or the king in person"—in any of a number of *fora*: "the king's superior courts of law, the itinerant justices, the county courts, the local or communal courts, and the private courts of lordships," intoned Pound mockingly.

The speaker's meaning was clear: England had come to its senses, and so should the American states.[27]

The court system in Alabama at the beginning of the twentieth century was a perfect example of the freewheeling growth Roscoe Pound had railed against that night. As Alabama's population had exploded, law-makers tried to lighten the courts' load by adding more of them. Persuaded again and again that the addition of just one more court would prove "of financial advantage," the legislators piled a labyrinth of inferior local courts on top of the twenty or so circuit courts that already crisscrossed the state: there were criminal courts and probate courts, justice-of-the-peace courts and chancery courts, courts of common pleas, and courts of law and equity. And while in theory each of these courts exercised its own little pocket of authority, in practice the tribunals often bumped up against each other in confused and confusing ways, leaning into and over each other in a jumble of roughly shared or closely guarded power.

By 1915, Alabama law-makers had lived with the complexities and expense of the judicial potpourri long enough. The time had come to prune.[28]

It was perhaps one of those things best described as "bad timing" that Hugo Black had taken office as county solicitor for Jefferson County, Alabama, only eight months before the General Assembly passed the Consolidated Court Act of 1915. Under the new law, state law-makers trimmed the excess from the state's bulging court system with the delicacy of a lopper. Turning their attention to Jefferson County, the legislators decreed that as of January 1, 1917, virtually all of the county's inferior courts, including the Criminal Court, before which Hugo Black prosecuted his cases, would be no more.

In retrospect, a lot of trouble might have been saved had the General Assembly simply timed the ending of the Jefferson County solicitor's position with the closing date of the court before which he practiced. But it did not. The Consolidated Court Act ordered the Criminal Court to close its doors at the beginning of January 1917, but another part of the law made clear that the county solicitor himself would not be out of a job until two years later, when his elected term came to an end on January 1, 1919. On that date, the county solicitor position would vanish forever, and all of Hugo

Black's open cases and prosecutorial authority would revert to the office of the *circuit* solicitor—Joe Tate.

As a result of all of the law-makers' shearing, all but the first eight months of Hugo Black's tenure as county solicitor was served in the shadow of an upraised axe. Black had won the office of county solicitor after a hard-fought, grass-roots campaign against a formidable incumbent, Harrington P. Heflin. The scrappy younger lawyer had challenged Heflin's seat by driving his Model T Ford "into the remote nooks of Jefferson County," shaking hands and passing out leaflets, pledging to bring down the crime rate, and attempting all the while to turn a negative—the lack of any official endorsements—into a positive. He had sought the support of no newspaper or monied interest! his campaign materials exclaimed. He owed favors to no one! The voters bit, electing him their new county solicitor on November 3, 1914. He took office two months later.[29]

It is hard to know whether Hugo Black would have bothered to run for the office had he known what was coming only eight months later: that the criminal court before which he and his assistants brought all of their cases would be closed as of New Year's Day 1917; that any case still pending on that date would be transferred to the Circuit Court; and that Joe Tate's office would regain its authority to prosecute criminal cases, the power that had been spirited away from Charles Ferguson back in 1887. For Black, the news must have been a terrible blow.

As the date for the closing of the Criminal Court approached, Birmingham reporters seemed suddenly to realize that when the General Assembly had decreed that that court be closed, it had left one question glaringly open: if the court before which Black prosecuted his cases was to be shut down, and all of its cases were to be transferred into the Circuit Court a full two years before his powers as county solicitor were set to lapse, where was Black expected to conduct his business?

One answer to that question—the one that appeared perfectly obvious to Black—was that the county solicitor would simply tag along with his cases into the Circuit Court and prosecute them there. Although the law-makers had ordered that all of the county's criminal files were to be transferred to the Circuit Court at the beginning of 1917, they had also made clear that Black would not lose his status as "chief prosecutorial officer" for the county until the end of his elected term in January 1919, Black explained to the reporters. The law-makers must have meant for him to prosecute his cases in the Circuit Court during his last two years, Black said.

The argument was reasonable, if not self evident, but the reporters guessed that Joe Tate would not take kindly to the idea of sharing his domain. "Who

Will Be Circuit Solicitor Jefferson County after Jan. 1?" prodded a banner headline of the *Birmingham News,* in plain anticipation of a clash between the two public officials.[30]

But if the newsmen hoped for histrionics from Joe Tate, the circuit solicitor disappointed them. Judging from years of coverage of the man, Joe Tate did not make it a practice to fight his battles in the columns of the local papers, perhaps especially when any statement he might make would leave him looking like some silly schoolboy reluctant to share his toys. So when the reporters asked him what he would do if Hugo Black showed up in the Circuit Court at the start of the year to prosecute his cases there, Joe Tate held his fire.

He would cross that bridge when he came to it, the prosecutor told them calmly.

Would he initiate a proceeding to oust the County Solicitor from his office?

No, Tate said. There was no need. Any test of their respective powers would occur naturally, once the transferred cases were docketed before the Circuit Court at the start of the year.[31]

It was an impressive display of self-restraint. But even if Joe Tate was never induced to admit it aloud, some part of the man must have recoiled at the idea of being shoved aside by the self-possessed Hugo Black from an inferior criminal court. Up until that time, as circuit solicitor, Tate had been the only official to represent the state's interest in cases litigated before the circuit's highest tribunal. By 1917, he had held the office for six years. He would have been accustomed to the unquestioned dominion he and his assistants had wielded there. Although during that time he had lacked the power to prosecute *criminal* cases, Tate had been the attorney of record for all other matters affecting the circuit. To Tate, the General Assembly had simply returned the power his office had lost when the criminal court and the county solicitor position were first created. So why should he care about Black's pending homelessness? Not that many years had passed since the General Assembly had stripped the circuit solicitor's office of its right to prosecute criminal cases, a windfall to the inaugural holder of Black's position. It must have seemed an act of karmic justice—as if the ghosts of the old circuit solicitors, John Lusk and Charles Ferguson, had finally exacted their revenge.

For all of Joe Tate's public reserve, it quickly became evident that the lawyer had no intention of letting the newly increased powers of his office slip by unused. Even if it turned out that Tate had no choice but to share the Circuit Court with Hugo Black until 1919, the new law made it clear that the Office of the Circuit Solicitor would regain its criminal division as of 1917, and it had authorized Tate to hire up to three assistants to handle that additional work. Tate launched a preemptive strike. Before the Birmingham courts had the chance to take up the question of which of the two solicitors would be top dog over the county's criminal cases for the next two years, Tate hired three men to serve as his deputies: James Davis, John P. McCoy and Wallace McAdory. The move proved to be inspired. Although it took another several months and two arguments before the Alabama Supreme Court to resolve the question of who would serve as Jefferson County's "chief prosecutorial officer" until 1919—Joe Tate or Hugo Black—the treasurer for the county wanted no part of paying for the salaries of *two* sets of assistant prosecutors—Joe Tate's three, and Hugo Black's two more.

Money talked. The county coffers would be stretched only so far. If Hugo Black insisted on using his own assistants rather than relying on the men Tate had hired, the treasurer told him, Hugo's men would have to work for free! Hugo Black was furious. He couldn't be forced to prosecute his cases with men chosen by Joe Tate, Black told the treasurer, and he filed a suit to prove it.[32] But ultimately, the Alabama Supreme Court sided with the county treasurer. Black could run the county's criminal prosecutions until 1919, it ruled. He could even prosecute his cases in the courtrooms of the Circuit Court of the Tenth Judicial Circuit, previously the exclusive territory of Joe Tate. But the county could not be forced to pay for Hugo Black's assistants as well as Joe Tate's, wrote the court. Tate's men would have to suffice.[33]

Black would not have it. He fired off a letter of resignation to the governor. If he was to be denied the ability to name his own assistants, Black wrote, the authority of the county solicitor was in name only: "I do not feel that I can perform the duties of my office satisfactorily to the people and in accord with my own conscience with these assistants." He would sooner step down than be forced to work with men of Joe Tate's choosing—and that is exactly what he did.[34]

Joe Tate had won.

Four years later, when Black agreed to represent Edwin Stephenson, he still remembered the defeat. The younger lawyer was not given to losing, and more often than not his considerable skills in the courtroom saved him that injury. The passage of time had not erased the wound of the other man's triumph. Looking back, even decades later, Black would describe the 1917 battle between himself and Joe Tate as "the worst political turmoil in his life."[35]

The defense strategy began to take shape shortly after the Birmingham papers broadcast the names of the four men hired to represent Stephenson.

Hugo and Josephine Black's delayed honeymoon trip in Colorado presented an immediate issue for the defense: the Blacks had only recently arrived in Colorado, and they had no intention of cutting their trip short. They were not due to be back for several more weeks, but Stephenson's preliminary hearing was scheduled to begin in a matter of days. The hurdle was hardly insurmountable—it was customary for a defendant to waive the preliminary hearing. Deliberations by the grand jury and rulings by a judge at a preliminary hearing were largely duplicative. When a grand jury returned an indictment (the formal name for a felony charge against a defendant) it was essentially deciding there was "probable cause" to believe that the defendant had committed some crime—the same legal question a judge at a preliminary hearing was asked to consider. Thus, once a grand jury indicted a case, there was no need for the judge to repeat the work. For this reason, preliminary hearings occurred only rarely. Accused men like Stephenson had a right to them, and hearing dates would be announced in open court. But due to the very great odds that a grand jury would have returned an indictment against them prior to that date, defendants typically waived the hearings, and concentrated their energies on either working out a plea with the prosecutor or awaiting the formal charge and preparing for trial.

Once Joe Tate announced that he would not call the Jefferson County grand jury immediately back to work to hear evidence concerning the death of Father Coyle, however, many of the reasons Stephenson might have had to waive his hearing simply vanished. Because of Tate's decision, the grand jury would not start to hear evidence related to the case until the same Tuesday that Stephenson's preliminary hearing was set to begin. This did not guarantee that the preliminary hearing would actually occur, of course. The grand jury was set to resume its work in the morning, while the preliminarily hearing would not start until later that afternoon; the prosecutor would have a head start. Quick work by Joe Tate before the grand jury might lead to an indictment before the hearing was called, in which case the judge assigned to conduct it, the Honorable H. B. Abernethy, would have no reason to proceed.

But if for some reason the grand jury moved more slowly, there was a chance that the hearing *would* proceed. The defense team decided to prepare for the possibility. With Hugo Black still out of town, the timing of such a hearing would be awkward, but Stephenson's lawyers agreed that it would be a mistake to sit on their hands while Joe Tate built his case against their client. They decided that Crampton Harris, Fred Fite, and John Arnold would appear at the hearing without Black, if necessary.

There is no record of how Joe Tate received word that the lawyers for Stephenson were refusing to waive the preliminary hearing. Perhaps he read about it as so many others did, under a taunting headline in one of the city's leading papers: "Early Showdown, Stephenson Plans," trumpeted the *Birmingham News*. Taking the offense, Stephenson's lawyers publically vowed to make every effort to ensure that the preliminary hearing occurred—to "force the state to show its hand," wrote one paper; to give the defense "information it would otherwise not obtain until the actual trial," wrote another. If the grand jury proceeding dragged on past the morning, the preliminary hearing would have to begin, and the prosecutor's resources would be split in two. While the grand jury occupied Tate's time, the defense lawyers told the reporters, his assistants would have no choice but to put on evidence in open court, giving the defense a rare pretrial look at the state's witnesses and theories, most of which were likely to reappear at trial. They might even have a few surprises for the prosecution at the hearing, Stephenson's lawyers hinted mysteriously.[36]

The newsmen smelled blood. They asked Joe Tate if the defense was entitled to such a hearing.

"If it desires it," Tate replied calmly, "provided the grand jury has not acted on the case before the preliminary hearing is called."

The prosecutor's answer projected an air of confidence that the grand jury would act quickly—that the defense's bluster was just that, bluster. But the reporters pressed him, asking if he had made a mistake not recalling the grand jury sooner to give the men more time?

Even if the hearing happened, Stephenson's lawyers would end up showing more of their hand than his men would, Tate answered. The standard of proof at a preliminary hearing was low: all the prosecution had to do was establish probable cause that Father Coyle was dead and that "Stephenson did the killing." There was no question that the priest was dead, and the minister had admitted that he killed him, Tate reminded them. And even if Stephenson entered a plea of self-defense, Tate continued, the law of Alabama put the burden on the accused to provide some evidence of that type of claim. It was what was known as an affirmative defense. That meant it was Stephenson's lawyers who would end up exposing their evidence, Tate said, not him.[37]

There was logic in the prosecutor's answers, but the newsmen sensed a hollowness in the explanation. They found it hard to believe that Joe Tate could be as indifferent to the prospect of his men holding a hearing in open court as he was trying to make out. The game may have just begun, but the defense appeared to have won an important round.[38]

———

By Tuesday, August 16, 1921, Ruth Stephenson Gussman was desperate. Five days had passed since the shooting; three since Mary Stephenson had refused to allow H. W. Schaefer of the *Age-Herald* to take some garments to her daughter. Over an inch of rain had fallen the day before, as the mercury climbed to 87 degrees by midafternoon. The city must have felt like a steam bath. Ruth needed fresh clothes, and if her mother wouldn't send them, she resolved to fetch them herself.

Judging from Mary Stephenson's cool reception when Ruth and a friend marched up to the Stephensons' porch on Seventh Avenue, it seems likely that Ruth had called ahead to advise her mother that she was on her way. The older woman was sitting like a sentinel on a swing near the front door.

The girl's arrival created quite a stir. She had been missing for days. Neighbors watched enthralled as Ruth and her unknown companion climbed the steps to the porch. Mary Stephenson's daughter didn't even bother to say hello to her mother, one of the neighbors told a reporter later. She just barked a demand, and her tone—so angry!

"I have come for my clothes, mother."

Mary Stephenson did not budge. "Your clothes are not here, Ruth," she said.

If the neighbors were bewildered that the woman did not rush from her seat to pull her missing daughter into her arms, they did not show it. It was Ruth's manner that they noticed—the teenager had addressed her mother in such an insolent way!

Ruth ignored her mother's answer. "I have come for my clothes and I mean to have them," she said again. She brushed past the seated woman and went into the house.

It must have been an uncomfortable moment for Ruth's friend, who trailed closely behind her. It was one thing for Ruth to defy her mother, but her companion was a stranger to the household. Mary Stephenson barked a question at young woman as she passed: "Who are you?"

Maybe the visitor had girded herself for some sort of confrontation. "That is none of your business," the neighbors heard her answer. "I have come with Ruth to get her clothes and we are going to have them."

"You won't find them," Mary Stephenson corrected her. "Ruth's clothes are in the wash."

The explanation must have sounded a bit too convenient, as if in the midst all of the turmoil that had subsumed the Stephenson household— a jailed husband, a missing daughter, both involved in the city's biggest scandal—Mary Stephenson could have felt a pressing need to send all of her daughter's things out for laundering.

Mary must have read the look of disapproval on the young woman's face. "Ruth can have the clothes when they come back home," she said defensively. "I have no desire to keep them."

Ruth's companion gave no reply; she just continued into the house. But the neighbors watched Mary Stephenson get up from her seat then and follow the women inside, where she was heard to say a second time that "she did not *want* to keep [Ruth's] clothing, but the way she was acting was killing her!"—inching closer and closer to confessing, even if unwittingly, that the fortuity of the missing apparel and her daughter's grievous behavior were linked in fact. That it was no accident that the things that the young bride needed the most *(not her mother or father, plainly!)*, the things that had finally forced her to return to her parents' home, were nowhere to be found. It was an act of pathetic retaliation. No longer able to command her daughter's conduct, Mary Stephenson had controlled what she could: the only objects Ruth seemed to care about.

Not long after, Ruth and her friend walked out of the house without a word, a neighbor said, the teenager carrying just a "small bundle." Apparently, after a search of the entire house, she had recovered only one useable dress.[39]

———

It can no longer be known who first proposed that the Alabama Ku Klux Klan fund the defense of Reverend Edwin Stephenson, but some years later, according to James Esdale, the head of Birmingham's Robert E. Lee Klavern No. 1 at the time, the Alabama forces of the Invisible Empire footed the entire bill. Certainly there would have been no way for Edwin Stephenson to afford the legal fees of his four prestigious lawyers himself. Even in good times, "the accused minister [was] a man of little or no means," and once behind bars, his meager finances worsened quickly. With no ability to chase down clients in the hallways of the courthouse, he was soon strapped for cash, and lawyers didn't come cheap. Stephenson's attorneys may have felt a special obligation toward the minister. Like their client, three of the four defense lawyers—Crampton Harris, Fred Fite, and John Arnold—were Klansmen, too. Only Hugo Black had yet to join the secret fraternal order. But there is no evidence that their common affinity for the Klan translated into a cut in the lawyers' rates. Not long after the men were retained, the *Birmingham Post* reported that a massive statewide drive was under way to raise money for the minister's defense.[40]

When local reporters tried to find out who was behind the fund-raising effort, all they could discover was that a group calling itself the Stephenson Defense Committee had been created, and that the group was "generally understood [to be] an anti-Catholic organization," the *Post*'s sources said. Members of the committee were visiting cities across the state on the hunt for contributions, and before long, money was flooding in: "Supporters of the movement claim[ed] that Montgomery, Mobile, Tuscaloosa, and Gadsden [had] been visited and considerable money secured." Two meetings in Gadsden lasting scarcely ten minutes each had raised $500 apiece, the *Post* reported. Anniston would be visited next.[41]

A day after the *Birmingham Post* revealed the existence of the Stephenson Defense Committee, John C. Johnson of 121 Twenty-first Street North issued a written statement declaring that he was the committee's chairman, and that he wanted to make it clear that the True Americans were not behind the fund-raising effort, as some seemed to believe. Since Coyle's funeral, where the Catholic bishop from Mobile "made the unwarranted statement that a certain society was responsible for the death of Priest Coyle, the press ha[d] sought to make his words true," Johnson wrote. But the suspicion was false. The True Americans were "not connected with this committee."[42]

But when it came to disclosing particulars about who *did* make up the group, Johnson was decidedly coy: "This committee, which is several hundred strong, is composed of friends of the minister, who may or may not belong to the various honored societies and fraternal orders of the city," he wrote. Johnson did declare, however, that Stephenson's friends were confident that he would be acquitted.

It would be many years before anyone associated with the Klan would publically admit that the Invisible Empire had been behind the successful fundraising campaign.[43]

SEVEN

The Engines of Justice Turn

THE THIRD AVENUE block buzzed with nervous energy as the grand jurors filed into the courthouse on the morning of August 23, 1921. Reporters had surrounded the building in anticipation of the men's arrival, and court-watchers, wagering that Joe Tate would not succeed in wangling an indictment from the group, had already begun to mill around the halls, waiting for the doors to Judge Abernathy's courtroom to be opened, realizing that only an early arrival would guarantee them a good seat. In 1921, the grand jury's eighteen members remained all white, and despite the recent successes of women's suffrage, all male as well. On the days they were scheduled to deliberate, the men climbed the steps into the three-story building, passing beneath the shrouded statue named "Lady Justice" that determinedly guarded the front entrance, legal scroll in one hand, sword in the other. There was an elevator inside, and the grand jury room was located on the second floor, but many visitors to the building opted for the stairs. Nearest the hand rail, the steps had been "worn to razor-edge thinness," clear proof of "the tramp of thousands of feet too impatient to wait" on the conveyor.[1]

On the morning of August 23, Joe Tate was also in a hurry. He had tried to put a brave face on it, but few believed that the prosecutor was as unconcerned about Stephenson's refusal to waive the preliminary hearing as he had tried to make out—a decision that threatened to force Tate's assistants to showcase the state's evidence before the swarm of curiosity seekers who would jam the courthouse corridors just a few hours later. Matters before the Jefferson County grand jury were conducted in secret—only the prosecutor, a stenographer, a bailiff, and the eighteen grand jurors were allowed inside the room when the witnesses testified—and afterward, none but the witnesses themselves could share what was said. But the newsmen had eyes, and considering the swift current of witnesses that streamed in and out of the room that morning, they readily gleaned that the prosecutor badly wanted the grand jury to return an indictment before noon. As the *Birmingham News* reported later that day, the prosecutor rushed his "witnesses through the mill, one after another, whipping up things all morning in an effort to complete the grand jury hearing and return an indictment before 2 o'clock, thus hoping to conceal the state's hand until the regular trial."[2]

There were other signs as well. The reporters would have had no occasion to see it, but if any uncertainty remained about Tate's desire that day, a review of the transcript of the proceeding would have removed it. Despite the grand jury's secrecy, records of its meetings were prepared, making it possible, decades later, when the document came to light, to witness the prosecutor's haste, like a fly on the wall. It must have been some comfort to Joe Tate to know that the job of convincing the grand jury to indict a man normally did not take that long. A judge would famously quip some years later that a "grand jury would indict a ham sandwich" if a prosecutor asked it to.[3] Though hyperbolic, the remark possessed more than a grain of truth: only rarely did a grand jury buck the wishes of a prosecutor. With no defense lawyers in the room to slow things down, it would not have been unusual for Joe Tate to have a number of indictments in hand well before lunch.

Even as the threat of the preliminary hearing loomed, Joe Tate needed to be patient. For eleven days, the local papers had printed and reprinted Stephenson's and his wife's excuses: that he had shot Coyle in self-defense, Edwin said; that the Catholics had tormented them for years, Mary cried. Undoubtedly, the grand jurors would have seen the publicity. Some of them might even have wanted to believe it. Before Joe Tate could ask the men to reject Stephenson's story, and ask them to indict the minister for murder in the first degree, he had to convince them that there was "probable cause" to believe that Stephenson had shot Coyle with "malice aforethought" and "premeditation." That required some proof that in advance of the shooting, the minister had turned the idea of killing the priest over in his mind; that he had thought about it ahead of time—perhaps when he went home to retrieve his gun and carried it back to the rectory, or maybe only in the fast-moving, adrenalin-filled seconds before he pulled the trigger, again and again and again, until he fired the fatal shot. Unlike at trial, the standard was not proof "beyond a reasonable doubt." It was enough to show that there was *reason* to think Stephenson had decided to kill the priest before he shot. Normally, proof that a man had carried a loaded gun to another man's home, pointed it at his head, and pulled the trigger sufficed.

The minister's claim of self-defense had added a wrinkle, however, with its suggestion that Stephenson had acted impulsively, rather than deliberatively. As Joe Tate had told the reporters, to be entitled to make such a claim, Alabama law required a defendant to produce some actual evidence of it first, on the reasoning that one who asserted such a self-serving thing should at least be able to offer up some proof of it before the state was forced to expend precious resources disproving it. That was certainly the rule at trial, and even the preliminary hearing. But proceedings before the grand jury were different. No matter the technicalities about who was supposed to produce evidence of it first, in the grand jury room, it was Joe Tate's job to make sure the men were not fooled by what they read in the papers. If the grand jurors had questions about whether the minister had shot the priest in self-defense, Tate had to dispel them. To do that, the circuit solicitor needed to convince the grand jurors that Stephenson had disliked Father Coyle long before the two men met on the porch that day, and that the unblessed wedding of his daughter to the Catholic Pedro Gussman had been all the excuse he needed to take the cleric's life. If the prosecutor could show the jurors that, they might see through the minister's claim.

Still, the task was delicate. Gossip that the priest had lured the Stephenson girl to convert to Catholicism and to marry a Catholic had been circulating around town from the time of the shooting. Even if Tate succeeded in convincing the grand jurors that Stephenson had had no reason to fear that Father Coyle was about to take his life when he shot, the men might still be reluctant to blame the minister if they thought the priest had wrongfully tried to seduce his daughter away from her rightful Protestant religion. Even if the law of Alabama did not countenance such a vengeance killing—the *unwritten law* might, Tate knew. Somehow, he had to show that the priest was innocent of that, too.

The choice of the prosecutor's first witness must have seemed clear.

———

Ruth Stephenson Gussman, "accompanied by two ladies, appeared at the courthouse at 9 o'clock," reported one of the local papers, and they carved a path through a crush of reporters on their way to the grand jury room on the second floor. There was no sign of her husband, though Pedro must have suspected that his wife's reception at the courthouse would be chaotic. The newsmen fired questions at Ruth as she passed, but the young woman gave them the cold shoulder, looking straight ahead: "head erect and eyes for no one."[4] Talking to the press had won Ruth Gussman few rewards, with one possible exception—two days after the *Age-Herald* printed its story about

Ruth's confrontation with Mary Stephenson at their home, her mother had decided she might have her clothes after all, the paper reported.

The decision had caused some bitterness within the family. A number of Mary Stephenson's relatives had tried to convince her that she owed Ruth nothing, that it was Pedro Gussman's job to clothe her. "Her husband should provide for her," they said.[5] A reporter had tracked Pedro down, hoping for a reaction, but the paperhanger knew better than to get into a war of words with his wife's family. "He did not care to discuss it."

By then, the groom's reserve had become standard fare. Pedro avoided the newsmen whenever he could, and even when they managed to corner him, he said very little, despite their efforts to draw him out. He could not have liked the way the newsmen portrayed his young wife in their columns, with their endless insinuations about her deficiencies as a daughter. The urge to come to her defense must have burned. But Pedro had lived in Birmingham long enough to understand the benefits of silence, especially when his own social footing in the town had grown suddenly precarious. The papers seemed never to tire of writing about the newlyweds, and increasingly, their references to him noted not only his religion—("Pedro Gussman, a Catholic") and place of birth ("Gussman, a Porto Rican") but his "pronounced foreign accent" and the hue of his skin as well. Pedro Gussman's "dark complexion" stood in stark contrast with the features of "his pretty little wife," wrote one, as if its readers could make sense of the shooting of Father Coyle only when armed with that additional biographical information about the groom.

"Where is your husband from?" the journalists asked the girl repeatedly.

"I believe he's a Spaniard," she said again and again. And, no, she could not tell them any more about his native country.[6]

It was a bad omen, and doubtless Pedro knew it. Newcomers to the United States in the early part of the twentieth century quickly learned the importance of cultural conformity. Little good came from a focus on all of the things that made them different from the country's "native white" stock. Years later, Greek children would tell of the beatings they took in the Birmingham public schools during the period, and the great number of times they endured the slur "dago"—treatment scarcely better than that given a Negro, they thought; "I was just like the little black boy," one said. "When they weren't picking on the black boy, they were picking on me." Italians who emigrated to the United States in the early part of the twentieth century recounted similar experiences, facing powerful demands that they sublimate their alien ways, that they assimilate, that they speak English. For a time, it seemed they couldn't do it quickly enough. Italian children learned to ignore a slate of vilifications—"dago," "fish-eater," "spaghetti-eater," "crossback"—and though permitted to enroll in the same schools and sit in the same restaurants as the native whites, they occupied a social stratum decidedly inferior: "The Italian was not regarded as the social equal of the white person," one student of the region wrote flatly. The company towns that flanked the city provided "a street for native whites," a "second street for Italians, and a third for Negroes," as if to communicate to the immigrants that if they were on the path to the privileges of whiteness, they certainly had not yet fully arrived.

In theory, the common marginalization of the new arrivals could have led them to forge some powerful coalitions among themselves. But more often than not, the opposite was true. Shared histories of oppression cemented no alliances between its victims. Instead, the Negroes of America and the hordes of early twentieth-century immigrants from southeastern Europe and beyond found themselves "divided by decades of fierce competition for a share of industrialism's dregs, a tortured history of mutual distrust, and the poison of the American racial ideal, which made even the swarthiest of immigrants desperate to prove himself a white man," a leading historian of the era wrote.[7] Thus, just as in earlier decades when Irish settlers in New York City had actively participated in the worst racial violence of the city's draft riots, when the Greeks of Birmingham began to enjoy a greater measure of acceptance some years later, few demanded justice for the city's Negroes. "We got it like we want it and nobody is bothering us," explained one. "We won't bother nobody else."[8] If no profile in courage, the mindset was understandable—at a time when one's whiteness was sliced into so "many gradations of unfreedom," the importance of being able at least to celebrate one's *nonblackness* was apparent to all.[9]

No doubt for many of these same reasons, in 1921, Pedro Gussman preferred anonymity to celebrity, and but for the inconvenience of finding himself at the center of the state's biggest scandal, there can be little question that the wallpaper hanger would have been content to live out his days in the soothing shadows of obscurity. Danger lurked between the lines of the reporters' articles—with their almost daily references to the island of his birth, "Porto Rico," and the "swarthy" tone of his skin, a description that brought him uncomfortably close to the degraded Negro—nothing good could come of it. So whenever the Birmingham newsmen managed to corner him, Pedro generally had "little to say," and when, on the morning of August 23, his wife left for the courthouse to give her testimony, he let her face down the hordes of her critics without him.

It can't be known if Pedro thought about the costs of such restraint—that his eighteen-year-old bride might not fully appreciate the reasons for his diffidence. For silence in the face of aggression subdues few bullies. And if not her husband, Ruth Stephenson Gussman may have thought to herself, then who *would* come to her defense?[10]

——

If the many published descriptions of Ruth Stephenson Gussman at the time can be taken seriously, unlike her husband, the bride shared no dislike of the limelight. She reveled in being the center of attention, the journalists thought, and one of the reporters who watched her as she sat outside the grand jury chamber that day was put off by the girl's demeanor. Mrs. Gussman appeared at the courthouse dressed in "a stylish blue voile dress" and a matching hat, "completely at ease," wrote the newsman irritably, "chatting gaily," even "laughing occasionally" with her two unidentified companions. By the time Joe Tate invited Ruth to step into the grand jury room, the journalist seemed convinced by this display that the teenager hadn't a care in the world.

But it is impossible to think that Ruth Gussman could have been as calm as the newsman suggested, or unaffected by the stares of the roomful of grown men who watched her enter. She may even have recognized some of them. All of the men lived and worked within the city confines: the foreman, Lynn Patton, ran an insurance business; others were carpenters, machinists, and salesmen; two of the men worked for the railroad; one was a business agent for an industrial concern; another operated the presses at one of the local newspapers. Solid men, all gainfully employed, most of them married, with children—the kind of men who probably looked ill on adolescent disobedience; who would find it difficult to look kindly on a daughter who would testify against her own father, a man facing the gallows.[11]

When Ruth took her seat, Joe Tate wasted no time. If she was to be any help to him, he had to put the bride in a better light. Tate moved swiftly through the preliminaries—the place of her family's residence, the name of her employer, her father's name, the length of her family's time in Birmingham—the kind of questions that can buy a nervous witness a little time to relax. But when he reached his first substantive question, the veteran prosecutor stumbled, as if the tension in the room had affected him, too, leaving him unsure of the best place to start.

"What treatment did you receive from your father when you were—during the—recently, before you married," Joe Tate asked, awkwardly.

"I have been punished severely," Ruth answered.

"Punished?"

"Yes, sir."

The word hung in the air, barren and cold, surrounded by no details to give it life. In 1921, parents often disciplined their unruly children. Without more particulars to show that her father's treatment had been excessive, the statement was worthless. But instead of asking Ruth to be more specific, Tate's next question—"Had you left home before?"—seemed disjointed, making matters worse. She had, Ruth admitted, a number of times. She had fled to Chattanooga the fall before, and stayed with friends, until her father had come for her. Another time she had stayed with a Mrs. Harris, there in Birmingham, she prattled on. And twice she had sought refuge at the home of her godfather, Fred Bender, when she feared going home—but each time, her parents had found her and brought her back.

Too much too soon, Joe Tate must have thought to himself, and again the information lacked the kind of vivid detail that might create sympathy for the girl's plight. The prosecutor decided to back up, to give his witness a chance to explain the context.

"Well, did you join the Catholic church?" he asked. Not artful perhaps, but the question at least moved in the right direction—backward—toward the source of the trouble in the girl's household.

"Yes, sir," Ruth replied.

"At what place?"

"At Our Lady of Sorrows Church, over on the Southside."

"Father Coyle about there when you joined?"

Father Coyle had presided over St. Paul's Church, not Our Lady of Sorrows, but he had also been the dean of Northern Alabama, which give him supervisory authority over all of the Catholic churches in the region. Joe Tate must have wanted the jurors to understand that, despite what they might have read, Father Coyle had had nothing whatever to do with the girl's conversion.

"No sir, I didn't see him at all."

"Who was the priest?"

"Father Kelley," she said.

"O'Kelley?" the prosecutor corrected her, revealing to anyone who might have doubted it that Ruth's testimony was no surprise to him.

"Yes," she said.

Tate asked his witness when she had joined the church.

"The tenth of April."

"This year?"

"Yes."

"And had you been attending the church?"

"Not regularly," she said.

"Did your father *know* that you had joined that church?"

"No sir, not then, but he found it out later."

If the grand jurors were to be persuaded that the minister's violence on August 11 resulted from his long-simmering resentment against the Catholics, the date of the minister's discovery of Ruth's conversion was important. "How long after you joined was that that he found it out?" he asked.

"About three or four weeks."

"Three or four weeks?" Tate echoed—an old trial lawyer's trick, repeating the witness's answer not to clarify what she had just said but to emphasize it—to plant the point firmly in the grand juror's minds.

"Yes, sir."

"He had known it then since May?"

"Yes, sir."

"First of May, about that," the prosecutor said again, beginning to find his rhythm, his transitions smoother: "Did you ever hear him express his feelings toward Father Coyle or any of these other priests?"

"Yes, sir, all my life."

"What would he say?"

"He said that he hated them," Ruth answered, "that Catholicism was rotten." Her mother had, too, she added, as if sensing where the prosecutor was going: "I have heard my mother say many a time that she would like to set a bomb under St. Paul Cathedral."

The context set, Joe Tate circled back around to the topic of Fred Bender, the furniture salesman whom Ruth had already testified had taken her into his home during two of her flights. Stephenson had been spreading rumors around town that the Catholics had kidnapped his daughter, that the police had discovered Fred Bender and his wife holding her captive in their home, under lock and key.

"[W]ho was your godfather when you joined the church?" Tate asked.

"Mr. Bender."

"And it was at his house that you had gone to?"

"Yes, sir."

"And how long did you stay over there at his house?"

Ruth explained that she had fled to the Bender's home twice: on "the Monday before the fifteenth of May"—after she learned that her father had discovered her conversion—and again, a second time, the following Sunday. "A friend of mine told me that if I went home that night that they might kill me, they were so highly incensed over it," she said. "I went over to Mr. Bender's and stayed Monday night and Tuesday night."

"How were you treated over there?"

"Just splendid," the teenager replied, a tad too airily. Her choice of words made it sound as though she had been off on a romp instead of hiding out in fear. H. W. Schaefer, a reporter for the *Age-Herald*, had been put off by the same breezy nonchalance when he interviewed Ruth Stephenson a little over a week before. It was the kind of reply adults considered the very mark of youth.

There can be little doubt that Tate noticed Ruth's poor wording. Even if the law acknowledged Ruth at age eighteen as being mature enough to make life-altering decisions—like the decision whether to marry—the grand jurors would be tempted to make their own judgments about that. The prosecutor decided to press on, trying to get the girl to state clearly that she had stayed with the Benders of her own free will: "Did they keep you locked up in a room?" he asked.

"Not at all," she replied, "I had the freedom of the whole place."

The tone of the answer was still not right, but at least the girl had confirmed that her stay with the Benders had been voluntary. With all the fears about Catholics kidnapping the children of Protestants, Tate wanted to be sure that the grand jurors understood that Ruth thought of the Bender house as a sanctuary, not a prison. If anything had been against her will, it was her retrieval from the house. He turned to that next: "Who was it came over there?"

A big crowd of men, Ruth said, piled all together in a big car. "They said that they were officers." The teenager's voice must have dropped as she recalled the moment—remembering how her father had stopped at nothing to bend her will to his, even called out reinforcements.

"Talk a little bit louder," said Tate gently. "When they got there, where were you?" he asked.

"I was upstairs," she said. "I locked myself in the closet to keep them from finding me."

"Bender nor his folks didn't keep you locked up?" Tate asked again.

"No, sir, not at all. I locked the doors myself after [Mr. and Mrs. Bender] went to go to town. When I saw these policemen coming, I locked myself in the closet to keep them from finding me."

To sympathetic ears, the image would have been powerful: the frightened girl, crouched inside the darkened closet, hoping in vain that her father and his friends would pass it by unchecked. Tate moved on, asking Ruth about the time she had left the train on the return trip from Texas. Ruth described how she had gotten off the train at Texarkana and how she had made her way to the Catholic hospital. But then her mother and some lawmen had found her and put her back on the train. No escape.

The testimony edged the prosecutor and his witness closer to August 11, the day Ruth and Pedro had eloped. The grand jury was not likely to approve of the teenager's decision to hide her intentions from her parents that day, Tate knew. But at age eighteen, the law entitled her to make the choice for herself.

"Had you talked about getting married to your mother?" Tate asked.

"No, sir."

"Or your father?"

"No, sir."

"You were eighteen?" he prompted, doing what he could to provide some defense for the girl's secrecy.

"Yes, sir."

Tate returned to the question of her relationship with the priest who had married them: "Now, had you ever been in the rectory here," he asked, "or had you ever had any conversation with Father Coyle in any way?"

She had visited with the priest at the rectory when she was twelve years old, she said.

"Twelve years old?"

"Yes, sir," Ruth replied. "I went to ask him," she hesitated, then started again: "I wanted to join the church *then*. I went to talk to him about it, and I was sitting on the front porch, and my father came up and stood at the gate and told me to come home. So I went with him. When I arrived home, he punished me for going there."

There was that word again—*punished*—troublingly vague. But Tate declined to ask his witness to be more precise. Maybe he thought that the grand jury could picture it for themselves—the enraged minister, towering over the frightened twelve-year-old—that they could imagine the punishment he would have inflicted for such a betrayal. Or maybe the prosecutor simply wanted to keep Ruth Gussman on track, to have her assert again that her only connection to Father Coyle had been *inconsequential*—a single conversation six years before, when the girl was twelve!—a contact far too fleeting for the slain priest to have exerted any real influence over her decision to convert, or to marry a Catholic.

"Was that the only time you ever talked with [Father Coyle] then?"

"Yes, sir," she answered.

Tate turned to the wedding: "On the day of your marriage, what time of day did you go there to him?"

"To Father Coyle?" she asked.

"Yes."

"I judge about four o'clock," she said. "Father Coyle was not at home, so we waited in the church until he came."

"What time was the ceremony performed?"

"At 5:30."

He asked what she and Pedro did afterward. They had called for a taxi, she said. When had they left the church?

"About a quarter to six."

The prosecutor shifted back to Ruth's relationship with her parents, asking her if she had promised her parents after they had learned about her baptism at Our Lady of Sorrows that she would not pursue Catholicism. Ruth admitted she had made the agreement, but she had had little choice, she said—"I knew I was in their power. I had to do exactly as they said." So she had agreed not to go to the Catholic church any more, in exchange for some promises from them: that they would move to a nicer part of town, that they would allow her some greater freedoms, "the amusements and enjoyment that a girl should have," she said. And her father told her that he would send her on a trip to Texas.

"However, that was"—she stopped then, not bothering to finish the thought: that the deal had been a Faustian bargain. That it had bestowed no lasting liberties, only more kinsmen to sit in judgment on her choices. "They wanted me to promise that I would not go to the church any more, [to] give up my religion in return for *that*," she finished, contempt nearly dripping from her lips.

Tate must have realized that most of the men in the room would have sided with Ruth's parents on the matter. He changed the subject: "Your father ever discuss his marksmanship with a pistol?"

"Oh, yes. Numbers of times," she said. "He was always practicing shooting, and always cleaning his guns, and keeping them in perfect shape. He was very proud of his physical well-being and the fact that he could defend himself in case of trouble."

"Did he ever make any threats to kill Father Coyle or any one connected with the church?"

"He said many times that he wished Father Coyle was dead," Ruth said. "He thought he was one of humanity's biggest enemies."

The answer was not directly responsive. Stephenson could have wished the priest dead without threatening to be the one to kill him. But the fact that he had ruminated on the priest's death long before the shooting made it more likely that Stephenson had shot Father Coyle not because the priest was threatening his life but he because detested everything about him: his prominence in the city; his towering church, a building whose shadows during certain hours of the day blotted out the sunlight along Third Avenue where the Stephensons had their home; his imagined role in Stephenson's waning influence over his only daughter. His Ruth! A girl more enraptured by the lies of the Catholics than the lessons Edwin and Mary Stephenson had taught her from the day she was born. Bitterness such as that, Tate knew, could lead a man to take the law into his own hands—to anoint himself with the authority to decide whether another man should live or die. Joe Tate knew that Edwin Stephenson had done that once before: "Do you know of his ever taking part in the lynching of anybody?" he asked the girl.

"Yes, sir," she said. He was actively involved "in the lynching of a Negro in Cedartown, Georgia in 1902."

"Do you know the Negro's name?"

"No, sir, I don't. I have heard him speak about it though, ever since I can remember."

The foreman of the grand jury, Lynn Patton, interrupted: "What was the Negro lynched for?" he asked, as though Tate and the girl had omitted an important piece of information that needed clearing up.

"For assaulting a white girl," Ruth replied simply.

"He was doing a noble deed then, wasn't he?" another juror said.

"He certainly was," chimed in a third.

Ruth did not answer; there must have seemed little need. Her interrogators had just declared her father's part in a lynching an act of heroism— "a noble deed." If the thought of a mob taking the life of a Negro did not repulse the men, what hope was there that they would think her father had gone too far in dealing with her?[12]

———

The Cedartown lynching had actually occurred two years later than Ruth Gussman remembered, in 1904 rather than 1902, though seven Negroes were lynched in Georgia in 1902 as well—John Wise, William Mobley, Walter Allen, Benjamin Brown, Arthur McCauly, John Brown, and Henry Young. Although the state of Georgia was one of the nation's leaders for mob violence, Polk County had only one recorded lynching: in Cedartown in 1904, where the Stephensons lived at the time. The violence occurred on a Monday, just seven days shy of Ruth Stephenson's second birthday, a few miles from the eastern border of Alabama.[13]

On August 22, 1904, word of a Negro's sexual assault on the thirteen-year-old daughter of Abner Reeves, a local farmer, spread across Cedartown like wildfire. Squads of men soon gave chase, scouring the fields and woods for the fugitive. They soon found James Glover, cowering in a cabin, near a slate quarry west of the town. The papers never reported Glover's age—but they included other descriptions, like the "burly, black Negro"; "the black fiend"; and the "Negro ravisher." And they printed vivid details of how the young girl had resisted his attack: she had been choked into "insensibility," one paper said. Her clothes were "bloody and torn," her neck red and swollen, and all around where the attack took place, the "ground showed evidence of a struggle, the weeds and corn were mashed down," reported another. Though only thirteen, the scratches and bruises on her body displayed the vehemence of her combat, the papers reported approvingly—the girl had done all that was expected of her: in the words of the law of rape at the time, resisting "to the utmost," following that "natural instinct of every proud female to resist," until, overpowered, she was unable to do more.[14] As the pursuers mounted their horses or set off after the criminal by foot, the attack on Reeves's daughter would have seemed as much an affront to southern white male chivalry as an assault on the girl herself. The *Cedartown Standard* had made it a point to warn rapists of their fate when caught: "The rapist will receive his reward from lynchers in one section of the country as well as the other," the paper promised. "This is a white man's country, and folks might just as well make up their minds to that fact now as hereafter."[15]

When the posse pulled James Glover from the cabin later that afternoon, he protested his innocence, and the clothes he wore did not fit the girl's description. But other garments found in the cabin matched closely enough, and when the mob hauled Glover back to her home, the teenager agreed that he was the man. Her identification prompted Glover to confess it—though he stated he must have "had a spell on him" to have done such a thing. Hearing his words, a mob "fully 2,500 strong" surged toward him, amid angry shouts: "Burn him!" "Shoot him!" "Like a cyclone," they marched the prisoner up Main Street to West Avenue, where someone chained him to an oak tree, while others piled wood all around his feet, ignoring his pleas to be taken to the county jail. A match was soon put to the kindling, but the fire was too slow to ignite, and "the discharge of a pistol proved the signal for a general fusillade." Within seconds "hundreds of shots perforated the body of the Negro," one newsman wrote later, a barrage that turned out misguided, for not all of the shooters were the marksmen they imagined themselves to be. The suspect was killed, certainly, but stray shots wounded six men in the crowd as well, and one, John Sexton, shot in the abdomen, died the next day. After the onslaught, some of the men, perhaps desirous of a souvenir of the event, cut off Glover's ears, nose, fingers, and toes, before pulling his mutilated corpse from the tree, and dragging it back to Main Street by a chain around the neck, where they burned it "to ashes."[16]

———

There is no saying what went through Joe Tate's mind when one of the jurors called Stephenson's role in the Cedartown lynching a "noble deed"— but he could not have considered it a good sign. By the minute, Ruth

Gussman's testimony against her father seemed only to be drawing her audience nearer to the jailed minister rather than rallying them against him. The prosecutor needed to get the witness out of the room. He raced through a few more questions: Had anyone persuaded her to join the Catholic Church? Absolutely not, she said. No one could persuade her to do anything she didn't want to do. (*Teenage braggadocio—was the girl trying to sink his case?*) Did she know that her father had gotten papers to put her in an insane asylum? asked Tate. Yes, she had learned about that. The prosecutor was nearly through: did her father have any other employment other than marrying folks around the courthouse? "No sir," she said, not since accidentally shooting himself in the foot, an injury that had ended his career as a barber.

One grand juror piped up, asking the witness, helpfully, if her father hadn't run into some trouble as well with the Barber's Union, for which he had served as secretary for a time. "Yes sir," the girl replied, her father had been accused of stealing money that didn't belong to him.

A small glimmer of hope—at least one of the jurors seemed to think that Stephenson had flaws worth noting. Tate tried to make some headway on the point: "[H]e was secretary, and had charge of the money?" he asked.

"Yes, sir."

"And came up short?"

"Yes, sir."

"To the Union?"

But before she could answer, the grand jury foreman interrupted, stopping the line of questioning in its tracks—as if he couldn't give a damn about applications to insane asylums, or Stephenson's shenanigans in the courthouse, or his supposed theft of union dues. The foreman brought the focus back to the matter of the girl's religion: "Mrs. Gussman, were you ever a member of the *Methodist* church?" Lynn Patton asked.

"Yes, sir."

"How did it happen that you left that church and joined the Catholic church?"

"Because I believed that was the only true way," she said, "the only way by which I could save my soul."

Joe Tate must have wondered if the girl could have said anything that would have offended the man more.

"You said nobody influenced you," the foreman continued, without comment. "You took it upon yourself to change?"

"Yes, sir."

"It is rather unusual," Patton retorted, skeptically.

"Yes, sir, I know it is unusual," Ruth conceded. "But I have read and studied the question for years, and finally decided it was the only thing that could satisfy me."

The foreman's silence must nearly have filled the room.

Until another grand juror asked about her husband's nationality.

"He is Spanish," she replied.

"Is he *full-blooded* Italian?" the juror followed up, as though Spanish and Italian were national equivalents. And then, before she could answer: "Belong to the *Caucasian race?*"

"Yes," she said.

"How long have you been knowing him?" asked another.

"Sir?"

"I say, how long have you been knowing him?"

"I have been knowing him about seven years," she told him, then Joe Tate's voice, mercifully, reached her ears—thanking her for her testimony, telling her she was excused.[17]

The reporters had jockeyed for position outside the grand jury door so that they would be ready to pounce when Pedro Gussman's bride exited, but even they must have been surprised when the door swung open so soon, only fifteen minutes after the girl had begun her testimony. They showered her with questions, but Ruth passed through the corridors and out the front door without saying a word.[18]

Joe Tate questioned twenty more witnesses that morning: Marcella Coyle and Stella Caruthers, the two women first to find Father Coyle's bloodied body; Officers Weir and Snow, the two men who had chased Stephenson down outside the courthouse and taken him into custody; Sheriff Chris Hartsfield and two of his deputies; a handful of men who worked for Lige Loy's funeral parlor; several people who had been close enough to the rectory to hear the shots, see Stephenson step off the porch, or both; and Russum, the coroner.

In a case where there had never been a question about the *identity* of Father Coyle's killer, the path to indictment should have been eased considerably. Several witnesses told the jurors that they saw Stephenson step off the porch immediately after firing the shots; Weir and Snow testified about chasing him down and pulling the gun from his hand; and according to the testimony of Deputy Steve Wiggins, Chief Deputy Fred McDuff, and Deputy Coroner George Moore, Stephenson himself had *confessed* that he was the shooter. With identity a nonissue, the only remaining questions were whether the minister had "premeditated" taking the priest's life, as required for first-degree murder, or whether, as he was saying, he had shot the cleric in self-defense.

Though hurried, Joe Tate approached the case methodically, piling fact on fact, inference on inference, in an effort to close off every means of escape to the minister—steering the grand jury toward the conclusion that he had either gone to the rectory with the specific purpose of killing Coyle or had decided to kill the priest after he arrived. And that, contrary to the prisoner's claims, there had been no fight. That was simply a ruse, a contrivance; the only thing the minister had been able to come up with to defend his act. As is typical for a grand jury transcript, the official record of the proceeding would include none of the colloquy that occurred between the prosecutor and grand jury members; only the questions to the witnesses and the witnesses' answers were recorded. But there can be no doubt that Joe Tate instructed the jurors that, legally, it made no difference whether Stephenson concocted his plan to kill the priest before he stepped onto the porch or decided to kill him after he got there. Alabama's highest court had generously interpreted the word "premeditated" in the first-degree murder statute to require only a show-ing that a slayer intended to strike the lethal blow before it "was delivered, though it be *for only an instant of time before.*" So long as Stephenson had pulled the trigger after thinking for "even a single moment" that shooting a bullet into the priest's head would kill him, the crime of premeditated murder was committed.[19]

Joe Tate suspected that Stephenson had thought about killing the priest for longer than a second. The prosecutor believed that the minister had learned about his daughter's marriage before going to the rectory—that someone had informed him about it before he marched to the priest's home with a loaded gun—his nephew, Ross Campbell, perhaps, after Ruth had called home. But even if Stephenson had only learned about it from the priest after reaching the porch, by Stephenson's own admission, the news had *enraged* him—a powerful motivator to kill. Deputy Sheriff Fred McDuff and Deputy Coroner George Moore testified that Stephenson had confessed to them about shouting at Coyle, after learning the news, "You've treated me like a dirty dog!" or "You're a dirty dog!"—clear evidence of his fury. Thus, whether the minister had learned about his daughter's marriage before or after he stepped onto the rectory porch was largely beside the point. Even if the grand jurors were unwilling to credit Ruth Gussman's testimony that her father had hated the priest for years, that he had wanted Coyle dead, and even if they were not persuaded that Stephenson had gone to the rectory intending to kill Father Coyle for marrying his daughter to a Catholic, the jurors could still conclude that he had premeditated the victim's death. For at the moment he shot, Stephenson was furious about the marriage.

Stephenson, however, without ever appearing before the grand jury had nonetheless managed to gum up the works with his highly convenient claim that he shot Father Coyle, not in anger but out of fear for his life. Stephenson had insisted to Joe Tate, Deputy McDuff, and Assistant Coroner Moore that he had shot Coyle only *after* the priest attacked him; *after* Coyle had hit him on the head, knocked him down, hurting his head and his side, Stephenson said; *after* the priest had reached for something in his pocket. McDuff and Moore dutifully relayed these claims to the grand jurors along with their other testimony.

Joe Tate thought there was paltry corroboration for Stephenson's story—not one of the witnesses who heard the blasts of Stephenson's gun had heard or seen a scuffle between the two men before the shots pierced the air. But the testimony of M. L. Easter that morning muddied things, providing needed wiggle room for the minister's claim. Easter had just come out of the Greek-owned fruit stand on the corner of Twenty-second and Third, he said, after buying an ice-cold Coca-Cola. He was standing at the hitching post across the street from the rectory, waiting for the Highland Avenue streetcar to arrive, when he heard the first shot. He looked over to the rectory porch and saw flashes erupting from Stephenson's gun, he said, each shot progressively higher than the last. "As he shot," Easter testified, "it looked like to me he was either getting up off of his knees or out of a chair."

The witness's description of Stephenson possibly on his knees immediately drew the attention of one of the grand jurors: "Did he seem to be down?" the juror asked.

"Looked just about in the position that you look now," Easter told the seated man.

"Then he got up?" the juror continued to press.

"A little higher," Easter said, "and then he shot."

"When he fired the third shot...?"

"...he was straight up"—the witness finished the juror's sentence.

"In other words, he was down straight, started to shooting, and kept rising and shooting?" another juror asked, eagerly.

"Yes, sir, that is..."

"As he kept rising, he kept shooting?"

"Yes, sir."

"Until he shot three times?"

"The shots were just like that," Easter said. "Father Coyle didn't get up."

The testimony was confusing. It was impossible to tell whether Easter was saying that Stephenson had taken Father Coyle by surprise, pulling his gun while the two men were still seated, or that Father Coyle had knocked

Stephenson to his knees before he had pulled and fired his gun. When more questions were put to the witness, it seemed that Easter was unsure himself, and follow-up questions did little to clear things up. As it was left, the witness's amorphous description could have been used to support either of the competing scenarios, depending on each grand juror's preference.

Before Easter was dismissed, one of the jurors pressed him about another matter, asking about the disheveled state of the minister's clothes. The two officers who had chased Stephenson down after the shooting had testified that they saw something out of place when they caught up to the shooter: Officer Snow thought it was a suspender or belt "hanging down" along Stephenson's side. Officer Weir concurred: "[O]ne of the two was broke loose and swinging down below his knee" when they caught up to the man. In addition, the minister's collar was turned up, Weir said. Easter told the grand jury that he saw the dangling object as well. When Stephenson stepped off the porch, Easter said he gave chase and pointed Stephenson out to Officer Weir, who was also in pursuit. In the process, Easter noticed "something hanging down to one of [Stephenson's] sides," he said, but he could not say for sure what the item was.

Joe Tate realized that the grand juror's questions to Easter about the minister's exact position on the porch and his wayward belt portended a receptiveness to the minister's protestations of self-defense. If the minister had been down "on his knees," as Easter said, wasn't that a sign that there had been a fight? And if his belt or suspender had been jarred loose, wasn't that an indication that Father Coyle had been besting Stephenson in that battle, at least until the minister answered with gunshots? Speculations of that sort were bolstered when several other witnesses testified about seeing one of the rocking chairs from the porch lying on its side on the rectory lawn after the shooting (*shoved there in the heat of battle, perhaps?!*), and the testimony of others that some time after the minister had turned himself into the Sheriff's office, they observed a knot on the side of the man's head.

Beating back such speculations was like boxing one's shadow. Tate suspected that Stephenson himself was the cause of not only the dislodged suspender or loosened belt but the bump on his head as well—that the minister had mussed his own clothing, either when he jerked his gun from its hiding place or when he hurdled the rectory hedge on his way to the courthouse, and that after Deputy Wiggins left him in his cell alone, Stephenson had slammed his head against something hard—perhaps the wall—to make it appear as though he had been hurt in a fight. The prosecutor did his best to poke holes in Stephenson's claim, asking Deputy Sheriff Wiggins, who had escorted the minister to the jail immediately after his surrender, if Stephenson had mentioned a fight with Father Coyle after telling Wiggins he had just shot him:

No, said Wiggins, "I asked him then, 'Are you hurt?' He said, 'Not to amount to anything.'"

"Did he say anything [about] a scuffle with the priest?" Tate asked.

"No, sir."

But one of the jurors jumped in: "Did he call for a doctor, shortly after that?" the juror asked.

"I don't know," Deputy Wiggins replied. "I just carried him to the door there and turned him over to the warden's office."

"Did you notice any knot on his head or anything like that?" another of the jurors pressed.

The deputy answered that he detected a bump "the next day"—"a little knot up there on the side of his head"—but that he had not noticed it at the time of Stephenson's surrender, no.[20]

Tate called another witness to refute the idea that the furniture on the porch had been scattered during the claimed fight. A man by the name of Joseph Adams testified that he was sitting on his own porch just one block away when he heard gunshots and joined the people running along Third Avenue toward the rectory. When he reached the rectory, he saw the priest lying in a pool of blood. Adams helped the ambulance workers put him on a stretcher. Did he notice any weapon that the priest might have used or a chair on the lawn? asked Tate. No, he saw no weapon near the fallen priest, nor a chair laying in the yard, but he thought one of the ambulance workers might have moved a chair out of the way after they got there.[21] Lige Jr. testified that he thought he might have been the one to toss the chair out of the way, in his hurry to reach Father Coyle and get him into the ambulance. Another witness thought he saw a bystander, a man named Greer, toss the rocking chair off the porch after Stephenson headed for the courthouse. But still the grand jurors remained unconvinced.

Hoping to put an end to the dispute about the displaced rocking chair once and for all, Tate called in, one by one, the two witnesses in the very best position to know about the state of the porch immediately after the shooting: Stella Caruthers and Marcella Coyle, who had raced onto the porch from inside the house just seconds after hearing the shots.

"Did you see any weapon, or any stick, or pistol, or knife, or anything out there when you got out there on the porch?" Tate asked Father Coyle's sixty-six-year-old housekeeper, Stella Caruthers.

"No, sir."

"Any rock, brick, or anything, that could have been used to fight with?"

"Nothing at all," she said; the only things on the porch besides the furniture were "Father Coyle's hat, his breviary, and some papers that he was correcting." When she went out on the porch after the gun blasts stopped, all of these items were still sitting undisturbed on the swing.

"Did you hear any noise just prior to the shooting?" he asked her.

"Nothing at all," Caruthers answered firmly.

"Anything like two men on a scuffle there in that house?" the prosecutor prompted.

"Nothing at all," she said again. "I didn't hear anything until I heard the shots."

"What was on the porch in the way of furniture?" he asked. Only the furniture normally kept there, she answered, "the swing, two rocking chairs, and the settee." He asked her to describe the condition of the porch when she reached it. Had there been anything unusual about the way the furniture appeared when she reached the porch? No, things were in their usual place. It wasn't until the ambulance arrived that someone moved the chairs and settee, to make it easier "to get the body out," Caruthers said.[22]

Marcella Coyle testified next. The slender woman was dressed in black, the color of mourning. Beneath her veil, one of the reporters who watched her in the anteroom noted a "faraway look in her eyes" as she fingered a subpoena and waited for her turn to address the grand jurors. Joe Tate guided her back to where she was when she first heard the shots.[23]

"I was in the back of the house, in the housekeeper's room, when I heard three shots fired," Marcella began. "And I went to the front, and, as I went through the hall, I saw a man walk down the steps. And when I pushed open the door, he was going in the direction of the courthouse, through the yard, not to the front gate. I turned to the swing and asked what that noise was, and I saw my brother on the floor."

"[O]ut there on the porch, did you see any pistol, stick, rock, brick, weapon of any kind that any one could use in fighting?" Joe Tate asked gently.

"No, sir," Marcella said.

"Had you heard any, you know, like scuffling or noise on the porch out there?"

"No, sir," she said.

"Just prior to the shooting?" he clarified.

"No, sir," she repeated firmly.

But one of the grand jurors interrupted: "Could there have been a little scuffle and noise out on the front porch, and you back in the rear, and you not heard it?" he asked.

It is not hard to imagine Father Coyle's sister wanting to shout at the man: *No! It was nearly ninety degrees! The windows were thrown wide open! If there had been a fight between my brother and Stephenson, I, or someone else, would have heard it! How convenient for Edwin Stephenson that no one did!* But Marcella Coyle held her tongue: "Yes, I suppose so," she said steadily. Perhaps she understood the way of such questions—designed less to gather facts than to trap the person who offered them. Maybe she understood that had she said *No, there couldn't have been a brawl between my brother and his killer without my hearing it,* the answer would simply have made more questions possible, ensnaring her in a web of progressively worsening follow-ups. Questions like: What other noises had she heard coming from outside the house as she sat in the room in the back? Or had she heard the argument between the motorists who had gotten into an accident half a block away? The streetcar speeding up to the rectory, the one that had screeched to a halt after the shots rang out? Had she even realized that her brother and Stephenson were talking to each other out on the porch? Or was it possible that the cacophony of the late afternoon's sounds—that endless droning noise most folks just learned to tune out—had prevented her from hearing any of it, including a fight?

Marcella Coyle's temperate reply eliminated the opportunity for such challenges, but it also left it to Joe Tate to offer other reasons why the grand jury should doubt that a fight between the men had occurred as Stephenson claimed. If the grand jurors were unprepared to rely on the woman's ears, perhaps they would be more generous toward her *eyes,* Tate must have thought.

"And what about other signs of a struggle?" he asked Marcella. "What furniture was there on the porch?"

"A swing and two chairs," she answered.

"Rocking chairs?" Tate prompted.

"Two rocking chairs," she confirmed, "and a bench."

"Were the chairs set between the swing and the bench?"

"Yes," Marcella replied. Everything was in its place.

Satisfied, Joe Tate excused her from the room. Surely the grand jury could have no remaining doubts about what had happened on that porch after hearing Caruthers and Marcella Coyle, the prosecutor must have thought to himself. Neither woman had heard the purported fight—no raised voices or sounds of a tussle, and the supposed combatants had left behind no trace of their battle: no scuff marks, no overturned chairs, no scattered papers, no amateurish weapons wielded or dropped in the heat of battle. When two grown men fought, there were always signs of it.

The coroner of Jefferson County entered the grand jury room next, and true to form, J.D. Russum minced no words. Yes, he had examined Father

Coyle's body on the night of the shooting, Russum told the grand jurors. The cause of death was a bullet to the priest's head. The bullet struck the priest right at the jawbone, Russum continued, near the side of the cleric's left ear. The ball of steel penetrated his brain and blew a hole through the back of his skull, toward the center of his head, just above the base of the brain.

"Did you go to the courthouse jail on the night of the shooting to see the prisoner?" Joe Tate asked Russum.

"Yes, sir," the coroner said.

"Did you examine his belt?"

"Yes, sir."

"Was it broken?"

"No, sir."

"Torn?"

"No sir."

"Any signs at all on it that it had been broken or torn?"

"No, sir," he answered, "none that I could tell."

A grand juror interrupted. "What about his suspenders? His suspenders broken?"

"No, sir," J. D. Russum said again.

Russum would have been one of the first people to see Stephenson after the minister surrendered to the sheriff's office. "Did you examine his head?" asked Tate.

"Yes, sir."

"Did you see any sign on his head?"

"Absolutely none."

Joe Tate clarified: "Did you see any discoloration on his head?"

"Absolutely no color at all," Russum said squarely.[24]

But despite Russum's testimony, for the remainder of the morning, the grand jury clung to Stephenson's self-defense claim, pouncing whenever any of Joe Tate's witnesses said anything that even remotely supported it, interrupting Tate's questioning again and again to ask the witnesses what they knew about a chair that might have been shoved off the rectory porch, or a lump on Stephenson's head, or the disheveled state of the minister's clothes after the shooting. The questions were a red flag—signaling that many of the grand jurors were discounting the testimony of the witnesses who testified about hearing the shots from Stephenson's gun, but no sounds of a fight before them, or who had testified about seeing no injury on the man *until after* he had been left alone in his cell.[25]

Joe Tate must have seen the writing on the wall. If members of the grand jury were predisposed to take the minister's side, they could use the testimony about displaced chairs, rumpled clothes, or the lump on Stephenson's head as an excuse to hold out against an indictment forever. Even as Tate elicited testimony that challenged the credibility of Stephenson's self-defense claim, it was plain that the prosecutor had decided to hedge his bets. If the priest had punched Stephenson, as the prisoner claimed, there was little reason to think that the priest would have enjoyed any significant advantage over the minister in such a fight, Tate knew. And the law of self-defense in Alabama was clear: a man could use force to protect himself against an unprovoked attack, but only *proportionate* force. A beating, even a bad one, would not have been enough to justify shooting the priest. The law entitled Stephenson to use *fatal* force to ward off the purported attack only if he reasonably feared that he was about to be *killed*.

Even had a fight occurred, there was little reason to think that the priest's skills in combat were so superior to those of the minister that they entitled Stephenson to shoot Coyle dead. Perhaps intuitively sensing this problem with Stephenson's claim, one of the grand jurors had asked Chief Deputy Sheriff McDuff about the relative sizes of the men: "What size man is this Coyle?" he had asked, hopefully.

"He is a pretty good size man, weigh about 180 or possibly ninety pounds," replied the chief deputy.

"A big man in other words?"

"Yes, sir."

"At least six feet tall?" another juror prompted.

"Yes, sir."

"What is Stephenson, is he a small man?" another juror leaped in.

"Stephenson, I suppose he is about five feet eight or nine inches high, and weigh about 145 or 150 pounds," the deputy estimated.

But even if the deputy's guess was right, according to the testimony of the priest's sister, Marcella, Father Coyle was not substantially larger: if Stephenson was five feet, eight or nine inches, her brother would have been only two or three inches taller. "About what was your brother's age?" Tate had asked the woman.

"He was forty-eight years old, last March," she said. Just three years younger than Stephenson. "Do you know how tall he was?"

"Five feet, eleven."

The prosecutor repeated the fact for emphasis—"Five feet, eleven."

"And how much would he have weighed?" Tate asked.

"About 156," Marcella Coyle answered.[26]

With no significant disparity existing between the two men that might have contributed to a fear on the part of Stephenson that he was in danger of being killed in the claimed fight with Coyle, it was no wonder that the minister had awkwardly expanded his story: alleging that in the middle of their conversation, Father Coyle had suddenly excused himself, gone inside the house, and come back out again, all before telling the minister that he had just officiated his daughter's wedding. For only by expanding his story in this nonsensical way was Stephenson able later to claim that he feared the priest had secured a weapon, for which Stephenson then saw him reach, he said, after the priest warned Stephenson not to repeat his yawp "You've treated me like a dirty dog!" The minister wanted the grand jury to believe that Stephenson's only choice had been to pull his gun to protect himself from Coyle's.

The problem was, of course, as Joe Tate showed through a number of witnesses—Stella Caruthers, Marcella Coyle, Joseph Adams, the lawmen who had scoured the porch for evidence, and even Easter—the priest had had no gun, or any other weapon. Every witness Tate asked about it said the same thing: no, they saw no weapon near the fallen priest, the only weapon was Stephenson's own, which he continued to clutch even after he left the porch.

Absent other forces at work, there can be no doubt that most grand juries would have heard enough. But despite the fierce pace of Joe Tate's interrogations, when the time came for the grand jury to break for lunch, the men let the prosecutor know that they were unprepared to indict the case. His hopes dashed, the circuit solicitor updated his assistants on the mornings events; the preliminary hearing would have to be held, he told them. He would continue to bring witnesses before the grand jury, while James G. Davis and John P. McCoy put on evidence before Judge Abernathy. As soon as the grand jury was persuaded to indict, the preliminary hearing could be halted, the three men agreed.

It cannot be known for sure whether the prosecutors also discussed the order of the witnesses to be called, but it seems likely that Tate advised Davis and McCoy against calling Ruth Gussman as their first witness. Best to keep her in reserve, Tate probably told them. With any luck, the grand jury would indict the case, and Davis and McCoy would not need to call her at all.[27]

———

As the afternoon wore on, Joe Tate must nearly have wanted to scream. When the grand jurors reconvened after lunch, they were no more inclined to return an indictment than they had been that morning. The afternoon testimony bogged down. All told, less than half the number of the witnesses who had testified during the morning session appeared in the afternoon, and though Tate continued to make progress, the tempo was slow and plodding, and at some points even confused. As the day wore on, a picture of the official investigation that took place immediately after the shooting began to emerge. Although Stephenson had turned himself in to the sheriff's office at the courthouse, the testimony of Officers E. J. Wall, S. E. Goad, and Dan Maloney made it clear that from the start, the Birmingham Police Department had been determined to keep its hand in the case. The Chief Deputy Sheriff McDuff had testified during the morning session that after Stephenson surrendered, he went to the rectory and took measurements of the bullet holes left on the porch and church. The shots had ranged downward, McDuff said. The highest shot had glanced off the church. The two bullets that entered the house arched progressively lower—each piercing the clapboards on the outside of the priest's house at a spot higher outside than where it had exited on the inside. But McDuff was unable to tell the prosecutor where the steel-jacketed bullets or their shells had gotten off to—someone else must have secured them.

Wall, Goad, and Maloney of the Birmingham Police Department solved the mystery when they testified in the afternoon. Officer Wall had removed one of the bullets, he said, from the hole on the porch farthest to the left-hand side (facing from the street)—"a .38 steel jacket," he said. "I have the bullet in my pocket," he added as though the terms "chain of custody," "securing the evidence," or "evidentiary integrity" had no meaning for him.[28] Officer Goad saw the bullet holes as well, he testified, but neither he nor Wall had bothered to take measurements of the holes or file a report about their findings. Two plainclothes detectives from the police force had been there before them—Detective Walton and Detective Granger—"so we didn't make any report," Goad said, as if that excused their omission.[29] Officer Maloney rounded out this sorry testimony with a statement that he had removed the second bullet that had entered the house from the porch, a steel-jacketed bullet that had passed through the wall and lodged in a bookcase inside, but no, he hadn't measured the height of the holes either. He was pretty sure the trajectory of its path was "straight," but "I didn't measure nothing." And no, he no longer had the bullet—he was sure he had given it to the coroner.[30] Altogether, a shoddy performance by the officers of the Birmingham Police Department—one that raised more questions than it answered.

Matters worsened for the prosecutor later that afternoon when Police Chief Shirley strode into the room. It was Shirley's men who had raced to the crime scene. "Detectives Walton and Granger were there," Shirley said, and "Ed Wall and Goad were up there," too; the chief himself "was up at the place that night" as well, he said, just as soon as he heard about the shooting. His men who had left the rectory with their pockets filled with bullets and shells, had taken no measurements, and had seen no need to file any reports setting out the results of their investigations. But if Police Chief Shirley was sheepish about the inept work of his department, he showed no sign of it.

The testimony Chief Shirley gave that afternoon, which filled three pages of single-spaced type, left little doubt about his purpose: what he most wanted the grand jurors to know was that Ruth Gussman was not to be trusted—and that Edwin and Mary Stephenson had not been too hard on the girl. If anything, they had been too soft. After taking a seat, Shirley immediately launched into a diatribe about his experiences with the Stephensons over the past year, beginning with Edwin Stephenson's plea for his help when Ruth ran off to Chattanooga the fall before. "He wanted me to give him a letter of introduction that would get him the courtesies of the police department up there in catching her. . . . I gave him a letter," said Shirley unapologetically, and "he went up there and brought her back."

But the girl just kept running off! The next time, she called her father after a day or so and told him that she had "joined the Catholic church," Shirley said, "and asked him if he was going to punish her." Stephenson told her "he never had punished her," and to come on home, the police chief continued. She did, but not long after that she disappeared again, and Stephenson came to him and told him "he thought the Catholics had her." A woman at Loveman, Joseph & Loeb—"some old woman down there was appointed her godmother—whatever that is," scoffed Shirley—had told a friend of Stephenson's that Ruth was up at Fred Bender's place on Red Mountain. So Stephenson and four of his men went to the house to get her, but they found it "locked up," so Stephenson and two of the men stayed there while the other two went down "to town after Bender." Fred Bender came back with them, opened up the house, and they found the girl," Shirley said. Later Bender complained to one of Shirley's officers that Stephenson was "up there punishing his daughter, had her locked up in the house, and she could not get away, and so forth . . . because she wanted to join the Catholics." Bender had wanted Stephenson arrested. But Shirley told the officer: "I knew about it, that they weren't punishing the girl, they were [just] keeping her in the house."

When things settled down a bit, Edwin Stephenson and his wife did all they could to reason with the girl, the police chief continued. They bought her "a new suit of clothes, a new hat," and agreed to move to a nicer place. Stephenson even "got down on his knees in front of her, sitting down there in the police roll call room, and told her he would put a thousand dollars to her checking account, to spend as she wished . . . and all that sort of stuff."

Shirley had not been impressed, and he let Edwin and Mary Stephenson know it: "You cannot manage this girl," he told them. "You have lost your hold. You have let her manage you. You will have to put her in somebody else's hands." If he were them, Shirley continued, "he would *tell* her what to do, and *make* her do it."

Then, Shirley said, he spoke directly to Ruth: "I told the little girl, 'If you was my little girl and treat me like you are treating your parents, you would *stand up* and eat your meals for a month.'"

The witness went on with his story: Mary Stephenson took Ruth to Texas after that, to spend some time with her uncle, but "I understand that she got away from her mother down there, some place, and jumped off the train." Her mother had to "come back on the next train" and "found her in some kind of Catholic institution down there." After that the Stephensons had had enough, they had the girl examined by a doctor, and got a certificate "to get her in the asylum." But then they decided not to put her there.

For the first time, Joe Tate interrupted the police chief's rant. Ruth had "appeared to be sane all right, didn't she?" he asked.

The question seemed to annoy the police chief. "She seemed to be about like a ten- or twelve-year-old child in her mind to me," Shirley retorted. "I would not pay any attention to anything she would say at all! I would not give any statement she would make any credit. She is a child in her mind, [an] imbecile" he raged on; "almost an imbecile."

Determined to say more, the witness turned to the day of the girl's wedding. On August 11, Stephenson had found out Ruth was missing from work. He came to the Police Department looking for Shirley's help in finding her. "He wanted me to cover all the trains, he thought they were trying to get away with her and take her off." He and his wife wanted Shirley's men to search the convent over on the West End. But without any evidence suggesting that the girl was actually there, Shirley said, he couldn't do it. "I got rid of him by telling him that I understood that the last legislature passed some kind of law that gave the Sheriff a right to inspect such places," so Stephenson left his office to go see Chris Hartsfield over at the courthouse. That was the last Shirley saw of the man before he heard about the shooting, he said.[31]

Tate let Shirley bluster away—insisting that Ruth Gussman could not be trusted, telling the jurors what he would have done to the girl if her fate had been in his hands. The police chief's contempt for the girl and the way he thought her parents coddled her could not have been any clearer. But the longer Shirley talked, the more his story converged with hers. Far from contradicting what she had told the grand jurors, Shirley had unwittingly attested to the girl's credibility: confirming her many attempts to escape, all foiled; the source of the fury in the Stephenson household; Ruth's desire to become a Catholic; her flights to the Benders and her telephone call back home; even her plea not to be punished—the same story the girl had told to the papers, the same story she had told again that morning to the jurors themselves.

Yet even after Shirley's telling display, the grand jury was not prepared to indict.

Late in the day, in a last-ditch effort to drag an indictment from the men, Tate decided to let them examine the porch and the pathways of Stephenson's bullets for themselves. A reporter from the *Age-Herald* spotted the group of men there at the rectory, eyeing the building's scars. Those familiar with normal grand jury procedure would have been surprised by the move: trial juries were known to visit crime scenes, but rarely grand juries. The prosecutor must have decided the men's resistance would not be overcome without taking special steps. But even after seeing the site, the men would not be hurried. "Grand Jury Recesses without any Action Regarding Preacher," boomed a headline in one of the local papers a day later.[32]

If grand juries would "indict a ham sandwich," this one had missed the memo.

| Black Robes, White Robes

W HEN JOE TATE was unable to secure an indictment before the scheduled time for the preliminary hearing, his senior assistants, James G.
Davis and John P. McCoy, had no choice but to begin calling witnesses in
a much more public forum: before Judge H. B. Abernethy in the Jefferson
County Court of Misdemeanors. The event had all the hallmarks of public spectacle. Hours before the courtroom's doors were scheduled to open, overeager
court watchers had flooded the second floor hallway outside Judge Abernethy's
courtroom in numbers so great that the deputies assigned to keep order worried whether they would be able "to restrain the throngs." Finally somebody
observed that the room normally occupied by Judge Abernethy was simply too
small, and hasty arrangements were made to channel the deluge upstairs, to
Circuit Judge Dan A. Greene's courtroom, one of the largest in the building.
Despite the move, in no time "every available seat was occupied," and hundreds
of would-be spectators had to be turned away. Yet some who were denied entry
refused to leave, contenting themselves with a small spot in the hall, "craning
their necks to catch a glimpse of the witnesses as they passed to and from the
witness stand, and of the accused man as he entered the courtroom."[1]

Stephenson was escorted into the room just minutes before 2:00 P.M. The
minister looked "a little haggard," a reporter for the *Age-Herald* thought, but
likely his spirits lifted some once he was surrounded by three of his lawyers,
his wife, and other family and friends who had come to offer their support.
Only Hugo Black, still in Colorado, was missing. Displaying a penchant for
promptness, Judge Abernethy called the case to order precisely on the hour.

James Davis and John McCoy were Joe Tate's two most senior assistants; the ones he had hired to beat Hugo Black out of becoming the lead

prosecuting attorney for the county. The men Black had resigned as county solicitor over, rather than be forced to accept as his assistants.[2] Whatever Black had thought of them back in 1917, by the time of Edwin Stephenson's preliminary hearing in the summer of 1921, Davis and McCoy had eight years of prosecutorial experience between them, and McCoy brought something else to the case as well—personal insight into the ill will so many Protestants harbored toward Catholics. Born and raised in Jefferson County, McCoy had close connections to the Methodist church: his father, William Clark McCoy, held a pastorate in the church, and his brother, James Henry McCoy, was a bishop in the M.E.C., South. To the extent that religious furor was behind the crush of observers who had flocked to the courtroom just to watch a preliminary hearing that day, Joe Tate's assistants were not likely to underestimate it.

The prosecutors had no intention of feeding the public's frenzy over the case any more than was necessary. The men had agreed that Davis would take the lead in questioning the witnesses, while McCoy made sure they were ready to go as soon as their names were called. Their plan was to keep the number of their witnesses to as few as possible, and their testimony succinct. Davis decided that the first order of business was to introduce into evidence Stephenson's confession that he had killed Father Coyle to eliminate any question about Stephenson's identity as Coyle's killer, leaving only the question of whether the minister had killed the priest intentionally and with premeditation to be addressed by other witnesses.

Davis called Sheriff Hartsfield to the stand and led him back to the early evening of August 11. Yes, he had been notified about the shooting shortly after arriving home, Hartsfield said. His chief deputy had called to tell him that Father Coyle had been shot. Yes, he had examined the priest's fatal wound over at Lige Loy's later that evening. But when Davis asked the sheriff about what he had heard Stephenson say in his jail cell that night, Crampton Harris rose to his feet, objecting. If Sheriff Hartsfield had only witnessed part of the interrogation, he could not know whether the minister's statements had been voluntary, Harris protested. The objection was well taken, and Judge Abernethy sustained it. Sheriff Hartsfield had not been in the cell with the others when Joe Tate first began questioning Stephenson. He couldn't say how the minister had been persuaded to talk.[3]

But the victory was short-lived. Davis immediately called Fred McDuff, the sheriff's chief deputy, to admit the confession through him. McDuff confirmed that he had entered Stephenson's cell with Joe Tate that night. Yes, he had stayed with the prosecutor for the duration of the questioning. Davis flew through the necessary preliminary questions: Had he offered the defendant any violence? No, sir. Had Mr. Tate? No, sir. Had either of them held out any hope of a reward or inducement to talk? No, sir. Threatened him in any way? No, sir. "What did he say to you in regard to this shooting?"

Before the chief deputy could answer, Crampton Harris was up again, saying he wanted the chance "to qualify the deputy" before the judge let him repeat the minister's statements. It was the trial lawyer's right. The rules of evidence permitted him an opportunity to confirm that McDuff had been in a position to observe what he was about to describe before he described it, and additional Alabama rules considered only statements deemed to have been made *voluntarily* as useable evidence. Still, Harris was walking a fine line. Objections could create the impression that a lawyer was afraid of what the court would learn if his opponent's witness was permitted to answer—that he was trying to hide the ball. Worse, efforts to undermine or disqualify a witness could backfire. Crampton Harris had wanted to show that Stephenson's statements that night had been "involuntary," but none of McDuff's answers seemed to support the claim. Four transcript pages of questions later, the lawyer had only succeeded in digging a hole for himself. Growing frustrated, he finally put the question to the deputy directly: didn't Joe Tate tell Stephenson that night that "it was *necessary* for him to make a statement?"

"I don't remember that," replied McDuff.

You couldn't say that Tate *didn't* tell him that, could you? Harris retorted.

"I wouldn't say he did or didn't say it; but I don't think he did," the deputy answered unhelpfully.

After several more tries, the best Harris was able to do was to get the chief deputy to agree that Stephenson had not *invited* Joe Tate, George Moore, and him into his cell that night—that the lawmen had come of their own accord—and that Tate had not warned Stephenson that his statements could be used against him. But in 1921, state prosecutors were not expected to wait for such an invitation, or to make such a disclosure, and every lawyer in the room would have known it. It was a sore spot with members of the criminal defense bar. Not until 1966 would the Supreme Court rule in *Miranda v. Arizona* that police and prosecutors had to give such a warning to make a defendant's statements useable at trial.

Crampton Harris finally retreated to his seat, tossing over his shoulder a dismissive "That's all"—as if to convey satisfaction with a line of questioning that had won him no ground at all.

At this point, James Davis sprang to his feet, and underscoring his opponent's failure, put the simple question to McDuff again: "What did he say?"

"He said he shot Father Coyle," the deputy replied flatly.

The prosecutor must have found it hard not to smile.

When the chief deputy testified more fully about what it was that Stephenson had actually said that night, however, the spectators in the room might reasonably have wondered why Crampton Harris had gone to such lengths to fight it. It was true that Stephenson had admitted to shooting the priest, but the rest of his claims were entirely exculpatory—tailored to justify the shooting, not admit to its wrongfulness—raising the question of whether it should have been the prosecution, not the defense who tried to keep the statements out of evidence.

But there is little reason to think that James Davis feared that the judge would be persuaded by the story the minister had told that night. If a story sounded too good to be true, more often than not it was. Defendants hung themselves with false exculpatory statements all the time, especially when other witnesses were available to contradict their claims. The court needed to hear the prisoner's story first though, before it could be discredited; so the prosecutor asked McDuff to tell the court all that Stephenson had said.

The chief deputy complied: Reverend Stephenson said that the priest had called out to him as he walked by the rectory, McDuff began, and that Father Coyle invited him up to the porch, so he went on up and took a seat "just as nice as he knew how." The deputy sheriff was plainly editorializing, but his characterization of the minister's statement drew no objection, and the witness continued: he said that after he took a seat, Father Coyle told him that he had married his daughter "to this Gussman." Stephenson said that he shouted at the priest then—"You dirty dog!" or that he had treated his family "like a dirty dog," or something to that effect—and that at some point Father Coyle had excused himself to go inside the house, McDuff recalled. He said the priest came back out again a little while later, and that when Stephenson shouted at him, the priest told Stephenson not to say it again; but that he did repeat it—telling Father Coyle he had treated him like a dirty dog!—at which point the priest hit him, Stephenson said, and caught him by the belt, and knocked him down, hurting his side and his foot. Then he said that the priest "put his hand to his hip pocket," so Stephenson pulled his own gun and shot, McDuff finished. James Davis was satisfied. With other witnesses waiting to take the stand, he turned McDuff over to his opponent.

On cross-examination, Crampton Harris tried to make some headway with his client's self-defense claim by asking the chief deputy about the disheveled state in which he had found the porch shortly after Stephenson had surrendered. He had gone over to the rectory porch to help with the investigation, hadn't he? Yes, he had, McDuff said, and yes he had noticed the state of the porch when he arrived. "How many chairs were on the porch when you went there?" One chair on the porch, and a settee against the wall. "Were there any other chairs around there anywhere?" "There was one chair laying out in the yard." How far from the steps of the porch? Maybe six to ten feet. "Was the chair sitting up as if somebody had been sitting in it out there in the yard, or was it thrown over or knocked over?" "Thrown over," McDuff said, "face downward." Crampton Harris walked the deputy sheriff back through Stephenson's statements again then, as if thinking that the story would become more plausible the more times it was repeated: about Father Coyle *inviting* him onto the porch, and him sitting convivially with the priest there until the shock of learning that the priest had married his Ruth to Gussman; about shouting at the priest; about Father Coyle going briefly inside the house, then outside again, then their heated words, and the priest striking Stephenson, and catching him by the belt, hurting his side.

"Did you notice the condition of Mr. Stephenson's belt?" Harris interrupted.

"Yes, sir; I noticed his belt."

But there must have been something in the deputy's voice that made the lawyer think twice about asking him to describe its condition. Harris took a different tack: did Stephenson complain about having been hit in the head? "Yes, sir." And did you see a bump? Later that night he did, McDuff said, when Joe Tate and he were talking with the minister, he had noticed a bump "right along on the side of his head."

James Davis wasn't troubled by McDuff's testimony about the bump on Stephenson's head. The chief deputy had said that he only saw it later that night, after Stephenson would have had time to inflict the injury on himself. As for the disordered state of the porch, the prosecutor had plans to let his other witnesses explain the chair McDuff had seen tossed out on the grass. But something McDuff said on cross-examination jarred Davis's memory of another thing the witness had told Davis about what he had noticed about the porch—something that might help to undercut the minister's assertions about a brawl. On redirect, Davis asked McDuff whether he had seen anything in the porch swing where Father Coyle had been sitting that night.

"As well as I remember, there was some papers and magazines and a testament," McDuff replied. They were all undisturbed.[4]

Because Joe Tate was still occupied by the grand jury that afternoon while his assistants handled the preliminary hearing, Tate would have had very little time, if any, to warn James Davis about the way his next intended witness, Easter, had muddled things before the grand jury that morning; it took Easter very little time to repeat the performance in open court. When Davis asked Easter to tell the court what he had seen on August 11 from where he stood across the street from St. Paul's rectory, the prosecutor must have felt his control slipping away. Yes, he had heard the shots, Easter testified, and when he looked up he saw a man shooting at another man. He could see the "bulk of both of them," he said. It looked "like they were sitting in a chair, or down on their knees on the floor." Then, after the last shot, Stephenson "raised right up and walked off from the porch, just as though he had been sitting down in a chair, getting up from his knees and walked over towards that building that they tore down." Incredible! Easter's garbled recollections were helping Stephenson's defense. Davis tried to repair the damage: "Did you see the men exchanging blows before the first shot?" No, "I didn't see anything until the first shot attracted my attention to it." Hadn't seen Father Coyle go in the house and come out again either? No, sir, Easter said.

But Crampton Harris saw his opportunity, and he went straight at it. Could you tell if Mr. Stephenson was on his knees or crouching when he shot? Harris asked on cross-examination. "He was down in *some* kind of a kneeling position," Easter said. But his voice must have wavered; the defense attorney urged him to say just a little more: "And it looked as if the men were grappling with each other, didn't it?" Harris nudged.

Before he could answer, James Davis brought the witness up short, objecting that Harris was mischaracterizing Easter's testimony. He hadn't said anything whatever about a fight, the prosecutor protested, and the judge sustained the objection.

Weren't they right up against each other? Harris pressed on, not yet ready to give up. But the witness's answers were becoming more equivocal by the second: "They looked to be a foot apart, or a foot and a half," Easter hedged; but "it was getting dark," and he "could just see the figures of them." The defense lawyer must have calculated that he was unlikely to get much more help from the man on the question of the alleged fight. More questions might even lead Easter to profess his uncertainty even more clearly. Harris shifted gears, asking Easter if he had noticed Stephenson's belt after the shooting stopped. "I saw something hanging down from beneath his coat." It might have been a belt; he couldn't be sure. It was not unequivocal. But the testimony provided some corroboration for Stephenson's claim that a fight between himself and Coyle had preceded the shooting. Good enough, Crampton Harris must have thought to himself. He returned to his seat.[5]

The prosecutors could not have been pleased.

Later in the afternoon Harris gained a little more ground when he questioned H. G. McClellan, who had testified on direct examination that he, too, heard the gunfire from across the street from the rectory, shortly after two cars had collided at the corner of Third Avenue and Twenty-second Street.

After hearing the shots, McClellan said, he watched the shooter step off the porch and start walking away. Then, when a woman screamed, McClellan had followed the two police officers who chased the shooter down near the side door of the courthouse. It was Reverend Edwin Stephenson, he said. A little while later, after walking with the officers and Stephenson to the sheriff's office, McClellan returned to the rectory, he said. The time line was murky—it would have taken some time for McClellan to go with the officers and then get back to the porch—but Crampton Harris decided to chance it. He asked McClellan whether he had noticed an overturned chair when he got back to the rectory porch. Yes, there was a chair lying in the yard. Harris followed up: "And that was before anybody had come on the porch at all," except for the woman who screamed? Yes, sir. "And you are positive there wasn't a single person standing on the porch except the lady?" Yes, sir, the witness said again. Harris turned to the matter of Stephenson's clothing then, asking whether McClellan had seen that Stephenson's belt had been torn loose. "There was something hanging down his leg," McClellan confirmed. "Did you notice that his coat had been pulled away?" It had been turned up, McClellan recalled.[6]

The prosecutor's heart must have sunk. Blowing smoke was a common defense tactic—befuddling things just enough to make a judge or jury lose their way. There were perfectly logical explanations for a chair flung onto the grass and a belt pulled free from its loops that had nothing to do with a fistfight. But witnesses like Easter and McClellan did little to illuminate them. Neither of the men had seen a fight, but the defense could twist what they had seen into support for the argument that one had occurred. To refute the suggestion, Davis decided to call Marcella Coyle and Stella Caruthers, who had been inside the rectory and had reached the porch before Easter, or McClellan, or anyone else.

Marcella and Stella repeated much of what they had said that morning in front of the grand jury: that they were reading in Stella's room at the back of the rectory when they heard the shots; that they ran to the porch and found Father Coyle lying in a pool of blood; that a man was walking slowly away—the defendant—toward the courthouse. Davis asked Marcella if she had heard anyone talking or arguing on the porch before the shots. "No, sir." Where was her brother? He was lying next to the swing, she said. His feet were near the swing his body was angled toward the wall. Could she tell if he was alive? Yes, she could hear him making noises. "Did you see any chairs on the porch there at that time?" "Yes, sir; two chairs." Facing what direction? The street, she said. Any in the yard? "No, sir." Did she know the man she saw walking away from the porch? "I knew him by seeing him."

"Is this the man?" asked Davis, pointing toward Stephenson.

Marcella looked at the minister seated at counsel table with his three attorneys. "Yes, sir," she said.

Incredibly, Crampton Harris interrupted then, asking the woman to be specific about which man at the defense table she was referring to, as if there could have been any doubt. The question might have made sense in a case where the witness had had very little exposure to the defendant facing charges. But Edwin Stephenson's picture had been plastered across the front pages for days on end. It was the kind of error a novice lawyer might make, giving the witness the opportunity to identify the accused not once, but twice. "The one next to you," Marcella Coyle said evenly.

James Davis returned to the question of the purported fight: "Did you hear any scuffling out there on the porch just before you heard the shooting?"

"No, sir."

Stella Caruthers confirmed it as well. There had been no sound of a fight.[7]

When cross-examining witnesses like Marcella Coyle or Stella Caruthers, often the best a trial lawyer will be able to do is to underscore what they had not been in a position to know—to "get in and out"—or even to decline to question the witnesses at all, in the hope of leaving the impression that what the witnesses had been able to say on direct was of no real consequence. At first it seemed that Crampton Harris would do just that when questioning the two women from St. Paul's rectory. He asked them about the distance between the porch and Stella Caruthers's bedroom, plainly hoping to show that there could have been a fight between Stephenson and Father Coyle without either of them hearing it. She and Mrs. Caruthers had been all the way at the back of the house, hadn't they? Harris asked Marcella. "Yes, sir" she said. And the door between the dining room and kitchen was partially closed, which would have made it harder for them to hear? "I suppose so." In fact, she hadn't even been aware that her brother had had a visitor, had she? "Did you know that anybody was out on the porch talking to your brother?" "No, sir."

But then Harris veered into dangerous territory, asking Marcella Coyle what she had done after she reached the porch. Why had she not run to her brother's body when she saw he was fallen? Why had she gone back inside? As though something important about the question of his client's guilt or innocence could be gleaned from the decision of the injured priest's sister to run to the phone instead of directly to him. "You saw him lying there, but didn't go to him?" "No, sir. I went to the phone to call a doctor." "But you didn't go to your brother's side at all?" "No, sir." "You saw him lying there after just hearing shots, but didn't go to him?" "No sir." "What did you do?" "I screamed," she said evenly. "Did you ask anyone to look after him?" "No, I screamed and ran for the phone."

The exchange was bizarre. But Crampton Harris repeated the same line of attack after Stella Caruthers testified on direct examination that she, too, had heard no conversation or sounds of a fight before hearing the gunshots. Through it all, James Davis sat quietly in his chair, interposing no objection. Whatever Crampton Harris was hoping to accomplish, he seemed to be doing his client more harm than good.

Later that afternoon, Davis called to the stand the two officers who had chased Stephenson down after the shooting, Snow and Weir, hoping to show that Stephenson was not only unhurt after shooting Father Coyle, but surprisingly calm for a man who claimed to have just survived a life-and-death battle with an unexpected assailant. Davis brought Snow back to the moment he and Weir caught up to Stephenson on the courthouse landing, asking him to tell the court what Stephenson had said to them. "He said, 'Don't bother me, gentlemen, I know what I am doing . . . I want to be locked up," Snow testified. "Did you notice anything about his appearance?" "Yes, something had fallen loose," he said, "a suspender or a belt, and was hanging down." "Notice any bruises on him?" "No, sir." "Any bumps on his head?" "No, sir." "Any injuries to his side, or foot?" Same answer. "Did he make any complaint to you about being hurt?" James Davis pressed. "No, sir," Snow repeated.

On cross, Crampton Harris tried to undo some of the damage by focusing once again on his client's dishevelment, but his questions were clumsy. Had Reverend Stephenson been walking at a natural pace? Harris asked. Snow said that he had been. "Did you notice the condition of his coat?" "No, sir." "Wasn't his collar all awry and pulled up?" Not that Snow remembered. "But you wouldn't say for sure it was not?" "No, sir."[8] Little help.

But Harris made some headway with Henry Weir, the officer on foot patrol who had helped Snow chase down the man walking away from the rectory still clutching a gun. Weir had noticed no injuries on the minister when they caught up with him, but he did seem to remember that Stephenson's coat collar had been "turned up like this," he gestured, and when Crampton Harris asked him about seeing a chair lying out in the yard after he had left Stephenson at the jail and returned to the rectory, Weir said yes, he had seen it.[9]

James Davis knew he had to do something to explain that chair.

As the afternoon grew late, the prosecutor called a pressman for the Dispatch Printing Company, T. E. Mitchell, who finally resolved the mystery of the wayward chair. Davis asked him where he was just before the shots were fired. He had been walking west along Third Avenue toward the rectory, Mitchell said. He had just reached the corner of St. Paul's Church when he heard the shots. "What did you do?" The safest thing he could think of: he pressed himself flat against the wall of the church and waited for the shots to stop. When things got quiet, he saw people running toward the rectory, he said, so he went up to the porch, too. "What did you see?" "Father Coyle lying there." "See a chair in the yard?" "Yes, sir, one chair from the porch. "Do you know how it got there?"

"Yes, sir. Some man throwed that out there after they come to get Father Coyle," Mitchell said.

The man's answer created quite a stir. Judge Abernathy leaned toward Mitchell then, wanting to be sure that the witness had actually watched someone throw the chair off the porch himself, and was not just repeating what someone else had told him. "Did you *see* that?" the judge asked.

"Yes, sir. I saw the chair thrown out," Mitchell told him. He did not know the name of the man who had thrown it, but he was certain that the chair had not gotten there in the frenzy of some purported brawl. Before returning to his seat, James Davis asked Mitchell to repeat his answer again, just to be sure: "You saw that, did you?" "Yes, sir."

This time Crampton Harris knew better than to push. On cross-examination, Harris got Mitchell to say that he wasn't able to pick out Stephenson as the shooter, and that he couldn't even say whether the man he saw walking away from the rectory had been carrying a gun. But on the critical question of how the chair ended up on the lawn, Harris had no intention of asking the witness to repeat his answer a fourth time. It was the first real blow to the defense's suggestion that Stephenson and Coyle had knocked the chair off the porch in the throes of a fight.[10]

Near the end of the afternoon, after eight witnesses had completed their testimony, John McCoy told the judge that the state intended to call only a few others, but that the officers out looking for the witnesses had not yet returned. Judges with crowded dockets frowned on such delays; some might even have demanded that the state rest its case if it had no other witnesses ready to take the stand. Judge Abernethy asked Crampton Harris if he wanted to go ahead with his defense. But Harris had no intention of helping the prosecutors out: "Not before they close their case," he said. The lawyer's swipe seemed to have its desired effect of putting the prosecutors back on their heels: "We have other witnesses, but they haven't come yet," McCoy explained again, weakly.

The prosecutors were lucky; the hour was growing late. Judge Abernethy let the lapse slide: "Have them here tomorrow," he warned Davis and McCoy, and rapped his gavel sharply against the hard wooden bench. "I'll adjourn until nine o'clock."

———

The crowd that jammed the courthouse corridors the next morning broke all county records. Overnight, a rumor that the prosecutors planned to call the minister's daughter to testify against her father had raced across the city. Although the source of the report was unclear, the city's morning paper predicted that Ruth Gussman would be "the state's ace in the hole," and the gossip swelled the ranks of the crowd that swarmed through the courthouse doors to watch the show. As on the day before, not all of the spectators landed a seat, and though some evidently would have been happy to stand, the judge ordered all of those left clogging the aisles ushered out of the room just before the hearing resumed. Ropes were stretched outside the room to hold back the great number of those ejected who, once again, refused to leave the building. Witnesses would need a clear path to reach the vacant chair at the head of the room; it would not do to have them tripping over friends or foes on their way to it.[11]

Though lightheartedness is hardly typical of one standing accused of murder, on the second day of the hearing, Stephenson appeared remarkably chipper. As the sheriff and two deputies walked their prisoner to the courtroom around 8:30 A.M., Stephenson smiled at the crowd and puffed contentedly on a cigar, one reporter wrote. He was "[d]ressed in his usual clerical garb"—black suit, white shirt, white tie, and a "bat wing" collar, looking "thoroughly ministerial" and even "refreshed from his night's sleep." After taking a seat, "he settled into an amiable chat with his wife, Mary, and a brother who sat close by," another wrote, and bid his lawyers a "cheery good morning" when they arrived shortly after.

It is possible that Stephenson's mood was simply a feint played out for the benefit of the onlookers, of course—for in some schools, the *appearance* of confidence was considered nearly as valuable as the genuine article. But the preacher's upbeat mood might also have been sincere. The news overnight had been bright: despite the torrent of Joe Tate's witnesses, the grand jury had adjourned without returning an indictment against him. Undoubtedly, Stephenson's lawyers would have advised him that such reticence from the grand jury was rare. Or maybe Stephenson's lightness of heart sprang out of the successes in Judge Abernethy's courtroom the day before. Through the befuddling recollections of some of the prosecutor's witnesses about flung chairs, loosened belts, and upturned collars, Crampton Harris had scored a few points on the question of self-defense, even without the help of his law partner Hugo Black. Things certainly could have gone worse; at a minimum, the defense was boxing the prosecution's witnesses in.

But if Stephenson entertained hope that morning that the wins of the day before would lead the court to order him released, there can be little doubt that his lawyers would have realized that the odds of defeating a prosecutor's case at the preliminary hearing stage were slim. As in the grand jury, the standard of proof at the hearing was considerably lower than the "proof beyond a reasonable doubt" standard that applied at trial. James Davis's evidence needed only to amount to "probable cause" to believe the defendant had committed the offense charged in the coroner's warrant to bind him over to await the grand jury's final action. And unlike the proceeding before the grand jury, it was a judge—a man trained in the law, not a group of laymen—who would make that judgment.

At Davis's request, Judge Abernethy briefly delayed the start of the proceeding to accompany the prosecutors and the defense lawyers two doors down to St. Paul's rectory, so that the judge might examine the porch and "the bullet holes in the wall" for himself. The reporters trailed after the small group of men, watching the prosecutors point out the gashes in the building and the normal placement of various chairs, while the men and women back in the courtroom waited patiently for their return, reluctant to lose their seats. The crowd's perseverance was rewarded when the hearing resumed a short while later and James Davis told the judge that he had but one witness more, the defendant's own daughter, Ruth.

"An intense silence" filled the room as Ruth Gussman made her way to the witness chair at the head of the room. With the exception of the clash with her mother over the matter of her clothes, the bride had not seen either of her parents since the ill-fated morning of her wedding. The reporters watched for any sign of warmth toward them, but Ruth ignored the table where her father sat with his lawyers and her mother close behind that, and kept her eyes locked on James Davis instead.

The prosecutor's task was delicate. Davis understood that little would be gained by keeping his witness on the stand any longer than necessary. His goal was to satisfy the probable cause standard—to show that Stephenson had a reason to kill Father Coyle—nothing more. Witnesses the day before had already established that Stephenson had shot Coyle, and Davis had done what he could to punch holes in the defendant's self-defense claim along the way. If the two men had fought, why had no one seen the blows? The only thing left for Davis to show was that there was reason to believe the minister had gone to the porch with a motive and an intent to kill the priest—that he had premeditated taking Father Coyle's life.

Davis got straight to the point, asking Ruth about her decision to convert to Catholicism months before her wedding, getting her to describe her parents' outrage over it. He then turned to the wedding itself: had her parents known about her plans to marry Pedro? No, they had not known, Ruth said. Had they ever met Pedro? Yes, Pedro had boarded with them on Third Avenue for nearly a week while he did work in the house about four years before. Had her father ever threatened Father Coyle?

"Yes," Ruth replied squarely, "he made threats in my presence many times."

What had he said that she found threatening?

Her father had asked her if she wanted to see Father Coyle and Fred Bender killed, Ruth said, and had said that she would see the priest dead if she kept going to the Catholic church.

The prosecutor was satisfied. Ruth's answers to just a few spare questions had revealed that her father's hostility against the priest had predated her nuptials, making it possible for Davis to argue that the shooting, far from being in self-defense, had been motivated by Stephenson's long-standing hatred of Father Coyle and his church, and his fury that his daughter had secretly joined it in disobedience of his and Mary's wishes. There was no need to go further, Davis decided, and every reason not to. He turned Ruth over to the defense.[12]

But if James Davis had hoped to limit Ruth Gussman's time on the stand by speeding through his own examination of the girl, Crampton Harris had no intention of following his opponent's example. If he managed things well, he might even make it appear as if it was Ruth Gussman on trial instead of her father. Harris asked Ruth to explain the circumstances under which she first began going to the Catholic church.

James Davis was on his feet then, objecting: the question was outside of the scope of his direct examination, he protested. But the judge allowed it. By asking Ruth about her conversion to Catholicism, Davis had "opened the door" to other related questions: about what had led her to that decision, and why she had been so determined to reject her parents' faith.

Harris fired off a barrage of questions, then—accusations really—hadn't Ruth's parents talked to her about their objections to the Catholic Church? Hadn't they begged her for years not to join it? Hadn't they told her that they "belonged to a different church" and that they wanted her to remain in the church of her birth, too? "Yes, sir," Ruth was forced to concede again and again, and each time she tried to provide a fuller explanation—"I understood their wishes on the matter, but I wanted to join the church from an early age—," the lawyer simply ignored her and continued his assault, asking her when she and her parents had first begun to quarrel over her interest in the Catholic religion. "When I was about twelve," Ruth said. "Hadn't your father been sending you to church and Sunday school before that?" "Yes." "What church and Sunday school?" "Methodist." Had he ever taken her to the Catholic church? "No." Then how had she begun going there? Ruth answered that, living so close to St. Paul's, she had watched the Catholics come and go, and over time she had come to want to go there, too. So she had just done what she had wanted to do? "Did you let your parents know at that age that you were going down to the Catholic church?" Harris asked, outraged.

"They knew it, and punished me for it."

Crampton Harris knew better than to dwell on the question of Edwin Stephenson's methods of disciplining his daughter. "But you kept on going, just the same," Harris fired back at her.[13]

The lawyer's questions were starting to irritate her. "No, I didn't keep on going," Ruth retorted, not until she had turned eighteen when she could choose for herself.[14]

Harris was plainly unimpressed by the girl's forbearance. "[T]hey told you that they didn't belong to that church, but belonged to a different church, and wanted you to go to the same church they did, didn't they?"[15]

"I know they told me that," Ruth began, "but that wasn't any reason why they should—"

"Just answer my question," Harris said, cutting her off. He had no intention of letting the girl describe her parents' supposed abuse of her. He repeated his question: hadn't her parents told her they wanted her to go to their church, the Methodist church?

"Yes, they told me that."

"And they begged and entreated you to stay in the same church they were members of, didn't they?" Harris flung at the girl. He turned to the question of Ruth's lack of trustworthiness: "And didn't you promise them that you wouldn't join the Catholic church?"[16]

When they had *forced* her to promise that, Ruth shot back.

And hadn't they offered her all kinds of things in exchange for her promise that she would not join the Catholic Church? That they would send her on a trip to Texas? And pay for her to attend college? That her mother would write off to the school and make the arrangements?

The lawyer was making her sound like a spoiled child. "She *said* that she had written them a letter, but she didn't say she had made any arrangements whatever," Ruth replied angrily, falling into Harris's trap.

"*You* didn't tell her that you were going to slip away and marry Mr. Gussman the first chance, did you?"

"No."[17]

They had even taken her off to Texas to get her away from the influences that were working on her there in Birmingham to join the Catholic Church, hadn't they? Harris continued.

They took me there, Ruth answered, but no one had influenced her to join the church, she added.

"There was no influence?" Harris scoffed.

The girl stood firm: "None whatever."[18]

Harris asked her to describe her relationship with Fred Bender.

"He was my godfather," she said.

"Your godfather in the *Catholic* Church?"

"Yes."

"Did you ever tell your father and mother that Fred Bender had been named your *Godfather*?"[19]

Ruth's reply was steely: when they had forced her to, she said.

"When did you tell them that?"

"When they had me locked up at home," Ruth began, but Harris changed the subject.

That was "after they found you locked up in a closet out at Bender's house," wasn't it? the lawyer fired back.

No one had locked her in, Ruth said, holding her ground. She had locked the door herself.[20]

Harris ignored her again. Fred Bender had helped her get ready to join the Catholic church, hadn't he?[21] Ruth denied it. "You went out and stayed at his house one night, didn't you?" "Yes." Without bothering to tell your parents that you were going to stay? Ruth replied she hadn't dared to go home for fear of what her father would do to her: "[A] friend of mine told me if I went home that night, my people would kill me for having joined the church."

So Fred Bender "*was* the man that was helping you join the Catholic church?" Harris pounced.

"He didn't help me," Ruth said again. "I joined of my own free will."[22]

Crampton Harris's questions were growing increasingly sarcastic: Hadn't anyone ever explained to her "the difference between the Catholic Church and the Protestant churches?"[23]

"I knew the difference," Ruth replied stonily.

"Who explained those differences to you?" Harris asked, implying again that someone must have influenced her to join the Catholic Church. But Ruth stuck to her guns: "I discovered it myself, by reading books and asking questions."

It was a mistake; the lawyer smelled blood. "What books? Name one book that you have read about the Catholic Church," he demanded. She couldn't remember their titles, Ruth said, flustered. "[Y]ou can't remember the name of a single one of them?" he asked disbelievingly. It was an old trial lawyer's trick. Put the witness on the defense until she said something she could not back up, then even the littlest things could be used to attack her credibility. Harris must have sensed that he had the girl against the ropes: "Who did you ask questions of" about the Catholic Church? A great number of Catholics. "Who were they?" Harris demanded: "Name them." Ruth was plainly frustrated: "It would be impossible to name the hundreds of people I know," she said, weakly. Name *some* of them, Harris fired back. "[T]he Sisters at the convent...over on the Southside," she said. "How many times had you talked to Mr. Bender and asked him questions about the Catholic church?" Harris asked. "Very few times," she said, "perhaps two or three..." Mrs. Bender? Never, Ruth said. Miss Marcella Coyle? "I have never spoken to her in my life."

Harris moved in for the kill: "How many times did you talk to Father Coyle and ask *him* questions about the Catholic Church?"[24]

"I never asked him but once in my life," Ruth replied hotly, and that was long "before I was married."

"How old were you?"

"Twelve."

Twelve! "How long did you talk to him?"

"Perhaps half an hour," she said, while they sat together out on the front porch of the rectory.

"Did he ask you to join the Catholic Church?"

The question was a blunder.

"He did not," she said squarely. Father Coyle had had nothing to do with her decision to convert.

Crampton Harris must have realized his mistake. He shifted to safer ground: Ruth's husband, firing off a series of questions: She and Pedro Gussman had not been engaged for long, had they? Only since late in July, the month before? After she had sent Pedro a letter suddenly accepting a proposal he had made to her when she was only just a teenager? And she had kept all that from her parents, too, hadn't she? Reluctantly, Ruth conceded each point.[25] "Who got you to write him that letter and tell him you were willing to marry him?"[26] "No one at all," she said. "I wrote it myself." Harris ignored her denial.

Mr. Gussman is a Porto Rican, isn't he?[27]

"He is a Spaniard," she answered.

"A man of very dark complexion, isn't he?"

"Yes."

"He doesn't speak very good English, does he?"

"No."

"It is rather difficult to understand his English, is it not?"

James Davis had had enough, objecting then—protesting that the question had no bearing on the killing at all—just as Ruth was heard to say, "No," that she was able to understand Pedro without trouble. But before the judge could rule on the objection, Harris fired off another question, returning to her husband's religion: "Mr. Gussman is a Catholic, too, isn't he?"

"Yes," said Ruth.

The lawyer could not resist a final query: "Did you tell your father that he was a Catholic, and that you were going to marry him?"

There had been no need. "He knew he was a Catholic," Ruth said, frostily.[28]

By the time he was done, Crampton Harris's questions to Ruth Gussman filled thirty pages, as the lawyer labored to paint the least flattering portrait of the girl possible—untrustworthy and disobedient; willfully resistant to her parents' good guidance; possessing the kind of temperament that left a girl vulnerable to those who preyed on such weakness. The men and women seated in the galley "hung on every word" of the heated exchange—enthralled, even occasionally amused, as the lawyer and witness sparred back and forth. But even as Harris landed his blows, it was difficult to see what many of his questions had to do with Stephenson's claim of self-defense. If anything, the entire line of questioning seemed to point to the conclusion that, after Ruth had rejected her parents' church and secretly joined the Catholics, her parents had been furious. "They told you that they didn't belong to that church!" Harris had flung at Ruth, like a dagger.[29]

Perhaps for that reason, James Davis sat silently at the prosecutor's table through almost all of Ruth Gussman's cross-examination, declining to object, letting the girl fend for herself. The prosecutor rose to his feet only once: when Harris veered away from Edwin Stephenson's anger over his daughter's attraction to the Catholics and began to ask questions about Pedro's "very dark complexion" and thick foreign accent. As far as Davis was concerned, Harris's examination of Ruth only made it more likely that the girl's rejection of her parents' faith and counsel had fanned Stephenson's rage, and that Father Coyle's act of marrying her to the Catholic Gussman on August 11 had been the final straw. Certainly nothing in the girl's testimony supported the defense's suggestion that Stephenson had sat down with Coyle to have an amiable chat.

So when Crampton Harris finished, Davis told Judge Abernethy that he had no further questions for the witness. "The state rests," the prosecutor said, and Ruth Gussman was permitted to stand down.

Judge Abernathy turned to Crampton Harris then, asking if the defense wished to put on evidence. For days, Stephenson's lawyers had staged a whisper campaign—the prosecutors would be in for "some surprises" at the hearing, they had told the reporters. At "least three witnesses" would testify that the minister had fired in self-defense.[30] But when the time had finally come to present such evidence, Harris told the judge he would call no witnesses. It was a defendant's right, no matter what his lawyers had promised the newsmen. The burden to satisfy the standard of proof in a criminal case remained ever on the state, even in its earliest stages. The defense was under no obligation to respond. But Harris's reply left Abernethy little choice but to rule. The judge hesitated, turning back to the prosecutors, as though reluctant to be the one to order the minister held. He asked Davis and McCoy whether the grand jurors had completed their deliberations.

Joe Tate's men must have been as surprised as the judge that their boss had not interrupted the hearing with the message that the grand jury had returned a "true bill." Grand juries were not normally known for their slow-footedness. John McCoy said he would check with Tate on its progress. Before long, he was back. The grand jury had not yet acted, he reported. Mr. Tate thought it would be necessary to call more witnesses; he did not expect that the grand jury would finish its deliberations for some days.

If Abernethy had hoped to avoid being the one to side with the prosecutors, the answer provided no help. "I order the defendant held for the action of the grand jury without bond," the judge said finally rising to his feet, as the sound of gavel against wood signaled the hearing's end. The ruling could not have been welcome news, but Edwin Stephenson "took the decision stoically," one of the local papers reported later that day—even "indifferently," wrote another. Immediately after hearing the judge's ruling, the minister and his attorneys huddled together in a brief private conference, while well-wishers interrupted them, trying to rally the man's nerve, pledging their support, until the sheriff's men interrupted the encouragements to escort the minister back to the county jail.[31]

In the meantime, news of the court's pronouncement reached Ruth Gussman and some friends who were still seated in the hallway just outside the courtroom. "When word that her father had been ordered held without bond was brought to her, Mrs. Gussman who had just completed her testimony for the state, sprang up, her face wreathed in smiles, and clapped her hands together," one reporter wrote. The newsman asked the girl if the ruling suited her.

It was fine, Ruth said. She was more than satisfied.

"Do you want him convicted?" the reporter asked.

Ruth must have detected the journalist's scorn. "Well, I'll say this," she answered carefully, "if he gets out of jail I'll have to move to some other town for self-protection. I will not be safe if he is freed."

Judging from the article he filed later that day, the reporter didn't think much of the girl's explanation. Perhaps he found the kind of fear to which Ruth alluded unimaginable. Or maybe he believed that no abuse by Stephenson, no matter how vile, could have deserved such a public retribution. Not by the man's own daughter. While the bride was "on the witness stand, she never once glanced at her father," the reporter wrote, as if the girl's treachery would have been vastly more palatable had Ruth given her testimony looking Edwin Stephenson dead in the eye. After she was informed of the judge's ruling, the newsman added, "she left the courthouse without making any effort to speak to him. Nor to her mother who had sat beside her husband throughout the hearing."

Never must the contrast between the two women have appeared so acute.

––––––

Later, Ruth insisted that the reporter got it wrong, that it was one of her friends who had clapped, not she. But newsmen from each of the city's three leading papers were in accord when it came to the question of the girl's celebratory attitude that day: "Mrs. Gussman...manifested much delight when the news was brought to her," reported the *Age-Herald*. "Girl's Testimony May Hang Her Own Father" blared a headline in the *Post*. "Daughter Laughs and Powders Nose as Father Is Being Tried for Life," a reporter from the *Birmingham News* wrote: "What Ruth was saying and laughing about those near them did not know, but it was evident that her thoughts were of herself, her clothes and the tip of her repeatedly powdered nose," he concluded, with no care for her father fighting for his life.

Seeing in Ruth's actions only childishness and vanity, defiance and betrayal, not one of the reporters contemplated another possibility: that Ruth Gussman might have surrounded herself with friends to buck up her nerve, or that among themselves they had exchanged little pleasantries, as friends will do, to keep Ruth from thinking back on Crampton Harris's jeering insults. Not a word about courage could be found in the columns—about the fortitude it takes to testify in front of a roomful of faultfinders; to endure a lawyer's ridicule and the snickers of an appreciative audience—save the courage of

Edwin and Mary Stephenson, of course, so poorly treated by their only child, a subject of which the newsmen never seemed to tire.

These scathing judgments must have given the prosecutors pause.

———

Even as local and national headlines spread the news that Ruth's testimony had secured her father's confinement, Pedro Gussman discovered he could no longer watch the events unfold from the shadows. The morning after the hearing, two detectives and an officer of the Birmingham Police Department tracked Gussman down at 820 Twentieth Street, North, at a house where Pedro was hanging wallpaper, dressed in painter's overalls and a white cloth cap. When the officers asked him to step outside, Pedro put down his brush and paper, and did as he was told. Outside, the lawmen frisked him and pulled a pair of shears from one of his pockets. They told him they had a warrant for his arrest, for an unsolved murder committed in Peoria, Illinois, ten months before, by a man with the same name as his. Pedro would have to come with them.

It can no longer be known exactly when the Peoria warrant reached the desk of Police Chief Shirley. Perhaps it arrived, as Shirley claimed, in the morning mail on August 25, 1921, the same day Shirley ordered his men to go bring Pedro Gussman in. If so, the postal service had taken a full twelve days to deliver the out-of-state request, and the fact that a Birmingham judge had bound over for trial Shirley's fellow Klansman Edwin Stephenson just the day before, was entirely coincidental. But it seems equally plausible that the request for an investigation had arrived earlier, and that Shirley, having reason to doubt that the two Pedro Gussmans were one and the same, had simply pocketed it. It is impossible to know for sure.

It is clear that the unsolved murder in Peoria was gruesome. The bloodied body of twenty-three-year-old Mrs. Pearl Gussman had been found late in the afternoon of November 8, 1920, sprawled across the bed in the room she and her husband had rented since mid-October. The Peoria authorities suspected the husband, a Mexican steelworker by the name of Pedro Gussman. Fellow boarders at the rooming house were far from shocked; they had heard the couple quarrel. And Pedro Gussman had been charged with attempting to murder Pearl before, just four months earlier, after striking his wife with a broken beer bottle. Had Pearl Gussman not taken pity on him then and refused to appear against him in the Peoria police court, she might have lived to see the end of that year. But likely he possessed that regrettable quality that some men have—the ability to convince their victims of their resolve to reform—so he paid a small fine for disorderly conduct and was released. Four months later to the day, when the police discovered Pearl Gussman's lifeless body, her head had been nearly severed from her body.

The couple's rented room bore signs of a ferocious struggle: scattered furniture and streaks of Pearl's blood splattered across the floor and walls. Her husband had vanished, leaving behind an unclaimed paycheck from his job at the Keystone Steel and Wire Company. The police launched an immediate search for him, with no luck. Ten months later, when the Peoria police superintendent read about the murder of Father Coyle in the *Chicago Tribune,* he sent a request to Shirley to investigate whether the Pedro Gussman who was wanted in Peoria for the murder of Pearl Gussman was the Pedro Gussman who had married Ruth Stephenson in Birmingham. The Illinois communication described the wanted man as Mexican, about thirty-seven years old, five feet six inches tall, weighing about 140 pounds, possibly bearing a mustache covering a hairlip scar.[32]

For his part, in Birmingham, Pedro Gussman believed that it was his marriage to Ruth Stephenson that supplied the reason for his arrest, not any sincere suspicion that he had killed some woman in Illinois. He had never been in Peoria in his life, he told the reporters. The newsmen had tracked down the paperhanger in the "Bertillon Room" at the Police Department, where an officer was recording his measurements for comparison with the man wanted in Peoria. Pedro Gussman was visibly upset.

Police forces in the United States had been slow to adopt the criminal identification system created by the French ethnologist Alphonse Bertillon in Paris in the 1880s. But by the time Shirley's men arrested Pedro Gussman in late August 1921, the term "Bertillon measurements" had become a household word, in the same way that fingerprinting, handwriting exemplars, and DNA swabs would years later. The aim of the Bertillon system was to identify criminals through the methodical recording of the measurements of select body parts and features. By age twenty, the human skeleton was fixed, Bertillon had argued—no two people presented the same combination of bodily characteristics. By taking the photograph of a suspect from the front and the side, Bertillon said, and carefully recording his skull width and limb span, the length of his trunk and his left middle finger, his hair and eye color, and the presence of tattoos, scars, and moles, habitual criminals might more easily be identified. By the turn of the century, Bertillon's identification method had become Europe's standard operating procedure. Authorities had gathered the images and measurements of over 150,000 offenders. There were even rumors that criminals had begun to flee to the West, where use of the Bertillon system was less prevalent. As of 1890, only one major city in the United States—Chicago—had adopted the Bertillon system; it took

New York City another decade to follow suit. But after that, its popularity spread quickly, eventually prompting calls for the establishment of a national identification office, a forerunner of the Federal Bureau of Investigation.[33]

Up until the day of his arrest, Pedro had done a fair job of ducking the newsmen. But now he spoke willingly. As a detective carefully recorded his measurements, Pedro told the journalists he could not have committed the crime. He had been in Birmingham on the day Pearl Gussman was killed. He had lived in the city for fourteen years; only rarely had he taken a day off from work. His supplier at Sherwin Williams could verify it. The only time he had been away since moving to the city was about ten years before, when he had taken his first wife back to Nashville, after she got sick. He had buried her there when she died, then returned to Birmingham, and had not been out of the city in the last three years.

"What is behind the charge against you then?" the reporters asked him.

Pedro shrugged his shoulders. "I don't know unless it is this marriage," he said.

The reporters took advantage of the opportunity to take stock of the man. "His complexion was not unusually dark," one observed, "and his features [were] finely chiseled in the Caucasian mold." A thick Spanish accent punctuated each word. They considered the description of the man wanted by Illinois authorities and began to focus on the dissimilarities between the two men. It was true that they shared a name, and both were also five feet, six inches tall. But the man in custody in Birmingham was forty-two, and weighed 105 pounds, making him five years older and thirty-five pounds lighter than the fugitive from Illinois. He had a barely noticeable scar on his right temple, but not a harelip cloaked by a mustache, like the man in Peoria.

The journalists pressed the Birmingham police officials about the discrepancies, but a spokesman for the department seemed unconcerned. It was possible for a person to change his appearance, he said. Gussman might have had a mustache and shaved it off, and if one looked very closely, it was also possible to detect a faint scar on the paperhanger's lip, he thought. There was also the matter of his demeanor, said the spokesman. According to one of the arresting officers, Gussman had been nervous when the police approached him at work. He had come along without once asking what he was wanted for.

What led Ruth Gussman to the doorstep of the law office of Horace C. Alford is no longer known, but the papers reported that she sought Alford's help immediately after she learned of Pedro's arrest. It is possible that she and the lawyer were previously acquainted. Horace Alford's youngest sister

Margaret was exactly Ruth's age. It is likely that the girls went to the same school, where Margaret Alford might have told Ruth that her oldest brother, Horace, was a lawyer, a piece of information that could have brought the panicked Ruth Gussman to his door on the day of her husband's arrest.

But even if Horace Alford had not been acquainted with Ruth Gussman before that day, the thick-set, solo practitioner with blond hair and brown eyes had to have recognized the girl—her picture had been plastered over the front pages of Birmingham's leading newspapers for weeks. A lawyer could make a name for himself in such a high-publicity case, especially if he was on the winning side, and from what Alford learned from Ruth that day, Pedro could not have murdered the Illinois woman. Her husband had never left the state, Ruth Gussman insisted. Horace Alford agreed to represent him.[34]

Not long after, Ruth Gussman and the lawyer walked over to the county jail, where they were permitted to meet with Pedro for a short time in the warden's office. When their time was up, Ruth kissed her husband affectionately, one paper wrote. Ruth told the newsmen who had gathered outside that she would stand behind Pedro, but if she hoped to win the same approval her mother had won for rallying behind Edwin, Ruth underestimated the reporters' ability to draw fine distinctions between such things. A reporter for the *Birmingham News* thought the girl's pronouncement of wifely support a mere "show of dramatics." He asked if she thought Pedro might be the man wanted in Peoria. "I don't believe any of the charges," Ruth said. Had she known about his prior marriage? Yes, Pedro had never kept that a secret. She had known for some time that Pedro had been married before and that his first wife had died in Nashville.[35]

It took Horace Alford less than a day to identify a number of alibi witnesses for Pedro, each of whom was willing publicly to attest to Pedro's presence in Birmingham during the month Pearl Gussman had been killed. Pedro had attended a dance at the Ben-Hur Dance Hall on the night of the murder, Mrs. Charles H. Kilgore said unequivocally. Three days before Pearl Gussman was murdered in Illinois, Pedro had paid his union dues in Birmingham, a labor official said, making any suggestion that he might have led a double life in a state over six hundred miles to the north entirely implausible. Pedro had been in the city throughout November, agreed the proprietor of a dry cleaning company: the launderer's books showed that the paperhanger had dropped off and picked up clothes shortly before and after the date the Peoria woman was killed.[36]

Yet Police Chief Shirley claimed to remain skeptical: "We can't give all the evidence we have, but I am almost convinced that Gussman is the man," Shirley said in answer to why the man had not been released. The department had at least two people who would swear that Pedro Gussman was *not* in the city on the day Pearl Gussman was murdered, the police chief said. What would be done with Pedro? a reporter asked him. He had wired the Peoria authorities earlier that day, informing them that he had Gussman in custody, and that the prisoner fit the culprit's "description fairly well," Chief Shirley said. Pedro Gussman's Bertillon measurements and mug shots had been sent to Illinois by mail. An Associated Press report later that day confirmed Peoria's receipt of the wire from Birmingham. If Pedro's picture bore any resemblance to the wanted man, a Peoria officer would come to retrieve Gussman straightaway, the AP report said.

Horace Alford had heard enough. He filed a habeas corpus petition in the Jefferson County court demanding that the Birmingham chief of police show legal cause why Pedro should not be immediately released, and a writ of injunction to bar anyone from hauling Gussman out of the county before the court had the chance to consider the matter. "The whole thing is a frame-up," Alford told reporters with certainty; "an attempt to get Gussman out of Birmingham"—away from his young wife, and the courtroom in which her father would soon be on trial.[37]

But the couple's troubles just worsened. The next day Alford amended his pleading, seeking to enjoin Police Chief Shirley and any other lawman in the state from interfering with Ruth Gussman as well. With her husband jailed and paltry few defenders left to come to her aid, Ruth Gussman was terrified that Shirley and other friends of her father's were planning to abduct her and have her committed in the insane asylum in Tuscaloosa, Alford's injunction papers said. Men had begun to loiter outside of the Gussmans' rooming house at all hours of the night, and his client had learned that a doctor in town had agreed to certify her incompetence, without even bothering to examine her. Pedro Gussman's arrest on the trumped up claim that he had murdered the tragic Pearl Gussman made it reasonable to conclude that Ruth Gussman's detractors would stop at nothing to aid her father's cause, including Birmingham's lawmen, whose responsibility it was to protect her. A week or so after her father's surrender, Ruth had sent a request to the police chief seeking his protection, her papers said. But witnesses had seen Shirley pound his desk when he received it and say: "I would not give Ruth Stephenson protection if I knew she would be killed within the next ten minutes!"

When reporters asked Shirley for a comment, the police chief denied the accusation. It was all false, he said; the only thing he knew about people wanting to put Ruth Gussman in the insane asylum was what her own parents had told him—"that they had the insanity papers prepared for their daughter."[38] A hearing to decide whether an injunction should be issued was scheduled for the next week.

On August 29, 1921, the same day Horace Alford filed the injunction papers to prevent Chief Shirley and his minions from seizing Ruth Gussman and tossing her into the insane asylum against her will, the bride quietly turned nineteen. With her husband in jail and strange men milling around her boardinghouse, the day likely came and went without much celebration. If any of the reporters were aware of the occasion, they let it pass without mention.

––––––

Pedro Gussman must have thought that things could hardly get worse; but then they did. The first postcard came through the mail, postmarked the evening of August 25, the same day as Pedro's arrest. Horace Alford found it waiting when he returned to his office the next morning. "You made a big mistake taking the Gussman case," the handwritten card snarled. "You and the X-backs can just go T' Hell." An inscription was scrawled on the bottom of the card—"The T.A.s"—followed by the final acid incrimination: "Gussman is a Portuguese Nigger—not a Porto Rican."

By 1921, nearly every adult in Birmingham knew that "T.A." was shorthand for the secretive, anti-Catholic group, the True Americans, and "X-back" simply a truncated rendering of "crossback," a favorite twentieth-century slur for Catholics. But the defamation "Portuguese Nigger" carried a less popularized meaning, though it is possible that Horace Alford, having grown up in St. Clair County, Alabama, was familiar with the expression. For decades, the phrase had been applied with some celebrity to a mysterious colony of olive-skinned people called the "Melungeons," a group of men, women, and children who had lived clustered in the lushly wooded Appalachian foothills of northeastern Tennessee. The Melungeons' ancestral origins were murky, leaving their racial makeup suspect. Some said they descended from Spanish or Portuguese explorers who had been shipwrecked in the sixteenth century. Others whispered of the progeny of Sir Francis Drake's long-lost colony of Roanoke. Still others thought them the offspring of Gypsies, or the ancient Phoenicians, or even one of the Lost Tribes of Israel. Consensus on the question was as elusive as the matter of their provenance itself. In an era where privileges and disadvantages were dispensed in step with one's place on the spectrum of whiteness, and its lack, uncertainty about a man's race had become intolerable. The inability of their neighbors to pinpoint the Melungeons' origins, clouded the issue of their rightful social place.

There was also the law to consider. Before the Civil War and the passage of the Eighteenth Amendment, the Tennessee constitution had banned nonwhites from voting. If the Melungeons weren't white, they couldn't vote. Even after the war, as the state and its neighbors began to pass Jim Crow laws, segregating Negroes from whites in public eateries and public schools, on streetcars and trains, and more, the question of the Melungeons' racial status assumed even greater importance. In 1890, a writer trying to find some clarity on the matter put the question directly to three members of the Tennessee state legislature—"What *is* a Melungeon?" she asked—and received a medley of replies:

"A dirty Indian sneak," said one law-maker, derisively.

"God only knows what he is," said another. "A Melungeon isn't a nigger, and he isn't an Indian, and he isn't a white man either," he added.

A Melungeon is *"a Portuguese nigger,"* a third legislator declared, and the colorful phrase stuck.[39]

Naturally, the Melungeons resented the characterizations. When permitted to self-identify, members of the clan tended to describe themselves as Indian, or Portuguese—"or as many pronounced it, 'Portyghee,'"—but never Negro. And owing to their most commonly described features—swarthy complexions, high cheekbones, and "jet black hair, generally straight but at times with a slight tendency to curl"—it was generally conceded that it was possible to visually distinguish the Melungeons from the Negroes. Nonetheless, over time, most of the Melungeons' white neighbors came to regard them as "a mixed race" at best: the descendents of a once noble group of Portuguese explorers perhaps, but whose godless "trampling on the marriage relation" and laxity toward the question of intermingling with Indians and Negroes had "mongrelized" any prior claim they might have had to whiteness. Hence, the slander "Portuguese nigger" was intended less as a slur on the Portuguese, than on those with whom they had deigned to consort after arriving on American shores.[40]

It is difficult to know whether the author of the card left at Horace Alford's law office was suggesting that Pedro Gussman was a Melungeon, or simply using "Portuguese nigger" loosely to accuse the paperhanger of having "mixed blood." The writer's very specific accusation that Gussman was *"not a Porto Rican"* could have been meant to suggest that he was instead a Melungeon. According to Pedro's own statements, before moving to Birmingham, he had lived in Tennessee for three years, not far from the Melungeon enclaves.

But it is also possible that, over time, the phrase "Portuguese nigger" had morphed into a more generic insult, ascribed to anyone whose ambiguous racial attributes created the danger that they might slip across the color line. "Passing as white" by fair-skinned Negroes was a practice closely policed in the early decades of twentieth-century America. The ubiquitous antimiscegenation laws insisted on it. Few greater dangers to the future of the nation could be conceived than the defilement of the white race by unwitting commingling with the Negro.

Whatever the meaning of the writer of the note, Horace Alford was plainly unnerved. Had he known that his representation of Pedro Gussman would invite such hostility, there can be little question that he would have turned his back on the whole mess. But he had already accepted a retainer in the case, and the ethical standards that governed attorney-client relationships obligated the lawyer to continue to assist him.

Nonetheless, over the next several days, Alford scrambled to distance himself from Pedro and Ruth Gussman in every way he could. The lawyer made it a point whenever speaking about the matter of Pedro's arrest to stress that his connection to the couple was strictly professional: "I have no connection with the Stephenson case," the lawyer repeatedly reminded reporters. Alford even wrote a formal statement, which the *Birmingham News* printed in full, underscoring that he was "a member of the *Baptist* Church"; that he "was born at Riverside, St. Clair County, Ala., of *Protestant* parents"; was "reared a Protestant, [was] still a Protestant, and always expect[ed] to be" a Protestant. He could hardly be faulted for complying with the rules of his profession, which demanded that he pursue his client's cause, Alford's statement said.[41]

Horace Alford was not the only one to receive a warning. Mrs. Charles Kilgore, one of Pedro's alibi witnesses, had also begun to feel the heat. The city's leading papers had all printed Kilgore's statement that Pedro had attended a dance in Birmingham on the day Pearl Gussman was butchered in Peoria. A letter mailed to Kilgore's home warned the woman to mind her own business: "Best thing for you to do is to keep your mouth shut," the unsigned letter read; "remember the tar and feathers, also [the] thrashing of [the] woman at 904 N. No. 13." The message couldn't have been clearer: Kilgore should just stay clear of the case involving Edwin Stephenson, and the same went for her "nigger friend, Gussman, and [e]special[ly] his wife," the letter added, darkly. "People in this good old U.S.A. won't put up with this stuff."

The situation was spiraling out of control, and Pedro Gussman knew it. It must have been hard to think which threat was graver: being tossed in jail for an out-of-state murder or having his racial identity opened up for public debate. The papers were printing things about him that were not true, he told the reporters. The man wanted in Illinois spelled his name with a double *s*, whereas the correct spelling of his name was with one *s*. And his parents *were* Spanish, Gussman protested. His father had been sent to Cuba from Spain, and had settled in Puerto Rico after the Spanish American War. Pedro had been born there, he said, in Guayama, Porto Rico.

It must have been a great relief when one of the accusations against him was cleared up two days after his arrest. Illinois authorities wired Police Chief Shirley that the jailed man in Birmingham was not the man who killed Pearl Gussman. "Peoria had no claim upon him," the telegram said. But even as Judge Abernethy ordered Pedro's release, the police chief continued to defend his decision to arrest him. Pedro Gussman and the man wanted in Peoria were identically named and the same height, Shirley said, ignoring, as did the papers, the question of the proper spelling of the man's name. They were also fairly close in age, said Shirley. "There was no choice but to arrest him."[42]

After Pedro's release from jail, questions about his race seemed to linger, until finally, the paperhanger who had once done his best to avoid the pressmen told them that he wanted to discuss the matter of his race to refute the lies being told about him. "I have been living in this country twenty-three years," Pedro said, "in Birmingham fourteen years. During that time no one has ever questioned my color until I became mixed up in this case. I am not a negro and have no negro blood in my veins. I have gone to dances with other white people and no question has been raised. I am a legally qualified voter in Jefferson County and have paid my poll tax. Anyone who wants my record for steadiness can get it [throughout the city] from north Birmingham to Glen Iris Avenue." All he wanted was that the lies being told about him stop.[43]

———

Very little could have caused more of a stir than the sudden disappearance of Ruth Gussman over Labor Day weekend, just days before the hearing was to be held on her motion to enjoin Chief Shirley from abducting her. Local reporters began to hear rumors on September 6 that the girl had boarded the Louisville & Nashville train the night before and fled, and they chased all over town trying to confirm it, but the details of her flight were sketchy. When they caught up with Pedro Gussman, the man verified that his wife had left, but he was at a loss to say where she had gone. Neither could the girl's mother, or her attorney, Horace Alford. If she had told a soul where she was headed, her confidant had yet to be found. Apparently only the owner of the rooming house where Ruth and Pedro had been staying and the taxi-cab driver who had shuttled her to the train station had witnessed her hasty departure. Hurried inquiries at the terminal revealed that the girl had purchased a ticket for passage on the late evening train headed north. But her final destination and the reason for her departure remained clouded. Had he and Ruth quarreled? the reporters pressed Pedro. No, he said. Then why had she deserted him? Pedro said he had no idea. He had taken the morning off and gone to East Lake Park, he said, where a Labor Day barbeque was under way. He had served as a member of the Birmingham Trade Council committee, and had helped plan the day's festivities. He had expected his wife to join him there, but she never showed up. He only learned later that she had packed all of her clothes and vanished.

The mystery deepened a couple of days later when Mrs. Ruth Campbell hand-delivered a letter from Ruth Gussman to reporters at the city's leading papers. The two Ruths—Ruth Campbell and Ruth Gussman—were close friends, at the time living on the same avenue only two blocks apart. Newsmen had frequently seen the two of them together. The letter stated that Ruth Gussman had left the city after concluding that Pedro was planning to betray her. Contrary to what her husband was telling them, she wrote, Ruth and Pedro had quarreled, when shortly after his release from jail she found Pedro in possession of a large sum of money and demanded to know where he had gotten it. Although he denied it, she had come to believe that her husband's captors had persuaded him to take her father's side against her at the trial, and paid him dearly for the pledge. In defense of her father! "The True Americans have bought him out" the letter read—all part of the anti-Catholic faction's plan to cause their marriage to fail. "Their object from the very first has been to separate me from my husband," she continued, so that she would be forced to return to her parent's home. "They threw [Pedro] in jail on a pretended charge" and threatened to commit her to an asylum; then, failing in that, they embarked on an even "baser" plan, tempting Pedro with large sums of money to spread falsehoods about her in the service of her father. She could conceive of no greater betrayal. Remaining with him was unfathomable. "As a Catholic, I do not believe in divorce," Ruth wrote, pledging to remain true to her faith. But she hoped that her friends would not be fooled by "the black lies" being spread about her.[44]

The reporters swarmed around Pedro like flies. They asked if there was truth to his wife's accusations. No, the man protested, he had no intention of testifying at her father's trial. Why would she write such a thing? He had no idea, Pedro said, the bills she had seen were his wages, not a payoff. He had worked every day since their wedding save one, when he was ill. He had done all he could think of to support her. She had fled without a word of explanation, he insisted.

It must have been difficult to know what to make of it all. It was possible that efforts had been made to convince Gussman of the benefits of aiding Stephenson's defense, or the perils of assisting Joe Tate. Immediately after Pedro's arrest the week before, reporters had seen city detectives walk Pedro over to the private office of Police Chief Shirley. What took place there would never be discovered. The newsmen had been barred from the room while Pedro was interrogated.

But Pedro Gussman insisted that he had no intention of participating in the Stephenson trial: "Rumors that I will testify and give sensational testimony are false," he said flatly. "Simply because I am a foreigner I am getting the hot end of this thing."

The newsmen asked him if he would take Ruth back.

Pedro was plainly at the end of his rope. His wife could do as she pleased, he answered, come back or stay away. "I have given her all that a man could give her.... She left me absolutely without cause." All he wanted was to be left alone.[45]

Horace Alford saw an opportunity in Ruth Gussman's flight from Birmingham. The lawyer had been looking for ways to separate himself from Ruth and Pedro, and the girl's departure seemed to provide it: a few days after Ruth sent her letter to the papers, Alford withdrew his motion for injunctive relief against Police Chief Shirley and the other officials, asserting that the request was mooted by his client's defection. The lawyer's desire to repair the damage done to his reputation could not have been clearer: "As a lawyer and as a Protestant, I sincerely trust that this full and complete statement will enable the critics who have criticized me for having represented Mrs. Gussman to understand that my connection with the case was solely that of a lawyer." He then terminated his attorney-client relationship with her, though not before telling reporters that he considered the girl's decision to leave her husband "more common sense" than she had displayed "at any previous time."[46]

———

It is difficult to stay hidden when entire neighborhoods are galvanized to the hunt. Ruth Gussman's letter made no mention of where she was staying, but the newsmen soon discovered it. One of the two suitcases the bride had hastily filled with clothes was missing a handle. It was hard to forget. The driver of the taxi who transported her to the train terminal and an employee who worked there had been forced to wrap their arms around the piece of luggage just to carry it. Follow-up questions to the cargo staff soon revealed that a suitcase of that description had been checked through to Loretto, Tennessee, a sleepy town located due north of Birmingham, not far from the border. A woman named Lenis Patt lived there with her husband Tony J. Patt, a blacksmith, and their four-year-old adopted daughter, Mamie Helen. Lenis Patt frequently traveled to Birmingham to visit with family and friends, including Ruth Campbell, who was Mamie Helen's biological mother—the same Ruth Campbell known to reporters as Ruth Stephenson's closest friend. On one of Lenis Patt's trips to the city that summer, she had met Ruth Gussman while visiting Ruth Campbell's home. Aware of the girl's troubles, Lenis had offered Ruth Gussman a place to stay in Loretto if events in Birmingham became unbearable.

Loretto was little more than a tavern made of logs with a stagecoach stop where travelers could bed down and rest their horses in the mid-1800s; but in the 1870s, German Catholics began to find their way there, in a roundabout flight from the *kulturkampf* campaign of Chancellor Otto von Bismarck. They took passage, paying $25 a head, on steamships from Hamburg to New York City, a voyage that could take anywhere from two weeks to three times that—"depending on conditions." Many did not survive it. Of the lucky ones, some made their way to a remote place in southern Tennessee called Glenrock, where they built farms and gristmills just six miles north of the Alabama state line. Sufficiently sheltered from the rising anti-Catholicism that bedeviled other localities not many miles away, these immigrants were emboldened to rename their little town Loretto, "for Saint Loretto, a Catholic nun," wrote a town historian many years later—though almost certainly the the nun had been given the name Loretto, after the birthplace of the Virgin Mary herself. The settlers quickly built a house of worship, the Sacred Heart Church, and a convent, and a Catholic school for their young, which with the help of a group of nuns and friars, one resident wrote, soon outstripped the neighboring county schools.[47]

After all of Ruth Gussman's troubles in Birmingham, the thought of the secluded Catholic enclave must have beckoned like a siren song. Remembering Lenis Patt's offer of sanctuary, Ruth boarded a train for Columbia, Tennessee, and on from there to Loretto.

After repeated calls from the press, town officials finally confirmed that a nineteen year-old visitor had in fact arrived there, midday on September 6. She was staying with Tony and Lenis Patt. The papers could scarcely contain their glee: "Ruth Gussman at Friend's Home in Loretto, Tennessee," boomed a headline of the *Birmingham Post* triumphantly, as if its staff reporters had unearthed the Holy Grail itself.[48]

| Trials and Tribulations

B Y 1921, BILLY PARKER had begun to spend several months of each
year at his home in Miami, but when the heat was too oppressive, the
publisher of the *New Menace* headed north for a home he still kept in Branson,
Missouri, where his printing presses churned out issue after issue warning its
readers about the Romanist Pope's most recent threats. Just a few days after
Reverend Edwin Stephenson shot and killed Father Coyle, the weekly paper
had run a half-page spread about the violence, leaving no mystery about
whose side the paper was on: "Ala. Priest Killed by Aggrieved Father," a
banner headline on the front page bellowed; "Daughter of Minister Inviegled
into Romanism by Papist Lover and Priests."[1]

The article's undisguised slant would neither have surprised nor disturbed
the paper's loyal readers. Since the founding of its predecessor, the *Menace,* in
1911, the popular anti-Catholic weekly had fostered a reputation for sensa-
tionalism, and its staff offered no apologies for it. Pressing dangers called for
blunt language, not "elegant diction and scholarly phrases," the editors and
writers thought. When face-to-face with "the unsavory record of Romanism," the reading public grew weary of such civilities.[2]

The *New Menace*'s hefty subscriber rolls appeared to confirm its readers'
appreciation of its journalistic excesses. Within a few years of its launch,
the paper had outgrown "the poor, humble little wooden building" where it
had begun and grown into the most successful anti-Catholic publication in
American history. At its height, with its "contemporary bustling printing
plant," it boasted over 1.6 million subscribers, a circulation figure "three
times greater than the largest daily papers in Chicago and New York City
combined" at the time, one religious historian calculated.

No doubt part of its appeal was consistency. Each issue could be counted on to sound the same fear-drenched alarms: the Romanists' conspiratorial plot to make the nation Catholic; the papists' determination to dupe Protestant children and women; the need for Protestant men to wake up and to answer the sinister threat in their midst.[3]

In the 1920s, if still popular the *New Menace*'s warnings were no longer new. During the nineteenth century, a number of celebrated anti-Catholic books pounding the same themes had won a wide readership, even while not always demonstrating a strict devotion to the truth. Among the most popular were two purported "escaped nun" memoirs, *The Awful Disclosures of Maria Monk* and Rebecca Reed's *Six Months in a Convent*. Published in the 1830s, the books were instant best sellers, recounting the supposed travails of two alliteratively named young women, Maria Monk and Rebecca Reed, both born into solid Protestant families, but then lured by financial need or brainwashing into Catholic convent life, the tell-all books said. Once there, the women were made into virtual prisoners, the memoirs claimed, where they witnessed (nearly) unspeakable acts—priest orgies, nuns as sex slaves, flagellation, and the murder of unwanted babies born of the secret copulations. In an age of repressed sexuality, bookshop owners could scarcely keep the salacious tomes on their shelves.[4]

Eventually, both supposed autobiographies were debunked as pure fiction "ghostwritten by male literary agents." After their true authors were exposed, the fabrications about the two "convent escapees" lay dormant for a time. But in 1919, the *Menace* saw fit to print a story attempting to resurrect and defend the Maria Monk mendacities: a girl claimed to have talked with a woman who claimed to have been the daughter of a woman who claimed to have known Maria Monk, and to have heard the awful story of her captivity directly from Monk herself.[5] Apparently, when real life failed to provide the desired evidence of the papists' depravities, such "verifications" would do just as well.[6]

Stories like that of Edwin Stephenson's experiences in Birmingham, however, could breathe new life into the pages of a publication like the *New Menace,* its publisher knew. Parker's staff could scarcely have scripted the Stephenson saga any better. The story had it all: the Catholics' multi-year seduction of the minister's only daughter, a girl roundly believed to be hobbled with an enfeebled mind; the battle waged by the minister and his wife against the assault against their home, until the "priest Coyle" defied their wishes a final time by marrying Ruth to the Catholic Pedro Gussman, a dark-skinned foreigner. Here was a real-life example of the *New Menace*'s greatest fears!

Reverend Edwin Stephenson "would rather have seen his daughter in her grave than a member of the papal church, married to a Catholic, destined to bring into the world a generation of half breed slaves to the papal system," a front-page article in Billy Parker's paper applauded. Far from a crime, it was an act of bravery, the editors of the *New Menace* wrote; an act for which the minister would not and "*should not* be punished." The only pity, the paper continued, was that Stephenson's self-defense claim would prove more of a hindrance than a help to airing the truth about the Romanists. A self-defense claim was too confining. It would bar his attorneys from introducing evidence about "the proselytizing tactics employed to rob his home of a cherished daughter," Parker's paper explained, as in a court of law, all testimony about the Catholics' scheming would be considered "irrelevant" to the narrow question of whether the priest physically attacked Stephenson on that porch. The defense being planned in Birmingham on Stephenson's behalf would make all evidence of the papists' year-after-year seduction of the girl entirely immaterial. The jury would be prevented from hearing a word about it. Something had to be done.[7]

Billy Parker decided to take a detour. On his way back home in August 1921, Parker stopped off in the Magic City to meet in person the imprisoned minister about whom his paper had already written so much. Parker and Stephenson conferred at the county jail for several hours, the *Birmingham News* reported, and though it couldn't be known precisely what the two men discussed during their private conference, undoubtedly Billy Parker assured the minister of the backing of his influential paper. The question of Stephenson's planned self-defense claim might just have come up as well.

———

With the headline-grabbing news of Pedro Gussman's arrest and release, Ruth Gussman's request for a protective order against the Birmingham chief of police, and the hullabaloo over the bride's abrupt flight from the state, several days passed in September 1921 with Birmingham reporters paying little attention to the matter of the grand jury's inaction in the Stephenson case. But as the other news of the case began to ebb, the reporters seemed suddenly to remember that a surprising number of days had passed since Joe Tate's last witness had testified before the grand jury regarding Stephenson's prosecution. There was still no word of a formal charge against him! Rumors began to race around town that the grand jurors were refusing to indict; that they would sooner let their session lapse than condemn the minister's act; that Joe Tate would have to present his case all over again, before a new group of jurors who would not be sworn in until the following month.[8]

In the end, the rumors proved exaggerated, though when the grand jury finally told the prosecutor of their decision—twenty-six days after the day of the shooting—Joe Tate might have wished that the men had simply deferred. The prosecutor could have his indictment, their answer came finally, but not on the charge he preferred. The grand jury returned an indictment for murder in the second degree instead: "Edwin R. Stephenson unlawfully and with malice aforethought killed James E. Coyle by shooting him with a pistol, but without premeditation or deliberation," the indictment read in full.

By itself the decision meant that Stephenson, if convicted, would not be hanged. Unlike murder in the first degree, the maximum penalty for second degree murder was not death but life imprisonment. More important, the grand jury's judgment sounded silent warnings for Joe Tate. If the members of the trial jury were anything like the men who had made up the grand jury, their sympathies might rest with the minister instead of the priest; and the girl at the center of the prosecution's case might elicit more resentment than compassion. If so, the higher standard of proof the prosecutors would be expected to satisfy at trial—evidence "beyond a reasonable doubt"—might be just too much for Tate to meet. Against the ropes only a few weeks earlier, Edwin Stephenson had plainly won his first major victory, and he had done it without a lawyer even in the room.

It is common practice in the halls of justice to rub the nose of one's opponent in his defeats, especially when a case is being tried as much in the court of public opinion as the inside of a courtroom. So when the news broke about the grand jury's charge, Edwin Stephenson's attorneys made no effort to contain their joy. They were "openly elated," the *Birmingham Post* reported. By contrast, Joe Tate was noticeably tight-lipped: "Any comment from him would be improper," the prosecutor told reporters. Even without admitting it, the newsmen sensed the circuit solicitor's disappointment. The *Birmingham News* summed it up this way: "Defense Pleased, State Silent."

For a time, some speculated that Joe Tate would reject the grand jury's decision and "nolle prosequi" the indictment—asking the court to dismiss it "without prejudice"—so that he could try again with the grand jury that would be seated in early October. Another group of men might be persuaded to see things differently. But in the end, Tate heeded the counsel of those who said he was lucky to get what he had. An unidentified source told one of the local reporters that the second-degree murder charge had been a "compromise decision." Some of the men on the grand jury had wanted to return a "no true bill," refusing to indict the minister at all. If Tate pushed his luck, he might end up with nothing.[9]

Undoubtedly with that in mind, the veteran prosecutor decided to proceed with what he had.

———

It is a delicate thing, recasting a criminal defense—like the childhood game of pickup sticks, where the removal of one timber can bring the rest of its neighbors crashing down. In a criminal case, the abrupt abandonment of protestations of self-defense can make other parts of an accused's story rickety as well. Especially when the abandoned claim has been trumpeted to the masses in newspaper headlines for weeks on end. Perhaps for that reason, when Stephenson's lawyers mulled over the possibility of adding another defense for their client's violence, they decided that rather than taking the first explanation back, to pile a second one directly on top of it.

For over a month, Stephenson and his lawyers had offered a single claim of self-defense to explain the shooting of Father Coyle. It was the only defense the minister himself had offered in the hours after his arrest. At the preliminary hearing, Crampton Harris had hewed closely to the claim as well, endlessly dwelling on supposed tossed chairs and a busted belt. For by 1921, the legal doctrine of self-defense in the state was well established: a man who reasonably feared he might die or be severely injured from an attack launched by another without provocation could lawfully take the life of his attacker rather than sacrificing his own. If persuasive, the defense conferred a blessing unqualified in its scope—absolute vindication from a charge of wrongdoing—entitling the accused not only to his freedom but to the approval of his peers as well. For civilized societies had long concurred that killing an unprovoked deadly assailant was not only excusable but, under the circumstances, the correct action to take.

It cannot be known for sure if it was Hugo Black or some other member of the defense team who first worried that the minister's claim of an unprovoked attack might not be strong enough to wager their client's entire defense on it. Acquittals for self-defense could be elusive. If a man's peers questioned whether it was reasonable for him to have believed that he was about to be killed, they could conclude that he acted too harshly, or too precipitously. Or they might doubt that he had acted for the reasons he was saying at all. They might decide he had acted not out of fear for his life but out of anger, or hatred, or vengeance for some perceived wrong, which in the eyes of the law was not self-defense at all but conduct of an entirely different (and punishable) order.

What is clear is that shortly after Hugo Black returned to Birmingham, the story offered to justify the minister's violence began noticeably to evolve, and rumors that Stephenson was considering claiming "temporary insanity" as an additional reason for an acquittal began to seep into the newspapers' columns. When the reporters asked Black point-blank about his client's intentions, however, the lawyer declined to broadcast the defense team's thinking: "It was too soon to say," he said vaguely, or "the matter had not yet been decided." Nevertheless, by September 9, both the *Post* and the *News* felt confident enough in their sources to report that the defense strategy had in fact expanded: the minister planned to plead "not guilty by reason of insanity," they wrote.[10]

The newsmen did not probe the wisdom or folly of offering the two separate explanations for Stephenson's act at once: self-defense *and* temporary insanity. Perhaps it seemed sufficient that Alabama's procedural rules permitted the choice, despite its vaguely schizophrenic feel. For considered side by side, the two legal claims seemed at war with each other. The first hypothesis suggesting that Stephenson had acted *rationally* on that porch; that his decision to shoot was well reasoned, the decision a "reasonable man" in his shoes would have made when faced with the priest's unprovoked threat of death; that the minister had been thinking clearly enough on the porch to have reasonably concluded that his life was being threatened. While the second imagined Stephenson's behavior as entirely *irrational*—the kind of unwilled impulse no reasonable man would have experienced, but only a person suffering from an enfeebled or demented mind; that the minister's thinking was so *unclear* and disordered as to have lost all ability to control his actions.

The strategy of arguing both things simultaneously was risky. Although the newsmen seemed to have missed the tension between the competing claims, there was no reason to think that the trial jurors would make the same mistake—especially as the prosecutors could be expected to point it out. If the jurors noticed the irreconcilability of the two defenses or, worse, felt insulted by the implication that they would miss it, they might in turn choose to reward the illogic or slight by rejecting them both.

In the end, Hugo Black and his co-counsel decided to risk it, and likely something besides the weakness of Stephenson's self-defense claim supplied the impetus for their gamble. As Billy Parker's paper had explained to its subscribers some weeks before, pursuing a solitary claim of self-defense at trial would erect an almost insurmountable evidentiary roadblock: there was no proper reason to allow testimony to be heard at trial that Stephenson had been locked in a battle with the Catholics over the soul of his daughter for years, if the only legal issue in the case was whether Father Coyle had been about to kill the minister at a particular moment on a particular porch. The *New Menace* had lamented the self-defense claim for precisely that reason, and after Stephenson's private meeting with the publisher of the anti-Catholic weekly, friends of the minister told a local reporter that the minister had "openly hinted that he [too] would like to have religious testimony creep into the trial."[11]

———

Toward the end of September, as the sun beat on the city's streets and alley-ways more warmly than fiercely, word from the lawyers about their plans grew quiet. With the slowing of the pace of the news, the papers dutifully published the growing lists of witnesses who had been subpoenaed to testify, and as new names were added, the reporters combed through the lineups for clues about the attorneys' trial strategies. Some of these subpoenaed wit-nesses had testified before the grand jury or at the preliminary hearing, but other names were new, and the fact that none of the identities of the men and women on the defense's list had ever been revealed before kept the newsmen scrambling for biographical crumbs that might impact the trial.

By far the greatest public interest still centered on Ruth and Pedro Gussman, both of whose names appeared on the prosecutor's witness list, though for weeks the lawyers for Edwin Stephenson insisted they had no interest in summoning either one. Three days before the start of the trial, however, Hugo Black reversed course and ordered a subpoena served on Pedro Gussman. The unexpected move sent ripples of excitement through the news corps; reporters pressed Black about what he expected Gussman to say, but the lawyer would not reveal his reasons, and the same question put to Gussman himself was no help in resolving the mystery. Pedro told the jour-nalists he had been surprised to receive the summons. He had no idea what Hugo Black's plan for him might be.[12]

Whatever motivated the defense lawyer, the step plainly unnerved Joe Tate and his men. After fleeing the city, Ruth Gussman had sent the news-papers a letter stating that she believed Pedro had betrayed her and was pre-paring to testify for the defense; that he would blacken her reputation, and attack the character of Father Coyle who could no longer speak for himself. The prosecutors had not appeared to put much stock in the bride's fears, but then the *New Menace* published an article filled with innuendos about a secret coupling between the dead priest and the "rather good-looking" Miss Ruth Stephenson. The relationship between the two was "so friendly and intimate and peculiar," claimed the *New Menace*, that it had aroused suspicion. Several taxi drivers in the city were prepared to attest to having spirited Ruth and the priest away "to several lonely places," the weekly paper wrote, all *before* her marriage to the Catholic Pedro Gussman.[13]

It seems unlikely that Joe Tate and his men would have credited many of the *New Menace*'s libels—its regard for truth was not its strongest selling point. But the prosecutors must have begun to worry that Ruth Gussman's suspicions might have had some grounding in truth. A day after the Birmingham papers spread the news about Hugo Black's subpoena of Pedro, John Morrow, one of Joe Tate's leading assistants, summoned Pedro Gussman to his office, where, in front of an official stenographer, Morrow questioned Pedro at length about his relationship with his wife: how Pedro had met the girl; whether anyone had influenced him to propose to her; whether Father Coyle had known Pedro had intended to marry her before the day they showed up at St. Paul's Rectory; whether any Catholic, including Ruth's godfather, Fred Bender, had influenced him in any way to marry her. No, sir. No, sir. No, sir. No, sir, Pedro Gussman repeated again and again. He had asked Ruth Stephenson to marry him because he had wanted to marry her. No one had influenced him to do it in any way. He had wanted to marry her for some years, but she was too young. They were forced to wait until she was old enough to make the decision on her own. What about Father Coyle's involvement? Morrow pressed. Father Coyle would never even have been involved with the wedding except that the priest in Bessemer had been away when he and Ruth had showed up there, Pedro told him. He had talked with Father Coyle about his plans to get married a couple of weeks earlier, but had never mentioned Ruth Stephenson by name. The priest only came to know that it was Ruth that Pedro wanted to marry when the two of them showed up at St. Paul's, he said.

Pedro's answers seemed to mollify the prosecutor, but he was taking no chances. John Morrow had graduated from the University of Alabama Law School in Tuscaloosa in 1913. He had been practicing law for eight years; long enough to have learned that it was always the question a witness was not asked that came back to haunt a lawyer. Ruth Gussman had believed her husband was preparing to testify for the defense in a way that would blacken her reputation. Morrow zeroed in on the issue that would have damaged the girl's reputation more than anything else:

"[W]as Ruth Stephenson a pure girl, so far as you ever knew?"

"I honestly believe she was," Pedro replied.

"You always thought so?"

"Yes, sir."

"You still think?"

"I still think so yet," Pedro affirmed.

"So far as you know then she was a virgin at the time you married her?"

Again, Pedro Gussman confirmed his bride's chastity: "At the time I married her," he said.

The assistant solicitor was satisfied. If Pedro Gussman intended to testify in favor of Edwin Stephenson and betray his young wife, he certainly had a funny way of showing it.[14]

Later the same day, as the muffled noises of dusk began to descend on the city, another young couple looking to get married ran into some trouble. Mr. J. M. Norris of Penelope, Texas, had been scheduled to arrive in Birmingham earlier in the day, one of the papers reported, but his train was delayed, leaving him and his betrothed, Miss Nannie Trice of Ensley, Alabama, scarcely enough time to get their desired marriage certificate from the probate office at the Jefferson County Courthouse before it closed its doors for the night. It was a Saturday, and the hour was late—too late, it seemed, to locate a minister or a judge to perform the ceremony. Then someone suggested (the paper did not say who) that the lovers solicit the services of Reverend Edwin Stephenson in the neighboring jail, provided, of course, that Sheriff Hartsfield agreed.

The assent of all concerned parties was soon procured, and in the waning light of October 15, 1921, Norris and Trice stood before the jailed "Marrying Parson" and exchanged their vows. For an event supposedly arranged on the fly, a group surprisingly robust in number witnessed the unlikely ceremony—four deputy sheriffs "and a number of others," the *Age-Herald* noted, without identifying them, and one of its own reporters as well. The paper did not say how its reporter had come to be invited to cover the nuptials; nor did it appear to suspect that the whole thing might just have been staged to place the minister, on the eve of trial, in a slightly more respectable light. For who could remain hardened against a man who came so willingly to the aid of young love?[15]

Ruth Stephenson may have disappeared, but the interest in the role she might play at the trial did not. Opinions on the question veered back and forth. The prosecutors had included her name on its list of witnesses, but Hugo Black had made clear that the defense had no interest in calling her, and despite Black's reversal of course regarding Pedro, the pressmen took him at his word. But as the trial drew near, the reporters began to question whether the prosecutor's subpoena would be enough to woo her back, despite her earlier vow to return. Their skepticism deepened the day before the trial when Ruth Gussman's friends confirmed that they still had not heard from her. Sources for the *Birmingham Post* insisted that not only was the girl not in the city, but the prosecutors had not heard from her either.[16]

But the report was mistaken. A day or so before the trial was scheduled to begin, Ruth Gussman had slipped back into the city unnoticed, eluding the journalists camped out at Birmingham's main train terminal by getting off the southbound train "at Boyles" instead, a less busy stop in the city's northeastern corner, where she was spirited into a waiting car and driven to the home of the baker Tom McGough by way of the narrow alleyway behind his house.

Little Helen McGough, the baker's eleven-year-old daughter, long remembered the commotion that had attended the young woman's arrival. Helen and her twin brother, Joe, had been explicitly warned: they mustn't say a word about Ruth being there, their parents told them. The children were made to "promise solemnly." With everyone in town "wondering aloud as to Ruth's whereabouts," it was a lot to ask of ones so young. The "weight of [their] secret was simply odious," Helen later wrote. Yet somehow it seems they managed it. Not a word about the bride hiding out at the McGough home for the duration of the trial was published until twenty-five years later.

Maybe the opportunity to observe their celebrity visitor up close provided some little compensation for the children's pact. Much ink had been spilled about the character of Ruth Gussman. The *Birmingham News* had concluded that she "like[d] newspaper notoriety." The *Birmingham Post* had portrayed her as childish and uncaring. With an age gap of eight years between Helen McGough and Ruth, the younger girl was transfixed. Some were even saying that Ruth Stephenson and her father had planned the whole thing, just to put Father Coyle in his grave. But "[i]f there was any deceit or cunning in Ruth's make up, it was entirely unapparent" to young Helen McGough. Contrary to the rumors being spread about town, Pedro Gussman's bride "seemed filled with genuine regret and remorse for the tragedy which she precipitated," Helen thought. If anything, the minister's daughter just seemed sad.[17]

―――――

Judge William E. Fort could not have been pleased that the eyes of the nation were set to fall on Birmingham for the "most sensational murder trial" in Alabama's history at a time when the courthouse sorely needed renovating or, better yet, knocking down. The Jefferson County Courthouse was a positive "disgrace," the judge had been heard to say. Earlier in the year, Judge Fort had exhorted the grand jury to investigate the building's inadequacies. When first built in 1887, the courthouse had been lauded as one of the most handsome buildings in the city. "That day has long since passed," Judge Fort told the grand jurors, flatly. The building was barely functional. It lacked chambers for the judges and their clerks, and a room where witnesses could gather before they were called to testify. And no one involved in the building's original design had seemed at all concerned with the special requirements of women. When women appeared as witnesses, they were "jumbled" into the same hall as the men, Judge Fort told the grand jury, allowing anyone who wanted to approach them to do so, and the only toilet facility provided for the ladies was a small screened-off area directly across from the elevator on the lower floor. It was "an outrage," Fort said. The satellite county courthouse in Bessemer was vastly superior. He pushed the men to study the problem and make some recommendations.[18]

The grand jurors set to work on the matter, but they were not miracle workers. There was no getting around the fact that the run-down Jefferson County courthouse would have to provide the venue for the trial of Reverend Edwin Stephenson for the murder of Father James E. Coyle, which would open on the morning of Monday, October 17, 1921. Since the start of the month, the morning air had been cool and dry, heralding the arrival of autumn, though by late afternoon on many days the temperatures still edged near or above eighty degrees, forcing the men and women of Birmingham to dress for two seasons at once. Some accomplished it better than others. One woman arrived at the courthouse with a dark fur stole draped over her shoulders, which she had pinned closed with a small bouquet of flowers. In the cool morning air, the wrap's warmth and opulence must have drawn some envious glances, but if not flung off by midafternoon, it would have drenched the poor lady in a pool of sweat.

Notwithstanding the unspoken "Sunday best" dress code, the courthouse was a circus. While the jury was being picked, deputies struggled to maintain order over the herd of men and women corralled just outside the courtroom doors. But the crowd grew restless and unruly, and after repeated failed attempts to quiet them, Judge Fort finally ordered the corridors cleared. The spectators would be permitted back inside the building only after the jury was chosen and the witnesses had been instructed, the bailiffs advised them.

Shortly after the shooting, Charles Sweeny, the freelance writer for the *Nation,* had exhorted his readers to follow the Stephenson trial closely, while placing some of the blame for Father Coyle's death on the shoulders of the pressmen who had permitted the toxic anti-Catholic atmosphere to exist without challenge. If journalistic neglect had been part of the problem in Birmingham before Coyle was shot, it was unapparent on the first morning of the trial of his killer. Birmingham reporters had to elbow for space with newsmen from outside the city, some of whom had traveled hundreds of miles to cover the long-anticipated trial. "Every newspaper agency of any prominence in the country had a special correspondent" there, and several newspapers sent staff reporters to attend the trial as well. Joseph Pulitzer's *New York World* dispatched a reporter to cover it in person, as did the *Macon News* of Georgia and Missouri's *New Menace.*[19]

To gain a slight advantage over its competitors, the *Birmingham News* arranged for its staff reporter, J. Fisher Rothermel, to record the proceedings with a "noiseless typewriter" provided by the Underwood Typewriter Company. Never before in the history of the state had such a sophisticated machine been used to cover a criminal trial, the paper boasted. "It would give the *Birmingham News* a distinct advantage," its editors thought, enabling Rothermel to transcribe the testimony "almost verbatim" without interfering with others' ability to hear what was being said. Rothermel set the typewriter up a few feet away from the lawyers.[20]

Sheriff Hartsfield's chief deputy, Fred McDuff, walked Stephenson, unhandcuffed, through the crowd and up to the broad wooden table where his lawyers had gathered. Two rectangular tables, with several chairs each, faced the empty jury box that stretched along the left wall of the courtroom, the nearest table reserved for the prosecutors, and behind that, one for the defense. The defendant appeared remarkably calm, chewing gum, staring absently at the ceiling, and giving his wife a reassuring pat on the arm. "Wearing a black coat with grey striped trousers, high collar and black ministerial tie, the defendant looked so confident, so refreshed after his stay in jail and so unworried that his appearance caused open comment," wrote a reporter for the *Birmingham Post*. Discordant peals of laughter wafted through the courtroom windows—the sound of Catholic schoolchildren at play behind St. Paul's rectory—in strangely joyous juxtaposition to the muted mood of the primarily Protestant audience that waited for the start of the trial of the man who had taken the life of the children's priest.[21]

Jefferson County had begun to prepare to select a jury for the trial of Edwin Stephenson a full two weeks in advance. The process of selecting the right group of deliberators (or more accurately, perhaps, avoiding the worst of the available choices) could be nerve-wracking. The names of well over one hundred registered voters had been selected from the Jefferson County rolls for jury duty. From that jury pool—known as the venire—the judge and the lawyers had to whittle the number down to just twelve men. After the pool of potential jurors was admitted to Judge Fort's courtroom, the bailiff called their names out loud until each was identified or determined missing. Women had won the right to vote the year before, but Stephenson's venire still remained all white and all male.[22]

Despite the advance planning, the entire morning and most of the afternoon were needed to complete the task of selecting the jury. Rules governing jury selection varied among court systems, but always the procedure involved putting a series of questions—called voir dire—to the men in the jury pool to determine whether they harbored any views or prejudices that would prevent them from deciding the case fairly. For that reason, the name of the process—"jury selection"—had always been a bit of a misnomer, as more often than not, the lawyers in the courtroom were less focused on whom to select than on whom to reject. Judges almost always began the questioning, though some courts permitted the lawyers to question the prospective jurors as well. But after conferring this allowance, many judges found it to be greatly time consuming—how the lawyers did go on!—and so a number of courts were led to ban the attorneys' participation, leaving the questioning in the hands of the judge alone. The criminal division of the Jefferson County Court appeared to be in that school.

Because juries were expected to be neutral arbiters of the facts, no person who revealed by his answers to the judge's questions that he could not be fair or impartial would be permitted to serve. For this reason, the number of prospective jurors the trial judge was authorized to strike from the pool—excusing them "for cause"—was unlimited. The total number of "for cause" strikes expanded or contracted with the number of men who had previously made up their minds about how the case should come out, which often correlated, in turn, with the prominence of the people involved in the dispute, or the notoriety of the case. The higher a case's profile, the longer it took to seat a jury. Judge Fort asked each prospective juror the same series of questions— "What is your occupation?" "Are you related to the defendant, or deceased, or any of the attorneys?" "Are you opposed to penitentiary punishment?" "Would you convict on circumstantial proof?" "Have you any interest, whatsoever, in the case?"—and if the man's answer suggested a potential cause for concern about his impartiality or intractability, the judge followed up with additional questions to probe it.

In addition to the judge's strikes, the lawyers were empowered to excuse a number of jurors as well. Each side was awarded a preset number of "peremptory challenges," which the parties could use to strike a worrisome prospective juror who had somehow survived the judge's "for cause" review. Selective frugality by trial lawyers in the use of their peremptory challenges was a time-honored tradition. With only a limited number of "peremptory challenges" each—in 1921, Jefferson County gave the prosecution seventeen and the defense thirty-four—it was not uncommon for lawyers to horde their own strikes, urging the judge to use his "for cause" authority instead, like the child who parts more easily with the pennies of his parent than his few precious own.

Before the trial began, the *Birmingham News* predicted a large number of men would be disqualified from the jury pool due to the great number of those in the city whose minds appeared made up about the morality of the shooting. But if the men in Stephenson's venire were predisposed to regard the case through a tainted lens, very few of them were prepared to admit it. Only seven of the seventy-one men questioned that morning gave replies that led Judge Fort to strike them "for cause": Edward H. Anderson, John C. Stapleton, and the farmer Dink McCormack, after admitting they were opposed to convicting a man on the basis of circumstantial evidence; and then John W. Webb, a merchant, P. C. Ratliff, an insurance agent, and S. P. Lacey, after confessing that their opinions about the case were already firmly fixed. A particularly improbable moment occurred when Fred Bender's name was called from out of the venire. The quiet in the room deepened as Judge Fort questioned the man who had become well known as the godfather of Ruth Gussman, and Bender's answers quickly put to rest any question about the matter of his ability to serve—his opinion about the shooting was indelibly fixed, Bender told the judge—and the furniture salesman who had helped Lige Loy's men lift Father Coyle's bloodied body onto their cot was excused "for cause."[23]

But considering that city residents had read about the headline story for months, a remarkably stout number of the prospective jurors claimed no dog in the fight and insisted they could be fair. By the end of the day, a total of sixty-four men had denied "any interest in the case whatsoever," a lack of self-weeding that left the attorneys the unenviable task of deciding which of them to believe. The papers did not publish the names of the men the lawyers struck off with their peremptory challenges, but the attorneys' strikes quickly evaporated. After hours of scrutiny, the first twelve men able to dodge both the judge's and the lawyers' strikes were moved into the jury box, and the remainder of the pool was excused.

As a group, the dozen survivors were noticeably young—"only one gray head in the bunch," one reporter wrote—though they represented a spectrum of professions and trades: Oscar J. Garrard, an auto mechanic; James A. Lay, Jr., a stenographer; Hubbard Stamps, a business manager; Charles M. G. Cheek, a printer; Robert G. McMahon, an agent for Birmingham-Southern College; P. A. Lappage, a traveling salesman; Ira Lollar, a farmer; H. F. Holley, a butcher; and four office clerks—Lucien E. Barr, C. R. Bitz, S. G. Lacy, and Ben P. Rogers.[24] It had taken the entire day to select them, and Judge Fort solemnly addressed the men before adjourning for the night. Their service was the very "test of good citizenship," he said—though it was a duty that would surely inconvenience them and even test their patience. To ensure that they were not tampered with, they would be housed at the Hillman Hotel for the duration of the trial, and "closely guarded to see that no one communicate[d] with [them] concerning the case," the judge told them, and as a rap of his gavel brought the proceeding to a close, the trial of Edwin Stephenson was at last under way.[25]

———

Judge William E. Fort was a stickler for order. When the trial of Edwin Stephenson began the next morning promptly at 9:30 A.M. before an overflowing crowd, he issued a warning to the men and women who had packed his courtroom: demonstrations of any kind would result in their ejection, he said. The audience had reason to think it no idle threat. A great number of would-be court watchers still jammed the corridor outside; no doubt many of them would have been pleased to win a seat yet, even if it meant the judge tossing one of their neighbors from the room.

The walls of the cavernous courtroom were drab, bare of any adornment, and the ceiling soared so high that the photographer from the Southern News Service who dared to snap a shot (and attracted a withering look from Judge Fort for his trouble) could not capture it. The jurors sat tucked into a corner along the left-hand wall at the front of the room, in three rows of four chairs each. The back two rows of chairs were positioned on narrow risers, stadium-style, so that their occupants could see above the heads of the men in front of them. Several industrial-looking light fixtures, painted white, hung from the ceiling like upside-down teacups on long metal rods. A large rectangular chalkboard, covered from edge to edge with dusty eraser marks, hung from the wall directly behind the jury box, as if the room's designer had not given a thought to how the lawyers would reach it or the jurors see it. A motley assortment of chairs—straight-backed, bow-backed, press-backed, and Windsors—filled every inch of vacant floor, maximizing the number of spectators, with the result that the voices of the witnesses and attorneys would easily have been lost whenever a spectator shifted in his or her seat, scraping a chair's legs against hard wood.

If there remained any uncertainty about the direction of Edwin Stephenson's defense, Hugo Black put it to rest in the opening seconds of the trial when the clerk called the case to order and Judge Fort asked for the defendant's plea. The minister's lead attorney rose from his chair: "The defendant pleads not guilty and not guilty by reason of insanity," Hugo Black said.

As it turned out, the real surprise of that day had nothing to do with the defendant's choice to add a claim of temporary insanity to his defense; the real surprise was how quickly the prosecution's "case-in-chief" was completed. In the weeks leading up to the trial, the names on the prosecution's witness list had multiplied, jumping from an original core of twenty-three to a final tally of seventy-four. The sheer number hinted that the prosecution's case would take some days to complete.[26]

The complement of the men from Joe Tate's office seated at the state's table suggested the same thing. Every one of the circuit solicitor's assistants had been given a role: Tate's top two men, John McCoy and John Morrow, would take the leading role in presenting the state's witnesses, though Tate planned to conduct some of the cross-examinations as well. His fourth assistant, James Davis, would assist them all by running interference and feeding them witnesses.

Because the prosecutors needed to prove the defendant's guilt beyond a reasonable doubt, Joe Tate and his men were entitled by law to call their witnesses first, in what was known as the prosecution's "case-in-chief." If there was a silver lining to the grand jury's decision to indict the minister for second-degree rather than first-degree murder, the lesser charge significantly reduced the amount of proof that would be needed to convict him. Alabama law defined second-degree murder as any homicide committed with "malice aforethought," removing the requirement to prove "premeditation" as well. In turn, "malice aforethought" could be shown with proof that Stephenson had *intended* to take the priest's life. In this case, where the victim had been killed with a "deadly weapon," an instruction would be given to the jury that stacked the odds in the prosecution's favor: the jury would be told that the law considered it fair to *presume* Stephenson had acted with "malice aforethought," and that if Stephenson failed to rebut that presumption with evidence of his own, the jury should convict.

This meant that Joe Tate and his assistants needed to prove two simple things—that Stephenson had caused Coyle's death, and that he had done it with a gun—and then the burden to come forward with evidence suggesting he had not intended to kill the priest shifted to Stephenson himself. Sometimes a defendant met that burden, perhaps by offering proof that his intent had been only to injure his victim, not to kill. But Father Coyle's wound had been a bullet to the head, making such a claim scarcely believable. And if for that reason Stephenson had essentially to concede that his intent had been to kill Coyle, to avoid being found guilty, his only remaining choice was to claim the act was justifiable (because in self-defense perhaps) or at least excusable (because the accused had no control over his faculties). But each of those claims demanded that Stephenson offer some proof in support of it as well, and the prosecutors were permitted to wait until he had done so before offering evidence in contradiction.

John McCoy understood all this, and from his first witness, he began laying the groundwork. The first step was to prove that Father James had died from a gunshot wound.

As Dr. James M. Mason took the stand in Judge Fort's courtroom, he may have wished he had been anywhere else than where he had been on the day Father Coyle was shot. On most afternoons, James Mason saw patients in his downtown office located in the Jefferson County Bank building. But on August 11, 1921, he had been the attending physician at St. Vincent's Hospital when two men from Lige Loy's ambulance company rushed the gurney carrying Father Coyle through the emergency entrance. Even in a city like Birmingham, where homicides still occurred with disturbing frequency, fatal bullet wounds were hard to forget. John Morrow quickly established that Dr. Mason remembered what had happened. Yes, he recalled it; it had been "just about dusk" when they wheeled the priest into the operating room. Yes, he saw wounds on Father Coyle's body.[27]

"Just describe those wounds to the jury, Doctor."

Dr. Mason turned to the jurors. "There were two wounds in his head, one just in the front of his left ear, just down in this position," he said gesturing with his hand, "and another one just about this position, in the back of his skull," he pointed, before turning back to John McCoy. What kind of a wound? "Bullet wound." Was he conscious or unconscious? "Unconscious." Did you operate? No, sir. Did he die? "He did, yes, sir." How many bullets did it take to create those two wounds? Just one. John McCoy shifted to the minister's claim that he had shot as the priest was attacking him: "Did you see any powder burns on Father Coyle?" "No, sir." "[A]nywhere around the bullet hole you mentioned a moment ago?" McCoy persisted. "No, sir, I looked and did not see any."

"In your judgment, was his death caused from that bullet wound?"

"Yes, sir."

It was all the prosecutor needed, and a little more besides. The doctor had established the cause of Father Coyle's death—one bullet, entering the left side of the priest's head and exiting the back of the skull—more than enough to trigger the deadly weapons doctrine that entitled the state to the helpful instruction to the jury that they could presume that Father Coyle's killer had acted with "malice aforethought." And the doctor's testimony that there were no powder burns on the priest physically refuted Stephenson's claim that he had fired in self-defense. With no gunshot residue to corroborate Stephenson's story that the priest had been bearing down on him, there was no reason to believe that the life-ending shot was necessary. McCoy turned the witness over to the defense for cross-examination.

A witness like Dr. James Mason put a defense attorney in a bind. Hugo Black had no intention of contesting that Stephenson's bullet had caused Coyle's death. Far more damaging was the part of the doctor's testimony that seemed to contradict his client's self-defense claim. "Did you probe that wound?" Hugo Black asked, rising to his feet. "No, sir." "Take an x-ray picture of it?" "Yes, sir." "Where is that picture?" "Back at St. Vincent's Hospital." Black pressed: "Did it show the path of the bullet?"

Dr. Mason did not miss the lawyer's implication—if more reliable photographic evidence of the priest's wound had been created, why would the prosecutor have the doctor testify about the injury from memory? But the open-ended question gave Mason a chance to refocus the jury's attention on the priest's dire condition: The picture is "very poor," he said, "on account of the restlessness of the patient, [his] vomiting and [our] inability to control him."

Black realized his mistake. "You did not probe it?" he asked again, back-peddling: "You do not *know* which direction it went?" "No, not absolutely, but I have a practical idea which way it went." Hugo Black knew better than to let the physician explain his conclusions. "I have no more questions," he said, and took his seat. But John McCoy was on his feet then, asking the doctor to give his judgment again about which direction the bullet had traveled; had it entered through the hole near the left temple or the one in the back of the skull? The bullet entered in the front of the left ear, and "the wound on the back of the skull was the exit," Mason replied with certainty. Why did you draw that conclusion? The hole in the back of Father Coyle's skull was "a little larger and more jagged"—a fact ordinarily consistent with an exit wound—"and some little particles of bones" around that hole "seemed to be turned out[ward]." Mason gestured again with his hands, painting more vividly the bullet's brutal debris, replicating the bullet's lethal path from front to back. Satisfied, the prosecutor had no further questions.

Neither did the defense. Hugo Black had been a trial lawyer for long enough to know to quit while he was behind.

With the cause of Father Coyle's death established—gunshot from a deadly weapon—John McCoy looked to his next witness to prove that Edwin Stephenson had inflicted that fatal wound. A deep quiet filled the room when the prosecutor called out the name "Marcella Coyle."

Father Coyle's sister wore all black, her only embellishment a "heavy veil," also in black, which cloaked her face and skimmed the graceful curve of her shoulders. The etiquette of wearing a mourning dress had been slowly changing in America, but in the early 1920s many women still wore them, for periods that varied with the nature of the bond they had shared with the deceased—most commonly, two years for widows, and one for sisters. The very sight of Marcella Coyle must have stirred the observers' sympathy. Even the man who had taken her brother's life seemed moved: Edwin Stephenson "did not look at her," the *Birmingham News* reported later.

"What is your name, please ma'am?" asked the prosecutor gently.

"Marcella Coyle."

"What relation were you to James E. Coyle?"

"His sister," she said.

McCoy took his witness back to the moment her brother was shot; sitting in the back of the house in Stella Caruthers's room; hearing a gun fire. How many shots? "Three shots," she said. Her voice must have dropped as she recalled it. McCoy asked if she could please talk just a little bit louder. What did she do when she heard the shots? She went to the front of the house, through the hall, and out the front door. "I saw a man standing in the yard." Yes, she could she identify him. Yes, she saw him in the courtroom. John McCoy walked over to Edwin Stephenson and pointed directly at him; Is this the man? Yes, "sitting right there, yes, sir," she said. She had first seen him while she was running up the hallway toward the front door. She saw him "go down the steps," and when she reached the porch she saw him walking through the yard toward the court-house. Did he have a gun? Marcella couldn't say. Where was her brother? "I saw him on the porch, lying"—she stopped midsentence. The prosecu-tor urged her to continue. "He was lying on the porch, just at the swing," she said finally. His feet were stretched out toward the flower box at the end of the porch nearest the church. His head was near the wall of the house.

John McCoy wanted the jurors to be able to picture it; where the swing was in relation to the steps where she had first seen Stephenson standing; how far away from each other the men must have been. He asked several questions to make sure that the jurors could understand the swing's placement, as well as other furniture on the porch. The swing was at the far end of the porch toward the church, she said. Next to it there was a rocking chair, and next to that a settee. Yes, there were windows looking out onto the porch—two, with blinds. Open or closed? Open; her brother was lying beneath one of them with his head in the direction of the courthouse. She had been the first to reach the porch.

"Did you see any blood there?" McCoy asked.

"No, sir," she answered.

It was a small blessing—other witnesses recalled a great deal of it. Either Marcella had arrived at the porch so quickly that the blood pooling beneath her brother's head was not yet visible or the woman's mind had simply refused to compute the worst of the realities of the scene enfolding before her. The prosecutor was almost done. He turned to Stephenson's story about a fight. Had she heard any sound before the shots? "No, sir."[28]

Cross-examining some witnesses can be an exercise fraught with peril, like playing to an inside straight. Just as the temptation to draw that last critical card can overpower one's assessment of the statistical odds of doing it, so, too, can the hope of leading a witness to make some important concession on the stand shroud the cross-examiner's chances as well. For this reason, perhaps especially when a lawyer is questioning a witness who evokes deep sympathy, the wisest approach is often to save one's thunder for a stronger hand.

Hugo Black understood this better than many members of the defense bar; he had no intention of letting Father Coyle's sister lead him down the garden path. He kept his questions streamlined. How far was your brother's head from the rectory door? She had not measured it, but she expected about "six or eight feet," she said; "probably a little more." No help—the reply situated the fallen priest quite a distance from where she had seen Stephenson standing after hearing the shots. The man who shot her brother was already walking away, correct? Yes, he "was leaving, going down the steps." Hugo Black pivoted, focusing on Marcella's distance from the porch, too far away to enable her to hear the fight, he hoped to argue: "This room you were in, was back in the back of the house?" "Yes, sir." "How far is that from the front porch, Miss Coyle?" She couldn't say precisely—"the full length of the house." How many rooms away from the porch?—laying the groundwork for the argument that the women had been too far away to hear the scuffle. "Four." Black echoed her answer: "Four rooms between you and the front porch?" "Yes, sir." How wide were those rooms? She did not know the exact dimension, she replied. Black tried to supply a reason for her failure to consider such things: She was preoccupied? "You were back there talking to Miss Caruthers?" Marcella corrected him: "No, I was back there reading." Stung, Hugo Black grasped for a strong way to end: "Of course when you came out, you did not look accurately at everything that was on the porch," he ventured, "you were troubled, you were excited?" "I remember distinctly—" Marcella started to contradict him again, but this time Hugo Black cut her off, revising his question to focus solely on the tumultuousness of the moment: "You were excited, wasn't you, Miss Coyle?"

It is not hard to imagine the steel in Marcella's voice as Black walked back to his seat: "Naturally," she said.[29]

John McCoy had no intention of conceding that there could have been a fight between Stephenson and Coyle that Marcella Coyle and Stella Caruthers had failed to hear, but he was prepared to hedge the point. For even if Coyle had been besting Stephenson in a fight, the law of self-defense did not condone a man's use of fatal force to protect against nonfatal force. Shooting the priest would only have been justifiable self-defense if the priest had been threatening the minister with death or serious bodily injury, and there was scant reason to think it. On redirect examination of Marcella Coyle, McCoy asked his witness about her brother's age and physical stature. He was forty-eight years old, about "five feet nine inches," and "between 155 and [1]60."

Judge Fort interjected, asking for clarification about the position of her brother's body on the porch then, and as John McCoy took Marcella slowly through a description of the position of the rectory relative to St. Paul's Church, and its location on Third Avenue, Joe Tate moved to the blackboard behind the jury box, where he sketched the buildings and the body's position on the porch as Marcella answered each of McCoy's questions: This is the church? "Yes, sir." This is the rectory? "Yes, sir." This is the avenue out in front? "Yes, sir." And this is the porch of the rectory? "Yes, sir." Where on Mr. Tate's chalked diagram was the door to the porch located? McCoy asked. On the far end of the porch, she said, the end farthest away from the church and the porch swing. Nearest the courthouse? the prosecutor clarified; "right about here?"—gesturing so that the jurors could follow the testimony. "Yes, sir," she said again, and then pointed out the position of the other furniture: the settee and two chairs. And where was your brother's body? McCoy asked again. Marcella repeated that his feet were near the swing, and that he had fallen behind one of the chairs, up against the porch wall—some distance away from where she had seen Stephenson standing. John McCoy was satisfied. He had no other questions for the witness, he told the judge, and Marcella Coyle was excused.

———

John McCoy called William D. Chiles as his next witness, the miner who had spent August 11, 1921, trudging the streets of the city with his brother-in-law, Edward McGinty, looking for work. The courtroom quieted as Chiles made his way to the stand. The man was young, only twenty-five, but he walked with a noticeable limp; his hair was blond, and he wore a soft-collared shirt with no tie, as if understanding that the formality of the trial required respectful attire but having few items in his wardrobe by which to oblige. Unlike Dr. Mason and Marcella Coyle, neither Chiles nor McGinty had testified at the preliminary hearing. Joe Tate had taken their secret grand jury testimony days after the preliminary hearing was over. So unless Hugo Black had a mole on the grand jury, the defense team could only guess about what Chiles would say.[30]

A few weeks before the start of Stephenson's trial, Chiles had succeeded in finding work, but it had required him to leave Alabama and move to

Bicknell, Indiana. Joe Tate's subpoena had tracked him down, demanding his return and presence at the minister's trial. John McCoy brought Chiles back to the moment he had heard the shots. He and his brother-in-law had been standing in front of the courthouse "about twenty-five feet away" from the rectory yard, watching a man trying to crank his car, when he heard the first shot, Chiles said. Where precisely, relative to the rectory? asked McCoy. Near the iron railing that wrapped around the front of the courthouse. Facing which way? Toward the rectory, said Chiles, he had looked up toward the sound after the first shot was fired.

"How many shots did you hear fired?"

"Three."

What happened then? McCoy asked

"Mr. Stephenson stood there," said Chiles, "looked to me like between two and three seconds," though he could not "say positive" exactly how long. "[T]hen he turned and walked off."

John McCoy asked Chiles if he had actually seen Stephenson on the porch.

"I saw his back, yes, sir."

"What position was he in?"

"He was standing up," Chiles said: "He was facing that way," Chiles gestured away from himself.

"Toward the church?"

"Toward the church, yes, sir."

"And he was standing up?" McCoy asked again—knowing what Chiles would say; knowing that it would contradict Stephenson's claim of a fight; that he had been knocked to his knees. "He was standing up, yes, sir," Chiles confirmed.

What then? asked McCoy. After firing three times, Stephenson had stood there for two or three seconds, then he "turned around" toward Chiles and Edward, and walked "toward the courthouse," Chiles said. No, he hadn't seen him shoot the first shot, but he had looked up then. "I was looking at him when he fired the last two shots." No, he had not seen anybody else on the porch, nor anyone near Stephenson when he fired his last shots. "No, sir, I didn't see no one."

The prosecutor had no other questions. He handed Chiles over to the defense.

Unlike the grieving sister of Father Coyle, there was nothing about William D. Chiles that called for gentle examination. Chiles was young, and no doubt fit from years of hard work in the coal mines, though probably he was also illiterate; like many other men, when Chiles had registered for the draft before the Great War, he signed the card with a simple X. Without being privy to the testimony Chiles and McGinty had given before the grand jury, Hugo Black was flying cold. He picked up where John McCoy had left off, asking Chiles if he could see the swing on the rectory porch when he heard the shots. "If I had paid any close attention I may have could have seen a corner of it," Chiles replied, a little too defensively. "You were not looking to see what he was shooting at?" "No, sir, I wasn't studying about what he was shooting at." "You stood and watched a man shoot on a front porch, and did not look to see whether he was shooting at a man or a dog?" "No, sir."

The lawyer switched gears. "You say you live in Indiana now?" "Certainly do." "What part of Indiana?" The court reporter thought he heard Chiles answer "Bickner, Indiana," but almost certainly the miner had said "Bicknell." The residents of Bicknell numbered only around four thousand at the time, but half of them were men like Chiles who worked the twenty or so mines open for business in the area. One of the mines had hired Chiles to load coal. "You came all the way from Indiana down here?" Black asked. "I did." "Who paid your expenses?" "I paid my own fare." "Who is going to pay them back to you?"

The prosecutors should have prepared W. D. Chiles for this kind of examination, but judging from his answers, they probably had not gotten around to it. A witness could be put on the defensive by such questions, designed to suggest that there was something shifty about a man being reimbursed for the costs of his travel to and from a trial. "I don't know," Chiles said vaguely. "Anybody promise to?" "Not that I know of."

Hugo Black had gotten lucky. As a former county prosecutor himself, he could guess that Joe Tate's men would have arranged to pay Chiles's expenses. There was nothing wrong with that. But witnesses frequently got themselves into trouble by thinking they should deny it, probably because questions about such things hinted that they were being bought off to testify in the way they were. "You mean to tell the jury you came all the way from Indiana down here without anybody promising to pay your expenses?" Black scoffed. "I paid my expenses," Chiles answered, digging in. "And you just came down here and paid your fare and don't expect to get it back from anybody?" "I may get it back." "Well, from whom?" "I don't know." Hugo Black repeated the question; "or is your mind blank about that?" "The State promised me," Chiles said, finally: he had received a telegraph summoning him to the trial with a promise that his expenses would be repaid.

Hugo Black shifted focus, wanting to suggest another reason for Chiles's willingness to return to Birmingham to testify besides money. "Your brother-in-law is Edward McGinty?" "That is correct." "Where does Mr. Edward

McGinty live?" "Pratt City." "Mr. Edward McGinty was standing there with you?" "Yes, sir." "Did you marry his sister?" "I certainly did," Chiles replied, his tone slightly defiant, as if sensing what was coming. "Do you belong to the Catholic Church?" "I do not." "She does?" "Yes, sir." "Does *Mr. Edward McGinty* belong to it?" "Yes, sir."

Hugo Black let the man's answers speak for themselves. Chiles may not have been Catholic himself, but he had *married* one. How credible could he or "*Mr. Edward McGinty*" be? Whose side in the case could the jurors expect Chiles to take, when he had done the same thing Ruth Stephenson had done—married outside of her faith; married a Catholic?[31]

Hugo Black switched gears again, firing a series of questions at Chiles about the day of the shooting. What had he and Edward done that day? Where had they been? What were they doing in the city on a workday, instead of being at work?—questions designed to paint Chiles and McGinty as shiftless, lazy, irresponsible, maybe even drunk. "Did you work that day?" "No, I didn't work that day." "Where were you that morning?" Chiles said he couldn't recall. "Were you at home?" "I might have been home for a while." "What time did you leave home?" "I don't know." "Where did you go?" "I come to town." "When? In the morning or afternoon?" "Sometime in the afternoon." "Where were you in the morning?" "I don't remember where I was at in the morning," Chiles shot back.

"Were you sober?" Hugo Black "fairly bellowed" the question, one reporter remembered later, causing the witness to redden.

"I reckon I was," Chiles replied, icily.

"Can't you tell the jury *something* about where you were that morning?" "Walking around town here," Chiles answered, plainly growing exasperated. "You are sure about that now?" "I wouldn't say for sure, but I was around town." "All you really know about it is you were *living* somewhere that morning?" Hugo Black asked, sarcastically. "I wasn't dead," Chiles fired back. "Were you asleep?" "No, I had one eye open any how." Well, "what place in Jefferson County was that eye looking at?" taunted the lawyer. "A ripple of laughter ran through the courtroom" as Judge Fort gaveled for quiet.

"Is your mind blank, entirely blank from the time you and Mr. McGinty left home in the morning until you were standing in front of the courthouse at six o'clock?" Hugo Black continued to pummel Chiles. "Can you tell the jury one single, solitary place under the shining sun that you were between the time in the morning you and Mr. McGinty are said to have left home, until you say you and Mr. McGinty stood and looked at the shooting?" Chiles could only say that they had caught the streetcar at "the Bottoms," which had brought them into the city. They had been searching for a man named McCormick who worked as a taxi driver in town, and sometimes parked his car on Third Avenue near the courthouse, in the hope of fares.

Finally, Hugo Black turned to the moment Chiles heard the shots from the rectory porch from where he stood near the courthouse. He asked Chiles how he just happened to be looking at the porch when the shooting began. "Just happened [to]," replied Chiles. "Just accidently, at the opportune moment, when the car cranked you were looking up on this porch?" Chiles said he had seen Stephenson at the steps of the porch before the car cranked, and that he had looked back at the porch again after hearing gun fire. Black knew better than to go back over what Chiles said he saw.

After the shooting, "you and McGinty went home?" "Shortly after," Chiles said. But his answer was vague, as if the miner was purposely holding something back. The lawyer bit, probably hoping to trap Chiles into making more inane statements about his and Edward's traipsing around that day. "How long after?" demanded Black. A half hour, maybe forty-five minutes. "What were you doing *that* time?"

It was a blunder—the trial lawyer's cardinal sin: asking a witness a question not knowing how he would answer. We were "at the priest's house," Chiles answered. The prosecutors must have sat a little taller in their chairs. John McCoy had not asked Chiles on direct examination what he and Edward McGinty had done after the shooting. McCoy may have been as in the dark as Hugo Black about his witness would say next. "You went there?" Hugo Black asked. (Another mistake.) Yes, I was the second one to reach the porch. Who was the first? Black asked skeptically. Chiles said he did not know the man's name. "What did he do?" (Strike three.) "When he walked up on the porch and saw the undertaker coming, he picked up a chair and throwed it out."

The prosecutors must have felt like hooting out loud! And Hugo Black's next question only made matter worse—another cardinal sin: asking the witness to repeat something that could only hurt, not help: "*What* did he do?" "He threw the chair outside for the undertakers to get in." Chiles seemed completely unaware that every time he referred to Lige Loy's men he used the word "undertaker" instead of "ambulance drivers," even though the priest had still been alive at the moment Chiles was describing. Probably it seemed a trifling distinction with the priest so near death. "Which chair?" Hugo Black demanded, trying to trip Chiles up, but the miner said he did not know. "Rocking chair, or straight chair?" "It looked like a rocking chair to me." "How many chairs did he throw out?" "Throwed one," Chiles replied with certainty.

Finally Hugo Black changed the subject, but the damage was done. Chiles had just undercut Stephenson's self-defense claim by testifying that the chair from the porch that others had seen lying in the yard had been tossed off *after* the shooting by someone trying to help the priest, not *during* some purported fight between Stephenson and Coyle. The only thing to do was to hope that the jury would reject the recollection of a man who could remember thrown chairs but not where he had been that day; a man who would marry a Catholic. Black turned back to the most fruitful part of his cross-examination, before taking his seat: "[S]ince you have had time to reflect, just as a last question, can you tell the jury where you and *Mr. Edward McGinty* were on the morning of the killing?" Chiles said again that he could not recall.

Edward McGinty took the stand next, and a reporter for the *Birmingham Post* later described the man's appearance: the miner wore a dark grey sweater coat, "hung carelessly open" the newsman thought, over "a striped shirt and a short blue tie," which he had "tucked into his bosom." He appeared to be around age twenty-five, with a "swarthy" complexion and "bushy hair." John McCoy quickly put McGinty through his paces, establishing that he lived in nearby Pratt City, worked as a coal miner, and could remember the day Father Coyle was shot. He and his brother-in-law were standing in front of the courthouse when he heard the first shot. It was coming from the parsonage. McGinty then repeated the story his brother-in-law had given: after hearing gunfire, he saw a man with his back turned toward him; the man was standing upright on the rectory porch; he fired two more shots, but McGinty could not tell at what or whom; he stood for a couple of seconds looking down at the floorboards of the porch before turning and walking toward the courthouse. It was all the prosecutor needed. McCoy handed McGinty over to Hugo Black.

The defense lawyer had been rudderless with Chiles, but not so with Edward McGinty. Chiles had mentioned during his testimony that he could recall the time of the shooting because he had looked up at the courthouse clock and noticed that it was around twenty minutes to seven. When McGinty gave the same explanation almost word for word, their testimony sounded rehearsed. "Did you and Chiles look up at it together by agreement?" asked Hugo Black. McGinty murmured something about Chiles asking him what time it was, so he had checked to see, and then told his brother-in-law the time, and Black pounced on the discrepancy: then Chiles had not looked at the clock himself? McGinty must have realized he was caught: "I don't think he did," he stammered, "he may have turned—"

It was a little thing—which one of them, Chiles or McGinty, had looked at the clock—and it made no difference to any important issue in the case.

But a talented defense lawyer could sometimes construct an argument out of a little thing—by pointing out, perhaps, that a witness who would shave the truth about the little things, after swearing an oath to tell the *whole* truth, certainly could not be trusted about the really big things. Not when a man's liberty was at stake.

As he had done with Chiles, Hugo Black tormented McGinty with a flurry of questions about what the two men had done in the city that day. When exactly had they left their home in Pratt City? How long after breakfast had they left to go to town? And when McGinty couldn't be sure: "As much as an hour?" "As much as two hours?" "Three?" "Four?" "As much as five?" Until McGinty tired of the pummeling and guessed that, yes, it was as much as five. "That is as close as you can get to it?" Black started in on him again. Where precisely had they gone? "Could you say where you were between seven and eight?" "At home, I guess," said McGinty, weakly. "Could you say where you were between eight and nine?" "No, sir." "Could you say where you were between nine and ten?" "No, sir." And on it went, until the man said that sometime around noon he remembered hanging around the courthouse on the lookout for the taxi driver McCormick. But where had they been before that? Black started back in again.

The lawyer was relentless, bearing down on McGinty, wearing him down, until finally demanding to know what the two had *really* been up to that day—"Is there anything secret about it?"—"Did you all play pool that morning?" "No, sir," McGinty protested. "Did you all take a drink?" McGinty denied it: "Mr Chiles took a drink of water or Coca-Cola on Fifth Avenue—" *Where was that?* The witness could not say for sure, and the battering began anew: "Whose place was it?" What place on Fifth Avenue? Was it below Twentieth Street? Above Twenty-first? How many drinks had they stopped for? Where had they stopped besides Fifth Avenue? "I don't know," McGinty said again and again, until it seemed that he could not remember anything they had done that day, or anywhere they had been.

On redirect examination, John McCoy asked McGinty about the tossed chair Hugo Black had stumbled over while questioning Chiles but then had conspicuously avoided asking McGinty anything about. McGinty confirmed that he, too, had seen a man throw a chair off the porch to get at the fallen priest. But on recross, Black ignored the topic of the chair and once again brought the focus back to the man's lack of recall about his and Chile's movements that morning, until the exasperated witness said, "I don't know where I was that morning!"

"And you were not drinking?" Black retorted.

"No, sir."

Black flung his last question at the man like a knife: "You are a Catholic, aren't you, Mr. McGinty?" As if being Catholic and drinking in the middle of a work day went together.

McGinty did not flinch: "Yes, sir."

The prosecution's last witness for the day, James F. Greer, put to bed the question of who threw the chair from the rectory porch—Greer said he had done it. He had been walking along Twenty-second Street, and was about a block away from the rectory when he heard the shots, said Greer. He started running toward the porch as soon as the firing stopped, and when he saw Father Coyle on the floorboards and heard the ambulance coming, he "moved a chair off of the porch" to clear a path for them. First he had tried to hand it to someone, he said, but when they wouldn't take it, he just "dropped it in the yard," so the ambulance workers could get at the priest. After the ambulance workers carried Father Coyle off, Greer noticed Father Coyle's hat lying undisturbed in the swing on top of some papers "in an orderly manner." McCoy asked what he meant by "orderly manner." Unscattered, "like they had been arranged," Greer said; it "did not look like they had been moved at all." Was the other furniture on the porch in an orderly state as well? "Yes, sir."

Hugo Black must have decided little was to be gained from questioning Greer about moving the chair. Some witnesses are better approached by innuendo; planting seeds of mistrust about who they are as people, in order to argue later that what they have said is not to be trusted. Maybe by emphasizing the circle of people with whom they associated. You recognized Fred Bender? Black asked. "Yes, sir." "Who else did you recognize?" Mr. McGough, from his bakery, and Father Coyle's housekeeper. "You knew her, did you?" He had seen her before at the rectory. "Had you been to the house before?" "Yes, sir." "How many times?" Greer couldn't say exactly. "I have been going over there ever since I was about ten or eleven years old." "You belong to that church?" "You have been going to this church ever since you were about eleven?" James Greer confirmed it again: "Yes, sir." Black must have concluded that the concession was all he needed; Greer was excused.

When Greer's testimony concluded at around 11:30 A.M. on the first day of testimony, John McCoy announced to Judge Fort that the state rested its case-in-chief, and would reserve all other of its witnesses for its rebuttal case, following whatever case the defense chose to offer. The announcement could not have been a bigger surprise. Only five witnesses! And with no hint of the girl at the heart of the case, Ruth Stephenson!

The spectators were not the only ones taken off guard. When Judge Fort turned to Hugo Black and asked if the defense was ready to call its witnesses, it was apparent that the lawyer had not prepared for this possibility. He needed more time to coordinate his witnesses, Black said. Judge Fort issued an order that all persons who had been subpoenaed by the defense who were present in the courthouse be ushered into the empty grand jury room to meet with Hugo Black and the defense team, before rapping his gavel against the wooded bench and declaring that the trial of Edwin Stephenson would resume at two o'clock that afternoon.[32]

| Shadowboxing

THE OLD WORRIES were back. When it took all of the prosecutors' witnesses less time to testify in its case-in-chief than it had taken the parties to seat the jury, some in Birmingham again began to doubt that the state wanted to see Edwin Stephenson convicted. Resting its case without calling the minister's daughter? Everyone knew that the girl's name had been included on the state's witness list, and although in the days just before the start of the trial the papers had printed Tate's warnings that he might not call her in the end, few must have taken him seriously. How could the prosecutor win his case without her? The prosecutor's pretrial reserve about calling Ruth, therefore, had struck most as mere subterfuge—a harmless attempt to hide the ball—and although the newsmen had not actually seen the girl back in Birmingham, the *Age-Herald* had publicized a rumor the day before the trial began that, despite previous reports to the contrary, "Mrs. Ruth Gussman, daughter of the accused minister, had been seen alighting from a southbound train in the outlying suburbs of the city."[1]

The decision to rest the case so quickly was so confounding that it seemed to sway the way some of the reporters graded how the prosecutors' witnesses had fared on the stand. The reviews of the state's decision and the performance of its witnesses were decidedly underwhelming: The "[c]losing of the case set a speed record for important criminal cases," one paper wrote, before highlighting Hugo Black's successes on his cross-examination. Black showed that Miss Marcella Coyle had been in the *back* of the house where she might have been unable to hear a brawl involving her brother, the paper reported, and that Mr. W. D. Chiles was unable to remember where he and his brother-in-law had been "up to a few minutes before the shooting."[2]

There was another way to regard the brevity of the state's case-in-chief. Combined, the state's five spare witnesses supplied a casebook example of how streamlined a prosecutor's proof of second-degree murder could be. Once the grand jury chose to indict Stephenson for second- rather than first-degree murder, to convict him, the prosecutors needed only to offer sufficient proof that he had killed the priest intentionally, rather than with premeditation. The combined testimony of Dr. Mason, Marcella Coyle, William Chiles, Edward McGinty and James Greer easily provided that: Mason proved that a bullet had caused Coyle's death; Marcella Coyle identified Stephenson as the shooter; Chiles and McGinty identified him as well. Because Stephenson had caused the priest's death with a gun, the jury would be instructed that they could presume from that fact alone that the defendant had intended to kill Coyle. As for the minister's claim of self defense, every one of the prosecution's witnesses had belied it: Mason had observed no powder burns on the victim, indicating that the two men were some distance apart when the gun discharged and among Marcella Coyle, Chiles, and McGinty—the people who had been closest to the scene—not one of them had heard sounds of the claimed fight. Greer undercut that claim even more by taking credit for the tossed chair. Check, checkmate.

The most plausible explanation for the newsmen's negative reviews of Tate's case, therefore, was that Hugo Black's insinuations while cross-examining witnesses like Chiles, McGinty, and Greer—Your wife "belongs to the Catholic church, Mr. Chiles? "You are a Catholic, aren't you, Mr. McGinty?" "You have been knowing [Father Coyle] ever since you were eleven years old," Mr. Greer?—influenced the newsmen's assessments of the witnesses, just as Black hoped they would influence the twelve jurors. Each of the state's witnesses was either Catholic (Marcella, McGinty, Greer) or closely associated with the Catholics (Chiles and Mason, who worked at the Catholic hospital). The unspoken accusation was clear: all of the state's witnesses were biased in favor of the Catholic priest and against the Protestant minister.[3]

––––––

Most of the spectators in Judge Fort's courtroom that afternoon probably did not realize how rare it was for a criminal defendant to call trial witnesses. Criminal defendants were entitled to sit silently—to force the state to prove the charges it had leveled against them—and most defendants were content to do that. Especially after their lawyers schooled them about how witnesses could blow up on the stand; how defendants testifying in their own defense frequently provided the prosecutors with exactly what they needed to convict; and that they had a right to remain silent at trial instead.

But some trials made it difficult for an accused not to offer at least some evidence in answer to the prosecution's proof, such as where the defendant claimed self-defense, or temporary insanity, or in Stephenson's case, both. In such cases, the defense was expected to present something in support of its claim before the state was obligated to rebut it.

Still, if the spectators at Edwin Stephenson's trial were expecting fireworks at the start of the defense case, they must have been disappointed. "Character witnesses" for the minister filled the remaining hours of that day, and much of the next as well—the kind of testimony almost guaranteed to lull a weary jury to sleep if the attorneys failed to liven things up. The testimony of character witnesses could be excruciatingly formulaic: *Do you know the defendant, sir? Yes, I do. How long have you known him? I've known him for twenty years. Are you familiar with his reputation in the community? Yes, I am. What is that reputation, sir, if you please? Why, his reputation is good—or peaceable, or law-abiding, or honest and upright:* whatever quality the defense most wanted the jury to believe the accused possessed; whatever characteristic that seemed most at odds with the criminal behavior the prosecutor had alleged. Because such testimony was fairly predictable, it was also rarely riveting. Its value was also strikingly limited, for almost always the character witness was placed in a no-win bind: if a witness said she knew that the accused's reputation in the community was good, almost invariably the prosecutor would ask questions that raised doubts about how familiar she could actually have been with the man's reputation—*did you know that complaints had been made that the defendant beat his wife?*—and if the witness stuck to her guns, claiming not to believe such slurs or slanders, the attorney could calmly ask if the witness's good regard for the defendant's reputation would change if such dishonorable acts were proved to be true. It was a trap. If the character witness said yes, her testimony amounted to little more than a *hope* that the accused would turn out to be as good she fancied him to be. If she stubbornly said no, that her good opinion of him would not change no matter what disreputable acts he was proved to have committed, her own credibility as a reliable judge of character would in the process be irreparably marred.

Despite these pitfalls, Stephenson's defense team must have decided that wrapping the minister in a blanket of proclamations about his good and decent character was worth the trouble and risk, for over the first two days of the defense's case, the great bulk of the witnesses called by Hugo Black were men and women of this variety: J. H. Rogers, a sales clerk in a hardware store in Talladega, who had known Stephenson for a decade or more; O. F. Staples, who had known the defendant for fifteen years, and had known his parents too; J. H. Burgess, a farmer from Cedartown, Georgia, who had known him before he relocated his family to Birmingham; J. N. Day, a train engineer from Heflin; J. L. York, an electrical engineer from North Birmingham; W. I. Morgan, an employee of the C. N. Boyd Perfume Company; E. M. Blanton, an undertaker; F. A. Farabee, a traveling salesman; J. C. Moore, a locomotive engineer; T. J. Williamson, a barber; two brothers, W. O. Watkins and D. O. Watkins, the secretary and president of the Birmingham Laundry, and more.[4] Hugo Black asked each of them in turn: Did you know his reputation in the community? Have an opinion about his character? Yes, Edwin Stephenson's character was good, they all said. No, they had never heard anything against him.

But, as occurs so often with character witnesses, none of them had any knowledge of the events that transpired between the priest and the minister on the rectory porch on August 11, so the force of their testimony was significantly diluted. When it was his turn, the superintendent of schools in nearby Heflin, Mr. G. B. Bowman, testified that he had known Stephenson for about twenty-five years, since before Edwin, Mary and Ruth had moved from Cedartown, Georgia (the village that had exacted its revenge on the Negro James Glover for his alleged assault on the daughter of Abner Reeves in 1904). On cross-examination, John Morrow, who took the lead in responding to the defense's witnesses, got Bowman to admit that he had not seen Stephenson "but once or twice a year" since the defendant had moved, and that Bowman could not say how the minister's neighbors regarded him in Birmingham. "You don't know they all say he is a thief, do you? That he stole some money from the barber's union?" Morrow asked Bowman. "No, sir—" "You don't know that he made his living by hanging around the courthouse here and marrying people, did you?" Bowman could say only that he had heard that Stephenson sometimes married people there, but not that "he made his living that way."[5]

So too Reverend Powell of the M.E.C., North took the stand to vouch for his parishioner's character as well, but John Morrow seized the chance to ask the minister about something he had heard about the defendant that was not so becoming: "Didn't you know or hear that Dr. Echols, the presiding elder in this district in the Methodist Episcopal Church South, came down and demanded his license because he was conducting himself in such a way as to disgrace the ministry?" Powell appeared taken off guard, enabling Morrow to back him into a series of disclaimers: no, he had not heard that, not until after the shooting, he said. And no, he did not know the reason Stephenson had left the M.E.C., South; there was something about "objections to his marrying folk—" No, he had never heard that Stephenson had been expelled from the barber's union for embezzling money. No, he had not known that some officials in the courthouse considered him a bit of a vagrant for his antics there. No, no, no. It is not hard to picture Powell's discomfort. He had agreed to testify on Stephenson's behalf—he was after all a member of Powell's church—but the line Powell was walking must have felt treacherous. It would not do to jeopardize the M.E.C., North's reputation, or to besmirch the good names of its other congregants.[6]

On redirect, Hugo Black tried to throw the preacher a lifeline, stressing that Joe Tate and John Morrow were the ones who carried the responsibility of charging a man with embezzlement or of vagrancy if they had the evidence to prove it. But that only gave Morrow on recross reason to linger a bit longer on the spectacle of the defendant turning the courthouse into a marriage mill, until Powell was forced to say that he had heard that part of the objections to Stephenson's wedding practices were based on the suspicion that his pastoral credentials were not even sufficient under the rules of the M.E.C. to empower him to perform such rites—that he had not actually ever been formally ordained! By the time Powell stepped down, the defense must have regretted calling him.[7]

Occasionally one of the character witnesses was able to refute with greater specificity one of the state's allegations against the minister. Mrs. L. W. Adkinson testified that she had lived with the Stephenson family from June of that year until a few days before the shooting and that she had never seen the minister mistreat his daughter—"Ruth was treated better than any girl she had ever seen." And W. R. Sulzer, a family friend, testified that he had known the defendant since 1909 and had visited with the family at their home many times, and had never seen any evidence that the girl had been beaten. But on cross, John Morrow chipped away at how sure the witnesses could be that the girl had *not* been beaten, establishing that Mrs. Adkinson had not lived with the family during the period when the minister's most brutal beatings of the girl were believed to have occurred—in mid-May, after he learned of Ruth's secret conversion to Catholicism—or when she was younger, when the family lived on Third Avenue, and Ruth first displayed her interest in Coyle's church; or when she had committed some other infraction: "Do you know whether or not he whipped his daughter last winter because she stayed out after 9:30?" asked John Morrow. "No sir, I do not," Sulzer reluctantly admitted. "Do you know whether or not, on the fifteenth day of May of this past year, he tied that girl to a bedpost and beat her with a razor strap?" "No sir, I do not." And so it went.[8]

The official witnesses did better. Joe Tate and his men had not called a single member of the police force in their truncated case-in-chief, but Hugo Black called six: three from the Birmingham Police Department—Officers

Jake F. McGill, R. G. Patton, and Henry H. Weir; and another three from the sheriff's office: Chief Deputy Fred McDuff and deputies Steve Wiggins and R. E. Smith. The fact that it was the defense, not the state, that called the officers and deputies to the stand spoke volumes about the unusual alliances afflicting the prosecution's case. The men whose job it was to gather criminal evidence normally helped to prove, not disprove, an accused's guilt. But as with so many other aspects of the case against Edwin Stephenson, up was down, and down was up.

The way the defense was using the lawmen was also a surprise. It quickly became apparent that Hugo Black was relying on them to lend support to Stephenson's claim that he had been rendered temporarily insane at the time that he shot Father Coyle—his normal mental faculties momentarily suspended by years of Catholic torment. John Morrow repeatedly protested that the lawmen were no experts in the study of the human mind; they were entirely unqualified to offer an opinion on the question of Stephenson's sanity, the prosecutor argued. But Judge Fort permitted them to testify anyway, equating worry with delirium, anxiety with madness— "an unsound mind is an abnormal mind," the judge said, overruling the objections—until over the next two days of testimony, Hugo Black had elicited from the officers and others a mountain of statements about what they had noticed about Stephenson's increasingly agitated state over his daughter, and what they knew about the tumult within the Stephenson household over Ruth's defiance of her parents' wishes, and its effect on Edwin Stephenson on August 11. On the day of the shooting, Stephenson "was very nervous, and wrought up considerably," said Officer McGill. "He talked very brokenly, and sometimes would break down and cry while he was talking," added a family friend, S. E. Willoughby—"very much broken up about the matter and disturbed."[9]

Unable to get the judge to exclude the laypersons' assessments of Stephenson's mental health, John Morrow did his best to undermine the testimony, asking each man whether he was prepared to swear that Edwin Stephenson was actually *insane* when he shot the priest. But the witnesses responded in largely the same way each time: "Well, I can't say about that," Jake McGill said, but "he was very excited" when he arrived at the police station and asked for help finding his daughter. "You didn't think that he was insane?" Morrow shot back. "Well, I couldn't answer that question," McGill said, "I just knew he was very wrought up."

"He seemed worried and excited," Deputy McDuff echoed.

"You don't think he was crazy, did you?" Morrow pushed again.

No, McDuff admitted, "I could not say that he was."

And after Deputy Wiggins told the jury about how distraught both Edwin and Mary Stephenson had been when they arrived at the sheriff's office that day, a skeptical John Morrow pushed him too: "Was he acting like a crazy man?"

"I am not the judge of crazy people," Wiggins tried to dodge.

Did you *think* he was insane? Morrow shot back.

"I did not," the deputy finally conceded.[10]

Yet despite the defense's inability to find a single witness who could state with any real authority that Edwin Stephenson was actually mentally ill at the moment he shot the priest, the loose way Judge Fort permitted the defense witnesses to testify about the minister's "abnormal," "excited," or "worried" state of mind created the misimpression that the law of Alabama considered such agitated emotions to be enough.

———

When Hugo Black called Mary Stephenson to the stand later that day, little question could have remained that the lawyer intended to put the Catholic Church itself on trial. He moved quickly through the preliminaries—was she the defendant's wife? How long had they been married? How many children did they have? How old was Ruth "at the time of this trouble?"—and reached the crux of the case in a matter of seconds.

"What church do you belong to, Mrs. Stephenson?"

"Methodist."

"Have you ever belonged to the Catholic?"

"No, sir."

"So far as you know, have any of your people ever belonged to the Catholic?"

"No, sir."

Black asked if she and her husband Edwin had been having trouble with their daughter Ruth over the question of religion. They had, Mary Stephenson said, and she told the jury about having to enlist the help of Police Chief Shirley to get the girl back from Fred Bender's house; about taking Ruth away to Texas to visit family, and her escape from the train at Texarkana on the way back home. "Where did you find her?"

"Found her in a Catholic hospital," came Mary Stephenson's terse reply.

Black turned to the day of the shooting and asked how she and Edwin had come to know that their daughter was missing again. A friend had called their home from the department store where Ruth was working at the time and told them that Ruth had not returned after lunch, so Edwin went to the store to get more information, and Mary had called Chief Shirley for help, she said. Had they known Ruth had run off to get married? No, sir, they had not. They hadn't had any idea that Ruth and Pedro were even involved with each other. They knew the paperhanger, but no, he had never come to visit Ruth at the house. Hugo Black dwelled awhile longer on the fact that Ruth Stephenson had kept her parents in the dark about her relationship with Gussman. Many of the jurors were family men, with children still at home— the kind of men unlikely to bless a child's silent acts of defiance. "Did you *let* him come there?" "No, sir." She hadn't had any idea that Gussman had been showing Ruth any attention at all. He had only come to the house to hang some wallpaper.

Without directly asking, Black pointed out a reason Edwin and Mary Stephenson would have had to resist Ruth's relationship with Pedro had the girl been less secretive: "Did you know whether he was a Greek, or Porta Rican, or Dago," asked the lawyer, "or *what* he was?" The popular slur passed through his lips without a whiff of conscience. "I looked on him as a servant," Mary Stephenson said dismissively: "half Greek." Hugo Black let the answer—"half Greek"—hang in the air, though a natural next question might reasonably have been *What thought you about the other half, Mrs. Stephenson?* Black had a plan to come back to it later, at a moment when its impact could be used to maximum effect. "Could he talk English?" "Not that I could hardly understand."

The lawyer moved on to the afternoon of the shooting, asking Mary Stephenson about their efforts to get help from the sheriff's office to find their missing daughter. "I talked to Mr. Cole about getting a warrant to search some places where I thought she might be." "What places?" "Some Catholic places." When the sheriff's deputies wouldn't seek a warrant on the information she and Edwin had to give them, she returned home, leaving Edwin at the courthouse. The next time she saw him was in the jail, Mary Stephenson said. Black skipped over the cause of her husband's incarceration and went directly to one of the prongs of his defense instead. Was he injured? Yes, there was a knot on the left side of his head, the minister's wife confirmed.[11]

On cross-examination, John Morrow tried to get Mary Stephenson to admit the supreme irony that her husband was known throughout Birmingham as "the Marrying Parson," but the woman's answers were slippery, and Hugo Black pelted the prosecutor with objections whenever Morrow tried to pin her down.

"What church was Mr. Stephenson pastor of?" John Morrow asked her.

"He is not pastor of any church now."

"Was he preaching for a living?"

"No."

"What did he do for a living?"

Hugo Black objected: Reverend Stephenson's occupation was "immaterial and irrelevant," he protested, but Judge Fort overruled the objection and allowed the prosecutor to proceed.

He did "different things," Mary Stephenson said then.

"Well, what were they?" Morrow pressed.

"He was a penmanship teacher, for one thing," the witness glared.

"Did he depend on that entirely?"

Not altogether, she replied.

"What else did he do?"

"He was a card writer to a certain extent."

"*That* all he did?"

"No."

"Well, what else did he do?"

Black objected again with the same result.

"Well, I could not say," Mrs. Stephenson prevaricated, "several little things..."

No matter how many times Morrow asked, Mary Stephenson simply refused to say that her husband supported the family by marrying couples at the courthouse.

Morrow refused to give up: "Have you named everything he did for a living, that you know of?"

"No."

"Well name the rest of them please, ma'am."

At which point the woman refused point blank to respond at all, as if she could choose between the questions she cared for and those she did not.

No answer.

"Do you understand my question?" Morrow asked, incredulously. "I asked have you named all the occupations that you knew of that he was engaged in?"

No answer.

Finally, Judge Fort leaned over and spoke to Mary Stephenson directly: "State all that you remember, please, and let's get on with the case."

"Judge, he did so many different things," Mary Stephenson looked up at him piteously, "I can't remember."

"Do you remember any more than what you have stated?" the judge asked gently.

"He done so many different things, I can't recall," she repeated.

"If you remember any others," Morrow jumped in, "please let us know what they were."

Black shouted another objection. Overruled, said the judge.

The prosecutor was losing his patience: "Can you answer that question?" No answer.

"I don't know whether she hears me or not, if the Court please," John Morrow said to the judge. "I would like to have a reply one way or the other."

Judge Fort faced the woman on the stand again: "Do you remember any more, is the question, Mrs. Stephenson?" he explained, as if the problem was a lack of comprehension rather than a matter of pure obstinacy. But still she refused to say a word.

Morrow had had enough: "Did he do any kind of work around the courthouse?" the prosecutor demanded.

But Hugo Black was on his feet again then, objecting to the question, suggesting that his opponent ought to be ashamed, "going into details of that kind"—as though a woman like Mary Stephenson could not be put upon to admit that what her husband really did for a living was marry people at the courthouse.

And this time, inexplicably, the judge sustained the objection.

John Morrow must have been shocked. "You don't want to answer my question, do you?" he fired at the woman, ignoring Judge Fort's ruling.

"Objection!" Black shouted, "on the ground it is not only incompetent, but wrong," he said, answering for Mary Stephenson, putting words in her mouth.

"Sustained," ruled Judge Fort again.

Morrow shifted: "You and your husband were embittered against the Catholic Church and the Catholic people, weren't you?"

If it was a fight John Morrow wanted over their feelings toward the Catholics, Mary Stephenson felt no need to hold back. "We were not members of that church," the minister's wife replied.

"I say you were embittered against it," Morrow shot back.

"We were embittered enough not to be members of it," she said, sensing she was on surer ground.

And you felt that way at the time of this killing, didn't you? demanded Morrow.

"What I know of them, I wouldn't hold with them," she said.

Whatever the papers had written about the woman's frailty, Mrs. Stephenson knew how to pick her battles, and Hugo Black must have agreed that Morrow's last questions to Mary helped rather than hurt his case. On redirect he let the woman's answers about her feelings about the Catholics stand, and turned his attention instead to the question of whether she or her husband had ever abused their daughter. Did "you all ever tie your daughter to a bed post, or beat her with a razor strap, or nail the windows down...so she couldn't get out, and shut her up in there?" Likely, the lawyer's tone was doubtful, as if it was hardly worth the effort to put the question into words.

"No, sir," Mary Stephenson replied as her husband's lawyer took his seat.[12]

————

When the Edwin Stephenson took the stand at 3:30 that afternoon, Hugo Black wasted no time. He asked a series of questions designed to put the minister at ease and to put him in a favorable light: How old was he? What was his profession? How long had he been a member of the Methodist church? He was fifty-one years old, Stephenson said. He was a Methodist minister, and a lifelong member of the "M.E. church." "Have you ever belonged to the Catholic Church?" Black asked. "No, sir." The lawyer dwelled on the denial, giving Stephenson a chance to punctuate it: "Have any of your people, so far as you know, back through the generations, as far as they can be traced, ever belonged to the Catholic Church?" Stephenson's two-word answer mimicked his lawyer's incredulity: "No, sir," he said, flatly.

Black turned to the question of Ruth, asking how many children they had. "One living," Stephenson said. "Have you ever mistreated her, Mr. Stephenson," the lawyer asked, "abused her and beat her, have you ever done that?" "No, sir." "Do you care for her?" "Sir?" Stephenson seemed to think that he must have misunderstood—the answer to the question being so obvious. "Do you love your daughter, Mr. Stephenson?" Black repeated. The minister smiled faintly then: "Yes, sir, with all my heart." *(Even after all she had put him through!)*

Black turned to the troubles Stephenson and his wife had experienced with their daughter. Yes, there had been trouble over the Catholic Church. No, he couldn't remember exactly when it had started. Yes, he remembered the time he and some officers had found his daughter over at Fred Bender's house. "Had you, in your home, tried to rear her as a Christian girl?" Hugo Black asked then, as if "Christian" and "Catholic" had no business in the same sentence. "Yes, sir," Stephenson answered steadily, his daughter had been a Methodist since she was a little over six years old, when the family lived in Talladega, he said.[13]

Black turned to the day of the shooting, after Stephenson and his wife learned that their daughter was missing from her job. They had learned of it from a friend, Stephenson confirmed, and yes, he and Mary had tried to find her. They sought help from the Birmingham police department and the county sheriff, but they weren't able to get a search warrant to look for her. When had he put his pistol in his pocket? Black asked, probably hoping to paint a picture of Stephenson's growing desperation as each of his efforts to rouse help from the city's officials failed. "When I was at home last," Stephenson said.

What had he done when he was unable to get a search warrant? Black asked. He had walked up Third Avenue, Stephenson said, to Fred Bender's store, and then he "came back down the street" to Lige Loy's place, where he used the phone to call a detective at the police station. But there was still no news, and the minutes were flying by! Each one chipping away at any chance they had to find her. So he had walked back down along Third Avenue, Stephenson said, and when he was directly in front of the Catholic rectory, the priest invited him to come in, he said, and asked him to have a seat. Black asked his client if he had ever talked to the priest before. Yes, two or three times, Stephenson said. Concerning what? "My daughter," Stephenson said—always his daughter. After the time she had been found at the Benders' he had called the priest, Stephenson said, and told Coyle it would be better "for his people and mine . . . not to try to induce my daughter any way whatever to belong to the Catholic church."

Black asked him what the priest had said, but he could not have wanted to linger on the claimed conversation for long—not when his client's statement could be considered a threat.

He said "he wasn't concerned about other people," and "if people wanted to become Catholics it didn't need to concern me."

Black turned back to the meeting between Stephenson and Coyle on the porch: "What was said by you and what was said by him?"

Stephenson said that he told the priest his daughter was missing and that he would appreciate his help finding her, to "keep her from going clear away"—emotion seemed to rob the minister of his voice for a moment—"and leaving her father and mother that love her more than their own lives—," he said finally. The court stenographer noted that the witness had started to cry: "He said, 'It isn't my place to look after other people's family affairs.'" Hugo Black urged his client to go on: "just a little bit louder, please." And Stephenson did, telling the jury that Father Coyle had asked him what he had against his daughter becoming Catholic. To which he had responded that he and his wife had reared Ruth to be a "good *Christian* girl"—that word again—and that the priest had then asked him: Did he know that Ruth had become a Catholic, and had been one for some time? To which Stephenson, growing angry, told the priest that no, "I didn't know it," and "she is *my* daughter, and under age, and I love her—!" Tears of pent-up rage and frustration spilled down Stephenson's cheeks—"and she has been living in *my* home, and *I* have been feeding her and caring for her!" But then the priest said to him "when your girl becomes married she isn't yours anymore," Stephenson went on, and "I says, "Well my daughter *isn't* married!" and that "she was home last night" and that "I had went with her to the store" where she worked "just that morning!" But then the priest broke in again, saying that Ruth *was* married, and that she was married to a Catholic, and that he had married her himself that evening!

Self-interest threaded through every line of the minister's testimony, and without a single witness to corroborate the supposed conversation (and several who contradicted it), it is doubtful that very much of his testimony was true. But the minister's anguish and ragged fury were almost certainly genuine. Even if it had not been the priest who told him about his daughter's marriage as he claimed on the stand, even if someone else had delivered word of it before Stephenson reached the rectory porch (his nephew Ross Campbell, perhaps, after Ruth phoned home), the news must have infuriated him. Not marriage! Stephenson had found ways to deal with his daughter's disobedience, but none of her prior willful conduct had carried the emancipating effects of marriage. Marriage held the power to sever Edwin Stephenson's control over Ruth once and for all. It is not difficult to imagine the feeling of despair that must have gripped him, or the way that despair might seek the relief of rage.

Black let the tension of the scene build, allowing Stephenson to recount the tale without interruption, until the account covered nearly two pages of the trial transcript. So carried away was the minister by his own emotion, however, that he forgot to tell the jurors the part about Father Coyle excusing himself, going into the house, and then coming back out again—the part of his story that had made it possible for Stephenson to claim that he believed the priest might be armed. Realizing his mistake, the minister circled back, groping for the right words: "Just *before* he said that, he said, 'Excuse me,'" Stephenson stammered, trying to repair the damage: "and [he] walked in the house for just a minute or two and came back, *before* he said she had..." he trailed off.

It can't be known whether the jurors noticed that the minister had botched the story, precisely at the point his account strained credulity the most: that the priest had gone into the house before the men came to blows—the only sequence that made it possible for Stephenson to claim that he had reason to think the priest might be armed. After an awkward pause, Stephenson fumbled on: "and he sit down on the swing and says, 'Your girl is a Catholic, and she is married, for I married her this evening.'

"—and I said, 'To whom?'

"—and he said, 'To Pedro Gussman, a Catholic.'

"—and I said, 'You have treated me as dirty as a dog!' and I rose to my feet, and my heart broke."

The court reporter noted that the minister was crying again.

"I says, 'You have ruined my home! That man is a Negro.'" Then Father Coyle hit him, Stephenson said, and called him a heretical son-of-a-bitch, and knocked him to his knees and against the post, and then he kicked him in his side, before catching him by his suspenders (*not belt!*) and jerking him back to his feet. (*Of course!—that was how Chiles and McGinty had seen him standing, not down. It explained the trajectory of the bullet, too—downward, not upward, because the priest had hauled him back to his feet!*) Then Father Coyle reached his hand "this way," Stephenson said, gesturing toward his pocket, "and then I fired." How many shots? Hugo Black asked.

"I couldn't tell." (*Not when having to remember so much else!*) "Only two or three—" he added.

"Any shots after he fell?"

"No, sir."

Joe Tate and his men must nearly have fallen out of their chairs. Father Coyle had pulled him back up! And Pedro Gussman a Negro! Edwin Stephenson was claiming that the Catholic priest had married his daughter not only to a Catholic but a Negro!

———

Hugo Black gave the prosecutors no time to digest the abrupt turn in his client's testimony. He turned to the court bailiff: "Call Pedro Gussman in." What happened next was extraordinary. The door at the back of the courtroom swung open, as if on the lawyer's cue, and a deputy marched Pedro Gussman up the center aisle, stopping at the railing that separated the lawyers' tables from the rows of seated spectators, whose audible gasp could be heard as Hugo Black's surprise move unfolded before them.

Black turned back to his client. "Is that Pedro Gussman?" he asked, in the manner in which a trial lawyer might ask a victim to identify his assailant.

Stephenson affirmed it.

The lawyer ordered Gussman brought forward then. "Bring him closer to the jury," a reporter heard Hugo Black say to the officer at Pedro Gussman's side, "let them look at his eyes." The man escorting Pedro complied, depositing him in front of the jury box, like a live physical exhibit, where the paperhanger stood, plainly ill at ease, as twelve pairs of eyes scrutinized him for the telltale signs of Negro blood. White southerners considered themselves good judges of such things, though a deliberate effort by one such as Gussman to conceal his true race was capable of deceiving his neighbors for a time—subterfuges that made the policing of racial lines all the more important.

Finally, Hugo Black was satisfied that the jurors had seen enough. "I just wanted you to see the man," he told them, his meaning clear. As the officer led Gussman back out into the hall, Hugo Black turned back to his client and asked if he had known that Pedro Gussman "had been going with" his daughter, or whether Stephenson had "ever seen him with her?"

Edwin Stephenson's answer was little more than a growl: "Never in my life."[14]

Many years later, after Hugo Black's career took off, one of the historians who studied Black's early days in Alabama asked a reporter who had sat through Stephenson's trial if he recalled the moment when Black called Pedro Gussman into the courtroom. J. Fisher Rothermel of the *Birmingham News* replied that he would never forget it. Before calling Pedro Gussman into the courtroom, the newsman said, Hugo Black had dimmed the lighting in the room by pulling the window shades low. The dull light accentuated the dark tones of Pedro's tanned skin, subliminally buttressing the defense's insinuation that the priest had married Stephenson's daughter not only to a Catholic, but a Negro.[15]

It is hard to know whether the reporters who witnessed the dramatic display accurately captured the moment in the columns of their papers. Certainly readers some decades later would easily spot the way some of the newsmen's descriptions reflected a deeply ingrained racialized thought pattern when they wrote about Pedro Gussman's reaction to being hauled before the jury box in the middle of Edwin Stephenson's testimony. "The man whom Atty. Black had previously referred to as 'a Greek, a dago, or a Porto Rican,'" wrote one, "looked around in wide-eyed amazement. Evidently he didn't understand what was wanted of him, but he seemed perfectly willing to do as told." "The astonished Porto Rican was marched to the front of the jury box. His eyes grew wider, his dark skin seemed to pale. His heavy, coal-black hair was combed straight back; his features showed amazement more than ever" as "[q]uizically, the jurors looked him over," until Hugo Black, content, dismissed him from the room.[16]

But even if the reporters' accounts of the unexpected twist in the defense's strategy revealed as much about their own racial assumptions as they did about the groundwork being laid for the defense's closing argument, in October 1921, their screaming headlines and their accompanying descriptions of the moment Pedro Gussman was paraded before the jury could not have failed to cement the minister's racial accusation even more deeply in their readers' minds.[17]

Pedro Gussman had not been in the courtroom when his father-in-law called him a Negro. Along with the other subpoenaed witnesses, he had waited outside until a deputy came to get him, a precaution generally adhered to at trials to prevent witnesses from molding their testimony to jibe with the statements made by others who preceded them. For this reason, of all the witnesses called to testify at Edwin Stephenson's trial, only Mary Stephenson had been permitted to stay in the courtroom and listen while others gave their testimony—the woman's special status as the minister's wife seemed to warrant this little indulgence, or so Hugo Black argued, and Judge Fort had agreed.

Without the benefit of hearing Stephenson's racial accusation, therefore, Pedro Gussman had to have been greatly surprised when he was marched into the overflowing room and found that instead of waiting empty for him, the chair at the front of the room was already occupied—by Edwin Stephenson! And like the victor in a game of "Ring around the Rosie," the minister gave no sign of relinquishing his berth. Instead, everyone in the room craned in their seats to catch a glimpse of Pedro, studying with a new curiosity every inch of his body, as Hugo Black ordered him brought not to the witness stand, but to a spot directly in front of the jury box. The wallpaper hanger must have felt like a man thrown suddenly into a lineup—only a lineup in which his accuser had not bothered to include any other suspects or decoys, making it virtually certain that he alone would be the one picked out.

When the door closed behind Gussman, Hugo Black had only a few more questions for his client. What did you do after firing the shots? "Come to the sheriff's office." Were you hurt? Yes. Where? "On my head." "Have you the suspenders that you had on that night?" "Yes, sir." "Let's see them." Stephenson held up a pair of broken suspenders, which he had brought to the witness stand unnoticed. This procedure was highly irregular. There are rules about the admissibility of physical evidence at trials. To be admitted, items like a pair of suspenders are normally required to be identified and safeguarded prior to trial; a precaution necessary to ensure that the object is what the witness claims it to be, rather than some look-alike substitute, and to provide assurance that the item has not been tampered with in the meantime, perhaps after the defendant turned himself in. There would have been nothing to prevent Stephenson from tearing the suspenders himself in support of his concocted justification for his actions on the rectory porch. Typically, a prosecutor would have taken the suspenders into custody as soon as it was clear that they were relevant to his investigation. But apparently Joe Tate had not done so when he met with Stephenson in his cell shortly after the shooting, probably because on that night Stephenson had claimed that it was his belt that had been damaged, not his suspenders. Nonetheless, for some reason, neither Joe Tate nor any of his assistants objected to the introduction of the suspenders when Hugo Black offered them into evidence.

Black had only a few more questions. Had Stephenson ever beaten his daughter with a razor strap? "No, sir." "Did you know that this fellow that has just been in here"—Black gestured, declining to say Pedro's name—"had ever been going with her at all?" Ever seen him with her?

"Never in my life."

At that, Hugo Black rested his case.

None of the reporters' accounts of the events in Judge Fort's courtroom that day probed the most compelling implications of Mary Stephenson's vague description of Pedro Gussman as "half Greek," and Edwin Stephenson's willingness to fill in the other half: "You've married my daughter to a Negro!" It is possible that the newsmen, swept away by the drama of the couple's testimonies, simply missed, swirling through the murky waters of their racial insinuations, that together the two had just labeled their daughter the witting or unwitting sexual partner of a man the law of Alabama declared to be her racial inferior; a man with whom she was forbidden to have any such interaction. If the jury was persuaded by these insinuations, they would have done untold damage to their daughter's reputation. In 1921, there existed no more "degrading slur": sex between a white woman and a Negro man being considered not only illegal and immoral—a form of "cultural and racial treason" even—but "unnatural" as well, not unlike an act of bestiality.[18]

It can't be known if Edwin Stephenson suffered qualms before declaring his daughter's husband to be a Negro, or whether Hugo Black, as his lawyer, had misgivings about eliciting such an accusation in a public courtroom teeming with reporters and the man's friends and neighbors as well. Looking back, the strategy seems tinged with a kind of desperation: a decision that the jury's antipathy toward marriage between a daughter of a Protestant minister and a Catholic might not be strong enough to save the minister from a conviction. A determination that the religious insult embodied by the priest's act when he married Ruth to Pedro, powerful as it was, could never be the equivalent of the racial injury Coyle would have inflicted on the Stephenson household by marrying Ruth to a supposed Negro—"You've treated my family like a dirty dog!" Stephenson had yelled at Coyle, immediately before firing his gun. If the jury's hoped-for anti-Catholicism had the power of three aces, Hugo Black and his client must have thought that only racism would deal the defense the fourth.

It is reasonable to think that Stephenson and his lawyer would have had some serious reservations about concluding the minister's testimony in the dramatic way they did, however. Pedro Gussman had been living in

Birmingham for over a decade without suffering the special diminishments bestowed daily on the city's Negroes. A few days after Hugo Black had him carted before the jury, Pedro wrote a letter to the *Birmingham News,* which the paper published, pointing out the very many reasons Stephenson and his lawyer had to know that their accusation was untrue, and that that knowledge might also perhaps have motivated the defense's decision not to put him in the witness stand, where he might have proved his "citizenship [and] membership in the white race."

"Having been called a Negro in the press this past week," Pedro wrote," I wish to say in self-defense that I am not," and Stephenson "was the last man expected" to accuse him of it. "I lived in the house with him about six years ago on Third Avenue...being paid in this way for some papering which I did for him." And when the minister was supporting his family on his wages as a barber, the letter went on, Pedro had been one of Stephenson's customers—a service the man would never have conferred had he truly considered Pedro to be a Negro. In 1921, it went without saying that white barbers did not shave Negro men, and everyone in Birmingham knew it. "I am a qualified voter," Pedro's letter continued, "living in a white rooming house," and an official representative of the paperhangers' union. Anyone questioning his racial bona fides needed only to ask his landlord, or the union president, or any other member of the union, who would willingly "testify that I am not a Negro" but a man "born in Porto Rico...of Spanish descent."[19]

Before diving into the quagmire created by Stephenson's claim about his son-in-law's race, Joe Tate and his men decided to start their cross examination of the defendant by focusing on irony: the irony that Reverend Edwin Stephenson, of all people, would claim that Father Coyle's decision to marry his daughter to Gussman was such an affront that it caused him (blessedly only temporarily!) to lose his senses and the control of his actions, when the minister himself, as Birmingham's "Marrying Parson," conducted similar ceremonies nearly every day without a care about the wishes of the parents of the spouses-to-be. But when John Morrow tried to get the minister to own up to the means of his livelihood, Stephenson proved as slippery as his wife had been, and Hugo Black pelted Morrow with objections, arguing that the matter was irrelevant; inexplicably, Judge Fort once again sustained them, directing Morrow to move on.[20]

Joe Tate's assistant complied, deciding to go straight at what the prosecutorial team deemed the real reason for the shooting—Edwin Stephenson's long-standing hatred of Father Coyle, his church, and all of those he had represented. Morrow put the question to Stephenson directly: "What's the state of your feeling toward the Catholic Church?"

"I have no objection to the—"

"Sir?" Morrow fired back, disbelievingly.

"I have no ill will toward them."

"You have no ill will toward the Catholic Church or Catholic people?"

"Catholic Church is what you asked me."

"Have you any ill will toward the Catholics in general?"

Stephenson hedged: "I don't know who you include in "in general."

The prosecutor asked Judge Fort to instruct the minister just to answer the question, and when, over another objection from Black, the judge did so, Morrow asked his question again: "Have you any ill will toward the Catholics?"

"As a class?"

Morrow had had enough, nearly shouting at Stephenson then, asking him whether he hadn't told his daughter from the time she was eleven or twelve that he hated Catholics; that he would like to see them all blown to hell; that he would like to be the one to put a bomb under Coyle's church; and that he hated Coyle—all years before he shot the priest to death. But Stephenson denied all of it, saying that he had never said any such things, no, sir, never.[21]

The prosecutor moved on to Stephenson's claims that the Catholics had been trying to convince Ruth to abandon her Protestantism, and had locked her up to do it. Stephenson had said during his direct examination that Fred Bender had confined the girl inside his house up on Red Mountain. Morrow asked him to name one time "that any Catholic ever confined the girl against her will?" He and the police chief's men had found her at Benders, Stephenson replied. Was the girl locked up over there? He couldn't say, replied Stephenson, the officers had gone inside the house without him. So you didn't know whether anybody had locked her up, or whether she locked herself up in there? Morrow fired back. "No, sir." Or that any other Catholic had ever confined her against her will? "No, sir." "Didn't you tell the officers they had her locked up out there at Fred Bender's house?"

Stephenson realized his mistake. "The officers found her locked up there."

After you told them that she was locked up, Morrow retorted, "didn't you tell them that?"

No answer.

Morrow asked the question again.

"I told people she was locked up out there," Stephenson conceded.

"Out where?"

"At Bender's house," came his exasperated reply.

Morrow asked if he had ever asked his daughter whether she had been locked in or locked herself in.

He didn't remember asking her one way or the other "who locked her up, or not," Stephenson replied.

"And yet you went all over Birmingham telling people they had her locked up out there at Mr. Bender's house, didn't you do that?"

Stephenson denied it, but the prosecutor had made his point. If Stephenson wanted to pretend under oath that he harbored no ill will against Catholics, Morrow would let the man's own actions prove that his words were a lie.[22]

The prosecutor turned his attention to the afternoon of the shooting. Stephenson had returned to his home to get his gun about four o'clock, hadn't he? About then. And the gun was loaded, wasn't it? He hadn't looked to see. Didn't he know it was loaded? Morrow fired back. "It generally stayed that way." After going to the sheriff's office, where he had gone? Up Third Avenue. For what purpose? "To see if I could find out anything about our daughter." Where had he gone up on Third Avenue? To "in front of Mr. Bender's store." Where had he gone after that? To Lige Loy's undertaking company, to use the phone. And after using the phone, he walked pretty fast back down to the gate of the Catholic rectory, didn't he? "Not that I know of," Stephenson replied vaguely, as if it were possible for him not to know. And it was Stephenson's testimony that Father Coyle had invited him in?

"He asked me in," Stephenson insisted.

"You mean he called to you as you passed on the street?" Morrow asked skeptically.

"Didn't holler at me out in the street."

"Had you started in the gate before he spoke to you at all, or not?" Morrow demanded.

"Started in the gate," Stephenson said.

Hadn't you made up your mind that you would go to the rectory and ask Coyle about your daughter?

No, sir.

When had he made up his mind to go in there?

"Just as I got to the gate and saw him sitting on the porch."

You had entered the gate of the rectory before the priest spoke to you, isn't that right?

"Yes, sir."

John Morrow took him through the story again: the purported conversation, all quite civil, until the priest swung at him, hitting him in the head, and side, knocking him against the post, onto his knees, then kicking him, and jerking him up by his suspenders. What about your belt? Morrow reminded him, "How did he take hold of your belt?" Stephenson demonstrated. "Something like this," he gestured. You mean to "tell this jury that he kicked you and grabbed that belt all at the same time?"

The defendant's story was becoming more convoluted by the second. Hugo Black objected that Stephenson had already answered, and the judge sustained the objection.

And when you got up, "he walked back toward the other end of the porch?" Morrow asked, as if trying to make sense of the nonsensical.

"He stepped back a step or two, and put his hand back in his pocket."

Did you see a pistol?

"He was trying to get one."

"You['re] tell[ing] the jury he was trying to get a pistol?"

"Well, he—."

"You saw it, did you?"

It was a trap, and Stephenson knew it. "It was a little dark on the porch," he hedged, "you couldn't tell for sure."

"You mean to say at 6:35 in August it was so dark you could not see—?"

"It wasn't daylight," Stephenson said weakly.

Morrow moved on to how far apart he and Coyle had been when he pulled his gun to shoot the priest.

Stephenson said he had just raised his gun, but had no intention to shoot him.

Morrow repeated what the minister had just said, incredulous: "You did not intend to shoot him?"

"I had no idea of hitting his body or head," Stephenson clarified.

"Where *did* you try to hit him?"

"I wasn't trying to hit him anywhere."

"You didn't try to hit him when he was supposedly trying to shoot you?"

"No, sir."

The answer made no sense. Not when Stephenson's entire self-defense claim was premised on the claim that the minister shot Father Coyle to prevent the priest from shooting him. The man's justification was spiraling out of control.

John Morrow turned to the most incendiary part of the minister's testimony. If Stephenson wanted, against all reason, to try to justify the shooting or excuse the temporary loss of his faculties on the connivance that he considered Pedro Gussman to be a Negro, John Morrow hoped to turn the tables on the man. Stephenson's claimed skepticism about Gussman's race, however ill-founded, could have given the minister a motive to kill Coyle once he heard of his daughter's marriage to the paperhanger, casting doubt on his claims of self-defense and insanity. There was an important difference between self-defense, which the law justified, insanity, which the law forgave, and revenge, which it punished. Stephenson might just have painted himself into a corner. If Stephenson insisted on the thing, Morrow thought he might just use the story to his advantage by turning Stephenson's excuse back on him and arguing that it gave him a motive to kill the priest.

"Is Pedro Gussman a Negro?" Morrow asked Stephenson.

"Yes, sir," Stephenson said, defiant, "I knew him when I seen him."

"You say he is a Negro?"

When the minister answered, his voice was suddenly low, one reporter noticed, suggesting that the prosecutor's question had put him back on his heels: "I say I *look* on him as such," Stephenson hedged.

"I asked whether or not you *know* he is a Negro?" Morrow demanded, trying to box the minister in.

Stephenson hesitated. In 1921, racial accusations were no small thing. It was even possible that he had discussed the dangers of making such a claim with his lawyers ahead of time. Men had been sued over such allegations, and if they could not be substantiated, wronged victims of such slanders had been known to demand great sums of money for the damage done to their reputations.[23] But Hugo Black was on his feet then, objecting:, telling Judge Fort that his client had just said that he *looked on* Gussman as a Negro—and "that is as far as a man can tell," Black vouched for Stephenson. "He could not *trace* his lineage," Black continued, "very difficult to trace some of them." Judge Fort agreed once again and sustained the objection.

John Morrow refused to give up: Stephenson had testified that he had told Father Coyle, "You have married my daughter to a Negro," hadn't he?

Stephenson replied that those had not been his exact words.

Well, "what were the exact words you used?" Morrow fired back.

Edwin Stephenson snapped. I said: "You have ruined my home! That man is a Negro."

Finally, the prosecution had got a clear statement of the last thing Edwin Stephenson claimed to have said before firing his gun, and—whatever the jurors themselves might think about Gussman's race—it amounted to a clear indication that Stephenson would have had a motive to kill.

ELEVEN

A Jury's Verdict

IT IS SOMETIMES difficult to know when to let something go; to look an affront in the eye and (as counseled by that childhood wisdom, *Sticks and stones may break my bones...*) to shrug it off, as a thing of little real consequence. In the heat of a trial, the exercise of such restraint is perhaps harder still.

Joe Tate faced such a moment at the trial of Edwin Stephenson. Shortly before Judge Fort told Stephenson that he could step down from the witness stand, Hugo Black asked his client several questions on redirect examination to show that when Joe Tate had interviewed Stephenson after the shooting, he had led Stephenson to believe that it was necessary for him to make a statement—that the man had no choice—and that Tate had not advised Stephenson that his statements could be used against him or that he was entitled to a lawyer. Until that moment of the minister's testimony, Joe Tate had been sitting silently at the prosecutor's table, allowing his assistants to handle the state's case-in-chief and cross-examination of the defense's witnesses. But he sprang to his feet then, in tandem with John Morrow, both men objecting at once. The law did not require such warnings, and unless Joe Tate had overborne Stephenson's will, causing him to give a statement involuntarily—an allegation that normally would have been fought out prior to the start of the trial—Tate had violated no right of Stephenson's, as Hugo Black knew. But once again, Judge Fort sided with the defense, allowing Stephenson to say, "No, sir," Joe Tate had not told him any of that.

It must have been galling. And just as Joe Tate had found it impossible to remain in his seat when the minister first flung this accusation from the witness chair, the prosecutor could not abide that the slander go uncontested after Stephenson stepped down.

As a rule, a prosecutor never spoke with a suspect like Edwin Stephenson alone—not so much out of fear for his physical safety but out of fear of making himself the sole witness to whatever might transpire during the conference. A companion was needed so that later the prosecutor could put someone else on the stand to tell the jury about what had happened. Two men had accompanied Joe Tate when he entered the minister's cell that night for that reason—Chief Deputy Fred McDuff and the assistant coroner, George Moore—either one of whom should have been able to show that Stephenson had lied on the stand.

Looking back at it, Joe Tate probably realized that, of all the things Stephenson had said on the stand that day, the lie about Tate's conduct in his cell paled against many of his other claims: he harbored no ill will against the Catholic Church! He considered Pedro Gussman a Negro! But in the swirl of emotions of a trial, such comparisons can be obscured. So at the start of the state's rebuttal case, after the defense had rested, Joe Tate rose to his feet and called Fred McDuff to the stand and remaining standing, signaled that he would handle the questioning of this witness himself.

Tate got straight to it, asking McDuff whether on the night of his arrest the minister had been "told to make a statement or was required to make a statement" in any way. "I don't remember anybody telling him he would have to make a statement," the chief deputy replied at first. But when Joe Tate asked him again, more to emphasize the lawman's answer than to clear up any confusion—"Did anybody tell him it would be necessary for him to make a statement?"—Fred McDuff professed a sudden bewilderment: "My mind isn't clear on that," he said.

Joe Tate must have thought that he had misheard McDuff; for when a witness suddenly and inexplicably turns on his examiner, there is an almost irresistible temptation to engage in wishful thinking—to convince oneself that the witness simply misunderstood—shoving aside the alternative unhappy explanation that the witness knows exactly what he is doing; that he is getting ready to sink his questioner's case.

"To refresh your recollection," Tate put his question to McDuff again: I am asking if Stephenson wasn't told "that he *did not have to* make a statement, but that it was necessary for us to investigate the killing?" "As well as I remember," Fred McDuff replied, "my memory wasn't hardly clear on that, but I have a faint recollection of somebody telling him—you, or Mr. Moore, one—it was necessary for him to make a statement. Which one [of you], I would not say."

"*Necessary* for him to make a statement?" Tate asked McDuff again in disbelief.

"Yes, sir."

"Or necessary for us to *investigate* this killing?" Tate asked, still refusing to accept what McDuff was saying. To which Fred McDuff allowed that Stephenson had been told that as well, that "the killing was being investigated."

Blinders finally off, Joe Tate railed at the witness then, each question increasingly hostile, summarizing in interrogatory form what had actually happened in that cell: wasn't it true that all he had told Stephenson was that he had to investigate; and wasn't it true that Stephenson had then claimed that he had shot the priest in self-defense after the priest had knocked him down, and that he had broken his *belt,* not his suspenders; and wasn't it true that when Tate examined the belt he had said to Stephenson, "Why, your belt *isn't* broken—"

Before McDuff could say a word, Hugo Black was on his feet too, shouting an objection: "If Mr. Tate wants to testify he could do it from the witness stand!"

But the circuit solicitor just kept on, fuming at McDuff: "—which called for a certain reply on his part—"

Hugo Black tried to shout over him: "We move to exclude that statement on the ground Mr. Tate isn't under oath and isn't a witness—!"

"—That after that, the defendant said, 'Well, it come loose,'" Tate mimicked the minister, "and that he didn't know whether it was broken or not"; ignoring Hugo Black.

The battle between the two lawyers for the upper hand swung back and forth until Judge Fort interrupted and ruled that the circuit solicitor had "no right to state what happened unless he was on the witness stand." At which point, Hugo Black asked the Court to exclude the entirety of what Joe Tate · had said, and to instruct the jurors that they were not to consider any of it. The judge did so.

Judge Fort turned back to Joe Tate, who had at last gone quiet. He told the prosecutor that he could ask the deputy whether it was him or the assistant coroner who had told Stephenson that he had to talk. But Joe Tate simply looked Fred McDuff in the eye and told him: "Come down."

"You don't care to ask that question?" Judge Fort asked.

"No, sir," Joe Tate replied, disgusted. "I ain't going to ask another question."

———

Joe Tate may have decided against asking any further questions of Fred McDuff, but his assistants were not about to let the misimpression created by his testimony stand unrefuted. They quickly decided that Joe Tate should take the stand himself, to get into the record what Edwin Stephenson and

Chief Deputy McDuff had claimed not to recall. After Joe Tate was sworn in, John Morrow asked him point-blank: "Did you tell this defendant it would be necessary for him to make a statement?"

"I did not," Joe Tate answered.

"Did you use the word 'necessary' in any way?"

"I told him we were investigating this killing," Tate said, "that it was our duty, and necessary for us to do it." At first Stephenson said that he did not care to talk, Tate continued, and "I told him he did not have to do it." But then the assistant coroner asked Stephenson a question, and the minister reached for his belt and said it had been broken in a fight with the priest.

Hugo Black objected, trying to stop the prosecutor from saying anything else, but Joe Tate kept right on: "I looked at his belt and examined it—."

"We object to that—."

"—*hole by hole.*"

Black pleaded with the judge to exclude the statements, arguing that Tate's testimony showed that his client's statements were not voluntary; that Stephenson had stated that he did not care to talk. But the law was against Black's argument. A suspect in custody could always change his mind and decide to talk, provided the officials questioning him did not compel him to do so. And even if the statements would have been inadmissible in the prosecution's case-in-chief, Judge Fort reminded Black, once Stephenson took the stand and testified, the prosecutors were entitled to use his prior statements to impeach the credibility of what he said. A defendant could not use his right not to be compelled to talk as a shield for perjury.

Before Joe Tate stepped down from the witness stand, he looked Hugo Black in the eye and said: "Do *you* want to ask me any questions?"

"No, sir," the lawyer replied. His mama hadn't raised no fools.

The prosecutors' witnesses filled the rest of that day, revealing that the decision to call only five witnesses in the case-in-chief had in fact been a strategic one, not a matter of a lack of evidence. The prosecutors had simply wanted to force Stephenson's lawyers to pick a defense, which they could then try to repudiate in their rebuttal case.

Anna Bender testified about her experiences with the Stephenson girl. Ruth Stephenson had come to the Benders' home twice in May, shortly after the girl had converted to Catholicism and Fred Bender had agreed to be her godfather. John Morrow wanted to show that the girl had not been influenced in reaching her decision. "Did you invite her out there?" Morrow asked. "No, sir, I did not." "Did you know she was coming?" "No, sir, I did not," Anna Bender repeated. "Did you lock her up in the house?" Here Judge Fort overruled an objection by Hugo Black, and the woman repeated firmly: "No, sir,

I did not." Ever lock her in the closet? No, sir. Was it even possible to lock the girl in the house from the outside? She explained that it was not. "The inside handle will open the door?" "Yes, sir." "Did you ever try to persuade her to join the Catholic Church?" Morrow asked finally, covering all the bases. No, sir, the witness said; she had never mentioned Catholicism at all.[1]

It was difficult to think how the woman's steady testimony could be discredited without compelling proof that she was lying. Hugo Black asked her a mere six questions on cross-examination, and landing no blows, took his seat.

Fred Bender followed his wife, echoing what Anna had said—that Ruth Stephenson had come to their house twice, both times uninvited, always of her own accord. The first time, he had urged Ruth to phone home to let her parents know that she would be staying with them overnight. It seemed "no more than right—" Bender started to say. Hugo Black cut him off—"I object to his philosophical observations"—and the judge told the witness to just answer the questions. The second time Ruth came, Bender continued, his wife called the Stephensons to let them know she was there, before the officers came to get her. "Did anyone lock her up in that house?" Morrow asked. "No, sir." Bender described the lock on the front door; it required a key to get inside, but anyone inside could simply turn the knob to go out. "And you were the godfather to this girl?" "Yes, sir." Had he ever asked her to join the Catholic Church? No, sir. Ever talk to her about joining? No, sir. Ever know of anybody who attempted to persuade her? No, sir. Morrow asked then how Bender had come to stand up for Ruth at her baptism. He had run into her at his church, Our Lady of Sorrows, before services one week. Ruth said hello and asked him about becoming a Catholic, but he had said: "I wouldn't have any intention of that, your parents are not Catholics, are they?" She said: "No, they are not." A week or so later, Ruth approached him in his store, and said she had decided to become a Catholic, and asked him if he would stand up for her at her baptism, and he had agreed to do it.

On cross-examination of Fred Bender, Hugo Black displayed why so many in town considered him one of the best trial attorneys in the state. Black wanted to show that Bender knew Ruth and her family well, from her frequent visits to his store when the Stephensons lived next door—well enough to know that Edwin and Mary Stephenson had not raised their daughter as a Catholic. But Bender resisted the suggestion that his contact with the family had been that plentiful, denying that the girl had visited his store that often. You saw her frequently in the neighborhood? Black retorted. Bender conceded it.

"And you knew her?"

"I met her, yes sir."

"And you knew who she was?" Black asked, leading the witness, dragging the point out.

"Yes, sir."

"You knew who her father was?"

"Yes, sir."

"You knew he was a Methodist?"

"No, sir," Bender balked, seeing where the lawyer was going.

Two words—"No, sir"—in answer to an inconsequential question. But the lawyer knew that more often than not it was a witness's answers to the little things that caused him the most harm.

"You did not have any idea of that?" Black asked, setting the trap.

"No, sir," Bender said more slowly then, as if it was dawning on him that he might have made a mistake: "I didn't know he was a minister—" he added, beginning to backpedal.

But Hugo Black had no intention of letting his quarry slip away: "You didn't know what *church* he belonged to?" he repeated.

"No, sir," said Bender, sticking with his original reply.

"Never did have any idea?" The lawyer's tone must have sent shivers up Bender's spine—the sound of a predator in a game of cat and mouse—toying with him, savoring the chase.

"No, sir."

"You did not have any idea what church she belonged to up to the time you became her godfather?" Black asked again incredulously, ready to spring the trap.

"No, sir."

"What made you tell her then when she asked you to be her godfather that her parents were not Catholics?"

Bender was caught. "I don't know," he stammered.

"You just *accidentally guessed* they were not Catholics?"

"Yes, sir," the poor man said, "I suppose so." Then: "I understood they were not Catholics."

"*How* did you understand it?" Black demanded.

"Didn't see them at church."

"You don't go to *all* the Catholic churches, do you?" Black scoffed.

"No, sir."

Black stared Bender down: "You didn't know her people were Protestants?"—more an accusation than a question.

"I knew they were not Catholics."

How? Black asked. Ruth Stephenson had told him so, Bender said. When? "The day she asked me to be the—." Black cut him off. Hadn't he just told John Morrow that when Ruth Stephenson first mentioned wanting to become Catholic, he had told her: "Your people are not Catholics?"

"Yes, sir."

"*Before* she said a word to you about it?" "How did you know they were not?"

The assault went on and on, until Bender finally snapped: "I just knew it by him marrying people out of the courthouse here!"

Black could not have expected the answer, nor liked that Bender had put the spotlight back on his client's antics in the courthouse. He bore down, recapturing his advantage: "Then you did know, when Ruth came to you, that her father was not a Catholic, didn't you?"

"Yes, sir," Bender said, "Yes, sir."

"You knew he was a Methodist preacher, didn't you?" Black demanded again.

"No, sir."

"*Didn't have any idea of it?*" (In a game of poker, a savvy player would have recognized the question as Hugo Black's "tell").

"I didn't inquire into anybody's affairs," Bender said petulantly.

"You didn't know he was a minister?"

"No, sir."

"But you knew he was marrying people?"

"Yes, sir."

"But didn't know he was a preacher?"

"No, sir."

"You knew he was a Protestant?"

Bender finally gave up: "Yes, sir," he said.

It was a ridiculous exchange. The kind of back-and-forth that must have had the prosecutors squirming in their seats. For by the end of it, Hugo Black had made Fred Bender look like a fool, over nothing—something that the man probably said out of sheer defensiveness after suffering weeks of criticism in the local papers about his role in Ruth Stephenson's conversion.

"What is a godfather?" Black asked.

"A mere witness to baptism," said Bender, "like a witness to a marriage."

"Just a witness?" Black asked, skeptically.

"Yes, sir."

Doesn't a godfather look after the spiritual and welfare and comfort of his godchild?

Only if the parents of the child died, Bender said, until the child was eighteen.

"Or if the parents don't belong to that church—?"

"No, sir," Bender held firm.

"Isn't it true that the godfather is supposed to be the spiritual advisor?" Black insisted.

But Bender was finally on solid ground. He was the Catholic, not Hugo Black: "I never had to advise anybody at all," Bender replied, and added for good measure that Ruth Stephenson "was eighteen years old, and her own boss"; there would have been no call for him to advise her at all.[2]

Hugo Black looked for a way to regain the upper hand. Sometimes the best way was just to sling mud and see what stuck. Edwin and Mary Stephenson had told Hugo Black that someone must have been giving Ruth money. There were rumors that someone had even promised to pay to send her to Europe. Black asked Fred Bender if he had paid for Ruth's trip to Loretto, Tennessee, to get her out of town. The man denied it. Had he "contribute[d] any money to her before she left here?" No, sir. Know who did? No, sir. "You have sold out your business, haven't you?" Black asked, sowing a seed of doubt.

Fred Bender had decided to take his family out of Birmingham the month before. "Yes, sir," he said.

"Haven't any business now?"

"No, sir."

"Are you going abroad?"

Bender replied that they were taking a vacation to Los Angeles.

"You don't expect to go abroad?"

"I never did intend to," Bender said, resentfully.

"But you have no business now?"

"No, sir," Bender said sadly, "not a bit in the world."[3]

With that, it appeared that the saga for the Benders was nearly done, but Hugo Black recalled Anna Bender to ask just a few more questions, including whether she had ever suggested to Ruth Stephenson that the girl go abroad. "No," Anna Bender said, "that is a falsehood."

"You all sold out your business?"

"Yes, sir."

"Going abroad?"

It must have been hard for the woman to keep from shouting at the man: "No, sir, we are not."

"Where are you going?"

Probably the last thing Mrs. Bender wanted at that point was all of Birmingham to know where she and her family were headed. "I don't know where," she said.

Hugo Black perked up: "Haven't any idea?"

"No, sir."

"Haven't any remote idea?"

Joe Tate and his men must have wanted to curl up and die.

"No, sir."

"Your husband hasn't told you?"

"No, sir, don't know where we are going."

"Just going somewhere?"

"Yes, sir," the woman said again, "we don't know where we are going."

For the rest of the afternoon, the prosecutors called character witnesses to whittle away at the notion that Reverend Edwin Stephenson's reputation in the community was as good as his character witnesses had claimed. One after another, Charlie Neuer, B. G. Lackey, and Burr Hamilton Bell stated that they were familiar with how the community regarded the minister; not one had anything good to say about the man. As with Hugo Black's character witnesses, the prosecutors' witnesses were not on the stand for long. But undermining the credibility of a witness who attests that a person's reputation is bad is somehow never as easy as subverting the claim that it is good. The "good reputation" witness needs to be asked only two questions to begin to corrode a jury's confidence in the witness's assessment of the community's view of the person in question. In a murder trial, for example, the two key questions might be phrased as follows: *Are you familiar, sir, with the views of those who believe that X killed a man in cold blood?* And: *If good evidence proved that he did that, would you still be of the opinion that his reputation is good?* But perhaps for the same reason that humans are more readily captured by bad news than good, the witness who declares at a trial that another person's reputation is bad delivers a blow not as easily blunted.

Joe Tate and his assistants sorely wanted the jury to hear that Edwin Stephenson had lost his position as treasurer of the barbers' union over a scandal involving Stephenson's suspected theft of the dues paid by the union members. But evidentiary rules prevented John Morrow from asking his character witnesses about the *reasons* they had for believing Stephenson's reputation was bad. So long as Hugo Black did not "open the door" to such proof, perhaps by asking the men himself about their reasons for disliking Stephenson, the jury would never hear about them.

For that reason, a lawyer while cross-examining such a witness will do everything possible to avoid bringing the topic up—preferring instead to make oblique suggestions about the motivations or character of the *character witness*—with the goal of taking the focus off what the lawyer's client might have done to earn such ill repute. Therefore, after John Morrow had established on direct examination that Neuer, Lackey, and Bell knew the minister's reputation in the community to be bad, and that no, they wouldn't believe a word he said under oath, Hugo Black was faced with the task, when he cross-examined each of these witnesses, of persuading the jurors that the men harbored some murky, small-minded dislike of Black's client.

"Are your feelings toward Mr. Stephenson good or bad?" Black asked Charlie Neuer.

"Perfectly neutral."

"You testify to the jury your feelings toward him are perfectly neutral?"

"Yes, sir."

"Have nothing against him?"

"Not a thing."

"*Not a thing on earth?*"

"No, sir."

"You don't like him," Black fired back, more a statement than a question.

"No, I don't like him."

"So, is it true that you don't like him," Black pounced, "or true that your feelings are neutral toward him?"

And so it went, with each of the prosecutor's character witnesses, and every time one of them tried to explain why he disliked the man (Charlie Neuer: "I liked him up to the time he—"), Hugo Black would cut him off, demanding that he answer Black's question and nothing else.[4]

Burr Hamilton Bell, the last of the character witnesses to face Black's fiery cross, held up fairly well. Bell was a night watchman for the American Steel & Wire Company by the time of the trial, but he had come to know Stephenson as a fellow member of the barber's union years before. "Do you like Mr. Stephenson?" Black asked Bell.

"No, sir," Bell said flatly, "I haven't got any use for him now."

"You are very bitter towards him now?" Black asked.

"I guess you could call it so."

Did you contact the prosecutors and volunteer to come and testify about the bitterness you hold toward my client?

"No, sir," said Bell. "I didn't want to be a witness," he added.

Hugo Black was annoyed: "Will you kindly just answer my questions from now on?"

"Yes, sir," he said, but something must have told Bell he had rattled the lawyer.

"You tell the jury you are testifying a man's character is bad," Black said, but "your feelings are very bitter towards that man?"

"Yes, sir," Bell replied calmly, "I ain't got—"

Likely, Bell was about to say again that he had no use for Stephenson, but Hugo Black pulled him up short: "I didn't ask you anything else, did I?"

Burr Bell must have smiled.

"And it is funny to you to testify that a man's character is bad?" the lawyer asked, as he walked past the prosecutor's table, toward his seat. But John Morrow stood up then and spoke directly to Black instead of the judge: "Would you object to him stating *why* his feelings are bitter toward him?" asked Morrow.

Hugo Black was livid: "I will ask the court to instruct [Mr. Morrow] to address his remarks to the court and not to me," he shouted—and ask his own questions, and leave the objecting to him. So John Morrow obliged him, springing to his feet, asking Burr Bell if his feelings toward Stephenson had always been bitter. "No, sir," Bell replied, "I was his friend once." "Until when?" And before Hugo Black could stop him, Bell got out five words: "Up until he went crooked!"

The defense attorney exploded, asking the judge to exclude the statement, and to instruct the jury to disregard it, which Judge Fort promptly did. But Joe Tate and his men must have found some small satisfaction in the exchange. A night watchman had finally gotten under Hugo Black's skin.[5]

Burr Bell's sparring with Hugo Black was entertaining, but nothing could have competed with the electric sensation that rippled across Judge Fort's courtroom when Joe Tate rose to his feet near the end of the state's rebuttal case and called out the name "Pedro Gussman." Just as his appearance had drawn a gasp from the crowd before, the sound of the paperhanger's name stirred the spectators up again, causing Judge Fort to bang his gavel against his bench, demanding order, threatening to toss the transgressors from the room. Hugo Black's unusual procedure of parading Gussman in front of the jury in the middle of Edwin Stephenson's testimony had enabled the defendant to make his racial accusation while depriving Gussman of the chance to address the matter himself.

There was no guarantee, of course, but had Hugo Black put Gussman on the stand, his noticeable Spanish accent and "finely chiseled" features (and perhaps with the blinds pulled up) might have been enough to persuade the jury that Stephenson's claim was just a self-interested lie. For the second time during the trial of Edwin Stephenson, Joe Tate decided to handle the questioning of a witness himself.

The circuit solicitor eased in, asking Gussman for his age, what he did for a living, how long he had lived in Birmingham. He was forty-one, Pedro said, he worked as a wallpaper hanger, he had lived in the city going on fifteen years. "What nationality are you?" "Spanish descent." "Where were your father and mother born, if you know?" Barcelona, Spain." How long have you lived in this country? Nearly twenty-four years. How long had he known Ruth Stephenson? About eight.

Joe Tate moved to the day of the shooting. Yes, he recalled it, Gussman said. Yes, that was the day he married Ruth Stephenson. "Who married you?" "Father Coyle." Tate gestured toward the church anchoring the other end of the block: "Right over there?" "Yes, sir." "That on the same day that he was killed?" "Yes, sir." Tate asked if Father Coyle had known he and Ruth were coming to get married that day? No sir. They had made no previous arrangements with him? No, none. Tate asked the question again, for emphasis: "Did he know anything about it until you got there, so far as you know?" "No, sir." Then a third time, the trial lawyer's mantra: "You hadn't spoken with him about it?" "No, sir," Pedro said firmly.

Satisfied, Joe Tate turned back to the prosecutors' table, and beyond that to where Hugo Black was seated with his client, "That's all," he said.[6]

There was a moment in the life of every trial lawyer when he had to decide how far he was willing to go in the service of his client. It can't be known if Hugo Black had given much thought to what he would do if Joe Tate decided to put Pedro Gussman on the stand. So he may have had only the short time it took Tate to move through his questions with Pedro to decide on his course. Or maybe the lawyer had already cast his die, at the moment he darkened the room before ordering Pedro hauled before the jury; or during John Morrow's cross-examination of Stephenson, when he had leaped to his client's defense, saying: "he could not trace his lineage!" and "very difficult to trace some of them!"

If any remnants of doubt remained about how far Hugo Black would go to persuade Edwin Stephenson's jury to acquit him, the lawyer's cross-examination of Pedro Gussman must surely have removed them.

"Where were you born?" Black asked, rising to his feet.

"Porto Rico," Pedro said.

"How do you know where your father and mother were born?"

(*How does anyone know?*) "It was told me so," he said simply.

The defense lawyer turned back to Judge Fort then, moving to exclude all of the witness's prior statements about where his parents had been born: "he can't know" for sure, Black argued. "Overruled," Judge Fort said.

Black turned back to Gussman: "Did you ever see either one of them in Spain?"

"No sir, I never seen Spain."

"Did you ever see either one of them in Barcelona?"

Pedro was annoyed: "I just got through telling you I never was in Spain."

Black marched to the witness stand then and handed Pedro a newspaper clipping: "Is that your picture?"

"That is supposed to be the picture they got when they arrested me," Pedro replied resentfully. The paper had printed one of the mug shots taken by Chief Shirley's men after they arrested him on the out-of-state warrant for the murder of Pearl Gussman, before he was vindicated and released. As with most mug shots, its subject was not at his best.

"That was the picture of you that was made before you were dressed up and had your hair worked on?" Black fired back, offering the paper into evidence. The picture was handed to the jury.

No answer.

"When that picture was taken you had not been to the barber shop just before," had you?

"No, sir, they took me from my work."

Black appraised the man on the stand: "You have had the curls worked out since then?"

"I had a haircut," Pedro replied.

"When?"

"Last Monday."

"What else did they do to your hair?"

"Nothing else."

"Didn't smooth it down?"

"No, sir."

"Has anything been done to your hair since that picture was made?"

"No, sir," Pedro said, "don't use anything on my hair."

"Nothing has been done to your hair since that picture was made?" Black repeated skeptically as he moved to take his seat.

Pedro stuck to his guns: "No, sir."

———

On redirect examination, Joe Tate gave Pedro a chance to repeat that his parents were Spanish, but both men knew a thing or two about the power of racial suspicion. Hugo Black's suggestion that Pedro had had the kinks straightened from his hair had likely done its damage, and the longer Tate and Pedro spent on the question, the more defensive they must have looked. By the afternoon of October 21, the last day of the trial, as Pedro Gussman stepped down from the stand, Joe Tate and his men must have felt their case slipping away.[7]

What they needed was a miracle.

———

It is sometimes said that miracles come in unexpected packages, and when Douglas White appeared out of nowhere in the waning days of Edwin

Stephenson's trial, the man must have seemed the physical embodiment of the point. There was nothing expected about the coal miner from Lehigh, Alabama.

A day or so after Joe Tate and his men rested their case-in-chief, word reached the prosecutors that a man named Douglas White had seen the whole thing—the minister and the priest on the porch, the shooting, everything— a claim so unexpected and tardy that at first the prosecutors doubted that it was a miracle at all. Joe Tate and his men had tracked down a great number of claims of supposed eyewitnesses since the day Father Coyle was killed, and more often than not, they had found them lacking. It was hard to let their hopes be raised again. When they first heard that Douglas White of Lehigh had told a man out near Mount Pinson that he had witnessed the shooting, they were skeptical. But Joe Tate sent his assistant James Davis to hunt down the man, just in case.

Joe Tate was surprised when Davis returned with the man in tow, he later told the court, but after questioning Douglas White himself, he decided to put him on the stand.

"What is your name?" Tate asked.

"Douglas White."

"Where do you live?"

"Lehigh, Alabama."

"How long have you lived up there?"

"Four years," White said.

"What do you do?"

"Drive in the mines," he said.

Tate moved to the day of the shooting, giving Hugo Black his first clue about what the man might be about to say next: "Do you remember the occasion of Father Coyle being shot over here near the church?" Tate gestured.

"Yes, sir," Douglas White replied, "I was down between the courthouse and that building that [was torn] down when it happened."

Douglas White must have meant the old church goods supply house, the building that had served as the Catholics' parish house before the larger brick church was completed. On the bishop's order, the small building had been torn down shortly after Father Coyle was killed in preparation for work on a new rectory.

"Did you see the man that shot him?" Tate asked.

"Yes, sir."

"Where did he come from?"

But Joe Tate got no farther. Hugo Black had heard enough. "Now, we object to any questions to this witness which are not clearly in rebuttal," the lawyer complained to the judge. "The law contemplates that the state shall put on its evidence, and the defendant shall then put on its evidence. It has never contemplated that a supposed eye witness to a murder...could be held back..." It wasn't fair, "—not proper rebuttal testimony at all."

Without knowing where the prosecutor was headed, it was difficult for the judge to tell if the witness's proposed testimony was proper or not. It was true that the rules of evidence limited a lawyer during his rebuttal case to challenging a claim that his opponent has made during his case. It would have been improper, therefore, for Joe Tate to call additional witnesses during rebuttal solely to bolster the evidence already offered in the prosecution's case-in-chief. If what Douglas White had to say did no more than reiterate the prosecution's theory about the shooting, rather than responding to or undermining in some way some claim made during Hugo Black's defense case, the objection was sound. Without more of an idea of what the witness would say, however, Judge Fort had no way of knowing whether Black was right or not, so he dodged, telling Joe Tate to "confine the witness to rebuttal testimony."

"Did you see him shoot Father Coyle?" Tate asked White.

Hugo Black interrupted again, before White could answer, arguing that the witness could have been called earlier; and that if White were allowed to testify, the defense would have no choice but to reopen its entire case in response. Judge Fort told the prosecutor again to stick to rebuttal testimony.

"Did you see him walk up to the porch?" Tate asked White, drawing another loud objection from Black, and Judge Fort finally asked Tate what it was the witness proposed to say.

If the defense would just let the witness answer, Joe Tate replied, he *would* confine himself to rebutting what had been said during the defense case. Douglas White would say that he saw Edwin Stephenson walk up to the rectory gate, through it, and on up to the porch, and that he saw Stephenson pull his gun straightaway—"about the time he got on the porch" Tate said. Stephenson had testified that there had been conversation; Douglas White would say there was no conversation; that Stephenson had started firing straightaway. So the testimony was proper rebuttal, Joe Tate argued; White's testimony was "in direct contradiction" to what Stephenson had said during the defense's case.

The prosecutor was simply trying to offer a "supposed eyewitness" who could have been called earlier, in the prosecution's case-in-chief, Hugo Black complained in response. "They can't split it up like that." The witness would simply be going back over ground already covered.

The objection was meritless, and Black must have known it. There was no rule of evidence that prohibited Tate from calling a witness who could undermine testimony Black himself had offered during the defense case just because the man could have been called earlier. If what Douglas White had to say rebutted something Stephenson had said on the stand—which Tate's proffer suggested it would—the testimony was proper. Stephenson had testified at great length about what had happened on the porch: that the priest had invited the minister to join him; that the two men had chatted; that the priest had gone back into the rectory, then back out again, all before telling Stephenson that he had married his daughter to Gussman; before hitting Stephenson, and knocking him to his knees, all after Stephenson had told Father Coyle that he had ruined his home. If Douglas White proposed to say that all that was a lie, that there had been no conversation, or fight, that the minister had fired his gun as soon as he reached the porch, it was hard to see how the testimony fell afoul of the rule restricting rebuttal evidence.

But Judge Fort sustained the objection.

Joe Tate must have thought he had heard wrong. The state is not going over ground already covered, he told the judge. None of our witnesses have been able to say what happened on the porch before hearing the shots. This was not covered ground!

If Douglas White "knew anything about it," Black replied skeptically, "he should have been put on in the beginning."

What he has to say, Tate fired back, "is in contradiction to the defendant."

But Judge Fort said again he would sustain the objection.

Tate couldn't believe it. Surely the judge had misunderstood. The witness will say "there were no licks passed between them," he told the judge. Joe Tate faced the man still seated in the witness stand then, refusing to accept defeat, and he put a question directly to White himself: "Did you see any licks passed between the defendant and Father Coyle?"

But Hugo Black shouted his objection before White could utter a word.

"Sustained," said Judge Fort.

Tate was livid. "[W]e did not get hold of this witness until the state had closed" its case-in-chief, he said.

Judge Fort hesitated, giving Tate a moment of hope.

Hugo Black must have noticed the judge's indecision. "That makes it worse than ever," Black replied, "one of those new discoveries."

We used "every diligence in the world," John Morrow said, jumping in then. When we heard that a man "up here in the country" was saying he had been standing near the rectory when the minister fired his gun, we began to investigate. But the news only reached us while we were completing their examination of the witnesses in their direct case.

Black objected to the prosecutor speaking in front of the jurors about what White would say, but John Morrow ignored him and plowed ahead: "As soon as I got word of that," he said, "I sent a man up there immediately to investigate that report and see if it was true. When he got there, he found it was true," the prosecutor went on, "and brought the witness back."

"When did you first see the witness?" Judge Fort asked.

When he first walked into our office yesterday morning, replied Morrow.

It didn't matter, Black argued. They had the information about him earlier than that even if they hadn't met with him.

We needed time to determine "whether there was some substance behind" the man's statement, Morrow shot back.

Judge Fort paused again: If the witness only arrived yesterday, that was after "the state had rested its case," he said to Black.

Morrow jumped in again, seizing his advantage, echoing what the judge had just said: "We rested it the day before." And we are offering Mr. White "to contradict the defendant about what he says happened on that porch," which we hadn't had "any way in the world to get at until we got this witness." If they had known that the report about White was right, they would have asked the court to hold the case up until they had a chance to bring him to Birmingham. "But in a case like this," Morrow went on, "we receive many reports, and when we run them down, some of them are found to be unfounded, and some to be true."

"I have had information like that from a great many other people," Morrow forged ahead, "and when I asked the people about it, I found it was a mistake, and for that reason I didn't think it necessary to ask the court to hold up this trial for a day or two until we could bring the man down here when we were not sure whether he saw [the shooting] or not."

The lawyers went back and forth, arguing for several more minutes, until Judge Fort seemed prepared to rule. "I think it is too late, gentlemen, to offer testimony that should have been offered originally."

So Douglas White got no further. The miner from Lehigh was told to step down from the stand.

It was a devastating blow. Until that point, some of Judge Fort's rulings had gone the prosecution's way; many more had not. But this ruling bore the qualities of a death knell. Joe Tate asked the court's permission to bring the jurors to the porch of the Catholic rectory so that they could see for themselves the wounds Stephenson's gun had left there, after which the state would rest, Tate said.[8]

It was nearly 4:30 P.M. on October 20, 1921, when the twelve men charged with deciding Edwin Stephenson's fate stepped onto the porch of St. Paul's rectory, accompanied by a bailiff. The judge had assented to the state's request that the jurors be given a slim metal wire to trace the path of Stephenson's bullets. The jurors were still making their investigation when the bells of St. Paul's began to toll. "By strange coincidence there was a funeral underway in the church next door," one paper later reported. A small crowd of passersby stopped to watch the men as the church bells showered them with low, mournful reverberations, as if beseeching them to remember the life that had been taken there.[9]

———

In 1921, judges who presided over criminal trials still allotted generous amounts of time for opposing lawyers to make their closing arguments. Judge Fort agreed to a total of five hours, to be split evenly between the prosecutors and the defense team. Because the prosecution carried the burden of proof, it was permitted to deliver its closing argument first and last, with the defense's closing argument sandwiched in between.

The only records that remain of the closing arguments made by the lawyers in the case against Edwin Stephenson are the newspaper accounts filed by the reporters who sat through the trial. Going first, John Morrow rose from his chair and turned toward the box of jurors, with the plan that Joe Tate would conclude the state's argument after the jury heard from the defense. For forty-five minutes, Morrow reviewed for the jury the evidence that proved Stephenson guilty of killing Father Coyle with malice aforethought, and that decimated each one of his excuses. The proof all pointed to one conclusion, Morrow said: that Stephenson had killed Father Coyle out of religious hatred. His claim of self-defense was meritless: "Can a man go into another man's house and create a situation in order to kill him, and then come into court of justice and ask for freedom?" Morrow asked. The law said he could not. The law said that a man lost whatever claim of self-defense he might have had if he himself provoked the affray, such as by going to another man's home, and calling him a dirty dog, or saying he had ruined his home—"a man shot down on his front porch without so much as a pocket knife on him!" That was not self-defense, Morrow said.

The jurors should not replicate Stephenson's bigotry. "The Protestants are in the majority in this community, and the Catholics are in the minority," John Morrow allowed. "It is now in the hands of the Protestants as to whether they will give the Catholics decent treatment. I belong to the majority, as you do," the prosecutor went on, "and I demand justice for all. What you and I demand, we ought to be willing to give in return." Morrow turned toward

Edwin Stephenson then, pointed at the man, and said: "Can you doubt that this man is a cold-blooded murderer?"

If the prosecutor hoped to get a rise from the minister, he was disappointed. Stephenson stared back at him "unflinchingly," one reporter wrote. John Morrow returned the favor: Can you doubt "that if you acquit him you will have turned loose one of the guiltiest men ever tried? He says he has no prejudice against the Catholics, but who on this jury believes that statement?" "When the time comes that Catholics and Protestants cannot get equal protection under the law," said the prosecutor, "let's tear down our courthouse and put every man on his guard."

Nearly finished, John Morrow looked over the twelve men seated in front of him: "The eyes of the world are on this jury," he warned them solemnly. "Men and women everywhere are waiting to see if twelve southern men will permit bigotry and religious prejudice to free a cold-blooded murderer." He pleaded with the men to erase prejudice from their minds: "When you render your verdict, gentlemen, be fair; be just to those people. Do not try to persecute them by crucifying one of their priests in this courtroom."[10]

The hour was getting late by the time John Morrow was done, so Judge Fort adjourned for the day. They would resume with counsel arguments the next morning, he said.

It can no longer be known how Ruth Gussman learned that the lawyers at her father's trial had finished introducing their proof and had moved on to closing arguments, and that she would not be called to testify. It is possible that one of the prosecutors informed her, or that she heard it from a friend after the trial adjourned that day. Or maybe she learned it from the early morning issue of the *Age-Herald* the next day. However she heard of it, it is not difficult to imagine the wave of disappointment that must have swept over her when she realized that Joe Tate and his men would not put her on the stand to tell her side of the story; that the official court record would include only her parents' account and the witnesses who had scrambled to aid them.

But if Birmingham had learned anything about the girl at the center of the violence at St. Paul's rectory in 1921, it was that she would find a way to make her feelings known. The prosecutors might have chosen to silence her, Ruth must have thought to herself, but they could not keep her from the room.

A tremor of excitement rippled across the courtroom the next morning when Ruth Gussman and her companion, Lenis Patt from Loretto, Tennessee, quietly entered. Ruth wore a lovely blue traveling suit, the papers noted, with a matching blue hat trimmed with a velvet ribbon and a tiny feather.

A pair of stylish brown pumps completed the ensemble. The outfit brought out the blue in the pretty girl's eyes, one reporter thought. What the reporters noticed most, though, was that Ruth Gussman had "bobbed her hair." The hairstyle, all the rage at the time in some cities, had yet to win the approval of Birmingham. "You look a fright with your hair bobbed, Ruth," one of the girl's aunts was overheard to whisper to her, but Ruth didn't reply.

As soon as the men in the press corps noticed them, the journalists made room for the two young women at their table, no doubt hoping for some publishable comment. The trial had not yet reconvened, and Ruth's parents had yet to arrive; the newsmen took advantage of the quiet to whisper a few questions to Pedro Gussman's bride. Ruth told them she had nothing to say at that time, but she promised to deliver a letter to the papers after the trial concluded, which she hoped they would publish in its entirety, she said. A few minutes later, her parents arrived, but neither appeared to notice their daughter. It wasn't until after the trial resumed that Mary Stephenson finally saw her. Mrs. Stephenson quickly looked away, one reporter noted, and did not look back at her daughter again. "Edwin Stephenson apparently did not see her at all."[11]

Throughout the morning, Fred Fite for the defense and John McCoy for the state squared off, leaving the last arguments to be made by Hugo Black and Joe Tate. Fred Fite walked the jurors methodically through the defendant's claims of insanity and self-defense, never once conceding the tension between the two arguments. "No man has a right," Fite bellowed, "to interfere with a father's management of his child and his wishes toward her religious belief. Is it natural for a child to go against her parents as Ruth did?" he asked them, as though the answer were perfectly clear. "Fred Bender knew when he acted as the godfather to Ruth that he was invading the sanctity of the Stephenson home"—though it made no difference who it was who took her; either way, "old man Stephenson was crazy" over it, Fite added. "When they come into his home, and take the last child he has—the only child the Lord has allowed him to rear—do you think he could be normal then?" When his only daughter was ripped from her home, "their hopes for her blasted?"

Nothing was off limits; Fred Fite swung back and forth between affirming the rule of patriarchy—a father's control over his home—and trying to evoke the jurors' sympathy for the loss of client's daughter. He implored them "to protect the homes of Alabama by clearing the man who had sought only to maintain and protect his home"—though no matter what they decided, Fite told them solemnly, no verdict could send the minister "back to his home." "The house where he lives is not a home anymore," he said, not with the daughter he so loved forever "gone." Tears glistened in the eyes of many in the courtroom as Fred Fite went on, one reporter wrote. "And this little woman here," the lawyer gestured toward Mary Stephenson seated just behind her husband, "a mother whose child is gone from her forever though she is not in her grave—she's been through the Gethsemane herself," Fite said, invoking the image of Jesus agonizing in the garden of Gethsemane. "Picture her going into the valley of the shadow to bring her child into the world," Fite continued, his remarks becoming increasingly pastoral; "picture her watching over the babe in its cradle, praying as only a mother can pray and looking forward to the day of her radiant womanhood."

"Did she or her kindly old husband ever think things would come to *this?*" Fite asked. "No!" the answer exploded from him, "either of them would say: 'Sooner than that, I would rather my child was in her grave!'"

Edwin Stephenson put his handkerchief to his eyes. His wife Mary bowed her head and wept.

"Does the law of God or the law of man give any man the right to take the child of another?" Fite asked them. "My religion teaches me that my child is my own."

"I want to tell you right here, gentlemen," he said gravely, looking each of the jurors in the eye, "the man who takes *my* child and constitutes himself as a godfather to direct her religious training has got to reckon with me. The man who robs my wife of her babe and daughter has got to reckon with me too."[12]

It must have been hard for Ruth to listen to Fite's arguments. According to the reporters, he appeared unaware of her presence in the courtroom—oblivious. Fite painted a picture of her to the jury—a silly, naïve girl, whose only smart decision had been to leave her Porto Rican husband—and then contrasted that with her parents: constant in their love, devoted to her welfare, tormented by those who would steal her away. It seems doubtful that Ruth could have anticipated the intensity of the lawyer's assault, or given thought to the fact that she would be given no chance to defend herself against it, with the lawyers' cases closed—that she could only sit there, in silence. When Fite finally finished, and the judge announced they would take a short break, Ruth had heard enough. She rose, and she and her companion began to make their way out of the room. But Ruth's mother stood up then, too, and faced her daughter, slowing her steps. The newsmen who later described the encounter seemed to remember it differently, but all of them wrote that, at the prodding of others in the room, Ruth went to her mother, took her briefly in her arms, and kissed her gently. And that after that, she kissed her father, too, the reporters wrote, although more reluctantly, even "perfunctorily," one thought, before quickly pulling away and walking to the hall and out of the building.

Some of the newsmen seemed so pleased with the idea of the family's reconciliation that they filled their columns the next day with sentimental gushings about the meeting between the Stephensons and their prodigal daughter. "Ruth and her Family Reconciled," boomed a banner headline of the *Post* the next day; "Girl Goes into Parents' Arms, All Three Weep." But J. Fisher Rothermel, the reporter who noticed how Hugo Black had darkened the courtroom before calling Pedro Gussman into the courtroom during Edwin Stephenson's testimony, was doubtful that the short interlude meant very much at all. "Was It Reconciliation?" wondered a headline of the *News,* over Rothermel's article about the family's chance meeting. "Not a word passed" between the girl and her parents, Rothermel wrote, and it had seemed to him that Ruth broke away from her father as soon as he had circled his arms around her and patted her back, and then Rothermel thought he noticed "a slight quiver to her lips" and "a look of pain in her eyes" as she walked away.[13]

When the closing arguments resumed, John McCoy went next, stressing as John Morrow had that there had never been more interest in a case in the state's history, and reminding the jury "that it had taken an oath, to try the case without malice or prejudice."[14] The evidence in the case clearly established Stephenson's guilt, he told the jurors: that Stephenson "had gone home on the afternoon of the shooting and gotten his pistol." The judge would instruct them, McCoy told them, that the law presumed malice from Stephenson's possession and use of that deadly weapon. They had all the evidence they needed to convict.

After Stephenson failed to get a search warrant to look for his daughter, McCoy continued, and despite the lack of any evidence that Father Coyle had interested himself in any way in Ruth's conversion, or any proof that "any Catholics were trying to take his daughter away from Protestantism," he reminded them, Stephenson's heart was filled with "prejudice and hate." And the defense had tried to exploit that prejudice as well, McCoy said, by interjecting race into the trial, insinuating that Pedro Gussman was a Negro, without offering an iota of proof. It was a lie, "and all the evidence on the point was to the contrary." It was hate, not fear or insanity, that had motivated Stephenson's act, McCoy told them—not one witness had "been able to swear on the witness stand that the defendant was crazy."

"The Protestant people of Birmingham, the judges and court officials, and yourselves are being tried today, as well as Mr. Stephenson," McCoy intoned, before taking his seat.

A crowd bigger than any other previous one filled Judge Fort's courtroom that afternoon to hear the final arguments of Hugo Black and Joe Tate. "An absolute quiet" filled the room as Hugo Black rose to his feet. The lawyer was slim and wiry, the energetic frame of a man with a lifelong passion for the game of tennis, and he spoke with the southern accent of his home state—an accent he would never fully lose, even after moving a few years later to Washington, D.C., after supporters elected him to the United States Senate, before he was appointed an associate justice of the United States Supreme Court.

As John Morrow, Fred Fite, and John McCoy had done before him, Hugo Black marched through the evidence, but he urged the jurors to see the proof in a different light. "There should be no halo of glory" perched on the heads of the prosecutors simply because they chose to prosecute the case, Black told the twelve men seated in the jury box—though judging from Mr. McCoy's and Mr. Morrow's speeches, the prosecutors seemed to think they were entitled to it. He reminded the jury that the burden of proof in a criminal case rested always on the state, and that the jury was required by law to presume his client innocent until the prosecutors proved him guilty beyond a reasonable doubt—which the prosecutors couldn't do, Black argued, if his client had been shown to have a valid defense.

The prosecutors have said that the defense hoped the jury would decide the case based on prejudice, said Black. Not true. "I have tried to be fair in my conduct of the case." The defense "had not appealed to any passion or prejudice." But the same could not be said about the prosecutors, he fumed. "It was the state, not the defense," that had introduced the issue of religion into the trial, he said, by making it known that the man who had died "was a priest of the Catholic Church, and the slayer was a Methodist minister."

The argument was nonsense—as if it would have been possible to try the case without bringing out the facts that Father Coyle was a Catholic priest—but the crowd was very still as the defense lawyer continued. The state's proof of his client's guilt was plainly insufficient, said Black. The prosecutors had based their case almost wholly on the testimony of Edwin McGinty and William D. Chiles—those "Siamese twins," he mocked—the only two witnesses who claimed to have seen Stephenson on the porch. These men were not to be believed, Black said; the inaccuracies in their accounts were so numerous they threw suspicion on every other part—they were "brothers in falsehood, as well as in faith," he said, reminding the jurors: Edward McGinty was a Catholic, and Chiles had married his Catholic sister. Of course they had flown to the defense of the priest who had married Stephenson's daughter to Pedro Gussman.

And as for Father Coyle himself, Hugo Black went on, "because a man becomes a priest does not mean that he is divine." "He has no more right to protection than a Protestant minister." Neither did he nor any of his friends have a right to tamper with another man's home: "A child of a Methodist does not suddenly depart from her religion unless someone has planted in her mind the seeds of influence!" It made no difference to him, Black said, whether Fred Bender had locked Ruth Stephenson up in his home or she had locked herself in: "There is such a thing as imprisonment of the human will by influence, vice and persuasion. When you find a girl who has been reared well, persuaded from her parents by some cause or person, that cause or person is wrong."

Finally, the lawyer turned once to the question of Pedro Gussman's race: "there are twenty mulattoes to every Negro in Porto Rico," Black told them. "If Pedro Gussman was as the state had said—of proud Castilian descent—he has descended a long way." And as for the eyes of the world—the men and women outside of Birmingham whom the prosecutors had suggested had an interest in the outcome of the case—only you have seen the evidence, Black said. You alone have considered the testimony of the witnesses. "I admit that there are certain localities where a verdict of guilty from this jury would be looked upon with favor," Black said, "but those eyes have nothing to do with the evidence in the case." You must "return a fair verdict without regard to any fear that Birmingham might receive a black eye" from the judgments of those not here to see the proof. If they had so much as a reasonable doubt, it was their obligation to acquit Stephenson.

"If the eyes of the world are upon the verdict of this jury," Black prodded them, "I would write that verdict in words that cannot be misunderstood, that the homes of the people of Birmingham cannot be touched. If that brings disgrace, God bring the disgrace."[15]

There is no record of Joe Tate's thoughts as he rose to give the last argument in the prosecution of Edwin Stephenson. But it is clear from his remarks that the prosecutor understood the powerful social commitments pulling at the twelve men in the jury box. Hugo Black and Fred Fite had tried to exploit each one: the father protecting his home against religious and racial assault; the mother victimized and abandoned by a wayward daughter, the wife tortured by the threat of losing her husband as well; the insidious, if amorphous, danger to all of their homes presented by that alien religion in their midst. It was smoke and mirrors—a defense designed to pull the jurors' focus away from the evidence and toward the fears and bigotry they might share in common with the minister; a defense that sought to make Edwin

Stephenson out as a guardian not simply of the welfare of his daughter but of their daughters as well.

Joe Tate reminded the jurors again that because the charge was murder in the second degree, not murder in the first degree, the law only required the state to prove that there had been a death, occasioned by the intentional act of the defendant. The state had done that, he told them. The minister himself had admitted on the stand that he killed Father Coyle with a gun, and the judge would instruct them that when death was brought about by the use of such a deadly weapon, they were entitled to presume that the killing was intentional. The state had met its burden, Tate told them, with the testimony of the defendant himself, who admitted that he shot Father Coyle, and the doctor who testified that Stephenson's bullet was the cause of the priest's death as well.

If there was insufficient proof in the case as Mr. Black said, Tate told the jurors, it was the weakness of the evidence offered by the defense in support of Stephenson's claims. Certainly none of it was enough to substantiate Edwin Stephenson's claim that he had been attacked, Tate argued. A plea of self-defense required that a defendant prove "that he was free from fault in bringing on the fight, that he was in imminent danger of death or bodily harm, and that there was no reasonable avenue of escape," the prosecutor reminded them. But the minister's claim was implausible. Edwin Stephenson had said that the priest had knocked him down, that he shot Coyle when the priest had hold of his suspenders. Impossible—there were no powder burns on the fallen rector. If the two men had been that close to each other, physical signs of it would have been left behind. There were none. No witness to the shots heard or saw a fight. The bump on Stephenson's head had only appeared after he had been left alone in his cell. The priest had been unarmed. And even had there been a fight, Tate went on, the law denied Stephenson the right to claim self-defense if he himself had provoked it, which he had done by his own admission—if one believed him—by calling the priest a dirty dog. Neither did the defendant's claim of temporary insanity jibe with the facts, Tate told them: not one of the defense's witnesses could testify that the man was crazy. Though wasn't it peculiar that both the city and county officials were all on the defendant's side?

The circuit solicitor's points were logical, his march through the evidence methodical. But the veteran prosecutor must have known that trials do not always turn on logic. He eyed the twelve men who would decide the minister's fate and reminded them that the case was bigger than the charge against Edwin Stephenson: "The law punishes murder to deter others from committing the crime. If you go into the jury room and kick out the evidence, gentlemen of the jury, and then render a verdict of not guilty, you will have all the narrow-minded, fuzzy-necked people come out and pat you on the back," Tate conceded; "but the remainder of your lives," he warned, "you will have your consciences to prick and sting you."

With that Joe Tate took his seat.

The rest did not take long. Judge Fort gave his charge to the jurors, explaining what the law demanded of the prosecutors to prove a second-degree murder charge and how the burden to provide evidence shifted to the defense to substantiate a claim of self-defense or a claim of insanity. The judge's description was as Joe Tate and his men had said it would be; the real issue was what the jurors would make of the evidence—which story about the events on the porch they would deem more persuasive. Judge Fort finished his instructions at 6:00 P.M. on Friday, October 21, 1921, and the jury retired to the deliberation room with a copy of the indictment, Stephenson's gun, and the pair of torn suspenders.

A little more than four hours later, the foreman of the jury sent a note to the judge saying the men had reached a verdict, and the defendant, the lawyers, and as many as of the press corps and spectators as could be found on short notice hurried back into the courtroom to hear their decision. Mrs. Stephenson was there, one paper reported, and a handful of others, but the room was largely vacant, "in strange contrast to its appearance during the trial" when it had been filled to over-capacity.

When the jurors were reassembled, Judge Fort turned to the foreman and asked if the men had reached a unanimous decision. "We have, your honor," T. A. Lappage replied, and he handed a slip of paper to the clerk, who brought it to the judge. Judge Fort read it silently, and then handed it back to the clerk to be returned to the foreman, who was asked to read it out loud: "We the jury find the defendant not guilty," he said.

The crowd in the courtroom may have been small, but their cheers filled the room, signaling their approval. Stephenson and his wife embraced, visible tears in their eyes. Fred Fite and Hugo Black shook Stephenson's hand in congratulations, as Judge Fort banged his gavel and shouted for order. When quiet was restored, the judge thanked the jury for their service, telling them they would probably never again be called on to decide a case attracting more public interest, and that though there were sure to be many who had felt otherwise, he considered their decision "the honest verdict of twelve honest men."

As the jurors filed out of the room, Edwin Stephenson grasped the hand of each man in turn, thanking them one by one. He then approached Judge Fort, still seated at the bench, "I am a broken hearted man," said Stephenson to the judge, "but I am going to try to live so that no man on the jury will ever be sorry for the verdict they rendered." Minutes later, the warden of the county jail noted in his register for October 21, 1921, that Edwin R. Stephenson was "released by acquittal," and Chief Deputy Fred McDuff drove the minister and his wife back to their home. As word of the verdict spread, friends and well-wishers soon descended on the Stephenson house and kept the two parents up well into the night.[16]

The deliberations of juries are never transcribed. The only clues about their secret discussions come from jurors' willingness to speak about them after the fact. Reporters from the *Age-Herald,* the *News,* and the *Post* persuaded the foreman of Stephenson's jury to say a few words about how the men had reached their verdict. Lappage was reluctant to comment on the specific things said during the jurors' deliberations, he said, but he told the newsmen that the men had given the matter careful and prayerful consideration. "The first thing we did when we got back from supper," said Lappage, "was to read several selections from the Bible...excerpts from the words of Jesus...read by one of our number, a fervent and upright Christian," the foreman assured the journalists. The ballot to free Stephenson was unanimous; no dissenters.[17]

Epilogue

RUTH STEPHENSON PUT an end to the press's premature celebrations of her supposed reconciliation with her parents the day after the jury returned its verdict. As promised, Ruth delivered a letter to the three local papers denying that she and her parents had patched up their disagreements. The journalists had seen only what they had wanted to see, she wrote. Her parents had abused her for the last seven years, and then denied to the world ever having done it. Only self-imposed blinders could have led the reporters to think she could so easily forgive the mistreatment.

At the request of the prosecutors, Ruth had been in the city since the evening before the trial began, she wrote. But Joe Tate and his men had declined to call her as a witness for reasons known only to them. She had wanted to testify, the letter said. She had wanted a chance to expose the events that had taken place inside her parents' home; to answer the "great misrepresentations" that were being heard at the trial, and the "common gossip" that had abounded from the time of the shooting. The prosecutor's refusal to call her stole any chance she had to reveal her parents' bitter punishments: "how they beat me, locked me in my room for days at a time, how they hounded me, humiliated me, and mistreated me." It was years of abuse that had caused her to lose respect for her parents' religion, she wrote, not the influence of any Catholic. And as for the love they professed for her—"if that is an example of their love, then I shall be much better off without it." She would leave Birmingham, Ruth's letter ended, and take the time she needed to forget.

It can't be known what spurred Douglas White to take the time to record in writing what he knew about the events of August 11, 1921, after Edwin Stephenson's trial was over. The minister was back at his home with his wife, and double jeopardy principles guaranteed that Stephenson would never again be tried for ending Father Coyle's life, no matter what new evidence came to light. So nothing Douglas White had to say could pose a legal threat to Stephenson, and likely White knew it.

Maybe White simply wanted to deny Stephenson's lawyer the satisfaction of silencing him outside of Judge Fort's courtroom, as well as in it. Or maybe he realized that his knowledge about Stephenson's act would soon be lost in the absence of some special effort to preserve it. Whatever his reason, about a month after the Stephenson jury returned its verdict, White memorialized his recollections of the events of August 11 in a sworn affidavit, attesting to the truth of his statements under penalty of law. And not long after, the Catholic newspaper *Daily American Tribune* learned about it and published the document in its entirety, extending the shelf life of the man's memories even further.

In his affidavit, White swore, in the presence of a notary public, that he "was in Birmingham, Alabama on the evening of August 11th, 1921," standing "in front of the Church Goods House of the Catholic Church" on Third Avenue, working on the headlights of his car, at a distance of "about sixty feet away from the rectory." He saw Reverend Stephenson pass by, open the gate to St. Paul's rectory, walk "into the yard and up the steps upon the porch, where Father Coyle was sitting in the swing." Once there, White swore, the minister pulled a gun and started firing without any warning: "as he went up the steps he pulled out of his rear or hip pocket a pistol and fired three shots in succession." There had been no fight. The minister began shooting as soon as he reached the porch. "I saw no scuffle between the Rev. Stephenson and Father Coyle," White swore. Father Coyle had never had a chance.

Criticism of the anti-Catholicism that corrupted Birmingham and other parts of the country in the early decades of the 1900s grew louder after Reverend Edwin Stephenson was acquitted in October 1921, although it took some time before publications like the *Menace* went out of vogue, and the anti-Catholic sentiments fostered by groups like the Ku Klux Klan and the True Americans lost their potency. (It is roundly acknowledged that Governor Alfred E. Smith's run for the presidency of the United States in 1928 was defeated due to his Catholicism.) The day after Stephenson's trial concluded, the governor of Alabama denounced the verdict in a speech given at the Tutwiler Hotel in downtown Birmingham before a large group of alumni of the University of Alabama. It would seem "that a jury in Jefferson County has made an open season in Alabama for the killing of Catholics," Governor Emmett O'Neil told his audience. But "no thoughtful citizen could but feel that human life had become cheaper and less secure in Alabama" after reading about Stephenson's acquittal. "We have not advanced far from savagery or barbarism if murder is to be justified on account of the religious creed of the victim," the governor said.

The laws of the state were not inadequate to meet such criminal acts, Governor O'Neil continued: It was the *administration* of the law that was deficient, he said, not the laws themselves. "Has not the time come in Alabama when we should adopt some method of securing stronger, abler and more courageous judges to enforce our criminal law?" he asked. "If a man is guilty and the evidence establishes his guilt, but "his release is demanded by a majority of the people, and the judge yields to public sentiment," O'Neil said, "he is unworthy of the office he holds."[1]

Judge William Fort could not have been pleased.

Despite the governor's criticism, Stephenson's acquittal also attracted ample support in the community. Following the verdict, the papers printed a flurry of letters whose authors evoked Christianity and the importance of guarding against miscegenistic marriage to defend the jury's decisions. "It was a fair trial, by an impartial jury," W. G. Black of Tuscaloosa insisted, "and the *News* smudges it own name by trying to fan the smoldering embers into a flame by the base defamation of the men who composed the jury. Birmingham has exonerated herself in the eyes of the Christian world by protecting the sanctity of its home and the chastity of its womanhood."[2] J. A. MacKnight of Birmingham concurred: "There was not a man on that jury who had not carefully weighed the provocation, the misery, the humiliation and outrage which Stephenson had suffered at the hands of the meddling priest," MacKnight wrote. "Every man among them felt that he would have gone to the priest just as Stephenson did, to ask where his daughter was being kept, and that when the priest insolently told him that his daughter was already married by him to a Negro, and started in to assault the protesting parent, that they might have defended themselves just as Stephenson did, even to the use of a deadly weapon."[3] Another writer, R. R. Stanfield of Attalla, Alabama, agreed, though he understood that, strictly speaking, the criminal law of the state could reasonably lead one to conclude that Stephenson's act was unjustifiable: "Possibly he wasn't, as far as self-defense was involved in the matter, or insanity," Stanfield conceded. But he had a perfect right to protect his home and family from Catholic influence if he so desired. When we are denied the right to protect our homes and families, Gabriel had better grab his trumpet, Stanfield warned.[4]

The prosecutor responsible for pursuing the prosecution of Reverend Edwin Stephenson may have felt the wrath of such letter writers in the voting booth. After years of service as circuit solicitor for Jefferson County, Joe

Tate was voted out of office in the next election. He was defeated a second time when he tried to regain his former job four years later.

Joe Tate's reasons for not calling Ruth Stephenson as a witness at her father's trial remain a secret of history. It is reasonable to think that the prosecutor sincerely believed that Ruth would do his case against the minister more harm than good. Nonetheless, fairly or not, rumors that Joe Tate had not wanted to convict the minister could still be heard in Birmingham years after the trial's conclusion, in part due to his decision not to call Ruth Stephenson Gussman as a witness.

Looking back with the advantage of time and distance, the suspicion seems unfounded. Joe Tate battled the grand jury behind closed doors for weeks in pursuit of an indictment against the minister. There would have been little reason for this perseverance save a genuine desire to see Stephenson charged. What's more, Joe Tate and Hugo Black had crossed swords before: they were hardly friends. Tate had stood at the center of what Black long remembered as "the worst political turmoil" of his life: the loss of his power as county solicitor four years before Stephenson's trial. There is little reason to believe that either of the men would have wanted to lose to the other. The most compelling proof of the desire of Tate and his men to see Stephenson convicted, though, is the manner in which they conducted the trial, stopping at nothing less than Joe Tate making himself a witness in the case. The passion threading through the prosecutors' closing statements urging the 1921 jury to convict the minister would also have been hard to fake.

There is no way of knowing whether the case could have been saved by calling Ruth Stephenson Gussman as a witness. It is possible. But there is good reason to doubt it. The numerous articles written about the bride in the lead-up to the trial revealed the city's poor regard for her: Ruth's choices collided with the most deeply engrained religious and gender expectations of the day. She was a pariah to her family and neighbors, and Joe Tate would have known it. Worse, by the start of the trial, her marriage to Gussman had already fallen apart, a point the defense undoubtedly would have used to ridicule the young woman's choices even more had she taken the stand. Probably there was little the prosecutors could have done at the time to win a conviction of Reverend Edwin Stephenson. It is even possible that the case was over from the moment the court swore in the jury—that no amount of prosecutorial evidence, no impoverishment in the defense's argument, would have been enough to persuade Stephenson's judges to side with the Catholic priest over one of their own.

Years later, when asked why he had agreed to defend Stephenson in 1921, Hugo Black claimed that when Crampton Harris had telephoned him in

Boulder asking if he would take the case, Black had been confused about the prisoner's identity, he said—he thought that another Birmingham minister named Stephenson had been the one arrested. True or not, the answer may hint at a particle of regret about his role in the case, although Black himself never confessed it.

After the trial, there was talk that secret hand gestures of the Ku Klux Klan had been exchanged during the closing arguments of Stephenson's trial; that the foreman of the jury was a Klansman, that other jurors were as well, even the presiding judge. It is known that three of Stephenson's four attorneys had been initiated into the secret fraternity prior to the trial—of the team, only Hugo Black had yet to join. Edwin Stephenson's noticeable calm during the trial may in part be explained by the odds having been stacked in his favor in this way. "Hugo didn't have much trouble winning that verdict," James Esdale, the head of the Alabama Klan, said later, smugly.[5]

Two years later, Hugo Black joined the Klan as well, at a huge ceremony held in Edgewood Park, where he donned the imperial empire's iconoclastic white robes and, placing his left hand over his heart while raising his right toward heaven, "palm downward in a fascist-like salute," he mouthed, in sync with fifteen hundred other new initiates, the Klan's oath of secrecy and lifelong brotherhood. When Hugo Black decided to run for the United States Senate four years after Stephenson's trial, the Klan's support helped the ambitious lawyer win the seat. The grand dragon of the Alabama Klan, James Esdale, assured Black before his run for the Senate that he would safeguard Hugo's letter of resignation from the Klan for the day Black needed it to assure the empire's critics that he was no longer a member. Grateful, Hugo Black tendered his resignation letter on Esdale's official letterhead on July 9, 1925, over the closing: "Yours, I.T.S.U.B. (Yours, In the Sacred Unfailing Bond), Hugo L. Black."[6]

For the remainder of his life, Hugo Black would be asked why he had joined the Ku Klux Klan. Over the years, he offered numerous explanations: he was just a "joiner," Black said one time—he joined all sorts of fraternal groups—it was helpful for networking. Or: no one who wanted to run for public office in Alabama at the time had a prayer of being elected without being in the Klan, he stated on another occasion, as if political ambition and expedience satisfactorily justified the thing. Even: the Klan was simply a fraternal organization at the time he joined it, not "anti-Catholic, anti-Jewish, or anti-Negro," he said. The justifications had the ring of defensiveness, and his decision to join the secret order would forever mar his legal career, despite its other soaring successes.[7]

Years after Black's election to the Senate, a fellow senator raised, during a public session, the question of Black's former membership in the Klan. But

Black dismissed the accusation as speculative. Public confirmation of it did not come to light until 1938, as a result of the persistent sleuthing of an investigative reporter for the *Pittsburgh Post Gazette,* Ray Sprigle, after President Franklin D. Roosevelt nominated Black for a seat on the United States Supreme Court. The disclosure of Black's Klan membership was an embarrassment, but he survived the scandal and was sworn in as associate justice.[8]

Three decades later, Justice Black was still sitting on the Supreme Court when a case fittingly named *Loving v. Virginia* challenged the constitutionality of a Virginia law that made it a crime for any white person to marry a black person. Hugo Black joined the Court's unanimous decision declaring the law unconstitutional.

It is perhaps no surprise that decisions such as that won Justice Black little praise from many of his former supporters back in Alabama. And over the decades of his tenure on the Court, as Hugo Black authored or signed on to a number of decisions that expanded the civil and criminal rights of African Americans, more than one of those former supporters told the native son of Alabama that he was a traitor to the white race. In 1954, when Justice Black joined the Supreme Court's unanimous decision in *Brown v. Board of Education* ordering the desegregation of public schools, his role in the decision created such a loud tumult back in Birmingham that his son, Hugo Black, Jr., was forced to move his family to Florida to escape it.

Shortly after the acquittal of Reverend Edwin Stephenson, the M.E.C. took up the question of the minister's continuing church status. At the Fifty-fifth Annual Meeting of the Alabama Conference, held on November 9, 1921, at the Simpson Church on Seventh Avenue and Twenty-fifth Street in downtown Birmingham, over one hundred church elders convened. They were to discuss revoking Stephenson's ordination as a minister of the church, on the charge that he had violated the Sixth Commandment—"Thou shalt not kill"—and thus was "unfit to serve." Shortly before the scheduled date of the conference, however, it was determined in an executive session meeting that the issue would not be taken up after all. The matter was rightly considered by Stephenson's local church, a spokesman for the church said. No church penalty was ever imposed on the minister for killing Father Coyle. There was also little evidence that Ruth's unblessed wedding to Pedro Gussman impacted Stephenson's thinking about performing the marriage rites of couples like them himself. Stephenson continued to marry couples for a fee for many more years. Stephenson died in Birmingham on August 4, 1956, at the age of eighty-six.[9]

Fifty-one years after Edwin Stephenson's death, in response to a research inquiry for this book, an archivist for the United Methodist Church verified that Stephenson had in fact been ordained in Newnan, Georgia, in 1905 by Bishop William W. Dunn as he claimed. According to the archivist, however, Stephenson had been ordained a "local deacon," not "a minister in full connection with the conference." Unlike full or "traveling ministers, who were empowered to perform ministerial functions (such as marrying people) wherever they happened to travel, a local deacon like Rev. Edwin Stephenson would have possessed the authority to marry couples in only one place: the local church in Georgia that had awarded him the designation "deacon."

Pedro Gussman and Ruth Stephenson Gussman never resumed their lives as husband and wife. Probably their marriage had been doomed from the start. Pedro remained in Birmingham, and quietly regained his life as a wallpaper hanger, while Ruth fled the city, as she had vowed. Ruth filed papers for a divorce two years later, alleging, without specification, Pedro's violence toward her person. Likely the accusation was merely a fiction. "No-fault" divorces would not exist for another fifty years, making some allegation of wrongdoing by one of the marriage partners a requirement for a divorce order—the most popular of which was "cruelty." Pedro did not contest his wife's request for a divorce, and a decree ending their marriage was signed on June 5, 1923.[10]

Seven years later, Pedro Gussman married again. Like his first and second wives, his third wife was white as well, and once again the antimiscegenation laws posed no obstacle to the union. All pretense about Gussman's racial ambiguity had vanished quickly after the trial. Four years later, at the age of fifty-six, on Valentine's Day, Gussman was fatally injured in a hit-and-run accident at Third Avenue and Twenty-second Street, just steps away from the spot where his former father-in-law had shot Father James E. Coyle. The driver was never apprehended.[11]

———

On Tuesday, March 3, 1931, the day Congress declared "The Star-Spangled Banner" the national anthem, Ruth Lamka was confined in the Seventh Ward of the Chicago Fresh Air Hospital, at 2451 Howard Street, her body consumed by the terrible wasting disease pulmonary tuberculosis, which would terrorize the country for yet another decade. For three months, her doctor had overseen her care at the sanitarium where Cook County patients were sequestered, either until they were no longer infectious or, more likely, dead.

There is no evidence that the physician knew or remembered anything about his patient's sensational past. The papers in Chicago had certainly written about her. But many years had passed since the ink on those stories had dried, and by the time the hospital admitted her in January 1931, her name was Lamka, not Stephenson or Gussman. So even had the doctor remembered the stories, there would have been little reason to put them together with the young woman who lay in the bed in the Seventh Ward.

The records do not show it, but it is reasonable to assume that the Ruth Lamka fought for her life. Even as a child, she had been a fighter. If mettle alone could have beaten the disease, good money was on her chances. But both doctor and patient must have known that no matter how great her temerity, her odds were not good. Before the discovery of streptomycin, the survival rate for pulmonary tuberculosis was grim. Without antibiotics, the afflicted were more likely to die than live; some sanitariums buried over 80 percent of their patients. Just as bad timing had stalked the woman's steps before, once again it would deprive her of the life she chose: she had contracted her illness over a decade before the discovery of that sorely needed serum.[12]

The real crime of it was that before Ruth's illness, things had actually begun to look hopeful. After her flight from Alabama, her recorded trail grows dim. Likely she strove to disappear. She may have spent some time in Loretto, Tennessee, where she had stayed in seclusion before her father's trial. She had friends there; it would have been a natural place for a daughter of the South to catch her breath before deciding on her next move.

By 1925, she had made her way farther north, to Chicago, and the midwestern city's big and impersonal temperament must have been a balm. A woman could be blessedly anonymous there, free from the prying questions of reporters, unfettered by the judgments of her neighbors. Avoiding the torments of the garment district, Ruth landed a job as a telephone operator for Western Union. She met a man—Charles Lamka—and they married. They set up house at 2147 North Clark Street, just a block or so from the lake, where they lived, quietly, until ten years after her escape from Birmingham, when Ruth met her final undoing by a foe more unexpected and lethal than any of those that had plagued her past. Ruth Lamka died, childless, on March 3, 1931, at the age of twenty-eight.[13]

On Wednesday, March 4, 1931, for reasons unknown, instead of burying his young wife near their home in Chicago, Charles Lamka arranged to have her body shipped back to her parents in Alabama. Perhaps the explanation was no more than money, for Lamka's wages would barely have covered their expenses, and finances must have grown even tighter when his wife became ill.

Whatever the reason, one of the Birmingham newspapers got wind of it. Mrs. Charles Lamka, "the girl who [was] once Miss Ruth Stephenson, is coming back to Birmingham, dead," the paper briefly reported; her body was to be interned in Elmwood Cemetery. Her father would preside over her burial. Even in death, Ruth had not ceased to be news. But when a reporter for the *Birmingham News* called on Mary and Edwin Stephenson at their home at

2126 Seventh Avenue seeking more information about the girl who had once been at the center of the state's biggest scandal, he hit a stone wall. Unlike in days past when Stephenson had regaled reporters from his jail cell, his fate no longer hinged on how the journalists treated him in their stories, and he had no desire to resurrect the tale that had consumed the city, and the nation, for three months in 1921.

"Don't rake up those old things," snapped Reverend Edwin R. Stephenson, and he refused to answer any questions.[14]

NOTES

Abbreviations

BAH   *The Birmingham Age-Herald*
BN   *The Birmingham News*
BP   *The Birmingham Post*
GJ Tr.   Grand Jury Transcript in *Alabama v. Edwin R. Stephenson,* Case no. 1710
PH Tr.   Preliminary Hearing Transcript in *Alabama v. E. R. Stephenson,* no. 6860
Trial Tr. Trial Transcript in *Alabama v. Edwin Stephenson*

Chapter 1

1. Code of Alabama of 1907, vol. 2, civil, sec. 4885.
2. Pedro Gusman, draft registration card, serial no. 2691, order no. 3189, roll 1509350, Draft Board 1. United States Selective Service System. *World War I, Selective Service System Draft Registration Cards, 1917–1918.* Washington, D.C.: National Archives and Records Administration.
3. Forty-one of the fifty states enacted such laws at some point. A ban on white-black marriage was the single common denominator among them. But seven states passed laws prohibiting whites from marrying people of Asian descent as well. Hrishi Karthikeyan and Gabriel J. Chin, "Preserving Racial Identity: Population Patterns and the Application of Anti-miscegenation Statutes to Asian Americans, 1910–1950," *Asian Law Journal* 9 (2002), 1.
4. Ibid., 7; *Fourteenth Census of the United States, Department of Commerce, State Compendium Idaho* 3 (1924).
5. Ibid.
6. Alabama State Constitution, sec. 102; and Code of Alabama, sec. 5001.
7. For a fine summary of the different racial groups reached by the antimiscegenation laws during the period, see Edward Byron Reuter, *Race Mixture: Studies in Intermarriage and Miscegenation* (New York: McGraw-Hill, 1931), 82–98.

8. State of Alabama, Tenth Judicial Circuit Court, Grand Jury Records 1921, 473 84–88 no. 30, Birmingham Public Library Archives, Dep't Nos. 1540–1766. State of Alabama v. Jim Rollins and Edith Labue (March 8, 1921) (grand jury minutes), 1202–3.

9. James R. Barrett and David Roediger, "Inbetween Peoples: Race, Nationality and the 'New Immigrant' Working Class," *Journal of American Ethnic History* 16 (spring 1997), 3.

10. Ian F. Haney Lopez, *White by Law* (New York: New York University Press, 1996); Noel Ignatiev, How the Irish Became White (New York: Routledge, 1995); David R. Roediger, The Wages of Whiteness: Race and the Making of the American Working Class, rev. ed. (London: Verso, 1991); Clare Sheridan, "'Another White Race': Mexican Americans and the Paradox of Whiteness in Jury Selection," *Law and History Review* 21 (2003), 109, 131–32.

11. Kathleen Neils Conzen, David A. Gerber, Ewa Morawska, George E. Pozzetta, and Rudolph J. Vecoli, "The Invention of Ethnicity: A Perspective from the U.S.A.," *Journal of American Ethnic History* 12 (fall 1992), 27.

12. The term "Native White Stock" was used in the United States census to distinguish native whites from nonnative whites.

13. One woman later confessed her love for Pedro to a reporter on condition of anonymity. "Mother and Aunt Plead for Return of Girl Who Wed Paperhanger of 42," *BN*, August 12, 1921, 1–2.

14. Pedro Gussman was a widower. He had already buried his first wife, with whom he had lived in Nashville, after she died of an illness.

15. "Mrs. Gussman Bitterly Assails Her Father," *BN*, August 24, 1921.

16. Helen McGough, "Things I Remember about Father Coyle, His Death, Twenty Years Afterwards," *Catholic Monthly*, August 1, 1941; "Stephenson Acted as 'Marrying Parson' and Spent His Time at the Courthouse," *BP*, August 12, 1921, 2; "Priest Shot through Head on Porch of His Third Avenue Home," *BAH*, August 12, 1921, 1.

17. "Stephenson Acted as 'Marrying Parson," *BP*, August 12, 1921, 2.

18. *Birmingham City Directory*, 1911, entry listing Edwin Stephenson as a "teacher," probably meaning "preacher."

19. R. Stephenson, GJ Tr., August 23, 1921, 1710; "Stephenson Acted as 'Marrying Parson,'" *BP*, August 12, 1921, 2; "Priest Shot through Head on Porch of His Third Avenue Home" *BAH*, August 12, 1921, 1; "'I'm Minister,' Slayer Claims," *BP*, August 12, 1921, 1.

20. "Not Southern Methodist," *BAH*, August 12, 1921, 1; "Dr. Echols Makes His Position Clear," *BN*, August 12, 1921, 2.

21. Ibid.

22. John M. Schnorrenberg, *Aspiration: Birmingham's Historic Houses of Worship* (Birmingham: Birmingham Historical Society, 2000), 7–9, 19–23.

23. James Bowron, "Autobiography," 3 vols., TS, 1:363–64, University of Alabama Library.

24. Carl V. Harris, Political Power in Birmingham, 1871–1921 (Knoxville: University of Tennessee Press, 1977), 53.

25. "Not Southern Methodist," *BAH*, August 12, 1921, 1.

26. Glenn Feldman, *Politics, Society, and the Klan in Alabama, 1915–1949* (Birmingham: University of Alabama Press, 1999), 58; Nancy MacLean, *Behind the Mask of Chivalry:*

The Making of the Second Ku Klux Klan (New York: Oxford University Press, 1995); Rowland T. Berthoff, "Southern Attitudes Toward Immigration, 1865–1914," *Journal of Southern History* 17, no. 3 (August 1951), 328–60. William R. Snell, "Masked Men in the Magic City: Activities of the Revised Klan in Birmingham, 1916–1940," *Alabama Historical Quarterly* 34 (fall–winter 1972), 206–7.

27. R. Stephenson, GJ Tr., August 23, 1921, 1710–17.

28. C. Vann Woodward and Tom Watson, *Agrarian Rebel* (New York: Macmillan, 1938; reprint, New York: Oxford University Press, 1963), 146–244, 418–22, 432.

29. John Higham, *Strangers in the Land* (New Brunswick, N.J.: Rutgers University Press, 1955), 180; Justin Nordstrom, *Danger on the Doorstep: Anti-Catholicism and American Print Culture in the Progressive Era* (Notre Dame, Ind.: University of Notre Dame Press, 2006), 86–91.

30. R. Stephenson, GJ Tr., August 23, 1921, 1710–1712; R. Stephenson, PH Tr., August 24, 1921, 144–77.

31. Robert B. Rackleff, "Anti-Catholicism and the Florida Legislature, 1911–1919," *Florida Historical Quarterly* 50 (April 1971), 352, 354.

32. Campaign ad for Sidney J. Catts, *Florida Times-Union*, October 8, 1914. General Act and Resolutions, Regular Sess., chap. 7378, no. 120 (1917).

33. Rackleff, "Anti-Catholicism and the Florida Legislature," 355; David P. Page, "Bishop 'Michael J. Curley and Anti-Catholic Nativism in Florida," *Florida Historical Quarterly* 45 (October 1966), 103; John R. Deal, Jr., "Sidney Johnston Catts, 'Stormy Petrel of Florida Politics'" (Master's thesis, University of Florida, 1949), 31.

34. Sadly, there are many sources evidencing these widely held and openly publicized views about Catholics in the early decades of the twentieth century. Leading examples include the overtly anti-Catholic publications the *New Menace* and Tom Watson's *Jeffersonian*. For some other sources the reader might consult MacLean, *Behind the Mask of Chivalry*, xi and 96; and Higham, *Strangers in the Land*, 79–87, 180, 292. See also Arthur Remillard, "The Unfinished South: Competing Civil Religions in the Post-Reconstruction Era, 1877–1920" (Ph.D. diss., Florida State University, 2006), chap. 5, 155–93.

35. R. Stephenson, GJ Tr., August 23, 1921, 1710; R. Stephenson, PH Tr., August 24, 1921, 144–77.

36. R. Stephenson, PH Tr., August 24, 1921, 144–77. E. R. Stephenson, Trial Tr., October 20, 1921, establishes his height. Numerous *BAH*, *BN*, and *BP* articles describe Ruth Stephenson, nearing age nineteen, as "petite."

37. *BAH*, August 14, 1921, 1.

38. Not long before the trial, Edwin Stephenson moved his family from Third Avenue to 2126 Seventh Avenue. *Fourteenth Census of the United States* (listing the Stephensons' address as 2126 Seventh Avenue); *Birmingham City Directory*, 1921.

39. For the non-Catholic reader, the stations of the cross are a series of pictures, fourteen in all, which traditionally line the interior walls of a Catholic church and depict the various sufferings of Christ, each one more grim than the last, starting with his condemnation to death, through the crucifixion, until in the final tableau, Christ is laid in the Tomb. For a description of St. Paul's Cathedral, see Rose Gibbons Lovett, *Catholic Church in the Deep South: The Diocese of Birmingham in Alabama, 1540–1976* (Birmingham, 1981); *The Cathedral of St. Paul, 1893–1993* [monograph] (Birmingham: Centennial Celebration Committee, 1993), 5–6.

40. R. Stephenson, GJ Tr., 1710–17; R. Stephenson, PH Tr., 144–77. E. R. Stephenson, Trial Tr.; "Could You Blame Him? Cries Mrs. Stephenson," *BAH*, August 12, 1921, 1.

41. Lovett, *Catholic Church in the Deep South*, 86.

42. Our Lady of Sorrows Baptismal Record for Mary Ruth Stephenson, April 10, 1921.

43. Roger K. Newman, *Hugo Black: A Biography* (New York: Fordham University Press, 1997), 72.

44. F. Bender, GJ Tr., 1745–47; A. Bender, Trial Tr., 443–447.

45. F. Bender, GJ Tr., 1745–47; F. Bender, Trial Tr., 423–43.

46. Hill Ferguson Papers, file 56, Department of Archives and Manuscripts, Birmingham Public Library, 61–62.

47. Glenn Feldman, *Politics, Society and the Klan in Alabama, 1915–1949* (Tuscaloosa: University of Alabama Press, 1999), 29.

48. Police Chief T. J. Shirley, GJ Tr., August 23, 1921, 1741–43; R. Gussman, PH Tr., 150–58.

49. John S. Hughes, "Insights into an Insane Asylum," *Alabama Heritage* 18 (spring 1994), 23, 25.

50. John S. Hughes, *The Letters of a Victorian Madwoman* (Columbia: University of South Carolina Press, 1993), 27.

51. Hughes, "Insights into an Insane Asylum," 19.

52. Ibid., 26.

53. Hughes, *Letters of a Victorian Madwoman*, 39.

54. Ibid, 23; see also *Reports on the Legislative Investigation of the Alabama Insane Hospitals in 1907* (Tuscaloosa: Hospital Print, 1907).

55. *Response of Doctor O. T. Dozier to Priest James E. Coyle* (Birmingham: self-published by O. T. Dozier, M.D., 1917) (copy on file with author), 7.

56. "Mrs. Gussman Bitterly Assails Her Father," *BP*, August 24, 1921.

57. On St. Aloysius, see Lovett, *Catholic Church in the Deep South*, 93–94. For Ruth and Pedro's plan see R. Gussman, P.H. Tr., 144–77. Also "Mrs. Gussman Bitterly Assails Her Father," *BP*, August 24, 1921.

Chapter 2

1. "Not Southern Methodist," *BAH*, August 12, 1921, 1.

2. Perkins J. Prewitt, "Making Birmingham Safe for Life and Property," *Birmingham* 1 (May 1925), 13.

3. Marjorie Longenecker White, *Downtown Birmingham: Architectural and Historical Walking Tour Guide* (Birmingham: Birmingham Historical Society, 1980), 69–70; Rose Gibbons Lovett, *Catholic Church in the Deep South: The Diocese of Birmingham in Alabama 1540–1976* (Birmingham, 1980), 55; *The Cathedral of St. Paul, 1893–1993* [monograph] (Birmingham: Centennial Celebration Committee, 1993), 6.

4. White, *Downtown Birmingham*, 69; *Cathedral of St. Paul, 1893–1993*, 5.

5. A collection of wonderful pictures can be found in Pierce Lewis and Marjorie Longenecker White, *Birmingham View: Through the Years in Photographs* (Birmingham: Birmingham Historical Society, 1996), 2–3.

6. Many excellent pictures of the priest are retained in archival sites across Alabama. Particularly good sources are kept at the Department of Archives and Manuscripts, Birmingham Public Library.

7. The hospital project started slowly as a simple clinic in the home of a prominent Catholic resident. After St. Vincent's Hospital officially opened its doors, epidemics continued to torment the young city, and accidents remained a daily occurrence. But St. Vincent's gave the ill and the wounded hope where before there had been little.

8. "Predecessor of Father Coyle Met Tragic Death Here," *BN*, August 12, 1921, 2; Rose Gibbons Lovett, obituary of Rev. Patrick Augustine O'Reilly, in author's files. Father O'Reilly was buried on the grounds of the hospital he founded with full military and church honors, with the honorary rank of major.

9. "The Very Rev. Dean James E. Coyle, Died for the Faith," *Catholic Monthly*, 260.

10. "James Edwin Coyle," in Thomas McAdory Owen, *Dictionary of Alabama Biography* (1921), 3:408. "Memoranda for Biographical Sketch of Coyle, Rev. James E.," handwritten entry for use by Owen, Thomas McAdory, "History of Alabama," in *Dictionary of Alabama Biography*, 3 (Montgomery: S.J. Clark Publishing, 1921), 408.

11. *1920 U.S. Federal Census Record, Mobile, Alabama; 1910 U.S. Federal Census Record, Mobile, Alabama.*

12. "Memoranda for Biographical Sketch of Coyle, Rev. James E.," handwritten entry for use by Owen, Thomas McAdory, "History of Alabama," in *Dictionary of Alabama Biography* (Montgomery: S.J. Clark Publishing, 1921), 408.

13. "Preacher Pastimes," *BAH*, copy found in volume 13 of the bound, unpublished handwritten notes of Fr. James E. Coyle located at St. Paul's Rectory, Birmingham, Alabama (hereafter "Parish Notes") Parish Notes, 13 (1916), 16.

14. "The Very Rev. Dean James E. Coyle, Died for the Faith," *Catholic Monthly*, 260; "Dead Priest Loved Boyhood Home," *BN*, August 12, 1921.

15. Vincent Joseph Scozzari, "Father James E. Coyle, Priest and Citizen" (Master's thesis, Notre Dame Seminary, New Orleans, 1963).

16. James E. Coyle, Parish Notes, 1 (1904), 10.

17. Ibid., 1:9.

18. Ibid., 1:9, 79.

19. John Higham, *Strangers in the Land: Patterns of American Nativism, 1860–1925* (New Brunswick, N.J.: Rutgers University Press, 1955), 169.

20. "Rev. R. L. Durant Makes a Vigorous Attack on Catholic Church in Pulpit," *BAH*, March 5, 1916, 1.

21. "Preparedness Is Applied to Church as Well as State, Dean Coyle Refers to Systematic Attacks Made on the Catholic Church," *BAH*, 1916, 1; copy in Coyle, Parish Notes, 13 (1916), 17.

22. "Memoranda for Biographical Sketch of Coyle, Rev. James E.," handwritten entry for use by Owen, Thomas McAdory, "History of Alabama," in *Dictionary of Alabama Biography* (Montgomery: S.J. Clark Publishing, 1921), 408.

23. Kenneth K. Bailey, *Southern White Protestantism in the Twentieth Century* (New York: Harper and Row, 1964), 7.

24. Ibid., 9, quoting W. T. Bolling, "Methodism and Ministerial Education," *Southern Methodist Review* 2 (March 1887), 58–59.

25. *Doctrines and Discipline of the M.E.C., South, 1898* (Nashville, 1898), 287–89.

26. Bailey, *Southern White Protestantism*, 8.

27. F. C. Woodward, "Methodism and Ministerial Education," *Southern Methodist Review* 1 (November 1886), 212.

28. L. Alberstadt, "Alexander Winchell's Preadamites: A Case for Dismissal from the Vanderbilt University," *Earth Sciences History* 13 (1994), 97–112.

29. Ibid., 97–112; Bailey, *Southern White Protestantism*, 9; *Nashville Christian Advocate*, July 13, 1878; *Popular Science Monthly* 13 (August 1878), 492–95.

30. William Heth Whitsitt, *A Question in Baptist History: Whether the Anabaptists in England Practiced Immersion before 1681?* (Louisville: Chas. T. Dearing, 1897), 5–8.

31. Bailey, *Southern White Protestantism*, 13–16.

32. Ibid., 8, quoting M.E.C., South, General Conference, *Journal*, 1906 (Nashville, 1906), 40.

33. Ibid., 9, quoting W. T. Bolling, "Methodism and Ministerial Education," *Southern Methodist Review* 2 (March 1887), 58–59.

34. "Formal Reply to Rev. Mr. Durant Made by Catholic," *BAH*, March 6, 1916, 1.

35. L. E. Brice, letter to the editor, *BAH*, March 7, 1916.

36. "Will Stand for No Unfairness," editorial, *BAH*, March 7, 1916; "Rev. R. L. Durant Submits His Reply to Father Coyle," *BAH*, March 8, 1916.

37. "Cardinal Quoted on Church Enemies, Father J. E. Coyle Preaches at St. Paul's," *BAH*; Parish Notes, 13 (1916), 225.

38. "Catholic Issue Elected Catts in Florida, He Says," *BAH* (morning ed.), December 14, 1916; "Catts Fervid in Telling Story of Fight in Florida Governorship, Sympathetic Audience Cheers as He Recites Fight Made on Anti-Catholic Issue," *BAH*, December 14, 1916, 1.

39. "Catts Fervid in Telling Story of Fight in Florida for Governorship," *BAH*, December 15, 1916, 1.

40. James E. Coyle, "Sums up Substance of Conditions Surrounding Offer Made by Catholic Organ," letter to the editor, *BAH*, February 2, 1917.

41. "Father Coyle Makes Reply to Sidney J. Catts," *BAH*, December 14, 1916, 1.

42. "Dr. Dozier Says He Has Proof," *BAH*, December 15, 1916, 1.

43. *Response of Doctor O. T. Dozier to Priest James E. Coyle, Pastor, St. Paul's Roman Catholic Church* (Birmingham: self-published by O. T. Dozier, M.D., 1917) (copy on file with author), 149–50.

44. Ibid., 150.

45. Ibid., 151.

46. Kay J. Blalock, *Shades of Green: Ethnic Diversity and Gender Considerations among the Irish in a Southern Industrial Community, 1871–1921* (Toledo, Ohio: University of Toledo Press, 1998), 193–95 and n. 58.

47. Coyle to Bishop Allen (February 16, 1917) referencing letter of Sterling Wood (copy on file with author); *Response of Doctor O. T. Dozier to Priest James E. Coyle.*

48. Henry M. Edmonds, "About the Catholics," *BAH*, February 4, 1917.

49. "Rev. R. L. Durant Answers Article by Dr. Edmonds," letter to the editor, *BAH*, February 5, 1917.

50. Charles P. Sweeney, "Bigotry in the South," *Nation* 112 (November 24, 1920), 585–86.

51. Lovett, *Catholic Church in the Deep South*, 81. Glenn Feldman, *Politics, Society and the Klan in Alabama, 1915–1949* (Tuscaloosa: University of Alabama Press, 1999), 58; Mary Jacq Trammell, "A Little Bit o' Ireland," *Birmingham*, March 1988, 43.

52. *BP*, January 28, 1921; *BAH*, January 28, 1921; *BN*, January 28, 1921. See also Feldman, *Politics, Society and the Klan in Alabama*, 17; William R. Snell, "Masked Men

in the Magic City: Activities of the Revised Klan in Birmingham, 1916–1940," *Alabama Historical Quarterly* 34 (fall–winter 1972), 207–8.

53. Feldman, *Politics, Society and the Klan in Alabama* 58; *BN*, April 22, 1921; Virginia Van der Veer Hamilton, *Hugo Black: The Alabama Years* (Baton Rouge: Louisiana State University Press, 1972), 84; Horace Wilkinson to Earl Pettus, September 19, 1921, KKK file, U.S. Department of Justice, National Archives, Washington, D.C.

54. William R. Snell, *The KKK in Jefferson County* (Master's Thesis, Samford University, 1967), 21–22; Hamilton, *Hugo Black: The Alabama Years*, 84; Snell, "Masked Men in the Magic City," 206–7.

55. "60 Cars of Ku Klux Members," *BP*, June 14, 1921, 8.

56. Snell, *KKK in Jefferson County*, 41, 49, 52.

57. "Father J. E. Coyle Is Amused and Amazed," *BAH*, February 17, 1916), 1.

58. *BAH*, September 12, 1917.

59. D. B. Grace, "Official Life of George B. Ward," unpublished manuscript, Tutwiler Collection of Southern History, Birmingham Public Library, 45, 47, and 144.

60. Carl V. Harris, *Political Power in Birmingham, 1871–1921* (Knoxville: University of Tennessee Press, 1977), 86; Howard S. Shirley (son of Thomas J. Shirley) to Hill Ferguson, September 8, 1958, Hill Ferguson Collection, vol. 48, Birmingham Public Library.

61. Helen McGough, "Things I Remember About Father Coyle, His Death, Twenty Years Afterwards," *Catholic Monthly* (August 1, 1941).

62. "$20,000 for Home, Jubilee Present to Father Coyle," *BAH*, June 28, 1921, 1.

63. *BAH*, August 14, 1921, 4, Beecher, letter to the editor, reprinted in *Catholic Monthly*, September 21, 1921, 327–36, 343.

64. Ibid.

Chapter 3

1. Marjorie Longenecker White, *The Birmingham District: An Industrial History and Guide* (Birmingham, 1981), 25.

2. Ibid., 24–26.

3. Ibid.

4. John C. Henley, Jr., *This Is Birmingham* (Birmingham: Southern University Press, 1960), 3–14.

5. White, *Birmingham District*, 43.

6. Ibid.

7. Ibid.

8. Henley, *This Is Birmingham*, 20.

9. White, *Birmingham District*, 42–44.

10. John C. Henley, Jr., *Early Days in Birmingham* (Birmingham: Southern University Press, 1968), 1–2.

11. Ibid.

12. Ibid.

13. Ibid.

14. Marjorie Longenecker White, *Downtown Birmingham: Architectural and Historical Walking Tour Guide* (Birmingham: Birmingham Historical Society, 1980), 5.

15. Henley, Early Days in Birmingham, 31–34.

16. *The Cathedral of St. Paul, 1893–1993* [monograph] (Birmingham: Centennial Celebration Committee, 1993), 3.

17. *Fourteenth Census of the United States: 1920—Population, Birmingham, Jefferson County.*

18. There is an excellent photograph of St. Paul's rectory as it looked on August 11, 1921, in *Cathedral of St. Paul, 1893–1993, 9.*

19. Photograph, *BN*, August 13, 1921, 14.

20. Rose Gibbons Lovett, *Catholic Church in the Deep South: The Diocese of Birmingham in Alabama 1540–1976* (Birmingham, 1980), 55.

21. Some years later, William Fex's daughter, Mrs. Elizabeth Fex Dudley, kindly provided a copy of the picture for publication in this book. It was the last photograph ever taken of Father Coyle.

22. The picture of Edwin Stephenson taken by the photographer of the *BAH* can be found in *BAH*, August 12, 1921, 1.

23. R. E. Hammett, GJ Tr., August 23, 1921, 1716–1717.

24. Alvin W. Hudson and Harold E. Cox, *Street Railways of Birmingham* (Birmingham: printed by Harold E. Cox, 1976), 70.

25. *BAH*, April 4, 1891, 1; *BN*, December 14, 1913, 1; Carl V. Harris, *Political Power in Birmingham, 1871–1921* (Knoxville: University of Tennessee Press, 1977), 200.

26. *Fourteenth Census of the United States: 1920—Population, Birmingham, Jefferson County;* Lynne B. Feldman, *A Sense of Place: Birmingham's Black Middle-class Community, 1890–1930* (Tuscaloosa: University of Alabama Press, 1999), 8.

27. See Kevin Boyle, *Arc of Justice* (New York: Holt, 2004), 14–15, for a beautiful description of the similar layout of residential areas for Detroit's black, immigrant, and native white populations.

28. Harris, *Political Power in Birmingham*, 25–27, 180, 188, 238.

29. Mitchell, Ph.D. dissertation, 67.

30. *The Fourteenth Census of the United States, vol. 3, Population,* 66; Blaine A. Brownell, *Birmingham*, "Alabama: New South City in the 1920s," *Journal of Southern History* 38:1 (February 1972), 21–48, 28.

31. Harris, *Political Power in Birmingham*, 200–201.

32. Mitchell, Ph.D. dissertation, 100–104; Harris, *Political Power in Birmingham*, 199.

33. W. D. Chiles, GJ Tr., August 23, 1921, 1750–51; E. McGinty, GJ Tr., August 23, 1921, 1751.

34. Before Kettering invented the starter, "it took considerable strength to turn the engine with the crank, and if the car backfired, the crank could suddenly turn with great force. Broken arms and other injuries were not uncommon." Kettering invented a number of other objects familiar today, including the spark plug, leaded gasoline, safety glass, four-wheel brakes, and Freon. He was a graduate of Ohio State University. Richard A. Wright, "Cadillac, the 'Standard of the World,'" *Detroit News*, November 22, 1999.

35. Ibid.

36. W. D. Childs, GJ Tr., 1749–51; Edwin McGinty, GJ Tr., 1751.

37. Perkins J. Prewitt, "Making Birmingham Safe for Life and Property," *Birmingham* 1 (May 1925), 13.

38. M. G. McClellan, GJ Tr., 1717.

39. H. H. Weir, draft registration card, World War I, June 5, 1917. United States Selective Service System. *World War I, Selective Service System Draft Registration Cards, 1917–1918.* Washington, D.C.: National Archives and Records Administration.

40. H. H. Weir, GJ Tr., August 23, 1921, 1722–27; H. H. Weir, PH Tr., August 23, 1921, 79–83.

41. See entries in *Birmingham City Directory*, 1921, for Richard and Dick Gayle, Jr.

42. R.W. Gayle, Sr., GJ Tr., 1709; Dick Gayle, Jr., GJ Tr., 1711.

43. Dick Gayle, Jr., GJ Tr., 1711–12.

44. R.W. Gayle, Sr., GJ Tr., 1709–10.

45. H. H. Weir, GJ Tr., 1724.

46. S. Caruthers, GJ Tr., 1733.

47. S. Caruthers, GJ Tr., 1733; M. Coyle, GJ Tr., 1735.

48. Ibid.

49. S. Caruthers, GJ Tr., 1733–34.

50. H. H. Weir, GJ Tr., 1724; M.L. Easter, GJ Tr., 1730; W. L. Snow, GJ Tr., 1728–30.

51. Dick Gayle, Jr., GJ Tr., 1711.

52. R.W. Gayle, Sr., GJ Tr., 1709; Dick Gayle, Jr., GJ Tr., 1711.

53. Brownell, *Birmingham*, 34–35; Ross W. Harris, *Traffic Survey on the Vehicular and Street Railway Traffic Situation in Birmingham*, 60–62, 57, copy in City Clerk's Office, Birmingham.

54. W. L. Snow, GJ Tr.1727; W.L. Snow, PH Tr., August 23, 1921, 50–59.

55. W. L. Snow, GJ Tr., 1727; W.L. Snow, PH Tr., 50–59; see also Dick Gayle, Jr., GJ Tr., 1711.

56. Dick Gayle, Jr., GJ Tr., 1711.

57. W. L. Snow, GJ Tr., 1728–30.

58. Ibid.

59. *Fourteenth Census of the United States, 1920,* entry for Fred Bender. *City Directory of Birmingham, 1921–1922; Birmingham City Directory*, 1920–1921, entry for F. J. Bender Furniture and Fixture, Co., 492. Fred Bender, draft registration card, United States Selective Service System. *World War I, Selective Service System Draft Registration Cards, 1917–1918*. Washington, D.C.: National Archives and Records Administration.

60. *Birmingham City Directory*, 1920–1921, entry for Lige Loy's Undertaking Company; Lige Loy, Jr., GJ Tr., 1714; R. E. Hammett, GJ Tr., 1716; F. Reed, GJ Tr., 1715.

61. Lige Loy, Jr., GJ Tr., 1714; R.E. Hammett, GJ Tr., 1716–17; F. Reed, GJ Tr., 1715.

62. R. E. Hammett, PH Tr., preliminary hearing trial, 116; M. L. Easter, PH Tr., 36.

63. Lige Loy, Jr., GJ Tr., 1714; R. E. Hammett, GJ Tr., 1717.

64. M. E. Brantley, GJ Tr., 1712.

Chapter 4

1. L. T. Beecher, "The Passing of Father Coyle," *Catholic Monthly*, September ?, 1921, 331–32; "Father Coyle's Death Leaves the Community Shocked and Benumbed," *BAH*, August 13, 1921, 1.

2. Helen McGough, "Things I Remember about Father Coyle, His Death, Twenty Years Afterwards," *Catholic Monthly*, August 1, 1941.

3. Beecher, "Passing of Father Coyle," 331–32; "Father Coyle Dies under Operation, Girl's Whereabouts Mystery," *BN*, August 12, 1921, 2; "Plans for Funeral of Priest Slain by Preacher, Awaiting Arrival of Bishop," *BN*, August 12, 1921, 2. "Last rites"

refers to the anointing of a person in grave danger of death with consecrated oil accompanied by a prayer for God's grace and the pardoning of sins.

4. Death certificate of James E. Coyle, August 11, 1921, Jefferson County Vital Records; *BN*, August 12, 1921, 2; J. M. Mason, GJ Tr., August 23, 1921, 1745.

5. Beecher, "Passing of Father Coyle," 331–32.

6. Editorial, *Mobile Register*, August 13, 1921, 4; "Father J. E. Coyle Former Mobilian Dies from Wounds, Methodist Minister Held in Connection with Shooting of Well Known Churchman," *Mobile Register*, August 12, 1921, 1.

7. Letters to Bishop Edward Allen, (1904 to 1921), Archives of the Archdiocese of Mobile (copy on file with author). The bishop read from a number of the telegrams he received at the Requiem High Mass held in Birmingham on Saturday, August 13, 1921.

8. *BAH*, August 12, 1921, 1.

9. "Coyle Tragedy Is Described by Man Who Saw Shooting," *BN*, August 12, 1921, 1.

10. James Roberson, deputy chief of police, Jefferson County, personal communication, June 18, 2007.

11. J. C. Hartsfield, GJ Tr., 1736; J. C. Hartsfield, PH Tr., 3–18.

12. Ibid.

13. Code of Alabama of 1907, sec. 6213, 270.

14. Code of Alabama of 1907, sec. 6214, 270.

15. J. C. Hartsfield, GJ Tr., 1736–37.

16. Ibid.; P. C. Cole, GJ Tr., 1738.

17. Code of Alabama of 1907, sec. 6213, 270.

18. P. C. Cole, GJ Tr., 1738.

19. S. Wiggins, GJ Tr., 1721.

20. *BAH*, 1 August 12, 1921; S. Wiggins, GJ Tr., 1721; S. Wiggins, PH Tr., 134.

21. S. Wiggins, GJ Tr., 1721.

22. "Tragedy at the Rectory," *BAH*, August 12, 1921, 1.

23. "Girl's Whereabouts Mystery," *BN*, August 12, 1921, 2; "Unable to Locate Girl Whose Marriage Caused Father to Shoot Priest," *BP*, August 12, 1921, 1–2; "No Trace of Daughter Who Eloped," *BP*, August 2, 1921, 1.

24. Marriage license issued to Pedro Gussman and Mary Ruth Stephenson, August 11, 192, Jefferson County Vital Records, Alabama, (certified copy in possession of author); "Got License in Bessemer," *BAH*, August 12, 1921, 1.

25. "Not Southern Methodist," *BAH*, August 12, 1921, 1.

26. John C. Henley, Jr., *This Is Birmingham* (Birmingham: Southern University Press, 1960), 38–40.

27. "Church Status of Stephenson," *BP*, August 13, 1921, 8.

28. Donald G. Mathews, *Slavery and Methodism: A Chapter in American Morality 1780–1845* (Westport, Conn.: Greenwood Press, 1965), 247.

29. *The History of American Methodism*, vol. 2 (New York: Abingdon Press, 1964), 22–46, 46–59.

30. *New York Herald*, May 24, 1844, 2; May 25, 1844, 1; Mathews, *Slavery and Methodism*, 246–82.

31. The Epistle of St. Paul the Apostle to Philemon; Iveson L. Brookes, *A Defense of Southern Slavery against the Attacks of Henry Clay and Alexander Campbell* (Hamburg, S.C.: Robinson and Carlisle, 1851), 4.

32. Gen. 9:22, 25–27.

33. *History of American Methodism*, 2:110.

34. Declaration of A. B. Longstreet of the Georgia Conference, *Journal of the General Conference*, June 5, 1844, 109.

35. "Dr. Echols Makes His Position Clear," *BN*, August 12, 1921, 2.

36. *BN*, August 12, 1921, 2.

37. Several papers in Ireland reported the news of Father Coyle's shooting. See *Mungret Annual* (Mungret College, Limerick County) 6, no. 1 (July 1922), 61.

38. John Bruce, "'The Flapjack Murder'—The Murder of Father Patrick E. Heslin—1921," in Marie F. Rodell, *San Francisco Murders* (New York: Duell, Sloan and Pearce, 1947), 175–233; *Chicago Tribune*, August 7, 1921; *New York Times*, August 12, 1921; *New York Times*, August 14, 1921; *Washington Post*, August 17, 1921.

39. Charles P. Sweeney, "Bigotry Turns to Murder," *Nation* 113, no. 29 (August 31, 1921), 232–33.

40. "Father Coyle's Tragic Death: The News Hopes Justice Will Prevail," editorial, *BN*, August 12, 1921.

41. "The Stephenson Case, Letter of George B. Ward," editorial, August 13, 1921.

42. P. Thornton Marye, "The New Terminal Station, Birmingham, Ala.," *American Architect* 96, no. 1751 (July 14, 1909), 13–17.

43. "Funeral of Father Coyle Probably Saturday; High Church Dignitaries Come," *BP*, August 12, 1921, 1–2; "Bishop Allen en Route to Birmingham to Probe Slaying of Rev. Father Coyle," *BN*, August 12, 1921, 2; "Bishop Allen Arrives Friday Night to Plan Funeral of Father Coyle," *BN*, August 12, 1921, 2.

44. "St. Paul's Crowded; Services Held for Late Father Coyle," *BAH*, August 14, 1921, 4.

45. Isabel G. Beecher, "A Tribute to Father Coyle," *BN*, August 14, 1921.

46. Ibid.

47. Ibid.

48. Beecher, "Passing of Father Coyle," 333.

49. Francis Mahon Shillingburg, interview by author, March 12, 2005, recording on file with author; *Fifteenth Census of the United States: 1930, Population Schedule,* sheet no. 31-A.

50. "Few Politicians Are Blamed for Death of Coyle, Bishop Declares Slaying Resulted from Propaganda," *BN*, August 13, 1921, 1.

51. Ibid.

52. Beecher, "Passing of Father Coyle," 340.

53. Ibid; Sig G. Bauer, "Forgive Them Is Funeral Text," *BN*, August 15, 1921, 2; "We Do Not Ask Vengeance, Is Priest's Word," *BP*, August 15, 1921, 2.

54. Beecher, "Passing of Father Coyle," 341.

55. "Stephenson Girl Reported to Have Attended Mass Said for Rev. Coyle," *BN*, August 13, 1921, 1.

Chapter 5

1. *BP*, August 25, 1921, 1.

2. "Father Coyle Dies," *BN*, August 12, 1921, 2; "Father Coyle's Death Leaves the Community Shocked and Benumbed," *BAH*, August 13, 1921, 1.

3. "Father Coyle Dies," *BN*, August 12, 1921, 2.

4. *BAH*, August 14, 1921, 1.

5. Barbara Overton Chandler and J. E. Howe, *History of Texarkana and Bowie and Miller Counties, Texas-Arkansas* (Texarkana, Tex.-Ark.: 1939); Lucile Couch, "A Tale of Two Cities (Not by Dickens), Texarkana, Arkansas, and Texarkana, Texas" (Master's thesis, University of Texas, 1934).

6. *Fourteenth United States Federal Census, 1920.*

7. Chandler and Howe, *History of Texarkana and Bowie and Miller Counties.*

8. "Declares She Has Given Interview to No One Save *Age-Herald* Reporter," *BAH*, August 14, 1921, 1.

9. Ibid.

10. Ibid.

11. *BAH*, August 14, 1921, 1.

12. *Fourteenth U.S. Federal Census, 1920* (entry giving age of Francis Marion Campbell); *Ninth U.S. Federal Census, 1870* (entry giving residence of William F. and Mary Stephenson, parents of Alice, age nine, and Edwin, age two months); family tree entry for Francis Marion Campbell and Alice Stephenson Campbell, Ancestry.com; *Twelfth U.S. Federal Census, 1900* (showing residence of Bud and Alice A. Danforth, and their children); *Fourteenth U.S. Federal Census, 1920* (showing Birmingham residence of Alace (*sic*) Danforth and her son Ross Campbell).

13. "Bride Had Not Heard," *BAH*, August 12, 1921, 1; "Father Coyle Dies," *BN*, August 12, 1921, 2; "Father Coyle's Death Leaves the Community Shocked and Benumbed," *BAH*, August 13, 1921, 1.

14. "Father Coyle Dies under Operation, Girl's Whereabouts Mystery," *BN*, August 12, 1921, 2; "Unable to Locate Girl Whose Marriage Caused Father to Shoot Priest," *BP*, August 12, 1921, 1–2.

15. A picture of Joseph R. Tate, provided to the author by his grandson, Robert G. Tate, depicts the way the prosecutor would have looked after the events of 1921, when Tate was slightly older, copy on file with author.

16. "Joseph R. Tate, County Native, Succumbs after Short Illness," *BN*; Robert G. Tate, grandson of Joseph R. Tate, interview by author, January 20, 2006, recording on file with author; Robert G. Tate, Jr., telephone conversation with author, December 22, 2005; *Fourteenth and Fifteenth U.S. Census*, entries for Joseph R. Tate and Paul A. Tate.

17. George R. Leighton, "Birmingham, Alabama: The City of Perpetual Promise," Harper's Magazine, CLXXV (August 1937), 239.

18. Nat'l Comm'n on Law Observance and Enforcement (The Wickersham Comm'n Report"), "Lawlessness in Law Enforcement," vol. 11 (1928–1931).

19. In 1993, James Cameron received an official pardon for the crime from the state; see *Brown v. Mississippi*, 297 U.S. 278, 285 (1936).

20. *Miranda v. Arizona*, 384 U.S. 436 (1966); Gary L. Stuart, *Miranda: The Story of America's Right to Remain Silent* (Tucson: University of Arizona Press, 2004).

21. F. McDuff, GJ Tr., 1718; G. Moore, GJ Tr.,1740.

22. "Stephenson's Statement," *BAH*, August 12, 1921.

23. "Search for Daughter," *BAH*, August 13, 1921, 1.

24. "Father Coyle's Death Leaves the Community Shocked and Benumbed," *BAH*, August 12, 1921, 1.

25. "Could You Blame Him? Cries Mrs. Stephenson," *BAH*, August 12, 1921, 1.

26. "Waits in Vain for Daughter," *BP*, August 13, 1921, 1.

27. "Stephenson Girl Reported to Have Attended Mass Said for Rev. Coyle," *BN*, August 13, 1921, 1.

28. Ibid.

29. "Could You Blame Him?" *BAH*, August 12, 1921, 1.

30. "Bride Had not Heard," *BAH*, August 12, 1921, 2.

31. "Mrs. Stephenson Not Willing to Discuss Thursday's Tragedy," *BAH*, August 14, 1921, 8.

32. "Waits in Vain for Daughter," *BP*, August 13, 1921, 1.

33. "Could You Blame Him? Cries Mrs. Stephenson," *BAH*, August 12, 1921, 1.

34. R. Gussman, GJ Tr., 1710–1717; *BAH*, August 14, 1921, 1.

35. *BAH*, August 14, 1921, 1.

36. Ibid.

Chapter 6

1. "Coroner Secretly Is Investigating Coyle Shooting," *BN*, August 12, 1921, 1.

2. Code of Alabama of 1907, vol. 3, chap. 235, sec. 681.

3. "Coroner Secretly Is Investigating Coyle Shooting," *BN*, August 12, 1921, 1; "Father Coyle's Tragic Death: The News Hopes Justice Will Prevail," editorial, August 12, 1921.

4. "Star Chamber Inquests," editorial, *BP*, August 13, 1921, 4.

5. Ibid.

6. Thomas McAdory, "History of Alabama," in *Dictionary of Alabama Biography*, 3 (Montgomery: S.J. Clark Publishing, 1921) (entry for J. D. Russum).

7. Ibid.; Jesse Daniel Russum, draft registration card, World War I. United States Selective Service System. *World War I, Selective Service System Draft Registration Cards, 1917–1918.* Washington, D.C.: National Archives and Records Administration.

8. Thomas McAdory, "History of Alabama," in *Dictionary of Alabama Biography*, 3 (Montgomery: S.J. Clark Publishing, 1921) (entry for J. D. Russum).

9. Ibid.

10. "Coroner Secretly Is Investigating Coyle Shooting," *BN*, August 12, 1921, 1.

11. "Selects His Counsel," *BN*, August 16, 1921, 1; Letter of Fr. Joseph Malone to Bishop Allen (copy on file with author).

12. Grand Jury Notes, Circuit Court of Tenth Judicial Circuit of Alabama, Criminal Division, Proceeding Jefferson County Grand Jury, Birmingham Division, January Term 1921, nos. 1014–1257, Department of Archives and Manuscripts, Birmingham Public Library, 11–13.

13. "Coroner Secretly Is Investigating Coyle Shooting," *BN*, August 12, 1921, 1; "Officials Consider Calling Grand Jury," *BAH*, August 13, 1921, 4.

14. "Stephenson Now Faces Formal Murder Charge," *BN*, August 13, 1921, 1.

15. *BN*, August 12, 1921, 2; "No Special Grand Jury to Investigate Killing," *BP*, August 13, 1921, 1.

16. Ibid.

17. "'I'm Minister,' Slayer Claims," *BP*, August 12, 1921, 1.

18. "Slayer of Priest Stays in Cell and Reads Bible," *BN*, August 15, 1921, 1; *BP*, August 16, 1921, 8.

19. Virginia Van der Veer Hamilton, *Hugo Black: The Alabama Years* (Baton Rouge: Louisiana State University Press, 1972), 18, 23.

20. Ibid.

21. Roger K. Newman, *Hugo Black: A Biography*, 49–53; Hamilton, *Hugo Black: The Alabama Years*, 79–83.

22. Ibid.

23. "Four Noted Criminal Lawyers to Defend Stephenson," *BP*, August 16, 1921, 1; "Four Lawyers to Defend Minister," *BAH*, August 17, 1921, 1; "Selects His Counsel," *BN*, August 16, 1921, 1.

24. An Act to Establish the Criminal Court of Jefferson County, Acts of the General Assembly of Alabama Passed at the Session of 1886–87 (Montgomery: W. D. Brown, 1887), no. 395, s. 121, sec. 15, 835, 839.

25. Thomas M. Owen, *Alabama Official and Statistical Register 1885* (Montgomery: Brown, 1885).

26. *Ex Parte Lusk*, 82 Ala. 519, 2 So. 140, 144 (May 12, 1887).

27. Roscoe Pound, *The Causes of Popular Dissatisfaction with the Administration of Justice* (Part I) *A.B.A. Rep.* 29 (1906), 395–417.

28. *Smith v. Stiles*, 195 Ala. 107 (1915); *Journal of the House of Representatives of the State of Alabama* (1919), 37; Thomas McAdory, "History of Alabama," in *Dictionary of Alabama Biography*, 1 (Montgomery: S.J. Clark Publishing, 1921), 261–64.

29. Hamilton, *Hugo Black: The Alabama Years*, 51–59.

30. "Who Will Be Circuit Solicitor Jefferson Courts after Jan 1?" *BAH*, November 3, 1916; "Courts Must Determine Status of Solicitors," *BAH*, January 17, 1917.

31. "Courts Must Determine Status of Solicitors," *BAH*, January 17, 1917.

32. "Supreme Court to Settle Solicitor's Status Tomorrow," *BAH*, February 14, 1917; "Office Title Suits Will Be Decided by Supreme Court," *BAH*, February 15, 1917, "Black and Tate within the Law, Is Word of Supreme Court," *BAH*, February 16/17; "Black Files Mandamus to Force Board to Pay His Assistants," *BAH*, February 21, 1917.

33. "Solicitor Black Argues His Own Case in Court," *BAH*, June 16, 1917; *State ex rel. Gaston v. Tate*, 199 Ala. 321 (1917); *Henry v. State ex rel. Welch*, 200 Ala. 475 (1917).

34. "Solicitor Black Sends Resignation to the Governor," *BAH*, July 13, 1917.

35. Newman, *Hugo Black*, 47.

36. "Early Showdown Stephenson Plans," *BN*, August 17, 1921, 15; "Want Preliminary Hearing for Him," *BAH*, August 18, 1921, 4; "Coyle Tragedy to Be Aired Tuesday," *BN*, August 21, 1921, 1.

37. "Coyle Tragedy to be Aired Tuesday," *BN*, August 21, 1921, 1.

38. "Want Preliminary Hearing for Him," *BAH*, August 18, 1921.

39. "Mrs. Gussman Goes Home, but for Clothes, Shows Anger for Mother," *BN*, August 17, 1921, 16.

40. Roger Newman, *Hugo Black*, 47; "Defense Body Raising Fund for Minister," *BP*, September 13, 1921, 1.

41. "Defense Body Raising Fund for Minister," *BP*, September 13, 1921, 1.

42. Ibid.

43. "Defense Fund Is Explained," *BP*, September 14, 1921, 1.

Chapter 7

1. "Tower atop Building Fast Disappearing," *BN*, 12/16, 1936; "Looking Back," *BN*, August 12, 1959; "Statue of Justice at Old Courthouse Will Have Another Resting Place," *BN*, January 3, 1937.

2. "Stephenson Wins as Tate Is Forced into Preliminary," *BN*, August 23, 1921, 1.

3. Sol Wachtler, chief judge of the New York Court of Appeals, interview by Marcia Kramer, *New York Daily News*, January 31, 1985.

4. "Stephenson's Daughter First Witness as Grand Jury Starts Killing Probe," *BP*, August 23, 1921, 1; "Stephenson Wins as Tate Is Forced into Preliminary," *BN*, August 23, 1921, 1.

5. "Stephenson Wins as Tate Is Forced into Preliminary," *BN*, August 23, 1921, 1.

6. Congress changed the name "Porto Rico" to "Puerto Rico" on May 17, 1932. E.g., "Gussman a Porto Rican," *BAH*, August 12, 1921, 2; "Daughter of Man Held for Priest's Death Found Here," *BN*, August 14, 1921, 1.

7. Kevin Boyle, *Arc of Justice* (New York: Holt, 2004), 204.

8. Sofia Lafakis Petrou, *A History of the Greeks in Birmingham, Alabama* (1979), 23, 43. Theresa Aguglia Beavers, *The Italians of the Birmingham District* (Master's thesis, Samford University, Birmingham, 1969), 70–71.

9. David R. Roediger, *The Wages of Whiteness: Race and the Making of the American Working Class*, rev. ed. (London: Verso, 1991), 25.

10. "Mrs. Stephenson at Jail, Visits Husband," *BAH*, August 18, 1921, 4.

11. "Stephenson's Daughter First Witness as Grand Jury Starts Killing Probe," *BP*, August 23, 1921 1; Grand Jury Notes, July Term 1921 Circuit Court of Tenth Judicial Circuit of Alabama, Criminal Division, Proceeding Jefferson County Grand Jury, Birmingham Division, January Term 1921, nos. 1014–1257, Department of Archives and Manuscripts, Birmingham Public Library.

12. R. Gussman, GJ Tr., August 23, 1921, 1710–17.

13. "Georgia's Lynching Victims," Cyndi's List, genealogy website, at www.cyndislist.com/ga.htm, accessed November 6, 2007.

14. W. Fitzhugh Brundage, *Lynching in the New South: Georgia and Virginia, 1880–1930* (Urbana: University of Illinois Press, 1993), 39–40. "White Girl Raped, and the Guilty Wretch Lynched and Burned," *Cedartown Standard*, August 25, 1904; "Negro Ravisher Riddled by Hundreds of Bullets and His Corpse Cremated," *Atlanta Constitution*, August 23, 1904, 1.

15. *Cedartown Standard*, August 25, 1904.

16. "White Girl Raped," *Cedartown Standard*, August 25, 1904, 1–2.

17. Ruth G., GJ Tr., August 23, 1921, 1710–17.

18. "Stephenson Wins as Tate Is Forced into Preliminary," *BN*, August 23, 1921, 1; "Father Coyle Case before Grand Jury," *BAH*, August 24, 1921, 1.

19. 1907 Code of Alabama, sec. 7084; *Daughdrill v. Alabama*, 21 So. 378, 385 (Sup. Ct. of Ala. 1897).

20. S. Wiggins, GJ Tr., August 23, 1921, 1721–22.

21. J. Adams, GJ Tr., August 23, 1921, 1707–09.

22. S. Caruthers, GJ Tr., August 23, 1921, 1733–35.

23. "Stephenson Wins as Tate Is Forced into Preliminary," *BN*, August 23, 1921, 1.

24. J. D. Russum, GJ Tr., August 23, 1921, 1736.

25. W. L. Snow, GJ Tr., August 23, 1921, 1729.

26. M. Coyle, GJ Tr., August 23, 1921, 1735–36.

27. "Stephenson's Daughter First Witness as Grand Jury Starts Killing Probe," *BP*, August 23, 1921, 1.

28. E. J. Wall, GJ Tr., August 23, 1921, 1738–39.

29. S. E. Goad, GJ Tr., August 23, 1921, 1739.

30. D. Maloney, GJ Tr., August 23, 1921, 1745–46.

31. T. J. Shirley, GJ Tr., August 23, 1921, 41–44.

32. *BAH*, August 25, 1921, 1.

Chapter 8

1. "Stephensons Wins as Tate Is Forced into Preliminary," *BN*, August 23, 1921, 1; "Stephenson Bound Over without Bond," *BN*, August 24, 1921, 1.

2. "Solicitor Black Sends Resignation to the Governor," *BAH*, July 13, 1917.

3. J. C. Hartsfield, preliminary hearing testimony, 3–18.

4. F. McDuff, PH Tr., 18–34.

5. M. L. Easter, PH Tr., 34–50.

6. H.G. McClellan, preliminary hearing testimony, 125–34.

7. Marcella Coyle, PH Tr., 59–61; Stella Caruthers, preliminary hearing testimony, 68–70.

8. W. L. Snow, PH Tr., 50–59.

9. H. H. Weir, PH Tr., 79–85.

10. T. E. Mitchell, PH Tr., 85–93.

11. "Stephenson Bound Over without Bond, BN, August 24, 1921, 1; "Dramatic Tenseness Marks Preliminary Hearing of Rev. Edwin Stephenson," BAH, August 24, 1921, 1.

12. Ruth Gussman, PH Tr., 144–47.

13. Ibid., 149–50.

14. R.Gussman, PH Tr., August 23, 1921, 149–51, 158–59.

15. Ibid., 159–60.

16. Ibid., 168.

17. Ibid., 167–68.

18. Ibid., 159.

19. Ibid., 157–58.

20. Ibid.

21. Ibid., 151–52.

22. Ibid., 151–58.

23. Ibid., 159–63.

24. Ibid., 161, 163.

25. Ibid., 168–71.

26. Ibid., 171.

27. Ibid., 176–77.

28. Ibid., 168–177.

29. Ibid., 159.

30. "Claim Three Witnesses Will Testify Minister Fired in Self-Defense," BP, August 22, 1921, 1.

31. "Stephenson Bound Over without Bond, BN, August 24, 1921, 1.

32. Ibid.

33. "Bertillon System Discussed," New York Times, February 13, 1896; H. T. F. Rhodes, Alphonse Bertillon: Father of Scientific Detection (London: Abelard-Schuman, 1956).

34. Horace Coleman Alford, draft registration card, WWI Draft Registration Cards, 1917–1918, St. Clair County, Alabama, roll 1509429, Draft Board O. United States Selective Service System. World War I, Selective Service System Draft Registration Cards, 1917–1918. Washington, D.C.: National Archives and Records Administration.; Fourteenth U.S. Federal Census, 1920, Birmingham, Jefferson County, Alabama, roll T625–23, p. 22A, enumerated district 39, image 507.

35. "Ruth Stephenson's Husband Arrested for Peoria Police," BN, August 25, 1921, 1; "Gussman Arrested on Murder Charge for Illinois Authorities," BAH, August 26, 1921, 1–2; "Pedro Gussman under Arrest; Charge Brutal Murder of Woman," BP, August 25, 1921, 1.

36. "Alibi of Gussman Good, Friends Say; Police Skeptical," BN, August 26, 1921, 1.

37. "Gussman Arrested on Murder Charge," BAH, August 26, 1921, 1.

38. "Police Chief Refused to Protect Her, Says Wife of Gussman," BN, August 30, 1921, 1; "Shirley Denies Allegation of Gussman Petition," BAH, August 31, 1921, 7; "Ruth Gussman Makes Charges against Chief," BP, August 30, 1921, 1.

39. Wayne Winkler, "A Brief Overview of the Melungeons," at www.melungeons.com. B. Kennedy, The Melungeons: The Resurrection of a Proud People—An Untold Story of Ethnic Cleansing in America (Macon, Ga.: 1997), 15.

40. Winkler, "Brief Overview," 4; Kathleen McGowan, "Where Do We Really Come From?" Discover 24, no. 5 (2003), 58. Kennedy, Melungeons, 15.

41. "Threats Sent to Alford for Part in Gussman Case," BN, August 29, 1921, 1.

42. "Gussman Is Not Man Wanted, Say Peoria Police," BN, August 27, 1921, 1; "Gussman Is Cleared of Suspicion," BP, August 27, 1921, 1; "Gussman, Not Man Wanted in Peoria, Is Released Here," BAH, August 28, 1921, 1.

43. "Mrs. Gussman Has Not Left Town Is Stated; Not Accused Husband," BAH, September 7, 1921, 1.

44. "Ruth Gussman Tells Why She Left City, 'Double Crossed' by Her Husband She Writes News," BN, September 7, 1921, 1; "'My Husband Sold Out to My Enemies,' Says Statement from Girl," BP, September 7, 1921, 1.

45. "Gussman Has Separated from Her Husband," BAH, September 6, 1921, 1; "Ruth Stephenson Deserts Husband Then Disappears," BN, September 6, 1921, 1.

46. BP, September 9, 1921, 2.

47. Esta Cole, History of Loretto, Tennessee Area (Lawrenceburg, Tenn.: Byler Press, 1997), 10–17.

48. BP, September 8, 1921, 1; Mamie Helen Priestly, telephone interview by author, notes on file with author.

Chapter 9

1. "Sees Stephenson, Publisher of 'The Menace,' Confers with Slayer of Priest in Cell," BN, September 19, 1921, 1. Justin Nordstrom, Danger on the Doorstep: Anti-Catholicism and American Print Culture in the Progressive Era (Notre Dame, Ind.: University of

Notre Dame Press, 2006). Robert Maury, *The Wars of the Godly* (New York: Robert M. McBride, 1928), 261–63.

2. Nordstrom, *Danger at the Doorstep*, 78–79.

3. Ibid., 9–10; 107–44.

4. Philip Jenkins, *The New Anti-Catholicism: The Last Acceptable Prejudice* (New York: Oxford University Press, 2003), 44.

5. "Maria Monk Story Confirmed," *Menace*, February 8, 1919, 2; Nordstrom, *Danger on the Doorstep*, 39.

6. Nordstrom, *Danger on the Doorstep*, 39.

7. *New Menace*, August 27, 1921, 1.

8. "Coyle Case to Be Passed by Jury," *BN*, September 6, 1921, 2.

9. "$10,000 Bond Set for Stephenson in Circuit Court," *BN*, September 7, 1921, 1.

10. "Stephenson May Make Insanity Plea to Open Way for Startling Testimony," *BP*, September 9, 1921, 1–2; "Stephenson Plans 'Not Guilty' Plea Based on Insanity," *BN*, September 9, 1921, 1.

11. "Ruth Gussman Fails to Answer as Witnesses against Father Are Called," *BP*, October 17, 1921, 1–2.

12. "Defense Is Silent in Gussman Move," *BN*, October 14, 1921, 1; "Gussman Called to Testify for Rev. Stephenson," *BP*, October 13, 1921, 1; "'I Know Nothing of Tragedy,' Gussman Tells Reporters for News," *BN*, October 14, 1921, 8.

13. "Sensation of the Stephenson Case Is Not the Killing of the Priest but the Facts Concerning His Relations with the Girl He Married to Gussman, Taxi Drives to Lonely Places Were Very Frequent," *New Menace*, October 8, 1921, 1.

14. Statement of Pedro Gussman, *Alabama v. Edwin Stephenson*, October 15, 1921 (copy on file with author).

15. "Stephenson Performs Marriage Ceremony at the County Jail," *BAH*, October 16, 1921, 5.

16. Ibid.

17. Helen McGough, "Things I Remember about Father Coyle, His Death, Twenty Years Afterward," *Catholic Weekly*, August 1, 1941; "Whereabouts of Gussman Girl Is Still Uncertain," *BN*, September 8, 1921, 1.

18. Grand Jury Notes, Circuit Court of Tenth Judicial Circuit of Alabama, Criminal Division, Proceeding Jefferson County Grand Jury, Birmingham Division, January Term 1921, nos. 1014–1257, Department of Archives & Manuscripts, Birmingham Public Library, 11–13.

19. "Both Sides Ready on Eve of Trial in Stephenson Case," *BN*, October 16, 1921, 1.

20. "Spectators Must Get Seats or Get Out, Judge Rules," *BN*, October 16, 1921, 1; "Hundreds Turned Away as Stephenson's Trial Opens," *BN*, October 17, 1921, 1.

21. "Ruth Gussman Fails to Answer as Witnesses against Father Are Called," *BP*, October 17, 1921, 1–2; "Setting of the Drama," *BP*, October 17, 1921, 1.

22. "Venire Drawn," *BP*, September 28, 1921, 7.

23. "Both Sides Ready on Eve of Trial in Stephenson Case," *BN*, October 16, 1921, 1; "Secures Jury the First Day in Trial of Rev. Stephenson for Death of Father Coyle," *BAH*, October 18, 1921, 1; "State Rests in Stephenson Trial," *BP*, October 18, 1921, 2.

24. Picture of courtroom, *BP*, October 18, 1921, 1; "Young Men Make Up Stephenson Jury," *BP*, October 18, 1921, 1.

25. "Secures Jury the First Day in Trial of Rev. Stephenson for Death of Father Coyle," *BAH*, October 18, 1921, 1.

26. "Subpoenas Issued Stephenson Case," *BAH*, September 25, 1921, 1; "Pedro Gussman Is to Testify in the Stephenson Trial," *BAH*, October 14, 1921, 5.

27. Dr. James M. Mason, trial testimony, October 18, 1921, 4–7; entry for Dr. James M. Mason, *Birmingham City Directory*, 1920–21, 1185.

28. John Morley, *Death, Heaven and the Victorians* (Pittsburgh: University of Pittsburgh Press, 1972); James J. Farrell, *Inventing the American Way of Death, 1830–1920* (Philadelphia: Temple University Press, 1980); "Prosecution Rests in Stephenson Case," *BN*, October 18, 1921, 1; Marcella Coyle, Trial Tr., direct examination, October 17, 1921, at 8–12.

29. Marcella Coyle, Trial tr., cross-examination, 13–15, October 18, 1921.

30. "State Rests in Stephenson Trial," *BP*, October 18, 1921, 2.

31. W. D. Chiles, Trial Tr., cross-examination, 4–18, October 18, 1921.

32. "State Rests in Stephenson Trial," *BP*, October 18, 1921, 1.

Chapter 10

1. "Stephenson Case Set for Trial Tommorow," *BAH*, October 16, 1921, 1.

2. Ibid.

3. *BP*, October 18, 1921; *BAH*, October 19, 1921, 1.

4. J. H. Rogers, Trial Tr., 48; O. F. Staples, Trial Tr., 51; G. B. Bowman, Trial Tr., 55; J. N. Day, Trial Tr., 67; J. H. Burgess, Trial Tr., 73; J. L. York, Trial Tr., 87; S. A. Owens, Trial Tr., 89; W. I. Morgan, Trial Tr., 128; E. M. Blanton, Trial Tr., 131; F. A. Farabee, Trial Tr., 132; J. C. Moore, Trial Tr., 146; W. R. Sulzer, Trial Tr., 153; T. J. Williamson, Trial Tr., 158; W. O. Watkins, Trial Tr., 206; D. O. Watkins, Trial Tr., 211.

5. G. B. Bowman, Trial Tr., 55–60, trial testimony.

6. W. I. Powell, Trial Tr., 61–68; cross-examination, 62–65.

7. W. I. Powell, Trial Tr., 61, redirect and re-cross-examination, 65–68.

8. L. W. Adkinson, Trial Tr., 142; W. R. Sulzer, Trial Tr., 154.

9. J. F. McGill, Trial Tr., 119–28 ; Officer R. G. Patton, Trial Tr., 148–53–; H. H. Weir, Trial Tr., 186–206–; F. H. McDuff, Trial Tr., 175–79; S. Wiggins, Trial Tr., 180–86; R. E. Smith, Trial Tr., 171–74.

10. S. E. Willoughby, Trial Tr., 101–3; J. F. McGill, Trial Tr., 119–21; F. H. McDuff, Trial Tr., 162, 164, and 169.

11. M. Stephenson, Trial Tr., 283–85, direct examination.

12. M. Stephenson, Trial Tr., redirect examination.

13. E. R. Stephenson, Trial Tr., direct examination, 320–326.

14. E. R. Stephenson, Trial Tr., cross-examination, 337–96.

15. Virginia Van der Veer Hamilton, *Hugo Black: The Alabama Years*.

16. "Gussman Shown Jury as Minister Tells Story," *BP*, August 20, 1921, 2; "Gussman's Race Brought into the Case," *BP*, October 20, 1921, 1.

17. "Surprise Sprung When State Holds Back for Rebuttal," *BN*, October 18, 1921, 1; "Defense Attorney Presents Gussman before the Jury, Courtroom Holds Breath While Man about Whom So Much Has Been Said Quietly Stands Battery of Hundreds of Eyes—'Wanted Jury 'to See Him,' said Judge Black," *BAH*, October 20, 1921, 1.

18. Kirsten Fischer, "White Reputations 'Blacken'd & Made Loose,'" chap. 4 of Fischer, *Suspect Relations: Sex, Race, and Resistance in Colonial North Carolina* (Ithaca, N.Y.: Cornell University Press, 2002), 156.

19. "A Statement By Pedro Gussman," *BN*, October 31, 1921, 4.

20. E. R. Stephenson, Trial Tr., 338–339.

21. E. R. Stephenson, Trial Tr., 339–41.

22. E. R. Stephenson, Trial Tr., 345–51.

23. "Gussman's Race Brought into the Case," *BP*, October 20, 1921, 1.

Chapter 11

1. A. Bender, Trial Tr., 417–22.

2. F. Bender, Trial Tr., 423–42.

3. Ibid.

4. C. Neuer, Trial Tr., 450–57; B. G. Lackey, Trial Tr., 460–68; and B. H. Burr, Trial Tr., 469–80.

5. B. H. Bell, Trial Tr., 469–80.

6. P. Gussman, Trial Tr., 481–83.

7. Ibid.

8. Douglas White, Trial Tr., 508–19; "Stephenson Jury Visits Scene of Recent Tragedy," *BAH*, October 21, 1921, 1.

9. "Jurors Examine Death Scene as Big Bell Tolls," *BP* October 21, 1921, 10.

10. "Stephenson a Murderer, Morrow Tells the Jury," *BP*, October 21, 1921, 12; "Stephenson Jury Visits Scene of Recent Tragedy," *BAH*, October 21, 1921, 1.

11. "Stephenson Declared Not Guilty by Jury," *BAH*, October 22, 1921, 1.

12. "Fite Brings Tears as He Pleads for Acquittal," *BP*, October 21, 1921, 10.

13. "Was It a Reconciliation?" *BN*, October 21, 1921, 2.

14. *BP*, October 21, 1921, 1.

15. "Arguments Near End in Stephenson Case," *BN*, October 21, 1921, 1.

16. "Stephenson Declared Not Guilty by Jury," *BAH*, October 22, 1921, 1; "Still Uncertain of Future Plans, Says Mrs. Stephenson," *BN*, October 22, 1921, 1. "Stephenson, Free, Waits to Welcome His Daughter Back," *BP*, October 22, 1921, 1.

17. "Prayer Invoked by Jury Which Freed Slayer of Priest," *BN*, October 22, 1921, 1; "On Knees, Jurors Prayed for Guidance in Verdict," *BP*, October 22, 1921, 1; "Stephenson Declared Not Guilty by Jury," *BAH*, October 22, 1921, 1.

Epilogue

1. "Stephenson Jury Verdict Scored," *BN*, October 23, 1921, 12; "Gov. O'Neal Talks on Acquittal of Rev. Stephenson," October 23, 1921, 5.

2. W. G. Black, letter to the editor, *BN*, October 27, 1921.

3. J. A. MacKnight, letter to the editor, *BN*, October 29, 1921.

4. R. R. Stanfield, letter to the editor, *BN*, October 28, 1921.

5. Roger K. Newman, *Hugo Black: A Biography* (New York: Pantheon, 1994), 86; Gerald T. Dunne, *Hugo Black and the Judicial Revolution* (New York: Simon and Schuster, 1977), 114. Virginia Van de Veer Hamilton, *Hugo Black: The Alabama Years* (Baton Rouge: Louisiana University Press, 1972).

6. Newman, *Hugo Black*, 91–92; Dunne, *Hugo Black and the Judicial Revolution*, 114.

7. Newman, *Hugo Black*, 96–100.

8. Ibid., 126–27, 247–63; Dunne, *Hugo Black and the Judicial Revolution*, 132.

9. "Church to Discuss Slayer of Priest," *BN*, October 30, 1921, 4; "Church Status of Stephenson Up at Meeting," *BP*, October 28, 1921, 1; "Stephenson Case Left to District M. E. Conference," November 1, 1921, 1. Correspondence of L. Dale Patterson, Archivist-Records Administrator, United Methodist Church with Ohio State University Moritz College of Law Librarian Linda Poe, dated October 4 and October 5, 2007 (copies on file with author); Minutes of the Annual Conference of the Methodist Episcopal Church, South (1905): 148–49.

10. Decree of Divorce, no. 11768, Circuit Court, Tenth Judicial Circuit of Alabama (June 5, 1923). During the period, upward of 70 percent of wives seeking divorces in the city of San Francisco claimed "cruelty" as the reason. Lawrence M. Friedman, *American Law in the Twentieth Century* (New Haven: Yale University Press, 2002), 435–36.

11. Marriage record, Pedro Gussman and Vera Hancock, May 28, 1930, Jefferson County, Alabama, Vital Records; Certificate of death, Pedro Gussman, Jefferson County Department of Health, Bureau of Health Statistics and Vital Records, Birmingham, February 14, 1934, Jefferson County Vital Records.

12. Standard Certificate of Death, Department of Public Health, Division of Vital Statistics, State of Illinois, registered no. 7102 23, filed in Cook County on March 4, 1931, for Mrs. Margaret Lamka, daughter of E. R. Stephenson and Mary Thompson Stephenson. Katherine Ott, *Fevered Lives: Tuberculosis in American Culture since 1870* (Cambridge, Mass.: Harvard University Press, 1999).

13. Ruth Stephenson Lamka's death certificate lists her address as 2149 N. Clark, but the *Chicago City Directory*, 1928–29, lists the home of Charles and Ruth Lamka as 2147 N. Clark Street.

14. *BAH*, March 5, 1931; *BP*, March 5, 1931; *BN*, March ?, 1931.

Acknowledgments

WRITERS OFTEN BEGIN acknowledgments in a book with an observation about how many souls were involved in bringing their work into being. I now understand why. There truly are so many to thank.

Rising Road would not have been possible without the support of The Ohio State University and the Moritz College of Law, of which I am privileged to be a part. My former Dean Nancy H. Rogers and my former Associate Dean for Faculty, Josh Stulberg, made professional and personal sacrifices to ensure that I had the funding to complete the research for the book and to provide me the time to write. Their faith in the project never wavered, and I am eternally grateful. Ohio State's president, Gordon Gee, encouraged my work on the book as well, and I thank him for his time, supportive ear, and able leadership. Many members of the Moritz Law family shared their time and thoughts about the manuscript along the way; too many to list, you know who you are. My dear friend and colleague, Professor Marc Spindelman, however, endured more than any other—countless conversations, a close read of each of the chapters, offering encouragement at every step. I will never be able to thank him enough.

Special thanks are also owed to the Kirwan Institute for the Study of Race and Ethnicity, which awarded me a Senior Faculty Fellowship, bestowing funding and that inestimable gift of time that every writer needs. Its outstanding staff, led by Director john a. powell, supported the book at every phase and provided a forum for me to discuss the story at an early stage. I am especially appreciative of the help of Kirwan's senior researcher, Tom Rudd.

So often the stars seemed to align, illuming my path toward others outside the law school, who selflessly gave their time and talents to the book.

Early in the research stage of the project, it was my very good fortune to befriend Kevin Boyle, a professor in Ohio State's history department, who at the time was still completing his book tour for *Arc of Justice*, winner of the 2004 National Book Award. Our friendship and his good counsel have sustained me through these last years.

The outstanding staff at Moritz Law contributed hundreds of hours of work to the book, tracking down obscure sources, arranging for their delivery, and cheerfully responding to an endless stream of requests for additional books and microfilm. Under the able leadership of its director, Bruce Johnson, the library never blinked. Katherine Hall was a fantastic resource in the early stages of the research and writing. And my most heartfelt thanks to Linda Poe for her extraordinary assistance and encouragement from the first page to the last—no request was too much trouble. I am indebted as well to Carol Peirano, Jenny Pursell, and Patricia Schirtzinger, whose administrative help with the manuscript and close attention to detail saved me from many embarrassments. It is an honor to be associated with professionals like these. Several research assistants provided invaluable support as well: Jared Klaus, Jeffrey Meade, Troy Sitzman, and the phenomenally talented Anna Scanlon.

My college professor and life-long mentor, Dean Alfange Jr., did me the tremendous favor of reading the manuscript and sharing his impressions. I am forever grateful. Thanks as well to friends inside and outside Ohio who have listened to me talk about this story for years, and who gently asked each time we met when the book would be finished: Nick Ackerman, Michelle Alexander, Sally Bloomfield, Kenneth Bravo, Susan Brown, Legan Burgin, Jonathan Coughlan, Joshua Dressler, A. J. Dupres, Yale Kamisar, Cindy Linninger, The Honorable Algernon Marbley, James K. L. Lawrence, Matt and Jody Miller, Kathy Northern, Jim Phillips, Suzanne Richards, Doug Rogers, Sandy and Carol Ross, Andy Taslitz, and Dale Woods. A special word of gratitude is owed to the law firm Vorys, Sater, Seymour, & Pease, and the family of the late John C. Elam, Esq., who funded and awarded me a professorship honoring John's memory. The standard of excellence he set served as a humbling inspiration. As has the remarkable work of historical and legal scholars such as Virginia Van der Veer Hamilton, Ian Haney Lopez, Roger Newman, David R. Roediger, and Frank Wu, all of whom have extended acts of kindness to me as well.

No book like *Rising Road* would be possible without heavy reliance on the carefully maintained collections of libraries. The Archives and Manuscript Department of the Birmingham Public Library played a particularly central role. Its director, James Baggett, lent invaluable assistance time and again. Norwood Kerr, director of Archival Reference, at the Alabama Department of Archives and History in Montgomery, helped greatly, as did

Mary Beth Newbill at Southern History Department. Auburn University's Archives, Sanford University's Special Collections, the University of Notre Dame Library, and the University of Alabama's collections in Birmingham and Tuscaloosa aided as well. I am also thankful for the opportunities the law faculties of the University of Alabama, the University of Iowa, and the University of Kentucky gave me to deliver talks about the book.

During the research process, Hugo Black Jr. granted me permission to comb through the papers of his father, former United States Supreme Court Justice Hugo L. Black, which are currently housed at the Library of Congress. With that permission, and unburdened by the restriction normally placed on researchers of the Black Papers, I found a copy of the preliminary hearing transcript of *Alabama v. Edwin Stephenson* long believed lost. Many thanks to the Library of Congress staff who patiently brought me box after box of the Black Papers. Professor Sheila Killian, great niece of Father James Coyle, extended support as well.

Before beginning work on the book, I had never traveled to Alabama. Now I am blessed with a number of friends there. The help of the Honorable William H. Pryor Jr., United States Court of Appeals for the Eleventh Circuit, has been a tremendous gift; I have benefitted immensely from years of conversation and correspondence with him. The work of Glenn Feldman, professor of history at the University of Alabama at Tuscaloosa, has been a constant inspiration; our friendship is very dear to me. Paul Pruitt, director of the Library at the University of Alabama, School of Law, and James Pinto Jr., the director of the Fr. James E. Coyle Memorial Project, lent time and support. I am proud to have come to know them. Molly Franklin also helped greatly, and William Dudley set aside other work to videotape my interviews with his mother, the late Elizabeth Fex Dudley, thank you also to Catherine Barrett, Peggy Beuerlein, Dan Jordan, Frances Shillingburg, and Bill and Dorothy Sullivan. I am grateful to them all.

The support of the Very Reverend Richard E. Donohoe, presiding rector of the Cathedral of St. Paul's in Birmingham, was instrumental to this book, along with his executive assistant Krista Rataj who answered so many of my questions. Father Donohoe opened the doors of the rectory of St. Paul's and allowed me to spend a whole week one summer scouring through nineteen bound volumes of Father James Coyle's handwritten notes. I am also grateful to the former archbishop of the Archdiocese in Mobile, Alabama, Oscar Hugh Lipscomb, and the archdiocese's extraordinary archivist, Richard Chastang, lovers of history both.

And then there is the matchless John Wright Jr.—never before has a man gone to greater lengths to assist a stranger's wish to write a book. I can scarcely believe the hundreds of e-mails John responded to; the countless packages he sent me. Father James Coyle has no better champion, and I no dearer friend in the Magic City. Words fail to express the depths of my debt to him.

At Oxford University Press, I am profoundly thankful for the patient and thoughtful contributions of my editor David McBride, who steered me clear of purple prose and believed in *Rising Road* from the very beginning. And a sincere thanks to my publisher Niko Pfund, whose interest and confidence in the project never waned, and to Oxford's terrifically talented production and marketing staffs who worked so hard and well on the book's behalf.

It is hard to overstate the critical role played by family and friends on the road to publication. When I dared not show the manuscript to anyone else, my sister Cynthia Cunha slid it lovingly from my hands. She read every new draft, providing outstanding editorial suggestions on each one, and rescued me in my darkest moments. Her encouragement and keen eye are gifts I will never be able to repay. My mother, Patricia Prescott, ever my greatest booster, never doubted that I could do this and reassured me in those moments when I needed it most. Her own life decisions—most especially her decision to marry Forrest Davies, my father, at a time when some states still called the act criminal—inspired this work. Thanks as well to my other siblings, Brian, Jeff, Sheila, and Doug, who never fail me. And my deepest love and thanks to Barbara and Roger Michaels, my beloved MIL and FIL, from whom I continue to learn so much.

From the distant hills of Massachusetts, John Kazar III, that musely Malfet, supplied a nudge whenever I needed it, and a troika of amazing friends in Ohio made sure that I kept moving each time the way ahead grew dim: Mary McGirl, who read and commented on the manuscript and by all rights should receive wages for all the publicity she has given it; Beth Kaufman, whose reaction to the early chapters gave me the confidence to continue and whose certainty in its worth never flagged; and Treva Roberts, who traveled by my side every step of the way, from Phoenix to San Diego, and ensured that I did not get turned around in Yuma.

Finally I give thanks to the three people who paid the steepest toll for my five-year-long obsession with a family in Alabama long since gone and a crime long since forgotten: my husband of twenty years, Alan Michaels, and our two incredible children, Heather and Tyler. I love you all beyond words. If a book has a heart, you three are it.

Ruth's injunction against chief, 193–94, 197, 203
and Ruth's mistreatment, 96
Birmingham Post
on Edwin Stephenson, 127, 128
on Father Coyle's murder, 74, 81, 89
as fledgling newspaper, 81
on Ku Klux Klan, 48
on Mary Stephenson, 114
post-trial letters to editor, 281
on preliminary hearing, 188
on Ruth Stephenson, 188–89, 200, 209, 210
Ruth Stephenson's letter to, 279
on search for Ruth and Pedro, 78–79
trial coverage, 121, 131, 140–41, 204, 206, 212, 226, 278
Birmingham Terminal Station, 28, 87–88
Bitz, C.R., 214
Black, Hugo, Jr., 284
Black, Hugo Lafayette
birth and early years, 129
career, 129–30, 274, 283
clash with Tate over county prosecutor position, 133–36, 170–71, 282
Ku Klux Klan membership, 283–84
marriage and honeymoon, 130, 137, 170
physical appearance, 274
preparing for trial, 205–6, 207
as Stephenson's defense lawyer, 129, 130–31, 136–38, 205–6, 207, 282–83
at Stephenson's trial, 218, 220, 223–29, 230, 234–38, 239, 240–46, 250, 251, 254, 255, 256–62, 263–64, 265–68, 274–75, 277
as Supreme Court justice, 129, 274, 284
See also trial of Edwin Stephenson
Black, Josephine Foster, 130, 137
Black, W.G., 281
Blanton, E.M., 233
Bowman, G.B., 233
Bowron, James, 12
Brady, Father Thomas F.
on day of murder, 65, 100, 101
as priest at St. Paul's, 57, 74
saying Mass after Father Coyle's murder, 89–90
Brantley, Marie E., 70
Brice, L.E., 40
Brown, Benjamin, 153

Browne, John J., 28
Brown, John, 153
Brown v. Board of Education, 284
Brown v. Mississippi, 108
Bryce Hospital, 23–26
Bryce, Peter, 23
Burgess, J.H., 232

Cahaba River, 53
California, marriage laws, 4
Callahan, George, 26, 99
Cameron, James, 107
Campbell, Alice, 102
Campbell, Ross, 102, 157
Campbell, Ruth, 198, 199–200
Cartwright, Thomas, 102–3
Caruthers, Stella
on day of murder, 65–66, 219
grand jury testimony, 156, 160–61, 165
as housekeeper for rectory, 57, 65
preliminary hearing testimony, 176, 177, 178
Catholic Church
education required for clergymen, 37–38
Elyton Land Company gift to, 57
See also anti-Catholicism
Catholic Monthly, 18, 33, 50
Catts, Sidney Johnston
anti-Catholicism of, 16, 35, 41, 42
Birmingham lecture, 41–43
election to governorship of Florida, 16, 41–42
Cedartown lynching, 153–54, 233
Cedartown Standard, 154
Chadwick, Mrs. J.M., 115
Cheek, Charles M.G., 214
Chicago Tribune, 84–85, 190
Chiles, William
on day of murder, 60, 62–63, 222
employment, 222–23
trial testimony, 221–26, 230, 274
Circuit Court of Jefferson County, 131
Civil War, 55, 82
Cole, Paul C., 77–78, 237
colored people
use of term by author, ix
See also African Americans; Negroes
Consolidated Court Act of 1915, 133–34
Coyle, James E.
birth and early years, 31–32
daily routine at rectory, 27, 46, 50

Coyle, James E. (*continued*)
 on day of murder, 57–59, 65–66, 69, 72
 death, 72
 death threats against, 13, 15, 46, 48, 50,
  73, 92
 as defender of Catholic faith, 17, 19,
  36–37, 39–40, 41–46, 73
 friendship with Michael Henry, 30, 31, 32,
  73–74
 influence of parents, 31–32, 37, 46
 marriage ceremony for Ruth and Pedro,
  73, 100–102, 263
 missionary work in Mobile, 29, 32, 73
 ordination, 32
 as pastor of St. Paul's, 13, 29–31, 32–33,
  38, 50–51, 89–90
 physical appearance, 29, 164, 221
 relationship with Ruth, 16–17, 185
 Silver Jubilee, 50–51
 tributes to, 87
 wake and funeral, 74, 91–94
 See also murder of Father Coyle
Coyle, Marcella
 acquaintance with Ruth, 101, 185
 on day of murder, 65–66, 70, 218–21
 grand jury testimony, 156, 160, 161–62,
  164, 165
 in mourning, 218–19
 preliminary hearing, 176–78
 reaction to brother's murder, 90–91
 as support for brother, 57, 65
 testimony at trial, 218–21, 230
Coyle, Margaret Durney, 31, 37
Coyle, Owen, 31, 37
Creek Indians, 53
Criminal Court of Jefferson County, 131–32,
  133–34
criminal trials
 cardinal sins for lawyers, 225
 changing defense strategy, 205
 and character witnesses, 260
 claims of self-defense at, 205, 206,
  220–21, 251, 269
 claims of temporary insanity at, 206, 251
 cross-examinations, 220, 260
 defendants' testimony, 255
 double jeopardy, 280
 dual claims of self-defense and temporary
  insanity, 206
 jury selection, 212–13
 prosecution's "case-in-chief," 216

 prosecution's interview of suspect, 253
 relationships between opposing counsel,
  204
 rules of evidence, 172, 245, 266, 267
 sequestering of witnesses, 245
 standard of proof in, 181
 suspect's right to remain silent, 106, 109,
  255
 witnesses for the defense, 231–32
 See also Alabama law; murder
Crockett, David, 53
Cronan, Aileen, 19–20, 22

Daily American Tribune, 280
Danforth, Amanda Alice, 115
Davis, James
 interview of Douglas White, 265
 as Joe Tate's assistant, 105, 136, 170–71,
  265
 at preliminary hearing, 165, 170–73,
  174–75, 176–77, 178–79, 181–82,
  186, 187
 at trial, 216
Day, J.N., 233
DeBardeleben, Pearce H., 47, 75
Dickinson, A.J., 42, 48–49
double jeopardy, 280
Dozier, Byron, 26
Dozier, Orion T.
 anti-Catholic publications, 19, 25–26,
  43–44, 45, 46
 as leader of True Americans, 49
 and Sidney Catts's speech, 41, 42
Drumpark National School, 31, 32
Dunn, William Wallace, 127
Durant, Robert L.
 attack on Henry Edmonds, 45, 46
 "Romanism v. Americanism" sermon,
  34–36, 39–40, 41
Durney, Francis, 31

Eagan, Martin, 50
Easter, M.L.
 on day of murder, 66, 69
 grand jury testimony, 158–59, 165
 preliminary hearing, 174–75
Echols, Robert
 confrontation with Stephenson, 10–12,
  80, 83, 127, 233
 rift with M.E.C., North, 80–81,
  83–84

burning of St. Catherine's Church, 46, 86
community leaders as members of, 105,
    189, 283
death threats against Father Coyle, 48
during Reconstruction, 47
Edwin Stephenson as member of, 1, 13,
    105, 140, 283
films about, 48
Hugo Black as member of, 283–84
initiation ceremony, 47
involvement in Stephenson trial, 140–41,
    283
presence in Birmingham, 13, 22, 46–48
recruitment efforts, 48
revival of, 13, 15
See also Robert E. Lee Klavern No. 1

Labue, Edith, 5–6
Lacey, S.P., 214
Lackey, B.G., 260–61
Lacy, S.G., 214
Lamka, Charles, 286
Lamka, Ruth. *See* Stephenson, Ruth
Lappage, P.A., 214, 277, 278
law. *See* Alabama law
Lay, James A., Jr., 214
Leland, Henry, 62
Lige Loy's Ambulance and Funeral Com-
    pany, 59, 69, 72, 91
Lollar, Ira, 214
Loretto, Tenn., 199–200
Loveman, Joseph & Loeb, 19, 22, 26, 96
Loving v. Virginia, 284
Loy, Lige, Jr.
    on day of murder, 69, 70, 72, 90–91
    grand jury testimony, 160
Lummus, A.J., 98
Lusk, John, 132
lynchings, 153–54, 233

MacKnight, J.A., 281
Macon News, 211
Mahon, Francis, 91
Mahon, Helen, 91
"malice aforethought"
    established in Stephenson trial, 217
    under Alabama law, 216
Malone, Joseph, 100, 101
Maloney, Dan, 166
marriage laws
    of Alabama, 3–4, 5, 79

based on age, 3–4
based on race, 4–5
Mason, James M., 72, 217–18, 221
Mathews, Ernest, 126, 128–29
McAdory, Wallace, 136
McCauly, Arthur, 153
McClellan brothers, 63, 64
McClellan, H.G., 175–76
McCormack, Dink, 214
McCoy, James Henry, 171
McCoy, John
    closing arguments, 273, 274
    family life, 171
    as Joe Tate's assistant, 105, 136, 170–71
    at preliminary hearing, 165, 170–71,
        179, 187
    at trial, 216–17, 218, 219–22, 225, 227,
        228
McCoy, William Clark, 171
McDuff, Fred
    after trial, 278
    grand jury testimony, 164, 166
    jailhouse interview of Stephenson, 107,
        109, 156, 157, 158, 253
    preliminary hearing testimony, 171–74
    trial testimony, 212, 235, 253–54
McGill Institute, 32, 73
McGill, Jake F., 235
McGinty, Edward
    as Catholic, 223–24
    on day of murder, 60, 62–63, 224–25
    physical appearance, 226
    trial testimony, 221, 224–25, 226–28, 274
McGough, Helen, 71–72, 210
McGough, Joe, 210
McGough, Thomas A., 71–72, 210
McMahon, Robert G., 214
Meagher, Michael, 98
M.E.C., North (Methodist Episcopal
        Church, North)
    condemnation of Stephenson, 84
    rift with M.E.C., South, 80–83
    Stephenson family as members of, 12, 80,
        81, 233–34
M.E.C., South (Methodist Episcopal
        Church, South)
    building of, 11
    McCoy family as members of, 171
    requirements for ministry, 38
    rift with M.E.C., North, 80–83
    rift with Stephenson, 10–12

Williamson, T.J., 233
Willoughby, S.E., 235
Wilson, Woodrow, 35
Winchell, Alexander,
38–39
Wise, John, 153
Wood, Sterling, 44–45, 46

Woodward, C. Vann, 14
World War I, 48, 61

"X-backs," 194

York, J.L., 233
Young, Henry, 153

THE NAVARRE BIBLE: STANDARD EDITION

SAINT MATTHEW'S GOSPEL

VOLUMES IN THIS SERIES

Standard Edition
NEW TESTAMENT
St Matthew's Gospel
St Mark's Gospel
St Luke's Gospel
St John's Gospel
Acts of the Apostles
Romans and Galatians
Corinthians
Captivity Letters
Thessalonians and Pastoral Letters
Hebrews
Catholic Letters
Revelation

OLD TESTAMENT
The Pentateuch
Joshua–Kings [Historical Books 1]
Chronicles–Maccabees [Historical Books 2]
The Psalms and the Song of Solomon
Wisdom Books
Major Prophets
Minor Prophets

Reader's (Omnibus) Edition
The Gospels and Acts
The Letters of St Paul

Compact Edition
New Testament

THE NAVARRE BIBLE

Saint Matthew's Gospel

in the Revised Standard Version and New Vulgate
with a commentary by members of the
Faculty of Theology of the University of Navarre

FOUR COURTS PRESS • DUBLIN
SCEPTER PUBLISHERS • NEW YORK

Nihil obstat: Stephen J. Greene, *censor deputatus*
Imprimi potest: Desmond, Archbishop of Dublin

Typeset by Carrigboy Typesetting Services for
FOUR COURTS PRESS LTD
7 Malpas Street, Dublin 8, Ireland
e-mail: info@four-courts-press.ie
http://www.four-courts-press.ie
Distributed in North America by
SCEPTER PUBLISHERS, INC.
P.O. Box 211, New York, NY 10018–0004
e-mail: general@scepterpublishers.org
http://www.scepterpublishers.org

The translation of introductions and commentary was made by Michael Adams.

A catalogue record for this title is available from the British Library.
First edition 1988; Second edition 1991, reprinted many times;
Third edition (reset and repaged) 2005
Reprinted 2007

ISBN 1–85182–900–8

Library of Congress Cataloging-in-Publication Data [for first volume in this series]

Bible. O.T. English. Revised Standard. 1999.
    The Navarre Bible. – North American ed.
       p.   cm
    "The Books of Genesis, Exodus, Leviticus, Numbers, Deuteronomy in the Revised
       Standard Version and New Vulgate with a commentary by members of the
       Faculty of Theology of the University of Navarre."
    Includes bibliographical references.
    Contents: [1] The Pentateuch.
    ISBN 1–889334–21–9 (hardback: alk. paper)
I. Title.
    BS891.A1   1999.P75   99–23033
    221.7'7—dc21   CIP

The title "Navarre Bible" is © Four Courts Press 2003.

ACKNOWLEDGMENTS
Quotation from Vatican II documents are based on the translation in *Vatican Council II:
The Conciliar and Post Conciliar Documents*, ed. A. Flannery, OP (Dublin 1981).

The New Vulgate text of the Bible can be accessed via
http://www.vatican.va.archive/bible/index.htm

Printed and bound in Great Britain by MPG Books, Bodmin, Cornwall.

Contents

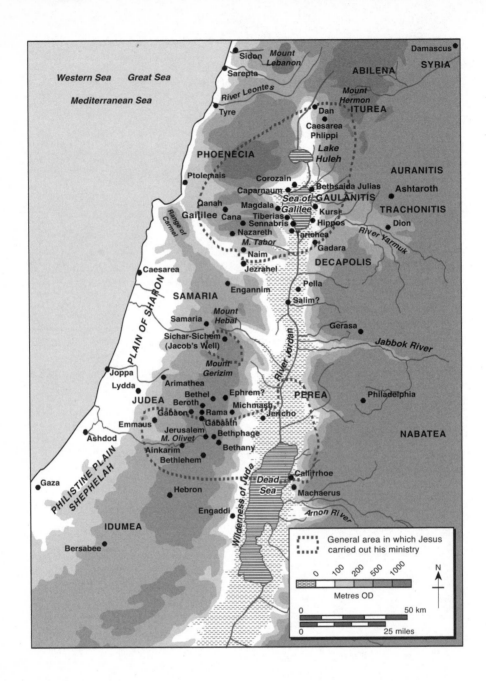

Palestine in the time of Jesus

Preface and Preliminary Notes

The English edition of *The Navarre Bible: New Testament* was published in twelve volumes in 1985–92. These books have been constantly reprinted and have obtained a very wide acceptance.

The project of a new Spanish translation of the Bible, with commentary, was originally entrusted to the faculty of theology at the University of Navarre by St Josemaría Escrivá, the founder of Opus Dei and the university's first chancellor. Because it involved making a new translation of the Bible from the original languages, the project was a much more substantial undertaking than might appear from the English edition.[1] The completion of the project was celebrated in Madrid in February 2005.

The main feature of the English edition, *The Navarre Bible*, is the commentary, that is, the notes and introductions provided by the editors; rarely very technical, these are designed to elucidate the spiritual and theological message of the Bible. Quotations from commentaries by the Fathers, and excerpts from other spiritual writers, not least St Josemaría Escrivá, are provided to show how they read Scripture and made it meaningful in their lives. The Standard Edition also carries the Western Church's official Latin version of the Bible, the *editio typica altera* of the New Vulgate (1986).

For the English edition we consider ourselves fortunate in having the Revised Standard Version as the translation of Scripture and wish to record our appreciation for permission to use that text.[2]

PRELIMINARY NOTES

The headings in the biblical text have been provided by the editors (they are not taken from the RSV); this is true also of the cross references in the marginal notes. These headings are listed in a section at the end of the book, to provide an overview of its content.

References in the margin of the biblical text or its headings point to parallel passages or other passages which deal with the same theme. With the exception of the New Testament and Psalms, the marginal references are to the New Vulgate, that is, they are not normally adjusted (where applicable) to the RSV.

---

1. *Sagrada Biblia: Antiguo Testamento. Libros poéticas y sapienciales* (Pamplona, 2001) at pp. 7–8 describes the principles governing its translation. **2.** Integral to which are the RSV footnotes, which are indicated by superior letters.

Preface

An asterisk in the biblical text refers the reader to the Explanatory Notes that appear in the RSV Catholic Edition of the Bible.

Abbreviations

Acts	Acts of the Apostles	1 Kings	1 Kings
Amos	Amos	2 Kings	2 Kings
Bar	Baruch	Lam	Lamentations
1 Chron	1 Chronicles	Lev	Leviticus
2 Chron	2 Chronicles	Lk	Luke
Col	Colossians	1 Mac	1 Maccabees
1 Cor	1 Corinthians	2 Mac	2 Maccabees
2 Cor	2 Corinthians	Mal	Malachi
Dan	Daniel	Mic	Micah
Deut	Deuteronomy	Mk	Mark
Eccles	Ecclesiastes (Qoheleth)	Mt	Matthew
Esther	Esther	Nah	Nahum
Eph	Ephesians	Neh	Nehemiah
Ex	Exodus	Num	Numbers
Ezek	Ezekiel	Obad	Obadiah
Ezra	Ezra	1 Pet	1 Peter
Gal	Galatians	2 Pet	2 Peter
Gen	Genesis	Phil	Philippians
Hab	Habakkuk	Philem	Philemon
Hag	Haggai	Ps	Psalms
Heb	Hebrews	Prov	Proverbs
Hos	Hosea	Rev	Revelation (Apocalypse)
Is	Isaiah	Rom	Romans
Jas	James	Ruth	Ruth
Jer	Jeremiah	1 Sam	1 Samuel
Jn	John	2 Sam	2 Samuel
1 Jn	1 John	Sir	Sirach (Ecclesiasticus)
2 Jn	2 John	Song	Song of Solomon
3 Jn	3 John	1 Thess	1 Thessalonians
Job	Job	2 Thess	2 Thessalonians
Joel	Joel	1 Tim	1 Timothy
Jon	Jonah	2 Tim	2 Timothy
Josh	Joshua	Tit	Titus
Jud	Judith	Wis	Wisdom
Jude	Jude	Zech	Zechariah
Judg	Judges	Zeph	Zephaniah

2. OTHER ABBREVIATIONS

ad loc.	*ad locum*, commentary on this passage	*Exhort.*	Exhortation
		f	and following (*pl.* ff)
AAA	*Acta Apostolicae Sedis*	ibid.	*ibidem*, in the same place
Apost.	Apostolic	in loc.	*in locum,* commentary on this passage
can.	canon		
chap.	chapter	loc.	*locum*, place or passage
cf.	*confer*, compare	par.	parallel passages
Const.	Constitution	Past.	Pastoral
Decl.	Declaration	RSVCE	Revised Standard Version, Catholic Edition
Dz-Sch	Denzinger-Schönmetzer, *Enchiridion Biblicum* (4th edition, Naples-Rome, 1961)	SCDF	Sacred Congregation for the Doctrine of the Faith
Enc.	Encyclical	sess.	session
		v.	verse (*pl.* vv.)

"Sources quoted in the Commentary", which appears at the end of this book, explains other abbreviations used.

Introduction to
the Gospel according to Matthew

With the help of God we are going to enter a golden city, more precious than all the gold the world contains. Let us notice what its foundations are made of, and find its gates to be composed of sapphires and precious stones. In Matthew we have the best of guides. Matthew is the door by which we enter, and we must enter eagerly, for if the guide notices that someone is distracted, he will exclude him from the city. What a magnificent and truly stately city it is; not like our cities, which are a mixture of streets and palaces. Here all are palaces. Let us, then, open the gates of our soul, let us open our ears, and as we prepare reverently to cross its threshold, let us adore the King who holds sway therein. What immense splendour shall we not find when we enter![1]

THE AUTHOR

As is the case with many other sacred books, the name of the author does not appear in the text of this Gospel. This fact is significant in itself: it indicates that the author was not writing a book of his own; he was bearing witness, briefly and in written form, to Jesus' life on earth, his teachings, his redemptive passion and death, and his glorious resurrection. He was seeking to show that Jesus of Nazareth, a descendant of David, a descendant of Abraham according to the flesh, who was virginally conceived in the pure womb of Mary by the working of the Holy Spirit, was the Messiah promised in the Old Testament prophecies; that he was the Incarnate Son of God, the Saviour of mankind, who had come to set men free from the slavery of sin, from the devil and from eternal death. In the presence of the divine and human majesty of Jesus Christ, St Matthew makes no appearance. Jesus is what matters, and what he said, and what he did.

However, the constant Tradition of the Church from earliest times identifies the human author of this Gospel as the apostle St Matthew, one of the first

1. St John Chrysostom, *Hom. on St Matthew*, 1, 8.

11

Twelve, whom Jesus himself called when he was working at his job as a "publican", that is, as a tax collector.

We have referred to St Matthew as being the "human author" of the first Gospel, the reason being that the principal author of the sacred books is God himself, who "inspired" the human authors, or hagiographers, in their literary work and "by supernatural power so moved and impelled them to write—he so assisted them when writing—that the things which he ordered, and those only, they, first, rightly understood, then willed faithfully to write down, and finally expressed in apt words and with infallible truth".[2]

However, when he communicates his grace to men, God, in his providence, does not destroy nature—in this case, the human qualities of the writers; rather, he raises nature on to a new level, perfects it and uses it to suit his purpose, in the same kind of way as a musician brings out all the qualities of a good violin. In two important respects, however, the comparison does not fit: firstly, because God, as well as using the writer as his instrument, also created him and endowed him with those qualities which he wanted him to have, to equip him to perform the task he planned for him; and secondly, because the sacred writer is not an inert instrument in God's hands: he is a living instrument, gifted with all his faculties. By virtue of this divine inspiration, a sacred book—in its entirety—is the end-product of close collaboration between God and the particular writer: each and every part of the book is really and in the proper sense of the word a work composed by God and a work composed by his instrument, the hagiographer; but, first and foremost, it is God's book, because God is its principal author.

St Matthew's Gospel, therefore—like any other biblical text—has characteristics of its own, which we will later examine. These help to identify the human author and they combine perfectly with the divine hallmark that is to be found in all the books of Holy Scripture.

Much less is known about St Matthew than about certain other New Testament authors, such as St Peter, St Paul and St John. We do know that very soon after being called to be an apostle, the immense joy he felt over his vocation led him to give a large dinner-party for his old friends and colleagues, a party attended by Jesus and by Matthew's new companions in the apostolate (cf. Mt 9:10–13; Mk 2:15–17; Lk 5:29–32). St Luke describes it as a "great feast" for "a large company": this shows that Matthew was well-to-do, had many friends and was held in high regard in Capernaum, despite the low opinion the Jews generally had of tax collectors.

St Matthew himself tells about how Jesus first called him (cf. Mt 9:9–12). When Jesus addressed him personally, in affectionate and at the same time imperative terms, Matthew immediately left his position as a tax collector and

2. Leo XIII, Enc. *Providentissimus Deus*.

"followed him" (cf. Mt 9:9; Mk 2:14; Lk 5:27). From St Luke (5:27) we learn that Matthew was also known as Levi, and St Mark (2:14) further specifies him as "Levi the son of Alphaeus".

Later on, St Matthew received a further call from our Lord: after spending a night in prayer Jesus chose him to be one of the twelve apostles (cf. Mt 10:1–14; Mk 3:13–19; Lk 6:12–16; 9:1–2; Acts 1:13). We find him involved in those episodes of our Lord's life where the Twelve are present—or the Eleven after Judas' betrayal. He was, therefore, an eye-witness of the life of Christ.

After the events reported in the Gospels and in the Acts of the Apostles, the New Testament tells us nothing further about Matthew's life. According to an ancient tradition reflected in Christian writers of the second to fourth centuries (St Irenaeus, Clement of Alexandria, Eusebius etc.), Matthew stayed in Palestine for some years, working with the other apostles, preaching the Gospel and ministering to the early Church. He would have written his Gospel towards the end of that period.

In later years he evangelized other countries, but no hard historical evidence is available in this connexion. Some documents speak of his ministering mainly in Abyssinia and Persia. The place, circumstances and date of his martyrdom are unclear.

DATE OF COMPOSITION

Written testimonies going back as early as the beginning of the second century assure us that St Matthew was the first to write down the Gospel of Jesus Christ "in the language of the Hebrews". This would have been the language spoken at that time by the Jews of Palestine; it is difficult to say exactly whether the evangelist used Hebrew or Aramaic, because no copy of the original text is extant nor any description of it—merely references to its existence. All we can say is that most scholars think that it must have been written in Aramaic. However, the Greek text of this Gospel was very soon accepted as canonical; Christian documents going back to the end of the first century show that it was widely known and used; these are: the *Didache*, written between AD 80 and 100; the *First Letter* of Pope St Clement of Rome, written between 92 and 101; the so-called *Letter of Barnabas*, written between 96 and 98; the *Letters* of St Ignatius of Antioch, martyred around the year 107; the writings of St Polycarp, who died in 156; etc.

We know that St Matthew wrote his (Aramaic) Gospel before the other evangelists wrote theirs; the estimated date is around the year 50. We do not know the date of composition of the Greek text, which is the one we have. Nor do we know whether the Greek editor was St Matthew himself or some other early Christian. The most likely date for this text is around the year 70. In any event, the original text (Aramaic or Hebrew) of St Matthew is to be dated prior to the destruction of Jerusalem (the year 70) and indeed prior to St Paul's journey to Rome (the year 60). In view of the general agreement among the Fathers and ancient ecclesiastical writers and the unanimous tradition of the Church from the beginning, our Greek Matthew, the only Matthew text used as canonical, is substantially identical with the original Matthew written in the language of the Jews.

AUTHENTICITY AND CANONICITY

The authenticity of the original Jewish-language text of St Matthew has never been questioned by the Church: in other words, it was always held that the apostle St Matthew is the author of the Gospel which bears his name. Similarly the Church has always regarded the Greek text as canonical.

THE PURPOSE OF THIS GOSPEL

The primary purpose of St Matthew's Gospel is identical with that of the other three. St John sums up this purpose very well in these words: "Now Jesus did many other signs in the presence of his disciples, which are not written in this book; but these are written that you may believe that Jesus is the Christ, the Son of God, and that believing you may have life in his name" (Jn 20:30–31). His purpose is also to show, in the first place, that Jesus of Nazareth is the Christ or Messiah promised and announced in the Old Testament, that is, that the ancient prophecies find their fulfilment in Christ; and that this messiahship consists in Jesus being the Son of God, that is, that Jesus Christ is God. This truth is illustrated and explained by providing a rich account of our Lord's teaching and reporting certain aspects or episodes of his life among men. Finally, "the Kingdom of God" or "the Kingdom of heaven", predicted in the Old Testament, has now come to pass and been made visible in the life of Jesus and in that of the messianic people he founded and convoked—the Church. That Church is the perfecting of the ancient people of God—Israel—and is the visible beginning of the definitive and perfect Kingdom of heaven, to which all are called; but only those will be finally chosen who have responded generously to God's call.

   To put it another way, the first Gospel sets out to proclaim in writing the "Good News", which the apostles preached orally—news to the effect that the salvation of Israel and of mankind, promised by God in the Old Testament, has now been brought into the world by Jesus Christ, the Messiah and the Son of God; men are enabled to know this by the marvellous account given in the Gospel, in which Jesus' words and works explain each other and reach their climax in his redemptive sacrifice, his passion and death, followed by his glorious resurrection.

CONTENT

In broad outline the content of the first Gospel can be summed up as follows: the birth and infancy of Jesus; the announcement by John the Baptist, the Precursor, that Christ is about to begin his mission; Jesus' public ministry in Galilee and the calling of the twelve apostles: here he begins to reveal his messiahship and divinity, through his teaching and miracles; journeys Jesus makes with his disciples, doing good, curing the sick, teaching—in other words fulfilling what the Old Testament prophecies said about him; the last stage of his public ministry in Judea and Jerusalem; the account of his passion and death; his glorious resurrection; and post-resurrection appearances.

An outstanding feature of this Gospel is its account of five long discourses of Jesus; these, and the narrative parts of the Gospel, shed light on each other and lead the reader into the drama of Christ's death and the joy of his resurrection.

It is really not possible to fit St Matthew's Gospel into any kind of rigid structure. However, the following outline may be of some help:

1. *Birth and infancy of Jesus* (chaps. 1–2). A selection of the basic historical facts which illustrate and explain the following truths of faith: Jesus is the Messiah descended from David, the Saviour promised in the Old Testament; the Son of God, conceived by the action of the Holy Spirit and born of the Virgin Mary; the *Emmanuel* or *God-with-us* prophesied by Isaiah, protected during his infancy by a special providence of God (the fatherly care given him by St Joseph and the maternal affection of the Blessed Virgin Mary); the King of Israel, adored even by Gentiles (the wise men). The sober accounts—simple yet profound—comprising these two chapters already bring in quite a number of the basic truths about the divine and human mystery of Jesus Christ.

2. *Prelude to the public ministry of Jesus* (3:1—4:11). This takes place in regions which for centuries lived in hope of salvation—the Judean desert and the river Jordan. Here we find the Baptist's prophetic announcement of the imminence of the Kingdom of God; his exhortation to conversion and

penance; the baptism of Jesus, accompanied by the revelation that he is the Son of God made man; and the temptations of Jesus in the wilderness.

PART ONE: JESUS' MINISTRY IN GALILEE
The beginnings of the message of salvation, the calling of the disciples and the convocation of the new people of God (4:12–25).
3. *The sermon on the mount.* Jesus, the supreme Teacher, Lawgiver and Prophet: the "discourse on the mount" (chaps. 5–7), the first of the five great discourses and a summary of the new Law of the Kingdom of God; Jesus, God made man, teaches a most sublime doctrine never heard before, in words simple yet totally demanding; this is the way of salvation which man must follow. This discourse is a kind of distillate of the teachings of Jesus the Messiah on evangelical holiness.

4. *The miracles of the Messiah* (chaps. 8–9). Following on these words or teachings, St Matthew's Gospel presents an array of miracles, whereby our Lord backs up his teaching with divine authority. These miracles also mean that the salvation promised in the Old Testament has come about in the person of Jesus. Also, the curing of the sick shows that men are being set free from sin, because sin is the ultimate cause of illness and mortality in man. These two chapters are, then, a kind of summary of "the words of the Messiah".

5. *From the old to the new people of God.* The first sending forth of the disciples, the "apostolic discourse", the hardening of the hearts of the religious leaders of Israel against Jesus' messiahship (chaps. 10–12); Jesus trains his twelve apostles for their immediate mission and for the future (chap. 10). In reaction to the proclamation of Jesus as Messiah—through his words and works and his convocation of the new messianic people (chaps. 3–10)—the Jewish leaders grow more and more opposed to him (chaps. 11–12). The scene is being set for their rejection of him, their plotting of his death, and the foundation of the Church as the new people of God.

6. *The parables of the Kingdom* (chap. 13). Despite this, Jesus continues to reveal to the people the mystery of the Kingdom of God, or Kingdom of heaven. This he does by means of parables—a teaching method suited to the capacity of his listeners. These parables contain a substantial proportion of his teaching concerning the Church which he will found; from a small beginning it will grow until the end of time. This "parabolic discourse" ends with a visit to Nazareth, where Jesus encounters the incredulity of his fellow-townsmen. This brings to an end what we might call the first part of St Matthew's Gospel.

7. *Jesus withdraws to the border country* (13:53—16:20). In view of the growing antagonism of the Jewish religious authorities and the martyrdom of John the Baptist, Jesus makes a series of evangelical journeys in the regions adjoining Israel. His disciples accompany him. These journeys are an advance indication of the universality of the Gospel; but they also act as a form of retreat, enabling Jesus to continue his ministry undisturbed, and to avoid precipitating his passion. Jesus teaches his disciples, with an eye to founding his Church. Outside Israel proper, in Caesarea Philippi, Peter makes a confession of faith in Jesus as Messiah, and Jesus promises to make Peter the head of his Church (Mt 16:13–20).

PART TWO: JESUS' MINISTRY ON THE WAY TO JERUSALEM
8. *Towards Judea and Jerusalem* (16:21—17:27). The transfiguration of Jesus and new teachings (chap. 17): Jesus' divinity is revealed to his disciples.

9. *The discourse on the Church* (chap. 18): so called because it contains specific teaching about the life of the future Church, and the authority of the apostles and their successors.

Various teachings of Jesus—on marriage and virginity, poverty, humility, etc. (chap. 19); the parable of the labourers in the vineyard; the third announcement of the Passion, etc. (chap. 20).

PART THREE: JESUS' MINISTRY IN JERUSALEM
10. *Cleansing of the temple. Controversies* (21:1—23:39). This begins with his messianic entry into the Holy City and the temple (21:1–17), followed by teaching concerning Christ's authority (21:18–27) and three great allegorical parables (21:28—22:14) on salvation history and the mystery of the Church. Then comes an account of controversies with the Pharisees (22:15–46) in which they bring up various questions in the hope that Jesus will provide them with grounds for indicting him. These events lead to Jesus' invective against the scribes and Pharisees ("Woe to him …": 23:13–36) and his lament over the destruction of Jerusalem (23:37–39).

11. *The eschatological discourse.* This section ends with Jesus' prophecies about the destruction of Jerusalem and the end of the world—the "eschatological discourse" (chaps. 24–25): the prophecies (24:1–36) are followed by teaching about the vigilance required of a Christian (24:37—25:30). Our Lord illustrates his teaching by three parables—that of the unjust servant (24:45–51), that of the ten virgins (25:1–13), and the parable of the talents (25:14–30). The eschatological discourse ends with teaching on the Last Judgment, where Jesus himself will be the judge (25:31–46).

12. *The passion, death and resurrection of Jesus* (chaps. 26–28). Like the other three Gospels, St Matthew's devotes considerable space to its account of the passion and death of the Son of God, which embraces the truths every Christian should know regarding the sacrifice of the Messiah. Two chapters cover the period from the anointing at Bethany (26:6–13), to the death of Jesus on the cross (27:45–56), his burial (27:57–61) and the placing of the guard over the tomb (27:62–66). At various points the Passion account throws light on Old Testament prophecies which predicted the Passion in one way or another.

Also like the other Gospels, St Matthew's ends with Jesus' victory over death through his glorious resurrection—a message of immense joy, hope and faith. It tells how the tomb was found to be empty (28:1–8, 11–15) and of the appearances of the risen Jesus to the holy women (28:9–10) and to the apostles (28:16–17). The Gospel ends with the proclamation of the absolute lordship of Jesus Christ, now glorified (28:18), and his charge to his disciples to preach the Gospel throughout the world, baptizing in the name of the three divine persons (28:19–20).

SPECIAL FEATURES

The Gospel of St Matthew is a divine and human work. God is the principal author of the book, and his purpose goes beyond that of the human author, his instrument. St Matthew—man, apostle and evangelist—does speak to us through these pages: but, above all, God himself is speaking. This means that no matter how much honest effort is put into studying and explaining this Gospel—or any other part of Holy Scripture—we can never grasp its full meaning. God's purpose in inspiring a particular man to write this book is to reveal to us something about himself and to entrust this text to his Church, which will make it comprehensible to us and helpful to our sanctification and eternal salvation. St Matthew's Gospel is one of the most precious of all the many gifts God has given us in Scripture; we should thank God for it, in the first instance; but we should also be grateful to the man who, with the help of divine inspiration, took pains to write it.

THE GOSPEL OF THE DISCOURSES OF THE LORD

St Matthew's Gospel has been called "the Gospel of the Discourses of the Lord" because of the five long discourses it contains. Through these we can hear Jesus' words and be present when he preaches. However, we should not forget that, since the Gospel was written under the inspiration of the Holy Spirit and has God as its principal author, the entire text—not just these discourses—is truly the word of God, and "all that the hagiographer (or sacred writer) affirms should be regarded as affirmed by the Holy Spirit".[3]

These five discourses are: the discourse on the mount (chaps. 5–7); the apostolic discourse (chap. 10); the parabolic discourse (chap. 13); the discourse on the Church (chap. 18); and the eschatological discourse (chaps. 24–25). There are also shorter discourses—such as Christ's indictment of the Pharisees and scribes (23:13–36) and some of his controversies with the Pharisees (12:25–45). Usually these discourses are preceded by other passages describing the development of events; the discourse part and narrative part of the account combine to help us understand the deep meaning of the works and words of Jesus.

THE GOSPEL OF FULFILMENT

Although each of the four Gospels was written for all men in all ages, God also wrote them for a particular immediate readership. In the case of Matthew, the text was obviously written in a manner suited to Christians of Jewish background—its immediate readers—as well as for later generations. Matthew, for example, is at pains to show that all the Old Testament finds its fulfilment in the person and work of Christ: at particularly important points in Jesus' life, the evangelist expressly points out that "this took place to fulfil what the Lord had spoken by the prophet" or words to that effect (cf., e.g., Mt 1:23; 2:6, 15, 17–18; 3:3–4; 4:4, 14–16; 5:17; 21:4–5, 16; 26:31; 27:9–10). This feature of his Gospel has led to its being called "the Gospel of fulfilment". Insight into the Old Testament in the light of the New is not unique to St Matthew's Gospel, for it was something Jesus was always teaching to his disciples and something that the Holy Spirit also revealed to them—it is the science of "understanding the Scriptures" (cf., e.g., Lk 24:32, 45; Acts 8:35)—but it was clearly an important factor in the evangelization of Jews and in their subsequent catechesis.

JESUS, THE REJECTED MESSIAH

In countless ways all the books of the New Testament show that Jesus is the promised Messiah, the Christ, the Lord (*Kyrios*) and the Son of God; and they also reveal the mystery of God, one essence and three persons.

But within this general teaching common to them all, it is clear from the particular accents it carries that Matthew's Gospel was addressed in the first instance to Christians of Jewish background. In keeping with what has been said about the "Gospel of fulfilment", it points out that the beginning of

---

3. Vatican II, *Dei Verbum*, 11.

Christ's public preaching is the dawn of messianic light (cf. Mt 4:13–17) foretold by the prophet Isaiah (cf. Is 8:23–9:1); similarly the first cures Jesus performs (cf. Mt 8:16–17) are presented as fulfilling the words of the prophets, particularly Isaiah (cf. Is 53:4–5).

And, above all, the first Gospel contains teaching and events which dramatically emphasize the mystery of the rejection of Jesus, the promised Messiah, by the rulers of the Jews, and by many of the people, whom those rulers succeeded in misleading. Guided by the light of divine inspiration, the evangelist confronts this mystery in various ways: sometimes, when reporting how the scribes, Pharisees and chief priests react against Jesus, or when narrating the way he suffers during his passion, he stresses that all this, far from frustrating God's plan, was foreseen and predicted by the Old Testament prophets and fulfils what they predicted would happen (cf. Mt 12:17; 13:35; 26:54, 56; 27:9; etc.). At other times he explains that this rejection of the Messiah by Israel is in line with and a culmination of a whole history of infidelity to God's generosity and love (cf., e.g., Mt 21:28–44; 23:9–33). In any event the Gospel shows the pain Christ feels over Israel's failure to respond to his love and the punishment that lies in store for it if it fails to mend its ways (cf. Mt 23:37–39).

THE GOSPEL OF THE KINGDOM

St Matthew refers 51 times to "the Kingdom", St Mark 14 times and St Luke 39. But whereas the two last-mentioned speak of "the Kingdom of God", Matthew on all but five occasions uses the phrase "the Kingdom of heaven". This must certainly have been the phrase Jesus normally used, given the Jewish custom of the time not to utter the name of God—out of respect—but instead to use other equivalent terms such as "of heaven". The Kingdom of God comes into being with the arrival of Christ (cf. note on Mt 3:2) and, especially in the parables, Jesus explains what its features are (cf. note on Mt 13:3). The first Gospel is called the "Gospel of the Kingdom" because it throws so much light on these features.

THE DIVINITY OF JESUS

Christ's divinity is affirmed in various ways in this Gospel. From the conception of Jesus by the action of the Holy Spirit (Mt 1:20) to the trinitarian formula for Baptism at the end (Mt 28:19), the first Gospel asserts and stresses that Jesus, the Christ, is the Son of God. In numerous passages it mentions the relationship between the Father and the Son: Jesus is the Son of the Father, the Father is God, and the Son is equal to the Father. Some passages also place the Father, the Son and the Holy Spirit on the same level (the most famous being that just mentioned: Mt 28:19). What this means is that the revelation of the Blessed Trinity, a revelation expressly made by Jesus Christ, is affirmed in St Matthew's Gospel by the revelation that Jesus is the Son of the Father, and God like him.

In the light of this essential truth, that Jesus is the Son of God, all the other messianic titles which the Old Testament used in prophecies about the Saviour fall into place—Son of David, Son of man, Messiah, Lord.

THE GOSPEL OF THE CHURCH

This Gospel has also been called the "ecclesiastical Gospel" or the "Gospel of the Church". One reason for this is that the actual word "church" appears three times (cf. Mt 16:18; 18:17 twice). Another is that the Church, even without being expressly named, can be seen to be in the background of the narrative: it is hinted at in different ways in quite a few parables; its foundation is announced and explicitly expressed when Peter is promised the primacy (cf. Mt 16:17–19); its beginning can in some way be seen in the discourse in chapter 18; it is figuratively depicted in some episodes such as that of the calming of the storm (cf. Mt 8:23–27); it is cast in the role of the new, true Israel in the parable of the wicked tenants of the vineyard (cf. Mt 21:33–45); and its role as universal vessel of salvation is based on the apostolic charge which our Lord gives at the end of the Gospel. In effect, the Church forms a background to the entire text of this Gospel and is ever-present in the mind and heart of the evangelist—as it is in the mind and heart of Jesus Christ.

LITERARY STYLE

From what has been said about its content and structure it can be seen that the Gospel also has strong literary unity: every paragraph is written in line with the writer's purpose; this affects both the content of the writing and the context in which it is placed. As the reader grows more familiar with the text he notices more hints, more symbolism and additional teaching developing themes already covered quite elaborately.

The precision with which Matthew articulates Jesus' teaching comes across very clearly. He writes in a concise, sober and thoughtful style, and a person making his way through the book will find that it enters into his soul and brings him face to face with the powerful yet tender mystery of Jesus Christ.

Many commentators have pointed out that St Matthew's particular style has the effect of making many of his phrases easy to recognize: we often find ourselves quoting Matthew's version in preference to other Gospel accounts. For this reason his Gospel has been called the first Gospel of Christian catechesis.

ST MATTHEW'S GOSPEL IN THE LIFE OF THE CHURCH

From the end of the first century—in references by Pope St Clement—there is overwhelming evidence of predominant use of the St Matthew text in the teachings of the Church's Magisterium. The early Fathers are forever quoting it and many later Fathers commented on it (for example, there are ninety long homilies by St John Chrysostom) as did the great teachers of the Middle Ages (for example, St Thomas Aquinas) and later ecclesiastical writers.

THE GOSPEL ACCORDING TO MATTHEW

The Revised Standard Version, with notes

1. BIRTH AND INFANCY OF JESUS

The ancestry of Jesus Christ

Lk 3:23–38
1 Chron 17:11
Gen 5:1; 22:1

1 ¹The book of the genealogy of Jesus Christ, the son of David, the son of Abraham.*

²Abraham was the father of Isaac, and Isaac the father of Jacob, and Jacob the father of Judah and his brothers, ³and Judah the father of Perez and Zerah by Tamar, and Perez the father of Hezron, and Hezron the father of Ram,ᵃ ⁴and Ramᵃ the father of Amminadab, and Amminadab the father of Nahson, and Nahson the father of Salmon, ⁵and Salmon the father of Boaz by Rahab, and Boaz the father of Obed by Ruth, and Obed the father of Jesse, ⁶and Jesse the father of David the king.

And David was the father of Solomon by the wife of Uriah, ⁷and Solomon the father of Rehoboam, and Rehoboam the father of Abijah, and Abijah the father of Asa,ᵇ ⁸and Asaᵇ the father of

Gen 21:3, 12;
25:26; 29:35;
49:10

1 Chron 1:34

1 Chron 2:5, 9
Gen 38:29f
Ruth 4:18–22
1 Chron 2:10f
Ruth 4:13–17

2 Sam 12:24

1 Chron
3:10–16

1:1. This verse is a kind of title to St Matthew's entire Gospel. The promises God made to Abraham for the salvation of mankind (Gen 12:3) are fulfilled in Jesus Christ, as is Nathan's prophecy to King David of an everlasting kingdom (2 Sam 7:12–16).

The genealogy presented here by St Matthew shows Jesus' human ancestry and also indicates that salvation history has reached its climax with the birth of the Son of God through the working of the Holy Spirit. Jesus Christ, true God and true man, is the expected Messiah.

The genealogy is presented in a framework of three series, each consisting of fourteen links which show the progressive development of salvation history.

For the Jews (and for other Eastern peoples of nomadic origin) genealogical trees were of great importance because a person's identity was especially linked to family and tribe, with place of birth taking secondary importance. In the case of the Jewish people there was the added

religious significance of belonging by blood to the chosen people.

In Christ's time each family still kept a careful record of its genealogical tree, since because of it people acquired rights and duties.

1:6. Four women are named in these genealogies—Tamar (cf. Gen 38; 1 Chron 2:4), Rahab (cf. Josh 2:6, 17). Bathsheba (cf. 2 Sam 11:12, 24) and Ruth (cf. Book of Ruth). These four foreign women, who in one way or another are brought into the history of Israel, are one sign among many others of God's design to save all men.

By mentioning sinful people, God's ways are shown to be different from man's. God will sometimes carry out his plan of salvation by means of people whose conduct has not been just. God saves us, sanctifies us and chooses us to do good despite our sins and infidelities—and he chose to leave evidence of this at various stages in the history of our salvation.

a. Greek *Aram* **b.** Greek *Asaph*

Jehoshaphat, and Jehoshaphat the father of Joram, and Joram the father of Uzziah, [9]and Uzziah the father of Jotham, and Jotham the father of Ahaz, and Ahaz the father of Hezekiah, [10]and Hezekiah the father of Manasseh, and Manasseh the father of Amos,[c] and Amos[c] the father of Josiah, [11]and Josiah the father of Jechoniah and his brothers, at the time of the deportation to Babylon.

[12]And after the deportation to Babylon: Jechoniah was the father of Shealtiel,[d] and Shealtiel[d] the father of Zerubbabel, [13]and Zerubbabel the father of Abiud, and Abiud the father of Eliakim, and Eliakim the father of Azor, [14]and Azor the father of Zadok, and Zadok the father of Achim, and Achim the father of Eliud,[15]and Eliud the father of Eleazar, and Eleazar the father of Matthan, and Matthan the father of Jacob, [16]and Jacob the father of Joseph the husband of Mary, of whom Jesus was born, who is called Christ.*

Ezra 1:32

1 Chron 3:17
Ezra 3:2

1:11. The deportation to Babylon, described in 2 Kings 24–25, fulfilled the prophets' warning to the people of Israel and their kings that they would be punished for their infidelity to the commandments of the Law of God, especially the first commandment.

1:16. Jewish genealogies followed the male line. Joseph, being Mary's husband, was the legal father of Jesus. The legal father is on a par with the real father as regards rights and duties. This fact provides a sound basis for recognizing St Joseph as Patron of the whole Church, since he was chosen to play a very special role in God's plan for our salvation; with St Joseph as his legal father, Jesus the Messiah has David as his ancestor.

Since it was quite usual for people to marry within their clan, it can be concluded that Mary belonged to the house of David. Several early Fathers of the church testify to this—for example, St Ignatius of Antioch, St Irenaeus, St Justin and Tertullian, who base their testimony on an unbroken oral tradition.

It should also be pointed out that when St Matthew comes to speak of the birth of Jesus, he uses an expression which is completely different from that used for the other people in the genealogy. With these words the text positively teaches that Mary conceived Jesus while still a virgin, without the intervention of man.

1:18. St Matthew relates here how Christ was conceived (cf. Lk 1:25–38): "We truly honour and venerate (Mary) as Mother of God, because she gave birth to a person who is at the same time both God and man" (St Pius V, *Catechism*, 1, 4, 7).

According to the provisions of the Law of Moses, engagement took place about one year before marriage and enjoyed almost the same legal validity. The marriage proper consisted, among other ceremonies, in the bride being brought solemnly and joyously to her husband's house (cf. Deut 20:7)

From the moment of engagement onwards, a certificate of divorce was needed in the event of a break in the relationship between the couple. The entire account of Jesus' birth teaches, through

---

c. Other authorities read *Amon* **d.** Greek *Salathiel*

¹⁷So all the generations from Abraham to David were fourteen generations, and from David to the deportation to Babylon fourteen generations, and from the deportation to Babylon to the Christ fourteen generations.

The virginal conception of Jesus, and his birth

¹⁸Now the birth of Jesus Christ[f] took place in this way. When his mother Mary had been betrothed to Joseph, before they came together she was found to be with child of the Holy Spirit; ¹⁹and her husband Joseph, being a just man and unwilling to put her to shame, resolved to send her away quietly. ²⁰But as he considered this, behold, an angel of the Lord appeared to him in a dream, saying, "Joseph, son of David, do not fear to take Mary your wife,

Lk 1:35

---

the fulfilment of the prophecy of Isaiah 7:14 (which is expressly quoted in vv. 22–23) that: 1) Jesus has David as his ancestor since Joseph is his legal father; 2) Mary is the Virgin who gives birth according to the prophecy; 3) the Child's conception without the intervention of man was miraculous.

1:19. "St Joseph was an ordinary sort of man on whom God relied to do great things. He did exactly what the Lord wanted him to do, in each and every event that went to make up his life. That is why Scripture praises Joseph as a 'just man' (Mt 1:19). In Hebrew a just man means a good and faithful servant of God, someone who fulfils the divine will (cf. Gen 7:1; 18:23–32; Ezek 18:5ff; Prov 12:10), or who is honourable and charitable towards his neighbour (cf. Tob 7:6; 9:6). So a just man is someone who loves God and proves his love by keeping God's commandments and directing his whole life towards the service of his brothers, his fellow men" (St Josemaría Escrivá, *Christ Is Passing By*, 40).

Joseph considered his spouse to be holy despite the signs that she was going

to have a child. He was therefore faced with a situation he could not explain. Precisely because he was trying to do God's will, he felt obliged to put her away; but to shield her from public shame he decided to send her away quietly.

Mary's silence is admirable. Her perfect surrender to God even leads her to the extreme of not defending her honour or innocence. She prefers to suffer suspicion and shame rather than reveal the work of grace in her. Faced with a fact which was inexplicable in human terms she abandons herself confidently to the love and providence of God. God certainly subjected the holy souls of Joseph and Mary to a severe trial. We ought not be surprised if we also undergo difficult trials in the course of our lives. We ought to trust in God during them, and remain faithful to him, following the example Mary and Joseph gave us.

1:20. God gives his light to those who act in an upright way and who trust in his power and wisdom when faced with situations which exceed human understanding. By calling him the son of David, the angel reminds Joseph that he is the prov-

---

f. Other ancient authorities read *of the Christ*

27

Lk 1:31; 2:21
Acts 4:12

Is 7:14
Lk 2:7

for that which is conceived in her is of the Holy Spirit; [21]she will bear a son, and you shall call his name Jesus, for he will save his people from their sins." [22]All this took place to fulfil what the Lord had spoken by the prophet:
[23]"Behold, a virgin shall conceive and bear a son,
and his name shall be called Emmanuel"

---

idential link which joins Jesus with the family of David, according to Nathan's messianic prophecy (cf. 2 Sam 7:12). As St John Chrysostom says: "At the very start he straightaway reminds him of David, of whom the Christ was to spring, and he does not wish him to be worried from the moment he reminds him, through naming his most illustrious ancestor, of the promise made to all his lineage" (*Hom. on St Matthew*, 4).

"The same Jesus Christ, our only Lord, the Son of God, when he assumed human flesh for us in the womb of the Virgin, was not conceived like other men, from the seed of man, but in a manner transcending the order of nature, that is, by the power of the Holy Spirit, so that the same person, remaining God as he was from eternity, became man, which he was not before" (St Pius V, *Catechism*, 1, 4, 1).

1:21. According to the Hebrew root, the name of Jesus means "saviour". After our Lady, St Joseph is the first person to be told by God that salvation has begun. "Jesus is the proper name of the God-man and signifies 'Saviour', a name given him not accidentally, or by the judgment or will of man, but by the counsel and command of God" [...]. All other names which prophecy gave to the Son of God—Wonderful Counsellor, Mighty God, Everlasting Father, Prince of Peace (cf. Is 9:6)—are comprised in this one name Jesus; for while they partially signified the salvation which he was to bestow

on us, this name included the force and meaning of all human salvation" (St Pius V, *Catechism*, 1, 3, 5 and 6).

1:23. "Emmanuel": the prophecy of Isaiah 7:14, quoted in this verse, foretold about seven hundred years in advance that God's salvation would be marked by the extraordinary event of a virgin giving birth to a child. The Gospel here, therefore, reveals two truths.

The first is that Jesus is in fact the God-with-us foretold by the prophet. This is how Christian tradition has always understood it. Indeed the Church has officially condemned an interpretation denying the messianic sense of the Isaiah text (cf. Pius VI, Brief *Divina*, 1779). Christ is truly God-with-us, therefore, not only because of his God-given mission but because he is God made man (cf. Jn 1:14). This does not mean that Jesus should normally be called Emmanuel, for this name refers more directly to the mystery of his being the Incarnate Word. At the Annunciation the angel said that he should be called Jesus, that is, Saviour. And that was the name St Joseph gave him.

The second truth revealed to us by the sacred text is that Mary, in whom the prophecy of Isaiah 7:14 is fulfilled, was a virgin before and during the birth itself. The miraculous sign given by God that salvation had arrived was precisely that a woman would be a virgin and a mother at the same time. "Jesus Christ came forth from his mother's womb without injury

(which means God with us). ²⁴When Joseph woke from sleep, he did as the angel of the Lord commanded him; he took his wife, ²⁵but knew her not until she had borne a son;* and he called his name Jesus.

---

to her maternal virginity. This immaculate and perpetual virginity forms, therefore, the just theme of our eulogy. Such was the work of the Holy Spirit, who at the conception and birth of the Son so favoured the Virgin Mother as to impart fruitfulness to her while preserving inviolate her perpetual virginity" (St Pius V, *Catechism*, 1, 4, 8).

1:25. St John Chrysostom, addressing himself to St Joseph, comments: "Christ's conception was the work of the Holy Spirit, but do not think this divine economy has nothing to do with you. For although it is true that you had no part in the generation of Christ, and that the Virgin remained inviolate, nevertheless, what pertains to a father (not injuring the honour of virginity) that do I give you— the naming of the child. For 'you shall call his name'. Although you have not generated him, you will act as a father to him. Hence it is that, beginning with giving him his name, I associate you intimately with the one who is to be born" (*Hom. on St Matthew*, 4).

Following the Greek text strictly, the New Vulgate version says: "et non cognoscebat eam, *donec* peperit filium". The literal English translation is: "and he knew her not *until* she had borne a son". The word "*donec*" (until) of itself does not direct our attention to what happened afterwards; it simply points out what has happened up to that moment, that is, the virginal conception of Jesus Christ by a unique intervention of God. We find the same word in John 9:18, where it says that the Pharisees did not believe in the miraculous cure of the man blind from

birth "until" (*donec*) they called his parents. However, neither did they believe afterwards. Consequently, the word "until" does not refer to what happens later.

The Vulgate adds after "*filium*" the words "*suum primogenitum*", which in the Bible simply means "the first son", without implying that there are any other children (cf. Ex 13:2). This Latin variant gives no ground whatsoever for thinking that our Lady had other children later. See the note on Lk 2:7.

The Church has always taught that the perpetual virginity of our Lady is a truth to be held by Catholics. For example, the following are the words of the Lateran Council of AD 649: "If anyone does not profess according to the holy Fathers, that in the proper and true sense, the holy, ever-virgin, immaculate Mary is the Mother of God, since in this last age not with human seed but of the Holy Spirit she properly and truly conceived the Divine Word, who was born of God the Father before all ages, and gave him birth without any detriment to her virginity, which remained inviolate even after his birth: let such a one be condemned" (can. 3).

St Jerome gives the following reasons why it was fitting that the Mother of God, as well as being a virgin, should also be married: first, so that Mary's child would be clearly a descendant of King David (through the genealogy of St Joseph); second, to ensure that on having a son her honour would not be questioned nor any legal penalty be imposed on her; third, so that during the flight into Egypt she would have the help and pro-

The adoration of the Magi

Lk 2:1–7

Num 24:17

2 ¹Now when Jesus was born in Bethlehem of Judea in the days of Herod the king, behold, wise men from the East came to Jerusalem, saying, ²"Where is he who has been born king of the Jews? For we have seen his star in the East, and have come to

---

tection of St Joseph. He even points to a fourth possible reason, expressly taken from St Ignatius Martyr, and to which he seems to give less importance—that the birth of Jesus would go unnoticed by the devil, who would have no knowledge of the virginal conception of our Lord (cf. *Comm. on Matthew*, 1, 1).

2:1. "King Herod": four different Herods are mentioned in the New Testament. The first is Herod the Great, referred to in this passage and in the next; the second, his son, Herod Antipas, who had St John the Baptist beheaded (Mt 14:1–12) and who abused our Lord during his passion (Lk 23:7–11); the third, Herod Agrippa I, a grandson of Herod the Great, who executed the apostle St James the Greater (Acts 12: 1–3), imprisoned St Peter (Acts 12:4–7), and died suddenly and mysteriously (Acts 12:20–23). The fourth, Herod Agrippa II, was Herod Agrippa I's son. It was before him that St Paul answered Jewish accusations when he was a prisoner in Caesarea (Acts 25:23).

Herod the Great, who appears here, was the son of non-Jewish parents. He came to power with the aid and as a vassal of the Romans. He was a consummate politician and among other things he rebuilt the temple in Jerusalem on a lavish scale. Herod the Great had a persecution complex; everywhere he saw rivals to his throne. He was notorious for his cruelty: he killed over half of his ten wives, some of his children and many people of standing. This information derives largely from the Jewish historian

Flavius Josephus, who wrote towards the end of the first century, and it confirms the cruel picture drawn in the Gospels.

"Wise men": these were learned men, probably from Persia, who devoted themselves to the study of the stars. Since they were not Jews, they can be considered to be the very first Gentiles to receive the call to salvation in Christ. The adoration of the wise men forms part of the very earliest documented tradition: the scene is already depicted at the beginning of the second century in the paintings in the catacombs of St Priscilla in Rome.

2:2. The Jews had made known throughout the East their hope of a Messiah. The wise men knew about this expected Messiah, king of the Jews. According to ideas widely accepted at the time, this sort of person, because of his significance in world history, would have a star connected with his birth. God made use of these ideas to draw to Christ these representatives of the Gentiles who would later be converted

"The star had been hidden from them so that, on finding themselves without their guide, they would have no alternative but to consult the Jews. In this way the birth of Jesus would be made known to all" (St John Chrysostom, *Hom. on St Matthew*, 7). Chrysostom also points out that "God calls them by means of the things they are most familiar with: and he shows them a large and extraordinary star so that they would be impressed by its size and beauty" (ibid., 6). God called the wise men in the midst of their ordinary occupations, and he still calls people in

worship him." ³When Herod the king heard this, he was troubled, and all Jerusalem with him; ⁴and assembling all the chief priests and scribes of the people, he inquired of them where the Christ was to be born. ⁵They told him, "In Bethlehem of Judea; for so it is written by the prophet:

Mic 5:2
Jn 7:42

---

that way. He called Moses when he was shepherding his flock (Ex 3:1–3), Elisha the prophet ploughing his land with oxen (1 Kings 19:19–20), Amos looking after his herd (Amos 7:15). ... "What amazes you seems natural to me: that God has sought you out in the practice of your profession! That is how he sought the first, Peter and Andrew, James and John, beside their nets, and Matthew, sitting in the custom-house. And—wonder of wonders!—Paul, in his eagerness to destroy the seeds of Christianity" (St Josemaría Escrivá, *The Way*, 799).

"Like the Magi we have discovered a star—a light and a guide in the sky of our soul. 'We have seen his star in the East and have come to worship him (Mt 2:2).' We have had the same experience. We too noticed a new light shining in our soul and growing increasingly brighter. It was a desire to live a fully Christian life, a keenness to take God seriously" (St J. Escrivá, *Christ Is Passing By*, 32).

2:4. In all Jewish circles at the time of Jesus, the hope was widespread that the Messiah would come soon. The general idea was that he would be a king, like a new and even greater David. Herod's worry is therefore all the more understandable: he governed the Jews with the aid of the Romans and cruelly and jealously guarded his crown. Due to his political ambition and his lack of religious sense, Herod saw a potential Messiah-King as a dangerous rival to his own worldly power.

In the time of our Lord, both Herod's monarchy and the occupying Romans (through their procurators) recognized the Sanhedrin as the representative body of the Jewish people. The Sanhedrin was, therefore, the nation's supreme council which ruled on day-to-day affairs, both religious and civil. The handling of the more important questions needed the approval of either the king (under Herod's monarchy) or the Roman procurator (at the time of the direct Roman occupation of Palestine). Following Exodus 24:1–9 and Numbers 11:16, the Sanhedrin was composed of seventy-one members presided over by the high priest. The members were elected from three groupings: 1) the chief priests, that is, the leaders of the principal priestly families; it was these families who appointed the high priest (the chief priests also included anybody who had formerly held the high priesthood); 2) the elders, or the leaders of the most important families; 3) the scribes, who were teachers of the Law or experts on legal and religious matters; the majority of these scribes belonged to the party or school of the Pharisees. In this passage of St Matthew only the first and third of the above groups are mentioned. This is understandable since the elders would have no authority in the matter of the birth of the Messiah—a purely religious question.

2:5–6. The prophecy referred to in this passage is Micah 5:1. It is worth noting that Jewish tradition interpreted this prophecy as predicting the Messiah's exact place of birth and as referring to a particular person. The second text thus teaches us once more that the prophecies of the Old Testament are fulfilled in Jesus Christ.

⁶'And you, O Bethlehem, in the land of Judah,
are by no means least among the rulers of Judah;
for from you shall come a ruler
who will govern my people Israel.'"

⁷Then Herod summoned the wise men secretly and ascertained from them what time the star appeared; ⁸and he sent them to Bethlehem, saying, "Go and search diligently for the child, and when you have found him bring me word, that I too may come and worship him." ⁹When they had heard the king they went their way; and lo, the star which they had seen in the East went before them, till it came to rest over the place where the child was. ¹⁰When they saw the star, they rejoiced exceedingly with great

---

2:8. Herod tried to find out exactly where the Child was—not, of course, to adore him, as he said, but to dispose of him. Such was Herod's exclusively political view of things. Yet neither his shrewdness nor his wickedness could prevent God's plans from being fulfilled. Despite Herod's ambition and his scheming, God's wisdom and power were going to bring salvation about.

2:9. "It might happen at certain moments of our interior life—and we are nearly always to blame—that the star disappears, just as it did to the wise kings on their journey. [...] What should we do if this happens? Follow the example of those wise men and ask. Herod used knowledge to act unjustly. The Magi use it to do good. But we Christians have no need to go to Herod nor to the wise men of this world. Christ has given his Church sureness of doctrine and a flow of grace in the sacraments. He has arranged things so that there will always be people to guide and lead us, to remind us constantly of our way" (St Josemaría Escrivá, *Christ Is Passing By*, 34).

2:10. "Why were they so happy? Because those who had never doubted received proof from the Lord that the star had not disappeared. They had ceased to contem-

plate it visibly, but they kept it always in their souls. Such is the Christian's vocation. If we do not lose faith, if we keep our hope in Christ who will be with us 'until the consummation of the world' (Mt 28:20), then the star reappears. And with this fresh proof that our vocation is real, we are conscious of a greater joy which increases our faith, hope and love" (*Christ Is Passing By*, 35).

2:11. The gifts they offered—gold, frankincense and myrrh—were those most valued in the East. People feel the need to give gifts to God to show their respect and faith. Since they cannot give themselves as a gift, which is what they would wish, they give instead what is most valuable and dear to them.

The prophets and the psalmists foretold that the kings of the earth would pay homage to God at the time of the Messiah (Is 49:23). They would offer him their treasures (Is 60:5) and adore him (Ps 72:10–15). Through this action of the wise men and the offering of their gifts to Jesus, these prophecies begin to be fulfilled.

The Council of Trent expressly quotes this passage when it underlines the veneration that ought to be given to Christ in the Eucharist: "The faithful of Christ venerate this most holy sacrament with

joy; [11]and going into the house they saw the child with Mary his
mother, and they fell down and worshipped him. Then, opening
their treasures, they offered him gifts, gold and frankincense and
myrrh. [12]And being warned in a dream not to return to Herod, they
departed to their own country by another way.

Ps 72:10–15
Is 60:6

The flight into Egypt. The massacre of the Innocents

[13]Now when they had departed, behold, an angel of the Lord
appeared to Joseph in a dream and said, "Rise, take the child and
his mother, and flee to Egypt, and remain there till I tell you; for
Herod is about to search for the child, to destroy him." [14]And he
rose and took the child and his mother by night, and departed to

Ex 2:15

---

the worship of latria which is due to the true God. [...] For in this sacrament we believe that the same God is present whom the eternal Father brought into the world, saying of him, 'Let all God's angels worship him' (Heb 1:6; cf. Ps 97:7). It is the same God whom the Magi fell down and worshipped (cf. Mt 2:11) and, finally, the same God whom the apostles adored and worshipped (cf. Mt 28:17)" (*De SS. Eucharistia*, chap. 5).

St Gregory Nazianzen has also commented on this verse, as follows: "Let us remain in adoration; and to him, who, in order to save us, humbled himself to such a degree of poverty as to take our flesh, let us offer him not only incense, gold and myrrh (the first as God, the second as king, and the third as one who sought death for our sake), but also spiritual gifts, more sublime than those which can be seen with the eyes" (*Oratio*, 19).

2:12. The involvement of the wise men in the events at Bethlehem ends with yet another act of respectful obedience and cooperation with God's plans. Christians also should be receptive to the specific grace and mission God has given them. They should persevere in this even if it means having to change any personal plans they may have made.

2:14. St John Chrysostom, commenting on this passage, draws particular attention to Joseph's faithfulness and obedience: "On hearing this, Joseph was not scandalized, nor did he say, 'This is hard to understand. You yourself told me not long ago that he would save his people, and now he is not able to save even himself. Indeed, we have to flee and undertake a journey and be away for a long time...'. But he does not say any of these things, because Joseph is a faithful man. Neither does he ask when they will be coming back, even though the angel had left it open when he said 'and remain there till I tell you'. This does not hold him back: on the contrary, he obeys, believes and endures all the trials with joy" (*Hom. on St Matthew*, 8).

It is worth noting also how God's way of dealing with his chosen ones contains light and shade: they have to put up with intense sufferings side by side with great joy: "It can be clearly seen that God, who is full of love for man, mixes pleasant things with unpleasant ones, as he did with all the saints. He gives us neither dangers nor consolations in a continual way, but rather he makes the lives of the just a mixture of both. This is what he did with Joseph" (ibid.).

Hos 11:1 Egypt, ¹⁵and remained there until the death of Herod. This was to fulfil what the Lord had spoken by the prophet, "Out of Egypt have I called my son."

¹⁶Then Herod, when he saw that he had been tricked by the wise men, was in a furious rage, and he sent and killed all the male children in Bethlehem and in all that region who were two years old or under, according to the time which he had ascertained

Jer 31:15 from the wise men. ¹⁷Then was fulfilled what was spoken by the prophet Jeremiah:

Gen 35:19 ¹⁸"A voice was heard in Ramah,
wailing and loud lamentation,
Rachel weeping for her children;
she refused to be consoled,
because they were no more."

Return to Nazareth
¹⁹But when Herod died, behold, an angel of the Lord appeared in
Ex 4:19 a dream to Joseph in Egypt, saying, ²⁰"Rise, take the child and his

---

2:15. The text of Hosea 11:1 speaks of a child who comes out of Egypt and is a son of God. This refers in the first place to the people of Israel whom God brought out of Egypt under Moses' leadership. But this event was a symbol or prefiguration of Jesus, the head of the Church, the new people of God. It is in him that this prophecy is principally fulfilled. The sacred text gives a quotation from the Old Testament in the light of its fulfilment in Jesus Christ. The Old Testament achieves its full meaning in Christ, and, in the words of St Paul, to read it without keeping in mind Jesus is to have one's face covered by a veil (cf. 2 Cor 3:12–18).

2:16–17. Concerning Herod, see the note on Matthew 2:1. God permitted Herod to be wicked and cruel in trying to kill the Child. His cruel behaviour also fulfils the prophecy of Jeremiah 31:15. The Church regards these children as the first martyrs to give their lives for Christ. Martyrdom brought them justification (that is, salvation) and gave them the same grace as

Baptism gives; their martyrdom is, in fact, Baptism by blood. St Thomas Aquinas comments on this passage in the following way: "How can it be said that they died for Christ, since they could not use their freedom? [...] God would not have allowed that massacre if it had not been of benefit to those children. St Augustine says that to doubt that the massacre was good for those children is the same as doubting that Baptism is of use to children. For the Holy Innocents suffered as martyrs and confessed Christ *non loquendo, sed moriendo*, not by speaking, but by dying" (*Comm. on St Matthew*, 2, 16).

2:18. Ramah was the city in which Nebuchadnezzar, king of Babylon, concentrated the Israelites he had taken prisoner. Since Ramah was in the land of Benjamin, Jeremiah puts this lament for the children of Israel in the mouth of Rachel, the mother of Benjamin and Joseph. So great was the misfortune of those exiled to Babylon that Jeremiah says poetically that Rachel's sorrow is too great to allow

mother, and go to the land of Israel, for those who sought the child's life are dead." ²¹And he rose and took the child and his mother, and went to the land of Israel. ²²But when he heard that Archelaus reigned over Judea in place of his father Herod, he was afraid to go there, and being warned in a dream he withdrew to the district of Galilee. ²³And he went and dwelt in a city called Nazareth, that what was spoken by the prophets might be fulfilled, "He shall be called a Nazarene."

Lk 1:26; 2:39
Is 11:1; 53:2
Jn 1:46

2. PRELUDE TO THE PUBLIC
MINISTRY OF JESUS

John the Baptist preaching in the wilderness

3 ¹In those days came John the Baptist, preaching in the wilderness of Judea, ²"Repent,* for the kingdom of heaven

Mk 1:2–8
Lk 3:3–18;
1:13; 4:17

---

of consolation. "Rachel was buried in the racecourse near Bethlehem. Since her grave was nearby and the property belonged to her son, Benjamin (Ramah was of the tribe of Benjamin), the children beheaded in Bethlehem could reasonably be called Rachel's children" (St John Chrysostom, *Hom. on St Matthew*, 9).

2:22. History tells us that Archelaus was ambitious and cruel like his father. By the time Joseph returned from Egypt, the new king was quite notorious. "In the different circumstances of his life, St Joseph never refuses to think, never neglects his responsibilities. On the contrary, he puts his human experience at the service of faith. When he returns from Egypt, learning 'that Archelaus reigned over Judea in place of his father Herod, he was afraid to go there'. In other words, he had learned to work within the divine plan. And to confirm that he was doing the right thing, Joseph received an instruction to return to Galilee" (St J. Escrivá, *Christ Is Passing By*, 42).

2:23. Nazareth, where the Annunciation had taken place (Lk 1:26), was a tiny and

insignificant Palestinian village. It was located in Galilee, the most northerly part of the country. The term "Nazarene" refers to Jesus' geographic origin, but his critics used it as a term of abuse when he began his mission (Jn 1:46). Even in the time of St Paul the Jews tried to humiliate the Christians by calling them Nazarenes (Acts 24:5). Many prophets predicted that the Messiah would suffer poverty and contempt (Is 52:2ff.; Jer 11:19; Ps 22) but the words "he shall be called a Nazarene" are not to be found as such in any prophetic text. They are, rather, as St Jerome points out, a summary of the prophets' teaching in a short and expressive phrase. However, St Jerome himself (cf. *Comm. in Isaiah*, 11:1) says that the name "Nazarene" fulfils the prophecy of Isaiah 11:1: Christ is the "shoot" (*nezer*, in Hebrew) of the entire race of Abraham and David.

3:1. The expression "in those days" does not specify the exact time of the event in question. It is sometimes used merely as an opening phrase to mark the beginning

Is 40:3
Jn 1:23

is at hand." ³For this is he who was spoken of by the prophet Isaiah when he said,

"The voice of one crying in the wilderness:
Prepare the way of the Lord,
make his paths straight."

---

of a new episode. In this case, in fact, it can be calculated that some twenty-five years have elapsed since the Holy Family's return from Egypt. This is only an estimate, because the exact date of their return has not been established.

On the date of the start of John the Baptist's preaching, see Luke 3:1–3.

The word "wilderness" has a wider meaning here than we give it today. It does not refer to a sandy or rocky desert, but rather to arid regions, low in vegetation.

3:2. "Repent": Christ's redeeming work ushers in a new era in the Kingdom of God. This brings such advance in salvation history, that what is required from now on is a radical change in man's behaviour towards God. The coming of the Kingdom means that God has intervened in a special way to save mankind, but it also implies that we must be open to God's grace and reform our ways. Christ's life on earth compels people to take a stand—either for God or against him ("He who is not with me is against me, and he who does not gather with me scatters": Lk 11:23). Given man's sinful state after original sin, the newly-arrived Kingdom requires that all men repent of their past life. To put it another way, they have to stop going away from God and instead try to get closer to him. Since sin hinders this conversion, it is impossible to turn back to God without performing acts of penance. Conversion is not simply a question of making a good resolution to mend our ways; we have to fulfil that resolution, even if we find it difficult. Penance grows only where there is hum-

ility—and everyone should admit sincerely that he is a sinner (cf. 1 Jn 1:8–10). Obedience also goes hand in hand with penance; everyone ought to obey God and keep his commandments (cf. 1 Jn 2:3–6).

The literal translation of the Greek is "Repent". But precisely because the very essence of conversion consists in doing penance, as we have said, the New Vulgate has *paenitentaim agite* ("do penance"). This translation conveys the deeper meaning of the text.

Man's whole life, in fact, consists in constantly correcting his behaviour, and therefore implies a continual doing of penance. This turning back to God was preached continually by the prophets in the Old Testament. Now, however, with the coming of Christ, this penance and turning to God are absolutely essential. That Christ took on our sins and suffered for us does not excuse us from making a true conversion; on the contrary, it demands it of us (cf. Col 1:24).

"Kingdom of heaven": this expression is identical to "Kingdom of God". The former is the one most used by St Matthew, and is more in line with the Jewish turn of phrase. Out of reverence, the Jews avoided pronouncing the name of God and substituted other words for it, as in this case. "Kingdom of God" or "Kingdom of heaven" was a concept used already in the Old Testament and in religious circles at the time of Christ. But it occurs particularly frequently in Jesus' preaching.

The phrase "Kingdom of God" can refer in a general way to God's dominion

⁴Now John wore a garment of camel's hair, and a leather girdle   2 Kings 1:18
around his waist; and his food was locusts and wild honey. ⁵Then
went out to him Jerusalem and all Judea and all the region about
the Jordan, ⁶and they were baptized by him in the river Jordan,
confessing their sins.*

over creatures; but normally, as in this text, it refers to God's sovereign and merciful involvement in the life of his people. Man's rebellion and sin broke the order originally established in creation. To re-establish it, God's intervention was needed again; this consisted in the redeeming work of Christ, Messiah and Son of God. It was preceded by a series of preliminary stages in salvation history throughout the Old Testament. Consequently, the Kingdom of God, announced as imminent by John the Baptist, is brought into being by Jesus. However, this is an entirely spiritual one and does not have the nationalistic dimension expected by Jesus' contemporaries. He comes to save his people and all mankind from the slavery of sin, from death and from the devil, thereby opening up the way of salvation.

In the period between the first and second comings of Christ, this Kingdom of God (or Kingdom of heaven) is, in fact, the Church. The Church makes Christ (and therefore also God) present among all peoples and calls them to eternal salvation. The Kingdom of God will be brought to completion only at the end of this world, that is, when our Lord comes to judge the living and the dead at the end of time. Then God will reign over the blessed in a perfect way.

In the passage we are considering, John the Baptist, the last of the Old Testament prophets, preaches the imminence of the Kingdom of God, ushered in by the coming of the Messiah.

3:3. By quoting Isaiah 40:3, St Matthew makes it clear that St John the Baptist has

a mission as a prophet. This mission has to purposes—first, to prepare the people to receive the Kingdom of God; second, to testify before the people that Jesus is the Messiah who is bringing that Kingdom.

3:4. The Gospel gives a brief outline of the extremely austere life of St John the Baptist. His style of life is in line with that of certain Old Testament prophets and is particularly reminiscent of Elijah (cf. 2 Kings 1:8; 2:8–13ff). The kinds of food and dress described are of the most rudimentary for the region in question. The locust was a kind of grasshopper; the wild honey probably refers to substances excreted by certain local shrubs rather than to bees' honey. In view of the imminent coming of the Messiah, John underlines, with his example, the attitude of penance preceding great religious festivals (similarly, in its Advent liturgy the Church puts John before us as a model and invites us to practise mortification and penance). In this way, the point made in the previous verse (concerning John's view of his mission as precursor of Christ) is fulfilled. A Christian's entire life is a preparation for his meeting with Christ. Consequently, mortification and penance play a significant part in his life.

3:6. John's baptism did not have the power to cleanse the soul from sin as Christian baptism does. The latter is a sacrament, a sign, which produces the grace it signifies. Concerning the value of John's baptism, see the note on Mt 3:11.

37

Gen 3:15

⁷But when he saw many of the Pharisees and Sadducees coming for baptism, he said to them, "You brood of vipers! Who warned you to flee from the wrath to come? ⁸Bear fruit that befits repentance, ⁹and do not presume to say to yourselves, 'We have Abraham as our father'; for I tell you, God is able from these stones to raise up children to Abraham. ¹⁰Even now the axe is laid to the root of the trees; every tree therefore that does not bear good fruit is cut down and thrown into the fire.

Rom 2:28f;
4:12
Jn 8:33, 39

Lk 13:7–9
Jn 15:6

Jn 1:15, 26f, 33

¹¹"I baptize you with water for repentance, but he who is coming after me is mightier than I, whose sandals I am not worthy

Acts 1:5

3:7. St John reproaches the Pharisees and Sadducees for their attitude towards him. His preaching and baptism are not simply one more purification rite Rather, they demand a true interior conversion of the soul, as a necessary predisposition to reach the grace of faith in Jesus. In the light of this explanation, we can understand why the prophetic words of St John the Baptist were so hard-hitting; as it turned out, most of these people did not accept Jesus as the Messiah.

"Pharisees": these constituted the most important religious group in Jesus' time. They kept the Law of Moses rigorously and also the oral traditions which had built up around it. They gave as much importance to these latter, indeed, as to the Law itself. They strongly opposed the influence of Greek paganism and totally rejected the homage paid to the Roman emperor. Among them there were men of great spiritual eminence and sincere piety; but there were many others who exaggerated pharisaical religiosity to the extreme of fanaticism, pride and hypocrisy. It was this perversion of the true Israelite religion that John the Baptist (and later our Lord) castigated.

"Sadducees": the Sadducees constituted a smaller religious group than the Pharisees, but they included many influential people, most of them from the main priestly families. They accepted the written Law, but, unlike the Pharisees, they rejected oral tradition. They also rejected certain important truths, such as the resurrection of the dead.

On the political front, they went along easily with the terms dictated by the Romans, and they acquiesced in the introduction of pagan customs into the country. Their opposition to Christ was even more pronounced than that of the Pharisees.

3:9–10. St John the Baptist's listeners believe their salvation is assured because they are descendants of Abraham according to the flesh. But St John warns them that to pass God's judgment it is not enough to belong to the chosen people; they must also yield the good fruit of a holy life. If they fail to do this, they will be thrown into the fire, that is, into hell, the eternal punishment, because they did not do penance for their sins. See the note on Mt 25:46.

3:11. St John the Baptist did not limit himself to preaching penance and repentance; he encouraged people to receive his baptism. This baptism was a way of interiorly preparing them and helping them to realize that the coming of Christ was imminent. By his words of encouragement and by their humble recognition of their sins, they were prepared to

to carry; he will baptize you with the Holy Spirit and with fire. ¹²His winnowing fork is in his hand, and he will clear his threshing floor and gather his wheat into the granary, but the chaff he will burn with unquenchable fire."

Jesus is baptized

¹³Then Jesus came from Galilee to the Jordan to John, to be baptized by him. ¹⁴John would have prevented him, saying, "I need to

Mk 1:9–11
Lk 3:21f
Jn 1:31–34

---

receive Christ's grace through Baptism with fire and the Holy Spirit. To put it another way, John's baptism did not produce justification, whereas Christian Baptism is the sacrament of initiation, which forgives sin and bestows sanctifying grace. The effectiveness of the sacrament of Christian Baptism is expressed in Catholic teaching when it says that the sacrament gives grace *ex opere operato*. This means that grace is given by virtue of Christ who acts through the sacrament, and not by virtue of the merits of either the minister or the recipient of the sacrament. "When Peter baptizes, it is Christ who baptizes [...]. When Judas baptizes, it is Christ who baptizes" (St Augustine, *In Ioann. Evang.*, 6).

The word "fire" points in a metaphorical way to the effectiveness of the Holy Spirit's action in totally wiping out sins. It also shows the life-giving power of grace in the person baptized. Foremost among the personal qualities of St John the Baptist is his remarkable humility; he resolutely rejects the temptation of accepting the dignity of Messiah which the crowds apparently wanted to bestow on him. Carrying the sandals of one's master was a job for the lowest of servants.

3:12. Verses 10 and 12 refer to judgment by the Messiah. This judgment has two parts: the first occurs throughout each man's life and ends in the Particular Judgment immediately after death; the

second occurs at the time of the Last Judgment. Christ is the judge in both instances. Let us remember the words of St Peter in Acts 10:42: "And he commanded us to preach to the people, and to testify that he [Jesus] is the one ordained by God to be judge of the living and the dead." The judgment will give to each person the reward or punishment merited by his good or bad actions.

It is worth noting that the word "chaff" does not refer only to bad deeds; it refers also to useless ones, for example, lives lacking in service to God and men. God will judge us, therefore, for our omissions and our lost opportunities.

"Don't let your life be barren. Be useful. Make yourself felt. Shine forth with the torch of your faith and your love. With your apostolic life, wipe out the trail of filth and slime left by the unclean sowers of hatred. And set aflame all the ways of the earth with the fire of Christ that you bear in your heart" (St Josemaría Escrivá, *The Way*, 1).

3:13. Jesus spent about thirty years (Lk 3:23) in what is normally called his "hidden life". We should marvel at the silence of the Incarnate Word of God during this period. There may be many reasons why he waited so long before beginning his public ministry, but one factor may have been the Jewish custom whereby rabbis did not carry out their function as teachers until they were thirty

be baptized by you, and do you come to me?" [15]But Jesus answered him, "Let it be so now; for thus it is fitting for us to fulfil all righteousness." Then he consented.* [16]And when Jesus was baptized, he went up immediately from the water, and behold, the heavens were opened[g] and he saw the Spirit of God descending like a dove, and alighting on him; [17]and lo, a voice from

1 Pet 4:14
Ezek 1:1

Mt 17:5
Ps 2:7

---

years old. Whatever the reason, by his long years of work beside St Joseph, our Lord teaches all Christians the sanctifying value of ordinary life and work.

The Baptist prepares the people to receive the Messiah, according to God's plan; and it is only then that Jesus commences his public life.

3:14. St. John's reluctance to baptize Jesus is not surprising since he had given such forthright witness to Him. Jesus did not need to be baptized by John since he had no sin, but he chose to receive this baptism (see the note on v. 15) before beginning to preach, so to teach us to obey all God's commands (he had already subjected himself to circumcision, presentation to the temple and being redeemed as the first-born). God wished to humble himself even to the extent of submitting to the authority of others.

3:15. "Righteousness" (or "justice") has a very deep meaning in the Bible; it refers to the plan which God, in his infinite goodness and wisdom, has marked out for man's salvation. Consequently, "to fulfil all righteousness" should be understood as fulfilling God's will and designs. Thus we could translate "fulfil all righteousness" as; "fulfil everything laid down by God". Jesus comes to receive John's baptism and hence recognizes it as a stage in salvation history—a stage foreseen by God as a final and immediate preparation for the messianic

era. The fulfilment of any one of these stages can be called an act of righteousness. Jesus, who has come to fulfil his Father's will (Jn 4:34), is careful to fulfil that saving plan in all its aspects. See the note on Mt 5:6.

3:16. Jesus possessed the fullness of the Holy Spirit from the moment of his conception. This is due to the union of human nature and divine nature in the person of the Word (the dogma of the hypostatic union). Catholic teaching says that in Christ there is only one person (who is divine) but two natures (divine and human). The descent of the Spirit of God spoken of in the text indicates that just as Jesus was solemnly commencing his messianic task, so the Holy Spirit was beginning his action through him. There are many texts in the Old Testament which speak of the showing forth of the Holy Spirit in the future Messiah. This sign of the Spirit gave St John the Baptist unmistakable proof of the genuineness of his testimony concerning Christ (cf. Jn 1:29–34). The mystery of the Holy Trinity is revealed in the baptism of Jesus: the Son is baptized; the Holy Spirit descends on him in the form of a dove; and the voice of the Father gives testimony about his Son. Christians must be baptized in the name of the three divine persons. "If you have sincere piety, the Holy Spirit will descend on you also and you will hear the voice of the Father saying to you from above: 'This was not

---

g. Other ancient authorities add *to him*   h. Or *my Son, my* (or *the*) *Beloved*

heaven, saying, "This is my beloved son,[h] with whom I am well pleased." Is 42:1

Jesus fasts and is tempted Mk 1:12f
Lk 4:1–13

4 ¹Then Jesus was led up by the Spirit into the wilderness to be tempted by the devil. ²And he fasted forty days and forty Heb 4:15
Ex 34:28
1 Kings 19:8

---

my son, but now after Baptism he has been made my son'" (St Cyril of Jerusalem, *De Baptismo*, 14).

3:17. Literally, as the RSV points out, "This is my Son, my (*or* the) Beloved". When the expression "the beloved" goes with "the son", normally it refers to an only son (cf. Gen 16; Jer 6:26; Amos 8:10; Zech 12:10). Repetition of the article and the solemnity of the passage show that, in the language of the Bible, Jesus is not just one more among the adopted sons of God, nor even the greatest of them. Rather, it declares strongly and correctly that Jesus is "the Son of God", the Only-begotten, who is totally different from other men because of his divine nature (cf. Mt 7:21; 11:27; 17:5; Jn 3:35; 5:20; 20:17; etc.).

Here we can see the fulfilment of the messianic prophecies, especially Isaiah 42:1, which is applied now to Jesus through the voice of the Father speaking from heaven.

4:1. Jesus, our Saviour, allowed himself to be tempted because he so chose; and he did so out of love for us and to instruct us. However, since he was perfect, he could only be tempted externally. Catholic teaching tells us that there are three levels of temptation: 1) suggestion, that is, external temptation, which we can undergo without committing any sin; 2) temptation, in which we take a certain delight, whether prolonged or not, even though we do not give clear consent; this level of temptation has now become

internal and there is some sinfulness in it; 3) temptation to which we consent; this is always sinful, and, since it affects the deepest part of the soul, is definitely internal. By allowing himself to be tempted, Jesus wanted to teach us how to fight and conquer our temptations. We will do this by having trust in God and prayer, with the help of God's grace and by having fortitude.

Jesus' temptations in the desert have a deep significance in salvation history. All the most important people throughout sacred history were tempted—Adam and Eve, Abraham, Moses, and the chosen people themselves. Similarly with Jesus. By rejecting the temptations of the devil, our Lord atones for the falls of those who went before him and those who come after him. He is an example for us in all the temptations we were subsequently to have, and also for the battles between the Church and the power of the devil. Later Jesus teaches us in the Our Father to ask God to help us with his grace not to fall at the time of temptation.

4:2. Before beginning his work as Messiah, that is, before promulgating the New Law or New Testament, Jesus prepares himself by prayer and fasting in the desert. Moses acted in the same way before proclaiming, in God's name, the Old Law on Mount Sinai (Ex 34:28), Elijah, too, journeyed for forty days in the desert to fulfil the Law (1 Kings 19:5–8).

The Church follows Jesus' footsteps by prescribing the yearly Lenten fast. We

41

Gen 3:1–7

nights, and afterward he was hungry. ³And the tempter came and said to him, "If you are the Son of God, command these stones to

Deut 8:3
Wis 16:26

become loaves of bread." ⁴But he answered, "It is written,

> 'Man shall not live by bread alone,
>> but by every word that proceeds from the mouth of God.'"

⁵Then the devil took him to the holy city, and set him on the pin-

Ps 91:11f

nacle of the temple, ⁶and said to him, "If you are the Son of God, throw yourself down; for it is written,

---

should practise Lent each year with this spirit of piety. "It can be said that Christ introduced the tradition of forty days fast into the Church's liturgical year, because he himself 'fasted forty days and forty night' before beginning to teach. By this Lenten fast the Church is in a certain sense called every year to follow her Master and Lord if she wishes to preach his Gospel effectively" (John Paul II, General Audience, 28 February 1979). In the same way, Jesus' withdrawal into the desert invites us to prepare ourselves by prayer and penance before any important decision or action.

4:3. Jesus has fasted for forty days and forty nights. Naturally he is very hungry and the devil makes use of this opportunity to tempt him. Our Lord rejects the temptation and in doing so he uses a phrase from Deuteronomy (8:3). Although he could do this miracle, he prefers to continue to trust his Father since performing the miracle is not part of his plan of salvation. In return for this trust, angels come and minister to him (Mt 4:11).

Miracles in the Bible are extraordinary and wonderful deeds done by God to make his words or actions understood. They do not occur as isolated outpourings of God's power but rather as part of the work of Redemption. What the devil proposes in this temptation would be for Jesus' benefit only and therefore could not form part of the plan for Redemption. This suggests that the devil, in tempting

him in this way, wanted to check if Jesus is the "Son of God". For, although he seems to know about the voice from heaven at Jesus' baptism, he cannot see how the Son of God could be hungry. By the way he deals with the temptation, Jesus teaches us that when we ask God for things we should not ask in the first place for what we can obtain by our own efforts. Neither should we ask for what is exclusively for our own convenience, but rather for what will help towards our holiness or that of others.

4:4. Jesus' reply is an act of trust in God's fatherly providence. God led him into the desert to prepare him for his messianic work, and now he will see to it that Jesus does not die. This point is underlined by the fact that Jesus' reply evokes Deuteronomy 8:3, where the sons of Israel are reminded how Yahweh fed them miraculously with manna in the desert. Therefore, in contrast to the Israelites who were impatient when faced with hunger in the desert, Jesus trustingly leaves his well-being to the Father's providence. The words of Deuteronomy 8:3, repeated here by Jesus, associate "bread" and "word" as having both come from the mouth of God: God speaks and gives his Law; God speaks and makes manna appear as food.

Also, manna is commonly used in the New Testament (see, for example, Jn 6:32–58) and throughout Tradition as a symbol of the Eucharist.

'He will give his angels charge of you,'

and

'On their hands they will bear you up,
lest you strike your foot against a stone.'"

⁷Jesus said to him, "Again it is written, 'You shall not tempt the Lord your God.'" ⁸Again, the devil took him to a very high mountain, and showed him all the kingdoms of the world and the glory

Deut 6:16

Deut 34:1
Rev 21:10

The Second Vatican Council points out another interesting aspect of Jesus' word when it proposes guidelines for international cooperation in economic matters: "In many instances there exists a pressing need to reassess economic and social structures, but caution must be exercised with regard to proposed solutions which may be untimely, especially those which offer material advantage while militating against man's spiritual nature and advancement. For 'man shall not live by bread alone, but by every word that proceeds from the mouth of God'" (*Gaudium et spes*, 86).

4:5. Tradition suggests that this temptation occurred at the extreme southeast corner of the temple wall. At this point, the wall was at its highest, since the ground beneath sloped away steeply to the Cedron river. Looking down from this point one could easily get a feeling of vertigo. St Gregory the Great (*In Evangelia homiliae*, 16) says that if we consider how our Lord allowed himself to be treated during his passion, it is not surprising that he allowed the devil also to treat him as he did.

4:6. "Holy Scripture is good, but heresies arise through its not being understood properly" (St Augustine, *In Ioann. Evang.*, 18, 1). Catholics should be on their guard against arguments which, though they claim to be founded on scripture, are nevertheless untrue. As we can see in this passage of the Gospel, the devil can also

set himself up at times as an interpreter of Scripture, quoting it to suit himself. Therefore, any interpretation which is not in line with the teaching contained in the Tradition of the Church should be rejected. The error proposed by a heresy normally consists in stressing certain passages to the exclusion of others, interpreting them at will, losing sight of the unity that exists in Scripture and the fact that the faith is all of a piece.

4:7. Jesus rejects the second temptation as he did the first; to do otherwise would have been to tempt God. In rejecting it, he uses a phrase from Deuteronomy (6:16): "You shall not put the Lord your God to the test". In this way he alludes also to the passage in Exodus where the Israelites demand a miracle of Moses. The latter replies, "Why do you put the Lord to the proof?" (Ex 17:2).

To tempt God is the complete opposite of having trust in him. It means presumptuously putting ourselves in the way of an unnecessary danger, expecting God to help us by an exceptional use of his power. We would also tempt him if, by our unbelief and arrogance, we were to ask him for signs of proof. The very first lesson from this passage of the Gospel is that if ever a person were to ask or demand extraordinary proofs or signs from God, he would clearly be tempting him.

4:8–10. The third temptation is the most pseudo-messianic of the three: Jesus is

43

Deut 6:13

of them; ⁹and he said to him, "All these I will give you, if you will fall down and worship me." ¹⁰Then Jesus said to him, "Begone, Satan! for it is written,

'You shall worship the Lord your God
and him only shall you serve.'"

Jn 1:51
Heb 1:6, 14

¹¹Then the devil left him, and behold, the angels came and ministered to him.

PART ONE

Jesus' ministry in Galilee

Mk 1:14f
Lk 4:14f
Jn 2:12; 4:43

Jesus begins to preach

¹²Now when he heard that John had been arrested, he withdrew into Galilee; ¹³and leaving Nazareth he went and dwelt in

---

urged to appropriate to himself the role of an earthly messianic king of the type so widely expected at the time. Our Lord's vigorous reply, "Begone, Satan!" is an uncompromising rejection of an earthly messianism—an attempt to reduce his transcendent, God-given mission to a purely human and political use. By his attitude, Jesus, as it were, rectifies and makes amends for the worldly views of the people of Israel. And, for the same reason, it is a warning to the Church, God's true Israel, to remain faithful to its God-given mission of salvation in the world. The Church's pastors should be on the alert and not allow themselves to be deceived by this temptation of the devil.

"We should learn from Jesus' attitude in these trials. During his life on earth he did not even want the glory that belonged to him. Though he had the right to be treated as God, he took the form of a servant, a slave (cf. Phil 2:6–7). And so the Christian knows that all glory is due to

God and that he must not make use of the sublimity and greatness of the Gospel to further his own interests or human ambitions.

"We should learn from Jesus. His attitude in rejecting all human glory is in perfect balance with the greatness of his unique mission as the beloved Son of God who takes flesh to save men […]. And the Christian, who, following Christ, has this attitude of complete adoration of the Father, also experiences our Lord's loving care: 'because he cleaves to me in love. I will deliver him; I will protect him, because he knows my name' (Ps 90:14)" (St Josemaría Escrivá, *Christ Is Passing By*, 62).

4:11. If we struggle constantly, we will attain victory. And nobody is crowned without having first conquered: "Be faithful unto death, and I will give you the crown of life" (Rev 2:10). By coming to minister to Jesus after he rejects the

Capernaum by the sea, in the territory of Zebulun and Naphtali,
[14]that what was spoken by the prophet Isaiah might be fulfilled:

> [15]"The land of Zebulun and the land of Naphtali,
>> toward the sea, across the Jordan, Galilee of the Gentiles
> —[16]the people who sat in darkness have seen a great light
> and for those who sat in the region and shadow of death
>> light has dawned."

[17]From that time Jesus began to preach, saying, "Repent, for the kingdom of heaven is at hand."

Is 8:23; 9:1
Jn 7:52

Lk 1:78f
Jn 1:9

---

temptations, the angels teach us the interior joy given by God to the person who fights energetically against the temptation of the devil. God has given us also powerful defenders against such temptations—our guardian angels, on whose aid we should call.

4:15–16. Here St Matthew quotes the prophecy of Isaiah 8:23–9:1. The territory referred to (Zebulun, Naphtali, the way of the sea, the land beyond the Jordan), was invaded by the Assyrians in the period 734–721 BC, especially during the reign of Tilgathpilneser III. A portion of the Jewish population was deported and sizeable numbers of foreigners were planted in the region to colonize it. For this reason it is referred to in the Bible henceforward as the "Galilee of the Gentiles".

The evangelist, inspired by God, sees Jesus' coming to Galilee as the fulfilment of Isaiah's prophecy. This land, devastated and abused in Isaiah's time, will be the first to receive the light of Christ's life and preaching. The messianic meaning of the prophecy is, therefore, clear.

4:17. See the note on Mt 3:2. This verse indicates the outstanding importance of the first step in Jesus' public ministry, begun by proclaiming the imminence of the Kingdom of God. Jesus' words echo John the Baptist's proclamation: the second part of this verse is the same, word for word, as Matthew 3:2. This underlines the role played by St John the Baptist as prophet and precursor of Jesus. Both St John and our Lord demand repentance, penance, as a prerequisite to receiving the Kingdom of God, now beginning. God's rule over mankind is a main theme in Christ's Revelation, just as it was central to the whole Old Testament. However, in the latter, the Kingdom of God had an element of theocracy about it: God reigned over Israel in both spiritual and temporal affairs and it was through him that Israel subjected other nations to her rule. Little by little, Jesus will unfold the new-style Kingdom of God, now arrived at its fullness. He will show it to be a Kingdom of love and holiness, thereby purifying it of the nationalistic misconceptions of the people of this time.

The King invites everyone without exception to this Kingdom (cf. Mt 22:1–14). The banquet of the Kingdom is held on this earth and has certain entry requirements which must be preached by the proponents of the Kingdom: "Therefore the eucharist celebration is the centre of the assembly of the faithful over which the priest presides. Hence priests teach the faithful to offer the divine Victim to God the Father in the sacrifice of the Mass, and with the Victim to make an offering of their whole lives. In the

The first disciples are called

Mk 1:16–20
Lk 5:1–11
Jn 1:40f

Ezek 47:10

Mt 19:27

[18]As he walked by the Sea of Galilee, he saw two brothers, Simon who is called Peter and Andrew his brother, casting a net into the sea; for they were fishermen. [19]And he said to them, "Follow me, and I will make you fishers of men." [20]Immediately they left their nets and followed him. [21]And going on from there he saw two other brothers, James the son of Zebedee and John his brother, in the boat with Zebedee their father, mending their nets, and he called to them. [22]Immediately they left the boat and their father, and followed him.

Mk 1:39
Lk 4:15, 44
Acts 10:38

[23]And he went about all Galilee, teaching in their synagogues and preaching the gospel of the kingdom and healing every disease and every infirmity among the people. [24]So his fame spread

---

spirit of Christ the pastor, they instruct them to submit their sins to the Church with a contrite heart in the sacrament of Penance, so that they may be daily more and more converted to the Lord, remembering his words: 'Repent, for the Kingdom of heaven is at hand'" (Vatican II, *Presbyterorum ordinis*, 5).

4:18–22. These four disciples had already met our Lord (Jn 1:35–42), and their brief meeting with him seems to have had a powerful effect on their souls. In this way Christ prepared their vocation, a fully effective vocation which moved them to leave everything behind so as to follow him and be their disciples. Standing out above their human defects (which the Gospels never conceal), we can see the exemplary generosity and promptness of the apostles in answering God's call.

The thoughtful reader cannot fail to be struck by the delightful simplicity with which the evangelists describe the calling of these men in the midst of their daily work. "God draws us from the shadows of our ignorance, our groping through history, and, no matter what our occupation in the world, he calls us in a loud voice, as he once called Peter and

Andrew" (St Josemaría Escrivá, *Christ Is Passing By*, 45).

"This divine and human dialogue completely changed the lives of John and Andrew, and Peter and James and so many others. It prepared their hearts to listen to the authoritative teaching which Jesus gave them beside the Sea of Galilee" (ibid., 108).

We should notice the words Sacred Scripture uses to describe the alacrity with which these apostles follow our Lord. Peter and Andrew "immediately" left their nets and followed him. Similarly, James and John "immediately" left their boats and their father and followed him. God passes by and calls us. If we do not answer him "immediately", he may continue on his way and we could lose sight of him. When God passes us by, he may do so rapidly; it would be sad if we were to fall behind because we wanted to follow him while still carrying many things that are only a dead weight and a nuisance.

Concerning Christ's call to men in the midst of their ordinary work, see the note on Mt 2:2.

4:23. "Synagogue": this word comes from the Greek and designates the build-

throughout all Syria and they brought him all the sick, those afflicted with various diseases and pains, demoniacs, epileptics, and paralytics, and he healed them. ²⁵And great crowds followed him from Galilee and the Decapolis and Jerusalem and Judea and from beyond the Jordan.

Mk 6:55

Mk 3:7f
Lk 6:17–19

3. THE SERMON ON THE MOUNT

The Beatitudes

5 ¹Seeing the crowds, he went up on the mountain, and when he sat down his disciples came to him. ²And he opened his mouth and taught them, saying:

Lk 6:20–49

---

ing where the Jews assembled for religious ceremonies on the sabbath and other feast days. Such ceremonies were non-sacrificial in character (sacrifices could be performed only in the temple of Jerusalem). The synagogue was also the place where the Jews received their religious training. The word was also used to designate local Jewish communities within and without Palestine.

4:24. "Epileptic" (or, in some translations, "lunatic"): this word was applied in a very general way to those who had illnesses related to epilepsy. The disease was popularly regarded as being dependent on the phases of the moon (Latin: *luna*).

4:23–25. In these few lines, the evangelist gives us a very fine summary of the various aspects of Jesus' work. The preaching of the gospel or "good news" of the Kingdom, the healing of diseases, and the casting out of devils are all specific signs of the Messiah's presence, according to Old Testament prophecies (Is 35:5–6; 61:1; 40:9; 52:7).

5:1. The discourse, or sermon, on the mount takes up three full chapters of St Matthew's Gospel—chapters 5–7. It is

the first of the five great discourses of Jesus which appear in this Gospel and contains a considerable amount of our Lord's teaching.

It is difficult to reduce this discourse to one single theme, but the various teachings it contains could be said to deal with these five points: 1) the attitude a person must have for entering the Kingdom of heaven (the Beatitudes, the salt of the earth, the light of the world, Jesus and his teaching, the fullness of the Law); 2) uprightness of intention in religious practices (here the Our Father would be included); 3) trust in God's fatherly providence; 4) how God's children should behave towards one another (not judging one's neighbour, respect for holy things, the effectiveness of prayer and the golden rule of charity); 5) the conditions for entering the Kingdom (the narrow gate, false prophets and building on rock).

"He taught them": this refers both to the disciples and to the multitude, as can be seen at the end of the Sermon (Mt 7:28).

5:2. The Beatitudes (5:3–12) form, as it were, the gateway to the Sermon on the Mount. In order to understand the Beatitudes properly, we should bear in mind

Matthew 5:3 *Hebrew* *Happy*

Is 57:15; 61:1
Mt 11:5
Lk 4:18

Ps 126:6
Is 61:2

Ps 37:11

³"Blessed are the poor in spirit, for theirs is the kingdom of heaven.

⁴"Blessed are those who mourn, for they shall be comforted.

⁵"Blessed are the meek, for they shall inherit the earth.

---

that they do not promise salvation only to the particular kinds of people listed here: they cover everyone whose religious dispositions and moral conduct meet the demands which Jesus lays down. In other words, the poor in spirit, the meek, those who mourn, those who hunger and thirst after righteousness, the merciful, the pure in heart, the peacemakers and those who suffer persecution in their search for holiness—these are not different people or kinds of people but different demands made on everyone who wants to be a disciple of Christ.

Similarly, salvation is not being promised to different groups in society but to everyone, no matter what his or her position in life, who strives to follow the spirit and to meet the demands contained in the Beatitudes.

All the Beatitudes have an eschatological meaning, that is, they promise us definitive salvation, not in this world, but in the next. But the spirit of the Beatitudes does give us, in this life, peace in the midst of tribulation. The Beatitudes imply a completely new approach, quite at odds with the usual way man evaluates things: they rule out any kind of pharisaical religiosity, which regards earthly happiness as a blessing from God and a reward for good behaviour, and unhappiness and misfortune as a form of punishment. In all ages the Beatitudes put spiritual good on a much higher plane than material possessions. The healthy and the sick, the powerful and the weak, the rich and the poor—all are called, independently of their circumstances, to the deep happiness that is experienced by those who live up to the Beatitudes which Jesus teaches.

The Beatitudes do not, of course, contain the entire teaching of the Gospel, but they do contain, in embryo, the whole programme of Christian perfection.

5:3. This text outlines the connexion between poverty and the soul. This religious concept of poverty was deeply rooted in the Old Testament (cf., e.g., Zeph 2:3ff). It was more to do with a religious attitude of neediness and of humility towards God than with material poverty: that person is poor who has recourse to God without relying on his own merits and who trusts in God's mercy to be saved. This religious attitude of poverty is closely related to what is called "spiritual childhood". A Christian sees himself as a little child in the presence of God, a child who owns nothing: everything he has comes from God and belongs to God. Certainly, spiritual poverty, that is, Christian poverty, means one must be detached from material things and practise austerity in using them. God asks certain people—religious—to be legally detached from ownership and thereby bear witness to others of the transitoriness of earthly things.

5:4. "Those who mourn": here our Lord is saying that those are blessed who suffer from any kind of affliction—particularly those who are genuinely sorry for their sins, or are pained by the offences which others offer God, and who bear their suffering with love and with a spirit of atonement.

"You are crying? Don't be ashamed of it. Yes, cry: men also cry like you, when they are alone and before God.

48

⁶"Blessed are those who hunger and thirst for righteousness, for they shall be satisfied.

⁷"Blessed are the merciful, for they shall obtain mercy.

⁸"Blessed are the pure in heart, for they shall see God.

Rev 7:16f

Jas 2:13

Ps 24:4; 51:10; 73:1
Jn 3:2f

Each night, says King David, I soak my bed with tears. With those tears, those burning manly tears, you can purify your past and supernaturalize your present life" (St J. Escrivá, *The Way*, 216).

The Spirit of God will console with peace and joy, even in this life, those who weep for their sins, and later he will give them a share in the fullness of happiness and glory in heaven: these are the blessed.

5:5. "The meek": those who patiently suffer unjust persecution; those who remain serene, humble and steadfast in adversity, and do not give way to resentment or discouragement. The virtue of meekness is very necessary in the Christian life. Usually irritableness, which is very common, stems from a lack of humility and interior peace.

"The earth": this is usually understood as meaning our heavenly fatherland.

5:6. The notion of righteousness (or justice) in Holy Scripture is an essentially religious one (cf. notes on Mt 1:19 and 3:15; Rom 1:17; 1:18–32; 3:21–22 and 24). A righteous person is one who sincerely strives to do the will of God, which is discovered in the commandments, in one's duties of state in life and through one's life of prayer. Thus, righteousness, in the language of the Bible, is the same as what nowadays is usually called "holiness" (1 Jn 2:29; 3:7–10; Rev 22:11; Gen 15:6; Deut 9:4).

As St Jerome comments (*Comm. on Matthew*, 5, 6), in the fourth Beatitude our Lord is asking us not simply to have a vague desire for righteousness: we should hunger and thirst for it, that is, we should

love and strive earnestly to seek what makes a man righteous in God's eyes. A person who genuinely wants to attain Christian holiness should love the means that the Church, the universal vehicle of salvation, offers all mean and teaches them to use—frequent use of the sacraments, an intimate relationship with God in prayer, a valiant effort to meet one's social, professional and family responsibilities.

5:7. Mercy is not just a matter of giving alms to the poor but also of being understanding towards other people's defects, overlooking them, helping them cope with them and loving them despite whatever defects they may have. Being merciful also means rejoicing and suffering with other people.

5:8. Christ teaches us that the source of the quality of human acts lies in the heart, that is, in a man's soul, in the depth of his spirit. "When we speak of a person's heart, we refer not just to his sentiments, but to the whole person in his loving dealings with others. In order to help us understand divine things, Scripture uses the expression 'heart' in its full meaning, as the summary and source, expression and ultimate basis, of one's thoughts, words and actions. A man is worth what his heart is worth" (St J. Escrivá, *Christ Is Passing By*, 164).

Cleanness of heart is a gift of God, which expresses itself in a capacity to love, in having an upright and pure attitude to everything noble. As St Paul says, "whatever is true, whatever is honourable, whatever is just, whatever is pure, whatever is lovely, whatever is gracious,

Rev 22:4
Heb 12:14
Sir 4:11

⁹"Blessed are the peacemakers, for they shall be called sons of God.

1 Pet 3:14

¹⁰"Blessed are those who are persecuted for righteousness' sake, for theirs is the kingdom of heaven.

1 Pet 4:14

¹¹"Blessed are you when men revile you and persecute you and utter all kinds of evil against you falsely on my account.

Jas 5:10
Heb 11:33–38

¹²"Rejoice and be glad, for your reward is great in heaven, for so men persecuted the prophets who were before you.

Salt of the earth and light of the world

Mk 9:50
Lk 14:34f

¹³"You are the salt of the earth; but if salt has lost its taste, how shall its saltness be restored? It is no longer good for anything except to be thrown out and trodden under foot by men.

---

if there is any excellence, if there is anything worthy of praise, think about these things" (Phil 4:8). Helped by God's grace, a Christian should strive to cleanse his heart and acquire this purity, the reward for which is the vision of God.

5:9. The translation "peacemakers" well conveys the active meaning of the original text—those who foster peace, in themselves and in others and, as a basis for that, try to be reconciled and to reconcile others with God. Being at peace with God is the cause and the effect of every kind of peace. Any peace on earth not based on this divine peace would be vain and misleading.

"They shall be called sons of God": this is an Hebraicism often found in Sacred Scripture; it is the same as saying "they will be sons of God". St John's first letter (3:1) provides a correct exegesis of this Beatitude: "See what love the Father has given us, that we should be called children of God; and so we are".

5:10. What this Beatitude means, then, is: blessed are those who are persecuted because they are holy, or because they are striving to be holy, for theirs is the Kingdom of heaven.

Thus, blessed is he who suffers persecution for being true to Jesus Christ and who does so not only patiently but joyfully. Circumstances arise in a Christian's life that call for heroism—where no compromise is admissible: either one stays true to Jesus Christ whatever the cost in terms of reputation, life or possessions, or one denies him. St Bernard (*Sermon on the Feast of All Saints*) says that the eighth Beatitude is as it were the prerogative of Christian martyrs. Every Christian who is faithful to Jesus' teaching is in fact a "martyr" (a witness) who reflects or acts in accordance with this Beatitude, even if he does not undergo physical death.

5:11–12. The Beatitudes are the conditions Jesus lays down for entering the Kingdom of heaven. This verse, in a way summing up the preceding ones, is an invitation to everyone to put this teaching into practice. The Christian life, then, is no easy matter, but it is worthwhile, given the reward that Jesus promises.

5:13–16. These verses are calling to that apostolate which is part and parcel of being a Christian. Every Christian has to strive for personal sanctification, but he also has to seek the sanctification of others. Jesus teaches us this, using the very expressive simile of salt and light. Salt preserves food from corruption; it

¹⁴"You are the light of the world. A city set on a hill cannot be hid. ¹⁵Nor do men light a lamp and put it under a bushel, but on a stand, and it gives light to all the house. ¹⁶Let your light so shine before men, that they may see your good works and give glory to your Father who is in heaven.

Jn 8:12
Rev 21:10f

Mk 4:21
Lk 8:16; 11:33

Eph 5:8f
1 Pet 2:12

Jesus and his teaching, the fullness of the Law

¹⁷"Think not that I have come to abolish the law and the prophets; I have come not to abolish them but to fulfil them.* ¹⁸For truly I

Lk 4:21
Rom 3:31; 10:4

---

also brings out its flavour and make it more pleasant; and it disappears into the food; the Christian should do the same among the people around him.

"You are salt, apostolic soul. '*Bonum est sal*: salt is a useful thing', we read in the holy Gospel; '*si autem sal evanuerit*: but if the salt loses its taste', it is good for nothing, neither for the land nor for the manure heap; it is thrown out as useless. You are salt, apostolic soul. But if you lose your taste …" (St Josemaría Escrivá, *The Way*, 921).

Good works are the fruit of charity, which consists in loving others as God loves us (cf. Jn 15:12). "I see now," St Thérèse of Lisieux writes, "that true charity consists in bearing with the faults of those about us, never being surprised at their weaknesses, but edified at the least sign of virtue. I see above all that charity must not remain hidden in the bottom of our hearts: 'nor do men light a lamp and put it under a bushel, but on a stand, and it gives light to all in the house.' It seems to me that this lamp is the symbol of charity; it must shine out not only to cheer up those we love best but all in the house" (*The Autobiography of a Saint*, chap. 9).

Apostolate is one of the clearest expressions of charity. The Second Vatican Council emphasized the Christian's duty to be apostolic. Baptism and Confirmation confer this duty, which is also a right (cf. *Lumen gentium*, 33), so much so that,

because the Christian is part of the Mystical Body, "a member who does not work at the growth of the body to the extent of his possibilities must be considered useless both to the Church and to himself " (*Apostolicam actuositatem*, 2). "Laymen have countless opportunities for exercising the apostolate of evangelization and sanctification. The very witness of a Christian life, and good works done in a supernatural spirit, are effective in drawing men to the faith and to God; and that is what the Lord has said: 'Let your light shine before men, that they may see your good works and give glory to your Father who is in heaven' " (ibid., 6).

"The Church must be present to these groups [those who do not even believe in God] through hose of its members who live among them or have been sent to them. All Christians by the example of their lives and the witness of their word, wherever they live, have an obligation to manifest the new man, which they put on in Baptism, and to reveal the power of the Holy Spirit by whom they were strengthened at Confirmation, so that others, seeing their good works, might glorify the Father and more perfectly perceive the true meaning of human life and the universal solidarity of mankind" (*Ad gentes*, 11; cf. 36).

5:17–19. In this passage Jesus stresses the perennial value of the Old Testament, it is the word of God; because it has a

Lk 16:17; 21:33 say to you, till heaven and earth pass away, not an iota, not a dot, will pass from the law until all is accomplished. ¹⁹Whoever then

Jas 2:10 relaxes one of the least of these commandments and teaches men
1 Cor 15:9 so, shall be called least in the kingdom of heaven; but he who does them and teaches them shall be called great in the kingdom of heaven. ²⁰For I tell you, unless your righteousness exceeds that of the scribes and Pharisees, you will never enter the kingdom of heaven.

Ex 20:13; 21:12 ²¹"You have heard that it was said to the men of old, 'You shall
Lev 24:17 not kill; and whoever kills shall be liable to judgment.' ²²But I say
Deut 17:8
1 Jn 3:15 to you that every one who is angry with his brotherⁱ shall be liable

---

divine authority it deserves total respect. The Old Law enjoined precepts of a moral, legal and liturgical type. Its moral precepts still hold good in the New Testament because they are for the most part specific, divine-positive, promulgations of the natural law. However our Lord gives them greater weight and meaning. But the legal and liturgical precepts of the Old Law were laid down by God for a specific stage in salvation history, that is, up to the coming of Christ; Christians are not obliged to observe them (cf. St Thomas Aquinas, *Summa theologiae*, 1–2, 108, 3 ad 3).

The law promulgated through Moses and explained by the prophets was God's gift to his people, a kind of anticipation of the definitive Law which the Christ or Messiah would lay down. Thus, as the Council of Trent defined, Jesus not only "was given to men as a redeemer in whom they are to trust, but also as law-giver whom they are to obey" (*De iustificatione*, can. 21).

5:20. "Righteousness": see the note on Mt 5:6. This verse clarifies the meaning of the preceding verses. The scribes and Pharisees had distorted the spirit of the Law, putting the whole emphasis on its

external, ritual observance. For them exact and hyper-detailed but external fulfilment of the precepts of the Law was a guarantee of a person's salvation: "if I fulfil this I am righteous, I am holy and God is duty bound to save me". For someone with this approach to sanctification it is really not God who saves: man saves himself through external works of the Law. That this approach is quite mistaken is obvious from what Christ says here; in effect what he is saying is: to enter the Kingdom of God the notion of righteousness or salvation developed by the scribes and Pharisees must be rejected. In other words, justification or sanctification is a grace from God; man's role is one of cooperating with that grace by being faithful to it. Elsewhere Jesus gives the same teaching in an even clearer way (cf. Lk 18:9–14, the parable of the Pharisee and the tax collector).

It was also the origin of one of St Paul's great battles with the "Judaizers" (see Gal 3 and Rom 2–5).

5:21–26. Verses 21–26 give us a concrete example of the way that Jesus Christ brought the Law of Moses to its fulfilment, by explaining the deeper meaning of the commandments of that law.

---

i. Other ancient authorities insert *without cause*

to judgment; whoever insults[j] his brother shall be liable to the council, and whoever says, 'You fool!' shall be liable to the hell[k] of fire. [23]So if you are offering your gift at the altar, and there remember that your brother has something against you, [24]leave your gift there before the altar and go; first be reconciled to your brother, and then come and offer your gift. [25]Make friends quickly with your accuser, while you are going with him to court, lest your accuser hand you over to the judge, and the judge to the guard, and you be put in prison; [26]truly, I say to you, you will never get out till you have paid the last penny.

Mk 11:25

Mt 18:35
Lk 12:58f
1 Pet 5:8

5:22. By speaking in the first person ("but I say to you") Jesus shows that his authority is above that of Moses and the prophets; that is to say, he has divine authority. No mere man could claim such authority.

"Insults": practically all translations of this passage transcribe the original Aramaic words, *raca* (cf. RSV note below). It is not an easy word to translate. It means "foolish, stupid, crazy". The Jews used it to indicate utter contempt; often, instead of verbal abuse they would show their feelings by spitting on the ground.

"Fool" translates an even stronger term of abuse than *raca*—implying that a person has lost all moral and religious sense, to the point of apostasy.

In this passage our Lord points to three faults which we commit against charity, moving from internal irritation to showing total contempt. St Augustine comments that three degrees of faults and punishments are to be noted. The first is the fault of feeling angry; to this corresponds the punishment of "judgment". The second is that of passing an insulting remark, which merits the punishment of "the council". The third arises when anger quite blinds us: this is punished by "the hell of fire" (cf. *De Serm. Dom. in monte*, 2, 9).

"The hell of fire": literally, "*Gehenna* of fire", meaning, in the Jewish language of the time, eternal punishment. This shows the gravity of external sins against charity—gossip, backbiting, calumny etc. However, we should remember that these sins stem from the heart; our Lord focusses our attention, first, on internal sins—resentment, hatred etc.—to make us realize that that is where the root lies and that it is important to nip anger in the bud.

5:23–24. Here our Lord deals with certain Jewish practices of his time, and in doing so gives us perennial moral teaching of the highest order. Christians, of course, do not follow these Jewish ritual practices; to keep our Lord's commandment we have ways and means given us by Christ himself. Specifically, in the New and definitive Covenant founded by Christ, being reconciled involves going to the sacrament of Penance. In this sacrament the faithful "obtain pardon from God's mercy for the offence committed against him, and are, at the same time, reconciled with the Church which they have wounded by their sins" (Vatican II, *Lumen gentium*, 11).

In the New Testament, the greatest of all offerings is the Eucharist. Although

j. Greek *says Raca to* (an obscure term of abuse)   k. Greek *Gehenna*

Ex 20:14
Job 31:1
2 Pet 2:14
Mt 18:8f
Mk 9:43, 47
Col 3:5

²⁷"You have heard that it was said, 'You shall not commit adultery.' ²⁸But I say to you that every one who looks at a woman lustfully has already committed adultery with her in his heart. ²⁹If your right eye causes you to sin, pluck it out and throw it away; it is better that you lose one of your members than that your whole

---

one has a duty to go to Mass on Sundays and holy days of obligation, an essential condition before receiving Holy Communion is that one be in the state of grace.

It is not our Lord's intention here to give love of neighbour priority over love of God. There is an order in charity: "You shall love the Lord your God with all your heart, with all your soul and with all your strength. This is the great and first commandment" (Mt 22:37–38). Love of one's neighbour, which is the second commandment in order of importance (cf. Mt 22:39), derives its meaning from the first. Brotherhood without parenthood is inconceivable. An offence against charity is, above all, an offence against God.

5:27–30. This refers to a sinful glance at any woman, be she married or not. Our Lord fills out the precepts of the Old Law, where only adultery and the coveting of one's neighbour's wife were considered sinful.

"Lustfully": feeling is one thing, consenting another. Consent presupposes that one realizes the evil of these actions (looking, imagining, having impure thoughts) and freely engages in them.

Prohibition of vices always implies a positive aspect—the contrary virtue. Holy purity, like every other virtue, is something eminently positive; it derives from the first commandment and is also directed to it: "You shall love the Lord your God *with all* your heart, *with all* your soul, and *with all* your mind" (Mt 22:37). "Purity is a consequence of the love that prompts us to commit to Christ

our soul and body, our faculties and senses. It is not something negative; it is a joyful affirmation" (St Josemaría Escrivá, *Christ Is Passing By*, 5). This virtue demands that we use all the resources available to us, to the point of heroism if necessary.

"Right eye", "right hand", refers to whatever we value most. Our Lord lays it on the line and is not exaggerating. He obviously does not mean that we should physically mutilate ourselves, but that we should fight hard without making any concessions, being ready to sacrifice anything which clearly could put us in the way of offending God. Jesus' graphic words particularly warn us about one of the most common occasions of sin, reminding us of how careful we need to be guarding our sight. King David, by indulging his curiosity, went on to commit adultery and crime. He later wept over his sins and led a holy life in the presence of God (cf. 2 Sam 11 and 12).

"The eyes! Through them many iniquities enter the soul. So many experiences like David's! If you guard your sight you will have assured the guard of your heart" (St Josemaría Escrivá, *The Way*, 183).

Among the ascetical methods of protecting the virtue of holy purity are: frequent Confession and Communion; devotion to our Lady; a spirit of prayer and mortification; guarding of the senses; flight from occasions of sin; and striving to avoid idleness by always being engaged in doing useful things. There are two further means which are particularly relevant today: "Decorum and modesty are younger brothers of purity" (ibid.,

body be thrown into hell.ᵏ* ³⁰And if your right hand causes you to sin, cut it off and throw it away; it is better that you lose one of your members than that your whole body go into hell.ᵏ

³¹"It was also said, 'Whoever divorces his wife, let him give her a certificate of divorce.' ³²But I say to you that every one who

Mk 10:4–12
Deut 24:1

---

128). Decorum and modesty are a sign of good taste, of respect for others and of human and Christian dignity. To act in accord with this teaching of our Lord, the Christian has to row against the current in a paganized environment and bring his influence for good to bear on it.

"There is need for a crusade of manliness and purity to counteract and undo the savage work of those who think that man is a beast. And that crusade is your work" (ibid., 121).

5:31–32. The Law of Moses (Deut 24:1), which was laid down in ancient times, had tolerated divorce due to the hardness of heart of the early Hebrews. But it had not specified clearly the ground on which divorce might be obtained. The rabbis worked out different sorts of interpretations, depending on which schools they belonged to—solutions ranging from very lax to quite rigid. In all cases, only husbands could repudiate wife, not vice versa. A woman's inferior position was eased somewhat by the device of a written document whereby the husband freed the repudiated woman to marry again if she wished. Against these rabbinical interpretations, Jesus re-establishes the original indissolubility of marriage as God instituted it (Gen 1:27; 2:24; cf. Mt 19:4–6; Eph 1:31; 1 Cor 7:10).

[The RSVCE carries a note which reads: "unchastity": The Greek word used here appears to refer to marriages which were not legally marriages, because they were either within the for-

bidden degrees of consanguinity (Lev 18:6–16) or contracted with a Gentile. The phrase "except on the ground of unchastity" does not occur in the parallel passage in Lk 16:18. See also Mt 19:9 (Mk 10:11–12), and especially 1 Cor 7:10–11, which shows that the prohibition is unconditional.] The phrase "except on the ground of unchastity" should not be taken as indicating an exception to the principle of the absolute indissolubility of marriage that Jesus has just re-established. It is almost certain that the phrase refers to unions accepted as marriage among some pagan peoples, but prohibited as incestuous in the Mosaic Law (cf. Lev 18) and in rabbinical tradition. The reference, then, is to unions radically invalid because of some impediment. When persons in this position were converted to the true faith, it was not that their union could be dissolved; it was declared that they had never in fact been joined in true marriage. Therefore, this phrase does not go against the indissolubility of marriage, but rather reaffirms it.

On the basis of Jesus' teaching and guided by the Holy Spirit, the Church has ruled that in the specially grave case of adultery it is permissible for a married couple to separate, but without the marriage bond being dissolved; therefore, neither party may contract a new marriage.

The indissolubility of marriage was unhesitatingly taught by the Church from the very beginning; she demanded practi-

---

k. Greek *Gehenna*

Lk 16:18
1 Cor 7:10f

divorces his wife, except on the ground of unchastity,* makes her an adulteress; and whoever marries a divorced woman commits adultery.

Ex 20:7
Lev 19:12
Num 30:2
Mt 23:16–22

33"Again you have heard that it was said to the men of old, 'You shall not swear falsely, but shall perform to the Lord what you have sworn.' 34But I say to you, Do not swear at all, either by

---

cal and legal recognition of this doctrine, expounded with full authority by Jesus (Mt 19:3–9; Mk 10:1–12; Lk 16:18) and by the apostles (1 Cor 6:16; 7:10–11, 39; Rom 7:2–8; Eph 5:31f). Here, for example, are just a few texts from the Magisterium on this subject: "Three blessings are ascribed to matrimony [...]. The third is the indissolubility of matrimony—indissoluble because it signifies the indivisible union of Christ with the Church. Although a separation from bed maybe permitted by reason of marital infidelity, nevertheless it is not permitted to contract another matrimony since the bond of a marriage lawfully contracted is perpetual" (Council of Florence, *Pro Armeniis*).

"If anyone says that the marriage bond can be dissolved by reason of heresy, domestic incompatibility, or willful desertion by one of the parties, let him be anathema" (Council of Trent, *De Sacram. matr.*, can. 5).

"If anyone says that the Church is in error when she has taught and does teach according to the doctrine of the Gospels and apostles that the marriage bond cannot be dissolved because of adultery on the part of either the husband or the wife; and that neither party, not even the innocent one who gave no cause for the adultery, can contract another marriage while the other is still living; and that adultery is committed both by the husband who dismisses the adulterous wife and marries again and by the wife who dismisses her adulterous husband and marries again: let him be anathema" (ibid., can. 7).

"Taking our starting point from that Encyclical, which is concerned almost entirely with vindicating the divine institution of matrimony, its dignity as a Sacrament, and its perpetual stability, let us first recall this immutable, inviolable and fundamental truth: matrimony was not instituted or re-established by men but by God; not men, but God, the Author of nature, and Christ our Lord, the restorer of nature, provided marriage with its laws, confirmed it and elevated it; and consequently those laws can in no ways be subject to human wills or to any contrary pact made even by the contracting parties themselves. This is the teaching of Sacred Scripture; it is the constant and universal Tradition of the Church; it is the solemnly defined doctrine of the Council of Trent, which uses the words of Holy Scripture to proclaim and establish that the perpetual indissolubility of the marriage bond, its unity and stability, derive from God himself" (Pius XI, *Casti connubii*).

"It is true that before the coming of Christ the perfection and strictness of the original law were modified to the extent that Moses, because of the hardness of their hearts, allowed even the members of God's people to give a bill of divorce for certain reasons. But Christ, by virtue of his power as supreme Lawgiver, revoked this concession and restored the law to its original perfection by those words which must never be forgotten: 'What God hath jointed together let no man put asunder'" (ibid.).

56

heaven, for it is the throne of God, [35]or by the earth, for it is his footstool, or by Jerusalem, for it is the city of the great King. [36]And do not swear by your head, for you cannot make one hair white or black. [37]Let what you say be simply 'Yes' or 'No'; anything more than this comes from evil.[1]

[38]"You have heard that it was said, 'An eye for an eye and a tooth for a tooth.' [39]But I say to you, Do not resist one who is evil.

Is 66:1
Acts 7:49
Ps 48:2

2 Cor 1:17
Jas 5:12

Lev 24:19f

Jn 18:22f

"For the good of the parties, of the children, and of society this sacred bond no longer depends on human decision alone. For God himself is the author of marriage [...]. The intimate union of marriage (as a mutual giving of two persons) and the good of the children demand total fidelity from the spouses and require an unbreakable unity between them" (Vatican II, *Gaudium et spes*, 48).

5:33–37. The Law of Moses absolutely prohibited perjury or violation of oaths (Ex 20:7; Num 30:3; Deut 23:22). In Christ's time, the making of sworn statements was so frequent and the casuistry surrounding them so intricate that the practice was being grossly abused. Some rabbinical documents of the time show that oaths were taken for quite unimportant reasons. Parallel to this abuse of oath-taking there arose no less ridiculous abuses to justify non-fulfilment of oaths. All this meant great disrespect for the name of God. However, we do know from Holy Scripture that oath-taking is lawful and good in certain circumstances: "If you swear, 'As the Lord lives', in truth, in justice, and in uprightness, then nations shall bless themselves in him, and in him shall they glory" (Jer 4:2).

Jesus here lays down the criterion that his disciples must apply in this connexion. It is based on re-establishing mutual trust, nobility and sincerity. The devil is "the father of lies" (Jn 8:44). Therefore, Christ's Church cannot permit human relationships to be based on deceit and insincerity. God is truth, and the children of the Kingdom must, therefore, base mutual relationships on truth. Jesus concludes by praising sincerity. Throughout his teaching he identifies hypocrisy as one of the main vices to be combatted (cf., e.g., Mt 23: 13–32), and sincerity as one of the finest of virtues (cf. Jn 1:47).

5:38–42. Among the Semites, from whom the Israelites stemmed, the law of vengeance ruled. It led to interminable strife and countless crimes. In the early centuries of the chosen people, the law of retaliation was recognized as an ethical advance, socially and legally: no punishment could exceed the crime, and any punitive retaliation was outlawed. In this way, the honour of the clans and families was satisfied, and endless feuds avoided.

As far as New Testament morality is concerned, Jesus establishes a definitive advance: a sense of forgiveness and absence of pride play an essential role. Every legal framework for combating evil in the world, every reasonable defence of personal rights, should be based on morality. The last three last verses refer to mutual charity among the children of the Kingdom, a charity which presupposes and enhances justice.

---

l. Or *the evil one*

Lev 19:18   But if any one strikes you on the right cheek, turn to him the other
1 Cor 6:7   also; ⁴⁰and if any one would sue you and take your coat, let him
have your cloak as well; ⁴¹and if any one forces you to go one
mile, go with him two miles. ⁴²Give to him who begs from you,
and do not refuse him who would borrow from you.

Lev 19:18   ⁴³"You have heard that it was said, 'You shall love your neigh-
Ex 23:4f   bour and hate your enemy.' ⁴⁴But I say to you, Love your enemies
Rom 12:14, 20 and pray for those who persecute you, ⁴⁵so that you may be sons
Lk 23:34
Acts 7:59   of your Father who is in heaven; for he makes his sun rise on the
Eph 5:1   evil and on the good, and sends rain on the just and on the unjust.
⁴⁶For if you love those who love you, what reward have you? Do
not even the tax collectors do the same? ⁴⁷And if you salute only
your brethren, what more are you doing than others? Do not even
Lev 19:2   the Gentiles do the same? ⁴⁸You, therefore, must be perfect, as
your heavenly Father is perfect.

5:43. The first part of this verse—"You shall love your neighbour"—is to be found in Leviticus 19:18. The second part—"hate your enemy"—is not in the Law of Moses. However, Jesus' words refer to a widespread rabbinical interpretation which understood "neighbours" as meaning "Israelites". Our Lord corrects this misinterpretation of the Law: for him everyone is our neighbour (cf. the parable of the Good Samaritan in Lk 10:25–37).

5:43–47. This passage sums up the teaching which precedes it. Our Lord goes so far as to say that a Christian has no personal enemies. His only enemy is evil as such—sin—but not the sinner. Jesus himself puts this into practice with those who crucified him, and he continues to act in the same way towards sinners who rebel against him and despise him. Consequently, the saints have always followed his example—like St Stephen, the first martyr, who prayed for those who were putting him to death. This is the apex of Christian perfection—to love, and pray for, even those who persecute and calumniate us. It is the distinguishing mark of the children of God.

5:46. "Tax collectors": the Roman Empire had no officials of its own for the collection of taxes; in each country it used local people for this purpose. These were free to engage agents (hence we find references to "chief tax collectors": cf. Lk 19:2). The global amount of tax for each region was specified by the Roman authorities; the tax collectors levied more than this amount, keeping the surplus for themselves: this led them to act rather arbitrarily, which was why the people hated them. In the case of the Jews, insult was added to injury by the fact that the chosen people were being exploited by Gentiles.

5:48. Verse 48 is, in a sense, a summary of the teaching in this entire chapter, including the Beatitudes. Strictly speaking, it is quite impossible for a created being to be as perfect as God. What our Lord means here is that God's own perfection should be the model that every faithful Christian tries to follow, even though he realizes that there is an infinite distance between himself and his Creator. However, this does not reduce the force of this commandment; it sheds more light

An upright intention in almsgiving, prayer and fasting

6 ¹"Beware of practising your piety before men in order to be seen by them; for then you will have no reward from your Father who is in heaven.

²"Thus, when you give alms, sound no trumpet before you, as the hypocrites do in the synagogues and in the streets, that they may be praised by men. Truly, I say to you, they have their reward. ³But when you give alms, do not let your left hand know what your right hand is doing, ⁴so that your alms may be in secret; and your Father who sees in secret will reward you.

⁵"And when you pray, you must not be like the hypocrites; for they love to stand and pray in the synagogues and at the street corners, that they may be seen by men. Truly, I say to you, they have their reward. ⁶But when you pray, go into your room and shut the

Rom 12:8

2 Sam 4:33
Is 26:20

an actor

---

on it. It is a difficult commandment to live up to, but also with this we must take account of the enormous help grace gives us to go so far as to tend towards divine perfection. Certainly, the perfection that we should imitate does not refer to the power and wisdom of God, which are totally beyond our scope; here the context seems to refer primarily to love and mercy. Along the same lines, St Luke quotes these words of our Lord: "Be merciful, even as your Father is merciful" (Lk 6:36; cf. the note on Lk 6:20–49).

Clearly, the "universal call to holiness" is not a recommendation but a commandment of Jesus Christ. "Your duty is to sanctify yourself. Yes, even you. Who thinks that this task is only for priests and religious? To everyone, without exception, our Lord said: 'Be ye perfect, as my heavenly Father is perfect'" (St J. Escrivá, *The Way*, 291). This teaching is sanctioned by chapter 5 of Vatican II's Constitution *Lumen gentium*, where it says (at no. 40): "The Lord Jesus, divine teacher and model of all perfection, preached holiness of life (of which he is the author and maker) to each and every one of his disciples without distinction: 'You, therefore, must be perfect,

as your heavenly Father is perfect' [...]. It is therefore quite clear that all Christians in any state or walk of life are called to the fullness of Christian life and to the perfection of love, and by this holiness a more human manner of life is fostered also in earthly society."

6:1–18. "Piety", here, means good works (cf. the note on Mt 5:6). Our Lord is indicating the kind of spirit in which we should do acts of personal piety. Almsgiving, fasting and prayer were the basic forms taken by personal piety among the chosen people—which is why Jesus refers to these three subjects. With complete authority he teaches that true piety must be practised with an upright intention, in the presence of God and without any ostentation. Piety practised in this way implies exercising our faith in God who sees us—and also in the safe knowledge that he will reward those who are sincerely devout.

righteousness & covenant behavior

6:5–6. Following the teaching of Jesus, the Church has always taught us to pray even when we were infants. By saying "you" (singular) our Lord is stating quite unequivocally the need for personal pray-

door and pray to your Father who is in secret; and your Father who sees in secret will reward you.*

Is 1:15

⁷"And in praying do not heap up empty phrases as the Gentiles do; for they think that they will be heard for their many words. ⁸Do not be like them, for your Father knows what you need before you ask him. ⁹Pray then like this:

---

er—relating as child to Father, alone with God.

Public prayer, for which Christ's faithful assemble together, is something necessary and holy; but it should never displace obedience to this clear commandment of our Lord: "When you pray, go into your room and shut the door and pray to your Father."

The Second Vatican Council reminds us of the teaching and practice of the Church in its liturgy, which is "the summit towards which the activity of the Church is directed; it is also the fount from which all her power flows [...]. The spiritual life, however, is not limited solely to participation in the liturgy. The Christian is indeed called to pray with others, but he must also enter into his bedroom to pray to his Father in secret; furthermore, according to the teaching of the apostle, he must pray without ceasing (1 Thess 5:17)" (*Sacrosanctum Concilium*, 10 and 12).

A soul who really puts his Christian faith into practice realizes that he needs frequently to get away and pray alone to his Father, God. Jesus, who gives us this teaching about prayer, practised it during his own life on earth: the holy Gospel reports that he often went apart to pray on his own: "At times he spent the whole night in an intimate conversation with his Father. The apostles were filled with love when they saw Christ pray" (St J. Escrivá, *Christ Is Passing By*, 119; cf. Mt 14:23; Mk 1:35; Lk 5:16; etc.). The apostles followed the Master's example, and

so we see Peter going up to the rooftop of the house to pray in private, and receiving a revelation (cf. Acts 10:9–16). "Our life of prayer should also be based on some moments that are dedicated exclusively to our conversation with God, moments of silent dialogue" (*Christ Is Passing By*, 119).

6:7–8. Jesus condemns the superstitious notion that long prayers are needed to attract God's attention. True piety is not so much a matter of the amount of words as of the frequency and the love with which the Christian turns towards God in all the events, great or small, of his day. Vocal prayer is good, and necessary; but the words count only if they express our inner feelings.

6:9–13. The Our Father is, without any doubt, the most commented-on passage in all Holy Scripture. Numerous great Church writers have left us commentaries full of poetry and wisdom. The early Christians, taught by the precepts of salvation, and following the divine commandment, centred their prayer on this sublime and simple form of words given them by Jesus. And the last Christians, too, will raise their hearts to say the Our Father for the last time when they are on the point of being taken to heaven. In the meantime, from childhood to death, the Our Father is a prayer which fills us with hope and consolation. Jesus fully realized how helpful this prayer would be to us. We are grateful to him for giving it to us,

Our Father who art in heaven,
Hallowed be thy name.
¹⁰Thy kingdom come,
Thy will be done,
On earth as it is in heaven.

Lk 11:2–4
Jn 17:6
Mt 7:11

Lk 22:42

to the apostles for passing it on to us and, in the case of most Christians, to our mothers for teaching it to us in our infancy. So important is the Lord's Prayer that from apostolic times it has been used, along with the Creed, the Ten Commandments and the Sacraments, as the basis of Christian catechesis. Catechumens were introduced to the life of prayer by the Our Father, and our catechisms today use it for that purpose. St Augustine says that the Lord's Prayer is so perfect that it sums up in a few words everything man needs to ask God for (cf. *Sermons*, 56). It is usually seen as being made up of an invocation and seven petitions—three to do with praise of God and four with the needs of men.

6:9. It is a source of great consolation to be able to call God "our Father"; Jesus, the Son of God, teaches men to invoke God as Father because we are indeed his children, and should feel towards him in that way.

"The Lord [...] is not a tyrannical master or a rigid and implacable judge; he is our Father. He speaks to us about our lack of generosity, our sins, our mistakes; but he does so in order to free us from them, to promise us his friendship and his love [...]. A child of God treats the Lord as his Father. He is not obsequious and servile, he is not merely formal and well-mannered: he is completely sincere and trusting" (St J. Escrivá, *Christ Is Passing By*, 64).

"Hallowed be thy name": in the Bible a person's "name" means the same as the person himself. Here the name of God

means God himself. Why pray that his name be hallowed, sanctified? We do not mean sanctification in the human sense—leaving evil behind and drawing closer to God—for God is holiness itself. God, rather, is sanctified when his holiness is acknowledged and honoured by his creatures—which is what this first petition of the Our Father means (cf. *St Pius V Catechism*, 4, 10).

6:10. "Thy kingdom come": this brings up again the central idea of the Gospel of Jesus Christ—the coming of the Kingdom. The Kingdom of God is so identical with the life and work of Jesus Christ that the Gospel is referred to now as the Gospel of Jesus Christ, now as the Gospel of the Kingdom (Mt 9:35). On the notion of Kingdom of God see the commentary on Matthew 3:2 and 4:17. The coming of the Kingdom of God is the realization of God's plan of salvation in the world. The Kingdom establishes itself in the first place in the core of man's being, raising him up to share in God's own inner life. This elevation has, as it were, two stages—the first, in this life, where it is brought about by grace; the second, definitive stage in eternal life, where man's elevation to the supernatural level is fully completed. We for our part need to respond to God spontaneously, lovingly and trustingly.

"Thy will be done": this third petition expresses two desires. The first is that man identify humbly and unconditionally with God's will—abandonment in the arms of his Father God. The second is that the will of God be fulfilled, that man

> [11] Give us this day our daily bread;[m]
> [12] And forgive us our debts,
>   As we also have forgiven our debtors;
> [13] And lead us not into temptation,
>   But deliver us from evil.[n]

Jn 17:11, 15

cooperate with it in full freedom. For example, God's will is to be found in the moral aspect of the divine law—but this law is not forced on man. One of the signs of the coming of the Kingdom is man's loving fulfilment of God's will. The second part of the petition, "on earth as it is in heaven", means that, just as the angels and saints in heaven are fully at one with God's will, so—we desire—should the same thing obtain on earth.

Our effort to do God's will proves that we are sincere when we say the words, "Thy will be done." For our Lord says, "Not every one who says to me, 'Lord, Lord' shall enter the kingdom of heaven, but he who does the will of my Father who is in heaven" (Mt 7:21). "Anyone, then, who sincerely repeats this petition, 'Fiat voluntas tua', must, at least in intention, have done this already" (St Teresa of Avila, *Way of Perfection*, chap. 36).

6:11. In making this fourth petition, we are thinking primarily of our needs in this present life. The importance of this petition is that it declares that the material things we need in our lives are good and lawful. It gives a deep religious dimension to the support of life: what Christ's disciple obtains through his own work is also something for which he should implore God—and he should receive it gratefully as a gift from God. God is our support in life: by asking God to support him and by realizing that it is God who is providing this support, the Christian

avoids being worried about material needs. Jesus does not want us to pray for wealth or to be attached to material things, but to seek and make sober use of what meets our needs. Hence, in Matthew as well as in Luke (Lk 11:2), there is reference to having enough food for every day. This fourth petition, then, has to do with moderate use of food and material things—far from the extremes of opulence and misery, as God already taught in the Old Testament: "Give me neither poverty nor riches; feed me with the food which is needful for me, lest I be full, and deny thee, and say, 'Who is the Lord?' or lest I be poor, and steal, and profane the name of my God" (Prov 30:8).

The Fathers of the Church interpreted the bread asked for here not only as material food but also as referring to the Blessed Eucharist, without which our spirit cannot stay alive.

According to the *St Pius V Catechism* (cf. 4, 13, 21) the Eucharist is called our daily bread because it is offered daily to God in the Mass and because we should worthily receive it, every day if possible, as St Ambrose advises: "If the bread is daily, why do you take it only once a year [...]? Receive daily what is of benefit to you daily! So live that you may deserve to receive it daily!" (*De Sacramentis*, 5, 4).

6:12. "Debts": clearly, here, in the sense of sin. In the Aramaic of Jesus' time the same word was used for offence and debt. In this fifth petition, then, we admit

---

m. Or *our bread for the morrow*

62

¹⁴For if you forgive men their trespasses, your heavenly Father also will forgive you; ¹⁵but if you do not forgive men their trespasses, neither will your Father forgive your trespasses.

Mk 11:25f

---

that we are debtors because we have offended God. The Old Testament is full of references to man's sinful condition. Even the "righteous" are sinners. Recognizing our sins is the first step in every conversion to God. It is not a question of recognizing that we have sinned in the past but of confessing our present sinful condition. Awareness of our sinfulness makes us realize our religious need to have recourse to the only One who can cure it. Hence the advantage of praying insistently, using the Lord's Prayer to obtain God's forgiveness time and again.

The second part of this petition is a serious call to forgive our fellow-men, for we cannot dare to ask God to forgive us if we are not ready to forgive others. The Christian needs to realize what this prayer implies: unwillingness to forgive others means that one is condemning oneself (see the notes on Mt 5:23–24 and 18:21–35).

6:13. "And lead us not into temptation": "We do not ask to be totally exempt from temptation, for human life is one continuous temptation (cf. Job 7:1). What, then, do we pray for in this petition? We pray that the divine assistance may not forsake us, lest having been deceived, or worsted, we should yield to temptation; and that the grace of God may be at hand to succour us when our strength fails, to refresh and invigorate us in our trials" (St Pius V, *Catechism*, 4, 15, 14).

In this petition of the Our Father we recognize that our human efforts alone do not take us very far in trying to cope with temptation, and that we need to have humble recourse to God, to get the strength we need. For, "God is strong enough to free you from everything and can do you more good than all the devils can do you harm. All that God decrees is that you confide in him, that you draw near him, that you trust him and distrust yourself, and so be helped; and with this help you will defeat whatever hell brings against you. Never lose hold of this firm hope […] even if the demons are legion and all kinds of severe temptations harass you. Lean upon Him, because if the Lord is not your support and your strength, then you will fall and you will be afraid of everything" (St John of Avila, *Sermons*, 9, First Sunday of Lent).

"But deliver us from evil": in this petition, which, in a way, sums up the previous petitions, we ask the Lord to free us from everything our enemy does to bring us down; we cannot be free of him unless God himself free us, in response to our prayers.

This sentence can also be translated as "Deliver us from the evil one", that is to say, the devil, who is in the last analysis the author of all evils to which we are prone.

In making this request we can be sure that our prayer will be heard because Jesus Christ, when he was on the point of leaving this world, prayed to the Father for the salvation of all men: "I do not pray that thou shouldst take them out of the world, but that thou shouldst keep them from the evil one" (Jn 17:15).

6:14–15. In vv. 14 and 15 St Matthew gives us a sort of commentary of our Lord on the fifth petition of the Our Father.

n. Or *the evil one*. Other authorities, some ancient, add, in some form, *For thine is the kingdom and the power and the glory, for ever. Amen*

Is 58:5–9

[16]"And when you fast, do not look dismal, like the hypocrites, for they disfigure their faces that their fasting may be seen by men. Truly, I say to you, they have their reward. [17]But when you fast, anoint your head and wash your face, [18]that your fasting may not be seen by men but by your Father who is in secret; and your Father who sees in secret will reward you.

Trust in God's fatherly providence

Lk 12:33f
Col 3:1f

[19]"Do not lay up for yourselves treasures on earth, where moth and rust[o] consume and where thieves break in and steal, [20]but lay up for yourselves treasures in heaven, where neither moth nor rust[o] consumes and where thieves do not break in and steal. [21]For where your treasure is, there will your heart be also.

Lk 11:34–36

[22]"The eye is the lamp of the body. So, if your eye is sound, your whole body will be full of light; [23]but if your eye is not

---

A God who forgives is a wonderful God. But if God, who is thrice-holy, has mercy on the sinner, how much more ought we forgive others—we sinners, who know from our own experience the wretchedness of sin. No one on earth is perfect. Just as God loves us, even though we have defects, and forgives us, we should love others, even though they have defects, and forgive them. If we wait to love people who have no defects, we shall never love anyone. If we wait until others mend their ways or apologize, we will scarcely ever forgive them. But then we ourselves will never be forgiven. "All right: that person has behaved badly towards you. But, haven't you behaved worse towards God?" (St Josemaría Escrivá, *The Way*, 686).

Thus, forgiving those who have offended us makes us like our Father, God: "In loving our enemies there shines forth in us some likeness to God our Father, who, by the death of his Son, ransomed from everlasting perdition and reconciled to himself the human race, which before was most unfriendly and hostile

to him" (St Pius V, *Catechism*, 4, 14, 19).

6:16–18. Starting from the traditional practice of fasting, our Lord tells us the spirit in which we should practise mortification of our senses: we should do so without ostentation, avoiding praise, discreetly; that way Jesus' words will not apply to us: "they have their reward"; it would have been a very bad deal. "The world admires only spectacular sacrifice, because it does not realize the value of sacrifice that is hidden and silent" (St Josemaría Escrivá, *The Way*, 185).

6:19–21. The idea here is very clear: man's heart yearns for a treasure that will give him security and happiness. However, every treasure in the form of earthly goods—wealth, property—becomes a constant source of worry, because there is always the risk we will lose it or because the effort to protect it is such a strain.

Against this, Jesus teaches us here that our true treasure lies in good works and an upright life, which will be eter-

o. Or *worm*

64

sound, your whole body will be full of darkness. If then the light in you is darkness, how great is the darkness!

Lk 16:9, 13

²⁴"No one can serve two masters; for either he will hate the one and love the other, or he will be devoted to the one and despise the other. You cannot serve God and mammon.* *(material)*

²⁵"Therefore I tell you, do not be anxious about your life, what you shall eat or what you shall drink, nor about your body, what you shall put on. Is not life more than food, and the body more than clothing? ²⁶Look at the birds of the air; they neither sow nor reap nor gather into barns, and yet your heavenly Father feeds them. Are you not of more value than they? ²⁷And which of you by being anxious can add one cubit to his span of life?ᵖ ²⁸And why are you anxious about clothing? Consider the lilies of the field, how they grow; they neither toil nor spin; ²⁹yet I tell you, even Solomon in all his glory was not arrayed like one of these. ³⁰But if God so

Lk 12:22–31
Phil 4:6
1 Pet 5:7
1 Tim 6:6
Heb 13:5

1 Kings 10

---

nally rewarded by God in heaven. That indeed is a treasure which one never loses, a treasure on which Christ's disciple should put his heart.

Jesus closes the teaching contained in the preceding verses with a kind of refrain (v. 21). He is not saying that people should be unconcerned about earthly things; what he does say is that no created thing can be "the treasure", the ultimate aim, of man. What man should do is make his way to God, sanctify himself and give all glory to God, by making right use of the noble things of the earth: "Whether you eat or drink, or whatever you do, do all to the glory of God" (1 Cor 10:31; cf. Col 3:17).

6:22–23. Here is another jewel of Jesus' wisdom teaching. It begins with a sentence that is then immediately explained. The Master uses the simile of the eye as a lamp which provides the body with light. Christian exegesis has seen this "eye", this "lamp", as meaning the motivation behind our behaviour. St Thomas explains it in this way: "The eye refers to

motive. When a person wants to do something, he first forms an intention: thus, if your intention is sound—simple and clear—that is to say, if it is directed towards God, your whole body, that is, all your actions, will be sound, sincerely directed towards good" (St Thomas Aquinas, *Comm. on St Matthew*, 6, 22–23).

6:24. Man's ultimate goal is God; to attain this goal he should commit himself entirely. But in fact some people do not have God as their ultimate goal, and instead choose wealth of some kind—in which case wealth becomes their god. Man cannot have two absolute and contrary goals.

6:25–32. In this beautiful passage Jesus shows us the value of the ordinary things of life, and teaches us to put our trust in God's fatherly providence. Using simple examples and comparisons taken from everyday life, he teaches us to abandon ourselves into the arms of God.

6:27. The word "span" could be translated as "stature", but "span" is closer to

p. Or *to his stature*

clothes the grass of the field, which today is alive and tomorrow is thrown into the oven, will he not much more clothe you, O men of little faith? [31]Therefore do not be anxious, saying, 'What shall we eat?' or 'What shall we drink?' or 'What shall we wear?' [32]For the Gentiles seek all these things; and your heavenly Father knows that you need them all. [33]But seek first his kingdom and his righteousness, and all these things shall be yours as well.

Rom 14:17
1 Kings 3:13f
Ps 37:4, 25

[34]"Therefore do not be anxious about tomorrow, for tomorrow will be anxious for itself. Let the day's own trouble be sufficient for the day.

Ex 16:19

Various precepts. Do not judge

Rom 2:1
1 Cor 4:5
Mk 4:24

7 [1]"Judge not, that you be not judged. [2]For with the judgment you pronounce you will be judged, and the measure you give

---

the original (cf. Lk 12:25). A "cubit" is a measure of length which can metaphorically refer to time.

6:33. Here again the righteousness of the Kingdom means the life of grace in man—which involves a whole series of spiritual and moral values and can be summed up in the notion of "holiness". The search for holiness should be our primary purpose in life. Jesus is again insisting on the primacy of spiritual demands. Commenting on this passage, Pope Paul VI says: "Why poverty? It is to give God, the Kingdom of God, the first place in the scale of values which are the object of human aspirations. Jesus says: 'Seek first his kingdom and his righteousness.' And he says this with regard to all the other temporal goods, even necessary and legitimate ones, with which human desires are usually concerned. Christ's poverty makes possible that detachment from earthly things which allows us to place the relationship with God at the peak of human aspirations" (General Audience, 5 January 1977).

6:34. Our Lord exhorts us to go about our daily tasks serenely and not to worry

uselessly about what happened yesterday or what may happen tomorrow. This is wisdom based on God's fatherly providence and on our own everyday experience: "He who observes the wind will not sow; and he who regards the clouds will not reap" (Eccles 11:4).

What is important, what is within our reach, is to live in God's presence and make good use of the present moment: "Do your duty 'now', without looking back on 'yesterday', which has already passed, or worrying over 'tomorrow', which may never come for you" (St Josemaría Escrivá, *The Way*, 253).

7:1. Jesus is condemning any rash judgments we make maliciously or carelessly about our brothers' behaviour or feelings or motives. "Think badly and you will not be far wrong" is completely at odds with Jesus' teaching.

In speaking of Christian charity St Paul lists its main features: "Love is patient and kind [...]. Love bears all things, believes all things, hopes all things, endures all things" (1 Cor 13:4, 5, 7). Therefore, "Never think badly of anyone, not even if the words or conduct of the person in question give you good

will be the measure you get. ³Why do you see the speck that is in your brother's eye, but do not notice the log that is in your own eye? ⁴Or how can you say to your brother, 'Let me take the speck out of your eye,' when there is the log in your own eye? ⁵You hypocrite, first take the log out of your own eye, and then you will see clearly to take the speck out of your brother's eye.

Respect for holy things

⁶"Do not give dogs what is holy; and do not throw your pearls before swine, lest they trample them under foot and turn to attack you.

Effectiveness of prayer

⁷"Ask, and it will be given you; seek, and you will find; knock, and it will be opened to you. ⁸For every one who asks receives,

Mk 11:24
Lk 11:9–13
Jer 29:13f
Jn 14:13; 16:23

---

grounds for doing so" (St Josemaría Escrivá, *The Way*, 442).

"Let us be slow to judge. Each one sees things from his own point of view, as his mind, with all its limitations, tells him, and through eyes that are often dimmed and clouded by passion" (ibid., 451).

7:1–2. As elsewhere, the verbs in the passive voice ("you will be judged", "the measure you will be given") have God as their subject, even though he is not explicitly mentioned: "Do not judge *others*, that you be not judged *by God.*" Clearly the judgment referred to here is always a condemnatory judgment; therefore, if we do not want to be condemned by God, we should never condemn our neighbour. "God measures out according as we measure out and forgives as we forgive, and comes to our rescue with the same tenderness as he sees us having towards others" (Fray Luis de León, *Exposición del Libro de Job*, chap. 29).

7:3–5. A person whose sight is distorted sees things as deformed, even though in fact they are not deformed. St Augustine gives this advice: "Try to acquire those virtues which you think your brothers lack, and you will no longer see their defects, because you will not have them yourselves" (*Enarrationes in Psalmos*, 30, 2, 7). In this connexion, the saying "A thief thinks that everyone else is a thief" is in line with this teaching of Jesus.

Besides: "To criticize, to destroy, is not difficult; any unskilled labourer knows how to drive his pick into the noble and finely-hewn stone of a cathedral. To construct: that is what requires the skill of a master" (St Josemaría Escrivá, *The Way*, 456).

7:6. Jesus uses a popular saying to teach discernment in the preaching of the word of God and distribution of the means of sanctification. The Church has always heeded this warning, particularly in the sense of respect with which she administers the sacraments—especially the Holy Eucharist. Filial confidence does not exempt us from the sincere and profound respect that should imbue our relations with God and with holy things.

7:7–11. Here the Master teaches us in a number of ways about the effectiveness of prayer. Prayer is a raising of mind and heart to God to adore him, to praise him,

and he who seeks finds, and to him who knocks it will be opened.
[9]Or what man of you, if his son asks him for bread, will give him

Jas 1:17

a stone? [10]Or if he asks for a fish, will give him a serpent? [11]If you
then, who are evil, know how to give good gifts to your children,
how much more will your Father who is in heaven give good
things to those who ask him!

Entire law of the gospel *underneath the moral lesson*

The golden rule *the love of the heavenly*

Lk 6:31
Rom 13:8–10

[12]So whatever you wish that men would do to you, do so to them;
for this is the law and the prophets.

The narrow gate

Lk 13:24
Jn 10:7, 9

[13]"Enter by the narrow gate; for the gate is wide and the way is
easy,[q] that leads to destruction, and those who enter by it are

---

to thank him and to ask him for what we need (cf. St Pius X, *Catechism*, 255). Jesus emphasizes the need for petitionary prayer, which is the first spontaneous movement of a soul who recognizes God as his Creator and Father. As God's creature and child, each of us needs to ask him humbly for everything.

In speaking of the effectiveness of prayer, Jesus does not put any restriction: "Every one who asks receives", because God is our Father. St Jerome comments: "It is written, to everyone who asks it will be given; so, if it is not given to you, it is not given to you because you do not ask; so, ask and you will receive" (*Comm. on Matthew*, 7). However, even though prayer in itself is infallible, sometimes we do not obtain what we ask for. St Augustine says that our prayer is not heard because we ask "aut mali, aut male, aut mala." "*Mali*" (= evil people): because we are evil, because our personal dispositions are not good; "*male*" (= badly): because we pray badly, without faith, not persevering, not humbly; "*mala*" (= bad things): because we ask for bad things, that is, things which are

not good for us, things which can harm us (cf. *De civitate Dei*, 20, 22 and 27; *De Serm. Dom. in monte*, 2, 27, 73). In the last analysis, prayer is ineffective when it is not true prayer. Therefore, "Pray. In what human venture could you have greater guarantes of success?" (St Josemaría Escrivá, *The Way*, 96).

7:12. This "golden rule" gives us a guideline to realize our obligations towards and the love we should have for others. However, if we interpreted it superficially it would become a selfish rule; it obviously does not mean "*do ut des*" ("I give you something so that you will give me something") but that we should do good to others unconditionally: we are clever enough not to put limits on how much we love ourselves. This rule of conduct will be completed by Jesus' "new commandment" (Jn 13:34), where he teaches us to love others as he himself has loved us.

7:13–14. "Enter": in St Matthew's Gospel this verb often has as its object the "Kingdom of heaven" or equivalent

---

q. Other ancient authorities read *for the way is wide and easy*

many. [14]For the gate is narrow and the way is hard, that leads to life, and those who find it are few.

Acts 14:22

False prophets

[15]"Beware of false prophets, who come to you in sheep's clothing but inwardly are ravenous wolves. [16]You will know them by their fruits. Are grapes gathered from thorns, or figs from thistles? [17]So, every sound tree bears good fruit, but the bad tree bears evil fruit. [18]A sound tree cannot bear evil fruit, nor can a bad tree bear good fruit. [19]Every tree that does not bear good fruit is cut down and thrown into the fire. [20]Thus you will know them by their fruits.

Acts 20:29

Gal 5:19–22
Jas 3:12

Jn 15:2, 6

---

expressions (life, the marriage feast, the joy of the Lord, etc.). We can interpret "enter" as an imperious invitation.

The way of sin is momentarily pleasant and calls for no effort, but it leads to eternal perdition. Following the way of a generous and sincere Christian life is very demanding—here Jesus speaks of a narrow gate and a hard way—but it leads to Life, to eternal salvation.

The Christian way involves carrying the cross. "For if a man resolve to submit himself to carrying this cross—that is to say, if he resolve to desire in truth to meet trials and to bear them in all things for God's sake, he will find in them all great relief and sweetness wherewith he may travel upon this road, detached from all things and desiring nothing. Yet, if he desire to possess anything—whether it comes from God or from any other source—with any feeling of attachment, he has not stripped and denied himself in all things; and thus he will be unable to walk along this narrow path or to climb upward by it" (St John of the Cross, *Ascent of Mount Carmel*, book 2, chap. 7, 7).

7:15–20. There are many references in the Old Testament to false prophets, perhaps the best-known being Jeremiah 23:9–40 which condemns the impiety of those prophets who "prophesied by Baal and led my people Israel astray"; "who prophesy to you, filling you with vain hopes; they speak visions of their own minds, not from the mouth of the Lord [...]. I did not send the prophets, yet they ran. I did not speak to them, yet they prophesied"; they "lead my people astray by their lies and their recklessness, when I did not send them or charge them; so that they do not profit this people at all".

In the life of the Church the Fathers see these false prophets, as of whom Jesus speaks, in heretics, who apparently are pious and reformist but who in fact do not have Christ's sentiments (cf. St Jerome, *Comm. on Matthew*, 7). St John Chrysostom applies this teaching to anyone who appears to be virtuous but in fact is not, and thereby misleads others.

How are false prophets and genuine prophets to be distinguished? By the fruit they produce. Human nobility and divine inspiration combine to give the things of God a savour of their own. A person who truly speaks the things of God sows faith, hope, charity, peace and understanding; whereas a false prophet in the Church of God, in his preaching and behaviour, sows division, hatred, resentment, pride and sensuality (cf. Gal 5:16–25). However, the main characteristic of a false prophet is that he separates the people of

Doing the will of God

Rom 2:13
Jas 1:22, 25; 2:14
1 Cor 12:3

Lk 13:25–27
1 Cor 13:1f
Jer 14:14; 27:15

2 Tim 2:19
Ps 6:8

[21]"Not every one who says to me, 'Lord, Lord,' shall enter the kingdom of heaven, but he who does the will of my Father who is in heaven. [22]On that day many will say to me, 'Lord, Lord, did we not prophesy in your name, and cast out demons in your name, and do many mighty works in your name?' [23]And then will I declare to them, 'I never knew you; depart from me, you evildoers.'

Building on rock

[24]"Every one then who hears these words of mine and does them will be like a wise man who built his house upon the rock; [25]and the rain fell, and the floods came, and the winds blew and beat

---

God from the Magisterium of the Church, through which Christ's teaching is declared to the world. Our Lord also indicates that these deceivers are destined to eternal perdition.

7:21–23. To be genuine, prayer must be accompanied by a persevering effort to do God's will. Similarly, in order to do his will it is not enough to speak about the things of God: there must be consistency between what one preaches—what one says—and what one does: "The kingdom of God does not consist in talk but in power" (1 Cor 4:20); "Be doers of the word, and not hearers only, deceiving yourselves" (Jas 1:22).

Christians, "holding loyally to the Gospel, enriched by its resources, and joining forces with all who love and practise justice, have shouldered a weighty task on earth and they must render an account of it to him who will judge all men on the last day. Not every one who says 'Lord, Lord' will enter the Kingdom of heaven, but those who do the will of the Father, and who manfully put their hands to the work" (Vatican II, *Gaudium et spes*, 93).

To enter the Kingdom of heaven, to be holy, it is not enough, then, to speak eloquently about holiness. One has to practise what one preaches, to produce fruit that accords with one's words. Fray Luis de León puts it very graphically: "Notice that to be a good Christian it is not enough just to pray and fast and hear Mass; God must find you faithful, like another Job or Abraham, in times of tribulation" (*Guide for Sinners*, book 1, part 2, chap. 21).

Even if a person exercises an ecclesiastical ministry that does not assure his holiness; he needs to practise the virtues he preaches. Besides, we know from experience that any Christian (clerical, religious or lay) who does not strive to act in accordance with the demands of the faith he professes, begins to weaken in his faith and eventually parts company also with the teaching of the Church. Anyone who does not live in accordance with what he says, ends up saying things that are contrary to faith.

The authority with which Jesus speaks in these verses reveals him as sovereign Judge of the living and the dead. No Old Testament prophet ever spoke with this authority.

7:22. "That day": a technical formula in biblical language meaning the day of the Judgment of the Lord or the Last Judgment.

upon that house, but it did not fall, because it had been founded on the rock. ²⁶And every one who hears these words of mine and does not do them will be like a foolish man who built his house upon the sand; ²⁷and the rain fell, and the floods came, and the winds blew and beat against that house, and it fell; and great was the fall of it."

Ezek 33:10f

Jesus teaches with authority

²⁸And when Jesus finished these sayings, the crowds were astonished at his teaching, ²⁹for he taught them as one who had authority, and not as their scribes.

Mk 1:22
Lk 4:32
Jn 7:46

1st person of authority

7:23. This passage refers to the Judgment where Jesus will be the Judge. The sacred text uses a verb which means the public proclamation of a truth. Since in this case Jesus Christ is the Judge who makes the declaration, it takes the form of a judicial sentence.

7:24–27. These verses constitute the positive side of the previous passage. A person who tries to put Christ's teaching into practice, even if he experiences personal difficulties or lives during times of upheaval in the life of the Church or is surrounded by error, will stay firm in the faith, like the wise man who builds his house on rock.

Also, if we are to stay strong in times of difficulty, we need, when things are calm and peaceful, to accept little contradictions with a good grace, to be very refined in our relationship with God and with others, and to perform the duties of our state in life in a spirit of loyalty and abnegation. By acting in this way we are laying down a good foundation, maintaining the edifice of our spiritual life and repairing any cracks that make their appearance.

7:28–29. Jesus' listeners could clearly see the radical difference between the style of teaching of the scribes and Pharisees, and the conviction and confidence with which Jesus spoke. There is nothing tentative about his words; they leave no room for doubt; he is clearly not giving a mere opinion. Jesus spoke with absolute command of the truth and perfect knowledge of the true meaning of the Law and the Prophets; indeed he often spoke on his own authority (cf. Mt 5:22, 28, 32, 38, 44), and with the very authority of God (cf. Mk 2:10; Mt 28:18). All this conferred a singular force and authority on his words, such as had never been known in Israel (cf. Lk 19:48; Jn 7:46).

Chapters 8 and 9 of St Matthew deal with a series of miracles worked by our Lord. The first Christians had vivid experience of the fact that the glorified Jesus was still present in his Church, confirming its teaching by signs, by miracles (Mk 16:20; Acts 14:3).

And so, St Matthew, after giving the nucleus of Jesus' public teaching in the Sermon on the Mount (chapters 5–7), goes on now to gather a number of miracles to support our Lord's words. Some commentators call this section— chaps. 8 and 9—"the works of the Messiah", parallelling what they called "the words of the Messiah" (the discourse on the mount). In chapters 5–7 we see Jesus as the supreme lawgiver and master who

4. MIRACLES OF THE MESSIAH

Curing of a leper

Mk 1:40–44
Lk 5:12–14

8 ¹When he came down from the mountain, great crowds followed him; ²and behold, a leper came to him and knelt before him, saying, "Lord, if you will, you can make me clean." ³And he stretched out his hand and touched him, saying, "I will; be clean." And immediately his leprosy was cleansed.* ⁴And Jesus said to him, "See that you say nothing to any one; but go, show yourself to the priest, and offer the gift that Moses commanded, for a proof to the people."ʳ

Mk 7:36
Lk 17:14
Lev 13:49;
14:2–32

The centurion's faith

Lk 7:1–10
Jn 4:47

⁵As he entered Capernaum, a centurion came forward to him, beseeching him ⁶and saying, "Lord, my servant is lying paralyzed at home, in terrible distress." ⁷And he said to him, "I will come and heal him." ⁸But the centurion answered him, "Lord, I am not

---

teaches with divine authority, a unique authority superior to that held by Moses and the prophets. Now, in chapters 8 and 9, he is shown as endowed with divine authority over disease, death, the elements and evil spirits. These miracles worked by Jesus Christ accredit the divine authority of his teaching.

8:1. The Gospel draws attention, for the third time, to the huge crowds that flocked to Jesus: literally, "many multitudes followed him". This shows the popularity he had achieved: he was so popular that the Sanhedrin (the great council of the Jewish nation) dared not arrest him for fear of what the people would do (cf. Mt 21:46; 26:5; Mk 14:2). Later on, they would accuse him before Pilate of stirring up the whole country from Judea to Galilee. And we will see Herod Antipas' eagerness to meet Jesus, of whom he has heard so much (cf. Mt 14:1). In contrast to this huge popularity, we find the elders opposing him and

deceiving the people into calling for Jesus' execution (cf. Mt 27:20–22).

8:2. The Fathers have taken the following meaning from this cure: leprosy is a vivid image of sin; it is ugly, disgusting, very contagious and difficult to cure. We are all sinners and we are all in need of God's forgiveness and grace (cf. Rom 3:23–24). The leper in the Gospel knelt down before Jesus, in all humility and trust, begging to be made clean. If we have recourse to our Saviour with that kind of faith, we can be sure that he will cure the wretchedness of our souls. We should often address Christ with this short prayer, borrowed from the leper: "Lord, if you will, you can make me clean."

8:4. According to the Law of Moses (Lev 14), if a leper is cured of his disease, he should present himself to a priest, who will register the cure and give him a certificate which he needs to be reintegrated into the civil and religious life of Israel.

r. Greek *to them*

worthy to have you come under my roof; but only say the word, and my servant will be healed. ⁹For I am a man under authority, with soldiers under me; and I say to one, 'Go,' and he goes, and to another, 'Come,' and he comes, and to my slave, 'Do this,' and he does it." ¹⁰When Jesus heard him, he marvelled, and said to those who followed him, "Truly, I say to you, not even[s] in Israel have I found such faith. ¹¹I tell you, many will come from east and west and sit at table with Abraham, Isaac, and Jacob in the kingdom of heaven, ¹²while the sons of the kingdom will be thrown into the outer darkness; there men will weep and gnash their teeth." ¹³And to the centurion Jesus said, "Go; be it done for you as you have believed." And the servant was healed at that very moment.

Lk 13:28f
Is 49:12; 59:19
Mal 1:11
Ps 107:3

Curing of Peter's mother-in-law

¹⁴And when Jesus entered Peter's house, he saw his mother-in-law lying sick with a fever; ¹⁵he touched her hand, and the fever left her, and she rose and served him.

Mk 1:29–34
Lk 4:38–41
1 Cor 9:5

Other cures

¹⁶That evening they brought to him many who were possessed with demons; and he cast out the spirits with a word, and healed

---

Leviticus also prescribes the purifications and sacrifice he should offer. Jesus' instruction to the leper is, then, in keeping with the normal way of fulfilling what the laws laid down.

8:5–13. "Centurion": an officer of the Roman army in control of one hundred men. This man's faith is still an example to us. At the solemn moment when a Christian is about to receive Jesus in the Blessed Eucharist, the Church's liturgy places on his lips and in his heart these words of the centurion, to enliven his faith: "Lord, I am not worthy …".

The Jews of this time regarded any Jew who entered a Gentile's house as contracting legal impurity (cf. Jn 19:28; Acts 11:2–3). This centurion has the deference not to place Jesus in an embarrassing position in the eyes of his fellow Israelites. He shows that he is convinced

that Jesus has power over disease and illness; he suggests that if Jesus just says the word, he will do what is needed without having actually to visit the house; he is reasoning, in a simple, logical way, on the basis of his own professional experience. Jesus avails of this meeting with a Gentile believer to make a solemn prophecy to the effect that his Gospel is addressed to the world at large; all men, of every nation and race, of every age and condition, are called to follow Christ.

8:14–15. After his body—or soul—is healed, everyone is called to "rise up" from his previous position, to serve Jesus Christ. No laments, no delays; instead one should make oneself immediately available to the Lord.

8:16–17. The expulsion of evil spirits is one of the main signs of the establish-

s. Other ancient authorities read *with no one*

[handwritten: 49 suffering servant chapter 49 servant song]

[handwritten margin: Is]

Is 53:4
Jn 1:29, 36

all who were sick. ¹⁷This was to fulfil what was spoken by the prophet Isaiah, "He took our infirmities and bore our diseases."

Following Christ is not easy

Mk 4:35
Lk 8:22

Lk 9:57–60

2 Cor 8:9

1 Kings 19:20

¹⁸Now when Jesus saw great crowds around him, he gave orders to go over to the other side. ¹⁹And a scribe came up and said to him, "Teacher, I will follow you wherever you go." ²⁰And Jesus said to him, "Foxes have holes, and birds of the air have nests; but the Son of man has nowhere to lay his head." ²¹Another of the disciples said to him, "Lord let me first go and bury my father." ²²But

[handwritten across page: Rabinic – calling himself Messiah]

ment of the Kingdom of God (cf. Mt 12:8). Similarly, the healing of diseases, which ultimately are the result of sin, is one of the signs of the "works of the Messiah" proclaimed by the prophets (cf. Is 29:18; 35:5–6).

8:18–22. From the very outset of his messianic preaching, Jesus rarely stays in the same place; he is always on the move. He "has nowhere to lay his head" (Mt 8:20). Anyone who desires to be with him has to "follow him". This phrase "following Jesus" has a very precise meaning: it means being his disciple (cf. Mt 19:28). Sometimes the crowds "follow him"; but Jesus' true disciples are those who "follow him" in a permanent way, that is, who keep on following him: being a "disciple of Jesus" and "following him" amount to the same thing. After our Lord's ascension, "following him" means being a Christian (cf. Acts 8:26). By the simple and sublime fact of Baptism, every Christian is called, by a divine vocation, to be a full disciple of our Lord, with all that that involves.

The evangelist here gives two specific cases of following Jesus. In the case of the scribe our Lord explains what faith requires of a person who realizes that he has been called; in the second case—that of the man who has already said "yes" to Jesus—he reminds him of what his com-

mitment entails. The soldier who does not leave his position on the battlefront to bury his father, but instead leaves that to those in the rearguard, is doing his duty. If service to one's country makes demands like that on a person, all the more reason for it to happen in the service of Jesus Christ and his Church.

Following Christ, then, means we should make ourselves totally available to him; whatever sacrifice he asks of us we should make: the call to follow Christ means staying up with him, not falling behind; we either follow him or lose him. In the sermon on the mount (Mt 5–7) Jesus explained what following him involves—a teaching that we find summarized in even the most basic catechism of Christian doctrine: a Christian is a man who believes in Jesus Christ—a faith he receives at Baptism—and is duty bound to serve him. Through prayer and friendship with the Lord every Christian should try to discover the demands which this service involves as far as he personally is concerned.

8:20. "The Son of man": this is one of the expressions used in the Old Testament to refer to the Messiah. It appeared first in Daniel 7:14 and was used in Jewish writings in the time of Jesus. Until our Lord began to preach, it had not been understood in all its depth. The title "the Son

Corporal work of mercy

Kingdom takes precedent

Jesus said to him, "Follow me, and leave the dead to bury their own dead."

Jn 1:43; 5:25
Rom 16:13

The calming of the storm

²³And when he got into the boat, his disciples followed him. ²⁴And behold, there arose a great storm on the sea, so that the boat was being swamped by the waves; but he was asleep. ²⁵And they went and woke him, saying, "Save, Lord; we are perishing." ²⁶And he said to them, "Why are you afraid, O men of little faith?" Then he rose and rebuked the winds and the sea; and there was a great calm. ²⁷And the men marvelled, saying, "What sort of man is this, that even winds and sea obey him?"

Mk 4:36–41
Lk 8:23–35
Ps 4:8

Ps 107:25ff

---

of man" did not fit in very well with Jewish hopes of an earthly Messiah; this was why it was Jesus' favourite way of indicating that he was the Messiah—thereby avoiding any tendency to encourage Jewish nationalism. In the prophecy of Daniel just mentioned this messianic title has a transcendental meaning; by using it Jesus was able discreetly to proclaim that he was the Messiah and yet avoid people interpreting his role in a political sense. After the Resurrection the apostles at last realized that "Son of man" meant nothing less than "Son of God".

8:22. "Leave the dead to bury their own dead": although this sounds very harsh, it is a style of speaking which Jesus did sometimes use. Here the "dead" clearly refers to those whose interest is limited to perishable things and who have no aspirations towards the things that last forever.

"If Jesus forbade him," St John Chrysostom comments, "it was not to have us neglect the honour due to our parents, but to make us realize that nothing is more important than the things of heaven and that we ought to cleave to these and not to put them off even for a little while, though our engagements be ever so indis-

pensable and pressing" (*Hom. on St Matthew*, 27).

8:23–27. This remarkable miracle left a deep impression on Jesus' disciples, as can be seen from the fact that the first three evangelists all report it. Christian Tradition has applied this miracle in various ways to the life of the Church and the experience of the individual soul. From earliest times Christian art and literature have seen the boat as representing the Church, which also has to make its way around hazards which threaten to capsize it. Indeed, very early on, Christians were persecuted in various ways by Jews of their time, and were misunderstood by the public opinion of a pagan society—which also began to persecute them. Jesus' sleeping through the storm has been applied to the fact that sometimes God seems not to come to the Church's rescue during persecution. Following the example of the apostles in the boat, Christians should seek Jesus' help, borrowing their words, "Save us, Lord; we are perishing". Then, when it seems we can bear it no longer, Jesus shows his power: "He rose and rebuked the winds and the sea; and there was a great calm"—but first rebuking us for being men of little faith. Quite often Gospel

The demoniacs of Gadara

Mk 5:1–17
Lk 8:26–37

Lk 4:41
2 Pet 2:4

²⁸And when he came to the other side, to the country of the Gadarenes,ᵗ two demoniacs met him, coming out of the tombs, so fierce that no one could pass that way. ²⁹And behold, they cried out, "What have you to do with us, O Son of God? Have you come here to torment us before the time?"* ³⁰Now a herd of many swine was feeding at some distance from them. ³¹And the demons begged him, "If you cast us out, send us away into the herd of swine." ³²And he said to them, "Go." So they came out and went into the swine; and behold, the whole herd rushed down the steep bank into the sea, and perished in the waters. ³³The herdsmen fled, and going into the city they told everything, and what had happened to the demoniacs. ³⁴And behold, all the city came out to

---

accounts are meant to serve as examples to us: they epitomize the future history of the Church and of the individual Christian soul.

8:28. Most Gospel codexes and the New Vulgate say "Gadarenes"; but the Vulgate and parallel texts in Mark and Luke have "Gerasenes". Both names are possible; the two main towns in the area were Gerasa and Gadara. The event reported here could have happened close to both towns (limits were not very well defined), though the swine running down into the lake or sea of Galilee makes Gadara somewhat more likely. "Gergesenes" was a suggestion put forward by Origen.

8:28–34. In this episode Jesus once more shows his power over the devil. That it occurred in Gentile territory (Gerasa and Gadara were in the Decapolis, east of Jordan) is borne out by the fact that Jews were forbidden to raise swine, which the Law of Moses declared to be unclean. This and other instances of expulsion of demons narrated in the Gospel are referred to in the Acts of the Apostles,

when St Peter addresses Cornelius and his household: "he went about doing good and healing all that were oppressed by the devil" (Acts 10:38). It was a sign that the Kingdom of God had begun (cf. Mt 12:28).

The attitude of local people towards this miracle reminds us that meeting God and living a Christian life require us to subordinate personal plans to God's designs. If we have a selfish or materialistic outlook we fail to appreciate the value of divine things and push God out of our lives, begging him to go away, as these people did.

9:1. "His own city": Capernaum (cf. Mt 4:13 and Mk 2:1).

9:2–6. The sick man and those who bring him to Jesus ask him to cure the man's physical illness; they believe in his supernatural powers. As in other instances of miracles, our Lord concerns himself more with the underlying cause of illness, that is, sin. With divine largesse he gives more than he is asked for, even though people do not appreciate this. St Thomas Aquinas says that Jesus Christ

---

t. Other ancient authorities read *Gergesenes*; some, *Gerasenes*

meet Jesus; and when they saw him, they begged him to leave their neighbourhood.

Curing of a paralyzed man

9 [1]And getting into a boat he crossed over and came to his own city. [2]And behold, they brought to him a paralytic, lying on his bed; and when Jesus saw their faith he said to the paralytic, "Take heart, my son; your sins are forgiven." [3]And behold, some of the scribes said to themselves, "This man is blaspheming." [4]But Jesus, knowing[u] their thoughts, said, "Why do you think evil in your hearts? [5]For which is easier, to say, 'Your sins are forgiven,' or to say, 'Rise and walk'? [6]But that you may know that the Son of man has authority on earth to forgive sins"—he then said to

Mk 2:1–12
Lk 5:16–26

Mk 2:7
Jn 2:25

---

acts like a good doctor: he cures the cause of the illness (cf. *Comm. on St Matthew*, 9, 1–6).

9:2. The parallel passage of St Mark adds a detail that helps us understand this scene better and explains why the text refers to "their faith": in Mark 2:2–5 we are told that there was such a crowd around Jesus that the people carrying the bed could not get near him. So they had the idea of going up onto the roof and making a hole and lowering the bed down in front of Jesus. This explains his "seeing their faith".

Our Lord was pleased by their boldness, a boldness which resulted from their lively faith which brooked no obstacles. This nice example of daring indicates how we should go about putting charity into practice—also how Jesus feels towards people who show real concern for others: he cures the paralytic who was so ingeniously helped by his friends and relatives; even the sick man himself showed daring by not being afraid of the risk involved.

St Thomas comments on this verse as follows: "This paralytic symbolizes the

sinner lying in sin"; just as the paralytic cannot move, so the sinner cannot help himself. The people who bring the paralytic along represent those who, by giving him good advice, lead the sinner to God" (*Comm. on St Matthew*, 9, 2). In order to get close to Jesus the same kind of holy daring is needed, as the saints show us. Anyone who does not act like this will never make important decisions in his life as a Christian.

9:3–7. Here "to say" obviously means "to say and mean it", "to say producing the result which your words imply". Our Lord is arguing as follows: which is easier—to cure the paralytic's body or to forgive the sins of his soul? Undoubtedly, to cure his body; for the soul is superior to the body and therefore diseases of the soul are the more difficult to cure. However, a physical cure can be seen, whereas a cure of the soul cannot. Jesus proves the hidden cure by performing a visible one.

The Jews thought that any illness was due to personal sin (cf. Jn 9:1–3); so when they heard Jesus saying, "Your sins are forgiven", they reasoned in their

u. Other ancient authorities read *seeing*

forgiveness of sin

the paralytic—"Rise, take up your bed and go home." [7]And he rose and went home. [8]When the crowds saw it, they were afraid, and they glorified God, who had given such authority to men.

The call of Matthew

Mk 2:13–17
Lk 5:27–32

[9]As Jesus passed on from there, he saw a man called Matthew sitting at the tax office; and he said to him, "Follow me." And he rose and followed him.

[10]And as he sat at table[v] in the house, behold, many tax collectors and sinners came and sat down with Jesus and his disciples.

---

minds as follows: only God can forgive sins (cf. Lk 5:21); this man says that he has power to forgive sins; therefore, he is claiming a power that belongs to God alone—which is blasphemy. Our Lord, however, forestalls them, using their own arguments: by curing the paralytic by just saying the word, he shows them that since he has the power to cure the effects of sin (which is what they believe disease to be), then he also has power to cure the cause of illness (sin); therefore, he has divine power.

Reconciliation

Jesus Christ passed on to the apostles and their successors in the priestly ministry the power to forgive sins: "Receive the Holy Spirit. If you forgive sins of any, they are forgiven; if you retain the sins of any, they are retained" (Jn 20:22–23). "Truly, I say to you, whatever you bind on earth shall be bound in heaven, and whatever you loose on earth shall be loosed in heaven" (Mt 18:18). Priests exercise this power in the sacrament of Penance: in doing so they act not in their own name but in Christ's—*in persona Christi*, as instruments of the Lord.

Hence the respect, veneration and gratitude with which we should approach Confession: in the priest we should see Christ himself, God himself, and we should receive the words of absolution firmly believing that it is Christ who is uttering them through the priest. This is why the minister does not say: "Christ absolves you ...", but rather "I absolve you from your sins ...": he speaks in the first person, so fully is he identified with Jesus Christ himself (cf. St Pius V, *Catechism*, 2, 5, 10).

9:9. "Tax office": a public place for the payment of taxes. On "following Jesus", see the note on Mt 8:18–22.

The Matthew whom Jesus calls here is the apostle of the same name and the human author of the first Gospel. In Mark 2:14 and Luke 5:27 he is called Levi the son of Alphaeus or simply Levi.

In addition to Baptism, through which God calls all Christians (cf. the note on Mt 8:18–22), the Lord can also extend, to whomever he chooses, a further calling to engage in some specific mission in the Church. This second calling is a special grace (cf. Mt 4:19–21; Mk 1:17-20; Jn 1:39; etc.) additional to the earlier calling through Baptism. In other words, it is not man who takes the initiative; it is Jesus who calls, and man who responds to this call by his free personal decision: "You did not choose me, but I chose you" (Jn 15:16).

---

v. Greek *reclined*

[11]And when the Pharisees saw this, they said to his disciples, "Why does your teacher eat with tax collectors and sinners?" [12]But when he heard it, he said, "Those who are well have no need of a physician, but those who are sick. [13]Go and learn what this means, 'I desire mercy, and not sacrifice.' For I came not to call the righteous, but sinners."

restoration of Gentiles

Lk 15:2

Hos 6:6
1 Sam 15:22
Mt 18:11

A discussion on fasting

[14]Then the disciples of John came to him, saying, "Why do we and the Pharisees fast,[w] but your disciples do not fast?" [15]And

Mk 2:18–22
Lk 5:33–38;
18:12

Matthew's promptitude in "following" Jesus' call is to be noted. When God speaks, a soul may be tempted to reply, "Tomorrow; I'm not ready yet." In the last analysis this excuse, and other excuses, are nothing but a sign of selfishness and fear (different from that fear which can be an additional symptom of vocation: cf. Jon 1). "Tomorrow" runs the risk of being too late.

As in the case of the other apostles, St Matthew is called in the midst of the ordinary circumstances of his life: "What amazes you seems natural to me: that God has sought you out in the practice of your profession! That is how he sought the first, Peter and Andrew, James and John, beside their nets, and Matthew, sitting in the custom-house. And—wonder of wonders!—Paul, in his eagerness to destroy the seeds of Christianity" (St Josemaría Escrivá, *The Way*, 799).

9:10–11. The attitude of these Pharisees, who are so prone to judge others and classify them as just men or sinners, is at odds with the attitude and teaching of Jesus. Earlier on, he said, "Judge not, that you be not judged" (Mt 7:1), and elsewhere he added, "Let him who is without sin among you be the first to throw a stone at her" (Jn 8:7). The fact is that all of us are sinners; and our Lord has come

to redeem all of us. There is no basis, therefore, for Christians to be scandalized by the sins of others, since any one of us is capable of committing the vilest of sins unless God's grace were to come to our aid.

9:12. There is no reason why anyone should be depressed when he realizes he is full of failings: recognition that we are sinners is the only correct attitude for us to have in the presence of God. He has come to seek all men, but if a person considers himself to be righteous, by so doing he is closing the door to God; all of us in fact are sinners.

9:13. Here Jesus quotes Hosea 6:6, keeping the hyperbole of the Semitic style. A more faithful translation would be "I desire mercy *more than* sacrifice". It is not that our Lord does not want the sacrifices we offer him: he is stressing that every sacrifice should come from the heart, for charity should imbue everything a Christian does—especially his worship of God (see 1 Cor 13:1–13; Mt 5:23–24).

9:14–17. This passage is interesting, not so much because it tells us about the sort of fasting practised by the Jews of the time—particularly the Pharisees and

w. Other ancient authorities add *much* or *often*

Jn 3:29

Jesus said to them, "Can the wedding guests mourn as long as the bridegroom is with them? The days will come, when the bridegroom is taken away from them, and then they will fast. ¹⁶And no one puts a piece of unshrunk cloth on an old garment, for the patch tears away from the garment, and a worse tear is made. ¹⁷Neither is new wine put into old wineskins; if it is, the skins burst, and the wine is spilled, and the skins are destroyed; but new wine is put into fresh wineskins, and so both are preserved."

Jn 1:17

The raising of Jairus' daughter and the curing of the woman with a hemorrhage

Mk 5:22–43
Lk 8:41–56

¹⁸While he was thus speaking to them, behold, a ruler came in and knelt before him, saying, "My daughter has just died; but come and lay your hand on her, and she will live." ¹⁹And Jesus rose and followed him, with his disciples.

²⁰And behold, a woman who had suffered from a hemorrhage for twelve years came up behind him and touched the fringe of his

---

John the Baptist's disciples—but because of the reason Jesus gives for not requiring his disciples to fast in that way. His reply is both instructive and prophetic. Christianity is not a mere mending or adjusting of the old suit of Judaism. The redemption wrought by Jesus involves a total regeneration. Its spirit is too new and too vital to be suited to old forms of penance, which will no longer apply.

We know that in our Lord's time Jewish theology schools were in the grip of a highly complicated casuistry to do with fasting, purifications etc, which smothered the simplicity of genuine piety. Jesus' words point to that simplicity of heart with which his disciples might practise prayer, fasting and almsgiving (cf. Mt 6:1–18 and notes to same). From apostolic times onwards it is for the Church, using the authority given it by our Lord, to set out the different forms fasting should take in different periods and situations.

9:15. "The wedding guests": literally, "the sons of the house where the wedding is

being celebrated"—an expression meaning the bridegroom's closest friends. This is an example of how St Matthew uses typical Semitic turns of phrase, presenting Jesus' manner of speech.

This "house" to which Jesus refers has a deeper meaning; set beside the parable of the guests at the wedding (Mt 22:1ff), it symbolizes the Church as the house of God and the body of Christ: "Moses was faithful in all God's house as a servant, to testify to the things that were to be spoken later, but Christ was faithful over God's house as a son. And we are his house if we hold fast our confidence and pride in our hope" (Heb 3:5–6). The second part of the verse refers to the violent death Jesus would meet.

9:18–26. Here are two miracles which occur almost simultaneously. From parallel passages in Mark (5:21–43) and Luke (8:40–56) we know that the "ruler" (of the synagogue) referred to here was called Jairus. The Gospels report Jesus raising three people to life— this girl, the son of the widow of Nain, and Lazarus.

garment; ²¹for she said to herself, "If I only touch his garment, I shall be made well." ²²Jesus turned, and seeing her he said, "Take heart, daughter; your faith has made you well." And instantly the woman was made well. ²³And when Jesus came to the ruler's house, and saw the flute players, and the crowd making a tumult, ²⁴he said, "Depart; for the girl is not dead but sleeping." And they laughed at him. ²⁵But when the crowd had been put outside, he went in and took her by the hand, and the girl arose. ²⁶And the report of this went through all that district.

Jn 11:11, 14, 25

Curing of two blind men. The dumb devil

²⁷And as Jesus passed on from there, two blind men followed him, crying aloud, "Have mercy on us, Son of David." ²⁸When he entered the house, the blind men came to him; and Jesus said to them, "Do you believe that I am able to do this?" They said to him, "Yes, Lord." ²⁹Then he touched their eyes, saying, "According to your faith be it done to you." ³⁰And their eyes were opened.

In each case the identity of the person is clearly given.

This account shows us, once again, the role faith plays in Jesus' saving actions. In the case of the woman with the hemorrhage we should note that Jesus is won over by her sincerity and faith: she does not let obstacles get in her way. Similarly, Jairus does not care what people will say; a prominent person in his city, he humbles himself before Jesus for all to see.

9:18. "Knelt before him": the eastern way of showing respect to God or to important people. In the liturgy, especially in the presence of the Blessed Eucharist, reverences are a legitimate and appropriate external sign of internal faith and adoration.

9:23. "The flute players": engaged to provide music at wakes and funerals.

9:24. "Depart, for the girl is not dead, but sleeping": Jesus says the same thing about Lazarus: "Our friend Lazarus has fallen asleep, but I go to awaken him" (Jn 11:11).

Although Jesus speaks of sleep, there is no question of the girl—or Lazarus, later—not being dead. For our Lord there is only one true death—that of eternal punishment (cf. Mt 10:28).

9:27–34. The evangelist shows people's different reactions to miracles. Everyone admits that God is at work in these events—everyone, that is, except the Pharisees who attribute them to the power of the devil. A pharisaical attitude so hardens a person's heart that he becomes closed to any possibility of salvation. The fact that the blind men recognize Jesus as the Messiah (they call him "Son of David": v. 27) may have exasperated the Pharisees. Despite Jesus' sublime teaching, despite his miracles, they remain entrenched in their opposition.

In the light of this episode it is easy enough to see that the paradox is true: there are blind people who in fact see God and seers who see no trace of him.

9:30. Why did our Lord not want them to publicize the miracle? Because his

And Jesus sternly charged them, "See that no one knows it." ³¹But they went away and spread his fame through all that district.

³²As they were going away, behold, a dumb demoniac was brought to him. ³³And when the demon had been cast out, the dumb man spoke; and the crowds marvelled, saying, "Never was anything like this seen in Israel." ³⁴But the Pharisees said, "He casts out demons by the prince of demons."

The need for good pastors

Mk 6:34

³⁵And Jesus went about all the cities and villages, teaching in their synagogues and preaching the gospel of the kingdom, and healing every disease and every infirmity. ³⁶When he saw the crowds, he had compassion for them, because they were harassed and help-

turning point: leadership comes after Jesus

---

plan was to gradually manifest himself as the Messiah, the Son of God. He did not want to anticipate events which would occur in their own good time; nor did he want the crowd to start hailing him as Messiah King, because their notion of messiah was a nationalistic, not a spiritual one. However, the crowd did in fact proclaim him when he worked the miracles of the loaves and the fish (Jn 6:14–15): "When the people saw the sign which he had done, they said, 'This is indeed the prophet who is to come into the world!' Perceiving then that they were about to come and take him by force to make him king, Jesus withdrew again to the hills by himself."

9:31. St Jerome (cf. *Comm. on Matthew*, 9, 31) says that the blind men spread the news of their cure, not out of disobedience to Jesus, but because it was the only way they could find to express their gratitude.

9:35. The Second Vatican Council uses this passage when teaching about the message of Christian charity which the Church should always be spreading: "Christian charity is extended to all without distinction of race, social condition or

religion, and seeks neither gain nor gratitude. Just as God loves us with a gratuitous love, so too the faithful, in their charity, should be concerned for mankind, loving it with that same love with which God sought man. As Christ went about all the towns and villages healing every sickness and infirmity, as a sign that the Kingdom of God had come, so the Church, through its children, joins itself with men of every condition, but especially with the poor and afflicted, and willingly spends herself for them" (*Ad gentes*, 12).

9:36. "He had compassion for them": the Greek verb is very expressive; it means "he was deeply moved". Jesus was moved when he saw the people, because their pastors, instead of guiding them and tending them, led them astray, behaving more like wolves than genuine shepherds of their flock. Jesus sees the prophecy of Ezekiel 34 as now being fulfilled; in that passage God, through the prophet, upbraids the false shepherds of Israel and promises to send them the Messiah to be their new leader.

"If we were consistent with our faith when we looked around us and contemplated the world and its history, we

Jesus the Good Shepherd because Pharisees failed

less, like sheep without a shepherd. [37]Then he said to his disciples, "The harvest is plentiful, but the labourers are few; [38]pray therefore the Lord of the harvest to send out labourers in to his harvest."

Num 27:17
Ezek 34:5
Lk 10:2

failed to find

Dan 7:13-14 / LK 19:10 -

HaKesh - (clickers)

5. FROM THE OLD TO THE NEW PEOPLE OF GOD

The calling of the twelve apostles

10 [1]And he called to him his twelve disciples and gave them authority over unclean spirits, to cast them out, and to heal every disease and every infirmity. [2]The names of the twelve apostles are these: first, Simon, who is called Peter, and Andrew his

Mk 6:7–13
Lk 9:1–5

Mk 3:14–19
Lk 6:13–16
Jn 1:40–49

---

would be unable to avoid feeling in our own hearts the same sentiments that filled the heart of our Lord" (St J. Escrivá, *Christ Is Passing By*, 133). Reflection on the spiritual needs of the world should lead us to be tirelessly apostolic.

9:37–38. After contemplating the crowds neglected by their shepherds, Jesus uses the image of the harvest to show us that that same crowd is ready to receive the effects of Redemption: "I tell you, lift up your eyes, and see now the fields are already white for harvest" (Jn 4:35). The field of the Jewish people cultivated by the prophets—most recently by John the Baptist—is full of ripe wheat. In farmwork, the harvest is lost if the farmer does not reap at the right time; down the centuries the Church feels a similar need to be out harvesting because there is a big harvest ready to be won.

However, as in the time of Jesus, there is a shortage of labourers. Our Lord tells us how to deal with this: we should pray God, the Lord of the harvest, to send the necessary labourers. If a Christian prays hard, it is difficult to imagine his not feeling urged to play his part in this apostolate. In obeying this commandment to pray for labourers, we should pray especially for there to be no lack of good shepherds, who will be able to equip others with the necessary means of sanctification needed to back up the apostolate.

In this connexion Paul VI reminds us: "the responsibility for spreading the Gospel that saves belongs to everyone— to all those who have received it! The missionary duty concerns the whole body of the Church; in different ways and to different degrees, it is true, but we must all of us be united in carrying out this duty. Now let the conscience of every believer ask himself: Have I carried out my missionary duty? Prayer for the Missions is the first way of fulfilling this duty" (Angelus Address, 23 October 1977).

10:1–4. Jesus calls his twelve apostles after recommending to them to pray to the Lord to send labourers into his harvest (cf. Mt 9:38). Christians' apostolic action should always, then, be preceded and accompanied by a life of constant prayer: apostolate is a divine affair, not a merely human one. Our Lord starts his Church by calling twelve men to be, as it were, twelve patriarchs of the new people of God, the Church. This new people is

brother; James the son of Zebedee, and John his brother; ³Philip and Bartholomew; Thomas and Matthew the tax collector; James the son of Alphaeus, and Thaddaeus;ˣ ⁴Simon the Cananaean, and Judas Iscariot, who betrayed him.

The apostles' first mission

Acts 13:46
Jer 50:6
Lk 10:9

⁵These twelve Jesus sent out, charging them, "Go nowhere among the Gentiles, and enter no town of the Samaritans,* ⁶but go rather

established not by physical but by spiritual generation. The names of those apostles are specifically mentioned here. They were not scholarly, powerful or important people: they were average, ordinary people who responded faithfully to the grace of their calling—all of them, that is, except Judas Iscariot. Even before his death and resurrection Jesus confers on them the power to cast out unclean spirits and cure illnesses—as an earnest of and as training for the saving mission which he will entrust to them.

The Church reveres these first Christians in a very special way and is proud to carry on their supernatural mission, and to be faithful to the witness they bore to the teaching of Christ. The true Church is absent unless there is uninterrupted apostolic succession and identification with the spirit which the apostles made their own.

"Apostle": this word means "sent"; Jesus sent them out to preach his Kingdom and pass on his teaching. The Second Vatican Council, in line with Vatican I, "confesses" and "declares" that the Church has a hierarchical structure: "The Lord Jesus, having prayed at length to the Father, called to himself those whom he willed and appointed twelve to be with him, whom he might send to preach the Kingdom of God (cf. Mk 3:13–19; Mt 10:1–10). These apostles (cf. Lk 6:13) he constituted in the form of

a college or permanent assembly, at the head of which he placed Peter, chosen from among them (cf. Jn 21:15–17). He sent them first of all to the children of Israel and then to all peoples (cf. Rom 1:16), so that, sharing in his power, they might make all peoples his disciples and sanctify and govern them (cf. Mt 28:16–20; Mk 16:15; Lk 24:45–48; Jn 20:21–23) and thus spread the Church and, administering it under the guidance of the Lord, shepherd it all days until the end of the world (cf. Mt 28:28)" (*Lumen gentium*, 19).

10:1. In this chapter St Matthew describes how Jesus, with a view to the spreading of the Kingdom of God which, he inaugurates, decides to establish a Church, which he does by giving special powers and training to these twelve men who are its seed.

10:5–15. After revealing his intention to found the Church by choosing the Twelve (vv. 1–4), in the present passage he shows that he intends to start training these first apostles. In other words, from early on in his public ministry he began to lay the foundations of his Church. Everyone needs doctrinal and apostolic training to follow his Christian calling. The Church has a duty to teach, and the faithful have a parallel duty to make that teaching their own. Therefore, every

x. Other ancient authorities read *Lebbaeus* or *Lebbaeus called Thaddaeus*

to the lost sheep of the house of Israel. ⁷And preach as you go, saying, 'The kingdom of heaven is at hand.' ⁸Heal the sick, raise the dead, cleanse lepers, cast out demons. You received without pay, give without pay. ⁹Take no gold, nor silver, nor copper in your belts, ¹⁰no bag for your journey, nor two tunics, nor sandals,

Acts 20:33

Lk 10:4
1 Tim 5:18

Christian should avail himself or herself of the facilities for training which the Church offers—which will vary according to a person's circumstances.

10:5–6. In his plan of salvation God gave certain promises (to Abraham and the patriarchs), a Covenant and a Law (the Law of Moses), and sent the prophets. The Messiah would be born into this chosen people, which explains why the Messiah and the Kingdom of God were to be preached to the house of Israel before being preached to Gentiles. Therefore, in their early apprenticeship, Jesus restricts the apostles' area of activity to the Jews, without this taking from the worldwide scope of the Church's mission. As we will see, much later on he charges them to "go and make disciples of all nations" (Mt 28:19); "Go into all the world and preach the Gospel to the whole creation" (Mk 16:16). The apostles also, in the early days of the spread of the Church, usually sought out the Jewish community in any new city they entered, and preached first to them (cf. Acts 13:46).

10:7–8. Previously, the prophets, when speaking of the messianic times, had used imagery suited to the people's spiritual immaturity. Now, Jesus, in sending his apostles to proclaim that the promised Kingdom of God is imminent, lays stress on its spiritual dimension. The powers mentioned in verse 8 are the very sign of the Kingdom of God or the reign of the Messiah proclaimed by the prophets. At first (chaps. 8 and 9) it is Jesus who exer-

cises these messianic powers; now he gives them to his disciples as proof that his mission is divine (Is 35:5–6; 40:9; 52:7; 61:1).

10:9. "Belts": twin belts, stitched together leaving space where coins and other small, heavy objects could be secreted and carried.

10:9–10. Jesus urges his disciples to set out on their mission without delay. They should not be worried about material or human equipment: God will make up any shortfall. This holy audacity in setting about God's work is to be found throughout the history of the Church: if Christians had bided their time, waiting until they had the necessary material resources, many, many souls would never have received the light of Christ. Once a Christian is clear in his mind about what God wants him to do, he should not stay at home checking to see if he has the wherewithal to do it. "In your apostolic undertakings you are right—it's your duty—to consider what means the world can offer you (2 + 2 = 4), but don't forget—ever!—that, fortunately, your calculations must include another term: God + 2 + 2 ..." (St Josemaría Escrivá, *The Way*, 471).

However, that being said, we should not try to force God's hand, to have him do something exceptional, when in fact we can meet needs by our own efforts and work. This means that Christians should generously support those who, because they are totally dedicated to the spiritual welfare of their brethren, have

85

Num 18:31

nor a staff; for the labourer deserves his food. ¹¹And whatever town or village you enter, find out who is worthy in it, and stay

Lk 10:5f

with him until you depart. ¹²As you enter the house, salute it. ¹³And if the house is worthy, let your peace come upon it; but if it

Lk 10:10–12
Acts 13:51;
18:6

is not worthy, let your peace return to you. ¹⁴And if any one will not receive you or listen to your words, shake off the dust from

Lk 20:47

your feet as you leave that house or town. ¹⁵Truly, I say to you, it shall be more tolerable on the day of judgment for the land of Sodom and Gomorrah than for that town.

Lk 10:3
Jn 10:12
Acts 20:29

Jesus' instructions to the apostles

Rom 16:19
Eph 5:15

¹⁶"Behold, I send you out as sheep in the midst of wolves; so be wise as serpents and innocent as doves. ¹⁷Beware of men; for they

Mk 13:9–13
Lk 21:12–17

will deliver you up to councils, and flog you in their synagogues,

Mt 24:9; 24:14
Acts 25:23; 27:24

¹⁸and you will be dragged before governors and kings for my

---

no time left over to provide for themselves: in this connexion see Jesus' promise in Mt 10:40–42.

10:11–15. "Peace" was, and still is, the normal Jewish form of greeting. On the apostles' lips it is meant to have a deeper meaning—to be a sign of God's blessing which Jesus' disciples, who are his envoys, pour out on those who receive them. The commandment our Lord gives here affects not only this specific mission; it is a kind of prophecy which applies to all times. His messenger does not become discouraged if his word is not well received. He knows that God's blessing is never ineffective (cf. Is 55:11), and that every generous effort a Christian makes will always produce fruit. The word spoken in apostolate always brings with it the grace of conversion: "Many of those who heard the word believed; and the number of the men came to about five thousand" (Acts 4:4; cf. 10:44; Rom 10:17).

Man should listen to this word of the Gospel and believe in it (Acts 13:48; 15:7). If he accepts it and stays faithful to it his soul is consoled, he obtains peace

(Acts 8:39) and salvation (Acts 11:4–18). But if he rejects it, he is not free from blame and God will judge him for shutting out the grace he was offered.

10:16–23. The instructions and warnings Jesus gives here apply right through the history of the Church. It is difficult for the world to understand the way of God. Sometimes there will be persecutions, sometimes indifference to the Gospel or failure to understand it. Genuine commitment to Jesus always involves effort—which is not surprising, because Jesus himself was a sign of contradiction; indeed, if that were not the experience of a Christian, he would have to ask himself whether he was not in fact a worldly person. There are certain worldly things a Christian cannot compromise about, no matter how much they are in fashion. Therefore, Christian life inevitably involves nonconformity with anything that goes against faith and morals (cf. Rom 12:2). It is not surprising that a Christian's life often involves choosing between heroism and treachery. Difficulties of this sort should not make us afraid: we are not alone, we can count on

sake, to bear testimony before them and the Gentiles. ¹⁹When they
deliver you up, do not be anxious how you are to speak or what
you are to say; for what you are to say will be given to you in that
hour; ²⁰for it is not you who speak, but the Spirit of your Father
speaking through you. ²¹Brother will deliver up brother to death,
and the father his child, and children will rise against parents and
have them put to death; ²²and you will be hated by all for my
name's sake. But he who endures to the end will be saved. ²³When
they persecute you in one town, flee to the next; for truly, I say to
you, you will not have gone through all the towns of Israel, before
the Son of man comes.

²⁴"A disciple is not above his teacher, nor a servant[y] above his
master; ²⁵it is enough for the disciple to be like his teacher, and the
servant[y] like his master. If they have called the master of the house
Beelzebul, how much more will they malign those of his household.

Lk 12:11f

Jn 14:26
1 Cor 2:4

Mic 7:6

Jn 15:21

Lk 6:40
Jn 13:16;
15:20
Mt 12:24

---

the powerful help of our Father God to
give us strength and daring.

10:20. Here Jesus teaches the completely supernatural character of the witness he asks his disciples to bear. The
documented accounts of a host of
Christian martyrs prove that he has kept
this promise: they bear eloquent witness
to the serenity and wisdom of often uneducated people, some of them scarcely
more than children. The teaching contained in this verse provides the basis for
the fortitude and confidence a Christian
should have whenever he has to profess
his faith in difficult situations. He will
not be alone, for the Holy Spirit will give
him words of divine wisdom.

10:23. In interpreting this text, the first
thing is to reject the view of rationalists
who argue that Jesus was convinced that
soon he would come in glory and the
world would come to an end. That interpretation is clearly at odds with many
passages of the Gospel and the New
Testament. Clearly, Jesus refers to him-

self when he speaks of the "Son of man",
whose glory will be manifested in this
way. The most cogent interpretation is
that Jesus is referring here, primarily, to
the historical event of the first Jewish war
against Rome, which ended with the
destruction of Jerusalem and of the
temple in the year 70, and which led to
the scattering of the Jewish people. But
this event, which would occur a few
years after Jesus' death, is an image or a
prophetic symbol of the end of the world
(cf. the note on Mt 24:1). The coming of
Christ in glory will happen at a time
which God has not revealed. Uncertainty
about the end of the world helps Christians and the Church to be ever-vigilant.

10:24–25. Jesus uses these two proverbs
to hint at the future that awaits his disciples: their greatest glory will consist in
imitating the Master, being identified
with him, even if this means being
despised and persecuted as he was before
them: his example is what guides a
Christian; as he himself said, "I am the
way, and the truth, and the life" (Jn 14:6).

y. Or *slave*

Lk 12:2–9
Mk 4:22
Lk 8:17

Jas 4:12

²⁶"So have no fear of them; for nothing is covered that will not be revealed, or hidden that will not be known. ²⁷What I tell you in the dark, utter in the light; and what you hear whispered, proclaim upon the housetops. ²⁸ And do not fear those who kill the body but cannot kill the soul; rather fear him who can destroy both soul and body in hell.ᶻ ²⁹Are not two sparrows sold for a penny? And not one of them will fall to the ground without your Father's will. ³⁰But even the hairs of your head are all numbered. ³¹Fear not, therefore; you are of more value than many sparrows. ³²So every one who acknowledges me before men, I also will acknowledge

---

Beelzebul (cf. Lk 11:15) was the name of the idol of the ancient Philistine city of Ekron. The Jews later used the word to describe the devil or the prince of devils (cf. Mt 12:24), and their hatred of Jesus led them to the extreme of applying it to him.

To equip them for the persecution and misunderstanding which Christians will suffer (Jn 15:18), Jesus encourages them by promising to stay close to them. Towards the end of his life he will call them his friends (Jn 15:15) and little children (Jn 13:33).

10:26–27. Jesus tells his disciples not to be afraid of calumny and detraction. A day will come when everyone will come to know the whole truth about everyone else, their real intentions, the true dispositions of their souls. In the meantime, those who belong to God may be misrepresented by those who resort to lies, out of malice or passion. These are the hidden things which will be made known.

Christ also tells the apostles to speak out clearly. Jesus' divine teaching method led him to speak to the crowds in parables so that they came to discover his true personality by easy stages. After the coming of the Holy Spirit (cf. Acts 1:8), the apostles would have to preach from

the rooftops about what Jesus had taught them.

We too have to make Christ's doctrine known in its entirety, without any ambiguity, without being influenced by false prudence or fear of the consequences.

10:28. Using this and other Gospel texts (Mt 5:22, 29; 18:9; Mk 9:43, 45, 47; Lk 12:5), the Church teaches that hell exists; there those who die in mortal sin suffer eternal punishment (cf. St Pius V, *Catechism*, 1, 6, 3), in a manner not known to us in this life (cf. St Teresa of Avila, *Life*, chap. 32). See the notes on Lk 16:19–31.

Therefore, our Lord warns his disciples against false fear. We should not fear those who can only kill the body. Only God can cast body and soul into hell. Therefore God is the only one we should fear and respect; he is our Prince and Supreme Judge—not men. The martyrs have obeyed this precept of the Lord in the fullest way, well aware that eternal life is worth much more than earthly life.

10:29–31. An *as* (translated here as "penny") was a small coin of very little value. Christ uses it to illustrate how much God loves his creatures. As St Jerome says (*Comm. on Matthew*, 10:29–31): "If little birds, which are of such

z. Greek *Gehenna*

88

before my Father who is in heaven; ³³but whoever denies me before men, I also will deny before my Father who is in heaven.

Lk 9:26

³⁴"Do not think that I have come to bring peace on earth; I have not come to bring peace, but a sword. ³⁵For I have come to set a man against his father, and a daughter against her mother, and a daughter-in-law against her mother-in-law; ³⁶and a man's foes will be those of his own household. ³⁷He who loves father or mother more than me is not worthy of me; and he who loves son or daughter

Lk 12:51–53

Mic 7:6

Deut 33:9
Lk 14:26f

---

little value, still come under the providence and care of God, how is it that you, who, given the nature of your soul, are immortal, can fear that you are not looked after carefully by him whom you respect as your Father?" Jesus again teaches us about the fatherly providence of God, which he spoke about at length in the Sermon on the Mount (cf. Mt 6:19–34).

10:32–33. Here Jesus tells us that public confession of our faith in him—whatever the consequences—is an indispensable condition for eternal salvation. After the Judgment, Christ will welcome those who have given testimony of their faith and condemn those whom fear caused to be ashamed of him (cf. Mt 7:23; 25:41; Rev 21:8). The Church honours as "confessors" those saints who have not undergone physical martyrdom but whose lives bore witness to the Catholic faith. Although every Christian should be ready to die for his faith, most Christians are called to be confessors of the faith.

10:34–37. Our Lord has not come to bring a false and earthly peace—the sort of tranquillity the self-seeking person yearns for; he wants us to struggle against our own passions and against sin and its effects. The sword he equips us with for this struggle is, in the words of Scripture, "the sword of the Spirit which is the word of God" (Eph 6:17), "lively and active, sharper than any two-edged

sword, piercing to the division of soul and spirit, of joints and marrow, and discerning the thoughts and intentions of the heart" (Heb 4:12).

The word of God in fact leads to these divisions mentioned here. It can lead, even within families, to those who embrace the faith being regarded as enemies by relatives who resist the word of truth. This is why our Lord goes on (v. 37) to say that nothing should come between him and his disciple—not even father, mother, son or daughter: any and every obstacle (cf. Mt 5:29–30) must be avoided.

Obviously these words of Jesus do not set up any opposition between the first and fourth commandments (love for God above all things and love for one's parents): he is simply indicating the order of priorities. We should love God with all our strength (cf. Mt 22:37), and make a serious effort to be saints; and we should also love and respect—in theory and in practice—the parents God has given us; they have generously cooperated with the creative power of God in bringing us into the world and there is so much that we owe them. But love for our parents should not come before love of God; usually there is no reason why these two loves should clash, but if that should ever happen, we should be quite clear in mind and in heart about what Jesus says here. He has in fact given us an example to follow on this point: "How is it that you sought me? Did you not know that I must

more than me is not worthy of me; [38]and he who does not take his
cross and follow me is not worthy of me. [39]He who finds his life
will lose it, and he who loses his life for my sake will find it.

[40]"He who receives you receives me, and he who receives me
receives him who sent me. [41]He who receives a prophet because
he is a prophet shall receive a prophet's reward, and he who
receives a righteous man because he is a righteous man shall
receive a righteous man's reward. [42]And whoever gives to one of
these little ones even a cup of cold water because he is a disciple,
truly, I say to you, he shall not lose his reward."

Messengers from John the Baptist

11 [1]And when Jesus had finished instructing his twelve disciples, he went on from there to teach and preach in their
cities.

Lk 17:33
Jn 12:25

Lk 10:16
Jn 12:44;
13:20

Mk 9:41

---

be in my Father's house?" (Lk 2:49)—his
reply when, as a youth, Mary and Joseph
found him in the temple of Jerusalem after
a long search. This event in our Lord's life
is a guideline for every Christian—parent
or child. Children should learn from it that
their affection for their parents should
never come before their love for God, particularly when our Creator asks us to
follow him in a way that implies special
self-giving on our part; parents should
take the lesson that their children belong
to God in the first place, and therefore he
has a right to do with them what he
wishes, even if this involves sacrifice,
even heroic sacrifice. This teaching of our
Lord asks us to be generous and to let
God have his way. In fact, however, God
never lets himself be outdone in generosity. Jesus has promised a hundredfold
gain, even in this life, and later on eternal
life (cf. Mt 19:29), to those who readily
respond to his holy will.

10:38–39. The teaching contained in the
preceding verses is summed up in these
two succinct sentences. Following Christ,
doing what he asks, means risking this
present life to gain eternal life.

"People who are constantly concerned with themselves, who act above
all for their own satisfaction, endanger
their eternal salvation and cannot avoid
being unhappy even in this life. Only if a
person forgets himself and gives himself
to God and to others, in marriage as well
as in any other aspect of life, can he be
happy on this earth, with a happiness that
is a preparation for, and a foretaste of, the
joy of heaven" (St Josemaría Escrivá;
Christ Is Passing By, 24). Clearly,
Christian life is based on self-denial:
there is no Christianity without the cross.

10:40. To encourage the apostles and to
persuade others to receive them, our Lord
affirms that there is an intimate solidarity,
or even a kind of identity, between himself and his disciples. God in Christ,
Christ in the apostles: this is the bridge
between heaven and earth (cf. 1 Cor
3:21–23).

10:41–42. A prophet's mission is not
essentially one of announcing future
events; his main role is that of communicating the word of God (cf. Jer 11:2; Is
1:2). The righteous man, the just man, is

²Now when John heard in prison about the deeds of the Christ, he sent word by his disciples ³and said to him, "Are you he who is to come, or shall we look for another?"* ⁴And Jesus answered them, "Go and tell John what you hear and see: ⁵the blind receive their sight and the lame walk, lepers are cleansed and the deaf hear, and the dead are raised up, and the poor have good news preached to them. ⁶And blessed is he who takes no offence at me."

⁷As they went away, Jesus began to speak to the crowds concerning John: "What did you go out into the wilderness to behold? A reed shaken by the wind? ⁸Why then did you go out? To see a manª clothed in soft raiment? Behold, those who wear soft raiment are in kings' houses. ⁹Why then did you go out? To see a prophet?ᵇ Yes, I tell you, and more than a prophet. ¹⁰This is he of whom it is written,

'Behold, I send my messenger before thy face,
who shall prepare thy way before thee.'

Lk 7:18–35
Mt 14:3
Mal 3:1
Dan 9:26
Is 35:5f; 61:1
Lk 4:18

Lk 1:76
Mal 3:1
Mk 1:2
Jn 3:28

---

he who obeys the Law of God and follows his paths (cf. Gen 6:9; Is 3:10). Here Jesus tells us that everyone who humbly listens to and welcomes prophets and righteous men, recognizing God in them, will receive the reward of a prophet and a righteous man. The very fact of generously receiving God's friends will gain one the reward that they obtain. Similarly, if we should see God in the least of his disciples (v. 42), even if they do not seem very important, they are important, because they are envoys of God and of his Son. That is why he who gives them a glass of cold water—an alms, or any small service—will receive a reward, for he has shown generosity to our Lord himself (cf. Mt 25:40).

11:1. In chapters 11 and 12 the Gospel records the obduracy of the Jewish leaders towards Jesus, despite hearing his teaching (chaps. 5–7) and seeing the miracles which bear witness to the divine nature of his person and his doctrine (chaps. 8–9).

11:2. John knew that Jesus was the Messiah (cf. Mt 3:13–17). He sent his disciples to him so that they could shed their mistaken notions about the kind of Messiah to expect, and come to recognize Jesus.

11:3–6. Jesus replies to the Baptist's disciples by pointing to the fact that they are witnessing the signs that the ancient prophecies said would mark the advent of the Messiah and his Kingdom (cf. Is 35:5, 61:1; etc.). He says, in effect, that he is the prophet who "was to come". The miracles reported in the Gospel (chaps. 8–9) and the teaching given to the people (chaps. 5–7) prove that Jesus of Nazareth is the expected Messiah.

11:6. Jesus here corrects the mistaken idea which many Jews had of the Messiah, casting him in the role of a powerful earthly ruler—a far cry from the humble attitude of Jesus. It is not surprising that he was a stumbling block to Jews (cf. Is 8:14–15; 1 Cor 1:23).

---

a. Or *What then did you go out to see? A man ...*   **b.** Other ancient authorities read *What then did you go out to see? A prophet?*

Lk 16:16;
13:24
Jn 6:15

Mal 3:23
Mt 17:10–13

Prov 29:9

[11]Truly, I say to you, among those born of women there has risen no one greater than John the Baptist; yet he who is least in the kingdom of heaven is greater than he. [12]From the days of John the Baptist until now the kingdom of heaven has suffered violence,[c] and men of violence take it by force. [13]For all the prophets and the law prophesied until John; [14]and if you are willing to accept it, he is Elijah who is to come. [15]He who has ears to hear,[d] let him hear.

Jesus reproaches his contemporaries

[16]"But to what shall I compare this generation? It is like children sitting in the market places and calling to their playmates,

[17] 'We piped to you, and you did not dance;
we wailed, and you did not mourn.'

11:11. With John the Old Testament is brought to a close and we are on the threshold of the New. The Precursor had the honour of ushering Christ in, making him known to men. God had assigned him the exalted mission of preparing his contemporaries to hear the Gospel. The Baptist's faithfulness is recognized and proclaimed by Jesus. The praise he receives is a reward for his humility: John, realizing what his role was, had said, "He must increase, but I must decrease" (Jn 3:30).

St John the Baptist was the greatest in the sense that he had received a mission unique and incomparable in the context of the Old Testament. However, in the Kingdom of heaven (the New Testament) inaugurated by Christ, the divine gift of grace makes the least of those who faithfully receive it greater than the greatest in the earlier dispensation. Once the work of our redemption is accomplished, God's grace will also be extended to the just of the Old Alliance. Thus, the greatness of John the Baptist, the Precursor and the last of the prophets, will be enhanced by the dignity of being made a son of God.

11:12. "The Kingdom of heaven has suffered violence": once John the Baptist announces that the Christ is already come, the powers of hell redouble their desperate assault, which continues right through the lifetime of the Church (cf. Eph 6:12). The situation described here seems to be this: the leaders of the Jewish people, and their blind followers, were waiting for the Kingdom of God the way people wait for a rightful legacy to come their way; but while they rest on the laurels of the rights and rewards they think their race entitles them to, others, the men of violence (literally, attackers) are taking it, as it were, by force, by fighting the enemies of the soul—the world, the flesh and the devil.

"This violence is not directed against others. It is a violence used to fight your own weaknesses and miseries, a fortitude, which prevents you from camouflaging your own infidelities, a boldness to own up to the faith even when the environment is hostile" (St Josemaría Escrivá, *Christ Is Passing By*, 82).

This is the attitude of those who fight their passions and do themselves violence, thereby attaining the Kingdom of

c. Or *has been coming violently*   **d.** Other ancient authorities omit *to hear*

[18]For John came neither eating nor drinking, and they say, 'He has a demon'; [19]the Son of man came eating and drinking, and they say, 'Behold, a glutton and a drunkard, a friend of tax collectors and sinners!' Yet wisdom is justified by her deeds."[e]

Jesus reproaches cities for their unbelief

[20]Then he began to upbraid the cities where most of his mighty works had been done, because they did not repent. [21]"Woe to you, Chorazin! woe to you, Bethsaida! for if the mighty works done in you had been done in Tyre and Sidon, they would have repented long ago in sackcloth and ashes. [22]But I tell you, it shall be more tolerable on the day of judgment for Tyre and Sidon than for you. [23]And you, Capernaum, will you be exalted to heaven? You shall

Lk 10:12–15

Jn 3:6

Is 14:13, 15

---

heaven and becoming one with Christ. As Clement of Alexandria puts it: "The Kingdom of heaven does not belong to those who sleep and who indulge all their desires, but to those who fight against themselves" (*Quis dives salvetur?*, 21).

11:14. John the Baptist is Elijah, not in person, but by virtue of his mission (cf. Mt 17:10–13; Mk 9:10–12).

11:16–19. Making reference to a popular song or a child's game of his time, Jesus reproaches those who offer groundless excuses for not recognizing him. From the beginning of human history the Lord has striven to attract all men to himself: "What more was there to do for my vineyard, that I have not done in it?" (Is 5:4), and often he has been rejected: "When I looked for it to yield grapes, why did it yield wild grapes?" (Is 5:4).

Our Lord also condemns calumny: some people do try to justify their own behaviour by seeing sin where there is only virtue. "When they find something which is quite obviously good," St Gregory the Great says, "they pry into it to see if there is not also some badness

hidden in it" (*Moralia*, 6, 22). The Baptist's fasting they interpret as the work of the devil; whereas they accuse Jesus of being a glutton. The evangelist has to report these calumnies and accusations spoken against our Lord; otherwise, we would have no notion of the extent of the malice of those who show such furious opposition to Him who went about doing good (Acts 10:38). On other occasions Jesus warned his disciples that they would be treated the same way as he was (cf. Jn 15:20).

The works of Jesus and John the Baptist, each in their own way, lead to the accomplishment of God's plan for man's salvation: the fact that some people do not recognize him does not prevent God's plan being carried into effect.

11:21–24. Chorazin and Bethsaida were thriving cities on the northern shore of the lake of Gennesaret, not very far from Capernaum. During his public ministry Jesus often preached in these cities and worked many miracles there; in Capernaum he revealed his teaching about the Blessed Eucharist (cf. Jn 6:51ff).

---

e. Other ancient authorities read *children* (Luke 7:35)

be brought down to Hades. For if the mighty works done in you had been done in Sodom, it would have remained until this day. [24]But I tell you that it shall be more tolerable on the day of judgment for the land of Sodom than for you."

Lk 10:21f
1 Cor 1:26–29
Sir 51:1
Acts 17:24
Jn 3:35; 17:2
Phil 2:9
Mt 16:7
Gal 1:15f
Mt 12:20
Jer 31:24

Jesus thanks his Father

[25]At that time Jesus declared, "I thank thee, Father, Lord of heaven and earth, that thou hast hidden these things from the wise and understanding and revealed them to babes; [26]yea, Father, for such was thy gracious will.[f] [27]All things have been delivered to me by my Father; and no one knows the Son except the Father, and no one knows the Father except the Son and any one to whom the Son chooses to reveal him.* [28]Come to me, all who labour and are

Tyre, Sidon, Sodom and Gomorrah, the main cities of Phoenicia—all notorious for loose living—were classical examples of divine punishment (cf. Ezek 26–28; Is 23).

Here Jesus is pointing out the ingratitude of people who could know him but who refuse to change. On the day of Judgment (vv. 22 and 24) they will have more explaining to do: "Every one to whom much is given, of him will much be required" (Lk 12:48).

11:25–26. The wise and understanding of this world, that is, those who rely on their own judgment, cannot accept the revelation which Christ has brought us. Supernatural outlook is always connected with humility. A humble person, who gives himself little importance, sees; a person who is full of self-esteem fails to perceive supernatural things.

11:27. Here Jesus formally reveals his divinity. Our knowledge of a person shows our intimacy with him, according to the principle given by St Paul: "For what person knows a man's thoughts except the spirit of the man which is in

him?" (1 Cor 2:11). The Son knows the Father by the same knowledge as that by which the Father knows the Son. This identity of knowledge implies oneness of nature; that is to say, Jesus is God just as the Father is God.

11:28–30. Our Lord calls everyone to come to him. We all find things difficult in one way or another. The history of souls bears out the truth of these words of Jesus. Only the Gospel can fully satisfy the thirst for truth and justice that sincere people feel. Only our Lord, our Master—and those to whom he passes on his power—can sooth the sinner by telling him, "Your sins are forgiven" (Mt 9:2). In this connexion Pope Paul VI teaches: "Jesus says now and always, 'come to me, all who labour and are heavy laden, and I will give you rest.' His attitude towards us is one of invitation, knowledge and compassion; indeed, it is one of offering, promise, friendship, goodness, remedy of our ailments; he is our comforter; indeed, our nourishment, our bread, giving us energy and life" (Homily on Corpus Christi, 13 June 1974).

f. Or *so it was well-pleasing before thee*

heavy laden, and I will give you rest. ²⁹Take my yoke upon you, and learn from me; for I am gentle and lowly in heart, and you will find rest for your souls. ³⁰For my yoke is easy, and my burden is light."

Sir 51:33f
Jer 6:16
1 Kings 12:4
Ps 2:3
1 Jn 5:3

The law of the sabbath

12 ¹At that time Jesus went through the grainfields on the sabbath; his disciples were hungry, and they began to pluck ears of grain and to eat. ²But when the Pharisees saw it, they said to him, "Look, your disciples are doing what is not lawful to do on the sabbath." ³He said to them, "Have you not read what David did, when he was hungry, and those who were with him: ⁴how he entered the house of God and ate the bread of the Presence, which

Mk 2:23–28
Lk 6:1–5
Deut 5:14;
23:26

Ex 20:10

1 Sam 21:7

Lev 24:9

"Come to me": the Master is addressing the crowds who are following him, "harassed and helpless, like sheep without a shepherd" (Mt 9:36). The Pharisees weighed them down with an endless series of petty regulations (cf. Acts 15:10), yet they brought no peace to their souls. Jesus tells these people, and us, about the kind of burden he imposes: "Any other burden oppresses and crushes you, but Christ's actually takes weight off you. Any other burden weighs down, but Christ's gives you wings. If you take a bird's wings away, you might seem to be taking weight off it, but the more weight you take off, the more you tie it down to the earth. There it is on the ground, and you wanted to relieve it of a weight; give it back the weight of its wings and you will see how it flies" (St Augustine, *Sermons*, 126). "All you who go about tormented, afflicted and burdened with the burden of your cares and desires, go forth from them, come to me, and I will refresh you and you shall find for your souls the rest which your desires take from you" (St John of the Cross, *Ascent of Mount Carmel*, book 1, chap. 7, 4).

12:2. "The sabbath": this was the day the Jews set aside for worshipping God.

God himself, the originator of the sabbath (Gen 2:3), ordered the Jewish people to avoid certain kinds of work on this day (Ex 20:8–11; 21:13; Deut 5:14) to leave them free to give more time to God. As time went by, the rabbis complicated this divine precept: by Jesus' time they had extended to thirty-nine the list of kinds of forbidden work.

The Pharisees accuse Jesus' disciples of breaking the sabbath. In the casuistry of the scribes and the Pharisees, plucking ears of corn was the same as harvesting, and crushing them was the same as milling—types of agricultural work forbidden on the sabbath.

12:3–8. Jesus rebuts the Pharisees' accusation by four arguments—the example of David, that of the priests, a correct understanding of the mercy of God and Jesus' own authority over the sabbath.

The first example, which was quite familiar to the people, who were used to listening to the Bible being read, comes from 1 Samuel 21:2–7: David, in flight from the jealousy of King Saul, asks the priest of the shrine at Nob for food for his men; the priest gave them the only bread he had, the holy bread of the Presence; this was the twelve loaves that were

Num 28:9

it was not lawful for him to eat nor for those who were with him, but only for the priests? ⁵Or have you not read in the law how on the sabbath the priests in the temple profane the sabbath, and are guiltless? ⁶I tell you, something greater than the temple is here.

Hos 6:6

⁷And if you had known what this means, 'I desire mercy, and not sacrifice,' you would not have condemned the guiltless. ⁸For the Son of man is lord of the sabbath.'"

Curing of the man with a withered hand

Mk 3:1–6
Lk 6:6–11;
14:3

⁹And he went on from there, and entered their synagogue. ¹⁰And behold, there was a man with a withered hand. And they asked him, "Is it lawful to heal on the sabbath?" so that they might accuse him. ¹¹He said to them, "What man of you, if he has one sheep and it falls into a pit on the sabbath, will not lay hold of it

Lk 14:5

and lift it out? ¹²Of how much more value is a man than a sheep! So it is lawful to do good on the sabbath." ¹³Then he said to the man, "Stretch out your hand." And the man stretched it out, and it

Jn 5:16

was restored, whole like the other. ¹⁴But the Pharisees went out and took counsel against him, how to destroy him.*

Jesus, the servant of God

Mk 3:7–12

¹⁵Jesus, aware of this, withdrew from there. And many followed him, and he healed them all, ¹⁶and ordered them not to make him

---

placed each week on the golden altar of the sanctuary as a perpetual offering from the twelve tribes of Israel (Lev 24:5–9). The second example refers to the priestly ministry to perform the liturgy, priests had to do a number of things on the sabbath but did not thereby break the law of sabbath rest (cf. Num 28:9). On the two other arguments, see the notes on Mt 9:13 and Mk 2:26–27, 28.

12:9–13. Jesus corroborates his teaching by performing this miracle: it is lawful to do good on the sabbath; no law should get in the way of doing good. He therefore rejects the interpretation given by the Pharisees; they are polarized on the letter of the law, to the detriment of God's honour and men's welfare. The very same people who are scandalized by

our Lord's miracle are quite ready to plot his death, even on the sabbath (v. 14).

12:17–21. Once again the sacred text points out the contrast between the contemporary mistaken Jewish notion of a spectacular messianic kingdom and the discernment which Jesus asks of those who witness and accept his teaching and miracles. By providing this long quotation from Isaiah (42:1–4), the evangelist is giving us the key to the teaching contained in chapters 11 and 12: in Jesus the prophecy of the Servant of Yahweh is fulfilled: the lovable and gentle teacher has come to bring the light of truth.

When narrating the passion of our Lord, the Gospels will once again remind us of the figure of the Servant of Yahweh, to show that in Jesus the suffering and

known. [17]This was to fulfil what was spoken by the prophet Is 42:1–4; 41:9
Isaiah:

[18]"Behold my servant whom I have chosen,
my beloved with whom my soul is well pleased.
I will put my Spirit upon him,
and he shall proclaim justice to the Gentiles.
[19]He will not wrangle or cry aloud,
nor will any one hear his voice in the streets;
[20]he will not break a bruised reed
or quench a smouldering wick,
till he brings justice to victory;
[21]and in his name will the Gentiles hope."

Allegations by the Pharisees. The sin against the Holy Spirit

Mk 3:22–30
Lk 11:14–26,
20, 32

[22]Then a blind and dumb demoniac was brought to him, and he healed him, so that the dumb man spoke and saw. [23]And all the people were amazed, and said, "Can this be the Son of David?" [24]But when the Pharisees heard it they said, "It is only by Beelzebul,* the prince of demons, that this man casts out demons." [25]Knowing their thoughts, he said to them, "Every kingdom divided against itself is laid waste, and no city or house divided against itself will stand; [26]and if Satan casts out Satan, he is divided against himself; how then will his kingdom stand? [27]And

---

expiatory aspect of the death of the Servant finds fulfilment (cf. Mt 27:30, with reference to Is 50:6; Mt 8:17 and Is 53:4; Jn 1:38 and Is 53:9–12; etc.).

12:17. Isaiah 42:1–4 speaks of a humble servant, beloved of God, chosen by God. And in fact Jesus, without ceasing to be the Son of God, one in substance with the Father, took the form of a servant (cf. Phil 2:6). This humility led him to cure and care for the poor and afflicted of Israel, without seeking acclaim.

12:18. See the note on Mt 3:16.

12:19. The justice proclaimed by the Servant, who is filled with the Holy Spirit, is not a noisy virtue. We can see the loving, gentle way Jesus worked his miracles, performing righteousness in all

humility. This is how he brings about the triumph of his Father's justice, his plan of revelation and salvation—very quietly and very effectively.

12:20. According to many Fathers, including St Augustine and St Jerome, the bruised reed and the smouldering wick refer to the Jewish people. They also stand for every sinner, for our Lord does not seek the sinner's death but his conversion, and his life (cf. Ezek 33:11). The Gospels often bear witness to this reassuring truth (cf. Lk 15:11–32, the parable of the prodigal son; Mt 18:12–24, the parable of the lost sheep; etc.).

12:22–24. Here is a case of possession by the devil. This consists in an evil spirit taking over a human body. Possession is normally accompanied by certain forms

if I cast out demons by Beelzebul, by whom do your sons cast them out? Therefore they shall be your judges. ²⁸But if it is by the Spirit of God that I cast out demons, then the kingdom of God has come upon you. ²⁹Or how can one enter a strong man's house and plunder his goods, unless he first binds the strong man? Then indeed he may plunder his house. ³⁰He who is not with me is against me, and he who does not gather with me scatters. ³¹Therefore I tell you, every sin and blasphemy will be forgiven men, but the blasphemy against the Spirit will not be forgiven.* ³²And whoever says a word against the Son of man will be forgiven; but whoever speaks against the Holy Spirit will not be forgiven, either in this age or in the age to come.

³³"Either make the tree good, and its fruit good; or make the tree bad, and its fruit bad; for the tree is known by its fruit. ³⁴You

Margin references:
1 Jn 3:8
1 Thess 2:16

Is 49:24
1 Jn 4:4

Mk 9:40
Jn 11:52

Heb 6:4, 6;
10:26
1 Jn 5:16

Lk 12:10
1 Tim 1:13

---

of illness or disease—epilepsy, dumbness, blindness .... Possessed people have lost their self-control; when they are in the trance of possession they are tools of the devil. The evil spirit who has mastery over them sometimes gives them supernatural powers; at other times he torments the person, and may even drive him to suicide (cf. Mt 8:16; 8:28–34; 17:14–21; Mk 1:26; Lk 7:21).

The expulsion of devils by invoking Jesus' name has special significance in the history of salvation. It proves that the coming of Jesus marks the beginning of the Kingdom of God and that the devil has been dispossessed of his territory (Jn 12:31). "The seventy returned with joy, saying 'Lord, even the demons are subject to us in your name!' And he said to them, 'I saw Satan fall like lightning from heaven'" (Lk 10:17–18). Ever since Christ's coming, the devil is on the retreat—which is not to say that there are not still instances of diabolic possession.

12:30. Here Jesus sums up his whole argument against the Pharisees: they are either for him or for the devil. He said the same thing in the Sermon on the Mount: "No one can serve two masters" (Mt

6:24). Those who are not united to Jesus through faith, hope and charity, are against him—and therefore they are on the side of the devil, Jesus' enemy.

Our Lord does not mince words when it comes to asking people to adopt an attitude to his person and his Kingdom. A Christian cannot temporize; if he wants to be a true Christian he must not entertain ideas or approaches which are not in keeping with the content of Revelation and with the teaching of the Church.

Therefore, we must not compromise on matters of faith, trying to adapt Jesus' teaching to suit our convenience or because we are afraid of how other people will react to it. Our Lord wants us to adopt a clear attitude to his person *and* to his teaching.

12:31–32. God wants all men to be saved (1 Tim 2:4) and he calls everyone to repentance (2 Pet 3:9). The Redemption won by Christ is superabundant: it atones for all sins and extends to every man and woman (Rom 5:12–21). Christ gave his Church the power to forgive sins by means of the sacraments of Baptism and Penance. This power is unlimited, that is to say, the Church can pardon all sins of

brood of vipers! how can you speak good, when you are evil? For out of the abundance of the heart the mouth speaks. ³⁵The good man out of his good treasure brings forth good, and the evil man out of his evil treasure brings forth evil. ³⁶I tell you, on the day of judgment men will render account for every careless word they utter; ³⁷for by your words you will be justified, and by your words you will be condemned."

Jn 8:43
Rom 8:7
Lk 6:45

The sign of Jonah

³⁸Then some of the scribes and Pharisees said to him, "Teacher, we wish to see a sign from you." ³⁹But he answered them, "An evil and adulterous generation seeks for a sign; but no sign shall be given to it except the sign of the prophet Jonah. ⁴⁰For as Jonah was three days and three nights in the belly of the whale, so will the Son of

1 Cor 1:22

Jn 2:1f

---

all the baptized as often as they confess their sins with the right disposition. This teaching is a dogma of faith (cf. Council of Trent, *De Paenitentia*, can. 1).

The sin Jesus speaks about here is termed "sin against the Holy Spirit", because external expressions of God's goodness are specially attributed to the third person of the Blessed Trinity. Sin against the Holy Spirit is said to be unforgivable not so much because of its gravity or malice but because of the subjective disposition of the sinner in this case: his attitude shuts the door on repentance. Sin against the Holy Spirit consists in maliciously attributing to the devil the miracles and signs wrought by Christ. Thus, the very nature of this sin blocks the person's route to Christ, who is the only one who can take away the sin of the world (Jn 1:29), and the sinner puts himself outside the range of God's forgiveness. In this sense the sins against the Holy Spirit cannot be forgiven.

12:33–37. Our Lord continues his case against the Pharisees: because he is evil, the devil cannot do good things. And if the works that I do are good, as you can see they are, then they cannot have been

done by the devil; "a sound tree cannot bear evil fruit, nor can a bad tree bear good fruit" (Mt 7:18).

As on other occasions Jesus reminds people that there is a Judgment. The Magisterium of the Church explains that there is a "particular" judgment immediately after one dies, and a "general" judgment at the end of the world (cf. Benedict XII, *Benedictus Deus*).

12:39–40. This sign the Jews were asking for would have been a miracle or some other prodigy; they wanted Jesus, incongruously, to confirm his preaching—given with such simplicity—by dramatic signs. Our Lord replies by announcing the mystery of his death and resurrection, using the parallel of the case of Jonah: "No sign shall be given to it except the sign of the prophet Jonah." Jesus' glorious resurrection is the "sign" *par excellence*, the decisive proof of the divine character of his person, of his mission and of his teaching.

When St Paul (1 Cor 15:3–4) confesses that Jesus Christ "was raised on the third day in accordance with the scriptures" (words that later found their way into the Nicene-Constantinopolitan Creed, the Creed used in the Mass), he

Jn 3:5

man be three days and three nights in the heart of the earth. ⁴¹The men of Nineveh will arise at the judgment with this generation and condemn it; for they repented at the preaching of Jonah, and behold, something greater than Jonah is here. ⁴²The queen of the South will arise at the judgment with this generation and condemn it; for she came from the ends of the earth to hear the wisdom of Solomon, and behold, something greater than Solomon is here.

1 Kings 10:1–10

⁴³"When the unclean spirit has gone out of a man, he passes through waterless places seeking rest, but he finds none. ⁴⁴Then he says, 'I will return to my house from which I came.' And when he comes he finds it empty, swept, and put in order. ⁴⁵Then he goes and brings with him seven other spirits more evil than himself, and they enter and dwell there; and the last state of that man becomes worse than the first. So shall it be also with this evil generation."

2 Pet 2:20

---

must have had this passage particularly in mind. We can see another allusion to Jonah in the words our Lord spoke shortly before his ascension: "Thus it is written, that the Christ should suffer and on the third day rise from the dead" (Lk 24:45–46).

12:41–42. Nineveh was a city in Mesopotamia (modern Iraq) to which the prophet Jonah was sent. The Ninevites did penance (Jn 3:6–9) because they recognized the prophet and accepted his message; whereas Jerusalem does not wish to recognize Jesus, of whom Jonah was merely a figure. The queen of the South was the queen of Sheba in southwestern Arabia, who visited Solomon (1 Kings 10:1–10) and was in awe of the wisdom with which God had endowed the King of Israel. Jesus is also prefigured in Solomon, whom Jewish tradition saw as the epitome of the wise man. Jesus' reproach is accentuated by the example of pagan converts, and gives us a glimpse of the universal scope of Christianity, which will take root among the Gentiles.

There is a certain irony in what Jesus says about "something greater" than Jonah or Solomon having come: really,

he is infinitely greater, but Jesus prefers to tone down the difference between himself and any figure, no matter how important, in the Old Testament.

12:43. Jesus says that when demons are driven out of men they retreat into the wilderness; but that if they repossess a man they torment him in a worse way. St Peter also says that the devil prowls around like a lion seeking someone to devour (1 Pet 5:8) and that people who have been converted and revert to the depravities of their past life become worse than they were before (2 Pet 2:20). Jesus is solemnly warning the Jews of his time that if they continue to reject the light they will end up worse than they were before. The same sad truth applies to the Christian who, after being converted and reconciled to God, allows the devil to enter his soul again.

12:46–47. "Brethren": ancient Hebrew, Aramaic and other languages had no special words for different degrees of relationship, such as are found in more modern languages. In general, all those belonging to the same family, clan and even tribe were "brethren".

The true kinsmen of Jesus

⁴⁶While he was still speaking to the people, behold, his mother and his brethren* stood outside, asking to speak to him.ᵍ ⁴⁸But he replied to the man who told him, "Who is my mother, and who are my brethren?"* ⁴⁹And stretching out his hand toward his disciples, he said, "Here are my mother and my brethren! ⁵⁰For whoever does the will of my Father in heaven is my brother, and sister, and mother."

Mk 3:31–35
Lk 8:19–21
Mt 13:55

Lk 2:49

Rom 8:29
Jn 15:14

6. THE PARABLES OF THE KINGDOM

Parable of the sower. The meaning of parables

13 ¹That same day Jesus went out of the house and sat beside the sea. ²And great crowds gathered about him, so that he got into a boat and sat there; and the whole crowd stood on the beach. ³And he told them many things in parables, saying: "A

Mk 4:1–20
Lk 8:4–15

In the particular case we have here, we should bear in mind that Jesus had different kinds of relatives, in two groups—some on his mother's side, others on St Joseph's. Matthew 13:55–56 mentions, as living in Nazareth, James, Joseph, Simon and Judas ("his brethren") and elsewhere there is reference to Jesus' "sisters" (cf. Mk 6:3). But in Matthew 27:56 we are told that the James and Joseph were sons of a Mary distinct from the Blessed Virgin, and that Simon and Judas were not brothers of James and Joseph, but seemingly children of a brother of St Joseph.

Jesus, on the other hand, was known to everyone as "the son of Mary" (Mk 6:3) or "the carpenter's son" (Mt 13:55).

The Church has always maintained as absolutely certain that Jesus had no brothers or sisters in the full meaning of the term: it is a dogma that Mary was ever-Virgin (cf. the note on Mt 1:25).

12:48–50. Jesus obviously loved his Mother and St Joseph. He uses this episode to teach us that in his Kingdom human ties do not take precedence. In Luke 8:19 the same teaching is to be found. Jesus regards the person who does the will of his heavenly Father as a member of his own family. Therefore, even though it means going against natural family feelings, a person should do just that when needs be in order to perform the mission the Father has entrusted to him (cf. Lk 2:49).

We can say that Jesus loved Mary more because of the bonds between them created by grace than because he was her son by natural generation: Mary's divine motherhood is the source of all our Lady's other prerogatives; but this very motherhood is, in its turn, the first and greatest of the graces with which Mary was endowed.

13:3. Chapter 13 of St Matthew includes as many as seven of Jesus' parables,

g. Other ancient authorities insert verse 47, *Some one told him "Your mother and your brothers are standing outside, asking to speak to you"*

sower went out to sow. [4]And as he sowed, some seeds fell along the path, and the birds came and devoured them. [5]Other seeds fell on rocky ground, where they had not much soil, and immediately they sprang up, since they had no depth of soil, [6]but when the sun rose they were scorched; and since they had no root they withered away. [7]Other seeds fell upon thorns, and the thorns grew up and choked them. [8]Other seeds fell on good soil and brought forth

---

which is the reason why it is usually called "the parable discourse" or the "parabolic discourse". Because of their similarity of content and setting these parables are often called the "Kingdom parables", and also the "parables of the Lake", because Jesus taught them on the shore of Lake Gennesaret. Jesus uses these elaborate comparisons (parables) to explain certain features of the Kingdom of God, which he has come to establish (cf. Mt 3:2)—its tiny, humble origins; its steady growth; its worldwide scope; its salvific force. God calls everyone to salvation but only those attain it who receive God's call with good dispositions and who do not change their attitude; the value of the spiritual benefits the Kingdom brings— so valuable that one should give up everything to obtain them; the fact that good and bad are all mixed together until the harvest-time, or the time of God's judgment; the intimate connexion between earthly and heavenly aspects of the Kingdom, until it reaches its point of full development at the end of time.

On Jesus' lips, parables are exceptionally effective. By using parables he keeps his listeners' attention, whether they are uneducated or not, and by means of the most ordinary things of daily life he sheds light on the deepest supernatural mysteries. He used the parable device in a masterly way; his parables are quite unique; they carry the seal of his personality; through them he has graphically shown us the riches of grace, the life of the Church, the demands of the faith and even the mystery of God's own inner life.

Jesus' teaching continues to provide every generation with light and guidance on moral conduct. By reading and reflecting on his parables one can savour the adorable humanity of the Saviour, who showed such kindness to the people who crowded around to hear him—and who shows the same readiness to listen to our prayers, despite our dullness, and to reply to our healthy curiosity when we try to make out his meaning.

13:3–8. Anyone who has visited the fertile plain to the west of the lake of Gennesaret will appreciate Jesus' touching description in the parable of the sower. The plain is crisscrossed by paths; it is streaked with rocky ground, often with the rocks lying just beneath the surface, and with the courses of rivulets, dry for most of the year but still retaining some moisture. Here and there are clumps of large thorn bushes. When the agricultural worker sows seed in this mixed kind of land, he knows that some seed will fare better than others.

13:9. Jesus did not explain this parable there and then. It was quite usual for parables to be presented in the first instance as a kind of puzzle to gain the listener's attention, excite his curiosity and fix the parable in his memory. It may well be that Jesus wanted to allow his more interested listeners to identify themselves by coming back to hear him again—as happened with his disciples.

grain, some a hundredfold, some sixty, some thirty. [9]He who has ears,[h] let him hear."

[10]Then the disciples came and said to him, "Why do you speak to them in parables?" [11]And he answered them, "To you it has been given to know the secrets of the kingdom of heaven, but to them it has not been given. [12]For to him who has will more be given, and he will have abundance; but from him who has not,

Mk 4:25
Lk 8:18

The rest—who listened out of idle curiosity or for too human reasons (to see him work miracles)—would not benefit from hearing a more detailed and deeper explanation of the parable.

13:10–13. The kind of kingdom Jesus was going to establish did not suit the Judaism of his time, largely because of the Jews' nationalistic, earthbound idea of the Messiah to come. In his preaching Jesus takes account of the different outlooks of his listeners, as can be seen in the attitudes described in the parable of the sower. If people were well disposed to him, the enigmatic nature of the parable would stimulate their interest; and Jesus later did give his many disciples a fuller explanation of its meaning; but there was no point in doing this if people were not ready to listen.

Besides, parables—as indeed any type of comparison or analogy—are used to reveal or explain something that is not easy to understand, as was the case with the supernatural things Jesus was explaining. One has to shade one's eyes to see things if the sun is too bright; otherwise, one is blinded and sees nothing. Similarly, parables help to shade supernatural brightness to allow the listener to grasp meaning without being blinded by it.

These verses also raise a very interesting question: how can divine revelation and grace produce such widely differing responses in people? What is at

work here is the mystery of divine grace —which is an unmerited gift—and of man's response to this grace. What Jesus says here underlines man's responsibility to be ready to accept God's grace and to respond to it. Jesus' reference to Isaiah (Mt 13:14–15) is a prophecy of that hardness of heart which is a punishment meted out to those who resist grace.

These verses need to be interpreted in the light of three points: 1) Jesus Christ loved everyone, including the people of his own hometown: he gave his life in order to save all men; 2) the parable is a literary form designed to get ideas across clearly: its ultimate aim is to teach, not to mislead or obscure; 3) lack of appreciation for divine grace is something blameworthy, which does merit punishment; however, Jesus did not come directly to punish anyone, but rather to save everyone.

13:12. Jesus is telling his disciples that, precisely because they have faith in him and want to have a good grasp of his teaching, they will be given a deeper understanding of divine truths. But those who do not "follow him" (cf. the note on Mt 4:18–22) will later lose interest in the things of God and will grow ever blinder: it is as if the little they have is being taken away from them.

This verse also helps us understand the meaning of the parable of the sower, a parable which gives a wonderful expla-

---

h. Other ancient authorities add here and in verse 43 *to hear*

[handwritten margin note: Schema — Hebrew — hear]

Deut 29:4

Is 6:9f *[handwritten: ~ 11]*

Jn 12:40

Acts 28:26f

even what he has will be taken away.* ¹³This is why I speak to them in parables, because seeing they do not see, and hearing they do not hear, nor do they understand. ¹⁴With them indeed is fulfilled the prophecy of Isaiah which says:

'You shall indeed hear but never understand,
and you shall indeed see but never perceive.
¹⁵For this people's heart has grown dull,
and their ears are heavy of hearing,
and their eyes they have closed,
lest they should perceive with their eyes,
and hear with their ears,
and understand with their heart,
and turn for me to heal them.'

[handwritten margin note: Covenant infidelity]

Lk 10:23f

¹⁶But blessed are your eyes, for they see, and your ears, for they hear. ¹⁷Truly, I say to you, many prophets and righteous men longed to see what you see, and did not see it, and to hear what you hear, and did not hear it.

---

nation of the supernatural economy of divine grace: God gives grace, and man freely responds to that grace. The result is that those who respond to grace generously receive additional grace and so grow steadily in grace and holiness; whereas those who reject God's gifts become closed up within themselves; through their selfishness and attachment to sin they eventually lose God's grace entirely. In this verse, then, our Lord gives a clear warning: with the full weight of his divine authority he exhorts us—without taking away our freedom— to act responsibly: the gifts God keeps sending us should yield fruit; we should make good use of the opportunities for Christian sanctification which are offered us in the course of our lives.

13:14–15. Only well-disposed people grasp the meaning of God's words. It is not enough just to hear them physically. In the course of Jesus' preaching the prophetic words of Isaiah come true once again.

However, we should not think that

not wanting to hear or to understand was something exclusive to certain contemporaries of Jesus; each one of us is at times hard of hearing, hard-hearted and dull-minded in the presence of God's grace and saving word. Moreover, it is not enough to be familiar with the teaching of the Church: it is absolutely necessary to put the faith into practice, with all that that implies, morally and ascetically. Jesus was fixed to the wood of the cross not only by nails and by the sins of certain Jews but also by our sins—sins committed centuries later but which afflicted the most sacred humanity of Jesus Christ, who bore the burden of our sins. See the note on Mk 4:11–12.

13:16–17. In contrast with the closed attitude of many Jews who witnessed Jesus' life but did not believe in him, the disciples are praised by our Lord for their docility to grace, their openness to recognizing him as the Messiah and to accepting his teaching.

He calls his disciples blessed, happy. As he says, the prophets and just men

¹⁸"Hear then the parable of the sower. ¹⁹When any one hears the word of the kingdom and does not understand it, the evil one comes and snatches away what is sown in his heart; this is what was sown along the path. ²⁰As for what was sown on rocky ground, this is he who hears the word and immediately receives it with joy; ²¹yet he has no root in himself, but endures for a while, and when tribulation or persecution arises on account of the word, immediately he falls away.ⁱ ²²As for what was sown among thorns, this is he who hears the word, but the cares of the world and the delight in riches choke the word, and it proves unfruitful. ²³As for what was sown on good soil, this is he who hears the word and understands it; he indeed bears fruit, and yields, in one case a hundredfold, in another sixty, and in another thirty."

1 Tim 6:9

The parable of the weeds

²⁴Another parable he put before them, saying, "The kingdom of heaven may be compared to a man who sowed good seed in his

---

and women of the Old Testament had for centuries lived in hope of enjoying one day the peace the future Messiah would bring, but they had died without experiencing this good fortune. Simeon, towards the end of his long life, was filled with joy on seeing the infant Jesus when he was presented in the temple: "he took him up in his arms and blessed God and said, 'Lord, now lettest thou thy servant depart in peace, according to thy word; for mine eyes have seen thy salvation'" (Lk 2:28–30). During our Lord's public life, his disciples were fortunate enough to see and be on close terms with him; later they would recall that incomparable gift, and one of them would begin his first letter in these words: "That which was from the beginning, which we have heard, which we have seen with our eyes, which we have looked upon and touched with our hands, concerning the word of life; [...] that which we have seen and heard we proclaim also to you, so that you may have fellowship with us;

and our fellowship is with the Father and with his Son Jesus Christ. And we are writing this that our [or: your] joy may be complete" (1 Jn 1:1–4).

This exceptional good fortune was, obviously, not theirs because of special merit: God planned it; it was he who decided that the time had come for the Old Testament prophecies to be fulfilled. In any event, God gives every soul opportunities to meet him: each of us has to be sensitive enough to grasp them and not let them pass. There were many men and women in Palestine who saw and heard the Incarnate Son of God but did not have the spiritual sensitivity to see in him what the apostles and disciples saw.

13:19. He does not understand because he does not love—not because he is not clever enough: lack of love opens the door of the soul to the devil.

13:24–25. "The situation is clear: the field is fertile and the seed is good; the

---

i. Or *stumbles*

field; ²⁵but while men were sleeping, his enemy came and sowed weeds among the wheat, and went away. ²⁶So when the plants came up and bore grain, then the weeds appeared also. ²⁷And the servants ʲ of the householder came and said to him, 'Sir, did you not sow good seed in your field? How then has it weeds?' ²⁸He said to them, 'An enemy has done this.' The servants ʲ said to him, 'Then do you want us to go and gather them?' ²⁹But he said, 'No; lest in gathering the weeds you root up the wheat along with them. ³⁰Let both grow together until the harvest; and at harvest time I will tell the reapers, Gather the weeds first and bind them in bundles to be burned, but gather the wheat into my barn.' "

Mk 4:30–32
Lk 13:18–19;
17:6

Ezek 17:23;
31:6

The mustard seed; the leaven

³¹Another parable he put before them saying, "The kingdom of heaven is like a grain of mustard seed which a man took and sowed in his field; ³²it is the smallest of all seeds, but when it has

---

Lord of the field has scattered the seed at the right moment and with great skill. He even has watchmen to make sure that the field is protected. If, afterwards, there are weeds among the wheat, it is because men have failed to respond, because they—and Christians in particular—have fallen asleep and allowed the enemy to approach" (St Josemaría Escrivá, *Christ Is Passing By*, 123).

13:25. This weed—cockle—looks very like wheat and can easily be mistaken for it until the ears appear. If it gets ground up with wheat it contaminates the flour and any bread made from that flour causes severe nausea when eaten. In the East personal vengeance sometimes took the form of sowing cockle among an enemy's wheat. Roman law prescribed penalties for this crime.

13:28. "When the careless servants ask the Lord why weeds have grown in his field, the explanation is obvious: '*inimicus homo hoc fecit*: an enemy has done this.'

We Christians should have been on guard to make sure that the good things placed in this world by the Creator were developed in the service of truth and good. But we have fallen asleep—a sad thing, that sluggishness of our heart! while the enemy and all those who serve him worked incessantly. You can see how the weeds have grown abundantly everywhere" (ibid., 123).

13:29–30. The end of this parable gives a symbolic explanation of why God allows evil to have its way for a time—and for its ultimate extirpation. Evil is to run its course on earth until the end of time; therefore, we should not be scandalized by the presence of evil in the world. It will be obliterated not in this life, but after death; at the Judgment (the harvest) the good will go to heaven and the bad to hell.

13:31–32. Here, the man is Jesus Christ and the field, the world. The grain of mustard seed is the preaching of the

j. Or *slaves*

106

grown it is the greatest of shrubs and becomes a tree, so that the
birds of the air come and make nests in its branches." ~Ps 104:12~

³³He told them another parable. "The kingdom of heaven is
like leaven which a woman took and hid in three measures of
meal, till it was all leavened." *disproportionate* (mother Theresa example) ~Lk 13:20f~

³⁴All this Jesus said to the crowds in parables; indeed he said
nothing to them without a parable. ³⁵This was to fulfil what was
spoken by the prophet:ᵏ ~Mk 4:33f~ ~Ps 78:2~

"I will open my mouth in parables,
I will utter what has been hidden
since the foundation of the world."

The parable of the weeds explained *speaks to the disciples*
³⁶Then he left the crowds and went into the house. And his disciples came to him, saying, "Explain to us the parable of the weeds
of the field." ³⁷He answered, "He who sows the good seed is the

Gospel and the Church, which from very small beginnings will spread throughout the world. The parable clearly refers to the universal scope and spread of the Kingdom of God: the Church, which embraces all mankind of every kind and condition, in every latitude and in all ages, is forever developing in spite of obstacles, thanks to God's promise and aid.

13:33. This comparison is taken from everyday experience: just as leaven gradually ferments all the dough, so the Church spreads to convert all nations. The leaven is also a symbol of the individual Christian. Living in the middle of the world and retaining his Christian quality, he wins souls for Christ by his word and example: "Our calling to be children of God, in the midst of the world, requires us not only to seek our own personal holiness, but also to go out onto all the ways of the earth, to convert them into roadways that will carry souls over all obstacles and lead them to the Lord. As we take part in all temporal

activities as ordinary citizens, we are to become leaven acting on the mass" (ibid., 120).

13:34–35. Revelation, God's plans, are hidden (cf. Mt 11:25) from those who are not disposed to accept them. The evangelist wishes to emphasize the need for simplicity and for docility to the Gospel. By recalling Psalm 78:2, he tells us once more, under divine inspiration, that the Old Testament prophecies find their fulfilment in our Lord's preaching.

13:36–43. While making its way on earth, the Church is composed of good and bad people, just men and sinners: they are mixed in with one another until the harvest time, the end of the world, when the Son of man, in his capacity as Judge of the living and the dead, will divide the good from the bad at the Last Judgment—the former going to eternal glory, the inheritance of the saints; the latter, to the eternal fire of hell. Although the just and the sinners are now side by side, the

k. Other ancient authorities read *the prophet Isaiah*

1 Cor 3:9

Son of man; ³⁸the field is the world, and the good seed means the sons of the kingdom; the weeds are the sons of the evil one, ³⁹and the enemy who sowed them is the devil; the harvest is the close of the age, and the reapers are angels. ⁴⁰Just as the weeds are gathered and burned with fire, so will it be at the close of the age. ⁴¹The Son of man will send his angels, and they will gather out of his kingdom all causes of sin and all evildoers, ⁴²and throw them into the furnace of fire; there men will weep and gnash their teeth. ⁴³Then the righteous will shine like the sun in the kingdom of their Father. He who has ears, let him hear.

Jn 15:6

Zeph 1:3
Mt 25:31–46;
7:23

Dan 12:3

The hidden treasure; the pearl; the net

Lk 14:33
Phil 3:7
Prov 2:4

⁴⁴"The kingdom of heaven is like treasure hidden in a field, which a man found and covered up; then in his joy he goes and sells all that he has and buys that field.

Prov 8:10f

⁴⁵"Again, the kingdom of heaven is like a merchant in search of fine pearls, ⁴⁶who, on finding one pearl of great value, went and sold all that he had and bought it.

Church has the right and the duty to exclude those who cause scandal, especially those who attack its doctrine and unity; this it can do through ecclesiastical excommunication and other canonical penalties. However, excommunication has a medicinal and pastoral function—to correct those who are obstinate in error, and to protect others from them.

13:44–46. In these two parables Jesus shows the supreme value of the Kingdom of heaven, and the attitude people need if they are to attain it. The parables are very alike, but it is interesting to note the differences: the treasure means abundance of gifts; the pearl indicates the beauty of the Kingdom. The treasure is something stumbled upon; the pearl, the result of a lengthy search; but in both instances the finder is filled with joy. Faith, vocation, true wisdom, desire for heaven, are things that sometimes are discovered suddenly and unexpectedly, and sometimes after much searching (cf. St Gregory the Great, *In Evangelia homiliae*, 11). However, the

man's attitude is the same in both parables and is described in the same terms: "he goes and sells all that he has and buys it": detachment, generosity, is indispensable for obtaining the treasure.

"Anyone who understands the Kingdom which Christ proposes realizes that it is worth staking everything to obtain it […]. The Kingdom of heaven is difficult to win. No one can be sure of achieving it, but the humble cry of a repentant man can open wide its doors" (St Josemaría Escrivá, *Christ Is Passing By*, 180).

13:47. "Fish of every kind": almost all the Greek manuscripts and early translations say "All kinds of things". A dragnet is very long and about two metres wide; when it is extended between two boats it forms double or triple mesh with the result that when it is pulled in it collects all sorts of things in addition to fish— algae, weeds, rubbish etc.

This parable is rather like the parable of the cockle, but in a fishing context: the net is the Church, the sea the world.

⁴⁷"Again, the kingdom of heaven is like a net which was thrown into the sea and gathered fish of every kind; ⁴⁸when it was full, men drew it ashore and sat down and sorted the good into vessels but threw away the bad. ⁴⁹So it will be at the close of the age. The angels will come out and separate the evil from the righteous, ⁵⁰and throw them into the furnace of fire; there men will weep and gnash their teeth.

⁵¹"Have you understood all this?" They said to him, "Yes." ⁵²And he said to them, "Therefore every scribe who has been trained for the kingdom of heaven is like a householder who brings out of his treasure what is new and what is old."

7. JESUS WITHDRAWS TO THE BORDER COUNTRY

No one is a prophet in his own country

⁵³And when Jesus had finished these parables he went away from there, ⁵⁴and coming to his own country he taught them in their

Mk 6:1–6
Lk 4:15–30

We can easily find in this parable the dogmatic truth of the Judgment: at the end of time God will judge men and separate the good from the bad. It is interesting to note our Lord's repeated references to the last things, especially Judgment and hell: he emphasizes these truths because of man's great tendency to forget them: "All these things are said to make sure that no one can make the excuse that he does not know about them: this excuse would be valid only if eternal punishment were spoken about in ambiguous terms" (St Gregory the Great, *In Evangelia homiliae*, 11).

13:52. "Scribe": among the Jews a scribe was a religious teacher, a specialist in Holy Scripture and its application to life. Our Lord here uses this old word to refer to the apostles, who will have the role of teachers in his Church. Thus, the apostles and their successors, the bishops, are the *Ecclesia docens*, the teaching Church; they have the authority and the mission to teach. The Pope and the Bishops exercise

this authority directly and are also helped in this by priests. The other members of the Church form the *Ecclesia discens*, the learning Church. However, every disciple of Christ, every Christian who has received Christ's teaching, has a duty to pass this teaching on to others, in language they can understand; therefore, he should make sure he has a good grasp of Christian doctrine. The treasure of Revelation is so rich that it can provide teaching that applies to all times and situations. It is for the word of God to enlighten all ages and situations—not the other way around. Therefore, the Church and its pastors preach, not new things, but a single unchanging truth contained in the treasure of Revelation: for the past two thousand years the Gospel has always been "good news".

13:53–58. The Nazarenes' surprise is partly due to people's difficulty in recognizing anything exceptional and supernatural in those with whom they have been on familiar terms. Hence the

109

synagogue, so that they were astonished, and said, "Where did this man get this wisdom and these mighty works? [55]Is not this the carpenter's son? Is not his mother called Mary? And are not his brethren James and Joseph and Simon and Judas? [56]And are not all his sisters with us? Where then did this man get all this?" [57]And they took offence at him. But Jesus said to them, "A prophet is not without honour except in his own country and in his own house." [58]And he did not do many mighty works there, because of their unbelief.

Jn 7:15, 52

Jn 4:44

The martyrdom of John the Baptist

Mk 6:14,
17–30
Lk 9:7–9; 3:19f

14 [1]At that time Herod the tetrarch heard about the fame of Jesus; [2]and he said to his servants, "This is John the Baptist, he has been raised from the dead; that is why these powers are at work in him." [3]For Herod had seized John and bound him and put him in prison, for the sake of Herodias, his brother Philip's wife;[1] [4]because John said to him, "It is not lawful for you to have her." [5]And though he wanted to put him to death, he feared the people, because they held him to be a prophet. [6]But when Herod's birthday came, the daughter of Herodias danced before the company, and pleased Herod, [7]so that he promised with an oath to give her whatever she might ask. [8]Prompted by her mother, she said, "Give me the head of John the Baptist here on a

Lev 18:16;
20:21

---

saying, "No one is a prophet in his own country." These old neighbours were also jealous of Jesus. Where did he acquire this wisdom? Why him rather than us? They were unaware of the mystery of Jesus' conception; surprise and jealousy cause them to be shocked, to look down on Jesus and not to believe in him: "He came to his own home, and his own people received him not" (Jn 1:11).

"The carpenter's son": this is the only reference in the Gospel to St Joseph's occupation (in Mk 6:3 Jesus himself is described as a "carpenter"). Probably in a town like Nazareth the carpenter was a general tradesman who could turn his hand to jobs ranging from metalwork to making furniture or agricultural implements.

For an explanation of Jesus' "brethren", see the note on Mt 12:46–47.

14:1. Herod the tetrarch, Herod Antipas (see the note on Mt 2:1), is the same Herod as appears later in the account of the Passion (cf. Lk 23:7ff). A son of Herod the Great, Antipas governed Galilee and Perea in the name of the Roman emperor; according to Flavius Josephus, the Jewish historian (*Jewish Antiquities*, 18, 5, 4), he was married to a daughter of an Arabian king, but in spite of this he lived in concubinage with Herodias, his brother's wife. St John the Baptist, and Jesus himself, often criticized the tetrarch's immoral life, which was in conflict with the sexual morality laid down in the Law (Lev 18:16; 20:21) and was a cause of scandal.

l. Other ancient authorities read *his brother's wife*

platter." [9]And the king was sorry; but because of his oaths and his guests he commanded it to be given; [10]he sent and had John beheaded in the prison, [11]and his head was brought on a platter and given to the girl, and she brought it to her mother. [12]And his disciples came and took the body and buried it; and they went and told Jesus.

First miracle of the loaves and fish *points to the Eucharist*

[13]Now when Jesus heard this, he withdrew from there in a boat to a lonely place apart. But when the crowds heard it, they followed him on foot from the towns. [14]As he went ashore he saw a great throng; and he had compassion on them, and healed their sick. [15]When it was evening, the disciples came to him and said, "This is a lonely place, and the day is now over; send the crowds away to go into the villages and buy food for themselves." [16]Jesus said, "They need not go away; you give them something to eat." [17]They said to him, "We have only five loaves here and two fish." [18]And he said, "Bring them here to me." [19]Then he ordered the crowds to sit down on the grass; and taking the five loaves and the two fish he looked up to heaven, and blessed, and broke and gave the loaves to the disciples, and the disciples gave them to the crowds. [20]And they all ate and were satisfied. And they took up twelve baskets full of the broken pieces left over. [21]And those who ate were about five thousand men, besides women and children.

Mk 6:31–44
Lk 9:10–17
Jn 6:1–13

12 tribes

2 Kings 4:44

Mk 6:45–56
Jn 6:15–21

14:3–12. Towards the end of the first century Flavius Josephus wrote of these same events. He gives additional information—specifying that it was in the fortress of Makeronte that John was imprisoned (this fortress was on the eastern bank of the Dead Sea, and was the scene of the banquet in question) and that Herodias' daughter was called Salome.

14:9. St Augustine comments: "Amid the excesses and sensuality of the guests, oaths are rashly made, which then are unjustly kept" (*Sermons*, 10). It is a sin against the second commandment of God's Law to make an oath to do something unjust; any such oath has no binding force. In fact, if one keeps it—as

Herod did—one commits an additional sin. The Catechism also teaches that one offends against this precept if one swears something untrue, or swears needlessly (cf. St Pius V, *Catechism*, 3, 3, 24). Cf. the note on Mt 5:33–37.

14:14–21. This episode must have occurred in the middle of springtime, because the grass was green (Mk 6:40; Jn 6:10). In the Near East loaves were usually made very thin, which meant it was easy to break them by hand and distribute them to those at table; this was usually done by the head of the household or the senior person at the meal. Our Lord follows this custom, and the miracle occurs when Jesus breaks the bread. The disciples then distribute it among the crowd.

Jesus walks on the water

Lk 6:12; 9:18

[22] Then he made the disciples get into the boat and go before him to the other side, while he dismissed the crowds. [23] And after he had dismissed the crowds he went up into the hills by himself to pray. When evening came, he was there alone, [24] but the boat by this time was many furlongs distant from the land,[m] beaten by the waves; for the wind was against them. [25] And in the fourth watch

Lk 24:37

of the night he came to them, walking on the sea. [26] But when the disciples saw him walking on the sea, they were terrified, saying, "It is a ghost!" And they cried out for fear. [27] But immediately he spoke to them, saying, "Take heart, it is I; have no fear."

[28] And Peter answered him, "Lord, if it is you, bid me come to you on the water." [29] He said, "Come." So Peter got out of the boat and walked on the water and came to Jesus; [30] but when he saw the wind,[n] he was afraid, and beginning to sink he cried out, "Lord, save me." [31] Jesus immediately reached out his hand and caught him, saying to him, "O man of little faith, why did you doubt?"

Here again we can see Jesus' desire to have people cooperate with him.

14:22–23. It has been a very full day, like so many others. First Jesus works many cures (14:14) and then performs the remarkable miracle of the multiplication of the loaves and the fish, a symbol of the future Eucharist. The crowds who have been following him were avid for food, teaching and consolation. Jesus "had compassion on them" (14:14), curing their sick and giving them the comfort of his teaching and the nourishment of food. He continues to do the same, down the centuries, tending to our needs and comforting us with his word and with the nourishment of his own body. Jesus must have been very moved, realizing the vivifying effect the Blessed Sacrament would have on the lives of Christians—a sacrament which is a mystery of life and faith and love. It is understandable that he should feel the need to spend some hours in private to speak to his Father. Jesus' private prayer, in an interlude between one demanding activity and another, teaches us that every Christian needs to take time out for recollection, to speak to his Father, God. On Jesus' frequent personal prayer see, for example, Mk 1:35; 6:47; Lk 5:16; 6:12. See the notes on Mt 6:5–6 and Mt 7:7–11.

14:24–33. This remarkable episode of Jesus walking on the sea must have made a deep impression on the apostles. It was one of their outstanding memories of the life they shared with the Master. It is reported not only by St Matthew, but also by St Mark (6:45–52), who would have heard about it from St Peter, and by St John (6:14–21).

Storms are very frequent on Lake Gennesaret; they cause huge waves and are very dangerous to fishing boats. During his prayer on the hill, Jesus is still mindful of his disciples; he sees them trying to cope with the wind and the

m. Other ancient authorities read *was out on the sea*   **n.** Other ancient authorities read *strong wind*

³²And when they got into the boat, the wind ceased. ³³And those in the boat worshipped him, saying, "Truly you are the Son of God."

Cures in Gennesaret

³⁴And when they had crossed over, they came to land at Gennesaret. ³⁵And when the men of that place recognized him, they sent round to all that region and brought to him all that were sick, ³⁶and besought him that they might only touch the fringe of his garment; and as many as touched it were made well.

Lk 6:19

The tradition of the elders. True cleanness

15 ¹Then Pharisees and scribes came to Jesus from Jerusalem and said, ²"Why do your disciples transgress the tradition of the elders? For they do not wash their hands when they eat." ³He answered them, "And why do you transgress the commandment of God for the sake of your tradition? ⁴For God commanded,

Mk 7:1–23
Deut 4:2
Lk 11:38

---

waves and comes to their rescue once he has finished praying. This episode has applications to Christian life. The Church, like the apostles' boat, also gets into difficulties, and Jesus who watches over his Church comes to its rescue also, after allowing it wrestle with obstacles and be strengthened in the process. He gives us encouragement: "Take heart, it is I; have no fear" (14:27); and we show our faith and fidelity by striving to keep an even keel, and by calling on his aid when we feel ourselves weakening: "Lord, save me" (14:30), words of St Peter which every soul uses when he has recourse to Jesus, his Saviour. Then our Lord does save us, and we urgently confess our faith: "Truly you are the Son of God" (14:33).

14:29–31. St John Chrysostom (*Hom. on St Matthew*, 50) comments that in this episode Jesus taught Peter to realize, from his own experience, that all his strength came from our Lord and that he could not rely on his own resources, on his own weakness and wretchedness.

Chrysostom goes as far as to say that "if we fail to play our part, God ceases to help us." Hence the reproach, "O man of little faith" (14:31). When Peter began to be afraid and to doubt, he started to sink, until again, full of faith, he called out, "Lord, save me." If at any time we, like Peter, should begin to weaken, we too should try to bring our faith into play and call on Jesus to save us.

14:34–36. Learning from the faith of these people on the shore of Lake Gennesaret, every Christian should approach the adorable humanity of the Saviour. Christ—God and Man—is accessible to us in the sacrament of the Eucharist. "When you approach the tabernacle remember that *he* has been awaiting you for twenty centuries" (St Josemaría Escrivá, *The Way*, 537).

15:3–4. "For God commanded": it is interesting to note the respect and formality with which Jesus refers to the commandments of the Law of God given through Moses—in this case, the fourth

Ex 20:12;
21:17
Deut 5:16 'Honour your father and your mother,' and, 'He who speaks evil of father or mother, let him surely die.' ⁵But you say, 'If any one tells his father or his mother, What you would have gained from me is given to God,° he need not honour his father.'* ⁶So, for the sake of your tradition, you have made void the wordᵖ of God.

Is 29:13 ⁷You hypocrites! Well did Isaiah prophesy of you, when he said:

⁸ 'This people honours me with their lips,

    but their heart is far from me;

⁹ in vain do they worship me,

    teaching as doctrines the precepts of men.' "

¹⁰And he called the people to him and said to them, "Hear and 1 Tim 4:4 understand: ¹¹not what goes into the mouth defiles a man, but what comes out of the mouth, this defiles a man." ¹²Then the disciples came and said to him, "Do you know that the Pharisees Jn 15:2 were offended when they heard this saying?" ¹³He answered, Lk 6:39
Jn 9:40
Rom 2:19 "Every plant which my heavenly Father has not planted will be rooted up. ¹⁴Let them alone; they are blind guides. And if a blind

---

commandment (cf. Ex 20:12; 21:17). Following its divine Master, the Church sees the ten commandments summing up all human and Christian morality, as the divine-positive formulation of basic natural law. Each and every one of the ten commandments of the Law of God should be lovingly kept, even if this calls for heroism.

15:5–6. Over the years teachers of the Law (scribes) and priests of the temple had distorted the true meaning of the fourth commandment. In Jesus' time, they were saying that people who contributed to the temple in cash or in kind were absolved from supporting their parents: it would be sacrilegious for parents to lay claim to this *corban* (offerings for the altar). People educated in this kind of thinking felt that they were keeping the fourth commandment—in fact, fulfilling it in the best way possible—and they were praised for their piety by the religious leaders of the

nation. But what in fact it meant was that, under the cloak of piety, they were leaving elderly parents to fend for themselves. Jesus, who is Messiah and God, is the one who can correctly interpret the Law. Here he explains the proper scope of the fourth commandment, exposing the error of Jewish practice at the time.

For Christians, therefore, the fourth commandment includes affectionate help of parents if they are old or needy, even if one has other family, social or religious obligations to attend to. Children should check regularly on whether they are looking after their parents properly.

15:6–9. Jewish man-made tradition was forever adding extra little precepts or interpretations onto the Law of God; by Jesus' time these constituted almost another law. This tradition was so incredibly detailed (and sometimes quite ridiculous) that it tended to suffocate the spirit of the Law of God instead of helping a

---

o. Or *an offering* **p.** Other ancient authorities read *law*

man leads a blind man, both will fall into a pit." [15]But Peter said to him, "Explain the parable to us." [16]And he said, "Are you also still without understanding? [17]Do you not see that whatever goes into the mouth passes into the stomach, and so passes on?q [18]But what comes out of the mouth proceeds from the heart, and this defiles a man. [19]For out of the heart come evil thoughts, murder, adultery, fornication, theft, false witness, slander. [20]These are what defile a man; but to eat with unwashed hands does not defile a man."

Gen 8:21

The Canaanite woman

[21]And Jesus went away from there and withdrew to the district of Tyre and Sidon. [22]And behold, a Canaanite woman from that region came out and cried, "Have mercy on me, O Lord, Son of David; my daughter is severely possessed by a demon." [23]But he did not answer her a word. And his disciples came and begged

Mk 7:24–30

---

person fulfil that Law. This is what our Lord is referring to here so bluntly. God himself, through Moses, sought to protect his Law by ordering that nothing be added to or taken from what he had commanded (cf. Deut 4:2).

15:10–20. Our Lord proclaims the true meaning of moral precepts and makes it clear that man has to answer to God for his actions. The scribes' mistake consisted in concentrating on externals and not giving pride of place to interior purity of heart. For example, they saw prayer in terms of exact recital of fixed forms of words rather than as a raising of the soul to God (cf. Mt 6:5–6). The same thing happened in the case of dietary regulations.

Jesus avails himself of the particular cases dealt with in this passage to teach us where to find the true centre of moral action: it lies in man's personal decision, good or evil, a decision that is shaped in his heart and then expressed in the form of action. For example, the

sins which our Lord lists are sins committed in the human heart prior to being acted out. In the Sermon on the Mount he already said this: "Every one who looks at a woman lustfully has already committed adultery with her in his heart" (Mt 5:28).

15:21–22. Tyre and Sidon were Phoenician cities on the Mediterranean coast, in present-day Lebanon. They were never part of Galilee but they were near its northwestern border. In Jesus' time they were outside the territory of Herod Antipas (see the note on Mt 2:1). Jesus withdrew to this area to escape persecution from Herod and from the Jewish authorities and to concentrate on training his apostles.

Most of the inhabitants of the district of Tyre and Sidon were pagans. St Matthew calls this woman a "Canaanite"; according to Genesis (10:15), this district was one of the first to be settled by the Canaanites; St Mark describes the woman as a "Syrophoenician" (Mk 7:26).

q. Or *is evacuated*

him, saying, "Send her away, for she is crying after us." [24]He answered, "I was sent only to the lost sheep of the house of Israel." [25]But she came and knelt before him, saying, "Lord, help me." [26]And he answered, "It is not fair to take the children's bread and throw it to the dogs." [27]She said, "Yes, Lord, yet even the dogs eat the crumbs that fall from their master's table." [28]Then Jesus answered her, "O woman, great is your faith! Be it done for you as you desire." And her daughter was healed instantly.

Curing of many sick people

Mk 7:31

Mk 3:10

[29]And Jesus went on from there and passed along the Sea of Galilee. And he went up into the hills, and sat down there. [30]And great crowds came to him, bringing with them the lame, the maimed, the blind, the dumb, and many others, and they put

Mk 7:37

them at his feet, and he healed them, [31]so that the throng wondered, when they saw the dumb speaking, the maimed whole, the lame walking, and the blind seeing; and they glorified the God of Israel.

Both Gospels point out that she is a pagan, which means that her faith in our Lord is more remarkable; the same applies in the case of the centurion (Mt 8:5–13).

The Canaanite woman's prayer is quite perfect: she recognizes Jesus as the Messiah (the Son of David)—which contrasts with the unbelief of the Jews; she expresses her need in clear, simple words; she persists, undismayed by obstacles; and she expresses her request in all humility: "Have mercy on me." Our prayer should have the same qualities of faith, trust, perseverance and humility.

15:24. What Jesus says here does not take from the universal reference of his teaching (cf. Mt 28:19–20; Mk 16:15–16). Our Lord came to bring his Gospel to the whole world, but he himself addressed only the Jews; later on he will charge his apostles to preach the Gospel to pagans. St Paul, in his missionary journeys, also adopted the policy of

preaching in the first instance to the Jews (Acts 13:46).

15:25–28. This dialogue between Jesus and the woman is especially beautiful. By appearing to be harsh he so strengthens the woman's faith that she deserves exceptional praise: "Great is your faith!" Our own conversation with Christ should be like that: "Persevere in prayer. Persevere, even when your efforts seem barren. Prayer is always fruitful" (St Josemaría Escrivá, *The Way*, 101).

15:29–31. Here St Matthew summarizes Jesus' activity in this border area where Jews and pagans were living side by side. As usual he teaches and heals the sick; the Gospel account clearly echoes the prophecy of Isaiah which Christ himself used to prove that he was the Messiah (Lk 7:22): "the eyes of the blind shall be opened, and the ears of the deaf unstopped ..." (Is 35:5). "They glorified the God of Israel": this clearly refers to the Gentiles, who thought that

Second miracle of the loaves and fish *another opportunity*

³²Then Jesus called his disciples to him and said, "I have compassion on the crowd, because they have been with me now three days, and have nothing to eat; and I am unwilling to send them away hungry, lest they faint on the way." ³³And the disciples said to him, "Where are we to get bread enough in the desert to feed so great a crowd?" ³⁴And Jesus said to them, "How many loaves have you?" They said, "Seven, and a few small fish." ³⁵And commanding the crowd to sit down on the ground, ³⁶he took the seven loaves and the fish, and having given thanks he broke them and gave them to the disciples, and the disciples gave them to the crowds. ³⁷And they all ate and were satisfied; and they took up seven baskets full of the broken pieces left over. ³⁸Those who ate were four thousand men, besides women and children. ³⁹And sending away the crowds, he got into the boat and went to the region of Magadan.

Mk 8:1–10

7 left over)

God could give the power to work miracles to Jews only. Once again the Gentiles are seen to have more faith than the Jews.

15:32. The Gospels speak of our Lord's mercy and compassion towards people's needs: here he is concerned about the crowds who are following him and who have no food. He always has a word of consolation, encouragement and forgiveness: he is never indifferent. However, what hurts him most are sinners who go through life without experiencing light and truth: he waits for them in the sacraments of Baptism and Penance.

15:33–38. As in the case of the first multiplication (14:13–20), the apostles provide our Lord with the loaves and the fish. It was all they had. He also avails of the apostles to distribute the food—the result of the miracle—to the people. In distributing the graces of salvation God chooses to rely on the faithfulness and generosity of men. "Many great things depend—don't forget it—on whether you and I live our lives as God wants" (St Josemaría Escrivá, *The Way*, 755).

It is interesting to note that in both miracles of multiplication of loaves and fish Jesus provides food in abundance but does not allow anything to go to waste. All Jesus' miracles, in addition to being concrete historical events, are also symbols of supernatural realities. Here abundance of material food also signifies abundance of divine gifts on the level of grace and glory: it refers to spiritual resources and eternal rewards; God gives people more graces than are strictly necessary. This is borne out by Christian experience throughout history. St Paul tells us that "where sin increased, grace abounded all the more" (Rom 5:20); he speaks of "the riches of his grace which he lavished upon us" (Eph 1:8) and tells his disciple Timothy that "the grace of our Lord overflowed for me with the faith and love that are in Christ Jesus" (1 Tim 1:14).

15:39. St Mark calls Magadan Dalmanutha (8:10). These are the only references to this place; we do not know its exact location.

The Pharisees and Sadducees try to test Jesus

Mk 8:11–21
Mt 12:38
Lk 12:54–56

16 ¹And the Pharisees and Sadducees came, and to test him they asked him to show them a sign from heaven. ²He answered them,[r] "When it is evening, you say, 'It will be fair weather; for the sky is red.' ³And in the morning, 'It will be stormy today, for the sky is red and threatening.' You know how to interpret the appearance of the sky, but you cannot interpret the signs of the times. ⁴An evil and adulterous generation seeks for a sign, but no sign shall be given to it except the sign of Jonah." So he left them and departed.

Jn 2:1
Mt 12:39f

⁵When the disciples reached the other side, they had forgotten to bring any bread. ⁶Jesus said to them, "Take heed and beware of the leaven of the Pharisees and Sadducees." ⁷And they discussed it among themselves, saying, "We brought no bread." ⁸But Jesus, aware of this, said, "O men of little faith, why do you discuss among yourselves the fact that you have no bread? ⁹Do you not yet perceive? Do you not remember the five loaves of the five thousand, and how many baskets you gathered? ¹⁰Or the seven loaves of the four thousand, and how many baskets you gathered? ¹¹How is it that you fail to perceive that I did not speak about

Lk 12:1

16:1–4. On Jesus' reply to the Pharisees and the meaning of the sign of Jonah, see the note on Mt 12:39–40.

16:3. "The signs of the times": Jesus uses man's ability to forecast the weather to speak about the signs of the advent of the Messiah.

He reproaches the Pharisees for not recognizing that the messianic times have in fact arrived: "For the Lord Jesus inaugurated his Church by preaching the Good News, that is, the coming of the Kingdom of God, promised over the ages in the Scriptures: 'The time is fulfilled, and the kingdom of God is at hand' (Mk 1:15; cf. Mt 4:17). This Kingdom shone out before men in the world, in the works and in the presence of Christ. The word of the Lord is compared to a seed that is sown in a field (Mk 4:14); those who hear it with faith and are numbered

among the little flock of Christ (Lk 12:32) have truly received the Kingdom. Then, by its own power the seed sprouts and grows until the harvest (cf. Mk 4:26–29). The miracles of Jesus also demonstrate that the Kingdom has already come on earth: 'If it be by the finger of God that I cast out demons, then the kingdom of God has come upon you' (Lk 11:20; cf. Mt 12:28). But principally the Kingdom is revealed in the person of Christ himself, Son of God and Son of man, who came 'to serve, and to give his life as a ransom for many' (Mk 10:45)" (Vatican II, *Lumen gentium*, 5).

16:13–20. In this passage St Peter is promised primacy over the whole Church, a primacy which Jesus will confer on him after his resurrection, as we learn in the Gospel of St John (cf. Jn 21:15–18). This supreme authority is given to Peter for

r. Other ancient authorities omit the following words to the end of verse 3

bread? Beware of the leaven of the Pharisees and Sadducees."
¹²Then they understood that he did not tell them to beware of the
leaven of bread, but of the teaching of the Pharisees and Sadducees.

Jn 6:27

Peter's profession of faith and his primacy

¹³Now when Jesus came into the district of Caesarea Philippi, he
asked his disciples, "Who do men say that the Son of man is?"
¹⁴And they said, "Some say John the Baptist, others say Elijah,
and others Jeremiah or one of the prophets." ¹⁵He said to them,
"But who do you say that I am?" ¹⁶Simon Peter replied, "You are
the Christ, the Son of the living God." ¹⁷And Jesus answered him,
"Blessed are you, Simon Bar-Jona! For flesh and blood has not
revealed this to you, but my Father who is in heaven. ¹⁸And I tell
you, you are Peter,ˢ and on this rockᵗ I will build my church, and
the powers of deathᵘ shall not prevail against it. ¹⁹I will give you
the keys of the kingdom of heaven, and whatever you bind on
earth shall be bound in heaven, and whatever you loose on earth
shall be loosed in heaven." ²⁰Then he strictly charged the disciples
to tell no one that he was the Christ.

Mk 8:27–30
Lk 9:18–21

Jn 6:69
Gal 1:15f
Mt 17:4–5
Jn 1:42
Eph 2:20
Job 38:17
Is 38:10
Ps 9:13;
107:18
Wis 16:30
Mt 18:18
Rev 1:18

---

the benefit of the Church. Because the Church has to last until the end of time, this authority will be passed on to Peter's successors down through history. The Bishop of Rome, the Pope, is the successor of Peter.

The solemn Magisterium of the Church, in the First Vatican Council, defined the doctrine of the primacy of Peter and his successors in these terms:

"We teach and declare, therefore, according to the testimony of the Gospel that the primacy of jurisdiction over the whole Church was immediately and directly promised to and conferred upon the blessed apostle Peter by Christ the Lord. For to Simon, Christ had said, 'You shall be called Cephas' (Jn 1:42). Then, after Simon had acknowledged Christ with the confession, 'You are the Christ, the Son of the living God' (Mt 16:16), it was to Simon alone that the solemn

words were spoken by the Lord: 'Blessed are you, Simon Bar-Jona. For flesh and blood has not revealed this to you, but my Father who is in heaven. And I tell you, you are Peter, and on this rock I will build my church, and the powers of hell shall not prevail against it. I will give you the keys of the kingdom of heaven, and whatever you bind on earth shall be bound in heaven, and what you loose on earth shall be loosed in heaven' (Mt 16:17–19). And after his resurrection, Jesus conferred upon Simon Peter alone the jurisdiction of supreme shepherd and ruler over all his fold with the words, 'Feed my lambs.... Feed my sheep' (Jn 21:15–17) [...].

"(Canon) Therefore, if anyone says that the blessed apostle Peter was not constituted by Christ the Lord as the Prince of all the apostles and the visible head of the whole Church militant, or that he received

s. Greek *Petros* **t.** Greek *petra* **u.** Greek *the gates of Hades*

119

PART TWO

Jesus' ministry on the way to Jerusalem

8. TOWARDS JUDEA AND JERUSALEM

Jesus foretells his passion and resurrection. The law of Christian renunciation

Mk 8:31–9:1
Lk 9:22–27
Mt 12:40
Jn 2:19

²¹From that time Jesus began to show his disciples that he must go to Jerusalem and suffer many things from the elders and chief

---

immediately and directly from Jesus Christ our Lord only a primacy of honour and not a true and proper primacy of jurisdiction: let him be condemned.

"Now, what Christ the Lord, supreme shepherd and watchful guardian of the flock, established in the person of the blessed apostle Peter for the perpetual safety and everlasting good of the Church must, by the will of the same, endure without interruption in the Church which was founded on the rock and which will remain firm until the end of the world. Indeed, 'no one doubts, in fact it is obvious to all ages, that the holy and most blessed Peter, Prince and head of the apostles, the pillar of faith, and the foundation of the Catholic Church, received the keys of the kingdom from our Lord Jesus Christ, the Saviour and the Redeemer of the human race; and even to this time and forever he lives', and governs, 'and exercises judgment in his successors' (cf. Council of Ephesus), the bishops of the holy Roman See, which he established and consecrated with his blood. Therefore, whoever succeeds Peter in this Chair holds Peter's primacy over the whole Church according to the plan of Christ himself [...]. For this reason, 'because of its greater sovereignty', it was always 'necessary for every church, that is, the faithful who are

everywhere, to be in agreement' with the same Roman Church [...].

"(Canon) Therefore, if anyone says that it is not according to the institution of Christ our Lord himself, that is, by divine law, that St Peter has perpetual successors in the primacy over the whole Church; or if anyone says that the Roman Pontiff is not the successor of St Peter in the same primacy: let him be condemned [...].

"We think it extremely necessary to assert solemnly the prerogative which the only-begotten Son of God deigned to join to the highest pastoral office. And so, faithfully keeping to the tradition received from the beginning of the Christian faith, for the glory of God our Saviour, for the exaltation of the Catholic religion, and for the salvation of Christian peoples, We, with the approval of the sacred council, teach and define that it is a divinely revealed dogma: that the Roman Pontiff, when he speaks *ex cathedra*, that is, when, acting in the office of shepherd and teacher of all Christians, he defines, by virtue of his supreme apostolic authority, doctrine concerning faith or morals to be held by the universal Church, possesses through the divine assistance promised to him in the person of St Peter, the infallibility with which the divine Redeemer willed his Church to be endowed in defining doctrine concerning faith or morals;

priests and scribes, and be killed, and on the third day be raised. ²²And Peter took him and began to rebuke him, saying, "God forbid, Lord! This shall never happen to you." ²³But he turned and said to Peter, "Get behind me, Satan! You are a hindrance^v to me; for you are not on the side of God, but of men."

²⁴Then Jesus told his disciples, "If any man would come after me, let him deny himself and take up his cross and follow me. ²⁵For whoever would save his life will lose it, and whoever loses his life for my sake will find it. ²⁶For what will it profit a man, if

Is 8:14

Jn 5:29
Rom 2:6

and that such definitions of the Roman Pontiff are therefore irreformable because of their nature, but not because of the agreement of the Church.

"(Canon) But if anyone presumes to contradict this our definition (God forbid that he do so): let him be condemned" (Vatican I, *Pastor aeternus*, chaps. 1, 2 and 4).

16:23. Jesus rejects St Peter's well-intentioned protestations, giving us to understand the capital importance of accepting the cross if we are to attain salvation (cf. 1 Cor 1:23–25). Shortly before this (Mt 16:17) Jesus had promised Peter: "Blessed are you, Simon"; now he reproves him: "Get behind me, Satan." In the former case Peter's words were inspired by the Holy Spirit, whereas what he says now comes from his own spirit, which he has not yet sloughed off.

16:24. "Divine love, 'poured into our hearts by the Holy Spirit who has been given to us' (Rom 5:5), enables lay people to express concretely in their lives the spirit of the Beatitudes. Following Jesus in his poverty, they feel no depression in want, no pride in plenty; imitating the humble Christ, they are not greedy for vain show (cf. Gal 5:26). They strive to please God rather than men, always ready to abandon everything for Christ (cf. Lk 14:26)

and even to endure persecution in the cause of right (cf. Mt 5:10), having in mind the Lord's saying: 'If any man wants to come after me, let him deny himself and take up his cross and follow me' (Mt 16:24)" (Vatican II, *Apostolicam actuositatem*, 4).

16:25. A Christian cannot ignore these words of Jesus. He has to risk, to gamble, this present life in order to attain eternal life: "How little a life is to offer to God!" (St Josemaría Escrivá, *The Way*, 420).

Our Lord's requirement means that we must renounce our own will in order to identify with the will of God; and so to ensure that, as St John of the Cross comments, we do not follow the way of those many people who "would have God will that which they themselves will, and are fretful at having to will that which he wills, and find it repugnant to accommodate their will to that of God. Hence it happens to them that oftentimes they think that that wherein they find not their own will and pleasure is not the will of God; and that, on the other hand, when they themselves find satisfaction, God is satisfied. Thus they measure God by themselves and not themselves by God" (*Dark Night of the Soul*, book 1, chap. 7, 3).

16:26–27. Christ's words are crystal-clear: every person has to bear in mind

v. Greek *stumbling block*

121

Ps 62:12
Prov 24:12

he gains the whole world and forfeits his life? Or what shall a man give in return for his life? ²⁷For the Son of man is to come with his angels in the glory of his Father, and then he will repay every man for what he has done. ²⁸Truly, I say to you, there are some standing here who will not taste death before they see the Son of man coming in his kingdom."

The transfiguration

Mk 9:2–13
Lk 5:28–36

2 Pet 1:16–18

17 ¹And after six days Jesus took with him Peter and James and John his brother, and led them up a high mountain apart. ²And he was transfigured before them, and his face shone like the sun, and his garments became white as light. ³And behold, there appeared to them Moses and Elijah, talking with him. ⁴And

---

the Last Judgment. Salvation, in other words, is something radically personal: "he will repay every man for what he has done" (v. 27).

Man's goal does not consist in accumulating worldly goods; these are only means to an end; man's last end, his ultimate goal, is God himself; he possesses God in advance, as it were, here on earth by means of grace, and possesses him fully and for ever in heaven. Jesus shows the route to take to reach this destination—denying oneself (that is, saying no to ease, comfort, selfishness and attachment to temporal goods) and taking up the cross. For no earthly—impermanent—good can compare with the soul's eternal salvation. As St Thomas expresses it with theological precision, "the least good of grace is superior to the natural good of the entire universe" (*Summa theologiae*, 1–2, 113, 9).

16:28. Here Jesus is referring not to his last coming (which he speaks about in the preceding verse) but to other events which will occur prior to that and which will be a sign of his glorification after death. The coming he speaks of here may refer firstly to his resurrection and his appearances thereafter; it could also refer

to his transfiguration, which is itself a manifestation of his glory. This coming of Christ in his Kingdom might also be seen in the destruction of Jerusalem—a sign of the end of the ancient people of Israel as a form of the Kingdom of God and its substitution by the Church, the new Kingdom.

17:1–13. Realizing that his death will demoralize his disciples, Jesus forewarns them and strengthens their faith. Not content with telling them in advance about his death and resurrection on the third day, he wants two of the three future pillars of the Church (cf. Gal 2:9) to see his transfiguration and thereby glimpse the glory and majesty with which his holy human nature will be endowed in heaven.

The Father's testimony (v. 5), expressed in the same words as he used at Christ's baptism (cf. Mt 3:17), reveals to the three apostles that Jesus Christ is the Son of God, the beloved Son, God himself. To these words—also spoken at Christ's baptism—he adds, "Listen to him", as if to indicate that Jesus is also the supreme prophet foretold by Moses (cf. Deut 18:15–18).

Peter said to Jesus, "Lord, it is well that we are here; if you wish,
I will make three booths here, one for you and one for Moses and
one for Elijah." ⁵He was still speaking, when lo, a bright cloud
overshadowed them, and a voice from the cloud said, "This is my
beloved Son,ʷ with whom I am well pleased; listen to him."
⁶When the disciples heard this, they fell on their faces, and were
filled with awe. ⁷But Jesus came and touched them, saying, "Rise,
and have no fear." ⁸And when they lifted up their eyes, they saw
no one but Jesus only.

⁹And as they were coming down the mountain, Jesus commanded them, "Tell no one the vision, until the Son of man is
raised from the dead." ¹⁰And the disciples asked him, "Then why
do the scribes say that first Elijah must come?" ¹¹He replied,
"Elijah does come, and he is to restore all things; ¹²but I tell you

Deut 18:15

Mal 3:23f

Lk 23:25

17:3. Moses and Elijah are the two most
prominent representatives of the Old
Testament—the Law and the Prophets.
The fact that Christ occupies the central
position points up his pre-eminence over
them, and the superiority of the New
Testament over the Old.

This dazzling glimpse of divine glory
is enough to send the apostles into a rap-
ture; so happy are they that Peter cannot
contain his desire to prolong this experience.

17:5. In Christ God speaks to all men;
through the Church his voice resounds in
all ages: "The Church does not cease to
listen to his words. She rereads them
continually. With the greatest devotion
she reconstructs every detail of his life.
These words are listened to also by non-
Christians. The life of Christ speaks,
also, to many who are not capable of
repeating with Peter, 'You are the Christ,
the Son of the living God' (Mt 16:16).
He, the Son of the living God, speaks to
people also as Man: it is his life that
speaks, his humanity, his fidelity to the
truth, his all-embracing love. Furthermore, his death on the Cross speaks—

that is to say the inscrutable depth of his
suffering and abandonment. The Church
never ceases to relive his death on the
Cross and his resurrection, which constitute the content of the Church's daily life
[...]. The Church lives his mystery,
draws unwearyingly from it and continually seeks ways of bringing this
mystery of her Master and Lord to humanity—to the peoples, the nations, the
succeeding generations, and every individual human being" (John Paul II,
Redemptor hominis, 7).

17:10–13. Malachi 4:5 (3:23 in the
Hebrew) speaks of the coming of Elijah
the prophet before "the great and terrible
day of the Lord", the Judgment Day.
When Jesus says that Elijah has already
come, he is referring to St John the
Baptist, whose mission it was to prepare
the way for the first coming of the Lord,
the same as Elijah will have to do prior to
his last coming. The scribes failed to
grasp the meaning of the prophecy of
Malachi; they thought it referred simply
to the coming of the Messiah, the first
coming of Christ.

w. Or *my Son, my* (or *the*) *Beloved*

that Elijah has already come, and they did not know him, but did
to him whatever they pleased. So also the Son of man will suffer

Lk 1:17

at their hands." [13]Then the disciples understood that he was speaking to them of John the Baptist.

Curing of an epileptic boy

Mk 9:14–29
Lk 9:37–42

[14]And when they came to the crowd, a man came up to him and
kneeling before him said, [15]"Lord, have mercy on my son, for he is
an epileptic and he suffers terribly; for often he falls into the fire,
and often into the water. [16]And I brought him to your disciples, and

Deut 32:5
Jn 14:9

they could not heal him." [17]And Jesus answered, "O faithless and
perverse generation, how long am I to be with you? How long am I
to bear with you? Bring him here to me." [18]And Jesus rebuked him,
and the demon came out of him, and the boy was cured instantly.
[19]Then the disciples came to Jesus privately and said, "Why could

Lk 17:16
Mk 11:23

we not cast it out?" [20]He said to them, "Because of your little faith.
For truly, I say to you, if you have faith as a grain of mustard seed,
you will say to this mountain, 'Move hence to yonder place,' and it
will move; and nothing will be impossible to you."[x]

Second announcement of the Passion. The temple tax

Mk 9:30–32
Lk 9:43–45
Mt 16:21

[22]As they were gathering[y] in Galilee, Jesus said to them. "The Son
of man is to be delivered into the hands of men, [23]and they will

---

17:14–21. This episode of the curing of the
boy shows both Christ's omnipotence and
the power of prayer full of faith. Because of
his deep union with Christ, a Christian
shares, through faith, in God's own omnipotence, to such an extent that Jesus actually
says on another occasion, "he who believes
in me will also do the works that I do; and
greater works than these will he do, because
I go to the Father" (Jn 14:12).

Our Lord tells the apostles that if they
had faith they would be able to work miracles, to move mountains. "Moving mountains" was probably a proverbial saying.
God would certainly let a believer move a
mountain if that were necessary for his
glory and for the edification of one's
neighbour; however, Christ's promise is

fulfilled everyday in a much more exalted
way. Some Fathers of the Church (St
Jerome, St Augustine) say that "a mountain is moved" every time someone is
divinely aided to do something which
exceeds man's natural powers. This clearly
happens in the work of our sanctification,
which the Paraclete effects in our souls
when we are docile to him and receive
with faith and love the grace given us in
the sacraments: we benefit from the sacraments to a greater or lesser degree depending on the dispositions with which we
receive them. Sanctification is something
much more sublime than moving mountains, and it is something which is happening every day in so many holy souls, even
though most people do not notice it.

---

x. Other ancient authorities insert verse 21, *But this kind never comes out except by prayer and fasting*
y. Other ancient authorities read *abode*

kill him, and he will be raised on the third day." And they were greatly distressed.

²⁴When they came to Capernaum, the collectors of the half-shekel tax went up to Peter and said, "Does not your teacher pay the tax?" ²⁵He said, "Yes." And when he came home, Jesus spoke to him first, saying, "What do you think, Simon? From whom do kings of the earth take toll or tribute? From their sons or from others?" ²⁶And when he said, "From others," Jesus said to him, "Then the sons are free. ²⁷However, not to give offence to them, go to the sea and cast a hook, and take the first fish that comes up, and when you open its mouth you will find a shekel; take that and give it to them for me and for yourself."

Ex 30:13

9. THE DISCOURSE ON THE CHURCH

The "little ones" and the Kingdom. On leading others astray. The lost sheep

18 ¹At that time, the disciples came to Jesus, saying, "Who is the greatest in the kingdom of heaven?" ²And calling to

Mk 9:33–47
Lk 9:46–48

The apostles and many saints down the centuries have in fact worked amazing material miracles; but the greatest and most important miracles were, are and will be the miracles of souls dead through sin and ignorance being reborn and developing in the new life of the children of God.

17:20. Here and in the parable of Matthew 13:31–32 the main force of the comparison lies in the fact that a very small seed—the mustard seed—produces a large shrub up to three metres (ten feet) high: even a very small act of genuine faith can produce surprising results.

17:21. See the RSV note and Mk 9:29.

17:24–27. "Half-shekel", or *didrachma*: a coin equal in value to the annual contribution every Jew had to make for the upkeep of the temple—a day's wage of a labourer. The shekel or stater which our Lord refers to in v. 27 was a Greek coin

worth two didrachmas. Jesus uses things great and small to get his teaching across to his disciples. Peter, who is to be the rock on which he will found his Church (Mt 16:18–19), he prepares by letting him see his dramatic transfiguration (17:1–8); now he gives Peter another inkling of his divinity through an apparently unimportant miracle. We should take note of Jesus' teaching method: after his second announcement of his passion, his disciples are downhearted (Mt 17:22–23); here he lifts Peter's spirits with this friendly little miracle.

17:26. This shows how conscientiously our Lord fulfilled his civic duties. Although the half-shekel tax had to do with religion, given the theocratic structure of Israel at the time payment of this tax also constituted a civic obligation.

18:1–35. The teachings of Jesus recorded in chapter 18 of St Matthew are often

Jn 3:3–5   him a child, he put him in the midst of them, ³and said, "Truly, I
say to you, unless you turn and become like children, you will
never enter the kingdom of heaven. ⁴Whoever humbles himself
like this child, he is the greatest in the kingdom of heaven.

---

called the "discourse on the Church" or "ecclesiastical discourse" because they are a series of instructions on the way in which his Church is to be administered.

The first passage (Mt 18:1–5), addressed to leaders, that is, the future hierarchy of the Church, warns them against natural tendencies to pride and ambition: even though they have positions of government, they must act with humility. In verses 6–10 Jesus emphasizes the fatherly care that pastors of the Church should have for the "little ones"—a term which covers everyone in need of special care for whatever reason (because they are recent converts, or are not well grounded in Church teaching, or are not yet adults, etc.). He makes a special point of warning them about the harm that scandal—leading others to commit sin— can do: Christians' fraternal charity requires that all, and particularly pastors, should avoid doing anything— even anything that in itself is quite legitimate— which could endanger the spiritual health of those who are less robust: God takes special care of the weak and will punish those who harm them.

Our Lord shows similar concern for those who are experiencing spiritual difficulties. Every effort, even an heroic effort, must be made to seek out the "lost sheep" (vv. 12–14). If the Church in general and each Christian in particular should be concerned to spread the Gospel, all the more reason for them to try and see that those who have already embraced the faith do not go astray.

The following passage (vv. 15–18) on fraternal correction has special doctrinal relevance: here Jesus uses the term "the

Church" in the sense of a social structure, an actual community, visible and compact, directly dependent on him and his twelve apostles and their successors, who have an all-embracing "power of the keys", a spiritual authority that God himself backs up. Among their powers is that of forgiving or retaining sins, of receiving people into the Church or cutting them off from communion with the Church—a remarkable divine power given by Jesus to the hierarchy and protected by a special kind of divine providence in the form of Jesus' continuous presence in the Church and the Holy Spirit's support of its hierarchical Magisterium.

This is followed by a passage (vv. 19–20) in which Jesus promises to be present whenever a number of Christians come together to pray (v. 20), and teaches the need to forgive any offences committed by one brother against another (vv. 21–22). The chapter ends with the parable of the unforgiving debtor (vv. 23–35), in which our Lord shows what forgiveness involves.

Thus, the whole of chapter 18, the "discourse on the Church", is a survey of the future history of the Church during its earthly stage, and a series of practical rules of conduct for Christians—a kind of complement to the Sermon on the Mount (chaps. 5–7), which is a "magna charta" for the new Kingdom established by Christ.

18:1–6. Clearly the disciples still suffer from human ambition: they want to occupy key positions when Jesus comes to establish his Kingdom on earth (cf. Acts 1:6). To correct their pride, our Lord

⁵"Whoever receives one such child in my name receives me; ⁶but whoever causes one of these little ones who believe in me to sin,ᶻ it would be better for him to have a great millstone fastened round his neck and to be drowned in the depth of the sea.

Jn 13:20

Lk 17:1f

---

shows them a child and tells them that if they want to enter the Kingdom of heaven, they must decide to be like children: children are incapable of hating anyone and are totally innocent of vice, particularly of pride, the worst vice of all. They are simple and full of trust.

Humility is one of the main pillars of the Christian life. "If you ask me", St Augustine says, "what is the essential thing in the religion and discipline of Jesus Christ, I shall reply: first humility, second humility and third humility" (*Letters*, 118).

18:3–4. Applying these words to our Lord's virtues, Fray Luis de Granada makes the point that humility is superior to virginity: "If you cannot imitate the virginity of the humble, then imitate the humility of the virgin. Virginity is praiseworthy, but humility is more necessary. The former is recommended to us, the latter is an obligation for us; to the former we are invited, to the latter we are obliged [...]. And so we see that the former is celebrated as a voluntary sacrifice, the latter required as an obligatory sacrifice. Lastly, you can be saved without virginity, but not without humility" (*Suma de la vida cristiana*, book 3, part 2, chap. 10).

18:5. Receiving a child in Jesus' name is the same as receiving Jesus himself. Because children reflect the innocence, purity, simplicity and tenderness of our Lord, "In children and in the sick a soul in love sees him" (St Josemaría Escrivá, *The Way*, 419).

18:6–7. The holy, pained indignation sounding in Jesus' words shows the seriousness of the sin of scandal, which is defined as "something said, done or omitted which leads another person to commit sin" (cf. St Pius X, *Catechism*, 417).

"Millstone": our Lord is referring to a form of punishment used in ancient times, which consisted in throwing a person into the sea with a heavy weight attached to his neck to prevent his body floating to the surface; this was regarded as a particularly ignominious form of death because it was inflicted only on the worst criminals and also because it meant deprival of burial.

Although Jesus affirms that people will cause others to sin, this does not mean that everyone, personally, should not ensure that this does not happen. Therefore, everyone who does cause another to sin is responsible for his action. Here he refers directly to scandal given to children—an action that is particularly malicious given the weakness and innocence of children. The evil of the world as enemy of the soul consists mainly in the harm it does in this way. Its evil maxims and bad example create an environment which draws people away from God, from Christ and from his Church.

The scandal given by those whose function it is to educate others is particularly serious. "If ordinary folk are lukewarm, that is bad; but it can be remedied, and the only one they harm is themselves; but if the teachers are lukewarm, then the Lord's 'Woe to the world'

z. Greek *causes ... to stumble*

⁷"Woe to the world for temptations to sin!ᵃ For it is necessary that temptations come, but woe to the man by whom the temptation comes! ⁸And if your hand or your foot causes you to sin,ᶻ cut it off and throw it from you; it is better for you to enter life maimed or lame than with two hands or two feet to be thrown into the eternal fire. ⁹And if your eye causes you to sin,ᶻ pluck it out and throw it from you; it is better for you to enter life with one eye than with two eyes to be thrown into the hellᵇ of fire.

Heb 1:14

¹⁰"See that you do not despise one of these little ones; for I tell you that in heaven their angels always behold the face of my Father who is in heaven.ᶜ ¹²What do you think? If a man has a hundred sheep, and one of them has gone astray, does he not leave the ninety-nine on the hills and go in search of the one that went

Lk 15:4–7

---

applies because of the great evil that results from this lukewarmness; this 'woe' threatens those lukewarm teachers who spread their lukewarmness to others and even suffocate their fervour completely" (St Augustine, *Sermons*, 55).

18:8–9. Entering life means entering the Kingdom of heaven. "The fire of hell": eternal punishment, merited by anyone who does not distance himself from what causes sin. Cf. the note on Mt 9:43.

18:8. Jesus is speaking figuratively. His teaching here can guide us in making moral decisions. If something or someone—however much we love them—is liable to cause us to commit sin, we have to stay away from them; it is as simple as that. "If thy right eye scandalize thee, pluck it out and cast it from thee! Your poor heart, that's what scandalizes you! Press it, squeeze it tight in your hands: give it no consolations. And when it asks for them, say to it slowly and with a noble compassion—in confidence, as it were: 'Heart, heart on the Cross, heart on the Cross!'" (St J. Escrivá, *The Way*, 163).

10. Jesus warns that giving scandal to little children is a very serious matter, for they have angels who guard them, who will plead a case before God against those who led them to commit sin.

In this context he speaks of children having guardian angels. However, everyone, adult or child, has a guardian angel. "By God's providence angels have been entrusted with the office of guarding the human race and of accompanying every human being so as to preserve him from any serious dangers [...]. Our heavenly Father has placed over each of us an angel under whose protection and vigilance we are" (St Pius V, *Catechism*, 4, 9, 4).

This means that we should have a trusting relationship with our guardian angel. "Have confidence in your guardian Angel. Treat him as a lifelong friend — that is what he is—and he will render you a thousand services in the ordinary affairs of each day" (*The Way*, 562).

18:11–14. This parable clearly shows our Lord's loving concern for sinners. It expresses in human terms the joy God feels when a wayward child comes back to him.

---

a. Greek *stumbling blocks* **z.** Greek *causes ... to stumble* **b.** Greek *Gehenna* **c.** Other ancient authorities add verse 11, *For the Son of man came to save the lost*

astray? [13]And if he finds it, truly, I say to you, he rejoices over it more than over the ninety-nine that never went astray. [14]So it is not the will of my[d] Father who is in heaven that one of these little ones should perish.

Fraternal correction. The apostles' authority

[15]"If your brother sins against you, go and tell him his fault, between you and him alone. If he listens to you, you have gained your brother. [16]But if he does not listen, take one or two others along with you, that every word may be confirmed by the evidence of two or three witnesses. [17]If he refuses to listen to them, tell it to the church; and if he refuses to listen even to the church, let him be to you as a Gentile and a tax collector. [18]Truly, I say to you, what-

Lev 19:17
Lk 17:3
Gal 6:1
Deut 19:15

1 Cor 5:13

Mt 16:19
Jn 20:23

Seeing so many souls living away from God, Pope John Paul II comments: "Unfortunately we witness the moral pollution which is devastating humanity, disregarding especially those very little ones about whom Jesus speaks.

"What must we do? We must imitate the Good Shepherd and give ourselves without rest for the salvation of souls. Without forgetting material charity and social justice, we must be convinced that the most sublime charity is spiritual charity, that is, the commitment for the salvation of souls. And souls are saved with prayer and sacrifice. This is the mission of the Church!" (Homily to the Poor Clares of Albano, 14 August 1979).

As the RSV points out, "other ancient authorities add verse 11, *For the Son of man came to save the lost*"—apparently taken from Lk 19:10.

18:15–17. Here our Lord calls on us to work with him for the sanctification of others by means of fraternal correction, which is one of the ways we can do so. He speaks as sternly about the sin of omission as he did about that of scandal (cf. Chrysostom, *Hom. on St Matthew*, 61).

There is an obligation on us to correct others. Our Lord identifies three stages in correction: 1) alone; 2) in the presence of one or two witnesses; and 3) before the Church. The first stage refers to causing scandal and to secret or private sins; here correction should be given privately, just to the person himself, to avoid unnecessarily publicizing a private matter and also to avoid hurting the person and to make it easier for him to mend his ways. If this correction does not have the desired effect, and the matter is a serious one, resort should be had to the second stage—looking for one or two friends, in case they have more influence on him. The last stage is formal judicial correction by reference to the Church authorities. If a sinner does not accept this correction, he should be excommunicated that is, separated from communion with the Church and sacraments.

18:18. This verse needs to be understood in connexion with the authority previously promised to Peter (cf. Mt 16:13–19): it is the hierarchy of the Church that exercises this power given by Christ to Peter, to the

d. Other ancient authorities read *your*

Mk 11:24

Jn 14:23

ever you bind on earth shall be bound in heaven, and whatever you loose on earth shall be loosed in heaven. [19]Again I say to you, if two of you agree on earth about anything they ask, it shall be done for them by my Father in heaven. [20]For where two or three are gathered in my name, there am I in the midst of them."

Forgiveness of injuries. Parable of the unforgiving servant

Lk 17:4

[21]Then Peter came up and said to him, "Lord, how often shall my brother sin against me, and I forgive him? As many as seven times?" [22]Jesus said to him, "I do not say to you seven times, but seventy times seven.[e]

[23]"Therefore the kingdom of heaven may be compared to a king who wished to settle accounts with his servants. [24]When he began the reckoning, one was brought to him who owed him ten thousand talents;[f] [25]and as he could not pay, his lord ordered him to be sold, with his wife and children and all that he had, and payment to be made. [26]So the servant fell on his knees, imploring him, 'Lord, have patience with me, and I will pay you everything.' [27]And out of pity for him the lord of that servant released him and forgave him the debt. [28]But that same servant, as he went out, came upon one of his fellow servants who owed him a hundred denarii;[g] and seizing him by the throat he said, 'Pay what you

---

apostles and their lawful successors—the Pope and the bishops.

18:19–20. "Ubi caritas et amor, Deus ibi est: where charity and love resides, there God is", the Holy Thursday liturgy entones, drawing its inspiration from the sacred text of 1 Jn 4:12. For it is true that love is inconceivable if there is only one person: it implies the presence of two or more (cf. St Thomas Aquinas, *Comm. on St Matthew*, 18:19–20). And so it is that when Christians meet together in the name of Christ for the purpose of prayer, our Lord is present among them, pleased to listen to the unanimous prayer of his disciples: "All those with one accord devoted themselves to prayer, together

with the women and Mary the mother of Jesus" (Acts 1:14). This is why the Church from the very beginning has practised communal prayer (cf. Acts 12:5). There are religious practices—few, short, daily "that have always been lived in Christian families and which I think are marvellous—grace at meals, morning and night prayers, the family rosary (even though nowadays this devotion to our Lady has been criticized by some people). Customs vary from place to place, but I think one should always encourage some acts of piety which the family can do together in a simple and natural fashion" (St Josemaría Escrivá, *Conversations*, 103).

---

e. Or *seventy-seven times* **f.** A talent was more than fifteen years' wages of a labourer **g.** The denarius was a day's wage for a labourer

owe.' ²⁹So his fellow servant fell down and besought him, 'Have patience with me, and I will pay you.' ³⁰He refused and went and put him in prison till he should pay his debt. ³¹When his fellow servants saw what had taken place, they were greatly distressed, and they went and reported to their lord all that had taken place. ³²Then his lord summoned him and said to him, 'You wicked servant! I forgave you all that debt because you besought me; ³³and should not you have had mercy on your fellow servant, as I had mercy on you?' ³⁴And in anger his lord delivered him to the jailers,ʰ till he should pay all his debt. ³⁵So also my heavenly Father will do to every one of you, if you do not forgive your brother from your heart."

Marriage and virginity

19 ¹Now when Jesus had finished these sayings, he went away from Galilee and entered the region of Judea beyond the Jordan; ²and large crowds followed him, and he healed them there.

Mk 10:1–12
Mt 7:28; 11:1;
13:53; 26:1

³And Pharisees came up to him and tested him by asking, "Is it lawful to divorce one's wife for any cause?" ⁴He answered, "Have you not read that he who made them from the beginning made them male and female, ⁵and said, 'For this reason a man shall leave

Gen 1:27

Gen 2:24
Eph 5:31

18:21–35. Peter's question and particularly Jesus' reply prescribe the spirit of understanding and mercy which should govern Christians' behaviour.

In Hebrew the figure of seventy times seven means the same as "always" (cf. Gen 4:24): "Therefore, our Lord did not limit forgiveness to a fixed number, but declared that it must be continuous and forever" (St John Chrysostom, *Hom. on St Matthew*, 6). Here also we can see the contrast between man's ungenerous, calculating approach to forgiveness, and God's infinite mercy. The parable also clearly shows that we are totally in God's debt. A talent was the equivalent of six thousand denarii, and a denarius a working man's daily wage. Ten thousand talents, an enormous sum, gives us an idea of the immense value attaching to the

pardon we receive from God. Overall, the parable teaches that we must always forgive our brothers, and must do so wholeheartedly.

"Force yourself, if necessary, always to forgive those who offend you, from the very first moment. For the greatest injury or offence that you can suffer from them is as nothing compared with what God has pardoned you" (St Josemaría Escrivá, *The Way*, 452).

19:4–5. "Marriage and married love are by nature ordered to the procreation and education of children. Indeed children are the supreme gift of marriage and greatly contribute to the good of the parents themselves. God himself said: 'It is not good that man should be alone' (Gen 2:18), and 'from the beginning (he) made

h. Greek *torturers*

131

his father and mother and be joined to his wife, and the two shall
become one'?[i] [6]So they are no longer two but one.[i] What therefore
God has joined together, let no man put asunder." [7]They said to
him, "Why then did Moses command one to give a certificate of
divorce, and to put her away?" [8]He said to them, "For your hardness of heart Moses allowed you to divorce your wives, but from
the beginning it was not so. [9]And I say to you: whoever divorces his
wife, except for unchastity,[j] and marries another, commits adultery;
and he who marries a divorced woman commits adultery."[k]

[10]The disciples said to him, "If such is the case of a man with
his wife, it is not expedient to marry." [11]But he said to them, "Not
all men can receive this precept, but only those to whom it is
given. [12]For there are eunuchs who have been so from birth, and
there are eunuchs who have been made eunuchs by men, and

1 Cor 7:10f

Deut 24:1

Lk 16:18

1 Cor 7:7, 17

---

them male and female' (Mt 19:4); wishing to associate them in a special way
with his own creative work, God blessed
man and woman with the words: 'Be
fruitful and multiply' (Gen 1:28). Without intending to underestimate the other
ends of marriage, it must be said that true
married life and the whole structure of
family life which results from it is
directed to disposing the spouses to
cooperate valiantly with the love of the
Creator and Saviour, who through them
will increase and enrich his family from
day to day" (Vatican II, *Gaudium et spes*,
50).

19:9. Our Lord's teaching on the unity
and indissolubility of marriage is the
main theme of this passage, apropos of
which St John Chrysostom comments
that marriage is a lifelong union of man
and woman (cf. *Hom. on St Matthew*,
62). On the meaning of "except for
unchastity", see the note on Mt 5:31–32.

19:11. "Not all men can receive this precept": our Lord is fully aware that the

demands involved in his teaching on
marriage and his recommendation of
celibacy practised out of love of God run
counter to human selfishness. That is
why he says that acceptance of this
teaching is a gift from God.

19:12. Our Lord speaks figuratively
here, referring to those who, out of love
for him, renounce marriage and offer
their lives completely to him. Virginity
embraced for the love of God is one of
the Church's most precious charisms (cf.
1 Cor 7); the lives of those who practise
virginity evoke the state of the blessed in
heaven, who are like the angels (cf. Mt
22:30). This is why the Church's Magisterium teaches that the state of virginity
for the sake of the Kingdom of heaven is
higher than the married state (cf. Council
of Trent, *De Sacram. matr.*, can. 10; cf.
also Pius XII, *Sacra virginitas*). On virginity and celibacy the Second Vatican
Council teaches: "The Church's holiness
is also fostered in a special way by the
manifold counsels which the Lord proposes to his disciples in the Gospel for

---

i. Greek *one flesh*   j. Other ancient authorities, after *unchastity*, read *makes her commit adultery*
k. Other ancient authorities omit *and he who marries a divorced woman commits adultery*

there are eunuchs who have made themselves eunuchs for the sake of the kingdom of heaven. He who is able to receive this, let him receive it."

Jesus blesses the children
¹³Then children were brought to him that he might lay his hands on them and pray. The disciples rebuked the people; ¹⁴but Jesus said, "Let the children come to me, and do not hinder them; for to such belongs the kingdom of heaven." ¹⁵And he laid his hands on them and went away.

Mk 10:13–16
Lk 18:15–17

The rich young man. Christian poverty and renunciation
¹⁶And behold, one came up to him, saying, "Teacher, what good deed must I do, to have eternal life?" ¹⁷And he said to him, "Why

Mk 10:17–31
Lk 18:18–30

---

them to observe. Towering among these counsels is that precious gift of divine grace given to some by the Father (cf. Mt 19:11; 1 Cor 7:7) to devote themselves to God alone more easily in virginity or celibacy [...]. This perfect continence for love of the Kingdom of heaven has always been held in high esteem by the Church as a sign and stimulus of love, and as a singular source of spiritual fertility in the world" (*Lumen gentium*, 42; cf. *Perfectae caritatis*, 12). And, on celibacy specifically, see Vatican II's *Presbyterorum ordinis*, 16 and *Optatam totius*, 10.

However, both virginity and marriage are necessary for the growth of the Church, and both imply a specific calling from God: "Celibacy is precisely a gift of the Spirit. A similar though different gift is contained in the vocation to true and faithful married love, directed towards procreation according to the flesh, in the very lofty context of the sacrament of Matrimony. It is obvious that this gift is fundamental for the building up of the great community of the Church, the people of God. But if this community wishes to respond fully to its vocation in Jesus Christ, there will also have to be

realized in it, in the correct proportion, that other gift, the gift of celibacy 'for the sake of the kingdom of heaven'" (John Paul II, *Letter to all priests*, 8 April 1979).

19:13–14. Once again (see Mt 18:1–6) Jesus shows his special love for children, by drawing them close and blessing them. The Church, also, shows special concern for children by urging the need for Baptism: "That this law extends not only to adults but also to infants and children, and that the Church has received this from Apostolic tradition, is confirmed by the unanimous teaching and authority of the Fathers.

"Besides, it is not to be supposed that Christ the Lord would have withheld the sacrament and grace of Baptism from children, of whom he said: 'Let the little children come to me, and do not hinder them; for to such belongs the kingdom of heaven' whom also he embraced, upon whom he imposed hands, to whom he gave his blessing" (St Pius V, *Catechism*, 2, 2, 32).

19:17. The Vulgate and other translations, supported by a good many Greek

Lk 10:26–28

Ex 20:12–16
Deut 5:17–20

Ex 20:12
Lev 19:18
Deut 5:16

Lk 12:33

Ps 62:9

Gen 18:14
Job 42:2
Zech 8:6

do you ask me about what is good? One there is who is good. If you would enter life, keep the commandments." [18]He said to him, "Which?" And Jesus said, "You shall not kill, You shall not commit adultery, You shall not steal, You shall not bear false witness, [19]Honour your father and mother, and, You shall love your neighbour as yourself." [20]The young man said to him, "All these I have observed; what do I still lack?" [21]Jesus said to him, "If you would be perfect, go, sell what you possess and give to the poor, and you will have treasure in heaven; and come, follow me." [22]When the young man heard this he went away sorrowful; for he had great possessions.

[23]And Jesus said to his disciples, "Truly, I say to you, it will be hard for a rich man to enter the kingdom of heaven. [24]Again I tell you, it is easier for a camel to go through the eye of a needle than for a rich man to enter the kingdom of God." [25]When the disciples heard this they were greatly astonished, saying, "Who then can be saved?" [26]But Jesus looked at them and said to them, "With men this is impossible, but with God all things are possible." [27]Then

---

codexes, fill this verse out by saying, "One alone is good, God."

19:20–22. "What do I still lack?" The young man kept the commandments that were necessary for salvation. But there is more. This is why our Lord replies, "if you would be perfect ..." that is to say, if you want to acquire what is still lacking to you. Jesus is giving him an additional calling: "Come, follow me"; he is showing that he wants him to follow him more closely, and therefore he requires him, as he does others (cf. Mt 4:19–22), to give up anything that might hinder his full dedication to the Kingdom of God.

The scene ends rather pathetically: the young man goes away sad. His attachment to his property prevails over Jesus' affectionate invitation. Here is sadness of the kind that stems from cowardice, from failure to respond to God's calling with personal commitment.

In reporting this episode, the evangelists are actually giving us a case-study which describes a situation and formulates a law, a case-study of specific divine vocation to devote oneself to God's service and the service of all men.

This young man has become a symbol of the kind of Christian whose mediocrity and shortsightedness prevent him from turning his life into a generous, fruitful self-giving to the service of God and neighbour. What would this young man have become, had he been generous enough to respond to God's call? A great apostle, surely.

19:24–26. By drawing this comparison Jesus shows that it is simply not possible for people who put their hearts on worldly things to obtain a share in the Kingdom of God. "With God all things are possible": that is, with God's grace man can be brave and generous enough to use wealth to promote the service of God and man. This is why St Matthew, in chapter 5, specifies that the poor *in spirit* are blessed (Mt 5:3).

19:28. "In the new world", in the "regeneration": a reference to the renewal

Peter said in reply, "Lo, we have left everything and followed you. What then shall we have?" ²⁸Jesus said to them, "Truly, I say to you, in the new world, when the Son of man shall sit on his glorious throne, you who have followed me will also sit on twelve thrones, judging the twelve tribes of Israel. ²⁹And every one who has left houses or brothers or sisters or father or mother or children or lands, for my name's sake, will receive a hundredfold,¹ and inherit eternal life. ³⁰But many that are first will be last, and the last first.

Lk 5:11

Lk 22:30
Dan 7:9–18

Heb 10:34

Lk 13:30

Parable of the labourers in the vineyard

20 ¹"For the kingdom of heaven is like a householder who went out early in the morning to hire labourers for his vineyard. ²After agreeing with the labourers for a denariusᵐ a day, he sent them into his vineyard. ³And going out about the third hour he saw others standing idle in the market place; ⁴and to them he said, 'You go into the vineyard too, and whatever is right I will give you.' So they went. ⁵Going out again about the sixth hour and

---

of all things which will take place when Jesus Christ comes to judge the living and the dead. The resurrection of the body will be an integral part of this renewal.

The ancient people of God, Israel, was made up of twelve tribes. The new people of God, the Church, to which all men are called, is founded by Jesus Christ on the twelve apostles under the primacy of Peter.

19:29. These graphic remarks should not be explained away. They mean that love for Jesus Christ and his Gospel should come before everything else. What our Lord says here should not be interpreted as conflicting with the will of God himself, the creator and sanctifier of family bonds.

20:1–16. This parable is addressed to the Jewish people, whom God called at an early hour, centuries ago. Now the Gentiles are also being called—with an equal

right to form part of the new people of God, the Church. In both cases it is a matter of a gratuitous, unmerited, invitation; therefore, those who were the "first" to receive the call have no grounds for complaining when God calls the "last" and gives them the same reward—membership of his people. At first sight the labourers of the first hour seem to have a genuine grievance—because they do not realize that to have a job in the Lord's vineyard is a divine gift. Jesus leaves us in no doubt that although he calls us to follow different ways, all receive the same reward—heaven.

20:2. "Denarius": a silver coin bearing an image of Caesar Augustus (Mt 22:19–21).

20:3. The Jewish method of calculating time was different from ours. They divided the whole day into eight parts, four night parts (called "watches") and four

l. Other ancient authorities read *manifold*   m. The denarius was a day's wage for a labourer

the ninth hour, he did the same. [6]And about the eleventh hour he went out and found others standing; and he said to them, 'Why do you stand here idle all day?' [7]They said to him, 'Because no one has hired us.' He said to them, 'You go into the vineyard too.' [8]And when evening came, the owner of the vineyard said to his steward, 'Call the labourers and pay them their wages, beginning with the last, up to the first.' [9]And when those hired about the eleventh hour came, each of them received a denarius. [10]Now when the first came, they thought they would receive more; but each of them also received a denarius. [11]And on receiving it they grumbled at the householder, [12]saying, 'These last worked only one hour, and you have made them equal to us who have borne the burden of the day and the scorching heat.' [13]But he replied to one of them, 'Friend, I am doing you no wrong; did you not agree with me for a denarius? [14]Take what belongs to you, and go; I choose to give to this last as I give to you. [15]Am I not allowed to do what I choose with what belongs to me? Or do you begrudge my generosity?'[n] [16]So the last will be first, and the first last."

Rom 9:16, 21

Mt 19:30

---

day parts (called "hours")—the first, third, sixth and ninth hour.

The first hour began at sunrise and ended around nine o'clock; the third ran to twelve noon; the sixth to three in the afternoon; and the ninth from three to sunset. This meant that the first and ninth hours varied in length, decreasing in autumn and winter and increasing in spring and summer and the reverse happening with the first and fourth watches.

Sometimes intermediate hours were counted—as for example in v. 6 which refers to the eleventh hour, the short period just before sunset, the end of the working day.

20:16. The Vulgate, other translations and a good many Greek codexes add: "For many are called, but few are chosen" (cf. Mt 22:14).

20:18–19. Once again our Lord prophesies to his apostles about his death and

resurrection. The prospect of judging the world (cf. Mt 19:28) might have misled them into thinking in terms of an earthly messianic kingdom, an easy way ahead, leaving no room for the ignominy of the cross.

Christ prepares their minds so that when the testing time comes they will remember that he prophesied his passion and not be totally scandalized by it; he describes his passion in some detail.

Referring to Holy Week, St Josemaría Escrivá writes: "All the things brought to our mind by the different expressions of piety which characterize these days are of course directed to the Resurrection, which is, as St Paul says, the basis of our faith (cf. 1 Cor 15:14). But we should not tread this path too hastily, lest we lose sight of a very simple fact which we might easily overlook. We will not be able to share in our Lord's Resurrection unless we unite ourselves with him in his Passion and Death. If we are to accom-

n. Or *is your eye evil because I am good?*

Third announcement of the Passion

¹⁷And as Jesus was going up to Jerusalem, he took the twelve disciples aside, and on the way he said to them, ¹⁸"Behold, we are going up to Jerusalem; and the Son of man will be delivered to the chief priests and scribes, and they will condemn him to death, ¹⁹and deliver him to the Gentiles to be mocked and scourged and crucified, and he will be raised on the third day."

Mk 10:32–34
Lk 18:31–33

Mt 16:21;
17:22f

The mother of the sons of Zebedee makes her request

²⁰Then the mother of the sons of Zebedee came up to him, with her sons, and kneeling before him she asked him for something. ²¹And he said to her, "What do you want?" She said to him, "Command that these two sons of mine may sit, one at your right hand and one at your left, in your kingdom." ²²But Jesus answered, "You do not know what you are asking. Are you able to drink the cup that I am to drink?" They said to him, "We are able." ²³He said to them, "You will drink my cup, but to sit at my right hand and at my left is not mine to grant, but it is for those for whom it has been prepared by my Father." ²⁴And when the ten heard it they were indig-

Mk 10:34–45
Mt 10:2

Mt 19:28

Jn 18:11

Acts 12:2
Rev 1:9

Lk 22:24–28

---

pany Christ in his glory at the end of Holy Week, we must first enter into his holocaust and be truly united to him, as he lies dead on Calvary" (*Christ Is Passing By*, 95).

20:20. The sons of Zebedee are James the Greater and John. Their mother, Salome, thinking that the earthly reign of the Messiah is about to be established, asks that her sons be given the two foremost positions in it. Christ reproaches them for not grasping the true —spiritual—nature of the Kingdom of heaven and not realizing that government of the Church he is going to found implies service and martyrdom. "If you are working for Christ and imagine that a position of responsibility is anything but a burden, what disillusionment awaits you!" (St Josemaría Escrivá, *The Way*, 950).

20:22. "Drinking the cup" means suffering persecution and martyrdom for following Christ. "We are able": the sons of

Zebedee boldly reply that they can drink the cup; their generous expression evokes what St Paul will write years later: "I can do all things in him who strengthens me" (Phil 4:13).

20:23. "You will drink my cup": James the Greater will die a martyr's death in Jerusalem around the year 44 (cf. Acts 12:2); and John, after suffering imprisonment and the lash in Jerusalem (cf. Acts 4:3; 5:40–41), will spend a long period of exile on the island of Patmos (cf. Rev 1:9).

From what our Lord says here we can take it that positions of authority in the Church should not be the goal of ambition or the subject of human intrigue, but the outcome of a divine calling. Intent on doing the will of his heavenly Father, Christ was not going to allocate positions of authority on the basis of human considerations but, rather, in line with God's plans.

nant at the two brothers. ²⁵But Jesus called them to him and said, "You know that the rulers of the Gentiles lord it over them, and their great men exercise authority over them. ²⁶It shall not be so among you; but whoever would be great among you must be your servant, ²⁷and whoever would be first among you must be your slave; ²⁸even as the Son of man came not to be served but to serve, and to give his life as a ransom for many."

Mk 9:35

Lk 22:27
Phil 2:7
1 Tim 2:6

Mk 10:46–52
Lk 18:35–43
Mt 15:22

Curing of the blind men of Jericho

²⁹And as they went out of Jericho, a great crowd followed him. ³⁰And behold, two blind men sitting by the roadside, when they heard that Jesus was passing by, cried out,^o "Have mercy on us, Son of David!" ³¹The crowd rebuked them, telling them to be silent; but they cried out the more, "Lord, have mercy on us, Son of David!" ³²And Jesus stopped and called them, saying, "What do you want me to do for you?" ³³They said to him, "Lord, let our eyes be opened." ³⁴And Jesus in pity touched their eyes, and immediately they received their sight and followed him.

20:26. Vatican II puts a marked emphasis on this *service* which the Church offers to the world and which Christians should show as proof of their Christian identity: "In proclaiming the noble destiny of man and affirming an element of the divine in him, this sacred Synod offers to co-operate unreservedly with mankind in fostering a sense of brotherhood to correspond to this destiny of theirs. The Church is not motivated by an earthly ambition but is interested in one thing only—to carry on the work of Christ under the guidance of the Holy Spirit, for he came into the world to bear witness to the truth, to save and not to judge, to serve and not to be served" (*Gaudium et spes*, 3; cf. *Lumen gentium*, 32; *Ad gentes*, 12; *Unitatis redintegratio*, 7).

20:27–28. Jesus sets himself as an example to be imitated by those who hold authority in the Church. He who is God and Judge of all men (cf. Phil 2:5–11; Jn 5:22–27; Acts 10:42; Mt 28:18) does not impose himself on us: he renders us loving service to the point of giving his life for us (cf. Jn 15:13); that is his way of being the first. St Peter understood him right; he later exhorted priests to tend the flock of God entrusted to them, not domineering over them but being exemplary in their behaviour (cf. 1 Pet 5:1–3); and St Paul also was clear on this *service*: though he was "free from all men", he became the servant of all in order to win all (cf. 1 Cor 9:19ff; 2 Cor 4:5).

Christ's "service" of mankind aims at salvation. The phrase "to give his life as a ransom for many" is in line with the terminology of liturgical sacrificial language. These words were used prophetically in chapter 53 of Isaiah.

Verse 28 also underlines the fact that Christ is a priest, who offers himself as priest and victim on the altar of the cross. The expression "as a ransom for many"

---

o. Other ancient authorities insert *Lord*

PART THREE

Jesus' ministry in Jerusalem

10. CLEANSING OF THE TEMPLE. CONTROVERSIES

The Messiah enters the Holy City

21 ¹And when they drew near to Jerusalem and came to Bethphage, to the Mount of Olives, then Jesus sent two disciples, ²saying to them, "Go into the village opposite you, and immediately you will find an ass tied, and a colt with her; untie them and bring them to me. ³If any one says anything to you, you shall say, 'The Lord has need of them,' and he will send them immediately." ⁴This took place to fulfil what was spoken by the prophet, saying,

Mk 11:1–10
Lk 19:29–38
Jn 12:12–19

---

should not be interpreted as implying that God does not will the salvation of all men. "Many", here, is used in contrast with "one" rather than "all": there is only one Saviour, and salvation is offered to all.

20:30–34. These blind men, who seize their opportunity as Christ is passing by, give us a lesson in the kind of boldness and persistence with which we should entreat God to listen to us (cf. commentary on the characteristics of petitionary prayer in note on the Sermon on the Mount: Mt 7:7–8). Chrysostom comments: "Clearly these blind men deserved to be cured: first, because they cried out; and then, because after they received the gift they did not hasten away, the way most people, in their ingratitude, are inclined to do once they have got what they wanted. No, they were not like that: they were both persevering before the gift and grateful after it, for they 'followed him' (*Hom. on St Matthew*, 66).

21:1–5. In his triumphant entry into Jerusalem Jesus reveals himself as the Messiah, as St Matthew and St John (12:14) stress by quoting the prophecy of Zechariah 9:9. Although the Latin translation says "mounted on a [female] ass", the original Hebrew text says "mounted on a [male] ass", and the latter is the text followed in this translation (in the Greek translation of the Septuagint no sex is specified). The other two Synoptic Gospels limit themselves to giving the key fact of Jesus' messianic entry into the Holy City mounted on the colt (Mk 11:2; Lk 19:30). St Matthew sees in the fact that the colt is with the ass a further detail of the prophecy, which refers to the colt being the foal of an ass (that seems to be why the ass is referred to throughout the account, the ass being with the colt, although Jesus was mounted only on the colt).

In the prophecy in Zechariah 9:9 (which in the original Old Testament text is longer than the quotation in Matthew) the future messianic king is described as

139

Zech 9:9
Is 62:11

⁵"Tell the daughter of Zion,
Behold, your king is coming to you,
humble, and mounted on an ass,
and on a colt, the foal of an ass.'"

⁶The disciples went and did as Jesus had directed them; ⁷they brought the ass and the colt, and put their garments on them, and

2 Kings 9:13

he sat thereon. ⁸Most of the crowd spread their garments on the road, and others cut branches from the trees and spread them on

Ps 118:25f
2 Sam 14:4

the road. ⁹And the crowds that went before him and that followed him shouted, "Hosanna to the Son of David! Blessed is he who comes in the name of the Lord! Hosanna in the highest!" ¹⁰And when he entered Jerusalem, all the city was stirred, saying, "Who is this?" ¹¹And the crowds said, "This is the prophet Jesus from Nazareth of Galilee."

Jesus in the temple

Mk 11:11–24
Lk 19:45–48
Jn 2:14–15

¹²And Jesus entered the temple of God^p and drove out all who sold and bought in the temple, and he overturned the tables of the money-changers and the seats of those who sold pigeons. ¹³He

---

"humble". The ass, originally a noble mount (cf. Gen 22:3; Ex 4:20; Num 22:21; Jud 5:10), was replaced by the horse in the period of the Israelite monarchy (cf. 1 Kings 4:26; 10:28; etc.). The prophecy, by referring to an ass, shows that the king of peace wins his victory by humility and gentleness, not by force of arms.

The Fathers have read a deeper meaning into this episode. They see the ass as symbolizing Judaism, for long subject to the yoke of the Law, and the foal, on which no one has ridden, as symbolizing the Gentiles. Jesus leads both Jews and Gentiles into the Church, the new Jerusalem.

21:9. The Hebrew word *"Hosanna"*, which the people use to acclaim our Lord, was originally an appeal to God meaning "Save us". Later it was used as a shout of joy, an acclamation, meaning something like "Long live ...". The people are demonstrating their enthusiasm by shouting, "Long live the Son of David!" The phrase "Blessed is he who comes in the name of the Lord" comes from Psalm 118:26 and is a jubilant and appreciative greeting to someone entrusted with a mission from God. The Church takes up these acclamations, incorporating them into the preface of the Mass, to proclaim the kingship of Christ.

21:12–13. Although God is present everywhere and cannot be confined within the walls of temples built by man (Acts 17:24–25), God instructed Moses to build a tabernacle where he would dwell among the Israelites (Ex 25:40). Once the Jewish people were established in Palestine, King Solomon, also in obedience to a divine instruction, built the temple of Jerusalem (1 Kings 6–8), where people went to render public worship to God (Deut 12).

Exodus (23:15) commanded the Israelites not to enter the temple empty-handed, but to bring some victim to be

said to them, "It is written, 'My house shall be called a house of prayer'; but you make it a den of robbers."

Is 56:7
Jer 7:11 –

¹⁴And the blind and the lame came to him in the temple, and he healed them. ¹⁵But when the chief priests and the scribes saw the wonderful things that he did, and the children crying out in the temple, "Hosanna to the Son of David!" they were indignant; ¹⁶and they said to him, "Do you hear what these are saying?" And Jesus said to them, "Yes; have you never read,

Ps 118:25

Ps 8:2

> 'Out of the mouth of babes and sucklings
> thou hast brought perfect praise'?"

¹⁷And leaving them, he went out of the city to Bethany and lodged there.

The cursing of the fig tree

¹⁸In the morning, as he was returning to the city, he was hungry. ¹⁹And seeing a fig tree by the wayside he went to it, and found nothing on it but leaves only. And he said to it, "May no fruit ever come from you again!" And the fig tree withered at once. ²⁰When the disciples saw it they marvelled, saying, "How did the fig tree

Lk 13:6

---

sacrificed. To make this easier for people who had to travel a certain distance, a veritable market developed in the temple courtyards with animals being bought and sold for sacrificial purposes. Originally this may have made sense, but seemingly as time went on commercial gain became the dominant purpose of this buying and selling of victims; probably the priests themselves and temple servants benefited from this trade or even operated it. The net result was that the temple looked more like a livestock mart than a place for meeting God.

Moved by zeal for his Father's house (Jn 2:17), Jesus cannot tolerate this deplorable abuse and in holy anger he ejects everyone—to show people the respect and reverence due to the temple as a holy place. We should show much greater respect in the Christian temple—Christian churches—where the eucharis-

tic sacrifice is celebrated and where Jesus Christ, God and Man, is really and truly present, reserved in the tabernacle. For a Christian, proper dress, liturgical gestures and postures, genuflections and reverence to the tabernacle etc. are expressions of the respect due to the Lord in his temple.

21:15–17. The children's acclamations please God and infuriate the proud. This episode fulfils something which Jesus said earlier: "I thank thee, Father, Lord of heaven and earth, that thou hast hidden these things from the wise and understanding and revealed them to babes" (Mt 11:25). Only an attitude of simplicity and humility can grasp the greatness of the King of peace and understand the things of God.

21:18–22. The cursing of the fig tree is a parable in action; Jesus acts in this dra-

---

p. Other ancient authorities omit *of God*

wither at once?" [21]And Jesus answered them, "Truly, I say to you, if you have faith and never doubt, you will not only do what has been done to the fig tree, but even if you say to this mountain, 'Be taken up and cast into the sea,' it will be done. [22]and whatever you ask in prayer, you will receive, if you have faith."

The authority of Jesus is questioned

Mk 11:27–33
Lk 20:1–8
Jn 2:18

Jn 1:25

[23]And when he entered the temple, the chief priests and the elders of the people came up to him as he was teaching, and said, "By what authority are you doing these things, and who gave you this authority?" [24]Jesus answered them, "I also will ask you a question; and if you tell me the answer, then I also will tell you by what authority I do these things. [25]The baptism of John, whence was it? From heaven or from men?" And they argued with one another, "If we say, 'From heaven,' he will say to us, 'Why then did you not believe him?' [26]But if we say, 'From men,' we are afraid of the multitude; for all hold that John was a prophet." [27]So they answered Jesus, "We do not know." And he said to them, "Neither will I tell you by what authority I do these things.

matic way to show people the power of faith. The disciples marvel not because he curses the fig tree but because it shrivels up instantly.

This is an example of God's omnipotence, which is something we should always keep before our minds. Jesus is explaining the enormous power of faith. A person with faith can do anything; he can do much more difficult things, such as moving a mountain. Jesus goes on to show that one effect of faith is that it makes prayer all-powerful. He also gives us a lesson on genuine and apparent faithfulness in the spiritual life. "I want you to make use of your time. Don't forget the fig tree cursed by our Lord. And it was doing something: sprouting leaves. Like you … Don't tell me you have excuses. It availed the fig tree little, relates the evangelist, that it was not the season for figs when our Lord came to it to look for them. And barren it remained for ever" (St Josemaría Escrivá, *The Way*, 354).

21:23–27. When the chief priests and elders ask "By what authority are you doing these things?" they are referring both to his teaching and to his self-assured public actions—throwing the traders out of the temple, entering Jerusalem in triumph, allowing the children to acclaim him, curing the sick, etc. What they want him to do is to prove that he has authority to act in this way or to admit openly that he is the Messiah. However, Jesus knows that they are not well-intentioned and he declines to give them a direct answer; he prefers to put a question to them that forces them to make their own attitude clear. He seeks to provoke them into examining their consciences and changing their whole approach.

21:32. St John the Baptist had shown the way to sanctification by proclaiming the imminence of the Kingdom of God and by preaching conversion. The scribes and Pharisees would not believe him, yet they

Parable of the two sons

28"What do you think? A man had two sons; and he went to the first and said, 'Son, go and work in the vineyard today.' 29And he answered, 'I will not'; but afterward he repented and went. 30And he went to the second and said the same; and he answered, 'I go, sir,' but did not go. 31Which of the two did the will of his father?" They said, "The first." Jesus said to them, "Truly, I say to you, the tax collectors and the harlots go into the kingdom of God before you. 32For John came to you in the way of righteousness, and you did not believe him, but the tax collectors and the harlots believed him; and even when you saw it, you did not afterward repent and believe him.

Lk 18:14

Lk 7:29

Parable of the wicked tenants

33"Hear another parable. There was a householder who planted a vineyard, and set a hedge around it, and dug a wine press in it, and built a tower, and let it out to tenants, and went into another country. 34When the season of fruit drew near, he sent his servants to the tenants, to get his fruit; 35and the tenants took his servants and beat one, killed another, and stoned another. 36Again he sent other servants, more than the first; and they did the same to them.

Mk 12:1–12
Lk 20:9–19
Mt 25:14
Is 5:1f

---

boasted of their faithfulness to God's teaching. They were like the son who says "I will go" and then does not go; the tax collectors and prostitutes who repented and corrected the course of their lives will enter the Kingdom before them: they are like the other son who says "I will not", but then does go. Our Lord stresses that penance and conversion can set people on the road to holiness even if they have been living apart from God for a long time.

21:33–46. This very important parable completes the previous one. The parable of the two sons simply identifies the indocility of Israel; that of the wicked tenants focusses on the punishment to come.

Our Lord compares Israel to a choice vineyard, specially fenced, with a watchtower, where a keeper is on the look-out to protect it from thieves and foxes. God has spared no effort to cultivate and embellish his vineyard. The vineyard is in the charge of tenant farmers; the householder is God, and the vineyard, Israel (Is 5:3–5; Jer 2:21; Joel 1:7).

The tenants to whom God has given the care of his people are the priests, scribes and elders. The owner's absence makes it clear that God really did entrust Israel to its leaders; hence their responsibility and the account he demands of them.

The owner used to send his servants from time to time to collect the fruit; this was the mission of the prophets. The second despatch of servants to claim what is owing to the owner—who meet the same fate as the first—refers to the way God's prophets were ill-treated by the kings and priests of Israel (Mt 23:37; Acts 7:42; Heb 11:36–38). Finally he sent his Son to them, thinking that they would have more respect for him; here we can see the difference between Jesus and the prophets, who were servants, not

[handwritten marginalia: God giving, or turning over, the work of the long-awaited, long-promised Old Testament prophet]

[handwritten marginalia: Christ entrusted his kingdom to the Church]

37Afterward he sent his son to them, saying, 'They will respect my son.' 38But when the tenants saw the son, they said to themselves, 'This is the heir; come, let us kill him and have his inheritance.' 39And they took him and cast him out of the vineyard, and killed him. 40When therefore the owner of the vineyard comes, what will he do to those tenants?" 41They said to him, "He will put those wretches to a miserable death, and let out the vineyard to other tenants who will give him the fruits in their seasons."

Ps 118:22f
Acts 4:11
Rom 9:33
1 Pet 2:6–8

42Jesus said to them, "Have you never read in the scriptures:
'The very stone which the builders rejected
has become the head of the corner;
this was the Lord's doing,
and it is marvellous in our eyes'?

Dan 2:34f; 44f

43Therefore I tell you, the kingdom of God will be taken away from you and given to a nation producing the fruits of it. 44And he who falls on this stone will be broken to pieces; but when it falls on any one, it will crush him."q

45When the chief priests and the Pharisees heard his parables, they perceived that he was speaking about them. 46But when they tried to arrest him, they feared the multitudes, because they held him to be a prophet.

"the Son": the parable indicates singular, transcendental sonship, expressing the divinity of Jesus Christ.

The malicious purpose of the tenants in murdering the son and heir to keep the inheritance for themselves is the madness of the leaders in expecting to become undisputed masters of Israel by putting Christ to death (Mt 12:14; 26:4). Their ambition blinds them to the punishment that awaits them. Then "they cast him out of the vineyard, and killed him": a reference to Christ's crucifixion, which took place outside the walls of Jerusalem.

Jesus prophesies the punishment God will inflict on the evildoers: he will put them to death and rent the vineyard to others. This is a very significant prophecy. St Peter later repeats it to the Sanhedrin: "this is the stone which was rejected by you builders, but which has become the head of the corner" (Acts 4:11; 1 Pet 2:4). The stone is Jesus of Nazareth, but the architects of Israel, who build up and rule the people, have chosen not to use it in the building. Because of their unfaithfulness the Kingdom of God will be turned over to another people, the Gentiles, who *will* give God the fruit he expects his vineyard to yield (cf. Mt 3:8–10; Gal 6:16).

For the building to be well built, it needs to rest on this stone. Woe to him who trips over it! (cf. Mt 12:30; Lk 2:34), as first Jews and later the enemies of Christ and his Church will discover through bitter experience (cf. Is 8:14–15).

Christians in all ages should see this parable as exhorting them to build faithfully upon Christ and make sure they do not fall into the sin of this Jewish genera-

q. Other ancient authorities omit verse 44

Parable of the marriage feast

22 ¹And again Jesus spoke to them in parables, saying, ²"The kingdom of heaven may be compared to a king who gave a marriage feast for his son, ³and sent his servants to call those who were invited to the marriage feast; but they would not come. ⁴Again he sent other servants, saying, 'Tell those who are invited, Behold, I have made ready my dinner, my oxen and my fat calves are killed, and everything is ready; come to the marriage feast.' ⁵But they made light of it and went off, one to his farm, another to his business, ⁶while the rest seized his servants, treated them shamefully, and killed them. ⁷The king was angry, and he sent his troops and destroyed those murderers and burned their city. ⁸Then he said to his servants, 'The wedding is ready, but those invited were not worthy. ⁹Go therefore to the thoroughfares, and invite to the marriage feast as many as you find.' ¹⁰And those servants went out into the streets and gathered all whom they found, both bad and good; so the wedding hall was filled with guests.

¹¹"But when the king came in to look at the guests, he saw there a man who had no wedding garment; ¹²and he said to him, 'Friend, how did you get in here without a wedding garment?'

Lk 14:16–24
Jn 3:29

---

tion. We should also be filled with hope and a sense of security; for, although the building—*the Church*—at some times seems to be breaking up, its sound construction, with Christ as its cornerstone, is assured.

22:1–14. In this parable Jesus reveals how intensely God the Father desires the salvation of all men—the banquet is the Kingdom of heaven—and the mysterious malice that lies in willingly rejecting the invitation to attend, a malice so vicious that it merits eternal punishment. No human arguments make any sense that go against God's call to conversion and acceptance of faith and its consequences.

The Fathers see in the first invitees the Jewish people: in salvation history God addresses himself first to the Israelites and then to all the Gentiles (Acts 13:46).

Indifference and hostility cause the Israelites to reject God's loving call and therefore to suffer condemnation. But the Gentiles also need to respond faithfully to the call they have received; otherwise they will suffer the fate of being cast "into outer darkness".

"The marriage", says St Gregory the Great (*In Evangelia homiliae*, 36) "is the wedding of Christ and his Church, and the garment is the virtue of charity: a person who goes into the feast without a wedding garment is someone who believes in the Church but does not have charity."

The wedding garment signifies the dispositions a person needs for entering the Kingdom of heaven. Even though he may belong to the Church, if he does not have these dispositions he will be condemned on the day when God judges all mankind. These dispositions essentially mean responding to grace.

And he was speechless. [13]Then the king said to the attendants, 'Bind him hand and foot, and cast him into the outer darkness; there men will weep and gnash their teeth.' [14]For many are called, but few are chosen."

Paying tax to Caesar

Mk 12:13–17
Lk 20:20–26
Jn 8:6
Mk 3:6
Jn 3:2

[15]Then the Pharisees went and took counsel how to entangle him in his talk. [16]And they sent their disciples to him, along with the Herodians, saying, "Teacher, we know that you are true, and teach the way of God truthfully, and care for no man; for you do not regard the position of men. [17]Tell us, then, what you think. Is it lawful to pay taxes to Caesar, or not?" [18]But Jesus, aware of their malice, said, "Why put me to the test, you hypocrites? [19]Show me the money for the tax." And they brought him a coin.[r] [20]And Jesus

Rom 13:7

said to them, "Whose likeness and inscription is this?" [21]They said, "Caesar's." Then he said to them, "Render therefore to

---

22:13. Vatican II reminds us of the doctrine of the "last things", one aspect of which is covered in this verse. Referring to the eschatological dimension of the Church, the Council recalls our Lord's warning about being on the watch against the wiles of the devil, in order to resist in the evil day (cf. Eph 6:11–13). "Since we know neither the day nor the hour, we should follow the advice of the Lord and watch constantly so that, when the single course of our earthly life is completed (cf. Heb 9:27), we may merit to enter with him into the marriage feast and be numbered among the blessed (cf. Mt 25:31–46) and not, like the wicked and slothful servants (cf. Mt 25:26), be ordered to depart into the eternal fire (cf. Mt 25:41), into the outer darkness where 'men will weep and gnash their teeth'" (*Lumen gentium*, 48).

22:14. These words in no way conflict with God's will that all should be saved (cf. 1 Tim 2:4). In his love for men, Christ patiently seeks the conversion of

every single soul, going as far as to die on the cross (cf. Mt 23:37; Lk 15:4–7). St Paul teaches this when he says that Christ loved us and "gave himself up for us, a fragrant offering and sacrifice to God" (Eph 5:2). Each of us can assert with the apostle that Christ "loved me and gave himself for me" (Gal 2:20). However, God in his infinite wisdom respects man's freedom: man is free to reject grace (cf. Mt 7:13–14).

22:15–21. The Pharisees and Herodians join forces to plot against Jesus. The Herodians were supporters of the regime of Herod and his dynasty. They were quite well disposed to Roman rule and, as far as religious matters were concerned, they held the same kind of materialistic ideas as the Sadducees. The Pharisees were zealous keepers of the Law; they were anti-Roman and regarded the Herods as usurpers. It is difficult to imagine any two groups more at odds with each other: their amazing pact shows how much they hated Jesus.

---

r. Greek *a denarius*

likeness - image (on the coin - ceaser)
we are created in the image + likeness of God.
(Pharasees)
Matthew 22:28

Caesar the things that are Caesar's, and to God the things that are God's." [22]When they heard it, they marvelled; and they left him and went away.

reminds they pay taxes) because they didn't give themselves to God.

Jn 8:9

The resurrection of the dead

[23]The same day Sadducees came to him, who say that there is no resurrection; and they asked him a question, [24]saying, "Teacher, Moses said, 'If a man dies, having no children, his brother must marry the widow, and raise up children for his brother.' [25]Now there were seven brothers among us; the first married, and died, and having no children left his wife to his brother. [26]So too the second and third, down to the seventh. [27]After them all, the woman died. [28]In the resurrection, therefore, to which of the seven will she be wife? For they all had her."

Mk 12:18–27
Lk 20:27–40
Acts 23:6, 8
Gen 38:8
Deut 25:5f

Had Jesus replied that it was lawful to pay taxes to Caesar, the Pharisees could have discredited him in the eyes of the people, who were very nationalistic; if he said it was unlawful, the Herodians would have been able to denounce him to the Roman authorities.

Our Lord's answer is at once so profound that they fail to grasp its meaning, and it is also faithful to his preaching about the Kingdom of God: give Caesar what is his due, but no more, because God must assuredly be given what *he* has a right to (the other side of the question, which they omitted to put). God and Caesar are on two quite different levels, because for an Israelite God transcends all human categories. What has Caesar a right to receive? Taxes, which are necessary for legitimate state expenses. What must God be given? Obviously, obedience to *all* his commandments—which implies personal love and commitment. Jesus' reply goes beyond the human horizons of these temptors, far beyond the simple yes or no they wanted to draw out of him.

The teaching of Jesus transcends any kind of political approach, and if the faithful, using the freedom that is

theirs, chose one particular method of solving temporal questions, they "ought to remember that in those cases no one is permitted to identify the authority of the Church exclusively with his own opinion" (Vatican II, *Gaudium et spes*, 43).

Jesus' words show that he recognized civil authority and its rights, but he made it quite clear that the superior rights of God must be respected (cf. Vatican II, *Dignitatis humanae*, 11), and pointed out that it is part of God's will that we faithfully fulfil our civic duties (cf. Rom 13:1–7).

22:23–33. The Sadducees argue against belief in the resurrection of the dead on the basis of the levirate law, a Jewish law which laid down that when a married man died without issue, one of his brothers, according to a fixed order, should marry his widow and the first son of that union be given the dead man's name. By outlining an extreme case the Sadducees make the law and belief in resurrection look ridiculous. In his reply Jesus shows up the frivolity of their objections and asserts the truth of the resurrection of the dead.

²⁹But Jesus answered them, "You are wrong, because you know neither the scriptures nor the power of God. ³⁰For in the resurrection they neither marry nor are given in marriage, but are like angels^s in heaven. ³¹And as for the resurrection of the dead, have

Ex 3:6

you not read what was said to you by God, ³²'I am the God of Abraham, and the God of Isaac, and the God of Jacob'? He is not God of the dead, but of the living." ³³And when the crowd heard it, they were astonished at his teaching.

The greatest commandment of all

Mk 12:28–31
Lk 10:25–28

³⁴But when the Pharisees heard that he had silenced the Sadducees, they came together. ³⁵And one of them, a lawyer, asked

---

22:30. Jesus explains quite unequivocally that the blessed have transcended the natural condition of man and the institution of marriage therefore no longer has any raison d'etre in heaven. The primary aim of marriage—the procreation and education of children—no longer applies because once immortality is reached there is no need for procreation to renew the human race (cf. St Thomas Aquinas, *Comm. on St Matthew*, 22:30). Similarly, mutual help—another aim of marriage—is no longer necessary, because the blessed enjoy an eternal and total happiness by possessing God.

22:34–40. In reply to the question, our Lord points out that the whole law can be condensed into two commandments: the first and more important consists in unconditional love of God; the second is a consequence and result of the first, because when man is loved, St Thomas says, God is loved, for man is the image of God (cf. ibid., 22:4).

A person who genuinely loves God also loves his fellows because he realizes that they are his brothers and sisters, children of the same Father, redeemed by the same blood of our Lord Jesus Christ: "this commandment we have from him, that he

who loves God should love his brother also" (1 Jn 4:21). However, if we love man for man's sake without reference to God, this love will become an obstacle in the way of keeping the first commandment, and then it is no longer genuine love of our neighbour. But love of our neighbour for God's sake is clear proof that we love God: "If anyone says, 'I love God', and hates his brother, he is a liar" (1 Jn 4:20).

"You shall love your neighbour as yourself ": here our Lord establishes as the guideline for our love of neighbour the love each of us has for himself; both love of others and love of self are based on love of God. Hence, in some cases it can happen that God requires us to put our neighbour's need before our own; in others, not: it depends on what value, in the light of God's love, needs to be put on the spiritual and material factors involved.

Obviously spiritual goods take absolute precedence over material ones, even over life itself. Therefore, spiritual goods, be they our own or our neighbour's, must be the first to be safeguarded. If the spiritual good in question is the supreme one of the salvation of the soul, no one is justified in putting his own soul into certain danger of being condemned in order to save another,

---

s. Other ancient authorities add *of God*

him a question, to test him. ³⁶"Teacher, which is the great commandment in the law?" ³⁷And he said to him, "You shall love the
Lord your God with all your heart, and with all your soul, and
with all your mind. ³⁸This is the great and first commandment.
³⁹And a second is like it, You shall love your neighbour as yourself. ⁴⁰On these two commandments depend all the law and the
prophets." *saying the some-thing*

Deut 6:5

Lev 19:18
Rom 13:10
Gal 4:14

The divinity of the Messiah

⁴¹Now while the Pharisees were gathered together, Jesus asked
them a question, ⁴²saying, "What do you think of the Christ?
Whose son is he?" They said to him, "The son of David." ⁴³He

Mk 12:25–37
Lk 20:41–44
Jn 7:42

because given human freedom we can never be absolutely sure what personal choice another person may make: this is the situation in the parable (cf. Mt 25:1–13), where the wise virgins refuse to give oil to the foolish ones; similarly St Paul says that he would wish himself to be rejected if that could save his brothers (cf. Rom 9:3)—an unreal theoretical situation. However, what is quite clear is that we have to do all we can to save our brothers, conscious that, if someone helps to bring a sinner back to the way, he will save himself from eternal death and cover a multitude of his own sins (Jas 5:20). From all this we can deduce that self-love of the right kind, based on God's love for man, necessarily involves forgetting oneself in order to love God and our neighbour for God.

22:37–38. The commandment of love is the most important commandment because by obeying it man attains his own perfection (cf. Col 3:14). "The more a soul loves," St John of the Cross writes, "the more perfect is it in that which it loves; therefore this soul that is now perfect is wholly love, if it may thus be expressed, and all its actions are love and it employs all its faculties and possessions in loving, giving all that it has, like the wise mer-

chant, for this treasure of love which it has found hidden in God [...]. For, even as the bee extracts from all plants the honey that is in them, and has no use for them for aught else save for that purpose, even so the soul with great facility extracts the sweetness of love that is in all the things that pass through it; it loves God in each of them, whether pleasant or unpleasant; and being, as it is, informed and protected by love, it has neither feeling nor taste nor knowledge of such things, for, as we have said, the soul knows naught but love, and its pleasure in all things and occupations is ever, as we have said, the delight of the love of God" (*Spiritual Canticle*, stanza 27, 8).

22:41–46. God promised King David that one of his descendants would reign forever (2 Sam 7:12ff); this was obviously a reference to the Messiah, and was interpreted as such by all Jewish tradition, which gave the Messiah the title of "Son of David". In Jesus' time this messianic title was understood in a very nationalistic sense: the Jews were expecting an earthly king, a descendant of David, who would free them from Roman rule. In this passage Jesus shows the Pharisees that the Messiah has a higher origin: he is not only "Son of David"; his nature is

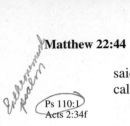

said to them, "How is it then that David, inspired by the Spirit,[t] calls him Lord, saying,

> [44]'The Lord said to my Lord,
>
> Sit at my right hand,
>
> till I put thy enemies under thy feet'?

[45]If David thus calls him Lord, how is he his son?" [46]And no one was able to answer him a word, nor from that day did any one dare to ask him any more questions.

Ps 110:1
Acts 2:34f

Jesus berates the scribes and Pharisees

Mk 12:38–40
Lk 20:45–47;
11:39–52

Mal 2:7f

23

[1] Then said Jesus to the crowds and to his disciples, [2]"The scribes and the Pharisees sit on Moses' seat; [3]so practise and observe whatever they tell you, but not what they do; for they

---

more exalted than that, for he is the Son of God and transcends the purely earthly level. The reference to Psalm 110:1 which Jesus uses in his argument explains that the Messiah is God: which is why David calls him Lord—and why he is seated at the right hand of God, his equal in power, majesty and glory (cf. Acts 33–36; 1 Cor 6:25).

23:1–39. Throughout this chapter Jesus severely criticizes the scribes and Pharisees and demonstrates the sorrow and compassion he feels towards the ordinary mass of the people, who have been ill-used, "harassed and helpless, like sheep without a shepherd" (Mt 9:36). His address may be divided into three parts: in the first (vv. 1–12) he identifies their principal vices and corrupt practices; in the second (vv. 13–36) he confronts them and speaks his famous "woes", which in effect are the reverse of the beatitudes he preached in chapter 5: no one can enter the Kingdom of heaven—no one can escape condemnation to the flames—unless he changes his attitude and behaviour; in the third part (vv. 37–39) he weeps over Jerusalem, so grieved is he

by the evils into which the blind pride and hardheartedness of the scribes and Pharisees have misled the people.

23:2–3. Moses passed on to the people the Law received from God. The scribes, who for the most part sided with the Pharisees, had the function of educating the people in the Law of Moses; that is why they were said to "sit on Moses' seat". Our Lord recognized that the scribes and Pharisees did have authority to teach the Law; but he warns the people and his disciples to be sure to distinguish the Law as read out and taught in the synagogues from the practical interpretations of the Law to be seen in their leaders' lifestyles. Some years later, St Paul—a Pharisee like his father before him—faced his former colleagues with exactly the same kind of accusations as Jesus makes here: "You then who teach others, will you not teach yourself? While you preach against stealing, do you steal? You who say that one must not commit adultery, do you commit adultery? You who abhor idols, do you rob temples? You who boast in the law, do you dishonour God by breaking the law?

---

t. Or *David in the Spirit*

preach, but do not practise. ⁴They bind heavy burdens, hard to bear,ᵘ and lay them on men's shoulders; but they themselves will not move them with their finger. ⁵They do all their deeds to be seen by men; for they make their phylacteries broad and their fringes long, ⁶and they love the place of honour at feasts and the best seats in the synagogues, ⁷and salutations in the market places, and being called rabbi by men. ⁸But you are not to be called rabbi, for you have one teacher, and you are all brethren. ⁹And call no man your father on earth, for you have one Father, who is in heaven. ¹⁰Neither be called masters, for you have one master, the Christ. ¹¹He who is greatest among you shall be your servant; ¹²whoever exalts himself will be humbled, and whoever humbles himself will be exalted.

Ex 13:9
Num 15:38f

Lk 14:7
Jn 5:44

Prov 29:23
Job 22:29
Ezek 21:26
Lk 18:14
1 Pet 5:5

For, as it is written, 'The name of God is blasphemed among the Gentiles because of you'" (Rom 2:21–24).

23:5. "Phylacteries": belts or bands carrying quotations from Holy Scripture which the Jews used to wear fastened to their arms or foreheads. To mark themselves out as more religiously observant than others, the Pharisees used to wear broader phylacteries. The fringes were light-blue stripes on the hems of cloaks; the Pharisees ostentatiously wore broader fringes.

23:8–10. Jesus comes to teach the Truth; in fact, he is the Truth (cf. Jn 14:6). As a teacher, therefore, he is absolutely unique and unparalleled. "The whole of Christ's life was a continual teaching: his silences, his miracles, his gestures, his prayer, his love for people, his special affection for the little and the poor, his acceptance of the total sacrifice on the cross for the redemption of the world, and his resurrection are the actualization of his word and the fulfilment of revelation. Hence for Christians the crucifix is one of the most sublime and popular images of Christ the Teacher.

"These considerations are in line with the great traditions of the Church and they all strengthen our fervour with regard to Christ, the Teacher who reveals God to man and man to himself, the Teacher who saves, sanctifies and guides, who lives, who speaks, rouses, moves, redresses, judges, forgives, and goes with us day by day on the path of history, the Teacher who comes and will come in glory" (John Paul II, *Catechesi tradendae*, 9).

23:11. The Pharisees were greedy for honour and recognition: our Lord insists that every form of authority, particularly in the context of religion, should be exercised as a form of service of others; it must not be used to indulge personal vanity or greed. "He who is greatest among you shall be your servant".

23:12. A spirit of pride and ambition is incompatible with being a disciple of Christ. Here our Lord stresses the need for true humility, for anyone who is to follow him. The verbs "will be humbled", "will be exalted" have "God" as their active agent. Along the same lines, St James preaches that "God opposes the proud, but gives

u. Other ancient authorities omit *hard to bear*

¹³"But woe to you, scribes and Pharisees, hypocrites! because you shut the kingdom of heaven against men; for you neither enter yourselves, nor allow those who would enter to go in.ᵛ ¹⁵Woe to you, scribes and Pharisees, hypocrites! for you traverse sea and land to make a single proselyte, and when he becomes a proselyte, you make him twice as much a child of hellʷ as yourselves.

¹⁶"Woe to you, blind guides, who say, 'If any one swears by the temple, it is nothing; but if any one swears by the gold of the temple, he is bound by his oath.' ¹⁷You blind fools! For which is greater, the gold or the temple that has made the gold sacred? ¹⁸And you say, 'If any one swears by the altar, it is nothing; but if any one swears by the gift that is on the altar, he is bound by his oath.' ¹⁹You blind men! For which is greater, the gift or the altar that makes the gift sacred? ²⁰So he who swears by the altar, swears

Ezek 29:37

---

grace to the humble" (Jas 4:6). And in the *Magnificat*, the Blessed Virgin explains that the Lord "has put down the mighty from their thrones, and exalted those of low degree [the humble]" (Lk 1:52).

23:13. Now comes our Lord's invective against the behaviour of the scribes and Pharisees: his "woes" condemn their past conduct and threaten them with punishment if they do not repent and mend their ways.

23:14. See the RSV note below. Our Lord is not reproaching them for praying long prayers but for their hypocrisy and cupidity. By going in for a lot of external religious practices, the Pharisees wanted to be recognized as devout men and then trade on that reputation particularly with vulnerable people. Widows, for example, would ask them to say prayers; the Pharisees in turn would ask for alms. What Jesus means here is that prayer should always come from an upright heart and a generous spirit. See the notes on Mt 6:5–8.

23:15. "Proselyte": a pagan convert to Judaism. The root of the word means "he who comes", he who—coming from idolatry—joins the chosen people in response to a calling from God. The Pharisees spared no effort to gain converts. Our Lord reproaches them not for this, but because they were concerned only about human success, their motivation being vainglory.

The sad thing about these proselytes was that, after receiving the light of Old Testament revelation, they remained under the influence of scribes and Pharisees, who passed on to them their own narrow outlook.

23:22. Our Lord's teaching about taking oaths is given in the Sermon on the Mount (Mt 5:33–37). Jesus does away with the nitpicking casuistry of the Pharisees by focussing directly on the uprightness of the intention of the oath-taker and by stressing the respect due to God's majesty and dignity. What Jesus wants is a pure heart, with no element of deceit. Our Lord

---

v. Other authorities add here (or after verse 12) verse 14, *Woe to you, scribes and Pharisees, hypocrites! for you devour widows' houses and for a pretence you make long prayers, therefore you will receive the greater condemnation* **w.** Greek *Gehenna*

by it and by everything on it; ²¹and he who swears by the temple, swears by it and by him who dwells in it; ²²and he who swears by heaven, swears by the throne of God and by him who sits upon it.

²³"Woe to you, scribes and Pharisees, hypocrites! for you tithe mint and dill and cummin, and have neglected the weightier matters of the law, justice and mercy and faith; these you ought to have done, without neglecting the others. ²⁴You blind guides, straining out a gnat and swallowing a camel!

Lev 27:30
Mic 6:8

²⁵"Woe to you, scribes and Pharisees, hypocrites! for you cleanse the outside of the cup and of the plate, but inside they are full of extortion and rapacity. ²⁶You blind Pharisee! first cleanse the inside of the cup and of the plate, that the outside also may be clean.

Mk 7:4

Tit 1:15
Jn 9:40

²⁷"Woe to you, scribes and Pharisees, hypocrites! for you are like whitewashed tombs, which outwardly appear beautiful, but within they are full of dead men's bones and all uncleanness. ²⁸So

Acts 23:2

---

particularly reproves any tendency to undermine the content of an oath, as the doctors of the Law tended to do, thereby failing to respect holy things and especially the holy name of God. He therefore draws attention to the commandment of the Law which says, "You shall not take the name of the Lord your God in vain" (Ex 20:7; Lev 19:12; Deut 5:11).

23:23. Mint, dill (aniseed) and cummin were herbs the Jews used in cooking or to perfume rooms. They were such insignificant items that they were not covered by the Mosaic precept on paying tithes (Lev 27:30–33; Deut 14:22ff); the precept did not apply to domestic animals and the more common agricultural products such as wheat, wine and olive oil. However, the Pharisees, being so intent on showing their scrupulous observance of the Law, paid tithes even of these herbs. Our Lord does not despise or reject the Law; he is simply telling people to get their priorities right: there is no point in attending to secondary details if one is neglecting what is really basic and important—justice, mercy and faith.

23:24. The Pharisees were so scrupulous about not swallowing any insect which the Law declared to be unclean that they went as far as to filter drinks through a linen cloth. Our Lord criticizes them for being so inconsistent—straining mosquitos, being so scrupulous about little things, yet quite happily "swallowing a camel", committing serious sins.

23:25–26. After reproaching the Pharisees for their hypocrisy in religious practice, our Lord now goes on to indict their twofacedness in matters of morality. The Jews used to perform elaborate washings of plates, cups and other tableware, in line with the regulations on legal cleansing (cf. Mk 7:1–4).

The example he chooses suggests a deeper level of meaning—concern for that moral purity which should characterize man's interior life. What is of prime importance is cleanness of heart, an upright intention, consistency between what one says and what one does, etc.

23:27–28. The Jews used to whitewash tombs annually, shortly before the feast of the Passover. The whitewash made the

153

Lk 16:15   you also outwardly appear righteous to men, but within you are full of hypocrisy and iniquity. ²⁹"Woe to you, scribes and Pharisees, hypocrites! for you build the tombs of the prophets and adorn the monuments of the right-eous, ³⁰saying, 'If we had lived in the days of our fathers, we would not have taken part with them in shedding the blood of the

Acts 7:52   prophets.' ³¹Thus you witness against yourselves, that you are sons of those who murdered the prophets. ³²Fill up, then, the measure of your fathers. ³³You serpents, you brood of vipers, how are you

1 Thess 2:15   to escape being sentenced to hell?ʷ ³⁴Therefore I send you prophets and wise men and scribes, some of whom you will kill and crucify, and some you will scourge in your synagogues and

Gen 4:8
2 Chron 24:20f
Mt 27:25   persecute from town to town, ³⁵that upon you may come all the righteous blood shed on earth, from the blood of innocent Abel to the blood of Zechariah the son of Barachiah, whom you murdered between the sanctuary and the altar. ³⁶Truly, I say to you, all this will come upon this generation.

---

tombs more visible and helped to avoid people brushing against them, which would have meant incurring legal uncleanness for seven days (Num 19:16; cf. Lk 11:44). In the sunlight, these tombs sparkled radiantly white, but inside they still held corruption.

23:29–32. Our Lord shows them that they are cut from the same cloth as their ancestors—not because they erect mau-soleums in honour of prophets and just men but because they are guilty of the same sin as those who killed the prophets. Hence their hypocrisy, which makes them even worse than their fathers. With pained irony Jesus tells them that they are com-pounding the sins of their ancestors.

Clearly this is referring to his passion and death: if the ancients killed the prophets, by causing him to suffer and die our Lord's contemporaries will be still more cruel.

23:34. The New Testament does in fact refer to prophets (cf. 1 Cor 12:28; Acts

13:1), wise men (cf. 1 Cor 2:6; Mt 13:52) and teachers (cf. Acts 13:1; 1 Cor 12:28), because the people in question are indeed full of the Holy Spirit and teach in Christ's name. The history of the Church shows that what Jesus says here came true, for it was in the synagogue that the first perse-cutions of the Christians occurred.

23:35. This Zechariah was different from the last but one of the main prophets. App-arently Jesus is referring to the Zechariah who suffered death by stoning during the reign of King Joash (2 Chron 24:16–22). "Between the sanctuary and the altar": within the sacred precincts, marked off by a wall, was the building which may be called the temple proper, in front of which was the great altar of holocausts.

23:37–39. Jesus' moving remarks seem almost to sum up the entire history of sal-vation and are a testimony to his divinity. Who if not God was the source of all these acts of mercy which mark the stages of the history of Israel? The image of

w. Greek *Gehenna*

Jerusalem admonished

³⁷"O Jerusalem, Jerusalem, killing the prophets and stoning those who are sent to you! How often would I have gathered your children together as a hen gathers her brood under her wings, and you would not! ³⁸Behold, your house is forsaken and desolate.^x ³⁹For I tell you, you will not see me again, until you say, 'Blessed is he who comes in the name of the Lord.'"

Lk 13:3f
Acts 7:59
1 Thess 2:15

Jer 22:5; 12:7
1 Kings 9:7f
Mt 21:9
Ps 118:26

11. THE ESCHATOLOGICAL DISCOURSE

Announcement of the destruction of the temple

24 ¹Jesus left the temple and was going away, when his disciples came to point out to him the buildings of the temple. ²But he answered them, "You see all these, do you not? Truly, I say to you, there will not be left here one stone upon another, that will not be thrown down."

Mk 13
Lk 21:5–36

Lk 19:44

---

being protected by wings, which occurs often in the Old Testament, refers to God's love and protection of his people. It is to be found in the prophets, in the canticle of Moses (cf. Deut 32:11), and in many psalms (cf. 17:8; 36:8; 57:2; 61:5; 63:8). "And you would not": the Kingdom of God has been preached to them unremittingly for centuries by the prophets; in these last few years by Jesus himself, the Word of God made man. But the "Holy City" has resisted all the unique graces offered it. Jerusalem should serve as a warning to every Christian: the freedom God has given us by creating us in his image and likeness means that we have this terrible capacity to reject him. A Christian's life is a continuous series of conversions—repeated instances of repentance, of turning to God, who, loving Father that he is, is ever ready to forgive.

24:1. In this discourse in which our Lord tells us about the last things, three prophecies seem to be interwoven—the destruction of Jerusalem (by the armies of

the Emperor Titus in the year 70); the end of the world; and the last coming of Christ. Our Lord invites us to be watchful and pray, as we await these three events.

The headings and side headings added into the Gospel text may be of some help in working out what Jesus is referring to at different stages in the discourse. It is quite easy to confuse the signs and times of the destruction of Jerusalem and those of the end of the world and the last coming—which is not all that surprising, given that the destruction of Jerusalem itself symbolizes the end of the world. Our Lord is speaking here very much in the style and language used by the prophets, who announced future events without specifying the order in which they would happen and who used a profusion of images and symbols. Every prophecy about the future seems quite obscure at first but as the events unfold everything fits into place. The Old Testament prophecies were not well understood until they were fulfilled during Christ's first coming; and the New Testament prophecies will

x. Other ancient authorities omit *and desolate*

The beginning of tribulations. Persecution on account of the Gospel

³As he sat on the Mount of Olives, the disciples came to him privately, saying, "Tell us, when will this be, and what will be the sign of your coming and of the close of the age?" ⁴And Jesus answered them, "Take heed that no one leads you astray. ⁵For many will come in my name, saying, 'I am the Christ,' and they will lead many astray. ⁶ And you will hear of wars and rumours of wars; see that you are not alarmed; for this must take place, but the end is not yet. ⁷For nation will rise against nation, and kingdom against kingdom, and there will be famines and earthquakes in various places: ⁸all this is but the beginning of the sufferings.

⁹"Then they will deliver you up to tribulation, and put you to death; and you will be hated by all nations for my name's sake. ¹⁰And then many will fall away,ʸ and betray one another, and hate one another. ¹¹And many false prophets will arise and lead many astray. ¹²And because wickedness is multiplied, most men's love will grow cold. ¹³But he who endures to the end will be saved. ¹⁴And this gospel of the kingdom will be preached throughout the

Margin references:
Jn 5:43
Acts 5:36f
1 Jn 2:18
Dan 2:28

Is 19:2
2 Chron 15:6
Mt 10:17–22
Jn 16:2
Dan 11:41
1 Jn 4:1

2 Thess 2:10
2 Tim 3:1–5
Mt 10:22
Rev 13:10

---

not become clear until his second coming. The notes which follow should be read against this background.

24:3. This dramatic prophecy makes such an impression on Christ's disciples that they want to know when it will happen; they see the end of the temple and the end of the world as coinciding (as yet the Holy Spirit has not yet come; he will make many things plain to them: cf. Jn 14:26).

24:4–14. Our Lord says that between then and the end of the world, the Gospel will be preached to every creature. In the intervening period, the Church will experience all kinds of tribulations. These are not signs of the end of the world; they are simply the normal context in which Christian preaching takes place.

24:15. "The desolating sacrilege": Jesus is referring to a prophecy in Daniel (Dan 9:27; 11:31; 12:11) where the prophet

foretold that the king (Antiochus IV) would occupy the temple and erect images of false gods on the altar of holocausts. This came to pass, and the idol was set up on the altar—a sign of "abomination" (idolatry) and desolation. Our Lord applies this episode in the history of Israel to the future destruction of Jerusalem—asking people ("let the reader understand") to pay more heed to the text in Daniel. Jesus tells them that a new abomination will occur, ruining the temple to make way for idolatrous worship—as happened in AD 70, when the Roman armies destroyed and profaned the temple, and later under Hadrian, who ordered the erection of a statue of Jupiter on the ruins.

"Having spoken of the ills that were to overtake the city, and of the trials of the apostles, and having said that they should remain unsubdued, and should conquer the whole world, he mentions again the Jews' calamities, showing that when the one [the Church] should be glorious,

y. Or *stumble*

whole world, as a testimony to all nations; and then the end will come.

The great tribulation

¹⁵"So when you see the desolating sacrilege spoken of by the prophet Daniel, standing in the holy place (let the reader understand), ¹⁶then let those who are in Judea flee to the mountains; ¹⁷let him who is on the housetop not go down to take what is in his house; ¹⁸and let him who is in the field not turn back to take his mantle. ¹⁹And alas for those who are with child and for those who give suck in those days! ²⁰Pray that your flight may not be in winter or on a sabbath. ²¹For then there will be great tribulation, such as has not been from the beginning of the world until now, no, and never will be. ²²And if those days had not been shortened, no human being would be saved; but for the sake of the elect those days will be shortened. ²³Then if any one says to you, 'Lo, here is the Christ!' or 'There he is!' do not believe it. ²⁴For false Christs and false prophets will arise and show great signs and wonders, so

Dan 9:27;
12:11

Lk 17:31

Acts 1:12

Dan 12:1
Joel 2:2

Deut 13:1–3
2 Thess 2:8f

---

having taught the whole world, the other [Israel] should suffer calamity" (St John Chrysostom, *Hom. on St Matthew*, 76).

24:15–20. People really did have to flee to escape the Romans (cf. Lk 21:20–21): the Christians had to leave the plains of Judea to take refuge in mountain caves. Many fled into present-day Transjordan (cf. Eusebius, *Ecclesiastical History*, 3, 5). Palestinian houses used to have a ladder directly from the terrace to the outside. On the sabbath, one was not allowed to walk more than two thousand paces—a little more than a kilometre (less than one mile).

Flavius Josephus, a contemporary Jewish historian, says that one million, one hundred thousand people died during the siege of Jerusalem in the year 70 (cf. *The Jewish War*, 6, 420)—which gives some idea of the scale of these events. The siege began when the city was full of pilgrims from all over the world, who had come to celebrate the Passover; therefore, Flavius Josephus' figure may not be all that far off the truth.

24:22. What salvation is our Lord referring to here? First, physical safety: if God in his mercy had not come to the rescue everyone would have died. Second, eternal salvation: this test will be so severe that God will have to cut the time short to avoid the elect being overcome by temptation, to ensure their salvation. We should bear in mind that tribulation has a physical dimension (earthquakes, upheavals, wars) and a spiritual one (false prophets, heresies, etc.).

24:23–28. Interwoven with the prophecy of the destruction of Jerusalem comes Jesus' announcement of his second coming. He uses mysterious words, whose meaning is obscure. Many events he speaks of in a very general way; they remain mere shadows.

The main thing we should do is grow in trust of Jesus and his teaching—"Lo, I have told you beforehand" (v. 25), as he has just said—and persevere until the end.

The same pattern as in vv. 4–13: between the fall of Jerusalem and the end

Lk 17:23–24
Job 39:30
Heb 1:18
Lk 17:37

Is 13:10; 34:4
2 Pet 3:10

as to lead astray, if possible, even the elect. [25]Lo, I have told you beforehand. [26]So, if they say to you, 'Lo, he is in the wilderness,' do not go out; if they say, 'Lo, he is in the inner rooms,' do not believe it. [27]For as the lightning comes from the east and shines as far as the west, so will be the coming of the Son of man. [28]Wherever the body is, there the eagles[z] will be gathered together.

The coming of the Son of man

Rev 1:7
Mt 26:64
Dan 7:13f
Zech 12:10ff
Rev 19:11

[29]"Immediately after the tribulation of those days the sun will be darkened, and the moon will not give its light, and the stars will fall from heaven, and the powers of the heavens will be shaken; [30]then will appear the sign of the Son of man in heaven, and then all the tribes of the earth will mourn, and they will see the Son of man coming on the clouds of heaven with power and great glory; [31]and he

---

of the world, Christians will experience suffering time and time again—persecution, false prophets, false messiahs who will lead others to perdition (vv. 23–24). Verse 28 is difficult to interpret; it looks like a proverb based on the speed with which birds of prey swoop down on their quarry. There may be a suggestion that at Christ's second coming all mankind will gather round him—good and bad, living and dead, all irresistibly attracted to Christ in triumph, some drawn by love, others forced by justice. St Paul has described the force of attraction in the Son of man when he says that the just "will be caught up ... in the clouds to meet the Lord in the air" (1 Thess 4:17).

24:29. Nature itself will tremble in the presence of this supreme Judge when he appears vested in all his power.

24:30. "The sign of the Son of man" has been traditionally interpreted as the cross in glory, which will shine like the sun (cf. St John Chrysostom, *Hom. on St Matthew*, 76). The liturgy of the cross contains the same interpretation: "this sign will appear in the heavens, when the Lord comes to

judge". This instrument of our Lord's passion will be a sign of condemnation for those who have despised it, and of joy for those who have borne a share of it.

24:32–35. Seeing in the destruction of Jerusalem a symbol of the end of the world, St John Chrysostom applies to it this parable of the fig tree: "Here he also foretells a spiritual spring and a calm which, after the storm of the present life, the righteous will experience; whereas for sinners there will be a winter after the spring they have had [...]. But this was not the only reason why he put before them the parable of the fig tree, to tell them of the interval before his coming; he wanted to show them that his word would assuredly come true. As sure as the coming of spring is the coming of the Son of man" (ibid., 77).

"This generation": this verse is a clear example of what we say in the note on Mt 24:1 about the destruction of Jerusalem being itself a symbol. "This generation" refers firstly to the people alive at the time of the destruction of Jerusalem. But, since that event is symbolic of the end of the world, we can say

z. Or *vultures*

will send out his angels with a loud trumpet call, and they will gather his elect from the four winds, from one end of heaven to the other.

1 Cor 15:52
1 Thess 4:16
Rev 8:1f
Is 27:13

The end will surely come. The lesson of the fig tree

[32]"From the fig tree learn its lesson: as soon as its branch becomes tender and puts forth its leaves, you know that summer is near. [33]So also, when you see all these things, you know that he is near, at the very gates. [34]Truly, I say to you, this generation will not pass away till all these things take place. [35]Heaven and earth will pass away, but my words will not pass away.

Deut 30:4

The time of the second coming of Christ

[36]"But of that day and hour no one knows, not even the angels of heaven, nor the Son,[a] but the Father only. [37]As were the days of

1 Thess 5:1f
Gen 6:11–13
Lk 17:26f

---

with St John Chrysostom that "the Lord was speaking not only of the generation then living, but also of the generation of the believers; for he knows that a generation is distinguished not only by time but also by its mode of religious worship and practice: this is what the Psalmist means when he says that 'such is the generation of those who seek him'(Ps 24:6)" (ibid.).

24:35. This is further confirmation that the prophecies he has just made will be fulfilled; it is as if he were saying: it is easier for heaven and earth, which seem so stable, to disappear, than for my words not to come true. Also he is making a formal statement about the value attaching to God's word: "heaven and earth, since they are created things, are not necessarily unchangeable: it is possible for them to cease to exist; whereas, Christ's words, which originate in eternity, have such power and force that they will last forever"(St Hilary, *In Matth.*, 26).

24:36. Every revelation about the end of the world is clothed in mystery; Jesus, being God, knows every detail of the plan

of salvation but he refrains from revealing the date of the Last Judgment. Why? To ensure that his apostles and disciples stay on the alert, and to underline the transcendence of this mysterious design. This phrase carries echoes of Jesus' reply to the sons of Zebedee: "to sit at my right hand and at my left is not mine to grant, but it is for those for whom it has been prepared by my Father" (Mt 20:23)—not because he does not know the details, but because it is not for him to reveal them.

"That day": the way the Bible usually refers to the day when God will judge all men (cf. Amos 2:26; 8:9, 12; Is 2:20; Mic 2:4; Mal 3:19; Mt 7:22; Mk 13:32; Lk 10:12; 2 Tim 1:12; etc.).

24:37–39. In a few strokes our Lord sketches man's perennial insensitivity and carelessness towards the things of God. Man thinks it is more important to eat and drink, to find a husband or wife; but if that is his attitude he is forgetting about the most important thing—eternal life. Our Lord also foretells that the end of the world will be like the great flood; the Son of man's second coming will happen

---

a. Other ancient authorities omit *nor the Son*

2 Pet 3:5f
Gen 7:7

Noah, so will be the coming of the Son of man. ³⁸For as in those days before the flood they were eating and drinking, marrying and giving in marriage, until the day when Noah entered the ark, ³⁹and they did not know until the flood came and swept them all away,

Lk 17:35f

so will be the coming of the Son of man. ⁴⁰Then two men will be in the field; one is taken and one is left. ⁴¹Two women will be grinding at the mill; one is taken and one is left. ⁴²Watch therefore,

Lk 12:39–46

for you do not know on what day your Lord is coming. ⁴³But know this, that if the householder had known in what part of the night the thief was coming, he would have watched and would not

Rev 16:15

have let his house be broken into. ⁴⁴Therefore you also must be ready; for the Son of man is coming at an hour you do not expect.

Parable of the faithful servant

⁴⁵"Who then is the faithful and wise servant, whom his master has set over his household, to give them their food at the proper time? ⁴⁶Blessed is that servant whom his master when he comes will find so doing. ⁴⁷Truly, I say to you, he will set him over all his

Eccles 8:11

possessions. ⁴⁸But if that wicked servant says to himself, 'My master is delayed,' ⁴⁹and begins to beat his fellow servants, and eats and drinks with the drunken, ⁵⁰the master of that servant will come on a day when he does not expect him and at an hour he does not know, ⁵¹and will punish^b him, and put him with the hypocrites; there men will weep and gnash their teeth.

---

unexpectedly, taking people by surprise, whether they are doing good or evil.

24:40. It is in the context of the ordinary affairs of life—farmwork, housework etc.—that God calls man, and man responds: that is where his eternal happiness or eternal punishment is decided. To be saved, one does not need to meet any special conditions, or to be in a special position in life: one simply has to be faithful to the Lord in the middle of ordinary everyday affairs.

24:42. Jesus himself draws from this revelation about the future the practical moral that a Christian needs to be on the watch,

living each day as if it were his last. The important thing is not to be speculating about when these events will happen and what form they will take, but to live in such a way that they find us in the state of grace.

24:51. "And will punish him [or, cut him in pieces]": this can be understood as a metaphor for "will cast him away". "Weeping and gnashing of teeth": the pains of hell.

25:1–46. The whole of chapter 25 is a practical application of the teaching contained in chapter 24. With these parables of the wise and foolish virgins and of the talents, and his teaching on the Last

b. Or *cut him in pieces*

Parable of the wise and foolish maidens

25 ¹"Then the kingdom of heaven shall be compared to ten maidens who took their lamps and went to meet the bridegroom.ᶜ ²Five of them were foolish, and five were wise. ³For when the foolish took their lamps, they took no oil with them; ⁴but the wise took flasks of oil with their lamps. ⁵As the bridegroom was delayed, they all slumbered and slept. ⁶But at midnight there was a cry, 'Behold, the bridegroom! Come out to meet him.' ⁷Then all those maidens rose and trimmed their lamps. ⁸And the foolish said to the wise, 'Give us some of your oil, for our lamps are going out.' ⁹But the wise replied, 'Perhaps there will not be enough for us and for you; go rather to the dealers and buy for yourselves.' ¹⁰And while they went to buy, the bridegroom came, and those who were ready went in with him to the marriage feast; and the door was shut. ¹¹Afterward the other maidens came also, saying, 'Lord, lord, open to us.' ¹²But he replied, 'Truly, I say to you, I do not know you.' ¹³Watch therefore, for you know neither the day nor the hour.

Lk 12:35f
Rev 19:7

Lk 13:25–27

Parable of the talents

¹⁴"For it will be as when a man going on a journey called his servants and entrusted to them his property; ¹⁵to one he gave five tal-

Lk 19:12–27

Judgment, our Lord is again emphasizing the need for vigilance (cf. the note on Mt 24:42). In this sense, chapter 25 makes chapter 24 more intelligible.

25:1–13. The main lesson of this parable has to do with the need to be on the alert: in practice, this means having the light of faith, which is kept alive with the oil of charity. Jewish weddings were held in the house of the bride's father. The virgins are young unmarried girls, bridesmaids who are in the bride's house waiting for the bridegroom to arrive. The parable centres on the attitude one should adopt up to the time when the bridegroom comes. In other words, it is not enough to know that one is "inside" the Kingdom, the Church: one has to be on the watch and be preparing for Christ's coming by doing good works.

This vigilance should be continuous and unflagging, because the devil is forever after us, prowling around "like a roaring lion, seeking someone to devour" (1 Pet 5:8). "Watch with the heart, watch with faith, watch with love, watch with charity, watch with good works […]; make ready the lamps, make sure they do not go out […], renew them with the inner oil of an upright conscience; then shall the Bridegroom enfold you in the embrace of his love and bring you into his banquet room, where your lamp can never be extinguished" (St Augustine, *Sermons*, 93).

25:14–30. A talent was not any kind of coin but a measure of value worth about fifty kilos (one hundred pounds) of silver.

In this parable the main message is the need to respond to grace by making a gen-

c. Other ancient authorities add *and the bride*

Rom 12:6

ents,[d] to another two, to another one, to each according to his ability. Then he went away. ¹⁶He who had received the five talents went at once and traded with them; and he made five talents more. ¹⁷So also, he who had the two talents made two talents more. ¹⁸But he who had received the one talent went and dug in the ground and hid his master's money. ¹⁹Now after a long time the master of those servants came and settled accounts with them. ²⁰And he who received the five talents came forward, bringing five talents more, saying, 'Master, you delivered to me five talents; here I have made five talents more.' ²¹His master said to him, 'Well done, good and faithful servant; you have been faithful over a little, I will set you over much; enter into the joy of your master.' ²²And he also who had the two talents came forward, saying, 'Master, you delivered to me two talents; here I have made two talents more.' ²³His master said to him, 'Well done, good and faithful servant; you have been faithful over a little, I will set you over much; enter into the joy of your master.' ²⁴He also who had received the one talent came forward, saying, 'Master, I knew you to be a hard man, reaping where you did not sow, and gathering where you did not winnow; ²⁵so I was afraid, and I went and hid your talent in the ground. Here you have what is yours.' ²⁶But his master answered him, 'You wicked and slothful servant! You knew that I reap where I have not sowed, and gather where I have not winnowed?

Lk 16:10
Heb 12:2

uine effort right through one's life. All the gifts of nature and grace which God has given us should yield a profit. It does not matter how many gifts we have received; what matters is our generosity in putting them to good use. A person's Christian calling should not lie hidden and barren: it should be outgoing, apostolic and self-sacrificial. "Don't lose your effectiveness; instead, trample on your selfishness. You think your life is for yourself? Your life is for God, for the good of all men, through your love for our Lord. Your buried talent, dig it up again! Make it yield" (St Josemaría Escrivá, *Friends of God*, 47).

An ordinary Christian cannot fail to notice that Jesus chose to outline his teaching on response to grace by using the simile of men at work. Here we have a reminder that the Christian normally lives out his vocation in the context of ordinary, everyday affairs. "There is just one life, made of flesh and spirit. And it is this life which has to become, in both soul and body, holy and filled with God. We discover the invisible God in the most visible and material things. There is no other way. Either we learn to find our Lord in ordinary, everyday life, or else we shall never find him" (St Josemaría Escrivá, *Conversations*, 114).

25:31–46. The three parables (Mt 24:42– 51; 25:1-13; and 25:14–30) are com- pleted by the announcement of a rigorous last judgment, a last act in a

d. A talent was more than fifteen years' wages of a labourer

²⁷Then you ought to have invested my money with the bankers, and at my coming I should have received what was my own with interest. ²⁸So take the talent from him, and give it to him who has the ten talents. ²⁹For to every one who has will more be given, and he will have abundance; but from him who has not, even what he has will be taken away. ³⁰And cast the worthless servant into the outer darkness; there men will weep and gnash their teeth.'

The Last Judgment

³¹"When the Son of man comes in his glory, and all the angels with him, then he will sit on his glorious throne. ³²Before him will be gathered all the nations, and he will separate them one from another as a shepherd separates the sheep from the goats, ³³and he will place the sheep at his right hand, but the goats at the left. ³⁴Then the King will say to those at his right hand, 'Come, O blessed of my Father, inherit the kingdom prepared for you from the foundation of the world; ³⁵for I was hungry and you gave me food, I was thirsty and you gave me drink, I was a stranger and you welcomed me, ³⁶I was naked and you clothed me, I was sick and you visited me, I was in prison and you came to me.' ³⁷Then the righteous will answer him, 'Lord, when did we see thee hungry and feed thee, or thirsty and give thee drink? ³⁸And when

Zech 14:5
Rev 20:11–33
Rom 14:10

Ezek 34:17

Is 58:7

---

drama, in which all matters of justice are resolved. Christian tradition calls it the Last Judgment, to distinguish it from the "Particular Judgment" which everyone undergoes immediately after death. The sentence pronounced at the end of time will simply be a public, formal confirmation of that already passed on the good and the evil, the elect and the reprobate.

In this passage we can discover some basic truths of faith: 1) that there will be a last judgment at the end of time; 2) the way Christ identifies himself with everyone in need—the hungry, the thirsty, the naked, the sick, the imprisoned; and 3) confirmation that the sinful will experience an eternal punishment, and the just an eternal reward.

25:31–33. In the Prophets and in the Book of Revelation the Messiah is depicted on a throne, like a judge. This is how Jesus will come at the end of the world, to judge the living and the dead. The Last Judgment is a truth spelt out in the very earliest credal statements of the Church and a dogma of faith solemnly defined by Benedict XII in the Constitution *Benedictus Deus* (29 January 1336).

25:35–46. All the various things listed in this passage (giving people food and drink, clothing them, visiting them) become works of Christian charity when the person doing them sees Christ in these "least" of his brethren.

Here we can see the seriousness of sins of omission. Failure to do something which one should do means leaving Christ unattended.

"We must learn to recognize Christ when he comes out to meet us in our

did we see thee a stranger and welcome thee, or naked and clothe thee? ³⁹And when did we see thee sick or in prison and visit thee?' ⁴⁰And the King will answer them, 'Truly I say to you, as you did it to one of the least of my brethren, you did it to me.' ⁴¹Then he will say to those at his left hand, 'Depart from me, you cursed, into the eternal fire prepared for the devil and his angels; ⁴²for I was hungry and you gave me no food; I was thirsty and you gave me no drink, ⁴³I was a stranger and you did not welcome me, naked and you did not clothe me, sick and in prison and you did not visit me.' ⁴⁴Then they also will answer, 'Lord, when did we see thee hungry or thirsty or a stranger or naked or sick or in prison, and did not minister to thee?' ⁴⁵Then he will answer them, 'Truly, I say to you, as you did it not to one of the least of these, you did it not to me.' ⁴⁶And they will go away into eternal punishment, but the righteous into eternal life."

Prov 19:17
Heb 2:11

Mt 7:23
Rev 20:10, 15

Jn 5:29
Dan 12:2

---

brothers, the people around us. No human life is ever isolated. It is bound up with other lives. No man or woman is a single verse; we all make up one divine poem which God writes with the cooperation of our freedom" (St Josemaría Escrivá, *Christ Is Passing By*, 111).

We will be judged on the degree and quality of our love (cf. St John of the Cross, *Spiritual Sentences and Maxims*, 57). Our Lord will ask us to account not only for the evil we have done but also for the good we have omitted. We can see that sins of omission are a very serious matter and that the basis of love of neighbour is Christ's presence in the least of our brothers and sisters.

St Teresa of Avila writes: "Here the Lord asks only two things of us: love for his Majesty and love for our neighbour. It is for these two virtues that we must strive, and if we attain them perfectly we are doing his will [...]. The surest sign that we are keeping these two commandments is, I think, that we should really be loving our neighbour; for we cannot be sure if we are loving God, although we may have good reasons for believing that we are, but we can know quite well if we

are loving our neighbour. And be certain that, the farther advanced you find you are in this, the greater the love you will have for God; for so dearly does his Majesty love us that he will reward our love for our neighbour by increasing the love which we bear to himself, and that in a thousand ways: this I cannot doubt" (*Interior Castle*, 5, 3).

This parable clearly shows that Christianity cannot be reduced to a kind of agency for "doing good". Service of our neighbour acquires supernatural value when it is done out of love for Christ, when we see Christ in the person in need. This is why St Paul asserts that "if I give away all I have ... but have not love, I gain nothing" (1 Cor 13:3). Any interpretation of Jesus' teaching on the Last Judgment would be wide of the mark if it gave it a materialistic meaning or confused mere philanthrophy with genuine Christian charity.

25:40–45. In describing the exigencies of Christian charity which gives meaning to "social aid", the Second Vatican Council says: "Wishing to come down to topics that are practical and of some urgency, the

12. THE PASSION, DEATH AND RESURRECTION OF JESUS

Last announcement of the Passion. The conspiracy against Jesus

26 ¹When Jesus had finished all these sayings, he said to his disciples, ²"You know that after two days the Passover is coming, and the Son of man will be delivered up to be crucified." ³Then the chief priests and the elders of the people gathered in the palace of the high priest, who was called Caiaphas, ⁴and took counsel together in order to arrest Jesus by stealth and kill him.

Mk 14:1f
Lk 22:1f
Mk 20:18

Council lays stress on respect for the human person: everyone should look upon his neighbour (without any exception) as another self, bearing in mind, above all, his life and the means necessary for living it in a dignified way 'lest he follow the example of the rich man who ignored Lazarus, the poor man' (cf. Lk 16:18–31).

"Today there is an inescapable duty to make ourselves the neighbour of every man, no matter who he is, and if we meet him, to come to his aid in a positive way, whether he is an aged person abandoned by all, a foreign worker despised without reason, a refugee, an illegitimate child wrongly suffering for a sin he did not commit, or a starving human being who awakens our conscience by calling to mind the words of Christ: 'As you did it to one of the least of these my brethren, you did it to me'" (*Gaudium et spes*, 27).

25:46. The eternal punishment of the reprobate and the eternal reward of the elect are a dogma of faith solemnly defined by the Magisterium of the Church in the Fourth Lateran Council (1215): "He [Christ] will come at the end of the world; he will judge the living and the dead; and he will reward all, both the lost and the elect, according to their works. And all these will rise with their own bodies which they now have so that they may receive according to their works, whether good or bad; the wicked, a perpetual punishment with the devil; the good, eternal glory with Christ."

26:1. The Gospel account of the Passion (Mt 26 and 27 and par.) is far more detailed than that of any other event in Christ's life—which is not surprising because the passion and death of our Lord are the culmination of his life on earth and his work of redemption; they constitute the sacrifice which he offers to God the Father to atone for our sins. Moreover, the terrible suffering he undergoes vividly demonstrates his infinite love for each and every one of us, and the gravity of our sins.

26:2. The Passover was the principal national festival, held to commemorate the liberation of Israel from slavery in Egypt and the protection Yahweh gave the Israelites when he castigated the Egyptians by causing their first born to die (cf. Ex 12). For a long time the festival was celebrated within the confines of the home, the essential ceremonies being the sacrifice of an unblemished lamb, whose blood was then smeared on the jambs and lintel of the front door of the house, and a thanksgiving meal. In our Lord's time the sacrifice was carried out

⁵But they said, "Not during the feast, lest there be a tumult among the people."

The anointing at Bethany. Judas betrays Jesus

Mk 14:3–9
Lk 7:36–50
Jn 12:18

⁶Now when Jesus was at Bethany in the house of Simon the leper, ⁷a woman came up to him with an alabaster jar of very expensive ointment, and she poured it on his head, as he sat at table. ⁸But when the disciples saw it, they were indignant saying, "Why this waste? ⁹For this ointment might have been sold for a large sum,

Lk 11:7

and given to the poor." ¹⁰But Jesus, aware of this, said to them, "Why do you trouble the woman? For she has done a beautiful

Deut 15:11

thing to me. ¹¹For you always have the poor with you, but you will not always have me. ¹²In pouring this ointment on my body she has done it to prepare me for burial. ¹³Truly, I say to you, wherever this gospel is preached in the whole world, what she has done

Mk 14:10f
Lk 22:3–6
Jn 11:57
Zech 11:12

will be told in memory of her."

¹⁴Then one of the twelve, who was called Judas Iscariot, went to the chief priests ¹⁵and said, "What will you give me if I deliver

---

in the temple of Jerusalem, while the meal took place in private houses, with the whole family attending.

Christ uses this to provide the setting for the new Passover, in which he himself will be the spotless lamb who will set all men free from the slavery of sin by shedding his blood on the cross.

26:3–5. This describes the rulers' final plot to do away with Jesus. The crime they are planning will provide the vehicle for Christ to fulfil to the very end his Father's plan of redemption (cf. Lk 24:26–27; Acts 2:23). This passage also shows that it was not the whole Jewish nation that plotted the death of the Lord, but only its leaders.

26:6. Bethany, where Lazarus and his sisters lived, was a small town to the east of the Mount of Olives, on the way from Jerusalem to Jericho. It is different from the other town of the same name where John the Baptist baptized people (cf. Jn 1:28).

26:8–11. The disciples criticize the generosity of this woman because they fail to understand the true meaning of poverty. They see her action as a waste of money—for, as St John tells us (12:5), the perfume cost more than three hundred denarii—that is, a labourer's annual earnings. They do not yet realize the love which motivated the woman's actions.

"The woman in the house of Simon the leper in Bethany, who anoints the Master's head with precious ointment, reminds us of our duty to be generous in the worship of God.

"All beauty, richness and majesty seem little to me. And against those who attack the richness of sacred vessels, of vestments and altars, stands the praise given by Jesus: '*opus enim bonum operata est in me*: she has acted well towards me' " (St Josemaría Escrivá, *The Way*, 527). See the note on Mt 21:12–13.

26:12. Wealthier Jews had bodies embalmed before burial, using rich ointments and perfumes. This woman is

him to you?" And they paid him thirty pieces of silver. [16]And from that moment he sought an opportunity to betray him.

1 Tim 6:9f

Preparations for the Last Supper and announcement of Judas' treachery

[17]Now on the first day of Unleavened Bread the disciples came to Jesus, saying, "Where will you have us prepare for you to eat the passover?" [18]He said, "Go into the city to such a one, and say to him, 'The Teacher says, My time is at hand; I will keep the passover at your house with my disciples.' " [19]And the disciples did as Jesus had directed them, and they prepared the passover.

Mk 14:12–16
Lk 22:7–13
Ex 12:18–20

[20]When it was evening, he sat at table with the twelve disciples;[e] [21]and as they were eating, he said, "Truly, I say to you, one of you will betray me." [22]And they were very sorrowful, and began to say to him one after another, "Is it I, Lord?" [23]He answered, "He who has dipped his hand in the dish with me, will betray me. [24]The Son of man goes as it is written of him, but woe to that man by whom the Son of man is betrayed! It would have

Mk 14:17–26
Lk 22:14–23
Jn 13:21–26

---

anticipating our Lord's death. She saw her action as a generous gesture and a recognition of Jesus' dignity; additionally it becomes a prophetic sign of his redemptive death.

26:15. It is disconcerting and sobering to realize that Judas Iscariot actually went as far as to sell the man whom he had believed to be the Messiah and who had called him to be one of the apostles. Thirty shekels or pieces of silver were the price of a slave (cf. Ex 21:32), the same value as Judas put on his Master.

26:17. This unleavened bread, azymes, took the form of loaves which had to be eaten over a seven-day period, in commemoration of the unleavened bread which the Israelites had to take with them in their hurry to leave Egypt (cf. Ex 12:34). In Jesus' time the passover supper was celebrated on the first day of the week of the Unleavened Bread.

26:18. Although the reference is to an unnamed person, probably our Lord gave the person's actual name. In any event, from what other evangelists tell us (Mk 14:13; Lk 22:10), Jesus gave the disciples enough information to enable them to find the house.

26:22. Although the glorious events of Easter have yet to occur (which will teach the apostles much more about Jesus), their faith has been steadily fortified and deepened in the course of Jesus' public ministry (cf. Jn 2:11; 6:68–69) through their contact with him and the divine grace they have been given (cf. Mt 16:17). At this point they are quite convinced that our Lord knows their internal attitudes and how they are going to act: each asks in a concerned way whether he will prove to be loyal in the time ahead.

26:24. Jesus is referring to the fact that he will give himself up freely to suffering

e. Other authorities omit *disciples*

been better for that man if he had not been born." ²⁵Judas, who betrayed him, said, "Is it I, Master?"ᶠ He said to him, "You have said so."

The institution of the Eucharist

1 Cor
11:23–25

²⁶Now as they were eating, Jesus took bread, and blessed, and broke it, and gave it to the disciples and said, "Take, eat; this is my body." ²⁷And he took a cup, and when he had given thanks he gave it to them, saying, "Drink of it, all of you; ²⁸for this is my

---

and death. In so doing he would fulfil the will of God, as proclaimed centuries before (cf. Ps 41:10; Is 53:7). Although our Lord goes to his death voluntarily, this does not reduce the seriousness of Judas' treachery.

26:25. This advance indication that Judas is the traitor is not noticed by the other apostles (cf. Jn 13:26–29).

26:26–29. This short scene, covered also in Mk 14:22–25, Lk 22:19–20 and 1 Cor 11:23–26, contains the essential truths of faith about the sublime mystery of the Eucharist—1) the institution of this sacrament and Jesus' real presence in it; 2) the institution of the Christian priesthood; and 3) the Eucharist, the sacrifice of the New Testament or the Mass.

1) In the first place, we can see the institution of the Eucharist by Jesus Christ, when he says, "This is my body … , this is my blood …". What up to this point was nothing but unleavened bread and wine, now—through the words and by the will of Jesus Christ, true God and true Man—becomes the true body and true blood of the Saviour. His words, which have such a realism about them, cannot be interpreted as being merely symbolic or explained in a way which obscures the mysterious fact that Christ is really present in the Eucharist: all we can

do is humbly subscribe to the faith "which the Catholic Church has always held and which she will hold until the end of the world" (Council of Trent, *De SS. Eucharistia*). Paul VI expresses this faith in these words in his encyclical letter *Mysterium fidei*, 5: "The continuous teaching of the Catholic Church, the traditions delivered to catechumens, the perception of the Christian people, the doctrine defined by the Council of Trent, and the very words of Christ as he instituted the most holy Eucharist, all insist that we profess: 'The Eucharist is the flesh of our Saviour Jesus Christ; the flesh which suffered for our sins and which the Father, of his kindness, brought to life.' To these words of St Ignatius of Antioch may be added the statement addressed to the people by Theodore of Mopsuestia, a faithful witness of the Church's belief on this subject: 'The Lord did not say: "This is the symbol of my body and this the symbol of my blood." He said: "This is my body and my blood".'"

This sacrament, which not only has the power to sanctify but actually contains the very Author of holiness, was instituted by Jesus Christ to be spiritual nourishment of the soul, to strengthen it in its struggle to attain salvation. The Church teaches that it also confers pardon of venial sins and helps the Christian not

---

f. Or *Rabbi*

blood of the[g] covenant, which is poured out for many for the forgiveness of sins. [29]I tell you I shall not drink again of this fruit of the vine until that day when I drink it new with you in my Father's kingdom."

Ex 24:8
Jer 31:31
Zech 9:11

The disciples' desertion foretold

Ps 113–118
Lk 22:39
Jn 18:1
Mk 14:27–31
Lk 22:31–34
Zech 13:7
Jn 16:32

[30]And when they had sung a hymn, they went out to the Mount of Olives. [31]Then Jesus said to them, "You will all fall away because of me this night; for it is written, 'I will strike the shepherd, and the

---

to fall into mortal sin: it unites us to God and thereby is a pledge of future glory.

2) In instituting the Blessed Eucharist our Lord laid down that it should be repeated until the end of time (cf. 1 Cor 11:24–25; Lk 22:19) by giving the apostles the power to perform it. From this passage, and the accounts in St Paul and St Luke (loc. cit.), we can see that Christ also instituted the priesthood, giving the apostles the power to confect the Eucharist, a power which they in turn passed on to their successors. This making of the Eucharist takes place at Mass when the priest, with the intention of doing what the Church does, says Christ's words of consecration over the bread and the wine. At this very moment, "a change takes place in which the whole substance of bread is changed into the substance of the body of Christ our Lord and the whole substance of the wine into the substance of his blood" (*De SS. Eucharistia*). This amazing change is given the name of "transubstantiation". Through transubstantiation the unleavened bread and the fruit of the vine disappear, becoming the body, blood, soul and divinity of Jesus Christ. Christ's real presence is to be found also in any little particles which become detached from the host, or the smallest drop from the chalice, after the consecration. It continues when the sacred species are reserved in the tabernacle, as long as the appearances (of bread and wine) last.

3) At the Last Supper, Christ—miraculously, in an unbloody manner—brought forward his passion and death. Every Mass celebrated from then on renews the sacrifice of our Saviour on the cross—Jesus once again giving his body and blood, offering himself to God the Father as a sacrifice on man's behalf, as he did on Calvary—with this clear difference: on the cross he gave himself shedding his blood, whereas on the altar he does so in an unbloody manner. "He, then, our Lord and our God, was once and for all to offer himself by his death on the altar of the cross to God the Father, to accomplish for them an everlasting redemption. But death was not to end his priesthood. And so, at the Last Supper, [...] in order to leave for his beloved spouse, the Church, a sacrifice that was visible, [...] he offered his body and blood under the species of bread and wine to God the Father and he gave his body and blood under the same species to the apostles to receive, making them priests of the New Testament at that time. This sacrifice was to represent the bloody sacrifice which he accomplished on the cross once and for all" (Council of Trent, *De SS. Missae sacrificio*, chap. 1).

The expression "which is poured out for many for the forgiveness of sins"

---

g. Other ancient authorities insert *new*

sheep of the flock will be scattered.' [32]But after I am raised up, I will go before you to Galilee." [33]Peter declared to him, "Though they all fall away because of you, I will never fall away." [34]Jesus said to him, "Truly, I say to you, this very night, before the cock crows, you will deny me three times." [35]Peter said to him, "Even if I must die with you, I will not deny you." And so did all the disciples.

Jn 13:38

Gethsemane—the agony in the garden

Mk 14:32–42
Lk 22:40–46

Heb 5:7

Ps 43:5
Jn 12:27

Jn 18:11
Heb 5:8

[36]Then Jesus went with them to a place called Gethsemane, and he said to his disciples, "Sit here, while I go yonder and pray." [37]And taking with him Peter and the two sons of Zebedee, he began to be sorrowful and troubled. [38]Then he said to them, "My soul is very sorrowful, even to death; remain here, and watch[h] with me." [39]And going a little farther he fell on his face and prayed, "My Father, if it be possible, let this cup pass from me; nevertheless, not as I will, but as thou wilt." [40]And he came to the disciples and found them sleeping; and he said to Peter, "So, could you not watch[h] with me

---

means the same as "which is poured out for all" (cf. the note on Mt 20:27–28). Here we have the fulfilment of the prophecies of Isaiah (chap. 53), which spoke of the atoning death of Christ for all men. Only Christ's sacrifice is capable of atoning to the Father; the Mass has this power because it is that very sacrifice: "The priest offers the Holy Sacrifice *in persona Christi*; this means more than offering 'in the name of' or 'in the place of' Christ. *In persona* means in specific sacramental identification with the eternal High Priest, who is the Author and principal Subject of this sacrifice of his, a sacrifice in which, in truth, nobody can take his place. Only he—only Christ—was able and is always able to be the true and effective 'expiation for our sins and ... for the sins of the whole world' (1 Jn 2:2; cf. 4:10)" (John Paul II, *Letter to all bishops*, on the Eucharist, 24 November 1980).

Finally, we should notice that this sublime sacrament should be received with proper dispositions of soul and body—in the state of grace, in a spirit of adoration, respect and recollection, for it is God himself whom one is receiving. "Let a man examine himself, and so eat of the bread and drink of the cup. For anyone who eats and drinks without discerning the body eats and drinks judgment upon himself" (1 Cor 11:28–29).

26:30–35. At the celebration of the Passover, Psalms 113–118 were recited: this is what the reference to the "hymn" means. Our Lord knows what is going to happen—the main events (his death and resurrection) and the lesser ones (such as Peter's denials).

Peter becomes so afraid that he denies his Master three times—a fall which Jesus allowed to happen in order to teach him humility. "Here we learn a great truth: that a man's resolution is not sufficient unless he relies on the help of God" (St John Chrysostom, *Hom. on St Matthew*, 83).

---

h. Or *keep awake*

one hour? [41]Watch[h] and pray that you may not enter into tempta- Heb 2:14; 4:15
tion; the spirit indeed is willing, but the flesh is weak." [42]Again, for
the second time, he went away and prayed, "My Father, if this
cannot pass unless I drink it, thy will be done." [43]And again he
came and found them sleeping, for their eyes were heavy. [44]So, 2 Cor 12:8
2 Sam 24:14
leaving them again, he went away and prayed for the third time,
saying the same words. [45]Then he came to the disciples and said to
them, "Are you still sleeping and taking your rest? Behold, the
hour is at hand, and the Son of man is betrayed into the hands of
sinners. [46]Rise, let us be going; see, my betrayer is at hand." Jn 14:31

Arrest of Jesus

[47]While he was still speaking, Judas came, one of the twelve, and Mk 14:43–50
Lk 22:47–53
with him a great crowd with swords and clubs, from the chief Jn 18:3–12
priests and the elders of the people. [48]Now the betrayer had given
them a sign, saying, "The one I shall kiss is the man; seize him."
[49]And he came up to Jesus at once and said, "Hail, Master!"[i] And

---

26:36–46. Here our Lord allows us to glimpse the full reality and exquisite sensitivity of his human nature. Strictly speaking, Christ, because he had complete self-control, could have avoided showing these limitations. However, by letting them express themselves, we are better able to understand the mystery of his genuine humanness—and to that extent, better able to imitate it. After tempting Jesus in the wilderness, the devil "departed from him until an opportune time" (Lk 4:13). Now, with the passion, he attacks again, using the flesh's natural repugnance to suffering; this is his hour "and the power of darkness" (Lk 22:53).

"Remain here": as if he did not want them to be depressed by seeing his agony; and "watch with me": to keep him company and to prepare themselves by prayer for the temptations that will follow. He goes a little farther away—about a stone's throw, St Luke tells us (22:41). Because there was a full moon, the apostles may have been able to see

Jesus; they may also have heard some words of his prayers; but that could hardly explain how they were able to report this scene in such detail. It is more likely that our Lord, after his resurrection, told his disciples about his agony (cf. Acts 1:3), as he must also have told them about the time he was tempted in the wilderness (Mt 4:1).

26:47–56. Jesus again demonstrates that he is giving himself up of his own free will. He could have asked his Father to send angels to defend him, but he does not do so. He knows why this is all happening and he wants to make it quite clear that in the last analysis it is not force which puts him to death but his own love and his desire to fulfil his Father's will. His opponents fail to grasp Jesus' supernatural way of doing things; he had done his best to teach them but their hardness of heart came in the way and prevented them from accepting his teaching.

i. Or *Rabbi* **j.** Or *do that for which you have come*

171

he kissed him. ⁵⁰Jesus said to him, "Friend, why are you here?"ʲ Then they came up and laid hands on Jesus and seized him. ⁵¹And behold, one of those who were with Jesus stretched out his hand and drew his sword, and struck the slave of the high priest, and cut off his ear.* ⁵²Then Jesus said to him, "Put your sword back into its place; for all who take the sword will perish by the sword. ⁵³Do you think that I cannot appeal to my Father, and he will at once send me more than twelve legions of angels? ⁵⁴But how then should the scriptures be fulfilled, that it must be so?" ⁵⁵At that hour Jesus said to the crowds, "Have you come out as against a robber, with swords and clubs to capture me? Day after day I sat in the temple teaching, and you did not seize me. ⁵⁶But all this has taken place, that the scriptures of the prophets might be fulfilled." Then all the disciples forsook him and fled.

Gen 9:6
Rev 13:10

Jesus before the chief priests

Mk 14:53–72
Lk 22:54–27
Jn 18:12–27

⁵⁷Then those who had seized Jesus led him to Caiaphas the high priest, where the scribes and the elders had gathered. ⁵⁸But Peter followed him at a distance, as far as the courtyard of the high priest, and going inside he sat with the guards to see the end. ⁵⁹Now the chief priests and the whole council sought false testimony against Jesus that they might put him to death, ⁶⁰but they found none, though many false witnesses came forward. At last two came forward ⁶¹and said, "This fellow said, 'I am able to destroy the temple of God, and to build it in three days.'" ⁶²And the high priest stood up and said, "Have you no answer to make?

Jn 2:19–21

26:50. To effect his betrayal Judas uses a sign of friendship and trust. Although he knows what Judas is about, Jesus treats him with great gentleness: he gives him a chance to open his heart and repent. This shows us that we should respect even people who harm us and should treat them with a refined charity.

26:61. As we know from St John's Gospel (2:19), Jesus had said, "Destroy this temple, and in three days I will raise it up", referring to the destruction of his own body, that is, his death and resurrection. They misunderstood him (Jn 2:20), thinking he referred to the temple of Jerusalem.

26:69. The houses of well-to-do Jews had a front lobby or porter's office; going through the lobby one came into a patio and by crossing the patio one could enter the rooms proper. Peter goes through the lobby but he is afraid to follow the mill of people around Jesus, so he stays in the patio, with the servants.

26:70–75. When they went to arrest Jesus in the Garden of Olives, Peter set about defending him and, sword in hand, he struck at the head of the first to lay a hand on his Master, but he only succeeded in cutting off his ear. Our Lord's reaction ("Put your sword back into its place": Mt 26:52) disconcerts Peter. His

What is it that these men testify against you?" [63]But Jesus was silent. And the high priest said to him, "I adjure you by the living God, tell us if you are the Christ, the Son of God." [64]Jesus said to him, "You have said so. But I tell you, hereafter you will see the Son of man seated at the right hand of Power, and coming on the clouds of heaven." [65]Then the high priest tore his robes, and said, "He has uttered blasphemy. Why do we still need witnesses? You have now heard his blasphemy. [66]What is your judgment?" They answered, "He deserves death." [67]Then they spat in his face, and struck him; and some slapped him, [68]saying, "Prophesy to us, you Christ! Who is it that struck you?"

Ps 110:1;
68:35
Mt 16:27;
24:30
Dan 7:13
Acts 7:56
Jn 10:33
Mk 16:19
Jn 19:7
Lev 24:16
Is 50:6

Peter's denials

[69]Now Peter was sitting outside in the courtyard. And a maid came up to him, and said, "You also were with Jesus the Galilean." [70]But he denied it before them all, saying, "I do not know what you mean." [71]And when he went out to the porch, another maid saw him, and she said to the bystanders, "This man was with Jesus of Nazareth." [72]And again he denied it with an oath, "I do not know the man." [73]After a little while the bystanders came up and said to Peter, "Certainly you are also one of them, for your accent betrays you." [74]Then he began to invoke a curse on himself and to swear, "I do not know the man." And immediately the cock crowed. [75]And Peter remembered the saying of Jesus, "Before the cock crows, you will deny me three times." And he went out and wept bitterly.

Jn 8:55

---

faith is not in doubt—Jesus himself had praised him above the other apostles (Mt 16:17)—but it is still too human and needs a profound purification. On Jesus' arrest, all the disciples flee in disarray; thereby the prophecy is fulfilled which says "Strike the shepherd, that the sheep may be scattered" (Zech 13:7). However, Peter keeps following our Lord, though at a distance (Mt 26:58); he is quite demoralized and disconcerted yet brave enough to enter Caiaphas' house, where Malchus, the man whose ear he cut off, works (Jn 18:10–11).

Peter's faith is put to the supreme test. A few hours before Jesus' arrest Peter had assured him, "Lord, I am ready to go with you to prison and to death" (Lk 22:33); and now, as Jesus predicted, he three times denies that he ever knew him. In the midst of his confusion, our Lord's serene glance reinforces his faith (Lk 22:61) and Peter's tears purify it. What our Lord had said a few hours earlier, in the intimacy of the Last Supper, has come true: "Simon, Simon, behold, Satan demanded to have you, that he might sift you like wheat, but I have prayed for you that your faith may not fail; and when you have turned again, strengthen your brethren" (Lk 22:31–32).

Peter has committed a grave sin, but his repentance also is deep. His faith, now put to the test, will become the basis

Jesus is brought before Pilate

Mk 15:1
Lk 22:66
Jn 18:28

Lk 23:1
Jn 18:31f

27 ¹When morning came, all the chief priests and the elders of the people took counsel against Jesus to put him to death; ²and they bound him and led him away and delivered him to Pilate the governor.

Judas' despair and death

³When Judas, his betrayer, saw that he was condemned, he repented and brought back the thirty pieces of silver to the chief priests and the elders, ⁴saying, "I have sinned in betraying innocent blood." They said, "What is that to us? See to it yourself."

Acts 1:18
2 Sam 17:23
Mk 12:41

⁵And throwing down the pieces of silver in the temple, he departed; and he went and hanged himself. ⁶But the chief priests, taking the pieces of silver, said, "It is not lawful to put them into the treasury, since they are blood money." ⁷So they took counsel, and bought with them the potter's field, to bury strangers in.

Acts 1:19

Zech 11:12f
Jer 32:6–9

⁸Therefore that field has been called the Field of Blood to this day. ⁹Then was fulfilled what had been spoken by the prophet Jeremiah, saying, "And they took the thirty pieces of silver, the price of him on whom a price had been set by some of the sons of Israel, ¹⁰and they gave them for the potter's field, as the Lord directed me."

---

on which Christ will build his Church (Mt 16:18).

As regards our own lives we should remember that no matter how low we may have fallen, God in his mercy, which is infinite, is ever ready to forgive us, because he does not despise a broken and contrite heart (Ps 51:19). If we sincerely repent, God will use us, sinners though we be, as his faithful instruments.

27:2. During this period the governor or procurator was the senior official in Judea. Although he was subordinate to the Roman legate in Syria, he had the *ius gladii*, the authority to condemn a criminal to death—which was why the Jewish leaders brought Jesus before Pilate: they were seeking a public sentence of death, to counteract Jesus' reputation and erase his teaching from people's minds.

27:3–5. Judas' remorse does not lead

him to repent his sins and be converted; he cannot bring himself to turn trustingly to God and be forgiven. He despairs, mistrusting God's infinite mercy, and takes his own life.

27:6. Once again the chief priests and elders show their hypocrisy. They behave inconsistently: they worry about exact fulfilment of a precept of the Law—not to put into the temple treasury money resulting from an evil action—yet they themselves have instigated that action.

27:9. By recalling the prophecy of Jeremiah (cf. Jer 18:2; 19:1; 32:6–15) and completing it with that of Zechariah (Zech 11:12–13), the Gospel shows that this incident was foreseen by God.

27:14. The evangelist possibly wishes to indicate that this silence was foretold in

Jesus' trial before Pilate

[11]Now Jesus stood before the governor; and the governor asked him, "Are you the King of the Jews?" Jesus said to him, "You have said so." [12]But when he was accused by the chief priests and elders, he made no answer. [13]Then Pilate said to him, "Do you not hear how many things they testify against you?" [14]But he gave him no answer, not even to a single charge; so that the governor wondered greatly.

[15]Now at the feast the governor was accustomed to release for the crowd any one prisoner whom they wanted. [16]And they had then a notorious prisoner, called Barabbas.[k] [17]So when they had gathered, Pilate said to them, "Whom do you want me to release for you, Barabbas[k] or Jesus who is called Christ?" [18]For he knew that it was out of envy that they had delivered him up. [19]Besides, while he was sitting on the judgment seat, his wife sent word to him, "Have nothing to do with that righteous man, for I have suffered much over him today in a dream." [20]Now the chief priests and the elders persuaded the people to ask for Barabbas and destroy Jesus. [21]The governor again said to them, "Which of the two do you want me to release for you?" And they said, "Barabbas." [22]Pilate said to them, "Then what shall I do with Jesus who is called Christ?" They all said, "Let him be crucified." [23]And he said, "Why, what evil has he done?" But they shouted all the more, "Let him be crucified."

Mk 15:2–5
Lk 23:2f
Jn 18:29–38
Mt 26:63
Is 53:7

Jn 19:9

Mk 15:6–15
Lk 23:13–25
Jn 18:29–19:1

Mt 31:38
Jn 11:47f;
12:19

Acts 7:9

---

the Old Testament when Isaiah 53:7 speaks of his being "afflicted, yet he opened not his mouth; like a lamb that is led to the slaughter, and like a sheep that before its shearers is dumb."

Sometimes the right thing for a Christian to do is to remain silent, bearing out what Isaiah says elsewhere: "in quietness and in trust shall be your strength" (Is 30:15).

"'Jesus remained silent. *Jesus autem tacebat.*' Why do you speak, to console yourself or to excuse yourself? Say nothing. Seek joy in contempt; you will always receive less than you deserve. Can you, by any chance, ask: '*Quid enim mali feci?* What evil have I done?'" (St Josemaría Escrivá, *The Way*, 671).

27:18. The chief priests and elders had seen how the crowd followed Jesus. This caused them to be envious of him, an envy which grew into a hatred that sought his death (Jn 11:47).

St Thomas observes that just as at the beginning it was envy that caused man's death (Wis 2:24), so it was envy that condemned Christ (cf. *Comm. on St Matthew*, 27:18).

Envy is indeed one of the causes of hatred (Gen 37:8). "So put away all malice and all guile and insincerity and envy and all slander" (1 Pet 2:1).

27:23. "It is hard to read that question of Pilate's in the holy Gospel: 'Whom do you wish me to release to you, Barabbas or Jesus, who is called Christ?' But it is

---

k. Other ancient authorities read *Jesus Barabbas*

Deut 21:6

²⁴So when Pilate saw that he was gaining nothing, but rather that a riot was beginning, he took water and washed his hands before the crowd, saying, "I am innocent of this righteous man's

Acts 5:28
Mt 23:35

blood;¹ see to it yourselves." ²⁵And all the people answered, "His blood be on us and on our children!" ²⁶Then he released for them Barabbas, and having scourged Jesus, delivered him to be crucified.

The crowning with thorns

Mk 15:16–19
Jn 19:2f

²⁷Then the soldiers of the governor took Jesus into the praetorium, and they gathered the whole battalion before him. ²⁸And they

---

more painful to hear the answer: 'Barabbas!' And more terrible still when I realize that very often by going astray I too have said 'Barabbas' and added 'Christ? ... *Crucifige eum!* Crucify him!' " (St Josemaría Escrivá, *The Way*, 296).

27:24. Pilate tries publicly to justify his lack of courage, even though he has all the material necessary for giving an honest verdict. His cowardice, which he disguises by this external gesture, ends up condemning Christ to death.

27:26–50. Meditation on the passion of our Lord has made many saints in the course of Church history. Few things are of more benefit to a Christian than contemplation—slow and devout, to the point of being amazed—of the saving events surrounding the death of the Son of God made man. Our mind and heart will be overwhelmed to see the suffering of him who created the angels, men, heaven and earth; who is the Lord of all creation; the Almighty who humbles himself to this extent (something quite unimaginable, were it not that it happened). He suffers in this way because of sin—the original sin of our first parents, the personal sins of all men, of those who have gone before us and those who will come after us, and each one's own sins. Christ's terrible sufferings

spell out for us, as nothing else can, the infinite gravity of sin, which has called for the death of God himself made man; moreover, this physical and moral suffering which Jesus undergoes is also the most eloquent proof of his love for the Father, which seeks to atone to him for man's incredible rebellion by the punishment inflicted on his own innocent humanity; and of his love for mankind, his brothers and sisters; he suffers what we deserve to suffer in just punishment for our sins. Our Lord's desire to atone was so great that there was no part of his body that he did not permit to be inflicted with pain—his hands and feet pierced by the nails; his head torn by the crown of thorns; his face battered and spat upon; his back pitted by the terrible scourging he received; his chest pierced by the lance; finally, his arms and legs utterly exhausted by such pain and weariness that he dies. His spirit, also, is saturated with suffering—the pain caused by his being abandoned and betrayed by his disciples, the hatred his own people turn on him, the jeers and brutality of the Gentiles, the mysterious way his divinity permits his soul to suffer.

Only one thing can explain why Christ undergoes this redemptive passion—love, immense, infinite, indescribable love. As he himself taught, the entire Law of God and the Prophets are sum-

l. Other ancient authorities omit *righteous* or *man's*

stripped him and put a scarlet robe upon him, ²⁹and plaiting a crown of thorns they put it on his head, and put a reed in his right hand. And kneeling before him they mocked him, saying, "Hail, King of the Jews!" ³⁰And they spat upon him, and took the reed and struck him on the head. ³¹And when they had mocked him, they stripped him of the robe, and put his own clothes on him, and led him away to crucify him.

Is 50:6

Mk 15:20–41
Lk 23:26,
33–49
Jn 19:16–30

The crucifixion and death of Jesus

³²As they were marching out, they came upon a man of Cyrene, Simon by name; this man they compelled to carry his cross. ³³And

---

med up in the divine comandment of love (cf. Mt 22:36–40).

The four evangelists have filled many pages with their account of the sufferings of our Lord. Contemplation of Jesus' passion, identification with the suffering Christ, should play a key role in the life of every Christian, if he is to share later in the resurrection of his Lord: "Don't hinder the work of the Paraclete: seek union with Christ, so as to be purified, and feel with him the insults, the spits, and the blows, and the thorns, and the weight of the cross ... , and the nails tearing through your flesh, and the agony of a forsaken death.

"And enter through our Lord's open side until you find sure refuge there in his wounded Heart" (St Josemaría Escrivá, *The Way*, 58).

27:27. A cohort, or battalion, consisted of some 625 soldiers. In Jesus' time there was always a cohort garrisoned in Jerusalem, quartered in the Antonia Tower, adjoining the temple. This reported to the governor and was recruited from non-Jewish inhabitants of the region.

27:28–31. The Gospel describes very soberly how Jesus puts up no resistance to being beaten and ridiculed; the facts are allowed to speak for themselves. He takes upon himself, out of love for the

Father and for us, the punishment we deserve to suffer for our sins. This should make us very grateful and, at the same time, cause us to have sorrow for sin, to desire to suffer in silence at Jesus' side and atone for our sins and those of others: Lord, I want never to sin again; but you must help me to stay true to you.

27:32. Seeing how much Jesus has suffered, the soldiers realize that he is incapable of carrying the cross on his own as far as the top of Golgotha. There he is, in the centre of the crowd, with not a friend in sight. Where are all the people who benefitted from his preaching and healing and miracles? None of them is there to help him. He had said, "If any man would come after me, let him deny himself and take up his cross and follow me" (Mt 16:24). But cowardice and fear have taken over. The soldiers resort to laying hold of a stranger and forcing him to carry the cross. Our Lord will reward this favour done to him: God's grace will come down on "Simon of Cyrene, ... the father of Alexander and Rufus" (Mk 15:21), who will soon be prominent members of the early Church. The experience of pain proves to be the best route to Christian discipleship.

Christ's disciples must try to ensure that cowardice does not undermine their

Ps 69:21
Ps 22:18

Ps 22:7;
109:25

Mt 26:61
Jn 2:19

when they came to a place called Golgotha (which means the place of a skull), ³⁴they offered him wine to drink, mingled with gall; but when he tasted it, he would not drink it. ³⁵And when they had crucified him, they divided his garments among them by casting lots; ³⁶then they sat down and kept watch over him there. ³⁷And over his head they put the charge against him, which read, "This is Jesus the King of the Jews." ³⁸Then two robbers were crucified with him, one on the right and one on the left. ³⁹And those who passed by derided him, wagging their heads ⁴⁰and saying, "You who would destroy the temple and build it in three days, save yourself! If you are the Son of God, come down from the cross." ⁴¹So also the chief priests, with the scribes and elders, mocked him, saying, ⁴²"He saved others; he cannot save himself.

---

commitment: "See how lovingly he embraces the Cross. Learn from him. Jesus carries the Cross for you: you … carry it for Jesus. But don't drag the Cross … Carry it squarely on your shoulder, because your Cross, if you carry it like that, will not be just any Cross.... It will be the Holy Cross. Don't carry your Cross with resignation: resignation is not a generous word. Love the Cross. When you really love it, your Cross will be … a Cross without a Cross" (St J. Escrivá, *Holy Rosary*, fourth sorrowful mystery).

27:33. On the outskirts of Jerusalem there was a little hill called "Golgotha", or "the place of a skull", as the evangelist expressly states. It was used as a site for executing criminals. The name "Golgotha" comes from a transcription of an Aramaic word meaning "head". The name "Calvary" comes from a Latin word with the same meaning.

27:34. They offered Jesus a drink consisting of a mixture of wine, honey and myrrh (cf. Mk 15:23); this was usually given to people condemned to death, as a narcotic to lessen the pain. Our Lord chooses not to take it, because he wants to suffer the full rigour of his passion.

"Let us drink to the last drop the chalice of pain in this poor present life. What does it matter to suffer for ten years, twenty, fifty … if afterwards there is heaven forever, forever … forever? And, above all—rather than because of the reward, *propter retributionem*—what does suffering matter if we suffer to console, to please God our Father, in a spirit of reparation, united to him on his cross; in a word: if we suffer for Love? …" (St Josemaría Escrivá, *The Way*, 182).

27:35. Some manuscripts add to this verse the following words taken from John 19:24: "This was to fulfil the scripture, 'They parted my garments among them, and for my clothing they cast lots'" (cf. Ps 22:18).

27:45. Approximately from twelve midday to three o'clock in the afternoon. See the note on Mt 20:3.

27:46. Words from Psalm 22:1, which our Lord uses to show the physical and moral pain he is suffering. In no sense should these words be taken as a complaint against God's plans. "Suffering does not consist in not feeling since that is proper to those who have no feelings;

178

He is the King of Israel; let him come down now from the cross, and we will believe in him. [43]He trusts in God, let God deliver him now, if he desires him; for he said, 'I am the Son of God.'" [44]And the robbers who were crucified with him also reviled him in the same way.

Ps 22:8
Wis 2:13,
18–20

[45]Now from the sixth hour there was darkness over all the land[m] until the ninth hour. [46]And about the ninth hour Jesus cried with a loud voice, "Eli, Eli, lama sabachthani?" that is, "My God, my God, why hast thou forsaken me?" [47]And some of the bystanders hearing it said, "This man is calling Elijah." [48]And one of them at once ran and took a sponge, filled it with vinegar, and put it on a reed, and gave it to him to drink. [49]But the others said, "Wait, let us see whether Elijah will come to save him."[n] [50]And Jesus cried again with a loud voice and yielded up his spirit.

Ps 22:1

Ps 69:21

---

nor does it lie in not showing that one feels pain: rather, suffering means that in spite of pain one does not set aside the law or obedience to God. For feeling is natural to the flesh, which is not like bronze; and so reason does not remove it, because reason gives to everything what its nature demands; and our sensitivity is very soft and tender; when it is wounded it of necessity feels, and when it feels it has to cry out" (Fray Luis de León, *Exposición del Libro de Job*).

In his agony in the garden (cf. note on Mt 26:36–46), Jesus experienced a kind of anticipation of the pain and abandonment he feels at this point in his passion. In the context of the mystery of Jesus Christ, God-and-Man, we should notice how his humanity—body and soul—suffers without his divinity assuaging that suffering, as it could have done. "Here before the cross, we should have sorrow for our sins and for those of all men, for they are responsible for Jesus' death. We should have faith to penetrate deep into this sublime truth which surpasses our understanding and to fill ourselves with amazement at God's love.

And we should pray so that Christ's life and death may become the model and motivation for our own life and self-giving. Only thus will we earn the name of conquerors: for the risen Christ will conquer in us, and death will be changed into life" (St Josemaría Escrivá, *Christ Is Passing By*, 101).

27:50. The phrase "yielded up his spirit" (literally, "released, exhaled") is a way of saying that Christ really died; like any other man, his death meant the separation of soul and body. The fact that he genuinely did die—something that everyone, even his enemies, acknowledged— will show that his resurrection was a real resurrection, a miraculous, divine fact.

This is the climax of Christ's surrender to the will of the Father. Here he accomplishes the salvation of mankind (Mt 26:27–28; Mk 10:45; Heb 9:14) and gives us the greatest proof of God's love for us (Jn 3:16). The saints usually explain the expiatory value of Christ's sacrifice by underlining that he voluntarily "yielded up his spirit". "Our Saviour's death was a sacrifice of holocaust which

---

m. Or *earth*   **n.** Other ancient authorities insert *And another took a spear and pierced his side, and out came water and blood*

Ex 26:31
Heb 10:19f

⁵¹And behold, the curtain of the temple was torn in two, from top to bottom; and the earth shook, and the rocks were split; ⁵²the tombs also were opened, and many bodies of the saints who had

Acts 26:23
Dan 12:2

fallen asleep were raised, ⁵³and coming out of the tombs after his resurrection they went into the holy city and appeared to many. ⁵⁴When the centurion and those who were with him, keeping watch over Jesus, saw the earthquake and what took place, they were filled with awe, and said, "Truly this was the Sonˣ of God!"

Lk 8:2f

⁵⁵There were also many women there, looking on from afar, who had followed Jesus from Galilee, ministering to him; ⁵⁶among whom were Mary Magdalene, and Mary the mother of James and Joseph, and the mother of the sons of Zebedee.

The burial of Jesus

Mk 15:42–47
Lk 23:50–55
Jn 19:38–42
Ex 34:25

⁵⁷When it was evening, there came a rich man from Arimathea, named Joseph, who also was a disciple of Jesus. ⁵⁸He went to Pilate and asked for the body of Jesus. Then Pilate ordered it to be

---

he himself offered to his Father for our redemption; for though the pains and sufferings of his passion were so great and violent that anyone else would have died of them, Jesus would not have died of them unless he so chose and unless the fire of his infinite charity had consumed his life. He was, then, himself the sacrificer who offered himself to the Father and immolated himself, dying in love, to love, by love, for love and of love" (St Francis de Sales, *Treatise on the Love of God*, book 10, chap. 17). This fidelity of Christ to the point of dying should be a permanent encouragement to us to persevere until the end, conscious of the fact that only he who is true until death will receive the crown of life (cf. Rev 2:10).

27:51–53. The rending of the temple veil indicates that the way to God the Father has been opened up to all men (cf. Heb 9:15) and that the New Covenant, sealed with the blood of Christ, has begun to operate. The other portents which attend

Jesus' death are signs of the divine character of that event: it was not just one more man who was dying, but the Son of God.

27:52–53. These events are undoubtedly difficult to understand. No explanation should say what the text does not say. Nor does any other part of Holy Scripture, or the Magisterium of the Church, help to clarify what actually happened.

The great Church writers have suggested three possible explanations. First: that it was not a matter of resurrections in the strict sense, but of apparitions of these dead people. Second: they would have been dead people who arose in the way Lazarus did, and then died again. Third: their resurrection would have been definitive, that is glorious, in this way anticipating the final universal resurrection of the dead.

The first explanation does not seem to be very faithful to the text, which does use the words "were raised" (*surrexerunt*). The third is difficult to recon-

x. Or *a son*

given to him. ⁵⁹And Joseph took the body, and wrapped it in a clean linen shroud, ⁶⁰and laid it in his own new tomb, which he had hewn in the rock; and he rolled a great stone to the door of the tomb, and departed. ⁶¹Mary Magdalene and the other Mary were there, sitting opposite the sepulchre.

Is 53:9

⁶²Next day, that is, after the day of Preparation, the chief priests and the Pharisees gathered before Pilate ⁶³and said, "Sir, we remember how that imposter said, while he was still alive, 'After three days I will rise again.' ⁶⁴Therefore order the sepulchre to be made secure until the third day, lest his disciples go and steal him away, and tell the people, 'He has risen from the dead,' and the last fraud will be worse than the first." ⁶⁵Pilate said to them, 'You have a guardᵒ of soldiers; go, make it as secure as you can.'ᴾ ⁶⁶So they went and made the sepulchre secure by sealing the stone and setting a guard.*

2 Cor 6:8

Dan 6:18

---

cile with the clear assertion of Scripture that Christ was the first-born from the dead (cf. 1 Cor 15:20; Col 1:18). St Augustine, St Jerome and St Thomas are inclined towards the second explanation because they feel it fits in best with the sacred text and does not present the theological difficulties which the third does (cf. *Summa theologiae*, 3, 53, 3). It is also in keeping with the solution proposed by the *St Pius V Catechism*, 1, 6, 9.

27:55–56. The presence of the holy women beside Christ on the cross gives an example of stoutheartedness to all Christians.

"Woman is stronger than man, and more faithful, in the hour of suffering: Mary Magdalene and Mary Cleophas and Salome! With a group of valiant women like these, closely united to our Lady of Sorrows, what work for souls could be done in the world!" (St Josemaría Escrivá, *The Way*, 982).

27:60. It was customary for well-to-do Jews to build tombs for themselves on their own property. Most of these tombs were excavated out of rock, in the form of a cavern; they would have had a small hall or vestibule leading to the tomb proper. At the end of the hall, which would only have been a few metres long, a very low doorway gave access to the burial chamber. The first entrance door, which was at ground level, was closed off by a huge stone which could be rolled (it was called a "gobel"), fitted into a groove to make rolling easier.

27:62. The Day of Preparation (the Greek word *parasceve* means "preparation") was the day prior to the sabbath (cf. Lk 23:54). It got its name from the fact that it was the day when everything needed for the sabbath was prepared, the sabbath being a day of rest, consecrated to God, on which no work was permitted.

27:66. All these preventive measures (sealing the entrance to the tomb, placing the guard there, etc.)—measures taken by Christ's enemies—became factors which helped people believe in his resurrection.

28:1–15. The resurrection of Jesus, which

o. Or *take a guard* p. Greek *know*

Jesus rises from the dead and appears to the women

Mk 16:1–10
Lk 24:1–10
Jn 20:1–18
Mt 27:61

Acts 1:10

Acts 2:36
Mt 26:32

28 *[1]Now after the sabbath, toward the dawn of the first day of the week, Mary Magdalene and the other Mary went to see the sepulchre. [2]And behold, there was a great earthquake; for an angel of the Lord descended from heaven and came and rolled back the stone, and sat upon it. [3]His appearance was like lightning, and his raiment white as snow. [4]And for fear of him the guards trembled and became like dead men. [5]But the angel said to the women. "Do not be afraid; for I know that you seek Jesus who was crucified. [6]He is not here; for he has risen, as he said. Come, see the place where he[q] lay. [7]Then go quickly and tell his disciples that he has risen from the dead, and behold, he is going before you to Galilee; there you will see him. Lo, I have told you." [8]So they departed quickly from the tomb with fear and great joy, and

happened in the early hours of the Sunday morning, is a fact which all the evangelists state clearly and unequivocally. Some holy women discover to their surprise that the tomb is open. On entering the hall (cf. Mk 16:5–6), they see an angel who says to them, "He is not here; for he has risen, as he said." The guards who were on duty when the angel rolled back the stone go to the city and report what has happened to the chief priests. These, because of the urgency of the matter, decide to bribe the guards; they give them a considerable sum of money on condition that they spread the word that his disciples came at night and stole the body of Jesus when they were asleep. "Wretched craftiness," says St Augustine, "do you give us witnesses who were asleep? It is you who are really asleep if this is the only kind of explanation you have to offer!" (*Enarrationes in Psalmos*, 63, 15). The apostles, who a couple of days before fled in fear, will, now that they have seen him and have eaten and drunk with him, become tireless preachers of this great event: "This Jesus", they will say, "God raised up, and of that we are all witnesses" (Acts 2:32).

Just as he foretold he would go up to Jerusalem and be delivered to the leaders of the Jews and put to death, he also prophesied that he would rise from the dead (Mt 20:17–19; Mk 10:32–34; Lk 18:31–34). By his resurrection he completes the sign he promised to give unbelievers to show his divinity (Mt 12:40).

The resurrection of Christ is one of the basic dogmas of the Catholic faith. In fact, St Paul says, "If Christ has not been raised, then our preaching is in vain and your faith is in vain" (1 Cor 15:14); and, to prove his assertion that Christ rose, he tells us "that he appeared to Cephas, then to the Twelve. Then he appeared to more than five hundred brethren at one time, most of whom are still alive, though some have fallen asleep. Then he appeared to James, then to all the apostles. Last of all, as to one untimely born, he appeared also to me" (1 Cor 15:5–8). The creeds state that Jesus rose from the dead on the third day (*Nicene Creed*), by his own power (Ninth Council of Toledo, *De Redemptione*), by a true resurrection of the flesh (*Creed* of St Leo IX), reunit-

q. Other ancient authorities read *the Lord*

ran to tell his disciples. [9]And behold, Jesus met them and said, "Hail!" And they came up and took hold of his feet and worshipped him. [10]Then Jesus said to them, "Do not be afraid; go and tell my brethren to go to Galilee; and there they will see me."

Heb 2:11
Gen 45:4;
50:19

The soldiers are bribed

[11]While they were going, behold, some of the guard went into the city and told the chief priests all that had taken place. [12]And when they had assembled with the elders and taken counsel, they gave a sum of money to the soldiers [13]and said, "Tell people, 'His disciples came by night and stole him away while we were asleep.' [14]And if this comes to the governor's ears, we will satisfy him and keep you out of trouble." [15]So they took the money and did as they were directed; and this story has been spread among the Jews to this day.

---

ing his soul with his body (Innocent III, *Eius exemplo*), and that this fact of the resurrection is historically proven and provable (St Pius X, *Lamentabili*).

"By the word 'resurrection' we are not merely to understand that Christ was raised from the dead ... but that he rose by his own power and virtue, a singular prerogative peculiar to him alone. Our Lord confirmed this by the divine testimony of his own mouth when he said: 'I lay down my life, that I may take it again.[...] I have power to lay it down: and I have power to take it up again' (Jn 10:17–18). To the Jews he also said, in corroboration of his doctrine: 'Destroy this temple, and in three days I will raise it up' (Jn 2:19–20) [...]. We sometimes, it is true, read in Scripture that he was raised by the Father (cf. Acts 2:24; Rom 8:11); but this refers to him as man, just as those passages on the other hand, which say that he rose by his own power, relate to him as God" (St Pius V, *Catechism*, 1, 6, 8).

Christ's resurrection was not a return to his previous earthly existence; it was a "glorious" resurrection, that is to say, attaining the full development of human life—immortal, freed from all limitations of space and time. As a result of the resur-

rection, Christ's body now shares in the glory which his soul had from the beginning. Here lies the unique nature of the historical fact of the resurrection. He could be seen not by anyone but only by those to whom he granted that grace, to enable them to be witnesses of this resurrection, and to enable others to believe in him by accepting the testimony of the seers.

Christ's resurrection was something necessary for the completion of the work of our redemption. For, Jesus Christ through his death freed us from sins; but by his resurrection he restored to us all that we had lost through sin and, moreover, opened for us the gates of eternal life (cf. Rom 4:25). Also, the fact that he rose from the dead by his own power is a definitive proof that he is the Son of God, and therefore his resurrection fully confirms our faith in his divinity.

The resurrection of Christ, as has been pointed out, is the most sublime truth of our faith. That is why St Augustine exclaims: "It is no great thing to believe that Christ died; for this is something that is also believed by pagans and Jews and by all the wicked: everyone believes that he died. The Christians' faith is in Christ's resurrection; this is

Appearance in Galilee. The mission to the world

Eph 1:20–22
Dan 7:14
Mk 16:15f

¹⁶Now the eleven disciples went to Galilee, to the mountain to which Jesus had directed them. ¹⁷And when they saw him they worshipped him; but some doubted. ¹⁸And Jesus came and said to them, "All authority in heaven and on earth has been given to me. ¹⁹Go therefore and make disciples of all nations, baptizing them in

---

what we hold to be a great thing—to believe that he rose" (*Enarrationes in Psalmos*, 120).

The mystery of the Redemption wrought by Christ, which embraces his death and resurrection, is applied to every man and woman through Baptism and the other sacraments, by means of which the believer is as it were immersed in Christ and in his death, that is to say, in a mystical way he becomes part of Christ, he dies and rises with Christ: "We were buried therefore with him by baptism unto death, so that as Christ was raised from the dead by the glory of the Father, we too might walk in newness of life" (Rom 6:4).

An ardent desire to seek the things of God and an interior taste for the things that are above (cf. Col 3:1–3) are signs of our resurrection with Christ.

28:16–20. This short passage, which brings to a close the Gospel of St Matthew, is of great importance. Seeing the risen Christ, the disciples adore him, worshipping him as God. This shows that at last they are fully conscious of what, from much earlier on, they felt in their heart and confessed by their words—that their Master is the Messiah, the Son of God (cf. Mt 16:18; Jn 1:49). They are overcome by amazement and joy at the wonder their eyes behold: it seems almost impossible, were he not before their very eyes. Yet he is completely real, so their fearful amazement gives way to adoration. The Master addresses them with the majesty proper to God: "All authority in heaven and on earth has been

given to me." Omnipotence, an attribute belonging exclusively to God, belongs to him: he is confirming the faith of his worshippers; and he is also telling them that the authority which he is going to give them to equip them to carry out their mission to the whole world, derives from his own divine authority.

On hearing him speak these words, we should bear in mind that the authority of the Church, which is given it for the salvation of mankind, comes directly from Jesus Christ, and that this authority, in the sphere of faith and morals, is above any other authority on earth.

The apostles present on this occasion, and after them their lawful successors, receive the charge of teaching all nations what Jesus taught by word and work: he is the only path that leads to God. The Church, and in it all Christian faithful, has the duty to proclaim until the end of time, by word and example, the faith that she has received. This mission belongs especially to the successors of the apostles, for on them devolves the power to teach with authority, "for, before Christ ascended to his Father after his resurrection, he […] entrusted them with the mission and power to proclaim to mankind what they had heard, what they had seen with their eyes, what they had looked upon and touched with their hands, concerning the Word of Life (1 Jn 1:1). He also entrusted them with the mission and power to explain with authority what he had taught them, his words and actions, his signs and commandments. And he gave them the Spirit

the name of the Father and of the Son and of the Holy Spirit,
²⁰teaching them to observe all that I have commanded you; and lo,   Jn 14:23
I am with you always, to the close of the age."

---

to fulfil their mission" (John Paul II, *Catechesi tradendae*, 1). Therefore, the teachings of the Pope and of the bishops united in communion with him should always be accepted by everyone with assent and obedience.

Here Christ also passes on to the apostles and their successors the power to baptize, that is, to receive people into the Church, thereby opening up to them the way to personal salvation.

The mission which the Church is definitively given here at the end of St Matthew's Gospel is one of continuing the work of Christ—teaching men and women the truths concerning God and the duty incumbent on them to identify with these truths, to make them their own by having constant recourse to the grace of the sacraments. This mission will endure until the end of time and, to enable the Church to do this work, the risen Christ promises to stay with it and never leave it. When Holy Scripture says that God is with someone, this means that that person will be successful in everything he undertakes. Therefore, the Church, helped in this way by the presence of its divine Founder, can be confident of never failing to fulfil its mission down the centuries until the end of time.

New Vulgate Text

EVANGELIUM SECUNDUM MATTHAEUM

[1] ¹Liber generationis Iesu Christi filii David filii Abraham. ²Abraham genuit Isaac, Isaac autem genuit Iacob, Iacob autem genuit Iudam et fratres eius, ³Iudas autem genuit Phares et Zara de Thamar, Phares autem genuit Esrom, Esrom autem genuit Aram, ⁴Aram autem genuit Aminadab, Aminadab autem genuit Naasson, Naasson autem genuit Salmon, ⁵Salmon autem genuit Booz de Rahab, Booz autem genuit Obed ex Ruth, Obed autem genuit Iesse, ⁶Iesse autem genuit David regem. David autem genuit Salomonem ex ea, quae fuit Uriae, ⁷Salomon autem genuit Roboam, Roboam autem genuit Abiam, Abia autem genuit Asa, ⁸Asa autem genuit Iosaphat, Iosaphat autem genuit Ioram, Ioram autem genuit Oziam, ⁹Ozias autem genuit Ioatham, Ioatham autem genuit Achaz, Achaz autem genuit Ezechiam, ¹⁰Ezechias autem genuit Manassen, Manasses autem genuit Amon, Amon autem genuit Iosiam, ¹¹Iosias autem genuit Iechoniam et fratres eius in transmigratione Babylonis. ¹²Et post transmigrationem Babylonis Iechonias genuit Salathiel, Salathiel autem genuit Zorobabel, ¹³Zorobabel autem genuit Abiud, Abiud autem genuit Eliachim, Eliachim autem genuit Azor, ¹⁴Azor autem genuit Sadoc, Sadoc autem genuit Achim, Achim autem genuit Eliud, ¹⁵Eliud autem genuit Eleazar, Eleazar autem genuit Matthan, Matthan autem genuit Iacob, ¹⁶Iacob autem genuit Ioseph virum Mariae, de qua natus est Iesus, qui vocatur Christus. ¹⁷Omnes ergo generationes ab Abraham usque ad David generationes quattuordecim; et a David usque ad transmigrationem Babylonis generationes quattuordecim; et a transmigratione Babylonis usque ad Christum generationes quattuordecim. ¹⁸Iesu Christi autem generatio sic erat. Cum esset desponsata mater eius Maria Ioseph, antequam convenirent inventa est in utero habens de Spiritu Sancto. ¹⁹Ioseph autem vir eius, cum esset iustus et nollet eam traducere, voluit occulte dimittere eam. ²⁰Haec autem eo cogitante, ecce angelus Domini in somnis apparuit ei dicens: «Ioseph fili David, noli timere accipere Mariam coniugem tuam. Quod enim in ea natum est, de Spiritu Sancto est; ²¹pariet autem filium, et vocabis nomen eius Iesum: ipse enim salvum faciet populum suum a peccatis eorum». ²²Hoc autem totum factum est, ut adimpleretur id, quod dictum est a Domino per prophetam dicentem: ²³*«Ecce, virgo in utero habebit et pariet filium, et vocabunt nomen eius Emmanuel»*, quod est interpretatum *Nobiscum Deus*. ²⁴Exsurgens autem Ioseph a somno fecit, sicut praecepit ei angelus Domini, et accepit coniugem suam; ²⁵et non cognoscebat eam, donec peperit filium, et vocavit nomen eius Iesum.   **[2]** ¹Cum autem natus esset Iesus in Bethlehem Iudaeae in diebus Herodis regis, ecce Magi ab oriente venerunt Hierosolymam, ²dicentes: «Ubi est, qui natus est, rex Iudaeorum? Vidimus enim stellam eius in oriente et venimus adorare eum». ³Audiens autem Herodes rex turbatus est et omnis Hierosolyma cum illo; ⁴et congregans omnes principes sacerdotum et scribas populi, sciscitabatur ab eis ubi Christus nasceretur. ⁵At illi dixerunt ei: «In Bethlehem Iudaeae. Sic enim scriptum est per prophetam: ⁶*“Et tu, Bethlehem* terra Iudae, / nequaquam *minima es in principibus Iudae; / ex te enim exiet dux, / qui reget populum meum Israel”»*. ⁷Tunc Herodes, clam vocatis Magis, diligenter didicit ab eis tempus stellae, quae apparuit eis, ⁸et mittens illos in Bethlehem dixit: «Ite et interrogate diligenter de puero; et cum inveneritis renuntiate mihi, ut et ego veniens adorem eum». ⁹Qui cum audissent regem, abierunt. Et ecce stella, quam viderant in oriente, antecedebat eos, usque dum veniens staret supra, ubi erat puer. ¹⁰Videntes autem stellam gavisi sunt gaudio magno valde. ¹¹Et intrantes domum viderunt puerum cum Maria matre eius, et procidentes adoraverunt eum; et apertis thesauris suis, obtulerunt ei munera, aurum et tus et myrrham. ¹²Et responso accepto in somnis, ne redirent ad Herodem, per aliam viam reversi sunt in regionem suam. ¹³Qui cum recessissent, ecce angelus Domini apparet in somnis Ioseph dicens: «Surge et accipe puerum et matrem eius et fuge in Aegyptum et esto ibi, usque dum dicam tibi; futurum est enim ut Herodes quaerat puerum ad perdendum eum». ¹⁴Qui consurgens accepit puerum et matrem eius nocte et recessit in Aegyptum ¹⁵et erat ibi usque ad obitum Herodis, ut adimpleretur, quod dictum est a Domino per prophetam dicentem: «*Ex Aegypto vocavi filium meum*». ¹⁶Tunc Herodes videns quoniam illusus esset a Magis, iratus est valde et mittens occidit omnes pueros, qui erant in Bethlehem et in omnibus finibus eius, a bimatu et infra, secundum tempus, quod exquisierat a Magis. [17]Tunc adimpletum est, quod dictum est per Ieremiam prophetam dicentem: [18]«*Vox in Rama audita est, / ploratus et ululatus multus: / Rachel plorans filios suos, / et noluit consolari, quia non sunt*». [19]Defuncto autem Herode, ecce apparet angelus Domini in somnis Ioseph in Aegypto [20]dicens: «Surge et accipe puerum et matrem eius et vade in terram Israel; defuncti sunt enim, qui quaerebant animam pueri». [21]Qui surgens accepit puerum et matrem eius et venit in terram Israel. [22]Audiens autem quia Archelaus regnaret in Iudaea pro Herode patre suo, timuit illuc ire; et admonitus in somnis, secessit in partes Galilaeae [23]et veniens habitavit in civitate, quae vocatur Nazareth, ut adimpleretur, quod dictum est per Prophetas: «Nazaraeus vocabitur».   [3] [1]In diebus autem illis venit Ioannes Baptista praedicans in deserto Iudaeae [2]et dicens: «Paenitentiam agite; appropinquavit enim regnum caelorum». [3]Hic est enim, qui dictus est per Isaiam prophetam dicentem: «*Vox clamantis in deserto: / "Parate viam Domini, / rectas facite semitas eius!"*». [4]Ipse autem Ioannes habebat vestimentum de pilis cameli et zonam pelliceam circa lumbos suos; esca autem eius erat locustae et mel silvestre. [5]Tunc exibat ad eum Hierosolyma et omnis Iudaea et omnis regio circa Iordanem, [6]et baptizabantur in Iordane flumine ab eo, confitentes peccata sua. [7]Videns autem multos pharisaeorum et sadducaeorum venientes ad baptismum suum, dixit eis: «Progenies viperarum, quis demonstravit vobis fugere a futura ira? [8]Facite ergo fructum dignum paenitentiae [9]et ne velitis dicere intra vos: "Patrem habemus Abraham"; dico enim vobis quoniam potest Deus de lapidibus istis suscitare Abrahae filios. [10]Iam enim securis ad radicem arborum posita est; omnis ergo arbor, quae non facit fructum bonum, exciditur et in ignem mittitur. [11]Ego quidem vos baptizo in aqua in paenitentiam; qui autem post me venturus est, fortior me est, cuius non sum dignus calceamenta portare; ipse vos baptizabit in Spiritu Sancto et igni, [12]cuius ventilabrum in manu sua, et permundabit aream suam et congregabit triticum suum in horreum, paleas autem comburet igni inexstinguibili». [13]Tunc venit Iesus a Galilaea in Iordanem ad Ioannem, ut baptizaretur ab eo. [14]Ioannes autem prohibebat eum dicens: «Ego a te debeo baptizari, et tu venis ad me?». [15]Respondens autem Iesus dixit ei: «Sine modo, sic enim decet nos implere omnem iustitiam». Tunc dimittit eum. [16]Baptizatus autem Iesus, confestim ascendit de aqua; et ecce aperti sunt ei caeli, et vidit Spiritum Dei descendentem sicut columbam et venientem super se. [17]Et ecce vox de caelis dicens: «Hic est Filius meus dilectus, in quo mihi complacui».   [4] [1]Tunc Iesus ductus est in desertum a Spiritu, ut tentaretur a Diabolo. [2]Et cum ieiunasset quadraginta diebus et quadraginta noctibus, postea esuriit. [3]Et accedens tentator dixit ei: «Si Filius Dei es, dic, ut lapides isti panes fiant». [4]Qui respondens dixit: «Scriptum est: / "*Non in pane solo vivet homo, / sed in omni verbo, quod procedit de ore Dei*"». [5]Tunc assumit eum Diabolus in sanctam civitatem et statuit eum supra pinnaculum templi [6]et dicit ei: «Si Filius Dei es, mitte te deorsum. Scriptum est enim: "*Angelis suis mandabit de te, / et in manibus tollent te, / ne forte offendas ad lapidem pedem tuum*"». [7]Ait illi Iesus: «Rursum scriptum est: "*Non tentabis Dominum Deum tuum*"». [8]Iterum assumit eum Diabolus in montem excelsum valde et ostendit ei omnia regna mundi et gloriam eorum [9]et dicit illi: «Haec tibi omnia dabo, si cadens adoraveris me». [10]Tunc dicit ei Iesus: «Vade, Satanas! Scriptum est enim: / "*Dominum Deum tuum adorabis / et illi soli servies*"». [11]Tunc reliquit eum Diabolus, et ecce angeli accesserunt et ministrabant ei. [12]Cum autem audisset quod Ioannes traditus esset, secessit in Galilaeam. [13]Et relicta Nazareth, venit et habitavit in Capharnaum maritimam [14]in finibus Zabulon et Nephthali, ut impleretur, quod dictum est per Isaiam prophetam dicentem: [15]«*Terra Zabulon et terra Nephthali, / ad viam maris, trans Iordanem, / Galilaea gentium; / [16]populus, qui sedebat in tenebris, / lucem vidit magnam, / et sedentibus in regione et umbra mortis / lux orta est eis*». [17]Exinde coepit Iesus praedicare et dicere: «Paenitentiam agite; appropinquavit enim regnum caelorum». [18]Ambulans autem iuxta mare Galilaeae, vidit duos fratres, Simonem, qui vocatur Petrus, et Andream fratrem eius, mittentes rete in mare; erant enim piscatores. [19]Et ait illis: «Venite post me, et faciam vos piscatores hominum». [20]At illi continuo, relictis retibus, secuti sunt eum. [21]Et procedens inde vidit alios duos fratres, Iacobum Zebedaei et Ioannem fratrem eius, in navi cum Zebedaeo patre eorum reficientes retia sua, et vocavit eos. [22]Illi autem statim, relicta navi et patre suo, secuti sunt eum. [23]Et circumibat Iesus totam Galilaeam, docens in synagogis eorum et praedicans evangelium regni et sanans omnem languorem et omnem infirmitatem in populo. [24]Et abiit opinio eius in totam Syriam; et obtulerunt ei omnes male habentes, variis languoribus et tormentis comprehensos, et qui daemonia habebant, et lunaticos et paralyticos, et curavit eos. [25]Et secutae sunt eum turbae multae de Galilaea et Decapoli et Hierosolymis et Iudaea et de trans Iordanem.   [5] [1]Videns autem turbas, ascendit in montem; et cum sedisset, accesserunt ad eum discipuli eius; [2]et aperiens os suum docebat eos dicens: [3]«Beati pauperes spiritu, quoniam ipsorum est regnum caelorum. [4]Beati, qui lugent, quoniam ipsi consolabuntur. [5]Beati mites, quoniam ipsi possidebunt terram. [6]Beati, qui esuriunt et sitiunt iustitiam, quoniam ipsi saturabuntur. [7]Beati misericordes, quia ipsi misericordiam consequentur. ⁸Beati mundo corde, quoniam ipsi Deum videbunt. ⁹Beati pacifici, quoniam filii Dei vocabuntur. ¹⁰Beati, qui persecutionem patiuntur propter iustitiam, quoniam ipsorum est regnum caelorum. ¹¹Beati estis cum maledixerint vobis et persecuti vos fuerint et dixerint omne malum adversum vos, mentientes, propter me. ¹²Gaudete et exsultate, quoniam merces vestra copiosa est in caelis; sic enim persecuti sunt prophetas, qui fuerunt ante vos. ¹³Vos estis sal terrae; quod si sal evanuerit, in quo salietur? Ad nihilum valet ultra, nisi ut mittatur foras et conculcetur ab hominibus. ¹⁴Vos estis lux mundi. Non potest civitas abscondi supra montem posita; ¹⁵neque accendunt lucernam et ponunt eam sub modio, sed super candelabrum, ut luceat omnibus, qui in domo sunt. ¹⁶Sic luceat lux vestra coram hominibus, ut videant vestra bona opera et glorificent Patrem vestrum, qui in caelis est. ¹⁷Nolite putare quoniam veni solvere Legem aut Prophetas; non veni solvere, sed adimplere. ¹⁸Amen quippe dico vobis: Donec transeat caelum et terra, iota unum aut unus apex non praeteribit a Lege, donec omnia fiant. ¹⁹Qui ergo solverit unum de mandatis istis minimis et docuerit sic homines, minimus vocabitur in regno caelorum; qui autem fecerit et docuerit, hic magnus vocabitur in regno caelorum. ²⁰Dico enim vobis: Nisi abundaverit iustitia vestra plus quam scribarum et pharisaeorum, non intrabitis in regnum caelorum. ²¹Audistis quia dictum est antiquis: *"Non occides*; qui autem occiderit, reus erit iudicio". ²²Ego autem dico vobis: Omnis, qui irascitur fratri suo, reus erit iudicio; qui autem dixerit fratri suo: "Racha", reus erit concilio; qui autem dixerit: "Fatue", reus erit gehennae ignis. ²³Si ergo offeres munus tuum ad altare, et ibi recordatus fueris quia frater tuus habet aliquid adversum te, ²⁴relinque ibi munus tuum ante altare et vade prius, reconciliare fratri tuo et tunc veniens offer munus tuum. ²⁵Esto consentiens adversario tuo cito, dum es in via cum eo, ne forte tradat te adversarius iudici, et iudex tradat te ministro, et in carcerem mittaris. ²⁶Amen dico tibi: Non exies inde, donec reddas novissimum quadrantem. ²⁷Audistis quia dictum est: *"Non moechaberis"*. ²⁸Ego autem dico vobis: Omnis, qui viderit mulierem ad concupiscendum eam, iam moechatus est eam in corde suo. ²⁹Quod si oculus tuus dexter scandalizat te, erue eum et proice abs te; expedit enim tibi, ut pereat unum membrorum tuorum, quam totum corpus tuum mittatur in gehennam. ³⁰Et si dextera manus tua scandalizat te, abscide eam et proice abs te; expedit enim tibi, ut pereat unum membrorum tuorum, quam totum corpus tuum abeat in gehennam. ³¹Dictum est autem: *"Quicumque dimiserit uxorem suam, det illi libellum repudii"*. ³²Ego autem dico vobis: Omnis, qui dimiserit uxorem suam, excepta fornicationis causa, facit eam moechari; et, qui dimissam duxerit, adulterat. ³³Iterum audistis quia dictum est antiquis: *"Non periurabis*; *reddes autem Domino iuramenta tua"*. ³⁴Ego autem dico vobis: Non iurare omnino, neque per *caelum*, quia *thronus Dei est*, ³⁵neque per *terram*, quia *scabellum est pedum eius*, neque per Hierosolymam, quia *civitas est magni Regis*; ³⁶neque per caput tuum iuraveris, quia non potes unum capillum album facere aut nigrum. ³⁷Sit autem sermo vester: "Est, est", "Non, non"; quod autem his abundantius est, a Malo est. ³⁸Audistis quia dictum est: *"Oculum pro oculo* et *dentem pro dente"*. ³⁹Ego autem dico vobis: Non resistere malo; sed si quis te percusserit in dextera maxilla tua, praebe illi et alteram; ⁴⁰et ei, qui vult tecum iudicio contendere et tunicam tuam tollere, remitte ei et pallium; ⁴¹et quicumque te angariaverit mille passus, vade cum illo duo. ⁴²Qui petit a te, da ei; et volenti mutuari a te, ne avertaris. ⁴³Audistis quia dictum est: *"Diliges proximum tuum* et odio habebis inimicum tuum". ⁴⁴Ego autem dico vobis: Diligite inimicos vestros et orate pro persequentibus vos, ⁴⁵ut sitis filii Patris vestri, qui in caelis est, quia solem suum oriri facit super malos et bonos et pluit super iustos et iniustos. ⁴⁶Si enim dilexeritis eos, qui vos diligunt, quam mercedem habetis? Nonne et publicani hoc faciunt? ⁴⁷Et si salutaveritis fratres vestros tantum, quid amplius facitis? Nonne et ethnici hoc faciunt? ⁴⁸Estote ergo vos perfecti, sicut Pater vester caelestis perfectus est.   **[6]** ¹Attendite, ne iustitiam vestram faciatis coram hominibus, ut videamini ab eis; alioquin mercedem non habetis apud Patrem vestrum, qui in caelis est.²Cum ergo facies eleemosynam, noli tuba canere ante te, sicut hypocritae faciunt in synagogis et in vicis, ut honorificentur ab hominibus. Amen dico vobis: Receperunt mercedem suam. ³Te autem faciente eleemosynam, nesciat sinistra tua quid faciat dextera tua, ⁴ut sit eleemosyna tua in abscondito, et Pater tuus, qui videt in abscondito, reddet tibi. ⁵Et cum oratis, non eritis sicut hypocritae, qui amant in synagogis et in angulis platearum stantes orare, ut videantur ab hominibus. Amen dico vobis: Receperunt mercedem suam. ⁶Tu autem cum orabis, intra in cubiculum tuum et, clauso ostio tuo, ora Patrem tuum, qui est in abscondito; et Pater tuus, qui videt in abscondito, reddet tibi. ⁷Orantes autem nolite multum loqui sicut ethnici: putant enim quia in multiloquio suo exaudiantur. ⁸Nolite ergo assimilari eis; scit enim Pater vester, quibus opus sit vobis, antequam petatis eum. ⁹Sic ergo vos orabitis: Pater noster, qui es in caelis, / sanctificetur nomen tuum, / ¹⁰adveniat regnum tuum, / fiat voluntas tua, / sicut in caelo, et in terra. / ¹¹Panem nostrum supersubstantialem da nobis hodie; / ¹²et dimitte nobis debita nostra, / sicut et nos dimittimus debitoribus nostris; / ¹³et ne inducas nos in tentationem, / sed libera nos a Malo. ¹⁴Si enim dimiseritis hominibus peccata eorum, dimittet et vobis Pater vester caelestis; ¹⁵si autem non dimiseritis hominibus, nec Pater vester dimittet peccata vestra. [16]Cum autem ieiunatis, nolite fieri sicut hypocritae tristes; demoliuntur enim facies suas, ut pareant hominibus ieiunantes. Amen dico vobis: Receperunt mercedem suam. [17]Tu autem cum ieiunas, unge caput tuum et faciem tuam lava, [18]ne videaris hominibus ieiunans sed Patri tuo, qui est in abscondito; et Pater tuus, qui videt in abscondito, reddet tibi. [19]Nolite thesaurizare vobis thesauros in terra, ubi aerugo et tinea demolitur, et ubi fures effodiunt et furantur; [20]thesaurizate autem vobis thesauros in caelo, ubi neque aerugo neque tinea demolitur, et ubi fures non effodiunt nec furantur; [21]ubi enim est thesaurus tuus, ibi erit et cor tuum. [22]Lucerna corporis est oculus. Si ergo fuerit oculus tuus simplex, totum corpus tuum lucidum erit; [23]si autem oculus tuus nequam fuerit, totum corpus tuum tenebrosum erit. Si ergo lumen, quod in te est, tenebrae sunt, tenebrae quantae erunt! [24]Nemo potest duobus dominis servire: aut enim unum odio habebit et alterum diliget aut unum sustinebit et alterum contemnet; non potestis Deo servire et mammonae. [25]Ideo dico vobis: Ne solliciti sitis animae vestrae quid manducetis, neque corpori vestro quid induamini. Nonne anima plus est quam esca, et corpus quam vestimentum? [26]Respicite volatilia caeli, quoniam non serunt neque metunt neque congregant in horrea, et Pater vester caelestis pascit illa. Nonne vos magis pluris estis illis? [27]Quis autem vestrum cogitans potest adicere ad aetatem suam cubitum unum? [28]Et de vestimento quid solliciti estis? Considerate lilia agri quomodo crescunt: non laborant neque nent. [29]Dico autem vobis quoniam nec Salomon in omni gloria sua coopertus est sicut unum ex istis. [30]Si autem fenum agri, quod hodie est et cras in clibanum mittitur, Deus sic vestit, quanto magis vos, modicae fidei? [31]Nolite ergo solliciti esse dicentes: "Quid manducabimus?", aut: "Quid bibemus?", aut: "Quo operiemur?". [32]Haec enim omnia gentes inquirunt; scit enim Pater vester caelestis quia his omnibus indigetis. [33]Quaerite autem primum regnum Dei et iustitiam eius, et haec omnia adicientur vobis. [34]Nolite ergo esse solliciti in crastinum; crastinus enim dies sollicitus erit sibi ipse. Sufficit diei malitia sua. [7] [1]Nolite iudicare, ut non iudicemini; [2]in quo enim iudicio iudicaveritis, iudicabimini, et in qua mensura mensi fueritis, metietur vobis. [3]Quid autem vides festucam in oculo fratris tui, et trabem in oculo tuo non vides? [4]Aut quomodo dices fratri tuo: 'Sine, eiciam festucam de oculo tuo', et ecce trabes est in oculo tuo? [5]Hypocrita, eice primum trabem de oculo tuo, et tunc videbis eicere festucam de oculo fratris tui. [6]Nolite dare sanctum canibus, neque mittatis margaritas vestras ante porcos, ne forte conculcent eas pedibus suis et conversi dirumpant vos. [7]Petite, et dabitur vobis; quaerite et invenietis; pulsate, et aperietur vobis. [8]Omnis enim qui petit, accipit; et, qui quaerit, invenit; et pulsanti aperietur. [9]Aut quis est ex vobis homo, quem si petierit filius suus panem, numquid lapidem porriget ei? [10]Aut si piscem petierit, numquid serpentem porriget ei? [11]Si ergo vos, cum sitis mali, nostis dona bona dare filiis vestris, quanto magis Pater vester, qui in caelis est, dabit bona petentibus se. [12]Omnia ergo, quaecumque vultis ut faciant vobis homines, ita et vos facite eis; haec est enim Lex et Prophetae. [13]Intrate per angustam portam, quia lata porta et spatiosa via, quae ducit ad perditionem, et multi sunt, qui intrant per eam; [14]quam angusta porta et arta via, quae ducit ad vitam, et pauci sunt, qui inveniunt eam! [15]Attendite a falsis prophetis, qui veniunt ad vos in vestimentis ovium, intrinsecus autem sunt lupi rapaces. [16]A fructibus eorum cognoscetis eos: numquid colligunt de spinis uvas aut de tribulis ficus? [17]Sic omnis arbor bona fructus bonos facit, mala autem arbor fructus malos facit: [18]non potest arbor bona fructus malos facere, neque arbor mala fructus bonos facere. [19]Omnis arbor, quae non facit fructum bonum, exciditur et in ignem mittitur. [20]Igitur ex fructibus eorum cognoscetis eos. [21]Non omnis, qui dicit mihi: "Domine Domine", intrabit in regnum caelorum, sed qui facit voluntatem Patris mei, qui in caelis est. [22]Multi dicent mihi in illa die: "Domine, Domine, nonne in tuo nomine prophetavimus, et in tuo nomine daemonia eiecimus, et in tuo nomine virtutes multas fecimus?". [23]Et tunc confitebor illis: Numquam novi vos; discedite a me, qui operamini iniquitatem. [24]Omnis ergo, qui audit verba mea haec et facit ea, assimilabitur viro sapienti, qui aedificavit domum suam supra petram. [25]Et descendit pluvia, et venerunt flumina, et flaverunt venti et irruerunt in domum illam, et non cecidit; fundata enim erat supra petram. [26]Et omnis, qui audit verba mea haec et non facit ea, similis erit viro stulto, qui aedificavit domum suam supra arenam. [27]Et descendit pluvia, et venerunt flumina, et flaverunt venti et irruerunt in domum illam, et cecidit, et fuit ruina eius magna? [28]Et factum est cum consummasset Iesus verba haec, admirabantur turbae super doctrinam eius; [29]erat enim docens eos sicut potestatem habens et non sicut scribae eorum.   [8] [1]Cum autem descendisset de monte, secutae sunt eum turbae multae. [2]Et ecce leprosus veniens adorabat eum dicens: «Domine, si vis, potes me mundare». [3]Et extendens manum, tetigit eum dicens: «Volo, mundare!»; et confestim mundata est lepra eius. [4]Et ait illi Iesus: «Vide, nemini dixeris; sed vade, ostende te sacerdoti et offer munus, quod praecepit Moyses, in testimonium illis». [5]Cum autem introisset Capharnaum, accessit ad eum centurio rogans eum [6]et dicens: «Domine, puer meus iacet in domo paralyticus et male torquetur». [7]Et ait illi: «Ego veniam et curabo eum». [8]Et respondens centurio ait: «Domine, non sum dignus, ut intres sub tectum meum, sed tantum dic verbo, et sanabitur puer meus. [9]Nam et ego homo sum sub potestate, habens sub me milites, et dico huic: "Vade", et vadit; et alii: "Veni", et venit; et servo meo: "Fac hoc", et facit». [10]Audiens autem Iesus, miratus est et sequentibus se dixit: «Amen dico vobis: Apud nullum inveni tantam fidem in Israel! [11]Dico autem vobis quod multi ab oriente et occidente venient et recumbent cum Abraham et Isaac et Iacob in regno caelorum; [12]filii autem regni eicientur in tenebras exteriores: ibi erit fletus et stridor dentium». [13]Et dixit Iesus centurioni: «Vade; sicut credidisti fiat tibi». Et sanatus est puer in hora illa. [14]Et cum venisset Iesus in domum Petri, vidit socrum eius iacentem et febricitantem; [15]et tetigit manum eius, et dimisit eam febris; et surrexit et ministrabat ei. [16]Vespere autem facto, obtulerunt ei multos daemonia habentes; et eiciebat spiritus verbo et omnes male habentes curavit, [17]ut adimpleretur, quod dictum est per Isaiam prophetam dicentem: *«Ipse infirmitates nostras accepit / et aegrotationes portavit»*. [18]Videns autem Iesus turbas multas circum se, iussit ire trans fretum. [19]Et accedens unus scriba ait illi: «Magister, sequar te quocumque ieris». [20]Et dicit ei Iesus: «Vulpes foveas habent et volucres caeli tabernacula, Filius autem hominis non habet, ubi caput reclinet». [21]Alius autem de discipulis eius ait illi: «Domine, permitte me primum ire et sepelire patrem meum». [22]Iesus autem ait illi: «Sequere me et dimitte mortuos sepelire mortuos suos». [23]Et ascendente eo in naviculam, secuti sunt eum discipuli eius. [24]Et ecce motus magnus factus est in mari, ita ut navicula operiretur fluctibus; ipse vero dormiebat. [25]Et accesserunt et suscitaverunt eum dicentes: «Domine, salva nos, perimus!». [26]Et dicit eis: «Quid timidi estis, modicae fidei?». Tunc surgens increpavit ventis et mari, et facta est tranquillitas magna. [27]Porro homines mirati sunt dicentes: «Qualis est hic, quia et venti et mare oboediunt ei?». [28]Et cum venisset trans fretum in regionem Gadarenorum, occurrerunt ei duo habentes daemonia, de monumentis exeuntes, saevi nimis, ita ut nemo posset transire per viam illam. [29]Et ecce clamaverunt dicentes: «Quid nobis et tibi, Fili Dei? Venisti huc ante tempus torquere nos?». [30]Erat autem longe ab illis grex porcorum multorum pascens. [31]Daemones autem rogabant eum dicentes: «Si eicis nos, mitte nos in gregem porcorum». [32]Et ait illis: «Ite». Et illi exeuntes abierunt in porcos; et ecce impetu abiit totus grex per praeceps in mare, et mortui sunt in aquis. [33]Pastores autem fugerunt et venientes in civitatem nuntiaverunt omnia et de his, qui daemonia habuerant. [34]Et ecce tota civitas exiit obviam Iesu, et viso eo rogabant, ut transiret a finibus eorum.   [9] [1]Et ascendens in naviculam transfretavit et venit in civitatem suam. [2]Et ecce offerebant ei paralyticum iacentem in lecto. Et videns Iesus fidem illorum, dixit paralytico: «Confide, fili; remittuntur peccata tua». [3]Et ecce quidam de scribis dixerunt intra se: «Hic blasphemat». [4]Et cum vidisset Iesus cogitationes eorum, dixit: «Ut quid cogitatis mala in cordibus vestris? [5]Quid enim est facilius, dicere: "Dimittuntur peccata tua", aut dicere: "Surge et ambula"? [6]Ut sciatis autem quoniam Filius hominis habet potestatem in terra dimittendi peccata — tunc ait paralytico—: Surge, tolle lectum tuum et vade in domum tuam». [7]Et surrexit et abiit in domum suam. [8]Videntes autem turbae timuerunt et glorificaverunt Deum, qui dedit potestatem talem hominibus. [9]Et cum transiret inde Iesus, vidit hominem sedentem in teloneo, Matthaeum nomine, et ait illi: «Sequere me». Et surgens secutus est eum. [10]Et factum est, discumbente eo in domo, ecce multi publicani et peccatores venientes simul discumbebant cum Iesu et discipulis eius. [11]Et videntes pharisaei dicebant discipulis eius: «Quare cum publicanis et peccatoribus manducat magister vester?». [12]At ille audiens ait: «Non est opus valentibus medico sed male habentibus. [13]Euntes autem discite quid est: *"Misericordiam volo et non sacrificium"*. Non enim veni vocare iustos, sed peccatores». [14]Tunc accedunt ad eum discipuli Ioannis dicentes: «Quare nos et pharisaei ieiunamus frequenter, discipuli autem tui non ieiunant?». [15]Et ait illis Iesus: «Numquid possunt convivae nuptiarum lugere, quamdiu cum illis est sponsus? Venient autem dies, cum auferetur ab eis sponsus, et tunc ieiunabunt. [16]Nemo autem immittit commissuram panni rudis in vestimentum vetus; tollit enim supplementum eius a vestimento, et peior scissura fit. [17]Neque mittunt vinum novum in utres veteres, alioquin rumpuntur utres, et vinum effunditur, et utres pereunt; sed vinum novum in utres novos mittunt, et ambo conservantur». [18]Haec illo loquente ad eos, ecce princeps unus accessit et adorabat eum dicens: «Filia mea modo defuncta est; sed veni, impone manum tuam super eam, et vivet». [19]Et surgens Iesus sequebatur eum et discipuli eius. [20]Et ecce mulier, quae sanguinis fluxum patiebatur duodecim annis, accessit retro et tetigit fimbriam vestimenti eius. [21]Dicebat enim intra se: «Si tetigero tantum vestimentum eius, salva ero». [22]At Iesus conversus et videns eam dixit: «Confide, filia; fides tua te salvam fecit». Et salva facta est mulier ex illa hora. [23]Et cum venisset Iesus in domum principis et vidisset tibicines et turbam tumultuantem, [24]dicebat: «Recedite; non est enim mortua puella, sed dormit». Et deridebant eum. [25]At cum eiecta esset turba, intravit et tenuit manum eius, et surrexit puella. [26]Et exiit fama haec in universam terram illam. [27]Et transeunte inde Iesu, secuti sunt eum duo caeci clamantes et dicentes: «Miserere nostri, fili David!». [28]Cum autem venisset domum, accesserunt ad eum caeci, et dicit eis Iesus: «Creditis quia possum hoc facere?». Dicunt ei: «Utique, Domine». [29]Tunc tetigit oculos eorum dicens: «Secundum fidem vestram fiat vobis». ³⁰Et aperti sunt oculi illorum. Et comminatus est illis Iesus dicens: «Videte, ne quis sciat». ³¹Illi autem exeuntes diffamaverunt eum in universa terra illa. ³²Egressis autem illis, ecce obtulerunt ei hominem mutum, daemonium habentem. ³³Et eiecto daemone, locutus est mutus. Et miratae sunt turbae dicentes: «Numquam apparuit sic in Israel!». ³⁴Pharisaei autem dicebant: «In principe daemoniorum eicit daemones». ³⁵Et circumibat Iesus civitates omnes et castella, docens in synagogis eorum et praedicans evangelium regni et curans omnem languorem et omnem infirmitatem. ³⁶Videns autem turbas, misertus est eis quia erant vexati et iacentes sicut oves non habentes pastorem. ³⁷Tunc dicit discipulis suis: «Messis quidem multa, operarii autem pauci; ³⁸rogate ergo Dominum messis, ut mittat operarios in messem suam». **[10]** ¹Et convocatis Duodecim discipulis suis, dedit illis potestatem spirituum immundorum, ut eicerent eos et curarent omnem languorem et omnem infirmitatem. ²Duodecim autem apostolorum nomina sunt haec: primus Simon, qui dicitur Petrus, et Andreas frater eius, et Iacobus Zebedaei et Ioannes frater eius, ³Philippus et Bartholomaeus, Thomas et Matthaeus publicanus, Iacobus Alphaei et Thaddaeus, ⁴Simon Chananaeus et Iudas Iscariotes, qui et tradidit eum. ⁵Hos Duodecim misit Iesus praecipiens eis et dicens: «In viam gentium ne abieritis et in civitates Samaritanorum ne intraveritis; ⁶sed potius ite ad oves, quae perierunt domus Israel. ⁷Euntes autem praedicate dicentes: «Appropinquavit regnum caelorum. ⁸Infirmos curate, mortuos suscitate, leprosos mundate, daemones eicite; gratis accepistis, gratis date. ⁹Nolite possidere aurum neque argentum neque pecuniam in zonis vestris, ¹⁰non peram in via neque duas tunicas neque calceamenta neque virgam; dignus enim est operarius cibo suo. ¹¹In quamcumque civitatem aut castellum intraveritis, interrogate quis in ea dignus sit; et ibi manete donec exeatis. ¹²Intrantes autem in domum, salutate eam; ¹³et siquidem fuerit domus digna, veniat pax vestra super eam; si autem non fuerit digna, pax vestra ad vos revertatur. ¹⁴Et quicumque non receperit vos neque audierit sermones vestros, exeuntes foras de domo vel de civitate illa, excutite pulverem de pedibus vestris. ¹⁵Amen dico vobis: Tolerabilius erit terrae Sodomorum et Gomorraeorum in die iudicii quam illi civitati. ¹⁶Ecce ego mitto vos sicut oves in medio luporum; estote ergo prudentes sicut serpentes et simplices sicut columbae. ¹⁷Cavete autem ab hominibus; tradent enim vos in conciliis, et in synagogis suis flagellabunt vos; ¹⁸et ad praesides et ad reges ducemini propter me in testimonium illis et gentibus. ¹⁹Cum autem tradent vos, nolite cogitare quomodo aut quid loquamini; dabitur enim vobis in illa hora quid loquamini. ²⁰Non enim vos estis, qui loquimini, sed Spiritus Patris vestri, qui loquitur in vobis. ²¹Tradet autem frater fratrem in mortem, et pater filium; et insurgent filii in parentes et morte eos afficient. ²²Et eritis odio omnibus propter nomen meum; qui autem perseveraverit in finem, hic salvus erit. ²³Cum autem persequentur vos in civitate ista, fugite in aliam; amen enim dico vobis: Non consummabitis civitates Israel, donec veniat Filius hominis. ²⁴Non est discipulus super magistrum nec servus super dominum suum. ²⁵Sufficit discipulo, ut sit sicut magister eius, et servus sicut dominus eius. Si patrem familias Beelzebul vocaverunt, quanto magis domesticos eius! ²⁶ Ne ergo timueritis eos. Nihil enim est opertum, quod non revelabitur, et occultum, quod non scietur. ²⁷Quod dico vobis in tenebris, dicite in lumine; et quod in aure auditis, praedicate super tecta. ²⁸Et nolite timere eos, qui occidunt corpus, animam autem non possunt occidere; sed potius eum timete, qui potest et animam et corpus perdere in gehenna. ²⁹Nonne duo passeres asse veneunt? Et unus ex illis non cadet super terram sine Patre vestro. ³⁰Vestri autem et capilli capitis omnes numerati sunt. ³¹Nolite ergo timere; multis passeribus meliores estis vos. ³²Omnis ergo qui confitebitur me coram hominibus, confitebor et ego eum coram Patre meo, qui est in caelis; ³³qui autem negaverit me coram hominibus, negabo et ego eum coram Patre meo, qui est in caelis. ³⁴Nolite arbitrari quia venerim mittere pacem in terram; non veni pacem mittere sed gladium. ³⁵Veni enim separare hominem *adversus patrem suum / et filiam adversus matrem suam / et nurum adversus socrum suam: /* ³⁶et inimici hominis domestici eius. ³⁷Qui amat patrem aut matrem plus quam me, non est me dignus; et, qui amat filium aut filiam super me, non est me dignus; ³⁸et, qui non accipit crucem suam et sequitur me, non est me dignus. ³⁹Qui invenerit animam suam, perdet illam; et, qui perdiderit animam suam propter me, inveniet eam. ⁴⁰Qui recipit vos, me recipit; et, qui me recipit, recipit eum, qui me misit. ⁴¹Qui recipit prophetam in nomine prophetae, mercedem prophetae accipiet; et, qui recipit iustum in nomine iusti, mercedem iusti accipiet. ⁴²Et, quicumque potum dederit uni ex minimis istis calicem aquae frigidae tantum in nomine discipuli, amen dico vobis: Non perdet mercedem suam». **[11]** ¹Et factum est cum consummasset Iesus praecipiens Duodecim discipulis suis, transiit inde, ut doceret et praedicaret in civitatibus eorum. ²Ioannes autem, cum audisset in vinculis opera Christi, mittens per discipulos suos ³ait illi: «Tu es qui venturus es, an alium exspectamus?». ⁴Et respondens Iesus ait illis: «Euntes renuntiate Ioanni, quae auditis et videtis: ⁵*caeci vident* et claudi ambulant, leprosi mundantur et surdi audiunt et mortui resurgunt et *pauperes evangelizantur;* ⁶et beatus est, qui non fuerit scandalizatus in me». ⁷Illis autem abeuntibus, coepit Iesus dicere ad turbas de Ioanne:

«Quid existis in desertum videre? Arundinem vento agitatam? ⁸Sed quid existis videre? Hominem mollibus vestitum? Ecce, qui mollibus vestiuntur, in domibus regum sunt. ⁹Sed quid existis videre? Prophetam? Etiam, dico vobis, et plus quam prophetam. ¹⁰Hic est, de quo scriptum est: *"Ecce ego mitto angelum meum ante faciem tuam, / qui praeparabit viam tuam ante te"*. ¹¹Amen dico vobis: Non surrexit inter natos mulierum maior Ioanne Baptista; qui autem minor est in regno caelorum, maior est illo. ¹²A diebus autem Ioannis Baptistae usque nunc regnum caelorum vim patitur, et violenti rapiunt illud. ¹³Omnes enim Prophetae et Lex usque ad Ioannem prophetaverunt; ¹⁴et si vultis recipere, ipse est Elias, qui venturus est. ¹⁵Qui habet aures, audiat. ¹⁶Cui autem similem aestimabo generationem istam? Similis est pueris sedentibus in foro, qui clamantes coaequalibus ¹⁷dicunt: "Cecinimus vobis, et non saltastis; / lamentavimus, et non planxistis". ¹⁸Venit enim Ioannes neque manducans neque bibens, et dicunt: "Daemonium habet!"; ¹⁹venit Filius hominis manducans et bibens, et dicunt: "Ecce homo vorax et potator vini, publicanorum amicus et peccatorum!". Et iustificata est sapientia ab operibus suis». ²⁰Tunc coepit exprobrare civitatibus, in quibus factae sunt plurimae virtutes eius, quia non egissent paenitentiam: ²¹«Vae tibi, Chorazin! Vae tibi, Bethsaida! Quia si in Tyro et Sidone factae essent virtutes, quae factae sunt in vobis, olim in cilicio et cinere paenitentiam egissent. ²²Verumtamen dico vobis: Tyro et Sidoni remissius erit in die iudicii quam vobis. ²³Et tu, Capharnaum, numquid *usque in caelum exaltaberis? Usque in infernum descendes!* Quia si in Sodomis factae fuissent virtutes, quae factae sunt in te, mansissent usque in hunc diem. ²⁴Verumtamen dico vobis: Terrae Sodomorum remissius erit in die iudicii quam tibi». ²⁵In illo tempore respondens Iesus dixit: «Confiteor tibi, Pater, Domine caeli et terrae, quia abscondisti haec a sapientibus et prudentibus et revelasti ea parvulis. ²⁶Ita, Pater, quoniam sic fuit placitum ante te. ²⁷Omnia mihi tradita sunt a Patre meo; et nemo novit Filium nisi Pater, neque Patrem quis novit nisi Filius et cui voluerit Filius revelare. ²⁸Venite ad me, omnes, qui laboratis et onerati estis, et ego reficiam vos. ²⁹Tollite iugum meum super vos et discite a me, quia mitis sum et humilis corde, et invenietis requiem animabus vestris. ³⁰Iugum enim meum suave et onus meum leve est». [12] ¹In illo tempore abiit Iesus sabbatis per sata; discipuli autem eius esurierunt et coeperunt vellere spicas et manducare. ²Pharisaei autem videntes dixerunt ei: «Ecce discipuli tui faciunt, quod non licet facere sabbato». ³At ille dixit eis: «Non legistis quid fecerit David, quando esuriit, et qui cum eo erant? ⁴Quomodo intravit in domum Dei et panes propositionis comedit, quod non licebat ei edere neque his, qui cum eo erant, nisi solis sacerdotibus? ⁵Aut non legistis in Lege quia sabbatis sacerdotes in templo sabbatum violant et sine' crimine sunt? ⁶Dico autem vobis quia templo maior est hic. ⁷Si autem sciretis quid est: *"Misericordiam volo et non sacrificium"*, numquam condemnassetis innocentes. ⁸Dominus est enim Filius hominis sabbati». ⁹Et cum inde transisset, venit in synagogam eorum; ¹⁰et ecce homo manum habens aridam. Et interrogabant eum dicentes: «Licet sabbatis curare?», ut accusarent eum. ¹¹Ipse autem dixit illis: «Quis erit ex vobis homo, qui habeat ovem unam et, si ceciderit haec sabbatis in foveam, nonne tenebit et levabit eam? ¹²Quanto igitur melior est homo ove! Itaque licet sabbatis bene facere». ¹³Tunc ait homini: «Extende manum tuam». Et extendit, et restituta est sana sicut altera. ¹⁴Exeuntes autem pharisaei consilium faciebant adversus eum, quomodo eum perderent. ¹⁵Iesus autem sciens secessit inde. Et secuti sunt eum multi, et curavit eos omnes ¹⁶et comminatus est eis, ne manifestum eum facerent, ¹⁷ut adimpleretur, quod dictum est per Isaiam prophetam dicentem: ¹⁸«*Ecce puer meus, quem elegi, / dilectus meus, in quo bene placuit animae meae; / ponam Spiritum meum super eum, / et iudicium gentibus nuntiabit. / ¹⁹ Non contendet neque clamabit, / neque audiet aliquis in plateis vocem eius. / ²⁰Arundinem quassatam non confringet / et linum fumigans non exstinguet, / donec eiciat ad victoriam iudicium; / ²¹et in nomine eius gentes sperabunt*». ²²Tunc oblatus est ei daemonium habens, caecus et mutus, et curavit eum, ita ut mutus loqueretur et videret. ²³Et stupebant omnes turbae et dicebant: «Numquid hic est filius David?». ²⁴Pharisaei autem audientes dixerunt: «Hic non eicit daemones nisi in Beelzebul, principe daemonum». ²⁵Sciens autem cogitationes eorum dixit eis: «Omne regnum divisum contra se desolatur, et omnis civitas vel domus divisa contra se non stabit. ²⁶Et si Satanas Satanam eicit, adversus se divisus est; quomodo ergo stabit regnum eius? ²⁷Et si ego in Beelzebul eicio daemones, filii vestri in quo eiciunt? Ideo ipsi iudices erunt vestri. ²⁸Si autem in Spiritu Dei ego eicio daemones, igitur pervenit in vos regnum Dei. ²⁹Aut quomodo potest quisquam intrare in domum fortis et vasa eius diripere, nisi prius alligaverit fortem? Et tunc domum illius diripiet. ³⁰Qui non est mecum, contra me est; et, qui non congregat mecum, spargit. ³¹Ideo dico vobis: Omne peccatum et blasphemia remittetur hominibus, Spiritus autem blasphemia non remittetur. ³²Et quicumque dixerit verbum contra Filium hominis, remittetur ei; qui autem dixerit contra Spiritum Sanctum, non remittetur ei neque in hoc saeculo neque in futuro. ³³Aut facite arborem bonam et fructum eius bonum, aut facite arborem malam et fructum eius malum: siquidem ex fructu arbor agnoscitur. ³⁴Progenies viperarum, quomodo potestis bona loqui, cum sitis mali? Ex abundantia enim cordis os loquitur. ³⁵Bonus homo de bono thesauro profert bona, et malus homo de malo thesauro profert mala. ³⁶Dico autem vobis: Omne verbum otiosum, quod locuti fuerint homines, reddent rationem de eo in die iudicii: ³⁷ex verbis enim tuis iustificaberis, et ex verbis tuis condemnaberis». ³⁸Tunc responderunt ei quidam de scribis et pharisaeis dicentes: «Magister, volumus a te signum videre». ³⁹Qui respondens ait illis: «Generatio mala et adultera signum requirit, et signum non dabitur ei nisi signum Ionae prophetae. ⁴⁰Sicut enim *fuit Ionas in ventre ceti tribus diebus et tribus noctibus*, sic erit Filius hominis in corde terrae tribus diebus et tribus noctibus. ⁴¹Viri Ninevitae surgent in iudicio cum generatione ista et condemnabunt eam, quia paenitentiam egerunt in praedicatione Ionae; et ecce plus quam Iona hic! ⁴²Regina austri surget in iudicio cum generatione ista et condemnabit eam, quia venit a finibus terrae audire sapientiam Salomonis; et ecce plus quam Salomon hic! ⁴³Cum autem immundus spiritus exierit ab homine, ambulat per loca arida quaerens requiem et non invenit. ⁴⁴Tunc dicit: 'Revertar in domum meam unde exivi'; et veniens invenit vacantem, scopis mundatam et ornatam. ⁴⁵Tunc vadit et assumit secum septem alios spiritus nequiores se, et intrantes habitant ibi; et fiunt novissima hominis illius peiora prioribus. Sic erit et generationi huic pessimae». ⁴⁶Adhuc eo loquente ad turbas, ecce mater et fratres eius stabant foris quaerentes loqui ei. ⁴⁷Dixit autem ei quidam: «Ecce mater tua et fratres tui foris stant quaerentes loqui tecum». ⁴⁸At ille respondens dicenti sibi ait: «Quae est mater mea, et qui sunt fratres mei?». ⁴⁹Et extendens manum suam in discipulos suos dixit: «Ecce mater mea et fratres mei. ⁵⁰Quicumque enim fecerit voluntatem Patris mei, qui in caelis est, ipse meus frater et soror et mater est». **[13]** ¹In illo die exiens Iesus de domo sedebat secus mare; ²et congregatae sunt ad eum turbae multae, ita ut in naviculam ascendens sederet, et omnis turba stabat in litore. ³Et locutus est eis multa in parabolis dicens: «Ecce exiit, qui seminat, seminare. ⁴Et dum seminat, quaedam ceciderunt secus viam, et venerunt volucres et comederunt ea. ⁵Alia autem ceciderunt in petrosa, ubi non habebant terram multam, et continuo exorta sunt, quia non habebant altitudinem terrae; ⁶sole autem orto, aestuaverunt et, quia non habebant radicem, aruerunt. ⁷Alia autem ceciderunt in spinas, et creverunt spinae et suffocaverunt ea. ⁸Alia vero ceciderunt in terram bonam et dabant fructum: aliud centesimum, aliud sexagesimum, aliud tricesimum. ⁹Qui habet aures, audiat». ¹⁰Et accedentes discipuli dixerunt ei: «Quare in parabolis loqueris eis?». ¹¹Qui respondens ait illis: «Quia vobis datum est nosse mysteria regni caelorum, illis autem non est datum. ¹²Qui enim habet, dabitur ei et abundabit; qui autem non habet, et quod habet, auferetur ab eo. ¹³Ideo in parabolis loquor eis, quia videntes non vident et audientes non audiunt neque intellegunt; ¹⁴et adimpletur eis prophetia Isaiae dicens: *"Auditu audietis et non intellegetis / et videntes videbitis et non videbitis. /* ¹⁵ *Incrassatum est enim cor populi huius, / et auribus graviter audierunt / et oculos suos clauserunt, / ne quando oculis videant / et auribus audiant / et corde intellegant et convertantur, / et sanem eos".* ¹⁶Vestri autem beati oculi, quia vident, et aures vestrae, quia audiunt. ¹⁷Amen quippe dico vobis: Multi prophetae et iusti cupierunt videre, quae videtis, et non viderunt, et audire, quae auditis, et non audierunt! ¹⁸Vos ergo audite parabolam seminantis. ¹⁹Omnis, qui audit verbum regni et non intellegit, venit Malus et rapit, quod seminatum est in corde eius; hic est, qui secus viam seminatus est. ²⁰Qui autem supra petrosa seminatus est, hic est, qui verbum audit et continuo cum gaudio accipit illud, ²¹non habet autem in se radicem, sed est temporalis; facta autem tribulatione vel persecutione propter verbum, continuo scandalizatur. ²²Qui autem est seminatus in spinis, hic est, qui verbum audit, et sollicitudo saeculi et fallacia divitiarum suffocat verbum, et sine fructu efficitur. ²³Qui vero in terra bona seminatus est, hic est, qui audit verbum et intellegit et fructum affert et facit aliud quidem centum, aliud autem sexaginta, porro aliud triginta». ²⁴Aliam parabolam proposuit illis dicens: «Simile factum est regnum caelorum homini, qui seminavit bonum semen in agro suo. ²⁵Cum autem dormirent homines, venit inimicus eius et superseminavit zizania in medio tritici et abiit. ²⁶Cum autem crevisset herba et fructum fecisset, tunc apparuerunt et zizania. ²⁷Accedentes autem servi patris familias dixerunt ei: "Domine, nonne bonum semen seminasti in agro tuo? Unde ergo habet zizania?". ²⁸Et ait illis: "Inimicus homo hoc fecit". Servi autem dicunt ei: "Vis, imus et colligimus ea?". ²⁹Et ait: "Non; ne forte colligentes zizania eradicetis simul cum eis triticum, ³⁰sinite utraque crescere usque ad messem. Et in tempore messis dicam messoribus: Colligite primum zizania et alligate ea in fasciculos ad comburendum ea, triticum autem congregate in horreum meum"». ³¹Aliam parabolam proposuit eis dicens: «Simile est regnum caelorum grano sinapis, quod accipiens homo seminavit in agro suo. ³²Quod minimum quidem est omnibus seminibus; cum autem creverit, maius est holeribus et fit arbor, ita ut volucres caeli veniant et habitent in ramis eius». ³³Aliam parabolam locutus est eis: «Simile est regnum caelorum fermento, quod acceptum mulier abscondit in farinae satis tribus, donec fermentatum est totum». ³⁴Haec omnia locutus est Iesus in parabolis ad turbas et sine parabola nihil loquebatur eis, ³⁵ut adimpleretur, quod dictum erat per prophetam dicentem: *«Aperiam in parabolis os meum, / eructabo abscondita* a constitutione mundi». ³⁶Tunc dimissis turbis venit in domum, et accesserunt ad eum discipuli eius dicentes: «Dissere nobis parabolam zizaniorum agri». [37]Qui respondens ait: «Qui seminat bonum semen, est Filius hominis; [38]ager autem est mundus; bonum vero semen, hi sunt filii regni; zizania autem filii sunt Mali; [39]inimicus autem, qui seminavit ea, est Diabolus; messis vero consummatio saeculi est, messores autem angeli sunt. [40]Sicut ergo colliguntur zizania et igni comburuntur, sic erit in consummatione saeculi: [41]mittet Filius hominis angelos suos, et colligent de regno eius omnia scandala et eos, qui faciunt iniquitatem, [42]et mittent eos in caminum ignis; ibi erit fletus et stridor dentium. [43]Tunc iusti fulgebunt sicut sol in regno Patris eorum. Qui habet aures, audiat. [44]Simile est regnum caelorum thesauro abscondito in agro, quem qui invenit homo abscondit et prae gaudio illius vadit et vendit universa, quae habet, et emit agrum illum. [45]Iterum simile est regnum caelorum homini negotiatori quaerenti bonas margaritas. [46]Inventa autem una pretiosa margarita, abiit et vendidit omnia, quae habuit, et emit eam. [47]Iterum simile est regnum caelorum sagenae missae in mare et ex omni genere congreganti; [48]quam, cum impleta esset, educentes secus litus et sedentes collegerunt bonos in vasa, malos autem foras miserunt. [49]Sic erit in consummatione saeculi: exibunt angeli et separabunt malos de medio iustorum [50]et mittent eos in caminum ignis; ibi erit fletus et stridor dentium. [51]Intellexistis haec omnia?». Dicunt ei: «Etiam». [52]Ait autem illis: «Ideo omnis scriba doctus in regno caelorum similis est homini patri familias, qui profert de thesauro suo nova et vetera». [53]Et factum est cum consummasset Iesus parabolas istas, transiit inde. [54]Et veniens in patriam suam, docebat eos in synagoga eorum, ita ut mirarentur et dicerent: «Unde huic sapientia haec et virtutes? [55]Nonne hic est fabri filius? Nonne mater eius dicitur Maria, et fratres eius Iacobus et Ioseph et Simon et Iudas? [56]Et sorores eius nonne omnes apud nos sunt? Unde ergo huic omnia ista?». [57]Et scandalizabantur in eo. Iesus autem dixit eis: «Non est propheta sine honore nisi in patria et in domo sua». [58]Et non fecit ibi virtutes multas propter incredulitatem illorum. **[14]** [1]In illo tempore audivit Herodes tetrarcha famam Iesu [2]et ait pueris suis: «Hic est Ioannes Baptista; ipse surrexit a mortuis, et ideo virtutes operantur in eo». [3]Herodes enim tenuit Ioannem et alligavit eum et posuit in carcere propter Herodiadem uxorem Philippi fratris sui. [4]Dicebat enim illi Ioannes: «Non licet tibi habere eam». [5]Et volens illum occidere, timuit populum, quia sicut prophetam eum habebant. [6]Die autem natalis Herodis saltavit filia Herodiadis in medio et placuit Herodi, [7]unde cum iuramento pollicitus est ei dare, quodcumque postulasset. [8]At illa, praemonita a matre sua: «Da mihi, inquit, hic in disco caput Ioannis Baptistae». [9]Et contristatus rex propter iuramentum et eos, qui pariter recumbebant, iussit dari [10]misitque et decollavit Ioannem in carcere; [11]et allatum est caput eius in disco et datum est puellae, et tulit matri suae. [12]Et accedentes discipuli eius tulerunt corpus et sepelierunt illud et venientes nuntiaverunt Iesu. [13]Quod cum audisset Iesus, secessit inde in navicula in locum desertum seorsum; et cum audissent, turbae secutae sunt eum pedestres de civitatibus. [14]Et exiens vidit turbam multam et misertus est eorum et curavit languidos eorum. [15]Vespere autem facto, accesserunt ad eum discipuli dicentes: «Desertus est locus, et hora iam praeteriit; dimitte turbas, ut euntes in castella emant sibi escas». [16]Iesus autem dixit eis: «Non habent necesse ire; date illis vos manducare». [17]Illi autem dicunt ei: «Non habemus hic nisi quinque panes et duos pisces». [18]Qui ait: «Afferte illos mihi huc». [19]Et cum iussisset turbas discumbere supra fenum, acceptis quinque panibus et duobus piscibus, aspiciens in caelum benedixit et fregit et dedit discipulis panes, discipuli autem turbis. [20]Et manducaverunt omnes et saturati sunt; et tulerunt reliquias fragmentorum duodecim cophinos plenos. [21]Manducantium autem fuit numerus fere quinque milia virorum, exceptis mulieribus et parvulis. [22]Et statim iussit discipulos ascendere in naviculam et praecedere eum trans fretum, donec dimitteret turbas. [23]Et dimissis turbis, ascendit in montem solus orare. Vespere autem facto, solus erat ibi. [24]Navicula autem iam multis stadiis a terra distabat, fluctibus iactata; erat enim contrarius ventus. [25]Quarta autem vigilia noctis venit ad eos ambulans supra mare. [26]Discipuli autem, videntes eum supra mare ambulantem, turbati sunt dicentes: «Phantasma est», et prae timore clamaverunt. [27]Statimque Iesus locutus est eis dicens: «Habete fiduciam, ego sum; nolite timere!». [28]Respondens autem ei Petrus dixit: «Domine, si tu es, iube me venire ad te super aquas». [29]At ipse ait: «Veni!». Et descendens Petrus de navicula ambulavit super aquas et venit ad Iesum. [30]Videns vero ventum validum timuit et, cum coepisset mergi, clamavit dicens: «Domine, salvum me fac!». [31]Continuo autem Iesus extendens manum apprehendit eum et ait illi: «Modicae fidei, quare dubitasti?». [32]Et cum ascendissent in naviculam, cessavit ventus. [33]Qui autem in navicula erant, adoraverunt eum dicentes: «Vere Filius Dei es!». [34]Et cum transfretassent, venerunt in terram Gennesaret. [35]Et cum cognovissent eum viri loci illius, miserunt in universam regionem illam et obtulerunt ei omnes male habentes, [36]et rogabant eum, ut vel fimbriam vestimenti eius tangerent; et, quicumque tetigerunt, salvi facti sunt. **[15]** [1]Tunc accedunt ad Iesum ab Hierosolymis pharisaei et scribae dicentes: [2]«Quare discipuli tui transgrediuntur traditionem seniorum? Non enim lavant manus suas, cum panem manducant». [3]Ipse autem respondens ait illis: «Quare et vos transgredimini mandatum Dei propter traditionem vestram?

[4]Nam Deus dixit: *"Honora patrem tuum et matrem"* et: *"Qui maladixerit patri vel matri, morte moriatur"*. [5]Vos autem dicitis: "Quicumque dixerit patri vel matri: Munus est, quodcumque ex me profuerit, [6]non honorificabit patrem suum"; et irritum fecistis verbum Dei propter traditionem vestram. [7]Hypocritae! Bene prophetavit de vobis Isaias dicens: [8] *"Populus hic labiis me honorat, / cor autem eorum longe est a me; / [9] sine causa autem colunt me, / docentes doctrinas mandata hominum"*». [10]Et convocata ad se turba, dixit eis: «Audite et intellegite: [11]Non quod intrat in os, coinquinat hominem; sed quod procedit ex ore, hoc coinquinat hominem!». [12]Tunc accedentes discipuli dicunt ei: «Scis quia pharisaei, audito verbo, scandalizati sunt?». [13]At ille respondens ait: «Omnis plantatio, quam non plantavit Pater meus caelestis, eradicabitur. [14]Sinite illos: caeci sunt duces caecorum. Caecus autem si caeco ducatum praestet, ambo in foveam cadent». [15]Respondens autem Petrus dixit ei: «Edissere nobis parabolam istam». [16]At ille dixit: «Adhuc et vos sine intellectu estis? [17]Non intellegitis quia omne quod in os intrat, in ventrem vadit et in secessum emittitur? [18]Quae autem procedunt de ore, de corde exeunt, et ea coinquinant hominem. [19]De corde enim exeunt cogitationes malae, homicidia, adulteria, fornicationes, furta, falsa testimonia, blasphemiae. [20]Haec sunt, quae coinquinant hominem; non lotis autem manibus manducare non coinquinat hominem». [21]Et egressus inde Iesus, secessit in partes Tyri et Sidonis. [22]Et ecce mulier Chananaea a finibus illis egressa clamavit dicens: «Miserere mei, Domine, fili David! Filia mea male a daemonio vexatur». [23]Qui non respondit ei verbum. Et accedentes discipuli eius rogabant eum dicentes: «Dimitte eam, quia clamat post nos». [24]Ipse autem respondens ait: «Non sum missus nisi ad oves, quae perierunt domus Israel». [25]At illa venit et adoravit eum dicens: «Domine, adiuva me!». [26]Qui respondens ait: «Non est bonum sumere panem filiorum et mittere catellis». [27]At illa dixit: «Etiam, Domine, nam et catelli edunt de micis, quae cadunt de mensa dominorum suorum». [28]Tunc respondens Iesus ait illi: «O mulier, magna est fides tua! Fiat tibi, sicut vis». Et sanata est filia illius ex illa hora. [29]Et cum transisset inde, Iesus venit secus mare Galilaeae et ascendens in montem sedebat ibi. [30]Et accesserunt ad eum turbae multae habentes secum claudos, caecos, debiles, mutos et alios multos et proiecerunt eos ad pedes eius, et curavit eos, [31]ita ut turba miraretur videntes mutos loquentes, debiles sanos, et claudos ambulantes, et caecos videntes. Et magnificabant Deum Israel. [32]Iesus autem convocatis discipulis suis dixit: «Misereor turbae, quia triduo iam perseverant mecum et non habent, quod manducent; et dimittere eos ieiunos nolo, ne forte deficiant in via». [33]Et dicunt ei discipuli: «Unde nobis in deserto panes tantos, ut saturemus turbam tantam?». [34]Et ait illis Iesus: «Quot panes habetis?». At illi dixerunt: «Septem et paucos pisciculos». [35]Et praecepit turbae, ut discumberet super terram; [36]et accipiens septem panes et pisces et gratias agens fregit et dedit discipulis, discipuli autem turbis. [37]Et comederunt omnes et saturati sunt; et, quod superfuit de fragmentis, tulerunt septem sportas plenas. [38]Erant autem, qui manducaverant, quattuor milia hominum extra mulieres et parvulos. [39]Et dimissis turbis, ascendit in naviculam et venit in fines Magadan.   **[16]** [1]Et accesserunt ad eum pharisaei et sadducaei tentantes et rogaverunt eum, ut signum de caelo ostenderet eis. [2]At ille respondens ait eis: «Facto vespere dicitis: 'Serenum erit, rubicundum est enim caelum'; [3]et mane: 'Hodie tempestas, rutilat enim triste caelum'. Faciem quidem caeli diiudicare nostis, signa autem temporum non potestis. [4]Generatio mala et adultera signum quaerit, et signum non dabitur ei nisi signum Ionae». Et, relictis illis, abiit. [5]Et cum venissent discipuli trans fretum, obliti sunt panes accipere. [6]Iesus autem dixit illis: «Intuemini et cavete a fermento pharisaeorum et sadducaeorum». [7]At illi cogitabant inter se dicentes: «Panes non accepimus!». [8]Sciens autem Iesus dixit: «Quid cogitatis inter vos, modicae fidei, quia panes non habetis? [9]Nondum intellegitis neque recordamini quinque panum quinque milium hominum, et quot cophinos sumpsistis? [10]Neque septem panum quattuor milium hominum, et quot sportas sumpsistis? [11]Quomodo non intellegitis quia non de panibus dixi vobis? Sed cavete a fermento pharisaeorum et sadducaeorum». [12]Tunc intellexerunt quia non dixerit cavendum a fermento panum, sed a doctrina pharisaeorum et sadducaeorum. [13]Venit autem Iesus in partes Caesareae Philippi et interrogabat discipulos suos dicens: «Quem dicunt homines esse Filium hominis?». [14]At illi dixerunt: «Alii Ioannem Baptistam, alii autem Eliam, alii vero Ieremiam, aut unum ex prophetis». [15]Dicit illis: «Vos autem quem me esse dicitis?». [16]Respondens Simon Petrus dixit: «Tu es Christus, Filius Dei vivi». [17]Respondens autem Iesus dixit ei: «Beatus es, Simon Bariona, quia caro et sanguis non revelavit tibi, sed Pater meus, qui in caelis est. [18]Et ego dico tibi: Tu es Petrus, et super hanc petram aedificabo Ecclesiam meam; et portae inferi non praevalebunt adversum eam. [19]Tibi dabo claves regni caelorum; et quodcumque ligaveris super terram, erit ligatum in caelis, et quodcumque solveris super terram, erit solutum in caelis». [20]Tunc praecepit discipulis, ut nemini dicerent quia ipse esset Christus. [21]Exinde coepit Iesus ostendere discipulis suis quia oporteret eum ire Hierosolymam et multa pati a senioribus et principibus sacerdotum et scribis et occidi et tertia die resurgere. [22]Et assumens eum Petrus coepit increpare illum dicens: «Absit a te, Domine, non erit tibi hoc». [23]Qui

conversus dixit Petro: «Vade post me, Satana! Scandalum es mihi, quia non sapis ea, quae Dei sunt, sed ea quae hominum!». ²⁴Tunc Iesus dixit discipulis suis: «Si quis vult post me venire, abneget semetipsum et tollat crucem suam et sequatur me. ²⁵Qui enim voluerit animam suam salvam facere, perdet eam; qui autem perdiderit animam suam propter me, inveniet eam. ²⁶Quid enim prodest homini, si mundum universum lucretur, animae vero suae detrimentum patiatur? Aut quam dabit homo commutationem pro anima sua? ²⁷Filius enim hominis venturus est in gloria Patris sui cum angelis suis, et tunc reddet unicuique secundum opus eius. ²⁸Amen dico vobis: Sunt quidam de hic stantibus, qui non gustabunt mortem, donec videant Filium hominis venientem in regno suo».   [17] ¹Et post dies sex assumit Iesus Petrum et Iacobum et Ioannem fratrem eius et ducit illos in montem excelsum seorsum. ²Et transfiguratus est ante eos; et resplenduit facies eius sicut sol, vestimenta autem eius facta sunt alba sicut lux. ³Et ecce apparuit illis Moyses et Elias cum eo loquentes. ⁴Respondens autem Petrus dixit ad Iesum: «Domine, bonum est nos hic esse. Si vis, faciam hic tria tabernacula: tibi unum et Moysi unum et Eliae unum». ⁵Adhuc eo loquente, ecce nubes lucida obumbravit eos; et ecce vox de nube dicens: «Hic est Filius meus dilectus, in quo mihi bene complacui; ipsum audite». ⁶Et audientes discipuli ceciderunt in faciem suam et timuerunt valde. ⁷Et accessit Iesus et tetigit eos dixitque eis: «Surgite et nolite timere». ⁸Levantes autem oculos suos, neminem viderunt nisi solum Iesum. ⁹Et descendentibus illis de monte, praecepit eis Iesus dicens: «Nemini dixeritis visionem, donec Filius hominis a mortuis resurgat». ¹⁰Et interrogaverunt eum discipuli dicentes: «Quid ergo scribae dicunt quod Eliam oporteat primum venire?». ¹¹At ille respondens ait: «Elias quidem venturus est et restituet omnia. ¹²Dico autem vobis quia Elias iam venit, et non cognoverunt eum, sed fecerunt in eo, quaecumque voluerunt; sic et Filius hominis passurus est ab eis». ¹³Tunc intellexerunt discipuli quia de Ioanne Baptista dixisset eis. ¹⁴Et cum venissent ad turbam, accessit ad eum homo genibus provolutus ante eum ¹⁵et dicens: «Domine, miserere filii mei, quia lunaticus est et male patitur; nam saepe cadit in ignem et crebro in aquam. ¹⁶Et obtuli eum discipulis tuis, et non potuerunt curare eum». ¹⁷Respondens autem Iesus ait: «O generatio incredula et perversa, quousque ero vobiscum? Usquequo patiar vos? Afferte huc illum ad me». ¹⁸Et increpavit eum Iesus, et exiit ab eo daemonium, et curatus est puer ex illa hora. ¹⁹Tunc accesserunt discipuli ad Iesum secreto et dixerunt: «Quare nos non potuimus eicere illum?». ²⁰Ille autem dicit illis: «Propter modicam fidem vestram. Amen quippe dico vobis: Si habueritis fidem sicut granum sinapis, dicetis monti huic: "Transi hinc illuc!", et transibit, et nihil impossibile erit vobis». ⁽²¹⁾ ²²Conversantibus autem eis in Galilaea, dixit illis Iesus: «Filius hominis tradendus est in manus hominum, ²³et occident eum, et tertio die resurget». Et contristati sunt vehementer. ²⁴Et cum venissent Capharnaum, accesserunt, qui didrachma accipiebant, ad Petrum et dixerunt: «Magister vester non solvit didrachma?». ²⁵Ait: «Etiam». Et cum intrasset domum, praevenit eum Iesus dicens: «Quid tibi videtur, Simon? Reges terrae a quibus accipiunt tributum vel censum? A filiis suis an ab alienis?». ²⁶Cum autem ille dixisset: «Ab alienis», dixit illi Iesus: «Ergo liberi sunt filii. ²⁷Ut autem non scandalizemus eos, vade ad mare et mitte hamum; et eum piscem, qui primus ascenderit, tolle, et aperto ore eius invenies staterem. Illum sumens, da eis pro me et te».   [18] ¹In illa hora accesserunt discipuli ad Iesum dicentes: «Quis putas maior est in regno caelorum?». ²Et advocans parvulum, statuit eum in medio eorum ³et dixit: «Amen dico vobis: Nisi conversi fueritis et efficiamini sicut parvuli, non intrabitis in regnum caelorum. ⁴Quicumque ergo humiliaverit se sicut parvulus iste, hic est maior in regno caelorum. ⁵Et qui susceperit unum parvulum talem in nomine meo, me suscipit. ⁶Qui autem scandalizaverit unum de pusillis istis, qui in me credunt, expedit ei, ut suspendatur mola asinaria in collo eius et demergatur in profundum maris. ⁷Vae mundo ab scandalis! Necesse est enim ut veniant scandala; verumtamen vae homini, per quem scandalum venit! ⁸Si autem manus tua vel pes tuus scandalizat te, abscide eum et proice abs te: bonum tibi est ad vitam ingredi debilem vel claudum, quam duas manus vel duos pedes habentem mitti in ignem aeternum. ⁹Et si oculus tuus scandalizat te, erue eum et proice abs te: bonum tibi est unoculum in vitam intrare, quam duos oculos habentem mitti in gehennam ignis. ¹⁰Videte, ne contemnatis unum ex his pusillis; dico enim vobis quia angeli eorum in caelis semper vident faciem Patris mei, qui in caelis est. ⁽¹¹⁾ ¹²Quid vobis videtur? Si fuerint alicui centum oves, et erraverit una ex eis, nonne relinquet nonaginta novem in montibus et vadit quaerere eam, quae erravit? ¹³Et si contigerit ut inveniat eam, amen dico vobis quia gaudebit super eam magis quam super nonaginta novem, quae non erraverunt. ¹⁴Sic non est voluntas ante Patrem vestrum, qui in caelis est, ut pereat unus de pusillis istis. ¹⁵Si autem peccaverit in te frater tuus, vade, corripe eum inter te et ipsum solum. Si te audierit, lucratus es fratrem tuum; ¹⁶si autem non audierit, adhibe tecum adhuc unum vel duos, *ut in ore duorum testium vel trium stet omne verbum*; ¹⁷quod si noluerit audire eos, dic ecclesiae; si autem et ecclesiam noluerit audire, sit tibi sicut ethnicus et publicanus. ¹⁸Amen dico vobis: Quaecumque alligaveritis super terram, erunt ligata in caelo, et quaecumque solveritis super terram, erunt soluta in caelo. ¹⁹Iterum dico vobis: Si duo ex vobis consenserint super terram de omni re, quamcumque petierint, fiet illis a Patre meo, qui in caelis est. [20]Ubi enim sunt duo vel tres congregati in nomine meo, ibi sum in medio eorum». [21]Tunc accedens Petrus dixit ei: «Domine, quotiens peccabit in me frater meus, et dimittam ei? Usque septies?». [22]Dicit illi Iesus: «Non dico tibi usque septies sed usque septuagies septies. [23]Ideo assimilatum est regnum caelorum homini regi, qui voluit rationem ponere cum servis suis. [24]Et cum coepisset rationem ponere, oblatus est ei unus, qui debebat decem milia talenta. [25]Cum autem non haberet, unde redderet, iussit eum dominus venumdari et uxorem et filios et omnia, quae habebat, et reddi. [26]Procidens igitur servus ille adorabat eum dicens: "Patientiam habe in me, et omnia reddam tibi". [27]Misertus autem dominus servi illius dimisit eum et debitum dimisit ei. [28]Egressus autem servus ille invenit unum de conservis suis, qui debebat ei centum denarios, et tenens suffocabat eum dicens: "Redde, quod debes!". [29]Procidens igitur conservus eius rogabat eum dicens: "Patientiam habe in me, et reddam tibi". [30]Ille autem noluit, sed abiit et misit eum in carcerem, donec redderet debitum. [31]Videntes autem conservi eius, quae fiebant, contristati sunt valde et venerunt et narraverunt domino suo omnia, quae facta erant. [32]Tunc vocavit illum dominus suus et ait illi: "Serve nequam, omne debitum illud dimisi tibi, quoniam rogasti me; [33]non oportuit et te misereri conservi tui, sicut et ego tui misertus sum?". [34]Et iratus dominus eius tradidit eum tortoribus, quoadusque redderet universum debitum. [35]Sic et Pater meus caelestis faciet vobis, si non remiseritis unusquisque fratri suo de cordibus vestris». **[19]** [1]Et factum est cum consummasset Iesus sermones istos, migravit a Galilaea et venit in fines Iudaeae trans Iordanem. [2]Et secutae sunt eum turbae multae, et curavit eos ibi. [3]Et accesserunt ad eum pharisaei tentantes eum et dicentes: «Licet homini dimittere uxorem suam quacumque ex causa?». [4]Qui respondens ait: «Non legistis quia, qui creavit ab initio, *masculum et feminam fecit eos* [5]et dixit: *"Propter hoc dimittet homo patrem et matrem et adhaerebit uxori suae, et erunt duo in carne una?"*. [6]Itaque iam non sunt duo sed una caro. Quod ergo Deus coniunxit, homo non separet». [7]Dicunt illi: «Quid ergo Moyses mandavit *dari libellum repudii et dimittere*?». [8]Ait illis: «Moyses ad duritiam cordis vestri permisit vobis dimittere uxores vestras; ab initio autem non sic fuit. [9]Dico autem vobis quia quicumque dimiserit uxorem suam, nisi ob fornicationem, et aliam duxerit, moechatur». [10]Dicunt ei discipuli eius: «Si ita est causa hominis cum uxore, non expedit nubere». [11]Qui dixit eis: «Non omnes capiunt verbum istud, sed quibus datum est. [12]Sunt enim eunuchi, qui de matris utero sic nati sunt; et sunt eunuchi, qui facti sunt ab hominibus; et sunt eunuchi, qui seipsos castraverunt propter regnum caelorum. Qui potest capere, capiat». [13]Tunc oblati sunt ei parvuli, ut manus eis imponeret et oraret; discipuli autem increpabant eis. [14]Iesus vero ait: «Sinite parvulos et nolite eos prohibere ad me venire; talium est enim regnum caelorum». [15]Et cum imposuisset eis manus, abiit inde. [16]Et ecce unus accedens ait illi: «Magister, quid boni faciam, ut habeam vitam aeternam?». Qui dixit ei: [17]«Quid me interrogas de bono? Unus est bonus. Si autem vis ad vitam ingredi, serva mandata». [18]Dicit illi: «Quae?». Iesus autem dixit: «*Non homicidium facies, non adulterabis, non facies furtum, non falsum testimonium dices,* [19] *honora patrem et matrem et diliges proximum tuum sicut teipsum*». [20]Dicit illi adulescens: «Omnia haec custodivi. Quid adhuc mihi deest?». [21]Ait illi Iesus: «Si vis perfectus esse, vade, vende, quae habes, et da pauperibus, et habebis thesaurum in caelo; et veni, sequere me». [22]Cum audisset autem adulescens verbum, abiit tristis; erat enim habens multas possessiones. [23]Iesus autem dixit discipulis suis: «Amen dico vobis: Dives difficile intrabit in regnum caelorum. [24]Et iterum dico vobis: Facilius est camelum per foramen acus transire, quam divitem intrare in regnum Dei». [25]Auditis autem his, discipuli mirabantur valde dicentes: «Quis ergo poterit salvus esse?». [26]Aspiciens autem Iesus dixit illis: «Apud homines hoc impossibile est, apud Deum autem omnia possibilia sunt». [27]Tunc respondens Petrus dixit ei: «Ecce nos reliquimus omnia et secuti sumus te. Quid ergo erit nobis?». [28]Iesus autem dixit illis: «Amen dico vobis quod vos, qui secuti estis me, in regeneratione, cum sederit Filius hominis in throno gloriae suae, sedebitis et vos super thronos duodecim, iudicantes duodecim tribus Israel. [29]Et omnis, qui reliquit domos vel fratres aut sorores aut patrem aut matrem aut filios aut agros propter nomen meum, centuplum accipiet et vitam aeternam possidebit. [30]Multi autem erunt primi novissimi et novissimi primi. **[20]** [1]Simile est enim regnum caelorum homini patri familias, qui exiit primo mane conducere operarios in vineam suam; [2]conventione autem facta cum operariis ex denario diurno, misit eos in vineam suam. [3]Et egressus circa horam tertiam vidit alios stantes in foro otiosos [4]et illis dixit: "Ite et vos in vineam; et, quod iustum fuerit, dabo vobis". [5]Illi autem abierunt. Iterum autem exiit circa sextam et nonam horam et fecit similiter. [6]Circa undecimam vero exiit et invenit alios stantes et dicit illis: "Quid hic statis tota die otiosi?". [7]Dicunt ei: "Quia nemo nos conduxit". Dicit illis: "Ite et vos in vineam". [8]Cum sero autem factum esset, dicit dominus vineae procuratori suo: "Voca operarios et redde illis mercedem incipiens a novissimis usque ad primos". [9]Et cum venissent, qui circa undecimam horam venerant, acceperunt singuli denarium. [10]Venientes autem primi arbitrati sunt quod plus essent accepturi; acceperunt autem et ipsi singuli denarium. [11]Accipientes autem murmurabant adversus patrem familias [12]dicentes: "Hi novissimi una hora fecerunt, et pares illos nobis fecisti, qui portavimus pondus diei et aestum!". [13]At ille respondens uni eorum dixit: "Amice, non facio tibi iniuriam; nonne ex denario convenisti mecum? [14]Tolle, quod tuum est, et vade; volo autem et huic novissimo dare sicut et tibi. [15]Aut non licet mihi, quod volo, facere de meis? An oculus tuus nequam est, quia ego bonus sum?". [16]Sic erunt novissimi primi, et primi novissimi». [17]Et ascendens Iesus Hierosolymam assumpsit Duodecim discipulos secreto et ait illis in via: [18]«Ecce ascendimus Hierosolymam, et Filius hominis tradetur principibus sacerdotum et scribis, et condemnabunt eum morte [19]et tradent eum gentibus ad illudendum et flagellandum et crucifigendum, et tertia die resurget». [20]Tunc accessit ad eum mater filiorum Zebedaei cum filiis suis, adorans et petens aliquid ab eo. [21]Qui dixit ei: «Quid vis?». Ait illi: «Dic ut sedeant hi duo filii mei unus ad dexteram tuam et unus ad sinistram in regno tuo». [22]Respondens autem Iesus dixit: «Nescitis quid petatis. Potestis bibere calicem, quem ego bibiturus sum?». Dicunt ei: «Possumus». [23]Ait illis: «Calicem quidem meum bibetis, sedere autem ad dexteram meam et sinistram non est meum dare illud, sed quibus paratum est a Patre meo». [24]Et audientes decem indignati sunt de duobus fratribus. [25]Iesus autem vocavit eos ad se et ait: «Scitis quia principes gentium dominantur eorum et, qui magni sunt, potestatem exercent in eos. [26]Non ita erit inter vos, sed quicumque voluerit inter vos magnus fieri, erit vester minister; [27]et, quicumque voluerit inter vos primus esse, erit vester servus; [28]sicut Filius hominis non venit ministrari sed ministrare et dare animam suam redemptionem pro multis». [29]Et egredientibus illis ab Iericho, secuta est eum turba multa. [30]Et ecce duo caeci sedentes secus viam audierunt quia Iesus transiret et clamaverunt dicentes: «Domine, miserere nostri, fili David!». [31]Turba autem increpabat eos, ut tacerent; at illi magis clamabant dicentes: «Domine, miserere nostri, fili David!». [32]Et stetit Iesus et vocavit eos et ait: «Quid vultis, ut faciam vobis?». [33]Dicunt illi: «Domine, ut aperiantur oculi nostri». [34]Misertus autem Iesus, tetigit oculos eorum; et confestim viderunt et secuti sunt eum.   [21] [1]Et cum appropinquassent Hierosolymis et venissent Bethfage, ad montem Oliveti, tunc Iesus misit duos discipulos [2]dicens eis: «Ite in castellum, quod contra vos est, et statim invenietis asinam alligatam et pullum cum ea; solvite et adducite mihi. [3]Et si quis vobis aliquid dixerit, dicite: "Dominus eos necessarios habet", et confestim dimittet eos». [4]Hoc autem factum est, ut impleretur, quod dictum est per prophetam dicentem: [5]«*Dicite filiae Sion*: / *Ecce Rex tuus venit tibi*, / *mansuetus et sedens super asinam* / *et super pullum filium subiugalis*». [6]Euntes autem discipuli fecerunt, sicut praecepit illis Iesus, [7]et adduxerunt asinam et pullum, et imposuerunt super eis vestimenta sua, et sedit super ea. [8]Plurima autem turba straverunt vestimenta sua in via; alii autem caedebant ramos de arboribus et sternebant in via. [9]Turbae autem, quae praecedebant eum et quae sequebantur, clamabant dicentes: «*Hosanna* filio David! *Benedictus, qui venit in nomine Domini! Hosanna* in altissimis!». [10]Et cum intrasset Hierosolymam, commota est universa civitas dicens: «Quis est hic?». [11]Turbae autem dicebant: «Hic est Iesus propheta a Nazareth Galilaeae». [12]Et intravit Iesus in templum et eiciebat omnes vendentes et ementes in templo, et mensas nummulariorum evertit et cathedras vendentium columbas, [13]et dicit eis: «Scriptum est: "*Domus mea domus orationis vocabitur*". Vos autem facitis eam *speluncam latronum*». [14]Et accesserunt ad eum caeci et claudi in templo, et sanavit eos. [15]Videntes autem principes sacerdotum et scribae mirabilia, quae fecit, et pueros clamantes in templo et dicentes: «Hosanna filio David», indignati sunt [16]et dixerunt ei: «Audis quid isti dicant?». Iesus autem dicit eis: «Utique; numquam legistis: "*Ex ore infantium et lactantium perfecisti laudem*"?». [17]Et relictis illis, abiit foras extra civitatem in Bethaniam ibique mansit. [18]Mane autem revertens in civitatem, esuriit. [19]Et videns fici arborem unam secus viam, venit ad eam; et nihil invenit in ea nisi folia tantum et ait illi: «Numquam ex te fructus nascatur in sempiternum». Et arefacta est continuo ficulnea. [20]Et videntes discipuli mirati sunt dicentes: «Quomodo continuo aruit ficulnea?». [21]Respondens autem Iesus ait eis: «Amen dico vobis: Si habueritis fidem et non haesitaveritis, non solum de ficulnea facietis, sed et si monti huic dixeritis: "Tolle et iacta te in mare", fiet. [22]Et omnia, quaecumque petieritis in oratione credentes, accipietis». [23]Et cum venisset in templum, accesserunt ad eum docentem principes sacerdotum et seniores populi dicentes: «In qua potestate haec facis? Et quis tibi dedit hanc potestatem?». [24]Respondens autem Iesus dixit illis: «Interrogabo vos et ego unum sermonem, quem si dixeritis mihi, et ego vobis dicam, in qua potestate haec facio: [25]Baptismum Ioannis unde erat? A caelo an ex hominibus?». At illi cogitabant inter se dicentes: «Si dixerimus: "E caelo", dicet nobis: "Quare ergo non credidistis illi?". [26]si autem dixerimus: "Ex hominibus", timemus turbam; omnes enim habent Ioannem sicut prophetam». [27]Et respondentes Iesu dixerunt: «Nescimus». Ait illis et ipse: «Nec ego dico vobis in qua potestate haec facio». [28]«Quid autem vobis videtur? Homo quidam habebat duos filios. Et accedens ad primum dixit: "Fili, vade hodie, operare in vinea". [29]Ille autem respondens ait: "Nolo"; postea autem paenitentia motus abiit. [30]Accedens autem ad alterum dixit similiter. At ille respondens ait: "Eo, domine"; et non ivit. ³¹Quis ex duobus fecit voluntatem patris?». Dicunt: «Primus». Dicit illis Iesus: «Amen dico vobis: Publicani et meretrices praecedunt vos in regnum Dei. ³²Venit enim ad vos Ioannes in via iustitiae, et non credidistis ei; publicani autem et meretrices crediderunt ei. Vos autem videntes nec paenitentiam habuistis postea, ut crederetis ei. ³³Aliam parabolam audite. Homo erat pater familias, qui *plantavit vineam et saepem circumdedit ei et fodit in ea torcular et aedificavit turrim* et locavit eam agricolis et peregre profectus est. ³⁴Cum autem tempus fructuum appropinquasset, misit servos suos ad agricolas, ut acciperent fructus eius. ³⁵Et agricolae, apprehensis servis eius, alium ceciderunt, alium occiderunt, alium vero lapidaverunt. ³⁶Iterum misit alios servos plures prioribus, et fecerunt illis similiter. ³⁷Novissime autem misit ad eos filium suum dicens: "Verebuntur filium meum". ³⁸Agricolae autem videntes filium dixerunt intra se: "Hic est heres. Venite, occidamus eum et habebimus hereditatem eius". ³⁹Et apprehensum eum eiecerunt extra vineam et occiderunt. ⁴⁰Cum ergo venerit dominus vineae, quid faciet agricolis illis?». ⁴¹Aiunt illi: «Malos male perdet et vineam locabit aliis agricolis, qui reddant ei fructum temporibus suis». ⁴²Dicit illis Iesus: «Numquam legistis in Scripturis: / "*Lapidem, quem reprobaverunt aedificantes, / hic factus est in caput anguli; / a Domino factum est istud / et est mirabile in oculis nostris*"? ⁴³Ideo dico vobis quia auferetur a vobis regnum Dei et dabitur genti facienti fructus eius. ⁴⁴Et, qui ceciderit super lapidem istum confringetur; super quem vero ceciderit, conteret eum». ⁴⁵Et cum audissent principes sacerdotum et pharisaei parabolas eius, cognoverunt quod de ipsis diceret; ⁴⁶et quaerentes eum tenere, timuerunt turbas, quoniam sicut prophetam eum habebant.　　**[22]** ¹Et respondens Iesus dixit iterum in parabolis eis dicens: ²«Simile factum est regnum caelorum homini regi, qui fecit nuptias filio suo. ³Et misit servos suos vocare invitatos ad nuptias, et nolebant venire. ⁴Iterum misit alios servos dicens: "Dicite invitatis: Ecce prandium meum paravi, tauri mei et altilia occisa, et omnia parata; venite ad nuptias". ⁵Illi autem neglexerunt et abierunt, alius in villam suam, alius vero ad negotiationem suam; ⁶reliqui vero tenuerunt servos eius et contumelia affectos occiderunt. ⁷Rex autem iratus est et, missis exercitibus suis, perdidit homicidas illos et civitatem illorum succendit. ⁸Tunc ait servis suis: "Nuptiae quidem paratae sunt, sed qui invitati erant, non fuerunt digni; ⁹ite ergo ad exitus viarum et quoscumque inveneritis, vocate ad nuptias". ¹⁰Et egressi servi illi in vias, congregaverunt omnes, quos invenerunt, malos et bonos; et impletae sunt nuptiae discumbentium. ¹¹Intravit autem rex, ut videret discumbentes, et vidit ibi hominem non vestitum veste nuptiali ¹²et ait illi: "Amice, quomodo huc intrasti, non habens vestem nuptialem?". At ille obmutuit. ¹³Tunc dixit rex ministris: "Ligate pedes eius et manus et mittite eum in tenebras exteriores: ibi erit fletus et stridor dentium". ¹⁴Multi enim sunt vocati, pauci vero electi». ¹⁵Tunc abeuntes pharisaei consilium inierunt, ut caperent eum in sermone. ¹⁶Et mittunt ei discipulos suos cum herodianis dicentes: «Magister, scimus quia verax es et viam Dei in veritate doces et non est tibi cura de aliquo; non enim respicis personam hominum. ¹⁷Dic ergo nobis quid tibi videatur: Licet censum dare Caesari an non?». ¹⁸Cognita autem Iesus nequitia eorum, ait: «Quid me tentatis, hypocritae? ¹⁹Ostendite mihi nomisma census». At illi obtulerunt ei denarium. ²⁰Et ait illis: «Cuius est imago haec et suprascriptio?». ²¹Dicunt ei: «Caesaris». Tunc ait illis: «Reddite ergo, quae sunt Caesaris, Caesari et, quae sunt Dei, Deo». ²²Et audientes mirati sunt et relicto eo abierunt. ²³In illo die accesserunt ad eum sadducaei, qui dicunt non esse resurrectionem, et interrogaverunt eum ²⁴dicentes: «Magister, Moyses dixit, *si quis mortuus fuerit non habens filios, ut ducat frater eius uxorem illius et suscitet semen fratri suo*. ²⁵Erant autem apud nos septem fratres: et primus, uxore ducta, defunctus est et non habens semen reliquit uxorem suam fratri suo; ²⁶similiter secundus et tertius usque ad septimum. ²⁷Novissime autem omnium mulier defuncta est. ²⁸In resurrectione ergo cuius erit de septem uxor? Omnes enim habuerunt eam». ²⁹Respondens autem Iesus ait illis: «Erratis nescientes Scripturas neque virtutem Dei; ³⁰in resurrectione enim neque nubent neque nubentur, sed sunt sicut angeli in caelo. ³¹De resurrectione autem mortuorum non legistis, quod dictum est vobis a Deo dicente: ³²"*Ego sum Deus Abraham et Deus Isaac et Deus Iacob*"? Non est Deus mortuorum sed viventium». ³³Et audientes turbae mirabantur in doctrina eius. ³⁴Pharisaei autem audientes quod silentium imposuisset sadducaeis, convenerunt in unum. ³⁵Et interrogavit unus ex eis legis doctor tentans eum: ³⁶«Magister, quod est mandatum magnum in Lege?». ³⁷Ait autem illi: «*Diliges Dominum Deum tuum in toto corde tuo et in tota anima tua* et in tota mente tua: ³⁸hoc est magnum et primum mandatum. ³⁹Secundum autem simile est huic: *Diliges proximum tuum sicut teipsum*. ⁴⁰In his duobus mandatis universa Lex pendet et Prophetae». ⁴¹Congregatis autem pharisaeis, interrogavit eos Iesus ⁴²dicens: «Quid vobis videtur de Christo? Cuius filius est?». Dicunt ei: «David». ⁴³Ait illis: «Quomodo ergo David in Spiritu vocat eum Dominum dicens: ⁴⁴"*Dixit Dominus Domino meo: Sede a dextris meis, / donec ponam inimicos tuos sub pedibus tuis*"? ⁴⁵Si ergo David vocat eum Dominum, quomodo filius eius est?». ⁴⁶Et nemo poterat respondere ei verbum, neque ausus fuit quisquam ex illa die eum amplius interrogare.　　**[23]** ¹Tunc Iesus locutus est ad turbas et ad discipulos suos [2]dicens: «Super cathedram Moysis sederunt scribae et pharisaei. [3]Omnia ergo, quaecumque dixerint vobis, facite et servate; secundum opera vero eorum nolite facere: dicunt enim et non faciunt. [4]Alligant autem onera gravia et importabilia et imponunt in umeros hominum, ipsi autem digito suo nolunt ea movere. [5]Omnia vero opera sua faciunt, ut videantur ab hominibus: dilatant enim phylacteria sua et magnificant fimbrias, [6]amant autem primum recubitum in cenis et primas cathedras in synagogis [7]et salutationes in foro et vocari ab hominibus Rabbi. [8]Vos autem nolite vocari Rabbi; unus enim est Magister vester, omnes autem vos fratres estis. [9]Et Patrem nolite vocare vobis super terram, unus enim est Pater vester, caelestis. [10]Nec vocemini Magistri, quia Magister vester unus est, Christus. [11]Qui maior est vestrum, erit minister vester. [12]Qui autem se exaltaverit, humiliabitur; et, qui se humiliaverit, exaltabitur. [13]Vae autem vobis, scribae et pharisaei hypocritae, quia clauditis regnum caelorum ante homines! Vos enim non intratis nec introeuntes sinitis intrare. (14) [15]Vae vobis, scribae et pharisaei hypocritae, quia circuitis mare et aridam, ut faciatis unum proselytum, et cum fuerit factus, facitis eum filium gehennae duplo quam vos! [16]Vae vobis, duces caeci, qui dicitis: "Quicumque iuraverit per templum, nihil est; quicumque autem iuraverit in auro templi, debet". [17]Stulti et caeci! Quid enim maius est: aurum an templum, quod sanctificat aurum? [18]Et: "Quicumque iuraverit in altari, nihil est; quicumque autem iuraverit in dono, quod est super illud, debet". [19]Caeci! Quid enim maius est: donum an altare, quod sanctificat donum? [20]Qui ergo iuraverit in altari, iurat in eo et in omnibus, quae super illud sunt; [21]et, qui iuraverit in templo, iurat in illo et in eo, qui inhabitat in ipso; [22]et, qui iuraverit in caelo, iurat in throno Dei et in eo, qui sedet super eum. [23]Vae vobis, scribae et pharisaei hypocritae, quia decimatis mentam et anethum et cyminum et reliquistis, quae graviora sunt legis: iudicium et misericordiam et fidem! Haec oportuit facere et illa non omittere. [24]Duces caeci, excolantes culicem, camelum autem glutientes. [25]Vae vobis, scribae et pharisaei hypocritae, quia mundatis, quod de foris est calicis et paropsidis, intus autem pleni sunt rapina et immunditia! [26]Pharisaee caece, munda prius, quod intus est calicis, ut fiat et id, quod de foris eius est, mundum. [27]Vae vobis, scribae et pharisaei hypocritae, quia similes estis sepulcris dealbatis, quae a foris quidem parent speciosa, intus vero plena sunt ossibus mortuorum et omni spurcitia! [28]Sic et vos a foris quidem paretis hominibus iusti, intus autem pleni estis hypocrisi et iniquitate. [29]Vae vobis, scribae et pharisaei hypocritae, qui aedificatis sepulcra prophetarum et ornatis monumenta iustorum [30]et dicitis: "Si fuissemus in diebus patrum nostrorum, non essemus socii eorum in sanguine prophetarum"! [31]Itaque testimonio estis vobismetipsis quia filii estis eorum, qui prophetas occiderunt. [32]Et vos implete mensuram patrum vestrorum. [33]Serpentes, genimina viperarum, quomodo fugietis a iudicio gehennae? [34]Ideo ecce ego mitto ad vos prophetas et sapientes et scribas; ex illis occidetis et crucifigetis et ex eis flagellabitis in synagogis vestris et persequemini de civitate in civitatem, [35]ut veniat super vos omnis sanguis iustus, qui effusus est super terram a sanguine Abel iusti usque ad sanguinem Zachariae filii Barachiae, quem occidistis inter templum et altare. [36]Amen dico vobis: Venient haec omnia super generationem istam. [37]Ierusalem, Ierusalem, quae occidis prophetas et lapidas eos, qui ad te missi sunt, quotiens volui congregare filios tuos, quemadmodum gallina congregat pullos suos sub alas, et noluistis! *[38]Ecce relinquitur vobis domus vestra deserta!* [39]Dico enim vobis: Non me videbitis amodo, donec dicatis: *"Benedictus, qui venit in nomine Domini!"*». **[24]** [1]Et egressus Iesus de templo ibat, et accesserunt discipuli eius, ut ostenderent ei aedificationes templi; [2]ipse autem respondens dixit eis: «Non videtis haec omnia? Amen dico vobis: Non relinquetur hic lapis super lapidem, qui non destruetur». [3]Sedente autem eo super montem Oliveti, accesserunt ad eum discipuli secreto dicentes: «Dic nobis: Quando haec erunt, et quod signum adventus tui et consummationis saeculi?». [4]Et respondens Iesus dixit eis: «Videte, ne quis vos seducat. [5]Multi enim venient in nomine meo dicentes: "Ego sum Christus", et multos seducent. [6]Audituri enim estis proelia et opiniones proeliorum. Videte, ne turbemini; oportet enim fieri, sed nondum est finis. [7]Consurget enim gens in gentem, et regnum in regnum, et erunt fames et terrae motus per loca; [8]haec autem omnia initia sunt dolorum. [9]Tunc tradent vos in tribulationem et occident vos, et eritis odio omnibus gentibus propter nomen meum. [10]Et tunc scandalizabuntur multi et invicem tradent et odio habebunt invicem; [11]et multi pseudoprophetae surgent et seducent multos. [12]Et, quoniam abundavit iniquitas, refrigescet caritas multorum; [13]qui autem permanserit usque in finem, hic salvus erit. [14]Et praedicabitur hoc evangelium regni in universo orbe in testimonium omnibus gentibus; et tunc veniet consummatio. [15]Cum ergo videritis *abominationem desolationis*, quae dicta est a Daniele propheta, stantem *in loco sancto*, qui legit, intellegat: [16]tunc qui in Iudaea sunt, fugiant ad montes; [17]qui in tecto, non descendat tollere aliquid de domo sua; [18]et, qui in agro, non revertatur tollere pallium suum. [19]Vae autem praegnantibus et nutrientibus in illis diebus! [20]Orate autem, ut non fiat fuga vestra hieme vel sabbato: [21]erit enim tunc *tribulatio* magna, *qualis non fuit ab initio mundi usque modo* neque fiet. [22]Et nisi breviati fuissent dies illi, non fieret salva omnis caro; sed propter electos breviabuntur dies illi. ²³Tunc si quis vobis dixerit: "Ecce hic Christus" aut: "Hic", nolite credere. ²⁴Surgent enim pseudochristi et pseudoprophetae et dabunt signa magna et prodigia, ita ut in errorem inducantur, si fieri potest, etiam electi. ²⁵Ecce praedixi vobis. ²⁶Si ergo dixerint vobis: "Ecce in deserto est", nolite exire; "Ecce in penetralibus", nolite credere: ²⁷sicut enim fulgur exit ab oriente et paret usque in occidentem, ita erit adventus Filii hominis. ²⁸Ubicumque fuerit corpus, illuc congregabuntur aquilae. ²⁹Statim autem post tribulationem dierum illorum, *sol obscurabitur, et luna non dabit lumen suum, et stellae cadent* de caelo, *et virtutes caelorum* commovebuntur. ³⁰Et tunc parebit signum Filii hominis in caelo, et tunc *plangent omnes tribus terrae* et videbunt *Filium hominis venientem in nubibus caeli* cum virtute et gloria multa; ³¹et mittet angelos suos cum tuba magna, et congregabunt electos eius a quattuor ventis, a summis caelorum usque ad terminos eorum. ³²Ab arbore autem fici discite parabolam: cum iam ramus eius tener fuerit, et folia nata, scitis quia prope est aestas. ³³Ita et vos, cum videritis haec omnia, scitote quia prope est in ianuis. ³⁴Amen dico vobis: Non praeteribit haec generatio, donec omnia haec fiant. ³⁵Caelum et terra transibunt, verba vero mea non praeteribunt. ³⁶De die autem illa et hora nemo scit, neque angeli caelorum neque Filius, nisi Pater solus. ³⁷Sicut enim dies Noe, ita erit adventus Filii hominis. ³⁸Sicut enim erant in diebus ante diluvium comedentes et bibentes, nubentes et nuptum tradentes, usque ad eum diem, quo introivit in arcam Noe, ³⁹et non cognoverunt, donec venit diluvium et tulit omnes, ita erit et adventus Filii hominis. ⁴⁰Tunc duo erunt in agro: unus assumitur, et unus relinquitur; ⁴¹duae molentes in mola: una assumitur, et una relinquitur. ⁴²Vigilate ergo, quia nescitis qua die Dominus vester venturus sit. ⁴³Illud autem scitote quoniam si sciret pater familias qua hora fur venturus esset, vigilaret utique et non sineret perfodi domum suam. ⁴⁴Ideo et vos estote parati, quia, qua nescitis hora, Filius hominis venturus est. ⁴⁵Quis putas est fidelis servus et prudens, quem constituit dominus supra familiam suam, ut det illis cibum in tempore? ⁴⁶Beatus ille servus, quem cum venerit dominus eius invenerit sic facientem. ⁴⁷Amen dico vobis quoniam super omnia bona sua constituet eum. ⁴⁸Si autem dixerit malus servus ille in corde suo: "Moram facit dominus meus venire", ⁴⁹et coeperit percutere conservos suos, manducet autem et bibat cum ebriis, ⁵⁰veniet dominus servi illius in die, qua non sperat, et in hora, qua ignorat, ⁵¹et dividet eum partemque eius ponet cum hypocritis; illic erit fletus et stridor dentium. **[25]** ¹Tunc simile erit regnum caelorum decem virginibus, quae accipientes lampades suas exierunt obviam sponso. ²Quinque autem ex eis erant fatuae et quinque prudentes. ³Fatuae enim, acceptis lampadibus suis, non sumpserunt oleum secum; ⁴prudentes vero acceperunt oleum in vasis cum lampadibus suis. ⁵Moram autem faciente sponso, dormitaverunt omnes et dormierunt. ⁶Media autem nocte clamor factus est: "Ecce sponsus! Exite obviam ei". ⁷Tunc surrexerunt omnes virgines illae et ornaverunt lampades suas. ⁸Fatuae autem sapientibus dixerunt: "Date nobis de oleo vestro, quia lampades nostrae exstinguuntur". ⁹Responderunt prudentes dicentes: "Ne forte non sufficiat nobis et vobis, ite potius ad vendentes et emite vobis". ¹⁰Dum autem irent emere, venit sponsus, et quae paratae erant, intraverunt cum eo ad nuptias; et clausa est ianua. ¹¹Novissime autem veniunt et reliquae virgines dicentes: "Domine, Domine, aperi nobis". ¹²At ille respondens ait: "Amen dico vobis: Nescio vos". ¹³Vigilate itaque, quia nescitis diem neque horam. ¹⁴Sicut enim homo peregre proficiscens vocavit servos suos et tradidit illis bona sua. ¹⁵Et uni dedit quinque talenta, alii autem duo, alii vero unum, unicuique secundum propriam virtutem, et profectus est. Statim ¹⁶abiit, qui quinque talenta acceperat, et operatus est in eis et lucratus est alia quinque; ¹⁷similiter qui duo acceperat, lucratus est alia duo. ¹⁸Qui autem unum acceperat, abiens fodit in terra et abscondit pecuniam domini sui. ¹⁹Post multum vero temporis venit dominus servorum illorum et ponit rationem cum eis. ²⁰Et accedens, qui quinque talenta acceperat, obtulit alia quinque talenta dicens: "Domine, quinque talenta tradidisti mihi; ecce alia quinque superlucratus sum". ²¹Ait illi dominus eius: "Euge, serve bone et fidelis. Super pauca fuisti fidelis; supra multa te constituam: intra in gaudium domini tui". ²²Accessit autem et qui duo talenta acceperat, et ait: "Domine, duo talenta tradidisti mihi; ecce alia duo lucratus sum". ²³Ait illi dominus eius: "Euge, serve bone et fidelis. Super pauca fuisti fidelis; supra multa te constituam: intra in gaudium domini tui". ²⁴Accedens autem et qui unum talentum acceperat, ait: "Domine, novi te quia homo durus es: metis, ubi non seminasti, et congregas, ubi non sparsisti; ²⁵et timens abii et abscondi talentum tuum in terra. Ecce habes, quod tuum est". ²⁶Respondens autem dominus eius dixit ei: "Serve male et piger! Sciebas quia meto, ubi non seminavi, et congrego, ubi non sparsi? ²⁷Oportuit ergo te mittere pecuniam meam nummulariis, et veniens ego recepissem, quod meum est cum usura. ²⁸Tollite itaque ab eo talentum et date ei, qui habet decem talenta: ²⁹omni enim habenti dabitur, et abundabit; ei autem, qui non habet, et quod habet, auferetur ab eo. ³⁰Et inutilem servum eicite in tenebras exteriores: illic erit fletus et stridor dentium". ³¹Cum autem venerit Filius hominis in gloria sua, et omnes angeli cum eo, tunc sedebit super thronum gloriae suae. ³²Et congregabuntur ante eum omnes gentes; et separabit eos ab invicem, sicut pastor segregat oves ab haedis, ³³et statuet oves quidem a dextris suis, haedos autem a sinistris. ³⁴Tunc dicet Rex his, qui a dextris eius erunt: "Venite, benedicti Patris mei; possidete paratum vobis regnum a constitutione mundi. [35]Esurivi enim, et dedistis mihi manducare; sitivi, et dedistis mihi bibere; hospes eram, et collegistis me; [36]nudus, et operuistis me; infirmus, et visitastis me; in carcere eram, et venistis ad me". [37]Tunc respondebunt ei iusti dicentes: "Domine, quando te vidimus esurientem et pavimus, aut sitientem et dedimus tibi potum? [38]Quando autem te vidimus hospitem et collegimus, aut nudum et cooperuimus? [39]Quando autem te vidimus infirmum aut in carcere et venimus ad te?". [40]Et respondens Rex dicet illis: "Amen dico vobis: Quamdiu fecistis uni de his fratribus meis minimis, mihi fecistis". [41]Tunc dicet et his, qui a sinistris erunt: "Discedite a me, maledicti, in ignem aeternum, qui praeparatus est Diabolo et angelis eius. [42]Esurivi enim, et non dedistis mihi manducare; sitivi, et non dedistis mihi potum; [43]hospes eram, et non collegistis me; nudus, et non operuistis me; infirmus et in carcere, et non visitastis me". [44]Tunc respondebunt et ipsi dicentes: "Domine, quando te vidimus esurientem aut sitientem aut hospitem aut nudum aut infirmum vel in carcere et non ministravimus tibi?". [45]Tunc respondebit illis dicens: "Amen dico vobis: Quamdiu non fecistis uni de minimis his, nec mihi fecistis". [46]Et ibunt hi in supplicium aeternum, iusti autem in vitam aeternam». **[26]** [1]Et factum est cum consummasset Iesus sermones hos omnes, dixit discipulis suis: [2]«Scitis quia post biduum Pascha fiet, et Filius hominis traditur, ut crucifigatur». [3]Tunc congregati sunt principes sacerdotum et seniores populi in aulam principis sacerdotum, qui dicebatur Caiphas, [4]et consilium fecerunt, ut Iesum dolo tenerent et occiderent; [5]dicebant autem: «Non in die festo, ne tumultus fiat in populo». [6]Cum autem esset Iesus in Bethania, in domo Simonis leprosi, [7]accessit ad eum mulier habens alabastrum unguenti pretiosi et effudit super caput ipsius recumbentis. [8]Videntes autem discipuli, indignati sunt dicentes: «Ut quid perditio haec? [9]Potuit enim istud venumdari multo et dari pauperibus». [10]Sciens autem Iesus ait illis: «Quid molesti estis mulieri? Opus enim bonum operata est in me; [11]nam semper pauperes habetis vobiscum, me autem non semper habetis. [12]Mittens enim haec unguentum hoc supra corpus meum, ad sepeliendum me fecit. [13]Amen dico vobis: Ubicumque praedicatum fuerit hoc evangelium in toto mundo, dicetur et quod haec fecit in memoriam eius». [14]Tunc abiit unus de Duodecim, qui dicebatur Iudas Iscariotes, ad principes sacerdotum [15]et ait: «Quid vultis mihi dare, et ego vobis eum tradam?». *At illi constituerunt ei triginta argenteos.* [16]Et exinde quaerebat opportunitatem, ut eum traderet. [17]Prima autem Azymorum accesserunt discipuli ad Iesum dicentes: «Ubi vis paremus tibi comedere Pascha?». [18]Ille autem dixit: «Ite in civitatem ad quendam et dicite ei: "Magister dicit: Tempus meum prope est; apud te facio Pascha cum discipulis meis"». [19]Et fecerunt discipuli, sicut constituit illis Iesus, et paraverunt Pascha. [20]Vespere autem facto, discumbebat cum Duodecim. [21]Et edentibus illis, dixit: «Amen dico vobis: Unus vestrum me traditurus est». [22]Et contristati valde, coeperunt singuli dicere ei: «Numquid ego sum, Domine?». [23]At ipse respondens ait: «Qui intingit mecum manum in paropside, hic me tradet. [24]Filius quidem hominis vadit, sicut scriptum est de illo; vae autem homini illi, per quem Filius hominis traditur! Bonum erat ei, si natus non fuisset homo ille». [25]Respondens autem Iudas, qui tradidit eum, dixit: «Numquid ego sum, Rabbi?». Ait illi: «Tu dixisti». [26]Cenantibus autem eis, accepit Iesus panem et benedixit ac fregit deditque discipulis et ait: «Accipite, comedite: hoc est corpus meum». [27]Et accipiens calicem, gratias egit et dedit illis dicens: «Bibite ex hoc omnes: [28]hic est enim sanguis meus novi testamenti, qui pro multis effunditur in remissionem peccatorum. [29]Dico autem vobis: Non bibam amodo de hoc genimine vitis usque in diem illum, cum illud bibam vobiscum novum in regno Patris mei». [30]Et hymno dicto, exierunt in montem Oliveti. [31]Tunc dicit illis Iesus: «Omnes vos scandalum patiemini in me in ista nocte. Scriptum est enim: *"Percutiam pastorem, et dispergentur oves gregis"*. [32]Postquam autem resurrexero, praecedam vos in Galilaeam». [33]Respondens autem Petrus ait illi: «Et si omnes scandalizati fuerint in te, ego numquam scandalizabor». [34]Ait illi Iesus: «Amen dico tibi: In hac nocte, antequam gallus cantet, ter me negabis». [35]Ait illi Petrus: «Etiam si oportuerit me mori tecum, non te negabo». Similiter et omnes discipuli dixerunt. [36]Tunc venit Iesus cum illis in praedium, quod dicitur Gethsemani. Et dicit discipulis: «Sedete hic, donec vadam illuc et orem». [37]Et assumpto Petro et duobus filiis Zebedaei, coepit contristari et maestus esse. [38]Tunc ait illis: «Tristis est anima mea usque ad mortem; sustinete hic et vigilate mecum». [39]Et progressus pusillum, procidit in faciem suam orans et dicens: «Pater mi, si possibile est, transeat a me calix iste; verumtamen non sicut ego volo, sed sicut tu». [40]Et venit ad discipulos et invenit eos dormientes; et dicit Petro: «Sic non potuistis una hora vigilare mecum? [41]Vigilate et orate, ut non intretis in tentationem; spiritus quidem promptus est, caro autem infirma». [42]Iterum secundo abiit et oravit dicens: «Pater mi, si non potest hoc transire, nisi bibam illud, fiat voluntas tua». [43]Et venit iterum et invenit eos dormientes: erant enim oculi eorum gravati. [44]Et relictis illis, iterum abiit et oravit tertio, eundem sermonem iterum dicens. [45]Tunc venit ad discipulos et dicit illis: «Dormite iam et requiescite; ecce appropinquavit hora, et Filius hominis traditur in manus peccatorum. [46]Surgite, eamus; ecce appropinquavit, qui me tradit». [47]Et adhuc ipso loquente, ecce Iudas, unus de Duodecim, venit et cum eo turba multa cum gladiis et fustibus, missi a principibus sacerdotum et senioribus populi. ⁴⁸Qui autem tradidit eum, dedit illis signum dicens: «Quemcumque osculatus fuero, ipse est; tenete eum!». ⁴⁹Et confestim accedens ad Iesum dixit: «Ave, Rabbi!» et osculatus est eum. ⁵⁰Iesus autem dixit illi: «Amice, ad quod venisti!». Tunc accesserunt et manus iniecerunt in Iesum et tenuerunt eum. ⁵¹Et ecce unus ex his, qui erant cum Iesu, extendens manum exemit gladium suum et percutiens servum principis sacerdotum amputavit auriculam eius. ⁵²Tunc ait illi Iesus: «Converte gladium tuum in locum suum. Omnes enim, qui acceperint gladium, gladio peribunt. ⁵³An putas quia non possum rogare Patrem meum, et exhibebit mihi modo plus quam duodecim legiones angelorum? ⁵⁴Quomodo ergo implebuntur Scripturae quia sic oportet fieri?». ⁵⁵In illa hora dixit Iesus turbis: «Tamquam ad latronem existis cum gladiis et fustibus comprehendere me? Cotidie sedebam docens in templo, et non me tenuistis». ⁵⁶Hoc autem totum factum est, ut implerentur scripturae Prophetarum. Tunc discipuli omnes, relicto eo, fugerunt. ⁵⁷Illi autem tenentes Iesum duxerunt ad Caipham principem sacerdotum, ubi scribae et seniores convenerant. ⁵⁸Petrus autem sequebatur eum a longe usque in aulam principis sacerdotum; et ingressus intro sedebat cum ministris, ut videret finem.

⁵⁹Principes autem sacerdotum et omne concilium quaerebant falsum testimonium contra Iesum, ut eum morti traderent, ⁶⁰et non invenerunt, cum multi falsi testes accessissent. Novissime autem venientes duo ⁶¹dixerunt: «Hic dixit: "Possum destruere templum Dei et post triduum aedificare illud"». ⁶²Et surgens princeps sacerdotum ait illi: «Nihil respondes? Quid isti adversum te testificantur?». ⁶³Iesus autem tacebat. Et princeps sacerdotum ait illi: «Adiuro te per Deum vivum, ut dicas nobis, si tu es Christus Filius Dei». ⁶⁴Dicit illi Iesus: «Tu dixisti. Verumtamen dico vobis: Amodo videbitis *Filium hominis sedentem a dextris Virtutis et venientem in nubibus caeli*». ⁶⁵Tunc princeps sacerdotum scidit vestimenta sua dicens: «Blasphemavit! Quid adhuc egemus testibus? Ecce nunc audistis blasphemiam. ⁶⁶Quid vobis videtur?». Illi autem respondentes dixerunt: «Reus est mortis!». ⁶⁷Tunc exspuerunt in faciem eius et colaphis eum ceciderunt; alii autem palmas in faciem ei dederunt ⁶⁸dicentes: «Prophetiza nobis, Christe: Quis est, qui te percussit?». ⁶⁹Petrus vero sedebat foris in atrio; et accessit ad eum una ancilla dicens: «Et tu cum Iesu Galilaeo eras!». ⁷⁰At ille negavit coram omnibus dicens: «Nescio quid dicis!». ⁷¹Exeunte autem illo ad ianuam, vidit eum alia et ait his, qui erant ibi: «Hic erat cum Iesu Nazareno!». ⁷²Et iterum negavit cum iuramento: «Non novi hominem!». ⁷³Post pusillum autem accesserunt, qui stabant et dixerunt Petro: «Vere et tu ex illis es, nam et loquela tua manifestum te facit». ⁷⁴Tunc coepit detestari et iurare: «Non novi hominem!». Et continuo gallus cantavit; ⁷⁵et recordatus est Petrus verbi Iesu, quod dixerat: «Priusquam gallus cantet, ter me negabis». Et egressus foras ploravit amare.

[27] ¹Mane autem facto, consilium inierunt omnes principes sacerdotum et seniores populi adversus Iesum, ut eum morti traderent. ²Et vinctum adduxerunt eum et tradiderunt Pilato praesidi. ³Tunc videns Iudas, qui eum tradidit, quod damnatus esset, paenitentia ductus, rettulit triginta argenteos principibus sacerdotum et senioribus ⁴dicens: «Peccavi tradens sanguinem innocentem». At illi dixerunt: «Quid ad nos? Tu videris!». ⁵Et proiectis argenteis in templo, recessit et abiens laqueo se suspendit. ⁶Principes autem sacerdotum, acceptis argenteis, dixerunt: «Non licet mittere eos in corbanam, quia pretium sanguinis est». ⁷Consilio autem inito, emerunt ex illis agrum Figuli in sepulturam peregrinorum. ⁸Propter hoc vocatus est ager ille ager Sanguinis usque in hodiernum diem. ⁹Tunc impletum est quod dictum est per Ieremiam prophetam dicentem: «*Et acceperunt triginta argenteos, pretium appretiati quem appretiaverunt a filiis Israel,* ¹⁰*et dederunt eos in agrum Figuli, sicut constituit mihi Dominus*». ¹¹Iesus autem stetit ante praesidem; et interrogavit eum praeses dicens: «Tu es Rex Iudaeorum?». Dixit autem Iesus: «Tu dicis». ¹²Et cum accusaretur a principibus sacerdotum et senioribus, nihil respondit. ¹³Tunc dicit illi Pilatus: «Non audis quanta adversum te dicant testimonia?». ¹⁴Et non respondit ei ad ullum verbum, ita ut miraretur praeses vehementer. ¹⁵Per diem autem sollemnem consueverat praeses dimittere turbae unum vinctum, quem voluissent. ¹⁶Habebant autem tunc vinctum insignem, qui dicebatur Barabbas. ¹⁷Congregatis ergo illis dixit Pilatus: «Quem vultis dimittam vobis: Barabbam an Iesum, qui dicitur Christus?». ¹⁸Sciebat enim quod per invidiam tradidissent eum. ¹⁹Sedente autem illo pro tribunali, misit ad illum uxor eius dicens: «Nihil tibi et iusto illi. Multa enim passa sum hodie per visum propter eum». ²⁰Principes autem sacerdotum et seniores persuaserunt turbis, ut peterent Barabbam, Iesum vero perderent. ²¹Respondens autem praeses ait illis: «Quem vultis vobis de duobus dimittam?». At illi dixerunt: «Barabbam!». ²²Dicit illis Pilatus: «Quid igitur faciam de Iesu, qui dicitur Christus?». Dicunt omnes: «Crucifigatur!». ²³Ait autem: «Quid enim mali fecit?». At illi magis clamabant dicentes: «Crucifigatur!». ²⁴Videns autem Pilatus quia nihil proficeret, sed magis tumultus fieret, accepta aqua, lavit manus coram turba dicens: «Innocens ego sum a sanguine hoc; vos videritis!». ²⁵Et respondens universus populus dixit: «Sanguis eius super nos et super filios nostros». ²⁶Tunc dimisit illis Barabbam; Iesum autem flagellatum tradidit, ut crucifigeretur. ²⁷Tunc milites praesidis suscipientes

Iesum in praetorio congregaverunt ad eum universam cohortem. [28]Et exuentes eum, clamydem coccineam circumdederunt ei [29]et plectentes coronam de spinis posuerunt super caput eius et arundinem in dextera eius et, genu flexo ante eum, illudebant ei dicentes: «Ave, rex Iudaeorum!». [30]Et exspuentes in eum acceperunt arundinem et percutiebant caput eius. [31]Et postquam illuserunt ei, exuerunt eum clamyde et induerunt eum vestimentis eius et duxerunt eum, ut crucifigerent. [32]Exeuntes autem invenerunt hominem Cyrenaeum nomine Simonem; hunc angariaverunt, ut tolleret crucem eius. [33]Et venerunt in locum, qui dicitur Golgotha, quod est Calvariae locus, [34]et *dederunt* ei vinum *bibere* cum *felle* mixtum; et cum gustasset, noluit bibere. [35]Postquam autem crucifixerunt eum, *diviserunt vestimenta* eius *sortem mittentes* [36]et sedentes servabant eum ibi. [37]Et imposuerunt super caput eius causam ipsius scriptam: «Hic est Iesus Rex Iudaeorum». [38]Tunc crucifiguntur cum eo duo latrones: unus a dextris et unus a sinistris. [39]Praetereuntes autem blasphemabant eum *moventes capita sua* [40]et dicentes: «Qui destruis templum et in triduo illud reaedificas, salva temetipsum; si Filius Dei es, descende de cruce!». [41]Similiter et principes sacerdotum illudentes cum scribis et senioribus dicebant: [42]«Alios salvos fecit, seipsum non potest salvum facere. Rex Israel est; descendat nunc de cruce, et credemus in eum. [43]*Confidit in Deo*; *liberet* nunc, *si vult eum*. Dixit enim: "Dei Filius sum"». [44]Idipsum autem et latrones, qui crucifixi erant cum eo, improperabant ei. [45]A sexta autem hora tenebrae factae sunt super universam terram usque ad horam nonam. [46]Et circa horam nonam clamavit Iesus voce magna dicens: «*Eli, Eli, lema sabacthani*?», hoc est: «*Deus meus, Deus meus, ut quid dereliquisti me*?». [47]Quidam autem ex illic stantibus audientes dicebant: «Eliam vocat iste». [48]Et continuo currens unus ex eis acceptam spongiam implevit aceto et imposuit arundini et *dabat* ei *bibere*. [49]Ceteri vero dicebant: «Sine, videamus an veniat Elias liberans eum». [50]Iesus autem iterum clamans voce magna emisit spiritum. [51]Et ecce velum templi scissum est a summo usque deorsum in duas partes, et terra mota est, et petrae scissae sunt, [52]et monumenta aperta sunt et multa corpora sanctorum, qui dormierant, surrexerunt [53]et exeuntes de monumentis post resurrectionem eius venerunt in sanctam civitatem et apparuerunt multis. [54]Centurio autem et, qui cum eo erant custodientes Iesum, viso terrae motu et his, quae fiebant, timuerunt valde dicentes: «Vere Dei Filius erat iste!». [55]Erant autem ibi mulieres multae a longe aspicientes, quae secutae erant Iesum a Galilaea ministrantes ei; [56]inter quas erat Maria Magdalene et Maria Iacobi et Ioseph mater et mater filiorum Zebedaei. [57]Cum sero autem factum esset, venit homo dives ab Arimathaea nomine Ioseph, qui et ipse discipulus erat Iesu. [58]Hic accessit ad Pilatum et petiit corpus Iesu. Tunc Pilatus iussit reddi. [59]Et accepto corpore, Ioseph involvit illud in sindone munda [60]et posuit illud in monumento suo novo, quod exciderat in petra, et advolvit saxum magnum ad ostium monumenti et abiit. [61]Erat autem ibi Maria Magdalene et altera Maria sedentes contra sepulcrum. [62]Altera autem die, quae est post Parascevem, convenerunt principes sacerdotum et pharisaei ad Pilatum [63]dicentes: «Domine, recordati sumus quia seductor ille dixit adhuc vivens: 'Post tres dies resurgam'. [64]Iube ergo custodiri sepulcrum usque in diem tertium, ne forte veniant discipuli eius et furentur eum et dicant plebi: 'Surrexit a mortuis', et erit novissimus error peior priore». [65]Ait illis Pilatus: «Habetis custodiam; ite, custodite, sicut scitis». [66]Illi autem abeuntes munierunt sepulcrum, signantes lapidem, cum custodia. **[28]** [1]Sero autem post sabbatum, cum illucesceret in primam sabbati, venit Maria Magdalene et altera Maria videre sepulcrum. [2]Et ecce terrae motus factus est magnus: angelus enim Domini descendit de caelo et accedens revolvit lapidem et sedebat super eum. [3]Erat autem aspectus eius sicut fulgur, et vestimentum eius candidum sicut nix. [4]Prae timore autem eius exterriti sunt custodes et facti sunt velut mortui. [5]Respondens autem angelus dixit mulieribus: «Nolite timere vos! Scio enim quod Iesum, qui crucifixus est, quaeritis. [6]Non est hic: surrexit enim, sicut dixit. Venite, videte locum, ubi positus erat. [7]Et cito euntes dicite discipulis eius: "Surrexit a mortuis et ecce praecedit vos in Galilaeam; ibi eum videbitis". Ecce dixi vobis». [8]Et exeuntes cito de monumento cum timore et magno gaudio cucurrerunt nuntiare discipulis eius. [9]Et ecce Iesus occurrit illis dicens: «Avete». Illae autem accesserunt et tenuerunt pedes eius et adoraverunt eum. [10]Tunc ait illis Iesus: «Nolite timere; ite, nuntiate fratribus meis, ut eant in Galilaeam et ibi me videbunt». [11]Quae cum abiissent, ecce quidam de custodia venerunt in civitatem et nuntiaverunt principibus sacerdotum omnia, quae facta fuerant. [12]Et congregati cum senioribus, consilio accepto, pecuniam copiosam dederunt militibus [13]dicentes: «Dicite: "Discipuli eius nocte venerunt et furati sunt eum, nobis dormientibus". [14]Et si hoc auditum fuerit a praeside, nos suadebimus ei et securos vos faciemus». [15]At illi, accepta pecunia, fecerunt, sicut erant docti. Et divulgatum est verbum istud apud Iudaeos usque in hodiernum diem. [16]Undecim autem discipuli abierunt in Galilaeam, in montem ubi constituerat illis Iesus, [17]et videntes eum adoraverunt; quidam autem dubitaverunt. [18]Et accedens Iesus locutus est eis dicens: «Data est mihi omnis potestas in caelo et in terra. [19]Euntes ergo docete omnes gentes, baptizantes eos in nomine Patris et Filii et Spiritus Sancti, [20]docentes eos servare omnia, quaecumque mandavi vobis. Et ecce ego vobiscum sum omnibus diebus usque ad consummationem saeculi».

Explanatory Notes

Asterisks in the text of the New Testament refer to these "Explanatory Notes" in the RSVCE.

THE GOSPEL ACCORDING TO MATTHEW

1:1: The genealogy is given to show that Jesus had the descent required for messiahship, i.e. from Abraham and, in particular, from David the king.

1:16: Joseph's, not Mary's, descent is given here, as the Jews did not usually reckon descent through the mother. Joseph was the legal and presumed father, and it was this fact that conferred rights of inheritance, in this case, the fulfilment of the messianic promises.

1:25: This means only that Joseph had nothing to do with the conception of Jesus. It implies nothing as to what happened afterwards.

3:2, *Repent* implies an internal change of heart.

3:6: Not Christian baptism but a preparation for it.

3:15: Though without sin, Jesus wished to be baptized by John, as this was the final preparation for his messianic mission.

5:17: Jesus came to bring the old Law to its natural fulfilment in the new while discarding what had become obsolete; cf. Jn 4:21.

5:29: An exaggeration to emphasize the need to avoid occasions of sin.

5:32, *unchastity*: The Greek word used here appears to refer to marriages which were not legally marriages, because they were either within the forbidden degrees of consanguinity (Lev 18:6–16) or contracted with a Gentile. The phrase *except on the ground of unchastity* does not occur in the parallel passage in Lk 16:18. See also Mt 19:9 (Mk 10:11–12), and especially 1 Cor 7:10–11, which shows that the prohibition is unconditional.

6:6: This does not, of course, exclude public worship but ostentatious prayer.

6:24, *mammon*: i.e., riches.

8:3: The miracles of Jesus were never performed to amaze people and shock them into belief. They were worked with a view to a real strengthening of faith in the recipient or beholder, from whom the proper dispositions were required.

8:29, *before the time:* Before the day of judgment the demons are permitted by God to tempt men and even to possess them.

10:5: The Gospel, the messianic salvation, had first to be preached and offered to the chosen people, Israel. Later it would be offered to the Gentiles.

11:3: The Baptist expected more obvious signs of the Messiah. By quoting the prophet Isaiah, Jesus showed that he was indeed inaugurating the messianic kingdom—but by doing good rather than by glorious manifestations or sudden punishments.

11:27: This shows a profound relationship between the Son and the Father, far superior to adoptive sonship.

12:14: The Pharisees regarded healing as work and so forbade it on the sabbath.

12:24, *Beelzebul:* Name of a Canaanite god meaning "the Prince-god." The Jews interpreted this name as "Prince of demons," because for them all false gods were demons.

12:31: To attribute to the devil the works of the Holy Spirit seems to imply a hardness of heart which precludes repentance.

12:46, *brethren*: The Greek word or its Semitic equivalent was used for varying degrees of blood relationship; cf. Gen 14:14; 29:12; Lev 10:4.

12:48: Jesus puts the work of salvation before family relationships. It is not said, however, that he refused to see them.

13:12: To those well-disposed Jews who have made good use of the old Covenant will now be given the perfection of the New. On the other hand, from those who have rejected God's advances will now be taken away even that which they have, because the old Covenant is passing away.

13:52: This is Matthew's ideal: that the learned Jew should become the disciple of Jesus and so add the riches of the new Covenant to those of the Old, which he already possesses; cf. verse 12.

Explanatory Notes

13:55: See note on Mt 12:46.

14:33: Their realization of his Godhead was the prelude to Peter's confession of faith at Caesarea Philippi (Mt 16:16).

15:5: By dedicating his property to God, i.e. to the temple, a man could avoid having to help his parents, without actually giving up what he had. The scribes held such a vow to be valid without necessarily approving it.

15:24: See note on 10:5.

16:14: The title of prophet had a messianic significance because the gift of prophecy, which had been extinct since Malachi, was expected to return at the beginning of the messianic era, especially by an outpouring of the Spirit as foretold by the prophet Joel and as realized in Acts 2:16.

16:16: The context shows that Peter recognizes the sonship of Jesus as divine and not adoptive like ours. Mark and Luke in the parallel passages mention only the confession of the messiahship.

16:18: The name "Peter" comes from the Greek word for "rock." Jesus makes him the foundation on which the Church is to be built. The word "church" means "assembly' or "society" of believers. The Hebrew equivalent is used in the Old Testament to indicate the chosen people. In applying it to the church Jesus shows it to be the messianic community foretold by the prophets. See note on Mt 18:18.

16:25, *life* (both times): A play on the word "life"—natural and supernatural; cf. Mk 8:35–36.

17:4: Peter thought the glorious messianic kingdom had come. In fact, Jesus allowed this glimpse of his glory to strengthen them for the coming passion.

18:9, *Gehenna* (see footnote b) was the name of a valley south of Jerusalem where human sacrifice had once been practised; cf. 2 Chron 33:6. Later it became a cursed place and refuse dump, and the name came to symbolize the Christian place of punishment.

18:18: To the other apostles is given a share in the authority given to Peter.

19:9: This appears to refer to the case in Mt 5:32, though the Greek word for "except" is different.

19:11–12: Jesus means that a life of continence is to be chosen only by those who are called to it for the sake of the kingdom of God.

21:9: The crowd openly recognize Jesus as the Messiah and he allows it for the first time.

21:23: They object to the assumption of authority implicit in the manner of his entry into the city and in his expulsion of the sellers from the temple.

21:33–44: This parable is really an allegory in which almost every detail represents something in God's dealings with Israel.

22:11: The wedding garment represents the dispositions necessary for admission to the kingdom.

23:5, *phylacteries*: Little leather boxes containing, on a very small scroll, the principal words of the law; cf. Deut 6:4–9. Taking the command literally, they fastened these to their arms and their foreheads.

23:9: i.e., "Do not use the title without reference to God's universal fatherhood." He cannot mean that the title is never to be used by a son to his father.

24:1–25:46: The "eschatological discourse," as it is called, deals with the fall of Jerusalem and the end of the world. The two themes seem to be inextricably intermingled in the Gospels as we now have it, but it is possible that originally they were in separate discourses. However, the fusion of the two does bring out their connexion. The one prefigures the other. Moreover, in the reverse direction, so to speak, the language used to describe the day of the Lord in Joel and elsewhere is here applied to the fall of Jerusalem, the details of which must therefore not be taken too literally (24:29).

25:29: See note on 13:12.

26:17: The Passover was celebrated this year on the Friday evening (Jn 18:28). Jesus must have anticipated the passover meal because he would be dead the following day and because the meal prefigured his death.

26:26: The details of the Eucharist are superimposed on the ritual of the Passover.

26:51: It was Peter, as John in his later Gospel tells us (Jn 18:10), though Matthew is reluctant to say so.

26:59: They sought evidence against him and this was necessarily false.

26:64–65: For the first time Jesus speaks clearly of his own identity. Caiaphas evidently understands him to claim divinity.

27:46: Jesus applies Psalm 22 (Vulgate 21) to himself.

27:66: The sealing and guarding only helped to make the subsequent resurrection more obvious.

28:1–20: The resurrection appearances. There are divergent traditions in the Gospels, Galilean and Judean. Paul adds his own record (1 Cor 15). The accounts do not easily fit together, but this is surely evidence of their genuineness. There is no attempt to produce an artificial conformity.

Explanatory Notes

Changes in the RSV for the Catholic Edition

	TEXT		FOOTNOTES	
	RSV	RSVCE	RSV	RSVCE
Mt 1:19	divorce her	send her away		
Mt 12:46,47 (note), 49	brothers	brethren		
Mt 13:31,34	brothers	brethren		
Mt 18:24			[f]Delete existing note and substitute:	[f]A talent was more than fifteen years' wages of a labourer
Mt 18:28			[g]Delete existing note and substitute:	[g]The denarius was a day's wage for a labourer
Mt 19:9		. . . commits adultery; and he who marries a divorced woman commits adultery."[k]		[k]Other ancient authorities omit *and he . . . adultery*
Mt 20:2			[m]Delete existing note and substitute:	[m]The denarius was a day's wage for a labourer
Mt 21:44		[q]+[44] And he who falls on this stone will be broken to pieces; but when it falls on any one, it will crush him		[q]Other ancient authorities omit verse 44
Mt 25:15			[d]Delete existing note and substitute:	[d]A talent was more than fifteen years' wages of a labourer
Mt 27:24		[l]this righteous man's blood		[l]Other ancient authorities omit *righteous* or *man's*

Headings added to the Biblical Text

Headings added to the Biblical Text

Part Two: Jesus' ministry on the way to Jerusalem

8. TOWARDS JUDEA AND JERUSALEM
Jesus foretells his passion and resurrection. The law of
Christian renunciation 16:21
The transfiguration 17:1
Curing of an epileptic boy 17:14
Second announcement of the Passion. The temple tax 17:22

9. THE DISCOURSE ON THE CHURCH
The "little ones" and the Kingdom. On leading others
astray. The lost sheep 18:1
Fraternal correction. The apostles' authority 18:15

Forgiveness of injuries. Parable of the unforgiving
servant 18:21
Marriage and virginity 19:1
Jesus blesses the children 19:13
The rich young man. Christian poverty and renunciation
19:16
Parable of the labourers in the vineyard 20:1
Third announcement of the Passion 20:17
The mother of the sons of Zebedee makes her request 20:20
Curing of the blind men of Jericho 20:29

Part Three: Jesus' ministry in Jerusalem

10. CLEANSING OF THE TEMPLE. CONTROVERSIES
The Messiah enters the Holy City 21:1
Jesus in the temple 21:12
The cursing of the fig tree 21:18
The authority of Jesus is questioned 21:23
Parable of the two sons 21:28
Parable of the wicked tenants 21:33
Parable of the marriage feast 22:1
Paying tax to Caesar 22:15
The resurrection of the dead 22:23
The greatest commandment of all 22:34
The divinity of the Messiah 22:41
Jesus berates the scribes and Pharisees 23:1
Jerusalem admonished 23:37

11. THE ESCHATOLOGICAL DISCOURSE
Announcement of the destruction of the temple 24:1
The beginning of tribulations. Persecution on account of
the Gospel 24:3
The great tribulation 24:15
The coming of the Son of man 24:29
The end will surely come. The lesson of the fig tree
24:32
The time of the second coming of Christ 24:36
Parable of the faithful servant 24:45

Parable of the wise and foolish maidens 25:1
Parable of the talents 25:14
The Last Judgment 25:31

12. THE PASSION, DEATH AND RESURRECTION OF JESUS
Last announcement of the Passion. The conspiracy
against Jesus 26:1
The anointing at Bethany. Judas betrays Jesus 26:6
Preparations for the Last Supper and announcement of
Judas' treachery 26:17
The institution of the Eucharist 26:26
The disciples' desertion foretold 26:30
Gethsemane—the agony in the garden 26:36
Arrest of Jesus 26:47
Jesus before the chief priests 26:57
Peter's denials 26:69
Jesus is brought before Pilate 27:1
Judas' despair and death 27:3
Jesus' trial before Pilate 27:11
The crowning with thorns 27:27
The crucifixion and death of Jesus 27:32
The burial of Jesus 27:57
Jesus rises from the dead and appears to the women 28:1
The soldiers are bribed 28:11
Appearance in Galilee. The mission to the world 28:16

Sources quoted in the Navarre Bible
New Testament Commentary

1. DOCUMENTS OF THE CHURCH AND OF POPES

Benedict XII
Const. *Benedictus Deus*, 29 January 1336
Benedict XV
Enc. *Humani generis redemptionem*, 15 June 1917
Enc. *Spiritus Paraclitus*, 1 September 1920
Clement of Rome, St
Letter to the Corinthians
Constantinople, First Council of
Nicene-Constantinopolitan Creed
Constantinople, Third Council of
Definitio de duabus
    in Christo voluntatibus et operationibus
Florence, Council of
Decree *Pro Jacobitis*
Laetentur coeli
Decree *Pro Armeniis*
John Paul II
Addresses and homilies
Apos. Exhort. *Catechesi tradendae*, 16 October
    1979
Apos. Exhort. *Familiaris consortio*, 22 November
    1981
Apos. Exhort. *Reconciliatio et paenitentia*, 2
    December 1984
Apos. Letter. *Salvifici doloris*, 11 February 1984
Bull, *Aperite portas*, 6 January 1983
Enc. *Redemptor hominis*, 4 March 1979
Enc. *Dives in misericordia*, 30 November 1980
Enc. *Dominum et Vivificantem*, 30 May 1986
Enc. *Laborem exercens*, 14 September 1981
Letter to all priests, 8 April 1979
Letter to all bishops, 24 February 1980
Gelasius I
Ne forte
Gregory the Great, St
Epistula ad Theodorum medicum contra
    Fabianum
Exposition on the Seven Penitential
Ne forte
In Evangelia homiliae
In Ezechielem homiliae
Moralia in Job

Regulae pastoralis liber
Innocent III
Letter *Eius exemplo*, 18 December 1208
John XXIII
Pacem in terris, 11 April 1963
Enc. *Ad Petri cathedram*, 29 June 1959
Lateran Council (649)
Canons
Leo the Great, St
Homilies and sermons
Licet per nostros
Promisisse mememeni
Leo IX
Creed
Leo XIII
Enc. *Aeterni Patris*, 4 August 1879
Enc. *Immortale Dei*, 1 November 1885
Enc. *Libertas praestantissimum*, 20 June 1888
Enc. *Sapientiae christianae*, 18 January 1890
Enc. *Rerum novarum*, 15 May 1891
Enc. *Providentissimus Deus*, 18 November 1893
Enc. *Divinum illud munus*, 9 May 1897
Lateran, Fourth Council of (1215)
De fide catholica
Lyons, Second Council of (1274)
Doctrina de gratia
Profession of faith of Michael Palaeologue
Orange, Second Council of (529)
De gratia
Paul IV
Const. *Cum quorumdam*, 7 August 1555
Paul VI
Enc. *Ecclesiam suam*, 6 August 1964
Enc. *Mysterium fidei*, 9 September 1965
Apos. Exhort. *Marialis cultus*, 2 February 1967
Apos. Letter *Petrum et Paulum*, 27 February 1967
Enc. *Populorum progressio*, 26 March 1967
Enc. *Sacerdotalis coelibatus*, 24 June 1967
Creed of the People of God: Solemn Profession
    of Faith, 30 June 1968
Apos. Letter *Octagesima adveniens*, 14 June
    1971

Sources quoted in the Commentary

Apos. Exhort. *Gaudete in Domino*, 9 May 1975
Apos. Exhort. *Evangelii nuntiandi*, 8 Dec. 1975
Homilies and addresses
Pius V, St
*Catechism of the Council of Trent for Parish
     Priests* or *Pius V Catechism*
Pius IX, Bl.
Bull *Ineffabilis Deus*, 8 December 1854
Syllabus of Errors
Pius X, St
Enc. *E supreme apostolatus*, 4 October 1903
Enc. *Ad Diem illum*, 2 February 1904
Enc. *Acerbo nimis*, 15 April 1905
Catechism of Christian Doctrine, 15 July 1905
Decree *Lamentabili*, 3 July 1907
Enc. *Haerent animo*, 4 August 1908
Pius XI
Enc. *Quas primas*, 11 December 1925
Enc. *Divini illius magistri*, 31 December 1929
Enc. *Mens nostra*, 20 December 1929
Enc. *Casti connubii*, 31 December 1930
Enc. *Quadragesimo anno*, 15 May 1931
Enc. *Ad catholici sacerdotii*, 20 December 1935
Pius XII
Enc. *Mystici Corporis*, 29 June 1943
Enc. *Mediator Dei*, 20 November 1947
Enc. *Divino afflante Spiritu*, 30 September 1943
Enc. *Humani generis*, 12 August 1950
Apost. Const. *Menti nostrae*, 23 September 1950
Enc. *Sacra virginitas*, 25 March 1954
Enc. *Ad caeli Reginam*, 11 October 1954
Homilies and addresses
Quierzy, Council of (833)
*Doctrina de libero arbitrio hominis et de
     praedestinatione*
Trent, Council of (1545–1563)
De sacris imaginibus

De Purgatorio
De reformatione
De sacramento ordinis
De libris sacris
De peccato originale
De SS. Eucharistia
De iustificatione
De SS. Missae sacrificio
De sacramento matrimonio
Doctrina de peccato originali
Doctrina de sacramento extremae unctionis
Doctrina de sacramento paenitentiae
Toledo, Ninth Council of (655)
De Redemptione
Toledo, Eleventh Council of (675)
De Trinitate Creed
Valence, Third Council of (855)
De praedestinatione
Vatican, First Council of the (1869–1870)
Dogm. Const. *Dei Filius*
Dogm. Const. *Pastor aeternus*
Vatican, Second Council of the
     (1963–1965)
Const. *Sacrosanctum Concilium*
Decree *Christus Dominus*
Decl. *Dignitatis humanae*
Decl. *Gravissimum educationis*
Decl. *Nostrae aetate*
Decree *Optatam totius*
Decree *Ad gentes*
Decree *Apostolicam actuositatem*
Decree *Perfectae caritatis*
Decree *Presbyterorum ordinis*
Decree *Unitatis redintegratio*
Dogm. Const. *Dei Verbum*
Dogm. Const. *Lumen gentium*
Past. Const. *Gaudium et spes*

Liturgical Texts

Roman Missal: Missale Romanum, editio typica altera (Vatican City, 1975)
The Divine Office (London, Sydney, Dublin, 1974)

Other Church Documents

Code of Canon Law
Codex Iuris Canonici (Vatican City, 1983)
Congregation for the Doctrine of the Faith
Declaration concerning Sexual Ethics,
     December 1975
Instruction on Infant Baptism, 20 October 1980
Inter insigniores, 15 October 1976
*Letter on certain questions concerning
     Eschatology*, 17 May 1979

Libertatis conscientia, 22 March 1986
Sacerdotium ministeriale, 6 August 1983
Libertatis nuntius, 6 August 1984
Mysterium Filii Dei, 21 February 1972
Pontifical Biblical Commission
Replies
New Vulgate
*Nova Vulgata Bibliorum Sacrorum editio typica
     altera* (Vatican City, 1986)

Sources quoted in the Commentary

2. THE FATHERS, ECCLESIASTICAL WRITERS AND OTHER AUTHORS

Alphonsus Mary Liguori, St
Christmas Novena
The Love of Our Lord Jesus Christ reduced to practice
Meditations for Advent
Thoughts on the Passion
Shorter Sermons
Sunday Sermons
Treasury of Teaching Material
Ambrose, St
De sacramentis
De mysteriis
De officiis ministrorum
Exameron
Expositio Evangelii secundum Lucam
Expositio in Ps 118
Treatise on the Mysteries
Anastasius of Sinai, St
Sermon on the Holy Synaxis
Anon.
Apostolic Constitutions
Didache, or *Teaching of the Twelve Apostles*
Letter to Diognetus
Shepherd of Hermas
Anselm, St
Prayers and Meditations
Aphraates
Demonstratio
Athanasius, St
Adversus Antigonum
De decretis nicaenae synodi
De Incarnatio contra arianos
Historia arianorum
Oratio I contra arianos
Oratio II contra arianos
Oratio contra gentes
Augustine, St
The City of God
Confessions
Contra Adimantum Manichaei discipulum
De Actis cum Felice Manicheo
De agone christiano
De bono matrimonii
De bono viduitatis
De catechizandis rudibus
De civitate Dei
De coniugiis adulterinis
De consensu Evangelistarum
De correptione et gratia
De doctrina christiana
De dono perseverantiae
De fide et operibus

De fide et symbolo
De Genesi ad litteram
De gratia et libero arbitrio
De natura et gratia
De praedestinatione sanctorum
De sermo Domini in monte
De spiritu et littera
De Trinitate
De verbis Domini sermones
Enarrationes in Psalmos
Enchiridion
Expositio epistulae ad Galatas
In I Epist. Ioann. ad Parthos
In Ioannis Evangelium tractatus
Letters
Quaestiones in Heptateuchum
Sermo ad Cassariensis Ecclesiae plebem
Sermo de Nativitate Domini
Sermons
Basil, St
De Spiritu Sancto
Homilia in Julittam martyrem
In Psalmos homiliae
Bede, St
Explanatio Apocalypsis
In Ioannis Evangelium expositio
In Lucae Evangelium expositio
In Marci Evangelium expositio
In primam Epistolam Petri
In primam Epistolam S. Ioanis
Sermon super Qui audientes gavisi sunt
Super Acta Apostolorum expositio
Super divi Iacobi Epistolam
Bernal, Salvador
Monsignor Josemaría Escrivá de Balaguer,
Dublin, 1977
Bernard, St
Book of Consideration
De Beata Virgine
De fallacia et brevitate vitae
De laudibus novae militiae
Divine amoris
Meditationes piissimae de cognitionis humanae conditionis
Sermons on Psalm 90
Sermon on Song of Songs
Sermons
Bonaventure, St
In IV Libri sententiarum
Speculum Beatae Virgine
Borromeo, St Charles
Homilies

Sources quoted in the Commentary

Catherine of Siena, St
Dialogue
Cano, Melchor
De locis
Cassian, John
Collationes
De institutis coenobiorum
Clement of Alexandria
Catechesis III, De Baptismo
Commentary on Luke
Quis dives salvetur?
Stromata
Cyprian, St
De bono patientiae
De dominica oratione
De mortalitate
De opere et eleemosynis
De unitate Ecclesiae
De zelo et livore
Epist. ad Fortunatum
Quod idola dii non sint
Cyril of Alexandria, St
Commentarium in Lucam
Explanation of Hebrews
Homilia XXVIII in Mattheum
Cyril of Jerusalem, St
Catecheses
Mystagogical Catechesis
Diadochus of Photike
Chapters on Spiritual Perfection
Ephraem, St
Armenian Commentary on Acts
Commentarium in Epistolam ad Haebreos
Eusebius of Caesarea
Ecclesiastical History
Francis de Sales, St
Introduction to the Devout Life
Treatise on the Love of God
Francis of Assisi, St
Little Flowers
Reflections on Christ's Wounds
Fulgentius of Ruspe
Contra Fabianum libri decem
De fide ad Petrum
Gregory Nazianzen, St
Orationes theologicae
Sermons
Gregory of Nyssa, St
De instituto christiano
De perfecta christiana forma
On the Life of Moses
Oratio catechetica magna
Oratio I in beatitudinibus
Oratio I in Christi resurrectionem

Hippolytus, St
De consummatione saeculi
Ignatius of Antioch, St
Letter to Polycarp
Letters to various churches
Ignatius, Loyola, St
Spiritual Exercises
Irenaeus, St
Against Heresies
Proof of Apostolic Preaching
Jerome, St
Ad Nepotianum
Adversus Helvidium
Comm. in Ionam
Commentary on Galatians
Commentary on St Mark's Gospel
Contra Luciferianos
Dialogus contra pelagianos
Expositio in Evangelium secundum Lucam
Homilies to neophytes on Psalm 41
Letters
On Famous Men
John of Avila, St
Audi, filia
Lecciones sobre Gálatas
Sermons
John Chrysostom, St
Ante exilium homilia
Adversus Iudaeos
Baptismal Catechesis
De coemeterio et de cruce
De incomprehensibile Dei natura
De sacerdotio
De virginitate
Fifth homily on Anna
Hom. De Cruce et latrone
Homilies on St Matthew's Gospel, St John's
Gospel, Acts of the Apostles, Romans,
Ephesians, 1 and 2 Corinthians, Colossians,
1 and 2 Timothy, 1 and 2 Thessalonians,
Philippians, Philemon, Hebrews
II Hom. De proditione Iudae
Paraeneses ad Theodorum lapsum
Second homily in praise of St Paul
Sermon recorded by Metaphrastus
John of the Cross, St
A Prayer of the Soul enkindled by Love
Ascent of Mount Carmel
Dark Night of the Soul
Spiritual Canticle
John Damascene, St
De fide orthodoxa
John Mary Vianney, St
Sermons

Sources quoted in the Commentary

Josemaría Escrivá, St
Christ Is Passing By
Conversations
The Forge
Friends of God
Furrow
Holy Rosary
In Love with the Church
The Way
The Way of the Cross
Josephus, Flavius
Against Apion
Jewish Antiquities
The Jewish War
Justin Martyr, St
Dialogue with Tryphon
First and Second Apologies
à Kempis, Thomas
The Imitation of Christ
Luis de Granada, Fray
Book of Prayer and Meditation
Guide for Sinners
Introducción al símbolo de la fe
Life of Jesus Christ
Sermon on Public Sins
Suma de la vida cristiana
Luis de Léon, Fray
Exposición del Libro de Job
Minucius Felix
Octavius
Newman, J.H.
Biglietto Speech
Discourses to Mixed Congregations
Historical Sketches
Origen
Contra Celsum
Homilies on Genesis
Homilies on St John
In Exodum homiliae
Homiliae in Iesu nave
In Leviticum homiliae
In Matth. comm.
In Rom. comm.
Philo of Alexandria
De sacrificio Abel
Photius
Ad Amphilochium
Polycarp, St
Letter to the Philippians
del Portillo, A.
On Priesthood, Chicago, 1974
Primasius
Commentariorum super Apocalypsim B. Ioannis libri quinque
Prosper of Aquitaine, St
De vita contemplativa

Pseudo-Dionysius
De divinis nominibus
Pseudo-Macarius
Homilies
Severian of Gabala
Commentary on 1 Thessalonians
Teresa of Avila, St
Book of Foundations
Exclamations of the Soul to God
Interior Castle
Life
Poems
Way of Perfection
Tertullian
Against Marcion
Apologeticum
De baptismo
De oratione
Theodore the Studite, St
Oratio in adorationis crucis
Theodoret of Cyrrhus
Interpretatio Ep. ad Haebreos
Theophylact
Enarratio in Evangelium Marci
Thérèse de Lisieux, St
The Autobiography of a Saint
Thomas Aquinas, St
Adoro te devote
Commentary on St John = Super Evangelium S. Ioannis lectura
Commentaries on St Matthew's Gospel, Romans, 1 and 2 Corinthians, Galatians, Ephesians, Colossians, Philippians, 1 and 2 Timothy, 1 and 2 Thessalonians, Titus, Hebrews
De veritate
Expositio quorumdam propositionum ex Epistola ad Romanos
On the Lord's Prayer
On the two commandments of Love and the ten commandments of the Law
Summa contra gentiles
Summa theologiae
Super Symbolum Apostolorum
Thomas More, St
De tristitia Christi
Victorinus of Pettau
Commentary on the Apocalypse
Vincent Ferrer, St
Treatise on the Spiritual Life
Vincent of Lerins, St
Commonitorium
Zosimus, St
Epist. Enc. "Tractoria" ad Ecclesias Orientales

217